ENVIRONMENTAL LAW HANDBOOK

Seventh Edition

J. Gordon Arbuckle, G. William Frick,
Ridgway M. Hall, Jr., Marshall Lee Miller,
Thomas F.P. Sullivan and Timothy A. Vanderver, Jr.

Government Institutes, Inc.
Rockville, MD
1983

NOTICE

This publication is designed to provide accurate and authoritative information with regard to the subject matter covered. It is sold with the understanding that the publisher is not engaged in rendering legal, accounting or other professional service. If legal advice or other expert assistance is required, the services of a competent professional person should be sought. -- From a Declaration of Principles jointly adopted by a Committee of the American Bar Association and a Committee of Publishers.

Publication of this book does not signify that the contents necessarily reflect the views and policies of Government Institutes, Inc.

Seventh Edition

May 1983

Published by
Government Institutes, Inc.
966 Hungerford Drive #24
Rockville, Maryland 20850
U.S.A.

PREFACE

A complex body of environmental laws, regulations, and decisions is now established in the United States. The environmental law segment which evolved quickly, now ranks with labor, tax, banking, communications, and several other fields as an accepted part of our legal system.

As the field has matured so have our publishing efforts. We at Government Institutes are extremely proud that our *Environmental Law Handbook*, the first such comprehensive text in the field and now in its seventh edition, has become a standard reference in the field. As the environmental law field has evolved so has our publishing activities, although this Handbook is the "flagship" of our environmental publishing efforts. We now offer a wide range of companion books. Two books, *Environmental Statutes* and *Environmental Glossary* are viewed as integral companions of this Handbook. The *Environmental Statutes* book reproduces all the major laws that are described and analyzed in this Handbook. The *Environmental Glossary* provides several thousand definitions from the statutes and Code of Federal Regulations (CFR). As you read this Handbook you will learn of the importance of definitions; in many cases the statutory or regulatory definition differs in some respect from the generally accepted meaning of a term. This *Environmental Glossary* has become an important reference with numerous definitions at your fingertips. I believe that those in the environmental field will find our series of three basic books--*Environmental Law Handbook, Environmental Statutes* and *Environmental Glossary*--invaluable desk references.

Inquiries on these books and our other publications in the field are invited because our job is to satisfy the informational needs of our clients.

I sincerely hope that our efforts help bring about a better understanding of the environmental laws, regulations and decisions. More importantly, we wish to encourage compliance with the spirit of the law so that public health and the environment are protected now and for future generations.

Thomas F. P. Sullivan
President
Government Institutes, Inc.

TABLE OF CONTENTS

Chapter 1 FUNDAMENTALS OF ENVIRONMENTAL LAW

TABLE OF CONTENTS

Chapter 2 NATIONAL ENVIRONMENTAL POLICY ACT

Chapter 3 WATER POLLUTION CONTROL

Chapter 4 AIR POLLUTION CONTROL

Chapter 5 RESOURCE CONSERVATION AND RECOVERY ACT

Chapter 6 TOXIC SUBSTANCES

Chapter 7 FEDERAL REGULATION OF PESTICIDES

Chapter 8 THE OCCUPATIONAL SAFETY AND HEALTH ACT

Chapter 9 NOISE

**Chapter 10 COMPREHENSIVE ENVIRONMENTAL RESPONSE
COMPENSATION AND LIABILITY ACT**

Chapter 11 ENVIRONMENTAL AUDITING

Chapter 12 LAND USE: MAJOR ISSUES IN THE CONTROL OF INDUSTRIAL DEVELOPMENT

Chapter 1

FUNDAMENTALS OF ENVIRONMENTAL LAW

Thomas F. P. Sullivan
Attorney & President
Government Institutes, Inc.
Rockville, MD

1.0 Introduction

The objective of this book is to satisfy the need for comprehensive and authoritative information on the major environmental
laws and regulations to those concerned with protecting public
health and the environment.

The attainment of this objective is a very difficult and challenging task, because our reading audience includes a broad
spectrum of educational backgrounds and degrees of experience.
Some readers will have little exposure to environmental law, while
others will be experienced practitioners of the law. This first
chapter is designed primarily for readers without legal training;
however, lawyers may find it to be an interesting review. This
chapter will provide the major fundamentals underlying and com-
plementing the environmental laws and regulations.

2.0 Lawyers and Laymen

Attorneys are professionally trained to provide advice on
"legal matters." However, some knowledge of environmental laws
and regulations is necessary for those non-lawyers who control the
operations and installations that are involved in environmental and
health protection.

A basic understanding of fundamental legal principles is also
beneficial to environmental managers when the need arises to work
with legal counsel. Non-lawyers who have environmental responsibilities should know something about environmental law to better
enable them to understand an environmental attorney's advice
regarding prevention of problems. This basic information can help a
non-lawyer to know when to seek counsel's advice and to even evaluate counsel's performance.

Violations of the law or the rights of others can mean loss of
time and money, personal embarrassment and possible disruption of

1

an on-going business. The information provided in this book will, we hope, help to avoid violations and expedite compliance.

This book is not intended to be another erudite tome but a useful text that will help those with responsibilities for environmental protection to comply with both the letter and the spirit of the law.

The reader should always be aware of the old axiom that a "little knowledge is dangerous." This chapter will present the fundamentals of environmental law. From these fundamentals can be derived many legal generalities. Generalities are difficult to sustain because the factual situation determines the actual application and, therefore, the results. It should always be remembered that exceptions are born of generalities. When generalities are applied to specific factual situations, the advice of competent counsel should be obtained. Also, the reader should be alert to the fact that this field is extremely dynamic. What is the "law" today changes with time as new laws and regulations are promulgated. In addition, the courts are regularly interpreting the application of the laws, regulations and legal principles in their decisions.

The majority of those who will read this book are not lawyers but have their training in the sciences or engineering. These readers should remember that scientists and lawyers deal with different kinds of laws. The laws of nature which the scientist tries to discover are inviolable. The law of gravitation, for example, or Newton's three laws of motion, cannot be disobeyed.

Human laws do not share this characteristic. The moral obligation imposed by man-made laws results precisely from the fact that it is possible to break them.

3.0 What Is Environmental Law?

Environmental law encompasses all the protections for our environment that emanate from the: (1) U.S. Constitution, (2) state constitutions, (3) Federal and state statutes and local ordinances, (4) regulations promulgated by Federal, state and local regulatory agencies, (5) court decisions interpreting these laws and regulations and, (6) common law.

This chapter covers the major legal fundamentals that are basic to the entire field of environmental law. In subsequent chapters, we will cover the areas that have been pre-empted by Federal legislation plus provide some analysis on the application of environmental law to facility siting and audits of industrial operations.

4.0 Environmental Law and the Courts

In order to gain the proper understanding of this field, a basic knowledge of the United States (U.S.) Court system is needed. As the courts interpret the environmental laws and regulations and apply them to specific factual situations, they are continually determining what the law means in actual cases.

The function of the U.S. Courts in our governmental organization is easy to understand when the federal structure is seen as a whole.

The Federal Government consists of three separate branches - the legislative, the executive, and the judicial. The U.S. Courts constitute the judicial branch. The authority of the U.S. Courts is limited to those powers (1) enumerated in Article III of the U.S. Constitution, and (2) not designated in the Constitution as responsibilities of the legislative or executive branches of the Federal Government.

4.1 States and United States Court Systems

Throughout the United States there are two sets of judicial systems: (1) the state and local courts, established in each state under the authority of the state government, and (2) U.S. Courts, set up under the authority of the Constitution by the Congress of the United States.

The state courts have general, unlimited power to decide almost every type of case, subject only to the limitations of state law. State and local courts are located in every town and county and are the tribunals with which citizens most often have contact. The great bulk of legal business concerning divorce, probate of estates, traffic accidents and all other matters except those assigned to the U.S. Courts is handled by these state and local courts.

The U.S. Courts, on the other hand, have the authority to hear and decide only selected types of cases which are specifically enumerated in the Constitution. The U.S. Courts are located principally in the larger cities while state and local courts are found throughout the country.

4.2 Cases Which the United States Courts Can Decide

The controversies which can be decided in the U.S. Courts are set forth in Section 2 of Article III of the United States Constitution.

These are first "Controversies to which the United States shall be a party." That is, cases in which the U.S. government itself or one of its officers is either suing someone else or is being sued by another party. Obviously, it would be inappropriate for the U.S. Government to depend upon the state governments to provide courts in which to decide controversies to which it is a party.

Secondly, the U.S. Courts have power to decide cases when state courts are inappropriate or might be suspected of partiality. Thus, Federal judicial power extends "to Controversies between two or more States; between a State and Citizens of another State; between Citizens of different States; between Citizens of the same State claiming Lands under Grants of different States . . . " If the State of Missouri sues the State of Illinois for pollution of the Mississippi River, a U.S. Court would be a more impartial forum than the courts of either Missouri or Illinois. Foreseeing the possibility of interstate rivalry, the drafters of the Constitution sought to avoid any suspicion of favoritism by vesting power to decide these controversies in the U.S. Courts.

State courts are also inappropriate in "Cases affecting Ambassadors, other public Ministers and Consuls" and in cases "between a State, or the Citizens thereof, and foreign States, Citizens, or Subjects." The United States Government has responsibility for diplomatic relations with other nations. Since cases involving representatives or citizens of other countries may affect our foreign relations, such cases are decided in the U.S. Courts.

And, thirdly, the Constitution provides that the judicial power extends "to all Cases, in Law and Equity, arising under this Constitution, the Laws of the United States, and Treaties made, or which shall be made, under their Authority" and "to all Cases of admiralty and maritime jurisdiction." Under these provisions, the U.S. Courts decide cases involving the Constitution, laws enacted by Congress, treaties, and laws relating to navigable waters. For example, in cases brought under provisions of the Clean Air Act, Clean Water Act, or other Federal statutes generally the appropriate forum is the U.S. Court system.

The Constitution declares what cases may be decided in the U.S. Courts. The Congress can and has determined that some of these cases may also be tried in state courts and that others may only be tried in U.S. Courts. Specifically, Congress has provided that, with some exceptions, cases arising under the Constitution or laws of the United States or between citizens of different states may be tried in the U.S. Courts only if the amount involved exceeds $10,000 and even then may be tried in either the state or the U.S. Courts. The Congress has also provided that maritime cases and suits against consuls can be tried only in the U.S. Courts. When a state court decides a case involving Federal law, it in a sense acts as a U.S. Court, and its decision on Federal law may be reviewed by the United States Supreme Court.

It should be clear from this discussion that the U.S. Courts cannot decide every case which arises, but only those which the Constitution and the laws enacted by Congress allot to them.

The question of which court has jurisdiction can be a complex issue. Also, the selection of the specific court in which a case is initiated is generally a key move in the overall strategy for winning a lawsuit. The selection of the specific court as a legal strategy is called "forum shopping." When bringing a case a good lawyer will evaluate which court is more inclined toward his client's position. For example the judges of the U.S. Courts in the District of Columbia are known for their pro-environmentalist record. So organizations such as the Environmental Defense Fund (EDF) and Sierra Club are inclined to initiate their lawsuits in the U.S. District Courts for the District of Columbia. Industrial firms are generally more inclined to file a lawsuit in a District Court in Louisiana or other such geographic area with a more conservative judicial record.

4.3 United States Court System

The structure of the U.S. Court system has evolved throughout the historical development of our country. The Constitution merely provides: "The Judicial Power of the United States, shall be vested in one Supreme Court, and in such inferior Courts as the Congress may from time to time ordain and establish." Thus, the only court which is constitutionally indispensable is the Supreme Court. The authority to establish and abolish other U.S. Courts is vested in and has been exercised by the Congress.

At the present time, the United States Court system is pyramidal in structure. At the apex of the pyramid stands the Supreme Court of the United States, the highest court in the land. On the next level stand the United States Courts of Appeals, 11 in all. On the next level down stand the United States District Courts, 94 in all, including the United States District Courts for the District of Columbia and Puerto Rico and the District Courts in the Canal Zone, Guam, and the Virgin Islands.

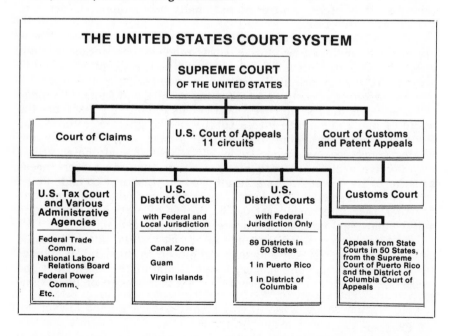

THE UNITED STATES COURT SYSTEM

	SUPREME COURT OF THE UNITED STATES	
Court of Claims	U.S. Court of Appeals 11 circuits	Court of Customs and Patent Appeals
U.S. Tax Court and Various Administrative Agencies	U.S. District Courts with Federal and Local Jurisdiction	U.S. District Courts with Federal Jurisdiction Only	Customs Court
Federal Trade Comm. National Labor Relations Board Federal Power Comm. Etc.	Canal Zone Guam Virgin Islands	89 Districts in 50 States 1 in Puerto Rico 1 in District of Columbia	Appeals from State Courts in 50 States, from the Supreme Court of Puerto Rico and the District of Columbia Court of Appeals

A person involved in a suit in a U.S. Court may proceed through three levels of decision. His case will first be heard and decided by one of the courts or agencies on the lower level. If either party is dissatisfied with the decision, he may usually have a right of review in one of the Courts of Appeals. Then, if he is still dissatisfied, he may petition for review in the Supreme Court of the United States. However, review is granted by the Supreme Court only in cases involving matters of great national importance.

This pyramidal organization of the courts serves two purposes. First the Supreme Court and the Courts of Appeals can correct errors which have been made in the decisions of the trial courts. Secondly, the higher courts can assure uniformity of decision by reviewing cases in which two or more lower courts have reached different decisions.

State courts have a similar pyramid structure with a basic court of original jurisdiction, an appellate court and then a supreme court, but often states do not call their highest court a Supreme Court. So, at the state level the nomenclature can be confusing.

4.4 Courts in Practical Perspective

From a practical viewpoint, when you hear of a judicial decision of interest to you, ask which court decided the case. If the Supreme Court of the U.S. decided the case, it is a very important decision for the entire country. If, however, a local court decided the case, it is of little interest nationally but of major interest to that local jurisdiction.

Also, be aware that courts do differ in their opinions. There are many examples of two lower courts reaching conflicting opinions on a point of law. This is an extremely difficult concept for many to accept. If you are originally trained in engineering or the sciences, you are probably accustomed to dealing in data and facts. To move into the realm of "ifs" and "yes, but" seems to be like going from the world of black and white into a total world of gray. For those who find this troubling, remember that in almost everything, we are talking about degrees of certitude. The field of environmental law may involve a higher degree of uncertitude than most other areas because of its newness. As a result, you do your best to understand what is the meaning of the laws, regulations and court opinions, and you then take into consideration the degree of certitude involved in a particular legal issue before proceeding to a decision.

Also, keep in mind that our U.S. court system, although hailed as one of the fairest systems ever developed by mankind, is subject to human frailties. The judges, lawyers, plaintiffs, defendants and jurors all involve human interactions, another source of uncertainties.

5.0 Common Law

Underlying the development of legal theory in the United States is a body of rules and principles relating to the government and security of persons and property which had its origin, development and formulation in England. Brought to the American colonies by peoples of Anglo-Saxon stock, these basic rules were formally adopted in the states in which they were in force after the American Revolution.   Known as the "common law," these principles are derived from the application of natural reason, an innate sense of justice, and the dictates of conscience.   The common law is not the result of legislative enactment.   Rather, its authority is derived solely from usages and customs which have been recognized, affirmed and enforced by the courts through judicial decisions.

It is important to realize that the "common law" is not a fixed or absolute set of written rules in the same sense as statutory or legislatively enacted law.   The unwritten principles of common law are flexible and adaptable to the changes which occur in a growing society.   New institutions and public policies; modifications of usage and practice; changes in mores, trade, and commerce; inventions; and increasing knowledge, all generate new factual situations which require application and reinterpretation of the fundamental principles of common law by the courts.

As the courts examine each new set of facts in the light of past precedent, an orderly development of common laws occurs through a slow and natural process.   Thus, the basic principles underlying American jurisprudence remain fundamentally constant, evolving slowly and progressively in scope as they absorb the surface ripples produced by the winds of social change.

The common law, so far as it has not been expressly abrogated, is recognized as an organic part of the jurisprudence of most of the states.   The major exception is Louisiana jurisprudence, which is based on Roman law – a relic of French rule prior to the Louisiana Purchase.   However, since the state court systems have functioned independently of each other, subject only to Federal review in cases of national importance, the common law varies slightly from state to state.

There is also a Federal common law which forms the basis for deciding cases in which a uniform standard is desirable for dealing with such claims as alleged Federal rights. 1/

The common law actions that we will discuss in subsequent sections are civil suits in which the plaintiff (the party bringing the lawsuit) seeks to remedy violation of a private right.   Civil actions are distinguished from criminal proceedings in which the state seeks to redress a breach of public or collective rights which are established in codified penal law.

Sections 7.1, 7.2 and 7.3 of this chapter review the three most frequently used types of common law actions that can be the basis of a lawsuit in the pollution control field: nuisance, trespass, and negligence.   After these three actions are described, collateral

---

1/   Illinois v. Milwaukee, 406 U.S. 91(1972), and a second opinion, U.S. Supreme Court 79-408, 28 April 1981.

matters are covered which should be of concern to industry and government officials responsible for operating facilities that have the potential of causing injury to human health or our environment.

6.0 Case Law

Because there is no unified codification of common law, we must look to the court records of actual judicial decisions to determine the application of common law rules and principles to a given set of facts.

To discover how the laws governing environmental controls are applied in a specific factual situation, it is necessary to analyze cases which arose from similar circumstances.

Since each case or factual situation is unique, the decisions reached in prior cases involving similar circumstances are valuable as precedents for points of law. A judicial opinion represents a synthesis of many factors such as: a careful examination of the facts, the weight of relevant precedent, the strength of the legal principles involved, the balance of equities in the case, and more.

Case law, then, is the aggregate of points of law derived from reported cases which forms the body of law established through judicial decisions. It is separate and distinct from statutory law, which is promulgated by legislative bodies.

6.1 Obiter Dicta

Obiter dicta is a Latin phrase used in the legal profession to refer to extraneous comments in a court's opinion. All that a court says is not law. A judicial opinion is, like evidence, only binding insofar as it is relevant. When a court's opinion touches upon points not at issue, the extraneous statements are not binding court opinions or precedents.

The obiter dicta in a court's opinion are not a compelling precedent. However, if the judge giving the decision is highly regarded as a legal scholar, his opinion - whether obiter dicta or not - may have some impact on succeeding cases.

7.0 Torts

In modern legal terminology, "tort" is the word used to denote a private wrong or wrongful act for which a civil action can be brought by the injured party. Thus, a tort is clearly distinguished from a criminal act which is an offense against statutorily established public rights and is prosecuted by the state in behalf of the citizenry.

A tort arises from the existence of a generalized legal duty to avoid causing harm to others, through acts of omission, as well as of commission. By virtue of citizenship, every adult person is obliged to fulfill a duty of care for the personal and property rights of others while engaged in daily life. Carelessness in exercising this responsibility may give rise to a cause of action (a lawsuit) by means of which the injured party may seek restitution. This duty is non-contractual; that is, it does not arise from an explicit promissary agreement between the parties to the action. So a tort is also distinguished from a contract right which is dependent upon the contract itself.

Tens of thousands of tort lawsuits have been filed against the major asbestos manufacturers resulting in Johns Manville and several other large corporations filing for bankruptcy. This has prompted some writers to allege that the 1980's will be the era of "toxic torts." It is clear that tort law will be of considerable interest to industry in the 80's as its role expands.

Torts are divided into two general classes: (1) property torts which involve injury or damage to property and (2) personal torts which involve injuries to a person, whether to the body, reputation or feelings.

7.1 Nuisance

The most common tort action in the field of environmental law is nuisance. Nuisance is defined as "the class of wrongs that arise from the unreasonable, unwarrantable or unlawful use by a person of his own property either real or personal, or from his own lawful personal conduct working an obstruction of or injury to the right of another or of the public and producing material annoyance, inconvenience, discomfort or hurt." 2/

The general rule is that a person may use his land or personal property in any manner he sees fit. However, this rule is subject to limitation: the owner must use his property in a reasonable manner. A nuisance arises whenever a person uses his property to cause material injury or annoyance to his neighbor.

In determining whether a given act constitutes a nuisance, the court considers the nature of the act itself, and the place and the circumstance surrounding the act. To be actionable, the injury or discomfort must amount to a material injury or annoyance. It must tangibly affect the physical comfort of ordinary people under normal circumstances or conditions.

7.1.1 Private or Public Nuisances

Nuisances may be private or public. A private nuisance may be abated by an injunction brought by the individual whose property or health is affected. A public nuisance is one which affects an indefinite number of persons in a community. A public official normally abates a public nuisance.

In the United States today, public nuisances are primarily defined by statute and ordinance. Regulation at the local level has

---

2/   Black, Law Dictionary (Revised 4th ed. 1968) 1214.

resulted in a great variety of specific provisions; for example, local ordinances generally prohibit making loud noises in the immediate vicinity of a hospital. Nearly all states have adopted broad criminal statutes covering public nuisances without attempting to define the specific acts which are covered by them. These have come to be construed as including anything that would have been a public nuisance at common law.

The distinction between public and private nuisance rests on a determination of whether the nuisance affects the rights of the public or the rights of an individual exclusively. The pollution of a stream which inconveniences one or two persons is considered a private nuisance, and the mere number of persons affected will not make it a public nuisance. 3/ But when the pollution kills the fish in a body of water used by the public, an interference with a public right occurs, and the action becomes a public nuisance. 4/

It is generally held that an individual acting privately cannot initiate a legal action for a purely public nuisance, unless his damage is in some way distinguished from that sustained by other members of the general public. The modern trend, however, is to eliminate this distinction between private and public nuisance and to allow private individuals to initiate legal actions whether the nuisance is private or public. 5/

A public nuisance is generally a crime. It may also be a tort or private nuisance if a plaintiff can prove that he has suffered some "special" or "particular" damage. The damage must be of a kind that is individual to the plaintiff as distinguished from that which he shares with the rest of the public.

In an Arkansas case, 6/ nine homeowners in the vicinity of a rendering plant brought suit to abate the odor nuisance created by operation of the plant. They claimed that odors from the rendering plant caused them to feel nausea and to lose sleep at night. On the witness stand, the plant manager admitted that operation of the plant violated existing law. The court found the plant to be a public nuisance, and the homeowners obtained a court order to close the

3/   Smith v. City of Sedalia, 152 Mo. 283, 53 S.W. 907 (1800)

4/   State ex rel. Wear v. Springfield Gas and Electric Co., 204 S.W. 942 (MO. App. 1918).

5/   Prosser, Private Action for Public Nuisance, 52 Va.L. Rev. 997 (1966).

6/   Ozark Poultry Products, Inc. v. Garmon, 251 Ark. 389, 472 S.W. 2d 714(1971).

plant unless conditions causing the nuisance were corrected within a time limit established by the court.

On appeal, the plant owner argued that the homeowners were not entitled to abatement of a public nuisance because they failed to show that they incurred damages beyond those sustained by the general public. The appeals court found that although the plant was found to be a public nuisance, this did not preclude it from also being a private nuisance with respect to the homeowners who brought suit. So the plant was declared a private nuisance by the appellate judge.

Some states have statutes which allow private individuals to sue in an attempt to abate a public nuisance.

7.1.2. Noise Nuisance

The most common form of environmental nuisance is noise pollution. Noise produced by human activities is a common environmental problem. In order to constitute a nuisance in the legal sense, noise must be of such magnitude and intensity as to cause actual or psychological discomfort to persons of ordinary sensibilities. Noise from the operation of an industrial plant constitutes an actionable nuisance only if it affects injuriously the health or comfort of ordinary people in the plant's vicinity to an unreasonable extent. There is not an absolute standard so this determination rests on the facts. 7/

O'Neil v. Carolina Freight Carriers Corporation 8/ is an example of a "noise nuisance" case in which a homeowner was awarded both an injunction and damages against the operators of a nearby business. In this case, the plaintiffs showed that they were ordinary people and that the noise from trucks and loading operations at a terminal located immediately adjacent to their home was unreasonable. It caused them loss of sleep and prevented general enjoyment of their home. The court ruled that the truck terminal noises between 11:00 p.m. and 6:00 a.m. were unreasonable and that every property owner must make reasonable use of his land so as not to cause unnecessary annoyance to his neighbors.

An example of noise conditions not held to be a nuisance is the case of Tortorella v. H. Traiser and Company. 9/ In the Tortorella case, the plaintiff owned a home about 80 feet from the defendant's cigar factory. The factory noise, between normal

---

7/   S. Dak. Comp. Law Ann. § 21-10-9. Wis. State § 280.02; Fla. Stat. § 60.05.

8/   156 Conn. 613, 244 A2d 372 (1968).

9/   284 Mass. 497, 188 N.E. 254 (1933).

working hours of 7:30 a.m. to 4:30 p.m., five days a week, was shown to be annoying to the plaintiff. However, since there was no proof that the plaintiff had suffered materially in comfort or health as a result of the noise, the court found no nuisance.

In the Tortorella case, the court applied a strict interpretation of the law of nuisance, because the plaintiff's request for an injunction against continued operation of the plant entailed a negative impact on local employment and economic conditions.

In the O'Neil case, the facts lead more readily to a conclusion of injury to health because the noise during the night could logically cause loss of sleep and resulting injury to health.

There is no fixed standard as to what degree or kind of noise constitutes a nuisance. The circumstances of each case must be considered independently, the key determination being whether or not the noise is unreasonable and causes some physical or psychological harm. This determination varies from one community to another and from one period of time to another depending on local attitudes and customs.

7.1.3 Other Nuisances

Smoke, dust, odors, other airborne pollutants, water pollutants and hazardous substances have also been held to be nuisances.

The Ozark Poultry Products case, previously cited (footnote 6), is an example of an odor being classed as a nuisance.

In a New York case, McCarty v. Natural Carbonic Gas Company, 10/ the plaintiffs owned a home adjacent to the defendant's manufacturing plant. The plaintiffs claimed that under specific wind conditions, black smoke settled about their home causing them discomfort, annoyance and injury. The court determined that the operation of the manufacturing plant resulted in an unreasonable use of the property, because all the damage could be avoided by the use of hard coal or by use of some modern emission control systems. Although either would involve an increase in expenses, the court held that the safety of persons, generally, is superior in right to a particular use of a single piece of property by its owner. So the court awarded the decision to the plaintiffs.

It should be noted that air pollutants only constitute a nuisance under certain circumstances. Normal air is usually considered as that common to a locality and so varies from one area to another. To be a nuisance, the air pollution must cause harm and discomfort to ordinary people to an unreasonable extent.

10/   189 N.Y. 40, 81 N.E. 549(1970).

In the case of Chicago v. Commonwealth Edison 11/ the court refused to issue an injunction against alleged air pollution. The court found that although the public had a right to clean air, the notion of pure air has come to mean clean air consistent with the character of the locality and the attending circumstances. The court ruled that "The City has failed to answer the threshold question of whether Commonwealth Edison's Indiana facility causes substantial harm so as to constitute an actionable invasion of a public right. In order to be entitled to injunctive relief a substantial harm or injury must be clearly demonstrated." This case is a strict interpretation of the law of nuisance because it was a request for an injunction to cease operation which would have a broad impact on employment and local economics. If the action had been for damages, the court may have decided it differently by not using a strict interpretation of the law.

In a 1973 case, Harrison v. Indiana Auto Shredders, 12/ the Seventh Circuit Court of Appeals also refused to permanently enjoin operation of an automobile shredding and recycling plant based on a nuisance action. The Court held that under the evidence presented and in the absence of an imminent hazard to health or welfare – none of which was established – the defendant could not be prevented from continuing to engage in its operation. In addition, the Court believed that the operation should be allowed a reasonable time to correct any defects not posing threats of imminent or substantial harm.

In essence, the courts were not convinced by the evidence presented in these cases that the harm caused by the alleged nuisance was so great as to justify forcing them to cease operation. If these facilities were shut down, many families would be injured by the forced unemployment. So the weighing of the equities by the Court resulted in a determination based on all the evidence presented in favor of allowing continued operations. This is generally called "balancing the equities."

An unusual type of nuisance case of considerable notoriety and interest involved the construction of the 110-story Sears building in Chicago. 13/ In this case, the plaintiffs requested an injunction to prevent completion of the building which they claimed would constitute a nuisance by distorting television reception in surrounding areas. The Court held that Sears had a legal right to use

---

11/   7 ERC 1480 (Ill. App. Ct. 1974).

12/   8 ERC 1569 (7th Cir. 1975).

13/   People ex rel Hoogasian v. Sears, Roebuck and Co., 52 Ill. 2d
       301, 287 N.E. 2d 677 (1972).

the airspace above its property, at least as much as it can occupy or use in connection with the land, subject only to legislative limitation. One can readily see the adverse consequences that such a theory could pose for solar energy.

The Earthline Corporation, a subsidiary of SCA Services, Inc., attempted to operate an industrial waste recovery, treatment, storage and disposal site on a 130-acre site in Illinois. Ninety acres are located within the Village of Wilsonville and the remaining acres adjacent to the village. The operation accepted hazardous wastes and toxic substances. The Village sued Earthline to stop the operation and also to require the removal of those hazardous wastes and toxic substances that had been deposited on the site. 14/ The court ruled that the site was a public/private nuisance, issued an injunction against Earthline's further operation of the site and required them to remove all wastes and contaminated soil.

It is most important to note that this case was decided against SCA even though they were in full compliance with government regulation. Compliance with government regulations was not an acceptable defense against a common law nuisance action. Also, the lower court decision emphasized the distinction between a nuisance and negligence action:

"Nuisance and negligence are distinct torts and except in the cases of nuisances created by negligence liability for nuisance does not depend upon the existence of negligence. Negligence is not an essential or material element of a cause of action for nuisance and need not be pleaded or proved especially where the thing complained of is a nuisance per se or a public nuisance or results from ultra-hazardous conduct on the part of the defendant. A nuisance is a condition and not an act or a failure to act on the part of the person responsible for the condition."

7.1.4 Some Defenses to Nuisance Actions

Nuisance actions have often come down to a question of balancing the equities (weighing the impact of the injuries to the respective parties involved in the litigation). In any balancing of the equities, the good faith efforts of the polluter, while not absolving him, would certainly be a factor if they exist. 15/

The availability of pollution control devices is, of course, a significant factor that can be considered by the court. For example,

---

14/   Village of Wilsonville v. SCA Services, Inc., 7 Ill. App. 3d 618, 396 N.E. 2d 522 (1979), aff'd 86 Ill. 2d1, 42 N.E. 2d 824 (1981).

15/   McElwain v. Georgia Pacific, 245 Ore. 247, 421 P. 2d 957.

in Renkin v. Harvey Aluminum, 16/ the court noted Harvey Aluminum's failure to keep pace with the technological advances in pollution controls.   In that case the court ordered adoption of such controls.

One of the reasons why nuisance actions have been of limited value for private relief is that if the nuisance affects the broad general public, it is considered a public nuisance. Theoretically only the proper public official can bring the action on behalf of the "public interest." The plaintiff cannot get damages unless he can show a special kind (not degree) of injury different from that of the general public.   In recent cases, such as the previously cited Ozark Poultry Products case, the distinction between public and private nuisance is being altered so that this distinction will probably be eliminated for practical purposes in the future. (See 7.1.1)

To bridge this gap between private and public nuisances, in those jurisdictions that do distinguish between the two, class actions have been attempted to emphasize to the courts the composite social cost to the victims compared with the cost of abating the pollution. The Supreme Court case of Snyder v. Harris 17/ (a stockholder's suit), however, limited the usefulness of bringing class actions in the Federal courts by not allowing the separate and distinct claimants to aggregate their respective claims to meet the $10,000 Federal jurisdictional amount.   In the Supreme Court decision Zahn v. International Paper Company, 18/ the Court upheld the Snyder ruling.   In Zahn, some owners of lake shore property charged that the defendant permitted discharges from its pulp and paper plant, thereby polluting the waters of Lake Champlain and damaging the value of surrounding properties. The Court held that the class action was not maintainable because the multiple plaintiffs had separate and distinct claims which did not each satisfy the $10,000 amount for suits in Federal courts.

In general, the courts are moving to strict liability for environmental nuisances so that practically speaking, there are no good defenses. The solution is: do not create nuisances.

7.1.5 Coming to a Nuisance

"Coming to a nuisance" is the phrase used to describe a defense that the complainant or plaintiff affected by the nuisance moved into the area where the "complained about activity" had already been in existence.

16/   226 F. Supp. 169 (D. Ore. 1963).

17/   394 U.S. 332 (1969).

18/   6 ERC 1120, 94 Sup. Ct. 505(1973).

An example of "coming to a nuisance" occurs when someone moves onto the property next to an airport or near an industrial complex and then complains of the nuisance that existed prior to his moving there. Generally, the fact that an individual purchases property with the knowledge of the existence of a nuisance or that he came to the nuisance will not defeat his right to the abatement of the nuisance or recovery of damages. 19/

However, some cases have held that if the complainant came to a nuisance, this constitutes a defense to a nuisance lawsuit. This minority view is probably a result of an old axiom of law that one who voluntarily places himself in a situation whereby he suffers an injury will not prevail. The test of liability in these cases is often the knowledge of the plaintiff regarding the consequences of his conduct.

The majority rule, however, is that the fact alone that a person moved into the vicinity of a nuisance by purchasing or leasing property in the area does not bar him from complaining in an action against the continued operation or maintenance of the nuisance. 20/ The majority rule is based on the theory that pure air and the comfortable enjoyment of property are as much rights belonging to it as the right of possession and occupancy. If population where there was none before approaches a nuisance, it is the duty of those liable to put an end to it.

7.2 Trespass

Nuisance is generally distinguished from trespass. A nuisance consists of a use of one's own property so as to cause injury, while a trespass involves a violation of the property rights of another.

In a general sense, an invasion of another's rights is a trespass. Usually, trespass is used in a more limited sense. It is to be understood as designating an injury to the person, property, or rights of another which is the immediate result of some unlawful act.

In order to constitute trespass, unlawful intent is not necessary. Intent or motive with which the act was done is immaterial except as far as it may affect the measure of damages. A person is liable even if he acted in good faith and with reasonable care.

Trespass is commonly divided into three types. These are:

19/ Fertilizing Co. V. Hyde Park, 97 U.S. 659; Rentz v. Roach, 154 Ga. 491: Vann v. Bowie 127 Tex. 97 are a few cases.

20/ A comprehensive article on this subject is found in 42 ALR 3d starting at page 344. This article includes a listing of cases by jurisdictions that recognize the majority rule.

1. **Trespass to personal property** is an injury to or interference with possession, with or without the exercise of physical force. This includes destruction of personal property as well as the taking from the possession of another, or a refusal to surrender possession.

2. **Trespass to the person** is an unlawful act committed on the person of another such as a vehicle impact or even an unauthorized operation. Mere words are not actionable trespass to the person.

3. **Trespass to realty** is an unlawful, forcible, entry on another's possession. An injury to the realty of another or an interference with his possession, above or below ground, is a trespass, regardless of the condition of the land and regardless of negligence.

Trespass to realty is the type of trespass action that is generally used in pollution control cases. In an action for trespass to realty, entry upon another's land need not be in person. It may be made by causing or permitting a thing to cross the boundary of the premises. The trespass may be committed by casting material upon another's land, by discharging water, soot or carbon, by allowing gas or oil to flow underground into someone else's land, but not by mere vibrations or light which are generally classed as nuisances. In the case of Martin v. Reynolds Metal Company, 21/ the deposit on Martin's property of microscopic fluoride compounds, which were emitted in vapor form from the Reynolds' plant, was held to be an invasion of this property – and so a trespass.

Cases have distinguished between trespass and nuisance and held that encroachment of the space above the land is a nuisance. Generally there must be physical invasion of the property to constitute a trespass.

Some courts have used trespass and private nuisance almost interchangeably. The end result is that the distinction between trespass and nuisance is somewhat clouded.

Negligence and trespass have also been used interchangeably as seen in the case of Stacy v. VEPCO. 22/ In this case, the court ruled that there was "negligence and/or trespass on the part of VEPCO" because of damage caused to Stacy's trees by the emissions from VEPCO's Mount Storm plant. It is interesting to note that the court in this case was convinced by the expert meteorologist's testimony that the emissions could travel the 22-mile distance from the plant to damage the trees. The important point to remember is that

21/ 221 Ore. 86, 342 P. 2d 790(1959), cert. denied, 362 U.S. 918 (1960).

22/ 7 ERC 1443 (D.C. EVa. 1975).

courts can and do minimize the concern with the form of the action but endeavor to do substantive justice based on all the evidence presented.

7.3 Negligence
Negligence is: (a) doing or omitting to do an act, (b) which a person owes to another by virtue of a legal duty imposed upon him by law, (c) thereby causing injury to the plaintiff or to his property. Negligence is that part of the law of torts which deals with acts not intended to inflict injury. If there is intent to inflict injury, then the case becomes one of criminal law. If an ordinary, prudent person under the same circumstances can foresee injury to the plaintiff, the defendant is negligent. The standard of care required by law is that degree which would be exercised by a person of ordinary prudence under the same circumstances. This is often defined as the "reasonable man" rule, namely what a reasonable person would do under all the circumstances.

In order to render the defendant liable, his act must be the proximate cause of the injury. Proximate cause is that which in the natural and continuous sequence, if unbroken by an efficient intervening act, produces injury and without which the result would not have happened.

An example of negligence action in a pollution case is Burgess v. Tamano. 23/ This case involved the July 1972 spill of more than 100,000 gallons of bunker oil from the tank ship Tamano into Maine's Casco Bay. Fishermen, boat owners, and property owners allegedly damaged by the spill brought suit against the Tamano, while Maine filed suit to recover damages sustained by the state as a result of the spill. Since the Federal Government has a great deal of money with which to pay damages, plaintiffs contended that the proximate cause of the escape and spread of oil from the Tamano was the Coast Guard's negligent conduct of its containment and cleanup operations. The court ruled that the United States, in undertaking any task such as buoyage or pollution abatement, is liable in tort for the consequences of its negligence to the same extent that a private person would be liable.

The evidence convinced the court that the Coast Guard caused injury, which could be foreseen, by its inadequate containment and cleanup operation. Since this conduct was the proximate cause of injury to the plaintiff, the court held that the Coast Guard was guilty of negligence.

Persons harmed as a result of careless and improper disposal or handling of hazardous waste can recover for their losses under a negligence cause of action. Indeed, state and Federal courts have

---

23/   5 ERC 1914 (D.C. Me. 1973) and 6 ERC 1380 (D.C. Me. 1974).

long recognized this common law theory of recovery against defendants who engage in the negligent disposal of pollutants such as hazardous waste. 24/ Where negligence can be established, it is no defense that the negligent action was in full compliance with all government regulations 25/ and permit conditions. 26/ On the other hand, noncompliance with regulations or a permit in some states may be prima facie evidence (that is, proof without any more evidence) of liability. 27/

7.3.1 Res Ipsa Loquitur

As a general rule, the mere fact that an accident occurs does not give rise to a presumption of negligence. Negligence must be proved by a preponderance of the evidence. The doctrine of res ipsa loquitur does not relieve the plaintiff of proving negligence but it does rearrange the method of establishing proof. Res ipsa loquitur means that the party claiming injury has produced sufficient facts to warrant an inference of negligence.

In order to rely on res ipsa loquitur, the plaintiff must show that the instrumentality which caused the injury was, to some extent, under the exclusive control of the defendant, and the injury was such that, in the ordinary course of things, it would not have occurred, if the one having control had used proper care.

The following is a hypothetical example of res ipsa loquitur:

> Smith is a passenger in the airplane of TransAm Company, a common carrier. In good flying weather, the plane disappears, and no trace of it is ever found. There is no evidence. Various explanations are possible, including mechanical failure which could not have been prevented by reasonable care, or bombs planted on the plane. In this case, however, it may be inferred by the jury that the most probable explanation for Smith's death is negligence on the part of TransAm Company

---

24/ See, e.g., Knabe v. National Supply Division of Armco Steel Corp., 592 F.2d 841 (5th Cir. 1979).

25/ Greater Westchester Homeowners Association v. City of Los Angeles, 26 Cal. 3d 86, 160 Cal. Rptr. 733, 603 P.2d 1329 (1978), cert. denied, 449 U.S. 820 (1980).

26/ Brown v. Petrolane, Inc., 102 Cal. App. 3d 720, 162 Cal. Rptr. 551 (1980); Belton V. Wateree Power Corp., 123 S.C. 291, 115 S.E. 587 (1922).

27/ See Martin v. Herzog, 126 N.E. 814 (N.Y. 1920).

under res ipsa loquitur because airplanes do not normally disappear and a logical explanation would be
mechanical failure. 28/

   In negligence cases involving pollution, it is generally difficult to link the activities of an alleged polluter with plaintiff's
claimed injury from the pollution. Res ipsa loquitur helps to eliminate this difficulty. The case of California Department of Fish and
Game v. SS Bournemouth 29/ presented such a case for use of res
ipsa. Officers of the California Fish and Game Department took oil
samples from an oil slick in a harbor and from the SS Bournemouth.
The court found a scientific probability that the two samples came
from the same source. The court also found, on the basis of evidence as to wind, current, and tide, that the slick could have come
from the ship. There was no other ship in the general area at the
relevant time. Then, the court applied the doctrine of res ipsa; the
oil spill probably could not have occurred unless someone was negligent; no other source of the spill was indicated; the plaintiff was not
negligent; the ship was under exclusive control of the defendant;
therefore, the burden of proof was shifted from the plaintiff to the
defendant based on res ipsa loquitur. Damages of the cost of cleaning up the spill were awarded against the vessel by the court.

7.3.2 Violation of a Statute or Ordinance
   Generally, the violation of a statute or ordinance which was
passed to promote safety is negligence. But the violation of such
law does not of itself give rise to civil liability. The plaintiff must
show that the violation of the law was the proximate cause of the
injury. The violation of a statute or ordinance, which is not designed
to prevent the sort of harm about which the plaintiff is complaining,
is not negligence.
   An example of the application of this doctrine in an environmental lawsuit is the 1975 case of Springer v. Schlitz Brewing Company. 30/ Mr. and Mrs. Springer owned a large farm downriver from
a newly constructed Winston-Salem, N.C., brewery of Schlitz. They
sued Schlitz for overloading the city's sewage treatment, causing it
to pollute the Yadkin river, resulting in fish kills and so interfering
with their riparian rights. In North Carolina, as in many other
states, a riparian landowner has a right to the agricultural, recreational and scenic use and enjoyment of the stream bordering his

---

28/   Restatement (Second) Torts, § 328D.

29/   318 F. Supp. 839 (C.D. Cal. 1970).

30/   7 ERC 1516 (4th Cir. 1975).

land. A city sewage ordinance prohibited the discharge of pollutants that interfere with the city's waste treatment process.

In this case the plaintiff did not, according to the Court's opinion, prove that Schlitz was negligent in the conventional sense. Instead, the Court looked to the theory that violation of a city sewage ordinance is negligence "per se." The appeals court directed that the jury should decide if Schlitz violated the city's ordinance. If the jury decides that the ordinance was violated, it is negligence per se and if the negligence proximately causes injury, then the industry is liable irrespective of any good faith efforts on the part of the defendant.

So, violations of environmental or pollution control statutes or ordinances which are generally designed to protect the public health or safety could result in a successful negligence lawsuit by the injured party even though there is no factual showing of negligence.

7.3.3 Dangerous Substances – Strict Liability

Courts have ruled that a person who keeps a potentially dangerous substance on his land which, if permitted to escape, is certain to injure others, must make good the damage caused by the escape of the substance, regardless of negligence on the defendant's part.

This strict liability theory is very old. It was used in a 1907 case where oil escaped into the Potomac River in Washington, D.C., and resulted in injury to some boats in a downstream boathouse. 31/ In this case, it was determined that a potentially dangerous substance is anything which, if permitted to escape, is certain to injure others. This description of a potentially dangerous substance is so broad as to include oil in the case under discussion plus thousands of other substances in subsequent litigation.

The reasoning for this strict liability standard is that, when persons suffer loss, no good reason can be found to charge the loss against anyone who did not contribute to it. If the defendant is engaged in an ultra-hazardous or dangerous activity for profit, he should bear the burden of compensating others who are harmed by his activities.

In making the determination of whether an activity is ultra-hazardous, courts have traditionally scrutinized six factors: (1) the existence of a high degree of risk, (2) the likelihood that the resultant harm will be great, (3) the ability to eliminate the risk by exercising reasonable care, (4) the extent to which the activity is not common in the community, (5) the appropriateness of the

---

31/ Brennan Construction Co. v. Cumberland, 29 U.S. App. D.C. 554(1907).

activity to the place where it is carried on, and (6) the activity's value to the community.

Not surprisingly, some courts have applied strict liability theories in cases involving the disposal of hazardous waste.

In spite of its rapid development in some jurisdictions, however, the doctrine of strict liability has not been applied to environmental torts in all states. Even those states which have adopted strict liability have not applied the theory in uniform fashion.

7.3.4 Defenses to an Action for Negligence

7.3.4.1 Contributory Negligence

Contributory negligence is an affirmative defense in some jurisdictions. The theory behind this concept is that a person is not entitled to benefit from his own wrong. Therefore, contributory negligence on the part of the plaintiff generally relieves the defendant of liability, unless he, the defendant, had the "last clear chance" of avoiding the accident.

The "last clear chance" doctrine 32/ presupposes a perilous situation created or existing through the negligence of both the plaintiff and the defendant. It assumes that there was a time, after such negligence has occurred, when the defendant could, and the plaintiff could not by the use of available means, avoid the accident. This doctrine is not applicable when the emergency is so sudden that there is no time to avoid it. Under the "last clear chance" doctrine, a negligent defendant is liable when he (aware of the plaintiff's peril, or unaware of it only through carelessness) had, in fact, a later opportunity than the plaintiff to avert the accident.

A comparative negligence concept (apportionment of responsibility or damages) is recognized in 12 states. 33/

7.3.4.2 Assumption of Risk

Generally any person who knows of a risk and assumes it is not permitted to recover for any injury sustained. This is based on the theory that a person should not be permitted to benefit from his own wrong. One of several exceptions to this rule is when the risk is assumed to save life.

7.3.4.3 Proving Negligence

Negligence actions in the pollution field are generally hampered by the plaintiff's difficulty in proving the defendant

---

32/   57 Am. Jur. 2d 796.

33/   Id. 846.

negligent. Also, the plaintiff must prove that the negligence of the defendant was the proximate cause of the plaintiff's injury. However, the increased availability to the public of plant records, monitoring, inspections and source emission data required under the various statutes and regulations will contribute to easing the evidentiary problems of proving a negligence case.

7.4 Sovereign Immunity and Torts

Theoretically, the law has granted immunity from tort liability to governments. Neither the United States nor any of the several states may be sued by a private citizen without the government's consent. The origin of this idea was the common law notion that "the King can do no wrong." But, it was not until the sixteenth century that this concept was fully established as law. When the individual sovereign was replaced by the broader concept of the modern state, the idea was carried over: that to allow a suit against a ruling government without its consent was inconsistent with the very idea of supreme executive power.

In most state jurisdictions, however, consent has been given, usually in a limited form by statutes, which provide for special procedure or create special courts of claims, or which authorize suits against the state in its own courts for particular causes of action. There is a good deal of variety to these statutes, and reference must be made to those of the particular jurisdiction.

In 1946, the United States waived its immunity, with certain exceptions, from liability in tort, and provided for litigation of tort claims against it in the Federal courts by the Federal Tort Claims Act. 34/

So, for anyone contemplating bringing a pollution lawsuit based on a tort action against a government entity, the first questions are: has sovereign immunity been waived, and what are the consent restrictions?

In regard to any suit against a state brought in a Federal court, the Eleventh Amendment to the U. S. Constitution states:

> "The Judicial power of the United States shall not be constructed to extend to any suit in law or equity commenced or prosecuted against one of the United States by Citizens of another State or by Citizens or subjects of any Foreign State."

While the Eleventh Amendment, by its own terms, does not bar suits against a state by its own citizens, the U.S. Supreme Court has consistently ruled that an unconsenting state is protected from

---

34/   28 U.S.C.A. §§ 1254 et seq.

suits brought in Federal courts by her own citizens as well as by citizens of another state. 35/ It is also well-settled law that even though a state is not named as a defendant, any judgment which must be paid from public funds of the state falls within the prohibitions of the Eleventh Amendment.

A successful example of the defense of sovereign immunity on the Federal level is found in an environmental case entitled Byram River v. Village of Port Chester. 36/ In this case, the plaintiffs were seeking to halt the depositing of allegedly inadequately treated sewage into the Byram River. The plaintiffs named a number of defendants, including the New York State Department of Environmental Conservation. The Court dismissed the action against New York State based on the defense of sovereign immunity as set forth in the Eleventh Amendment.

8.0 Constitutional Law

8.1 Constitution and Government Authority

The Federal Government was created to be a government of limited authority. The powers granted to the Federal Government are those enumerated in the U.S. Constitution. Although the Federal Government's authority is theoretically limited to only those enumerated, in practice these powers have been so expanded in scope by judicial interpretation that it is hard to conceive of any environmental laws being beyond the Federal authority. So this section will not review the general question of the theoretical basis of Federal power but, instead, focus on the specific Constitutional limits to this authority.

These limits appear to be of more pragmatic interest and concern today because they are the issues raised in lawsuits against the abuse of governmental authority.

8.2 Limits on Governmental Action

8.2.1 Search Warrants and the Fourth Amendment

The Fourth Amendment of the U.S. Constitution provides that:

"The right of the people to be secure in their persons, houses, papers, and effects, against unreasonable searches and seizures shall not be violated, and no

---

35/   Hans v. Louisiana, 134 U.S. 1(1890); Edelman v. Jordan, 415 U.S. 651 (1974).

36/   7 ERC 1970 (S.D.N.Y. 1975).

Warrants shall issue, but upon probable cause, supported by oath or affirmation and particularly describing the place to be searched and the persons or things to be seized."

One of the most common abuses of governmental authority is in the collection or obtaining of evidence. Evidence is necessary for any civil or criminal enforcement program. However, Federal evidence collection is limited by these Fourth Amendment prohibitions.

The courts have held that the Fourth Amendment applies to the corporate entity as well as to the private citizen. The Supreme Court has held that the requirement for a search warrant even applies to routine administrative inspections. 37/ In the Camara case, the Court held that the warrant requirement applied to a municipal health inspector's search of a private residence. A similar conclusion was reached with respect to a fire inspector's attempted search of a commercial warehouse. 38/ In these cases, the Court indicated that a lesser degree of "probable cause" would be required for an administrative search warrant than for the typical criminal search warrant. So there can be routine periodic searches of all structures in a given area based on an appraisal of conditions in the area as a whole rather than on a knowledge of conditions in a particular building. The reasonableness of such inspections is to be weighed against the invasion of rights that the search entails.

Generally warrants are only sought after entry is refused because there is no need for a search warrant when the owner or operator has given his consent.

To avoid this need for search warrants, the Congress has authorized warrantless searches in some statutes. In the famous Barlow case 39/ the constitutionality of these legislative waivers was reviewed by the Supreme Court. The Court held that Section 8 of the Occupational Safety and Health Act (OSHA) authorizing warrantless inspections violated the Fourth Amendment prohibition against warrantless searches and was unconstitutional. How does this affect you? Probably it doesn't affect you directly, but it does

---

37/   Camara v. Municipal Court, 387 U.S. 523 (1967).

38/   See v. City of Seattle, 387 U.S. 541 (1967).

39/   Marshall v. Barlow's Inc., 436 U.S. 307 (1978).

put some restraint on the Federal Government not to harass businesses with needless inspections. 40/

The Environmental Protection Agency (EPA) has avoided the test of the constitutionality of the warrantless search authorizations given to them by Congress in the Noise Control Act and the Resource Conservation and Recovery Act by not challenging the issue. If an EPA inspector is refused admission, EPA, as standard procedure, will then obtain a search warrant and not even try to use the statutory authority. This avoids the constitutional confrontation.

It is common, in the field of environmental law, to find exceptions to the general rules. An example of an exception to the search warrant requirement is the so-called "open fields" exception described in the Supreme Court case, Air Pollution Variance Board v. Western Alfalfa. 41/ In this case, an inspector of a Division of the Colorado Department of Health entered the premises of Western Alfalfa Corporation without its knowledge or consent to make a Ringelmann reading of plumes of smoke being emitted from the company's chimneys. The Western Alfalfa Corporation claimed that the inspection violated the Fourth Amendment by entering its property to collect evidence without a search warrant. The U.S. Supreme Court ruled that the inspector was within an exception to the Fourth Amendment and had not violated the rights of the Western Alfalfa Corporation. The Court held the general rule to be that the act of conducting tests on a defendant's premises without either a warrant or the consent of defendant constitutes an unreasonable search within the Fourth Amendment. However, in this case the inspector did not enter the plant or offices. Basically he sighted what anyone in the area near the plant could see in the sky. He was on the defendant's property but there was no showing that he was on premises from which the public was excluded. The Court held that there is an "open fields" exception to the constitutional requirement for a search warrant which was applicable in this case.

In the vast majority of practical situations, consent is given for collection of evidence. The consent may be oral or written, with the latter being more desirable, because it simplifies subsequent problems of proof. The consent is commonly given by employees simply admitting the inspectors to the company premises or giving answers to oral or written questions by government employees.

40/ For a thorough review of the Barlow Case and its impact, see "The Barlow Case and OSHA Inspections" by Marshall Lee Miller in Occupation Health & Safety Regulations (Government Institutes, Washington, D.C., June 1978). pages 147-154.

41/ 6 ERC 1571 (U.S. Sup. Ct. 1974).

One method of avoiding the necessity of obtaining a search warrant is to require the owner or operator of the pollution source to get a permit or license to operate. Then, a condition is included in the permit, allowing inspections without warrants. The United States Supreme Court has not yet ruled on the constitutionality of this method. Since permit systems are now being used more and more by Federal, state and local agencies to control pollution, this method of obtaining desired evidence will be the trend of the future and provides the government with the consent needed.

See Section 11 of this chapter for more on evidence.

8.2.2 Prohibition Against Self-Incrimination: The Fifth Amendment

The Fifth Amendment to the U.S. Constitution prohibits compulsory self-incrimination. It is limited in that it only applies to criminal cases. If the government agency collecting the evidence will use it only for civil actions, such as injunctions, the Fifth Amendment is not applicable. In addition, the Fifth Amendment applies only to persons and not to corporations or partnerships.

Most environmental statutes provide penalties for both individuals and corporations. Therefore, in a case where the evidence or samples taken might be used in a criminal action, the person in authority at the place where the evidence is to be taken should be advised of his rights to remain silent, to an attorney, and that any evidence taken may be used against him in a subsequent criminal action. If these rights are not formally observed, the evidence so collected may not be admissible in a criminal action.

8.2.3 Due Process, the Fifth and Fourteenth Amendments

The requirement that government entities not deprive anyone of due process of law is found in the Fifth and Fourteenth Amendments.

Due process is a very basic principle of our system of laws:

The Fifth Amendment to the U.S. Constitution says: "No person shall..., nor be deprived of life, liberty, or property, without due process of law; nor shall private property be taken for public use, without just compensation."

The Fourteenth Amendment to the U.S. Constitution states: "Section 1... No State shall make or enforce any law which shall abridge the privileges or immunities of citizens of the United States; nor shall any State deprive any person of life, liberty, or property without due process of law; nor deny to any person within it jurisdiction the equal protection of the law."

The Fifth Amendment prohibition applies to the Federal Government and the Fourteenth applies to the states. These protections guarantee to a person the right not to be deprived of his life, liberty or property without due process of law. Simply stated due process means the law of the land, that is, according to settled usage and mode of proceeding. As long as the law preserves the fundamental rights of a person according to the law of the land, the novelty of the law does not invalidate it.

An example of the application of the legal concept of due process is found in the case, Construction Industry v. Petaluma. 42/ In this case the Court held that a city ordinance that limits issuance of new building permits to achieve a goal of preserving "small town" character, open spaces and low density population does not violate the due process clause of the Fourteenth Amendment. The Court's opinion explained that zoning regulations must find their justification in some aspect of the police power asserted for the public welfare to satisfy the due process mandate. The Court found that the concept of the public welfare is sufficiently broad to uphold Petaluma's desire to preserve its small town character, open spaces and low density population.

The due process argument was used against the beverage container ordinance of the City of Bowie, Maryland. 43/ The Court ruled that there was not a violation of due process because there was not a showing that the police power was exercised arbitrarily, oppressively or unreasonably. The opinion also reasoned that a law should not be held void, if there are any considerations relating to the public welfare by which it can be supported.

8.2.4 Police Power and Due Process

Police power is the inherent right of a government to pass laws for the protection of the health, welfare, morals, and property of the people within its jurisdiction. In a sense, police power is but another name for the power of the government. Police power may not be bartered away by contract. It extends to all public needs. It may be put forth in the aid of what is sanctioned by usage or held by prevailing opinion to be greatly or immediately necessary for public welfare. By the exercise of reasonable police power, a government may regulate the conduct of individuals and of the use of their property and, in some instances, take property without compensation.

Although the police power of a state is very broad, it is not without limitation. It is always within the power of the court to

---

42/   8 ERC 1001 (9th Cir. 1975).

43/   Bowie Inn v. City of Bowie, 7 ERC 2083 (1975).

declare a law void which, although enacted as a police regulation, is not justified as such. In other words, a law enacted as a police regulation must be reasonable. If the law is unreasonable or exercised in an arbitrary manner, it is taking life, liberty, or property without due process of law.

Two examples of the allowable exercise of police powers are given in Section 8.2.3.

Another example of the valid exercise of police power which did not violate the due process principle was in the Supreme Court case, Village of Belle Terre v. Borass. 44/ In this case a New York village ordinance restricted land use to one-family houses and precluded occupancy by more than two unrelated persons. The Court held this ordinance to be a valid exercise of the city's police power, stating:

> A quiet place where yards are wide, people few, and motor vehicles restricted are legitimate guidelines in a land use project addressed to family needs. The police power is not confined to elimination of filth, stench, and unhealthy places. It is ample to lay out zones where family values, youth values, and the blessings of quiet seclusion and clean air make the area a sanctuary for people.

8.2.5 Prohibition Against Taking Property Without Compensation

The Fifth Amendment to the Constitution states that ". . . nor shall private property be taken for public use, without just compensation."

Despite numerous court opinions on this issue, the line between "takings" which require compensation and valid exercise of the "police power" which do not require compensation has never been clearly drawn. It is difficult to predict the outcome when the principles in this area are applied to factual situations. 45/

It may be said that the state takes property by eminent domain because it is useful to the public. This taking requires compensation. When the state takes property because it is harmful, it is done under the police power and does not require compensation. What is useful to one person may be harmful to another. So,

---

44/   416 U.S. 1 (1974).

45/   In July 1973, the Council on Environmental Quality in Washington, D.C., published a study entitled, "The Taking Issue," which is an analysis of the constitutional limits of land use control for those interested in a detailed analysis of this area of the law.

the perspective of all the conditions and circumstances is often the determining factor in choosing between useful and harmful.

The problem often comes down to one of degree. In both circumstances damages result. If the damage is suffered by many similarly situated and is in the nature of a restriction on use and ought to be borne by the individual as a member of society for the good of the public, it is a reasonable exercise of the police power not requiring compensation. However, if the damage is so great to the individual that he ought not to bear it under contemporary standards, then courts are inclined to treat it as a "taking" or unreasonable exercise of police power requiring compensation.

This taking issue has been in the forefront of noteworthy litigation. One important case involved the denial of operational drilling permits in the Santa Barbara Channel and was entitled Union Oil v. Morton. 46/ In this case the Court reviewed the question of the degree to which the government may interfere with the enjoyment of private property by exercise of its police power without having to pay compensation and concluded that there was not a simple answer to this question. The courts under a variety of tests have recognized that regulation of private property can become so onerous that it amounts to a taking of that property. The Court in this case held that a permanent unconditional suspension of permits to install drilling platforms is a taking that requires compensation or violates the Fifth Amendment.

A series of cases have held that airport noise can constitute a taking of property rights. In the landmark case of United States v. Causby, 47/ the Supreme Court held that frequent low flights over the Causby's land by military aircraft landing at a nearby airport operated by the United States constituted a taking of the Causby's property without compensation in violation of the Fifth Amendment of the U.S. Constitution. The noise from the aircraft rendered it impossible to continue the use of the property as a commercial chicken farm. Although the flights did not completely destroy the enjoyment and use of the land, they were held to be so low and frequent as to constitute a direct and immediate interference with the full enjoyment of the land, limiting the utility of the land and causing a diminution in its value, and therefore constituted a taking under the Fifth Amendment.

46/   7 ERC 1587 (9th Cir. 1975).

47/   328 U.S. 256 (1946).

In another major Supreme Court decision on this issue, Griggs v. Allegheny County, 48/ the Court held that Allegheny County, which owned and operated the Greater Pittsburgh Airport, was liable for a taking of property under the Fifth Amendment where the noise from taking off and landing at the airport on flight paths over the Griggs' property rendered the property undesirable and unbearable for residential use. The Court saw no difference between the county's responsibility to pay for the land on which the runways were built and its responsibility for the air easements necessary for operation of the airport. The glide path for the northwest runway is as necessary for the operation of the airport as is a surface right-of-way, wrote the Court.

A Federal Circuit Court has narrowly interpreted Causby and Griggs to mean that there is not taking under the Fifth Amendment unless the aircraft invade the air space directly over the plaintiff's property and the property is rendered uninhabitable. 49/ However, several states have interpreted their own constitutions to require compensation under less strict circumstances when the noise from aircraft has diminished the market value of the homeowner's property. The interference must be substantial and sufficiently direct in the majority of jurisdictions.

8.2.6 Commerce Clause Limitations

The Constitution grants to Congress the authority ". . . to regulate Commerce with foreign Nations and among the several States and with the Indian Tribes." So, if state statutes or regulations are found by the courts to be an impermissible burden upon interstate commerce, then they are unconstitutional and unenforceable.

It is well settled that a state regulation validly based on the police power does not impermissibly burden interstate commerce where the regulations neither discriminate against interstate commerce nor operate to disrupt its required uniformity. Where there is a reasonable basis to protect the social, as distinguished from the economic, welfare of a community, the courts will not deny this exercise of sovereign power and hold it to violate the Commerce Clause.

An example of a Commerce Clause case involved a challenge against New Jersey's Waste Control Act. 50/ This law barred disposal within the state of solid waste originating or collected outside

---

48/   369 U.S. 84 (1962).

49/   7 ERC (9th Cir. 1975).

50/   City of Philadelphia v. New Jersey, 437 U.S. 617 (1978).

the state's territorial borders. The U.S. Supreme Court opinion held that this statute does violate the Commerce Clause of the U.S. Constitution.

The Supreme Court held that all objects of interstate trade merit Commerce Clause protection and none is excluded from the definition of "commerce" including "valueless" out-of-state wastes. The Court ruled that the New Jersey statute was basically an economic protectionist measure, and thus virtually per se invalid, and not a law directed at legitimate local concerns that had only incidental effects on interstate commerce.

Another Commerce Clause case involved the Chicago ordinance banning the sale of detergents containing phosphates. 51/ The Seventh Circuit Court of Appeals held that the ordinance did not violate the Commerce Clause because, although it had some minor effect on interstate commerce, the benefits far outweighed these effects and the ordinance was a reasonable method to achieve a legitimate goal of improving Lake Michigan.

A similar result favorable to the legislators was reached in Oregon when the constitutionality of the famous Oregon "bottle-bill" which in essence banned the sale of non-returnable beverage containers was upheld. 52/

The trend is definitely one of the courts trying to uphold environmental legislation with the rationale being based on a balancing of the equities, namely weighing the benefits against the detrimental effect.

8.2.7 Equal Protection of the Laws

Section 1 of the Fourteenth Amendment to the U.S. Constitution prohibits the states from denying to any person the equal protection of the laws.

Does a state noise law which exempts construction equipment where there is no exemption for mining equipment deny equal protection? The Illinois Supreme Court held no in a suit entitled Illinois Coal Operators Association v. Illinois Pollution Control Board. 53/

The courts generally hold that for a classification to violate the constitutional guarantee of equal protection, there must be a showing that there is no reasonable basis for the distinction. A law is presumptively valid. Unless clear and convincing proof demonstrates that a law is arbitrary and unreasonable, the law must be

---

51/ Procter and Gamble v. Chicago, 7 ERC 1328 (7th Cir. 1975).

52/ American Can Co. v. Oregon Liquor Control Commission, 517 P2d 691, 4 ERC 1584 (1973).

53/ 7 ERC 1315 (1974).

upheld. The result is that few laws are ever held to violate the
equal protection clause.

8.3 Constitutional Protection of the Environment

Three major claims have been proposed to protect the environment which are based on the U.S. Constitution.

The Ninth Amendment of the Constitution has been alleged to
include a right to protect the public from unreasonable environmental degradation. The Ninth Amendment states: "The enumer-
ation in the Constitution of certain rights, shall not be construed to
deny or disparage others retained by the people." The theory is that
one of these other retained rights is the protection of natural
resources or an environment free of pollution.

The other constitutional claims come under the general
heading of "due process" and are based on the due process requirements of the Fifth and Fourteenth Amendments.

In the case of Hagedorn v. Union Carbide, 54/ the plaintiffs
who were residents of the county in which a Union Carbide plant was
located, complained about alleged air pollution from Union Carbide's
plant which:

> "deprived them of the following rights guaranteed by
> the Constitution:
> '(A) The right to breathe clean air and live in a decent
> environment including the fundamental human right of
> survival granted and protected by the Ninth Amend-
> ment.
> '(B) The right to their life, health and property and to
> full use and enjoyment thereof granted and protected by
> the Fifth Amendment.' "

The Court in its opinion held:

> "These and similar claims have been widely advanced
> but regularly rejected by the Federal courts. Indeed,
> the Fourth Circuit in Ely v. Velde, 451 F2d 1130 (3 ERC
> 1280) (1971), emphatically declined...to elevate to a
> constitutional level the claimed right to be protected
> from unnecessary and unreasonable environmental
> degradation and destruction. While a growing number of
> commentators argue in support of a constitutional
> protection for the environment, this newly-advanced
> constitutional doctrine has not yet been accorded judi-
> cial sanction...

54/   5 ERC 1755, 363 F. Supp. 1061 (N.D. W.Va. 1973).

This Court considers itself bonded by the clear language of Ely v. Velde, which is buttressed by the heavy weight of the emerging case law."

In another case entitled Environmental Defense Fund v. Corps of Engineers of the U.S. Army, 55/ the plaintiffs, in seeking to enjoin the damming of an Arkansas river, relied upon the Fifth, Ninth and Fourteenth Amendments. The Court declared that it was not within the province of a district court to bestow Constitutional protection to the environment.

"Those who would attempt to protect the environment through the courts are striving mightily to carve out a mandate from the existing provisions of our Constitution...such claims, even under our present Constitution, are not fanciful and may, indeed, some day, in one way or another, obtain judicial recognition. But, as stated by Judge Learned Hand in Spector Motor Service, Inc. v. Walsh, 139 F2d 809 (2 Cir. 1944): 'Nor is it desirable for a lower court to embrace the exhilarating opportunity of anticipating a doctrine which may be in the womb of time, but whose birth is distant.'

"The Ninth Amendment may well be as important in the development of constitutional law during the remainder of this century as the Fourteenth Amendment has been since the begining of the century. But the Court concludes that the plaintiffs have not stated facts which would under the present state of the law constitute a violation of their constitutional rights..."

In Tanner v. Armco Steel Corporation, 56/ the plaintiff-family alleged specific injuries from air pollutants from defendants' petroleum refineries and plants. The husband claimed that the pollution caused him pulmonary damage with consequent medical expense and loss of income. Damage to plaintiffs' homestead and lands was also alleged. The plaintiffs, the Tanners, sought relief under the Fifth, Ninth and Fourteenth Amendments. The Courts, however rejected the Constitutional claims, holding that:

"No legally enforceable right to healthful environment, giving rise to an action for damages, is guaranteed by

---

55/   2 ERC 1260, 325 F. Supp. 726 (E.D. Ark. 1971).

56/   3 ERC 1968, 340 F. Supp. 532 (S.D. Tex. 1972).

the Fourteenth Amendment or any other provision of
the Federal Constitution. As the United States Supreme
Court recently observed in rejecting a similarly imaginative constitutional claim, 'the Constitution does not
provide judicial remedies for every social and economic
ill. Lindsey v. Normet, 405 U.S. 56, 92 S. Ct. 862, 31 L.
Ed. 2d 36 (1972)."

These opinions clearly document the position of the courts
today that the Fifth, Ninth and Fourteenth Amendments of the U.S.
Constitution do not currently include these enforceable environmental rights.

9.0 Defenses

9.1 Generally
Some of the defenses available against civil lawsuits have
already been considered under the discussions of nuisance and negligence. Others not previously covered are considered in this section.
Generally, it is not a defense to an action for pollution that
the defendant was not negligent; nor that he used due care; nor that
his method of operation was customary.
Some courts have taken into consideration the relative importance of the interests of the parties and have refused to abate
pollution or to grant an injunction against a plant but have relegated
the plaintiff to an action for damages. 57/ This approach is based on
the concept that closing a plant could cause more harm than good.
The question of how far individual rights must yield to the
public good is a complex issue. Some courts have held that an
injunction will be granted to restrain pollution without regard to the
magnitude of the interest enjoined.
Stanley W. Schroeder in his article, "Pollution in Perspective"
for The Natural Resources Lawyer, 58/ sounds a note of concern
regarding defenses when he states:

"Not only in the pollution field, but in other social areas
there appears to be an effort to shift the basis of liability away from the traditional concept of the nature
of the wrong committed toward a concern for the
nature of the harm done. Under the common law,
whether one had a cause of action was a question of

57/   61 Am. Jur. 2d 977.

58/   Schroeder, Stanley E. "Pollution in Perspective," The Natural
Resources Lawyer, Vol. IV, No. 2, 381 (Apr. 1971).

whether 'duty owed' by the wrong-doer had been established. Today, not only is the duty expanded by strict and far-reaching statutory or regulatory standards, but as the Court said in Westchester Homeowners v. Los Angeles, 'The test of liability is coming to be the reasonable expectation of the person injured by the act of another to be free from such injury. The status and relationship of the parties have become important considerations in determinining liability.'

"Carried to their logical conclusion these trends would make futile any hope of a defense. The situation would be tantamount to strict liability, which, although helpful to aggrieved parties will certainly facilitate claims; if monitoring devices remove the questions of wrong from the case the only issues left would be causation and damages."

The current situation is a balancing of the equities involved or comparing the injuries between the parties involved in the lawsuit but the trend is definitely toward the strict liability concept.

9.2 Laches

The term "laches" is generally applied to describe the defense that is based on the failure of the plaintiff to do something which should have been done or to claim or enforce a right at a proper time. Generally, there are three criteria for the equitable doctrine of laches: (a) the defendant must show a delay in asserting a right or claim, (b) the delay was not excusable and (c) there was undue prejudice to the party against whom the claim is asserted.

The defense of laches was successfully used in the Michigan Supreme Court case Thompson v. Enz. 59/ In that case defendants had obtained formal approval for a lake-front development project from all locally concerned governmental agencies, and at least tacit approval from the state. The defendants made a substantial investment in initiating the project. After all of these efforts and investments by the defendants, the plaintiff initiated a lawsuit to stop the development. The Court ruled that the plaintiff would not be allowed to stop the completion of the project because of the defense of laches. The plaintiffs had allowed the defendants to proceed, and in the Court's opinion, they should have filed their lawsuit in the very beginning of the project. The Court indicated that it might have enjoined the project had it been promptly brought to its attention.

59/   2 ERC 1842, 188 N.W. 2nd 579.

Laches is determined in the light of all existing circumstances and requires, generally, that the delay be unreasonable. The mere lapse of time is not sufficient.

The equitable defense of laches should see increased service to put a reasonable time limit on efforts to obtain injunctions in environmental cases.

9.3 Contractual Authorization

The right to pollute the air or a stream may be acquired by grant or license as against the grantor or licensor. A case that is an example of this defense involved oil pollution in Texas. It was ruled in this case that a release given to an oil company by a rancher for all claims arising from the operation of the oil wells on his property barred recovery of damages by the rancher for harm caused by crude oil leaking onto his property. 60/

Some contract clauses go too far in waiving rights, and are then generally ruled void, as being against public policy. This rule of voidness would probably be applicable to many pollution cases because it could be shown as against public policy to contract away environmental rights.

9.4 Public Authorization

In some jurisdictions, legislative authorization of the cause of the pollution might be a defense against liability. There is authority, that a cause of action for abatement of a public nuisance does not arise, if the plant or establishment causing the pollution has legislative or administrative approval. 61/

A legislative license to create a nuisance by pollution must be given in express terms or by necessary implications. A private nuisance may arise, even though the facility has legislative sanction.

However, authority to build sewers is not authority to pollute a stream. Also, the legislature has no power to authorize the taking of property by pollution without just compensation.

9.5 Vagueness

One defense attempted against new statutory and regulatory prescriptions has been to attack them on the grounds of vagueness. However, the courts have not been responsive to this argument in pollution cases.

60/   Jackson v. Marathon Oil Co., 2 ERC 1533, 441 F.2d 511 (5th Cir. 1971).

61/   61 Am. Jr. 2d 983.

In Houston Compressed Steel v. Texas, 62/ the Texas Clean Air Act's broad definition of "air pollution" was upheld by the Texas Court of Civil Appeals as not to be too vague to be employed against a scrap metal company that burned railroad boxcars outdoors. The opinion stated that "since the science of air pollution control is new and inexact, and these standards are difficult to devise, if they are to be effective, they must be broad." The Texas Court also felt that an air polluter should not escape the consequences of his act merely because he is able to make his contaminants difficult to measure or control.

In Air Commission v. Coated Materials, 63/ the Pennsylvania Air Pollution Control Act's definition of air pollution, as some substance "which unreasonably interferes with the comfortable enjoyment of life and property" was found to be uncertain, and was susceptible to acceptable standards of proof "since the language employed in the statute is equivalent to the definition of nuisance which is certainly established in the law."

Similarly, the Connecticut General Statutes were found not unconstitutionally vague when they required every motor vehicle to be so equipped and adjusted as to prevent excessive fumes or exhaust smoke, since any ordinary and interested person would have no difficulty in determining whether or not a motor vehicle put out offensive or excessive exhaust fumes. 64/

Based on a review of the current case law, the argument of vagueness as a potential defense does not appear to offer a probability for success.

9.6 Unreasonableness and Impossibility of Performance

The courts do consider the reasonableness of duties imposed by statutes, regulations, standards and even court orders. An example is found in Pennsylvania v. Pennsylvania Power, 65/ where the Court ruled that the regulations requiring compliance with Pennsylvania's sulfur dioxide emission standards were unreasonable because the technology adequate to meet the standards did not exist and the company acted in good faith.

62/   456 S.W. 2d 768 (1970)

63/   778 C.D. 1969 (Pa. Ct. Com. Pls. 1970).

64/   Connecticut v. Schuster's Express, 6 Conn. Cir. Ct. 108 (1970).

65/   6 ERC 1328. See also previous contempt litigation [5 ERC 1373] 301 A. 2d 280 (1973).

The Court stated:

"To impose sanctions on PPC in an attempt to force it to perform an impossible act would be both meaningless and unjust.

"It has been held that where the defendant cannot perform the duty ordered, and where that inability is not due to actions of the defendant himself that impossibility is a defense. F.T.C. v. Plaine, 308 F. Supp. 932 (N.D. Ga. 1970)."

The courts have held in other cases that rules and regulations must be reasonable before the courts will enforce them.

However, the availability of the defense of economic and technological infeasibility in cases arising under the Clean Air Act resulted in contrary or partially contrary decisions in the Federal Circuit Courts. So, the question was resolved by the Supreme Court. The question in issue was: Is technological or economic feasibility a defense against compliance with a State Implementation Plan (SIP) for air pollution control?

The U.S. Supreme Court in a landmark decision decided June 25, 1976 said no on this key issue but also provided some additional guidance in this area of the law. In the case of Union Electric Co. v. EPA 66/ Mr. Justice Marshall writing for a unanimous Court said:

"After reviewing the relevant provision of the Clean Air Act Amendments of 1970 and their legislative history, we agree that Congress intended claims of economic and technological infeasibility to be wholly foreign to the Administrator's consideration of a state implementation plan.

"These requirements are of a technology-forcing character and are expressly designed to force regulated sources to develop pollution control devices that might at the time appear to be economically or technologically infeasible.

"This approach is apparent on the face of §110(a)(2). The provision sets out eight criteria that an implementation plan must satisfy, and provides that if these criteria are met and if the plan was adopted after reasonable notice and hearing, the Administrator 'shall approve' the proposed state plan. The mandatory 'shall' makes it quite clear that the Administrator is not to be concerned with factors other than those specified, and

---

66/   8 ERC 2143 (U.S. Sup. Ct. 1976).

none of the eight factors appears to permit consideration of technological or economic infeasibility."

However, the opinion continues by setting forth that claims
of infeasibility can be relevant. This infeasibility issue should be
raised before the particular state agency while formulating the
SIP. If the industry is not exempted in the original plan, then a
variance may be submitted as a revision to the SIP. An industry
denied exemption may take its claims of infeasibility to the state
courts. Also, a state governor may request an extension or postponement based on infeasibility grounds. Finally, claims of technological or economic feasibility are relevant to fashioning an
appropriate compliance order between EPA and the operator in
controversies arising under the Clean Air Act.

10.0 Parties
Parties to a lawsuit are classified as nominal, necessary and
indispensable. Nominal parties are those who have some interest in
the subject matter of the suit but are not affected by the judgment. Necessary parties are those who may be indirectly affected
by the judgment and should be made parties (if they can be served
with a subpoena to appear in court) but whose interests are separate
from the others. Indispensable parties are those without whom the
court cannot enter a valid judgment. Indispensable parties must be
joined in the suit and must be served with process.

10.1 Standing, or Who May Sue
One of the most basic questions regarding parties that is
normally asked is who may sue or in "lawyerese," the question of
which parties have "standing" to file a lawsuit. This question was in
the forefront of early environmental litigation.
Standing, strictly speaking, differs from who may sue. Theoretically speaking, anyone who has the fee to pay for filing a lawsuit
may initiate a lawsuit. Where a party has a sufficient interest in a
controversy to obtain judicial resolution of the controversy is what
is traditionally referred to as the question of "standing to sue."
The general rule of law under the Administrative Procedure
Act is that standing exists only when a plaintiff can satisfactorily
demonstrate that (a) the agency action complained of will result in
an injury in fact and that (b) the injury is to an interest "arguably
within the zone of interests to be protected" by the statute in question.
The leading cases addressing the "injury in fact" question are
cases involving the National Environmental Policy Act and environmental impact statements. The key case is the Supreme Court

decision in Sierra Club v. Morton. 67/ This case involved the recreational development of the Mineral King Valley. The question in
Sierra v. Morton was, what must be alleged by persons who claim
injury of a non-economic nature to widely shared interests to give
them standing. The Court recognized that environmental well-
being, like economic well-being, is an important ingredient of our
society. The fact that environmental interests are shared by the
many rather than few does not make them less deserving of legal
protection. But the "injury in fact" test, according to the Court,
requires that the party seeking review be himself among the injured. The Sierra Club did not allege and show that it or its
members would be affected in any of their activities or pastimes by
the development. So, the Court ruled against them. However, this
has since proven to be an easy matter to remedy, by the plaintiffs
alleging that an aesthetic or other non-economic interest was
injured. So, the Sierra Club established in this case decision that
environmental interests could be the basis for standing. This was a
major development in the law.

In a subsequent Supreme Court case, SCRAP v. U.S., 68/ the
Supreme Court gave some law students standing to sue the I.C.C. in
a rate increase case involving recyclables. The Supreme Court ruled
that standing to sue was demonstrated by the students, showing that
they used the forest and streams in the Washington, D.C. area for
camping and hiking and that this was disturbed by the adverse environmental impact, caused by the nonuse of recyclable goods, brought
on by the I.C.C. rate increase on recyclable commodities.

The rule appears now that injury to a non-economic interest
such as scenery, natural and historic objects and wildlife is a sufficient injury in fact to be a basis for a suit by a person or group who
will suffer the injury directly. This covers a broad range of potential plaintiffs and cases. As a result the issue regarding standing has
now shifted from the "injury in fact" question to the "zone of interests to be protected" by the statute involved in the litigation.

Citizens are given standing or access to the Federal Courts
explicitly in the Federal Water Pollution Control Act, the Clean Air
Act, the Noise Act, and many other statutes. This question of
standing is only relevant when statutory authority is not available.

10.2 Class Actions

Since many environmental lawsuits are brought as class
actions, the basis for these is set forth in this section.

67/   3 ERC 2039, 405 U.S. 345 (1972).

68/   412 U.S. 669 (1974).

One or more members of a class may sue or be sued as representative parties on behalf of all, only if, as a general rule:

1. The class is so numerous that a uniting in the pleadings of all members is impractical.
2. There are questions of law, or fact, common to the class.
3. The claims or defenses of the representative parties are typical of the claims or defenses of the class.
4. The representative parties will fairly and adequately protect the interests of the class.

In a true class suit, plaintiffs stand in judgment for the class. A judgment for or against the plaintiffs benefits or binds each member of the class personally under the principles of res judicata. The members of the class must, therefore, be capable of definite identification, as being either in or out of the class.

11.0 Evidence

Evidence is the legal means, exclusive of arguments, for proving or disproving any <u>fact</u>, the truth of which is submitted to investigation. Since evidence is so critical to many issues in the environmental field, some key points of interest will be presented in the following sections. Evidence is an extremely complex area of the law. So, this is intended only as a brief review to give non-lawyers some basic concepts.

Please note that the law of evidence is known for its exceptions to general rules.

11.1 Burden of Proof

In the law of evidence, the phrase burden of proof is used to denote the duty of affirmatively proving the facts in dispute on an issue raised between the parties.

This burden of proof rests throughout the trial, upon the party asserting the affirmative of the issue.

The burden of proof is generally distinguished from the burden of proceeding. The duty of proceeding with a case is called the burden of proceeding, and shifts between the plaintiff and defendant during the trial.

11.2 Judicial Notice

As a general rule, a party must prove everything he alleges. The exceptions to this general rule are (1) things admitted in the pleadings, (2) things stipulated by the parties, or (3) judicial notice.

Judicial notice means that the court will take cognizance of certain facts without requiring proof. An example of judicial notice is that January 9, 1983 is a Sunday. Many facts of common indisputable knowledge need not be proven by evidence because the courts take judicial notice of this information so as not to waste time.

11.3 Presumptions
A presumption is a conclusion, which is drawn from other facts already proved. Presumptions are either (1) conclusive - which are rules of law and may not be rebutted or (2) rebuttable - presumptions which can be overcome by evidence.

11.4 Admissions
An admission is a voluntary acknowledgement of the existence of or the truth of certain facts. An admission will be recognized in court, if made by an employee against an employer within the scope of employment. As a general rule, an admission made by a party to a suit is admissible no matter when or where made. One exception to this general rule is when the admission is made in an offer to compromise. An admission made during a telephone conversation may be admissible if there is collaborating testimony or evidence.
An admisson of guilt in a criminal case is a confession.

11.5 Questions Of Law and Fact
Questions arising during the course of a trial are either: questions of law or questions of fact. Generally, questions of law are decided by the court. Questions of fact are decided by a jury. One exception to that division of duties is whether a witness is an expert, which is determined by the court.

11.6 Relevant and Material
Two of the most commonly used words in the area of evidence are relevant and material. The facts or testimony presented in court must be relevant and material to the issue in question, or these irrelevant and immaterial facts or testimony are subject to exclusion. Whether the facts or testimony are relevant and material is a question of law, and so these are decided by the judge.

11.7 Res Inter Alios Acta
The Latin phrase res inter alios acta is used to denote the general rule that prior acts of a defendant or subsequent acts of precaution are not admitted in evidence, because they tend to multiply the issues or may be unfairly prejudical. There are a number of exceptions which have severely eroded this general rule.

11.8 Hearsay
Hearsay is that evidence which depends solely for its truth or falsity upon statements of a person other than the witness. Hearsay, in itself, has no evidentiary value. The witness cannot be cross-

examined regarding hearsay, because the statements are those of
another. Generally, hearsay is inadmissible, but there are numerous
exceptions. An interesting example of inadmissible hearsay is found
in the case Bebbington v. California Western States Life Insurance
Company. 69/ In this case the suit was brought by the beneficiary of
a life insurance policy against the insurance company (defendant).
The policy provided that it was void, if the insured died in a plane
crash. The insurance company in trying to prove that the decedent
died in a plane crash, introduced a letter from a friend of the
deceased, a telegram of condolence, and a newspaper clipping each
telling of the plane accident. The Court ruled that these were all
written hearsay, and so inadmissible. (The insurance company should
have proved the accident by an eyewitness or official records).

Usually in the case of documents, a statute provides for an
official custodian or witness who will certify to their authenticity or
validity to overcome the hearsay objection.

11.9 Opinion Evidence

Generally, the testimony of a witness is confined to a statement of concrete facts based upon his own observation or
knowledge. Expert opinion evidence is admissible when it concerns
scientific or technical knowledge. Non-expert witnesses may be
asked to express an opinion to help understand what was observed,
but conjecture is not admissible. The problem with experts is that
you can generally find one on either side of a case. For example the
prosecutor will have his psychiatrist testify that the defendant is
sane while the defendant's psychiatrist is testfying he is insane.

11.10 Best Evidence Rule

The "best evidence rule" simply states that unless a sufficient
reason is given, proof of the contents of a writing must be made by
producing the original evidence, or at least a certified copy of the
original. The best evidence possible must be submitted to the court,
or the evidence is inadmissible.

11.11 Parol Evidence Rule

The general rule is that parol (oral) evidence is not admissible
to vary, add to, take away from or contradict the terms of a written
instrument. There are exceptions, such as explaining an ambiguity,
showing a condition precedent, showing fraud and others.

11.12 Witnesses

Generally, all persons are competent to testify, but their
credibility can be attacked. Leading questions (ones which suggest

---

69/   30 Cal. 2d 157 (1947).

an answer), may generally only be asked of unwilling witnesses or adverse parties. A witness must answer all questions asked, which will provide information on the issue under investigation – unless this testimony may subject the witness to criminal prosecution. The opposing party has a right to cross-examine the witness. If the witness refuses to answer a question on cross-examination, his entire testimony may be expunged from the record. Generally, cross-examinations are limited to facts, on which a witness testified during direct examination.

11.13 Privileged Communications

Privilege is an exception to the rule that the public has the right to know every man's evidence. The reason for the exception is public policy.

At common law there was privilege only between an attorney and client, but by statutes and judicial decisions this has been extended to others such as physician and patient, clergy and laymen.

In environmental lawsuits, the concern is with the attorney-client relationship. It is the duty of a lawyer to preserve his client's confidences. This duty outlasts the lawyer's employment.

Nicholas A. Robinson, a New York City attorney, in a presentation before the International Pollution Engineering Congress stated an interesting concept regarding the use of privileged communications by industry:

"If a company does not know exactly the nature, volume, frequency, and sources of its emissions, it should find out. And since such knowledge may reveal that the company is in violation of different laws, it should be careful how it finds out. A company may wish to use the 'attorney-client privilege' to learn such facts without fear that they will fall into the hands of prosecutors or other plaintiffs.

"The attorney-client privilege in law provides such protection. If a company, as client, seeks advice on pollution liability from an attorney, that attorney can hire experts or consultants to run tests and determine the facts about the company's pollution. He can then evaluate the legal consequence of these facts and advise the company. Courts have held such investigative findings and legal analysis must be kept secret from both government and private parties. [See e.g., Radiant Burners, Inc. v. Am. Gas Corp., 320 F 2d 314 (7th Cir. 1963) and D. Simon, 'The Attorney-Client Privileges As Applied to Corporations,' 65 Yale Law Journal, 953 (1956).] If the company hired the experts on its own, there would be usually no way to prevent a prosecutor or a private plaintiff from obtaining the data. Only

when the facts are known can a company prepare for
and avoid liability."

11.14 Your Own Reports as Evidence Against You
Many of the new laws and regulations require reports or data
to be filed with the government. The laws governing occupational
health, waste and air pollution all require reports. Even the reports
to the Securities and Exchange Commission require disclosure of
information on pollution. Most of these reports are available to the
public and to competitors.

The extent to which the results of an investigation or inspection are available in private liability litigation remains uncertain. A
corporation is not protected by the Fourth and Fifth Amendments to
the Constitution. It may not object to the production of its books to
be used as evidence against it. 70/

11.15 Samples or Physical Evidence
One of the common evidentiary problems raised in court
cases is that involving physical evidence. In environmental cases the
evidence is often a sample or some data. Some of the key issues
normally involved with physical evidence are: (1) has the evidence
or data been altered or contaminated, (2) was the equipment used in
evidence collection properly calibrated, (3) were scientifically
acceptable and standard methods of analysis used in evaluation and
(4) who has handled the evidence (chain of custody)?

In order to lay a proper foundation for the admission of
evidence, an attorney should be able to present the principals in the
"chain of custody" to testify as to their involvement and appropriate
expertise in the proper handling of the evidence. The courts will
frequently require the parties to stipulate as to the authenticity of
the evidence to avoid this tedious form of proof. In legal terminology, "to stipulate" is to agree initially on conduct or evidence for
the purpose of shortening the legal proceedings.

11.16 Evidence Collection and Constitutional Rights
A problem that may arise in the collection of evidence concerns the Fourth Amendment or Constitutional rights of corporate
entities and private persons.

The Fourth Amendment to the U.S. Constitution prohibits all
unreasonable searches and requires a search warrant for most investigations.   However, no search warrant is needed in three basic
situations: (1) when there is an emergency, (2) when the owner or
operator gives his consent, or (3) when the samples could be taken

---

70/   Essgee Co. v. U.S., 262 U.S. 151.

from outside of the property (open fields exception). Search warrants are described in detail in Section 8.2.1.

In most states, search warrants are used for searches for the implements or fruits of a crime and not for mere investigation of conditions which may lead to either civil or criminal penalties. A few states authorize a special kind of search warrant, sometimes called an inspection warrant, which may be used to investigate conditions.

The Fifth Amendment prohibition against criminal self-incrimination was described earlier in Section 8.2.2. In evidence collection involving criminal charges against private parties, this Fifth Amendment right must be properly observed or the courts will not allow evidence to be introduced in the case. The Fifth Amendment protections apply only to private persons and not corporations or partnerships.

12.0 Administrative Law

12.1 Generally

Governments are customarily divided into executive, legislative and judicial branches. The executive branches function through a system of administrative agencies. These are the governmental officials with whom environmental managers are in the most contact on a regular basis. The operations of these administrative agencies are regulated by the field of administrative law. We will briefly identify some major points in administrative law which may be of interest to environmental managers.

12.2 Powers of Governmental Agencies

Rules, regulations and general orders promulgated by an administrative agency, pursuant to its delegated powers, have the force and effect of law. They are binding on all persons subject to them without notice, and the courts take judicial notice of them. However, the power to promulgate regulations is not a power to change the law.

In order for a regulation to be the basis of a crime, it is necessary that sufficient statutory authority exists for declaring any act or omission a criminal offense. A breach of a departmental regulation is not a crime, unless made so by the legislature. Regulations prescribed by the President of the United States and heads of departments, under authority granted by Congress, may be regulations prescribed by law. However, it does not follow that an act or omission constitutes a criminal offense when the statute does not make it so. An administrative agency may not provide for penalties or criminal liability unless specifically provided by statute.

An administrative agency has limited jurisdiction, depending entirely on that given to it by the statute.

12.3 Procedures

The procedures to be followed before an administrative agency are usually prescribed by the statute creating the agency. If the statute fails to prescribe the procedure, then the fundamental principle is that the regulations must preserve the requirements of fair play.

In general, an administrative agency is not bound by the technical or formal rules of procedure which govern trials before a court. While the constitutional guaranty of due process of law applies to an administrative agency as well as a court, due process is not necessarily judicial process. All the formalities of a judicial proceeding are not essential to constitute due process of law in an administrative proceeding. Neither the Fifth Amendment nor the Fourteenth Amendment of the Federal Constitution guarantee any particular form of procedure. In administrative proceedings due process signifies a right to be heard before a final order becomes effective.

It is not within the power of any tribunal to make a binding adjudication of the rights of any party not brought before it. Consequently, a party is entitled to notice, when a constitutional right is in question, and sufficient time to enable him to prepare a defense.

As in a judicial proceeding, notice by publication may be prescribed by statute and will sustain the jurisdiction. Consequently, it is generally held that a corporation doing business in a state, even though it has not applied for permission to do business in the state, consents to abide by the state laws, including service of notice in a proceeding before an administrative body.

12.4 Evidence in Administrative Law

As a general rule, an administrative agency is not bound by the strict rules of evidence, which must be observed in the trial of cases in courts of law. However, unless a statute provides rules of evidence for the agency, the latter, in the exercise of its quasi-judicial powers, must provide rules of evidence which preserve fair play, such as the right of cross-examination of witnesses and the right to subpoena witnesses and documents. But the mere fact that certain evidence which would be inadmissible in a court of law is admitted at a hearing before an administrative agency does not invalidate such administrative proceedings.

Under the Administrative Procedure Act, 71/ generally hearsay evidence is admissible, but no order can issue, unless it is supported by and in accordance with reliable, probative, and substantive evidence.

71/   5 U.S.C. §§ 551 et seq.

12.5 Hearings

Not every administrative determination for private individuals requires notice and hearing. In order to comply with due process, notice and hearing are required only when some constitutional right is claimed to have been violated.

When the purpose of an administrative determination is to decide whether a right or privilege, which a person does not have, shall be granted or withheld in the exercise of its discretion, it is not necessary to have a notice and hearing in the absence of a statutory provision.

The constitutional guarantee of a trial by jury does not apply to an administrative hearing. Determination of facts may be left to an administrative tribunal. It is common practice to have testimony taken before an examiner, who reports the facts to the tribunal. Exceptions may be taken to the report, and argument may be had before the deciding body. The recommendation in the report is not binding on the determining body, if it is charged with the duty of making final decisions.

12.6 Judicial Review

What decisions an administrative agency makes depends on the statute. It is common for a Federal agency to have the power to issue a cease and desist order, and in many instances an agency has the power to take affirmative action. An administrative order cannot be enforced in a court without an express provision in the statute.

Generally, before a person is able to have a court review an administrative action, he must exhaust all his administrative remedies because courts are normally reluctant to interfere with administrative action before it is completed. Once the administrative remedies have been exhausted, then the matter is considered "ripe" for judicial review.

Theoretically, the courts will not review the facts in the case but limit themselves to questions of law, or whether there has been abuse of authority and disregard of due process.

Recent cases are worthy of examination because basic concepts are being challenged in this area of administrative law as the trend develops for the courts to interject themselves more and more into examining the operation of administrative agencies.

In one case the manufacture of a mercury fungicide (use of which was ordered suspended by the Secretary of Agriculture, based on a single abnormal incident without a hearing), was reviewed by a Federal District Court. The review was undertaken by the Court based on the argument that the agency order was arbitrary and

capricious since there was only one incident and a hearing was not
held by the Department of Agriculture. 72/

On the state level in a case before the Pennsylvania Court of
Common Pleas of Dauphin County, there was a challenge of the
findings of the Pennsylvania Air Pollution Commission that a coil
coating plant emitted odorous gases in violation of the state Air
Pollution Control Act. The Court said that it could not modify the
finding on the ground of credibility of evidence. 73/ The Court said
it only considered whether the Air Pollution Commission was arbitrary, and left credibility of the evidence to the Commission. This
limited review is the usual approach taken by a court when considering an appeal from an administrative agency.

In the case of the Environmental Defense Fund v. Hardin, 74/
the Secretary of Agriculture's failure to act promptly on a conservation group's request for interim suspension of the registration of a
pesticide to protect the public from an "imminent hazard" was held
by the U.S. Court of Appeals for D.C. to be tantamount to an order
denying suspension and was, therefore, ripe for judicial review. The
Court held that even a temporary refusal results in irreparable
injury on a massive scale, and is thus a final disposition of such
rights as plaintiffs and the public may have to interim relief. In a
subsequent court action on the same controversy the Court's opinion
was critical of the handling of the case by the Department of Agriculture. The Court stated that for years courts have "treated
administrative policy decisions with great deference," but they no
longer will "bow to the mysteries of administrative expertise." One
judge disagreed and wrote a dissenting opinion charging that "the
Court is undertaking to manage the Department of Agriculture."
These majority and dissenting comments show two views on review
by the courts of administrative decisions.

If you are involved in a dispute with an administrative
agency, usually you must exhaust all available administrative remedies before you can initiate court action.

Generally, in the judicial review process, the courts first
determine whether or not the agency acted within the scope of its
authority. If this question is answered in the affirmative, then there
must be a finding whether the choice made was arbitrary, capricious
or not in accordance with law. The standard of review then becomes

---

72/ Nor-Am Agricultural Products, Inc., v. Hardin, 435 F2d 1133
(7th Cir. 1970).

73/ Air Commission v. Coated Materials, 778 C.D. 1969 (Pa. Ct.
Comm. Pls. 1970).

74/ 428 F. 2d 1093 (1970).

a determination whether the decision was based on a consideration of the relevant factors and whether there has been a clear error of judgment. The courts are not empowered to substitute their judgment for that of the agency.

13.0 Attorneys' Fees – New Concepts

One of the basic traditions of who pays the lawyers has been significantly modified in recent years. This trend is worthy of description in this book because the award of these fees may be a significant factor in an environmental lawsuit.

Generally, under the so-called "American Rule" the winning party in a lawsuit is awarded costs but these costs do not include attorneys' fees. The result is that each party normally is responsible for their respective attorneys' fees.

Several statutes have created exceptions to this rule by authorizing the award of attorneys' fees. These statutes include the Clean Air Act. Successful plaintiffs were awarded attorneys' fees in several environmental lawsuits during the past few years. The matter was becoming confused with various court interpretations of the law. However, the Supreme Court has spoken on the subject of award of attorneys' fees to clarify the situation. In Alyeska v. Wilderness Society, 75/ the Supreme Court ruled that in the absence of statutory authorization or an enforceable contract, litigants must pay their own attorneys' fees.

Congress while fully recognizing this general rule has made specific and explicit provisions for the allowance of attorneys' fees in some statutes. If a statutory provision is not involved, the courts generally will not order payment of attorney fees.

14.0 Criminal and Civil Liability

The environmental laws and regulations provide for a wide range of civil and criminal penalties for failure to comply.

Now, there is a quiet evolution taking place. The courts are no longer holding only a corporation liable under the statutes for a fine but are holding individuals personally liable in their corporate roles.

The U.S. Supreme Court case of U.S. v. Park 76/ is a landmark case in this area. In this case the Court held that a corporate officer could be criminally liable under the Food, Drug and Cosmetic Act if he had the corporate authority and responsibility for preventing violations of the statute but failed to do so.

75/   7 ERC 1849 (U.S. Sup. Ct. 1975).

76/   421 U.S. 658 (1975).

Park, the president of Acme Markets, was convicted of violating the Federal Food, Drug, and Cosmetic Act. It states that "any person who violates a provision of [the Act] . . . shall be imprisoned for not more than one year or fined not more than $1,000, or both." Park was charged with causing interstate food shipments, being held for sale in an Acme Baltimore warehouse, to become adulterated by exposure to rat poison. Park had received notice that there was a violation in Acme's Baltimore warehouse. He had delegated responsibility for remedying the situation to some employees. The trial court was of the opinion that because he knew of a previous violation in a Philadelphia warehouse that had been ineffectively remedied and he had delegated responsiblity to the same people, his delegation in the Baltimore case (which also turned out to be ineffective) was not a sufficient attempt to remedy the problem. He was convicted on five counts.

The trial court judge said that Park could be found guilty "even if he did not consciously do wrong" and even if he had not "personally participated in the situation," if it were proved beyond a reasonable doubt that he "had a responsible relationship" to the situation.

Generally, criminal violation requires some element of conscious wrong-doing or some criminal intent. In this case the Supreme Court upheld Park's conviction based on his being the responsible corporate official. This means that corporate officers can be held legally liable for their subordinates' actions or inactions in a broad range of cases.

The Supreme Court noted that a finding of guilt cannot be based solely on the officer's position in the company. There should be some measure of "blameworthiness." The test which the Supreme Court used was that a corporate officer could be held criminally responsible if such officer had, "by reason of his position in the corporation, responsibility and authority either to prevent in the first instance, or promptly to correct, the violation complained of, and that he failed to do so." 77/

Criminal liability under other environmental laws is generally not as broad as under the Food, Drug and Cosmetic Act because the other laws use a term such as "knowing" before the proposed violation to require some willfulness or intent.

Another example of the new criminal liability trend is the criminal conspiracy indictments in the now famous Kepone incident.

Governmental officials are also subject to criminal indictment. The Watergate cases give a famous example of the highest government officials being convicted of crimes for their actions or inactions.

77/   Ibid. at 672.

Civil penalties are a definite deterrent but criminal penalties can literally destroy individuals from both a social and economic viewpoint.

In a speech before a bar association meeting 78/ James W. Moorman, Assistant Attorney General of the U.S. Department of Justice, stated the government's position on strict criminal enforcement against corporate officials in the environmental field:

"Many failures to comply have simply been the result of bumbling or ignorance. For this category of noncompliance, EPA and Justice have sought, and will continue to seek, civil remedies from the courts in the form of monetary penalties and injunctions.

"There is a second form of resistance, however, which involves more deplorable conduct: willful, substantial violations of the pollution control laws of a criminal nature. For these transgressions, the Department of Justice has begun to invoke grand jury investigations both against corporations and against individuals. The Department will prosecute criminal conduct in this areas.

"The Congress has signaled its intention that vigorous criminal enforcement occur by providing strict and stringent criminal statutes. Under the Water Act, "any person who wilfully or negligently" violates the conditions of a permit or who discharges without a permit is exposed to criminal liability for fines up to $25,000 per day and imprisonment up to 1 year. That is for a first offense. Further offenses are punishable by fines of $50,000 per day of violation and jail terms of up to 2 years. The making of false applications or reports under the act is punishable by a $10,000 fine and 6 months imprisonment. Under the Air Act, there are similar penalties for knowing violations of the requirements of the Act, for false statements and for tampering with monitoring equipment. Other pollution control laws governing pesticides, toxic substances, and so forth, likewise have criminal provisions.

"I also invite your attention to the fact that violations of pollution control laws can often be crimes under the more general provisions of the criminal code found in Title 18, Section 1001, which covers false

---

78/ Statement of James W. Moorman, Assistant Attorney General, Department of Justice. February 10, 1978 before ALI-ABA in Washington, D.C.

statements to government agencies, and Section 1341, the mail fraud statutes, are two examples of such provisions.

"It should be evident to all here that the price paid for criminal misconduct can be quite high. · Many of those who have chosen to violate or who will be tempted to violate the pollution control laws are professional and business people. These are people for whom an indictment alone, not to mention conviction or imprisonment, can be a catastrophe. As a consequence, I believe a policy of vigorous criminal enforcement will be truly effective as a deterrent and will result in a higher degree of pollution control."

These trends toward increased severity in punishment for violation of the law should make everyone more conscious of their legal and social duties.

Chapter 2

NATIONAL ENVIRONMENTAL POLICY ACT

Timothy A. Vanderver, Jr.
Attorney
Patton, Boggs & Blow
Washington, DC

1.0 Introduction

The National Environmental Policy Act of 1969 1/ commonly referred to as "NEPA," was signed into law by President Nixon on New Year's Day, 1970. NEPA is a short, general statute: it declares a national environmental policy and promotes consideration of environmental concerns by federal agencies. Despite its relative brevity and generality, however, NEPA is one of only a few statutes that have had a significant effect on the federal decisionmaking process.

In great measure, NEPA's disproportionate impact has resulted from the vast amount of litigation it precipitated. Indeed, NEPA may have led to more lawsuits than all our other environmental laws combined. Consequently, a large body of NEPA case law has been developed, fleshing out and giving specific force to NEPA's general provisions. In response, even recalcitrant federal agencies have incorporated NEPA requirements into their routine procedures, and the early flurry of NEPA litigation has abated. The Reagan Administration, however, is seeking to reduce NEPA's importance, and this undoubtedly will again increase the level of NEPA-related litigation. What ultimate effect this will have on the law of NEPA remains to be seen.

1/   Pub. L. No. 91-190, 42 USC §§ 4321-4347, as amended by Pub. L. No. 95-52 (July 3, 1975) (appropriations) and Pub. L. No. 94-83 (August 9, 1975) (delegation to States to prepare environmental impact statements in certain limited cases). For a discussion of the latter amendment, see Part 4.4.1 of this chapter.

2.0 Overview

NEPA is divided into two titles. Title I declares a national environmental policy and goals, provides a method for accomplishing those goals and includes some guidance on the fundamental question of how NEPA relates to other federal law. Title II creates the Council on Environmental Quality (CEQ) and defines its responsibilities.

2.1 Title I: Policy and Goals

The national environmental policy declared in Title I of NEPA is the first ever enacted by Congress. It announces a general commitment to "use all practicable means" to conduct federal activities in a way that will promote "the general welfare" and be in "harmony" with the environment. NEPA's six related goals are set with an eye toward assuring "safe, healthful, productive and esthetically and culturally pleasing surroundings" for all generations of Americans.

2.1.1 Enforceability of Title I Policy and Goals

An important practical question about the policy and goals embodied in NEPA is whether they create any enforceable "substantive rights." Although there was once a split of opinion in the U.S. Courts of Appeals on this question, two recent U.S. Supreme Court decisions have resolved that conflict.

In Vermont Yankee Nuclear Power Corp. v. NRDC, 2/ the Court found that although "NEPA does set forth significant substantive goals for the Nation, . . . its mandate to the agencies is essentially procedural." And in Strycker's Bay Neighborhood Council v. Karlen, 3/ the Court reversed a Second Circuit decision that looked to the provisions of NEPA for the substantive standards necessary to review the merits of agency decisions. In so doing, the Court ruled that:

> [O]nce an agency has made a decision subject to NEPA's procedural requirements, the only role for a court is to insure that the agency has considered the environmental consequences; it cannot "interject itself within the area of discretion of the executive as to the choice of action to be taken." 4/

2/   435 U.S. 519 (1978).

3/   444 U.S. 223 (1980).

4/   444 U.S. at 227 (Citations and footnote omitted).

Thus, the Supreme Court has twice held that the policy and goals set forth in Title I of NEPA create no judicially enforceable substantive rights, but impose only a procedural duty on federal agencies to consider NEPA's aims when making decisions. So, although federal agencies are free to exercise their decisionmaking discretion in ways that are consistent with NEPA's ends, NEPA does not require agencies to make decisions promoting the preservation or protection of the environment.

2.1.2 The Environmental Impact Statement

Because NEPA has been found to create no new substantive rights, NEPA's importance today stems almost entirely from its environmental impact statement (EIS) provisions—procedural provisions designed to insure that agencies do in fact consider the environmental consequences of federal actions before they are taken.

With few exceptions, NEPA requires every federal agency to prepare an EIS detailing the environmental impact of, and alternatives to, every proposal for a major federal action significantly affecting the quality of the human environment. A number of lawsuits have involved questions regarding the precise perimeters of this requirement, and federal courts have played a leading role in defining what constitutes compliance with it.

U.S. Courts of Appeals in each Circuit have addressed the question of what standard of judicial review should be used to determine whether agencies have met NEPA's requirements. The standard has been stated in various ways, and legalistic differences may exist, but the common thread running through the opinions is this: federal courts will take a "hard look" to determine: (1) whether the federal agency reached its decision after giving full, good faith consideration to environmental factors, and (2) whether the agency's decision was arbitrary or gave insufficient weight to those environmental factors. The courts will not, however, simply substitute their own judgment for those of the agencies.

Federal courts have also contributed significantly to striking a balanced relationship between NEPA requirements and those of other federal law.

2.2 Title II: Council on Environmental Quality

CEQ, established under Title II of NEPA, is charged with monitoring progress toward achieving our national environmental goals as set forth in Section 101 of NEPA. The specific statutory duties of CEQ are set out in Section 204 of NEPA. CEQ is to "assist and advise the President in the preparation of the Environmental Quality Report." Issues as broad as its title implies are addressed in this annual report, and an analysis of the need for any further legislation is specifically required to be included in it by Section 201. It is also the duty of CEQ to gather environmental information and to conduct studies on the conditions and trends in environmental quality. Moreover, CEQ is charged with developing and recommending to the President national policies and legislation to protect the environment.

The various members of the Council have worked diligently since its inception to solidify its role as the first and foremost advisor to the President on environmental policy. Although there are grounds for doubting the degree to which its advice was heeded and, indeed, even sought during the Nixon and Ford Administrations, CEQ played a much more significant role under President Carter. The Reagan Administration, however, through budget and staff cuts, has once again relegated the Council to an advisory role of little significance.

There has been a wide range of opinion concerning CEQ's performance. It has been lauded for its efforts, derided for being ineffective, chastised for failing to achieve its potential, and praised or criticized for intervening in decisionmaking processes when significant environmental impacts were involved. Although these views are certainly colored by the perspectives of their holders, there is no doubt that CEQ has performed unevenly in its advisory role.   It is nevertheless true that CEQ studies of particular environmental problems have sometimes been the forerunners to major changes or developments in policy and legislation.   Good examples are its reports on offshore drilling, toxic substances, and marine pollution.

In addition to its role as advisor to the President on environmental issues, CEQ has also been afforded the duty of providing guidance to other federal agencies on compliance with NEPA. Part 4.1 of this chapter discusses the way in which CEQ has discharged this duty.

3.0 How NEPA Relates to Other Federal Law

One of the most fundamental questions about NEPA concerns its relationship with other federal law.   More specifically, the question is this: What effect does NEPA have on other federal laws that govern the way federal agencies operate?

Although the Supreme Court has held that a final EIS need not be prepared until an agency makes a recommendation or report on a proposal, 5/ NEPA requires all federal agencies to consider environmental impacts at every important stage in the decisionmaking process. This requirement is not explicitly set forth in

---

5/   Aberdeen & Rockfish R.R. Co. v. Students Challenging Regulatory Agency Procedures (SCRAP II), 422 U.S. 289 (1975), reaffirmed in dicta in Kleppe v. Sierra Club, 427 U.S. 390 (1976).

NEPA, but it is implicit in its various provisions. And, it is a rule of law that received the best of imprimaturs by being announced in the early, yet still most definitive, judicial interpretation of NEPA— Calvert Cliffs' Coordinating Committee v. AEC. 6/

Calvert Cliffs' involved Atomic Energy Commission (AEC) rules implementing NEPA, which, in part, provided that if no party to a proceeding raised any environmental issue, environmental issues would not be considered in the decisionmaking process. In reviewing this rule, the U.S. Court of Appeals for the D.C. Circuit said, "We believe that the Commission's crabbed interpretation of NEPA makes a mockery of the Act," 7/ and proceeded to wonder out loud what possible purpose there could be in requiring an EIS to "accompany the proposal through the existing agency review process" or, indeed, in requiring EIS's at all, if agencies could simply ignore their contents. The Court then found that:

> [NEPA] requires[s] the . . . agencies to consider environmental issues just as they consider other matters within their mandate. 8/

Thus, Calvert Cliffs' added NEPA's environmental impact provisions to the decisionmaking criteria set forth in other federal law.

If NEPA requires agencies to consider environmental factors when making decisions, does NEPA then expand the authority of federal agencies beyond what is granted them under other federal law? There is no case holding that NEPA gives an agency any direct authority not otherwise afforded it by other federal law. NEPA, however, was clearly enacted in order to provide federal agencies with a new tool for protecting the environment, and the authority to deny agency approval of actions that would result in unacceptable environmental consequences is implicit in the requirement that agencies consider the environmental consequences of an action before deciding to proceed with it. Thus, an agency's authority does appear to be expanded under NEPA, for an agency might well decide not to proceed with an entire project because of environmental concerns that, but for NEPA, might be found to be beyond the agency's power to consider.

6/   449 F. 2d 1109 (D.C. Cir. 1971), cert. denied, 404 U.S. 942 (1972).

7/   449 F. 2d at 1117.

8/   449 F. 2d at 1112 (Emphasis supplied).

A related question is this: What happens when an agency believes, on the basis of an EIS or otherwise, that on balance it should grant its approval if certain conditions are satisfied, but the agency does not have the regular, i.e., non-NEPA based, statutory authority to impose such conditions. For example, the U.S. Environmental Protection Agency once conditioned a grant to Sussex County, Delaware for the construction of a sewage-treatment facility on the County's agreement to halt all rezoning plans (thus effectively blocking major planned construction) until a comprehensive land-use plan was completed. Did NEPA grant EPA the authority to lawfully withhold its approval until this condition was satisfied? The issue was never litigated. How far an agency can go in expanding its authority under the aegis of NEPA, then, remains an open question of considerable importance.

The third and final basic question in this regard is this: Does NEPA override another federal law when the two are in irreconcilable conflict? Sections 102(1), 103, 104 and 105 of NEPA all bear on this question. Section 102 "authorizes and directs that, to the fullest extent possible: (1) the policies, regulations, and public laws of the United States shall be interpreted and administered in accordance with the policies set forth in this Act." Section 103 required all federal agencies to recommend to the President by July 1, 1971, the changes necessary to bring their authority and policies into conformity with NEPA. 9/ Section 104 provides that nothing in Sections 102 or 103 changes the specific statutory obligations of any federal agency to comply with other laws protecting the environment, to coordinate or consult with other federal or state agencies, or to act in accordance with the recommendations or certifications of any other federal or state agency. Section 105 simply states that the policies and goals set forth in NEPA are "supplementary" to the existing authorizations of federal agencies. These are the statutory provisions upon which the Supreme Court has twice rested decisions finding that NEPA does not override another federal law when the two conflict.

At issue in United States v. Students Challenging Regulatory Agency Procedures (SCRAP I) 10/ was a District Court decision

---

9/   The response of the Federal agencies as a whole to Section 103 was less than enthusiastic. Indeed, environmentalists have described it as a classic example of bureaucrats exalting form over substance. After July 1971, however, Federal courts began to find many necessary changes in agency authority that were not otherwise listed in agency Section 103 recommendations.

10/   412 U.S. 669 (1973).

concerning the Interstate Commerce Commission's (ICC) authorization, without first preparing an EIS, of a railroad surcharge. The
District Court held that NEPA empowered it to issue an injunction
against the Commission's action, notwithstanding another federal
law vesting sole and exclusive power to temporarily enjoin collection
of rates in the ICC itself and withdrawing such power from the
judiciary. Reversing that decision, the Supreme Court held:

> The statutory language, in fact, indicates that NEPA
> was not intended to repeal by implication any other
> statute. Thus, . . . [Section 105] specifies that "[t]he
> policies and goals set forth in [NEPA] are supplementary
> to those set forth in existing authorizations of Federal
> agencies," and . . . [Section 104] instructs that the Act
> "shall [not] in any way affect the specific statutory
> obligations of any Federal agency . . ." Rather than
> providing for any wholesale overruling of prior law,
> [Section 103 of] NEPA requires all Federal agencies to
> review their "present statutory authority, administra-
> tive regulations, and current policies and procedures for
> the purpose of determining whether there are any
> deficiencies or inconsistencies therein which prohibit
> full compliance with the purposes and provisions of
> [NEPA] and shall propose to the President . . . such
> measures as may be necessary to bring their authority
> and policies into conformity with the intent, purposes,
> and procedures set forth in [NEPA]. . . . It would be
> anamolous if Congress had provided at one and the same
> time that Federal agencies, which have the primary re-
> sponsibility for the implementation of NEPA, must
> comply with the present law and ask for any necessary
> new legislation, but that the courts may simply ignore
> what we described in [the previous] Arrow [case] as "a
> clear congressional purpose to oust judicial power . . ."
> 11/

In Flint Ridge Development Co. v. Scenic Rivers Association,
et al., 12/ the Supreme Court reached the same result on the question of irreconcilable conflict between NEPA and another federal
law, but this time relied entirely on Section 102.

Flint Ridge addressed the claim of environmental organizations that an EIS was required for approval of a land development
project on which an antifraud disclosure document had been filed

---

11/   412 U.S. at 694-695 (Emphasis supplied and footnote omitted).

12/   426 U.S. 776 (1976).

with the Department of Housing and Urban Development pursuant to the Interstate Land Sales Full Disclosure Act. That Act provides that disclosure documents automatically become effective thirty days after filing (thus allowing sales in interstate commerce), unless suspended because of inadequate disclosure. The document at issue was not found to be an inadequate disclosure, nor was it disputed that an EIS could not be prepared within the thirty day period. Nevertheless, the environmental groups successfully argued in the lower courts that NEPA empowered, and indeed required, a suspension beyond the statutory thirty day period until an EIS was prepared.

The Supreme Court reversed. Relying upon the principle announced in SCRAP I and the language in Section 102, stating that "to the fullest extent possible" (emphasis supplied) all federal agencies shall comply with NEPA's requirements, the court concluded:

> Section 102 recognizes . . . that where a clear and un-
> avoidable conflict in statutory authority exists, NEPA
> must give way.

Thus, it is clear that NEPA will not prevail when it is in irreconcilable conflict with another federal law.

4.0 Environmental Impact Statements

4.1 Background: CEQ's NEPA Regulations

CEQ originally issued advisory "Guidelines on the Preparation of Environmental Impact Statements" 13/ in order to assist federal agencies with the procedural aspects of NEPA. The various federal agencies then developed their own regulations for the implementation of the EIS requirement. These regulations and agency practice, however, did not necessarily adhere closely to the guidelines.

Pursuant to President Carter's Executive Order No. 11991, CEQ itself promulgated regulations implementing NEPA's procedural provisions on November 29, 1978. 14/ These regulations are binding on all federal agencies, replace over 70 different sets of agency

---

13/   Former 40 CFR Parts 1500 et seq.

14/   43 FR 55978.

regulations on NEPA, and provide uniform standards applicable throughout the federal government for the conduct of environmental reviews. 15/ In promulgating its NEPA regulations, CEQ announced that it hoped to accomplish three principal aims: to reduce paperwork, to reduce delays, and to produce better decisions in furtherance of the national environmental policy.

Perhaps the most notable effort toward reducing paperwork, in light of the inordinate length and encyclopedic nature of many early EISs, is the regulation limiting an EIS to 150 pages or, for proposals of unusual scope or complexity, 300 pages. 16/ Another important part of the effort to reduce paperwork was the creation of a "scoping" procedure, 17/ which has the objective of assisting agencies in deciding what the central issues are, how long the EIS will be, and how the responsibility for preparation of the EIS will be allocated among the lead agency 18/ and cooperating agencies.

The regulations also establish a number of measures designed to reduce delay. Lead agencies are encouraged to set time limits on the NEPA process and are required to do so when requested to by an applicant. 19/ In addition, the regulations seek to reduce significant time delays by providing for the integration of EIS requirements

---

15/ The importance of the old guidelines is an issue that is open to disagreement. Almost every court that has had an opportunity to do so has said that the guidelines are "entitled to great weight" in interpreting the EIS requirement. The guidelines also were important for collecting in one place much relevant information on how to prepare an EIS, and they helped to bring about much needed standardization in EIS procedures among the Federal agencies. On the other hand, the guidelines were often of extremely limited utility in providing sound answers to questions regarding the applicability of EIS requirements to a given case. Indeed, if the guidelines had addressed some categories of close cases, at least a few of the many expensive and delay-producing NEPA lawsuits might have been avoided. Further, as noted above, they were not binding, so agencies could go their own way.

16/ 40 CFR § 1502.7.

17/ 40 CFR § 1501.7.

18/ See Part 4.4.2 of this chapter for a discussion of the lead agency system.

19/ 40 CFR §§ 1501.8(a) and (b).

with other environmental review requirements, by emphasizing inter-agency cooperation, and by avoiding legal delays.

In order to foster agency decisions reflecting an increased sensitivity to environmental concerns, the regulations require the lead agency to produce a concise decisionmaking record, indicating how the EIS was used in arriving at the final decision on agency action. 20/ This provision was designed to ensure that an agency considers the EIS that it is required to prepare.

In August of 1981, CEQ requested public comment on how the various federal agencies are implementing its NEPA regulations. 21/ In general, those comments indicated that the regulations have led to more efficient and effective compliance with NEPA requirements. In certain areas, however, agencies were thought to be in need of further CEQ guidance. As a result, CEQ is considering ways in which to (1) improve agency management of the scoping process; (2) ensure appropriate analysis of alternatives in permitting situations, as opposed to situations in which the agency is undertaking activity at its own initiative; (3) promote agency adoption of analyses prepared by other federal and state agencies; (4) reduce repetitious analyses in environmental documents by promoting the proper use of tiering; and (5) define the circumstances under which an agency may charge an applicant for EIS preparation. How, if at all, CEQ will amend its regulations to achieve these ends remains to be seen.

4.2 Proposed Actions Requiring an EIS
Section 102(2)(C) requires that an EIS shall be "include[d] in every recommendation or report on proposals for legislation and other major federal actions significantly affecting the quality of the human environment."

Because NEPA makes no pretense of applying its requirements to other than federal agencies, perhaps the best first step toward deciding whether an EIS is required is to determine whether "federal" action is involved. Federal action obviously includes what is undertaken directly by the federal agencies, including operation of programs, construction of facilities, and the provision of funding

---

20/ 40 CFR § 1505.2.

21/ 46 FR 41131 (August 14, 1981).

to others. 22/ Federal action also clearly includes a federal agency's
decision on whether to grant its required permission for activities of
others, such as private businesses or state or local governments.

In addition to federal involvement, there must also be a
"proposal" for action before preparation of an EIS will be required.
The Supreme Court made this clear in Kleppe v. Sierra Club. 23/
There, the Sierra Club contended that Interior Secretary Kleppe was
required to prepare an EIS on coal development in the Northern
Great Plains region of the country. The Supreme Court carefully
reviewed Interior's past and contemplated actions. It found that
there was no proposal for regional action concerning coal development. All Interior proposals were for actions that were either local
or national in scope, even though such actions affected the Northern
Great Plains region. Thus, because there was no proposal for
regional action, the Court held no EIS was required on coal development in the Northern Great Plains region.

The Supreme Court has also held that federal agencies are
not required by Section 102(2)(C) to prepare an EIS to accompany
appropriation requests as such requests do not constitute "proposals"
for legislation or for major federal action. 24/ In so ruling, the
court noted that the language of Section 102(2)(C) is best interpreted as applying to those recommendations or reports that
actually propose programmatic actions, rather than to those that
merely suggest how such actions may be funded.

There are a multitude of cases on the question of whether a
given federal action is "major" and/or "significantly affects" the
quality of the human environment within the meaning of NEPA.
Almost all of these cases, as well as the CEQ regulations, however,
avoid the futile effort of trying to define the amorphous words

---

22/   General revenue sharing has been held not to require an EIS
      because it is not sufficiently Federal in nature. Carolina
      Action v. Simon, 389 F. Supp. 1244 (M.D.N.C. 1975), aff'd, 522
      F. 2d 295 (4th Cir. 1975). This holding is specifically supported
      by the CEQ regulations. 40 CFR § 1508.18 (a). On the other
      hand, block grants for more specific projects have been held to
      require an EIS. See, e.g., Ely v. Velde, 451 F.2d 1130(4th Cir.
      1971).

23/   427 U.S. 390 (1976).

24/   Andrus v. Sierra Club, 442 U.S. 347 (1979).

"major" and "significantly." 25/ The few cases where definition is
attempted shed no more light on the issue than does the dictionary.
The usual long analysis of those NEPA cases interpreting the meaning of "major" and "significantly affects" is therefore omitted here.
Such an analysis yields no valid criterion for deciding whether any
other federal action is "major" or "significantly affects" the environment.

Practically speaking, the initial decision of whether to prepare an EIS for any given proposed project lies within the sound
discretion of the various federal agencies. 26/ Accordingly, in the
last few years, increasing attention has been given to "findings of no
significant impact" or "negative declarations." 27/

4.2.1 Findings of No Significant Impact

The CEQ regulations define a "finding of no significant impact" (FONSI) as "a document prepared by a federal agency briefly
presenting the reasons why an action, not otherwise excluded . . . ,

---

25/ The regulations do provide some limited guidance as to what is
"significant" in this context. 40 CFR § 1508.27.

26/ There has been a split in the Circuits of the U.S. Courts of
Appeals as to the appropriate standard to employ in reviewing
an agency's "threshold decision" not to prepare an EIS for a
given project. Some Circuits have adopted an "arbitrary and
capricious" standard, others have employed a "reasonableness"
standard. See Aertsen v. Landrieu, 488 F. Supp. 314 (D. Mass.
1980) for a discussion of this difference of opinion. Although
the level of judicial scrutiny differs in some measure as a
result of choosing one standard rather than the other, it is
generally true that reviewing courts will simply look for an
administrative record that evidences a rational basis for the
agency's determination on the issue of whether or not to
prepare an EIS on a particular project.

27/ The CEQ regulations prescribe the use of the term "finding of
no significant impact" for such documents.   40 CFR
§ 1508.13. Before the promulgation of the regulations, these
documents were most frequently called "negative declarations."   The two terms are used interchangeably in this
chapter.

28/ will not have a significant effect on the human environment and for which an environmental impact statement therefore will not be prepared." 29/ The regulations further provide that a FONSI must include an environmental assessment or a summary of one. 30/ Although a federal agency need not itself prepare that environmental assessment, the agency is responsible for its content, for if the environmental assessment prepared in connection with the issuance of a FONSI does not provide sufficient evidence to support the agency's finding of no significant impact, that finding will be stricken by a federal Court in which review is sought.

Thus, a FONSI can avoid the lengthy EIS process if properly substantiated. As Professor Rodgers has pointed out, however, the cases "offer many examples of agency negative declarations being repudiated in the courts after a thorough inquiry into what often turns out to be an embarrassingly thin administrative effort." 31/ This is changing somewhat as agencies become more familiar with what is legally required for a FONSI and with the substantiation necessary to support one.

4.2.2 EIS Requirements for Special Types of Federal Action

Some particular types of federal agency actions merit special mention in connection with the EIS requirement. One is the preparation of an EIS in connection with legislation. In view of the unique nature of legislative recommendations and reports, CEQ's regulations provide for certain special features for EISs that

---

28/ There are a few exemptions from the EIS requirement. Most notable are the statutory exemptions for U.S. Environmental Protection Agency actions under most provisions of the Clean Water Act and under all Clean Air Act provisions. 33 USC § 1371 (c)(1); 15 USC § 793 (c)(1). In addition, special exemptions are occasionally granted by Congress for some Federal agency projects and for a few private projects that involve some Federal agency action. See, e.g., 15 USC § 793 (d). See also, 40 CFR § 1508.4.

29/ 40 CFR § 1508.13.

30/ Id.

31/ W. H. Rodgers, Environmental Law (1977) (Footnote and citations omitted).

accompany legislative proposals. 32/ First, the statement may be transmitted to the Congress up to thirty days after submission of the proposal in order to allow time for the preparation of an accurate and complete EIS. Second, a legislative EIS is to be prepared in the same manner as an ordinary draft EIS. 33/ Draft and final statements are required only in certain limited circumstances. Finally, comments on a legislative EIS are to be collected by the lead agency and forwarded to the Congress, together with the agency's responses to the comments.

A second type of federal agency action that merits special mention in connection with EIS requirements is the agency "program." Agency programs can be viewed as being of two principal types: (1) future development oriented, such as the liquid metal fast breeder reactor demonstration program; and (2) ongoing, such as natural resources management.

Although NEPA does not specifically require the preparation of "programmatic" EIS, the courts have required such EISs in certain circumstances. Scientists' Institute for Public Information v. Atomic Energy Commission, 34/ is a leading case dealing with EIS requirements for agency programs relating to future developments. In that case, the Commission had concluded that it did not need to prepare a programmatic EIS before deciding to proceed with its liquid metal fast breeder reactor demonstration program because the environmental impact of that program would be evaluated in EISs on each demonstration plant. The Court, looking to environmental effects that today's decisions on development of technology may have years hence, held that a programmatic EIS was indeed required. Although the courts have had considerable difficulty in deciding issues relating to the proper scope of a programmatic EIS, one simple way to state the EIS requirements for a program involving future developments is to say that a programmatic EIS must be prepared if institution of the program will foreclose decisions on whether to approve individual projects that would in themselves require EISs.

The applicability of the EIS requirement to ongoing federal agency programs is demonstrated by Minnesota Public Interest

---

32/   40 CFR § 1506.08.

33/   For a discussion of draft EIS requirements, see Part 4.3 of this chapter.

34/   481 F. 2d 1079 (D.C. Cir. 1973).

Research Group v. Butz, 35/ which held that the cumulative environmental impact of Forest Service decisions on the management of
timber in a certain area required a programmatic EIS on what
amounted to an ongoing but apparently ad hoc management plan.
The applicability of the EIS requirement to ongoing federal agency
programs appears to have significant potential for those--both
environmentalists and private interests--who seek to change what
are to them unacceptable, yet entrenched federal agency policies
and practices.

4.3 Procedure and Time of Required Issuance
As noted above, Section 102(2)(C) requires that an EIS be
"include[d] in" every recommendation or report on proposals for
major federal action significantly affecting the environment. That
section also requires an agency, prior to preparing its EIS, to consult
with and obtain the comments of any other federal agency that has
either jurisdiction by law or special expertise with respect to any
environmental impact involved. Further, copies of the EIS, federal
agency comments on it, and the views of appropriate state and local
agencies must be made available to the President, CEQ, and the
public and must accompany the proposal through the existing agency
review process. No mention is made of a "draft" EIS.
The concept of preparing and circulating for comment a draft
EIS is embodied in the CEQ regulations where EIS preparation procedures are set out: the draft is to be prepared "early enough so
that it can serve . . . as an important contribution to the decisionmaking process" 36/ and circulated as required for comment for not
less than forty-five days. 37/ The regulations also provide that, as a
general rule, no agency action should occur earlier than ninety days
after the draft EIS or thirty days after the final EIS is made available to CEQ and the public. 38/
In the SCRAP II case, 39/ the Supreme Court rejected the
holding of several Courts of Appeals that a final EIS must be prepared prior to agency hearings on an applicant's request for federal

---

35/ 498 F. 2d 1314 (8th Cir. 1974).

36/ 40 CFR § 1502.5.

37/ Id. § 1506.10 (c)

38/ Id. § 1506.10(b).

39/ Aberdeen & Rockfish RR. Co. v. Students Challenging
Regulatory Agency Procedures (SCRAP II), 422 U.S. 289 (1975),
reaffirmed in dicta in Kleppe v. Sierra Club, 427 U.S. 390
(1976).

action or at other times before the agency actually takes a position on a proposal. The Supreme Court made it clear that "the time at which the agency must prepare the final [EIS] is the time at which it makes 'recommendation or report' on a proposal." Thus, the holding in SCRAP II is strong precedent for requiring a federal agency to issue a final EIS, if one must be prepared, at the time it proposes regulations by publication in the Federal Register.

4.4 Who Can Prepare the EIS and the Lead Agency System

4.4.1 Delegation

It is strongly implied, but not explicitly stated, in Section 102(2)(C) that the federal agency or the "responsible federal official" proposing to take action is charged with preparing the requisite EIS. Early in NEPA's history, several Court of Appeals decisions addressed the question of whether, and, if so, to what extent, a federal agency can lawfully delegate responsibility for preparing an EIS. The issue divided the courts into three camps: (1) those disallowing any delegation of responsibility; 40/ (2) those allowing some delegation, but requiring the responsible federal official to significantly and actively participate in the preparation of the EIS 41/ and (3) those permitting extensive delegation of responsibility, followed only by review and adoption by the agency. 42/ In August of 1975, Congress enacted Pub. L. No. 94-83, adding to Section 102(2) a new subsection that settled the delegation question with respect to state officials and agencies, but left open issues involving delegation to private consultants.

The new subsection, which is designated as Section 102(2)(D), provides that an EIS "for any major federal action funded under a program of grants to States shall not be deemed to be legally insufficient solely by reason of having been prepared by a state agency or official," if (1) the state agency or official has state-wide jurisdiction and is responsible for the action, and (2) the responsible federal official (a) furnishes guidance and participates in the preparation of the EIS, (b) independently evaluates it prior to its approval and adoption, and (c) provides early notice to, and solicits

---

40/ See, e.g., Green County Planning Board v. Federal Power Commission, 455 F. 2d 412 (2d Cir. 1972), cert. denied, 409 U.S. 849 (1972).

41/ See, e.g., Life of the Land v. Brinegar, 485 F. 2d 460 (9th Cir. 1973), cert. denied, 416 U.S. 961 (1974).

42/ See, e.g., Citizens Environmental Council v. Volpe, 484 F. 2d 870 (10th Cir. 1973), cert. denied, 461 U.S. 936 (1974).

the view of, any other state or any federal land management entity on any action or alternatives thereto which may affect their responsibilities. The responsible federal official must also prepare a written assessment of the impacts on other agencies' responsibilities for incorporation into the EIS if there is any disagreement. Section 102(2)(D) goes on to state it does not relieve the federal official of responsibility for the scope, objectivity and content of an EIS or any other responsibilities under NEPA. The provisions of Section 102(2)(D) have been of primary importance in situations involving federal grants to states for highway construction. 43/

Thus, Congress rejected the per se no delegation rule of Green County in the case of projects involving grants to states and adopted the views expressed by those courts taking the middle course, allowing delegation, but requiring significant, active participation by the responsible federal agency. The law with regard to delegation to private consultants, however, remains unsettled.

4.4.2 The Lead Agency System

Projects requiring "major actions" by more than one federal agency are not uncommon. The concept of a "lead agency" to prepare or to supervise the preparation of an EIS for such an action was developed in order to satisfy the requirements of NEPA in the most efficient manner possible. CEQ's regulations incorporate that concept and require that a "lead agency" be designated to supervise the preparation of an EIS in such circumstances. 44/

Involved agencies are to determine which shall be the lead agency on the basis of five enumerated factors (listed in order of descending importance):

(1) magnitude of agency's involvement;
(2) project approval/disapproval authority;
(3) expertise concerning the action's environmental effects;
(4) duration of agency's involvement; and
(5) sequence of agency's involvement. 45/

43/ Congress enacted a special total delegation of responsibility provision for preparing an EIS to applicants under the Community Development Block Grant Program established in the Housing and Community Development Act of 1974. 42 USC § 5304(h).

44/ 40 CFR § 1501.5(a).

45/ 40 CFR § 1501.5(c).

CEQ will designate the lead agency if there is no consensual selection. 46/

4.5 Contents

The broad outline of an EIS is set forth in Section 102(2)(C). The EIS must be a "detailed" statement which is issued only after consultation with other appropriate government agencies and which addresses the environmental impact of the proposed action, unavoidable adverse environmental effects, alternatives, the relationship between local short-term uses of the environment and the maintenance and enhancement of long-term productivity and irreversible and irretrievable commitments of resources. Obviously, what a particular EIS must include depends on the proposal and the facts surrounding it.

The federal courts have supplemented the statutory requirements on a case-by-case basis. Although each of the cases concerns a particular EIS and surrounding facts, an individualized analysis with a composite overview reveals these useful guidelines: 1) the EIS must be a self-contained document written in language that is understandable to the layman yet allows for meaningful consideration by decisionmakers and scientists; and 2) it must also be responsive to opposing opinions, and of sufficient depth to permit a reasoned choice.

A fatally defective EIS is usally characterized by one or more of the following: sweeping conclusions unsupported by the facts, vagueness as to important issues, internal contradiction, disregard for local land use planning requirements, cursory treatment of secondary and cumulative environmental impacts and a failure to include sufficient information on the environmental impact of realistic and plausible alternatives and to make an unbiased comparison of them with the proposal. Because the consideration of alternatives is accorded the role of "linchpin" of the EIS, it merits some further mention.

The requirement to consider alternatives embodies the simple principle that a rational decision requires a knowledge of the available choices and their ramifications. The alternative of no action must always be discussed. NEPA does not, however, require that the consideration of alternatives be a "crystal ball" inquiry. 47/ Detailed discussion and consideration of alternatives that are remote or speculative are not required. Yet, an alternative may not be given short shrift because it is outside the jurisdiction of the

---

46/   40 CFR § 1501.5(e) and (f).

47/   Natural Resources Defense Council, Inc. v. Morton, 458 F. 2d 827, 837 (D.C. Cir. 1972).

agency or because it is contrary to existing agency policy. Simply put, the agency's consideration of alternatives must be reasonable. 48/

5.0 "International" Environmental Statements

There is nothing in Section 102(2)(C) to indicate that actions having international ramifications are to be treated any differently than others subject to the EIS requirement. Further, there is precedent for applying the EIS requirement to international programs. 49/ Nevertheless, federal agencies with international responsibilities expressed concern that compliance with EIS requirements could interfere with foreign policy objectives. As a consequence, these agencies and CEQ developed a program designed to accommodate these concerns while meeting the objectives of NEPA. In January of 1979, President Carter approved this program and issued Executive Order No. 12114. 50/

Although Executive Order No. 12114 is not formally based on NEPA, its objective is to further the purposes of the Act. It is designed to insure that federal decisionmakers are informed of pertinent environmental considerations concerning actions having effects outside the geographical boundaries of the United States, and that such considerations are taken into account when decisions are made. The Order prescribes the circumstances under which its requirements are applicable and also specifies a number of procedures that must be followed. Affected agencies are further required to develop their own implementing procedures.

Because it is not feasible, from a foreign policy viewpoint, to perform environmental reviews in connection with every action that has environmental impacts outside the United States, specific types of actions are exempted from the requirements of the Order. Examples are intelligence activities, arms transfers and disaster and emergency relief action. Finally, the order specifically does not create any right of judicial review.

In the few years since its issuance, the Order has had little effect. Its lack of impact has been primarily due to three factors: (1) excepted actions far outnumber the actions to which the Order's

---

48/ See, Vermont Yankee Nuclear Power Corp. v. NRDC, 435 U.S. 519 (1978).

49/ See, e.g., Sierra Club v. Coleman, 405 F. Supp. 53 (D.D.C. 1975), in which an EIS was required for preliminary construction activities by the Federal Highway Administration in connection with a highway through Panama and Columbia.

50/ 44 FR 1957 (January 9, 1979).

prescriptions are applicable; (2) even those agency actions to which the Order does apply are not judicially reviewable; and (3) the Reagan Administration has demonstrated very little interest in enforcing its provisions.

6.0 Applicants' Environmental Reports

In situations where the federal action involved is federal agency approval of a non-federal party's proposal, the agency is virtually certain to require an environmental report. The required contents of such a report prepared by an applicant for a permit or other authorization will vary, but are generally spelled out by the federal agency.

In practice, the agency's environmental assessment on which a FONSI may be based is often a rehash of the applicant's environmental report. And, as a practical matter, an EIS itself is often only as good as the applicant's environmental report. Thus, it is apparent that this report is critical to the EIS process and is a document on which the applicant should spend much care and effort.

Despite this, frequent difficulties arise from flawed environmental reports. A variety of problems stem from the frequent failure of such a report to reflect a thorough knowledge and appreciation of the law of NEPA. These problems are avoidable to a great extent. In particular, two potentially serious problems can readily be avoided.

The first problem arises from a failure to write carefully, or to think all the way through the practical or legal ramifications of an issue or position. It should be understood at the outset that an applicant's environmental report must state the relevant information in an honest and straightforward manner. 51/ Too often, though, a careful examination of an applicant's environmental report reveals language that is an overstatement, understatement or mistatement of the facts and conclusions. This is damaging to the applicant, for reviewing courts look to the information that was before the agency when its decisions were made and will not themselves undertake to build a more accurate factual record supporting the agency action. Thus, the agency's decision is apt to stand or fall on the accuracy of the applicant's environmental report.

The second problem that can arise in connection with applicants' environmental reports involves the ability of those who conduct the studies and analyses and prepare parts of the report to also serve as convincing expert witnesses if an agency hearing or court action arises at some point. No attempt will be made here to tell an applicant how to select an environmental consultant. Yet it

---

51/ There are very few instances of an applicant or an environmental consultant intentionally attempting to deceive.

can be a crucial flaw in some cases to discover too late that you have a barely qualified or an inexperienced expert witness or one who is unconvincing or offensive in oral presentations under pressure. Thus, it may be prudent for an applicant to make a careful assessment of the qualifications and the demeanor of the environmental consultant's personnel, particularly those who will be doing the actual work and thus would be the strongly preferred expert witnesses if the need arose.

7.0 The Seven Other "Action-Forcing" Provisions

In addition to NEPA's EIS requirements, there are seven other "action-forcing" provisions in Section 102(2). They require federal agencies to: (A) utilize an interdisciplinary approach to planning and decisionmaking; (B) insure appropriate consideration of unquantified environmental values; (E) study and develop alternatives to proposals involving unresolved conflicts over use of resources; (F) recognize the worldwide and long-range character of environmental problems; (G) make usable environmental information generally available; (H) initiate ecological information for resource-oriented projects; and (I) assist the CEQ. These sections are discussed briefly below with a view to neither ignoring nor overstating their individual and cumulative potential for important practical significance in the years ahead.

The seven "other" provisions of Section 102(2) are often thought of as relatively unimportant appendages to the EIS requirement. There is, however, a body of case law indicating that courts view at least some of these provisions as imposing on federal agencies duties that are both independent of and wider in scope than NEPA's EIS requirement. This view suggests that increased attention to these provisions could cause a significant change in the nature and extent of scientific data and information that must be compiled by the agencies in order to comply with NEPA. For, as the boundaries of environmental science continue to expand, national concern over mitigation measures and post-operational monitoring programs is likely to increase concomitantly. Thus, the extra-EIS provisions of Section 102(2) may come to play an ever more important role in the law of NEPA, serving as the legal basis for requiring agencies to secure more and better scientific data on environmental impacts both before and after federal action is taken, whether or not an EIS is required.

Section 102(2)(A) authorizes and directs all agencies to "utilize a systematic, inter-disciplinary approach" in planning and decisionmaking through an integrated use of natural and social sciences and environmental design arts. This section has been held to apply to all federal decisions that may have an impact on the environment, even those that do not themselves require the preparation of EIS. 52/   Professor Rodgers has perhaps best stated the requirements of Section 102(2)(A):

> Section 102(2)(A) lends strength to the argument that the agency must disclose and consider responsible opposing scientific opinions, coordinate expertise within the agency, expand its staff to accommodate environmental evaluations, respond to concerns raised by experts it retains, sponsor research on important issues either as a precondition or concurrently with implementation of a project, answer or perhaps even defer to expert criticism or recommendations from other agencies, actively seek out (as distinguished from passively absorbing) expert advice on opposing opinions or engage in actual consultation with other agencies. On the other hand, the agency need not be paralyzed by conflicting expert opinions, so long as they are fully disclosed; or undertake long-range research commitments as a precondition of actions; or hire a full stable of experts to consider a project or prepare an environmental impact statement so long as its doors are open to expert advice. 53/

Thus, Section 102(2)(A) has been found to have force independent of NEPA's EIS requirements. Its provisions might also be used in conjunction with the EIS requirement to produce greater court scrutiny of federal agency decisions. A court's "hard look" at the EIS should generally reveal whether Section 102(2)(A) has been complied with, but drawing the court's attention to that section might help to bring the agency's actual approach to planning and decisionmaking into focus. The result could well be judicial opinions compelling a significantly more systematic and integrated disciplinary approach to planning and decisionmaking, an approach that employs "state-of-the-art" scientific techniques.

Section 102(2)(B) directs federal agencies to "identify and develop methods and procedures . . . which will insure that presently unquantified environmental amenities and values may be given appropriate consideration in decisionmaking along with economic and technical considerations." What Section 102(2)(B) does and does not do is described very well in the Tennessee-Tombigbee decision:

52/   McDowell v. Schlesinger, 404 F. Supp. 212 (D.C. Mo. 1975).

53/   W.H. Rodgers, Environmental Law, pp. 719-21 (1977) (Citations to cases omitted).

[Section 102(2)(B)] cannot be fairly read to command an agency to develop or define any general or specific quantification process . . . [I]t requires no more than that an agency search out, develop and follow procedures reasonably calculated to bring environmental factors to peer status with dollars and technology in their decisionmaking. 54/

Section 102(2)(B) clearly adds to the list of factors that must be considered in the agency decisionmaking process, and thus also provides an additional basis upon which to review agency action.

Section 102(2)(E) 55/ requires all federal agencies to "study, develop, and describe appropriate alternatives to recommended courses of action in any proposal which involves unresolved conflicts concerning alternative uses of available resources." 56/ This section, like Section 102(2)(A), has been held to impose duties on federal agencies that are independent of NEPA's EIS requirements. For example, in Trinity Episcopal School Corp. v. Romney, 57/ the Court of Appeals for the Second Circuit reversed and remanded to HUD an agency decision to proceed with a low income housing project in New York City because HUD had not fully considered alternative sites for the project. The Court came to this conclusion despite the fact that HUD's decision not to prepare an EIS for the project went unchallenged. The potential significance of this finding is great indeed, for it is now possible to argue that the provisions of Section 102(2)(E) are applicable even to those Environmental Protection Agency actions under the Clean Air Act and the Clean Water Act that are categorically exempted from the EIS requirement.

54/ Environmental Defense Fund, Inc. v. Corps of Engineers, 429 F. 2d 1123, 1133 (5th Cir. 1974); see also, Hanly v. Kliendienst, 471 F. 2d 823 (2nd Cir. 1972), cert. denied, 412 U.S. 908 (1973).

55/ This provision was originally Section 102(2)(D). It was redesignated when NEPA was amended by Pub. L. No. 94-83 (1975).

56/ The last part of Section 102(2)(E) appears to limit its application to only those proposals which involve unresolved conflicts concerning alternative uses of available resources. It is difficult, however, to conjure up good examples of choices involving environmental impact that are clearly outside the apparent limitation.

57/ 523 F. 2d 88 (2d Cir. 1975).

Section 102(2)(F) requires all federal agencies to "[r]ecognize the worldwide and long-range character of environmental problems" and to lend such support as is consistent with our foreign policy to international efforts to protect the world environment. 58/ This section has received almost no attention from the federal courts. It could in the future, however, provide a basis for claims that agencies must develop and consider more scientific data and information in order to assess "long-range" effects of federal actions. It may also be used to buttress efforts to develop more comprehensive policies on international environmental protection issues.

Section 102(2)(G) requires all federal agencies to "[m]ake available to States, counties, municipalities, institutions, and individuals, advice and information useful in restoring, maintaining and enhancing the quality of the environment." This section has been of extremely limited practical utility with respect to particular projects. It does not require by its own terms disclosure of information different from that obtainable under the provisions of the Freedom of Information Act, nor does it add much, if anything, to the Administrative Procedure Act requirement that an agency be fair with public participants and disclose the basis for its decisions.

Another "action-forcing" provision that has received only limited attention to date, but which has great potential significance, is Section 102(2)(H). This section provides that all federal agencies shall "[i]nitiate and utilize ecological information in the planning and development of resource-oriented projects." The usual agency practice, evidenced in many EISs, is to make decisions simply on the best available information at the time. The requirement to "initiate" ecological information, then, could be used to require agencies themselves to generate additional information on particular projects before reaching a final decision to proceed.

Section 102(2)(I) simply requires federal agencies to assist the Council on Environmental Quality. At most, this section slightly strengthens the hand of CEQ (which has relatively little funding or staff) when it wants the cooperation of other federal agencies in undertaking a major examination of an environmental problem area.

8.0 Who Can Sue for Alleged Violations of NEPA

The question of who can sue, called "standing" by lawyers, is one that has received a great deal of attention from the U.S. Supreme Court since 1970. In general, the court's opinions on the issue are in conflict and a lengthy analysis of them yields little of

---

58/ For a discussion of "international" EISs, see Part 5.0 of this chapter.

predictive value. 59/ When environmental interests are a stake, however, the Court has consistently left the door to the courthouse wide open. A brief examination of the two leading Supreme Court decisions on standing in environmental cases reveals the limits to which the court's liberal stand on this issue goes.

Sierra Club v. Morton 60/ is the only major decision denying standing to a litigant in a case involving environmental interests. It involved a challenge to agency approval of construction of the Mineral King Resort in the Sequoia National Forest. Sierra Club treated the action as a test case, seeking to establish the principle that a membership organization with a "special interest" in the environment has standing to challenge action that would adversely affect the environment. Accordingly, Sierra Club intentionally failed to allege that it or any of its members actually used the Mineral King Valley for recreational purposes. Although the Court held that asthetic or environmental harm could constitute "injury in fact" sufficient to confer standing, it denied standing in this case because the Club had not pleaded facts establishing any such injury. The mere fact that the Club had a "special interest" in protecting the environment was not sufficient to allow the Club to challenge the agency action concerned.

The other leading Supreme Court decision on standing in the environmental area is United States v. Students Challenging Regulatory Agency Procedures (SCRAP I). 61/ SCRAP I is generally considered to be among the most liberal standing cases. There an unincorporated association of law students sued the Interstate Commerce Commission for failing to prepare an EIS before allowing railroads to collect a surcharge on freight. They claimed to be "injured in fact" by the Commission's order because they used national parks and forests, and the order would raise the price of recycled materials thereby discouraging the use of such materials, leading in turn to increased mining operations, which would consequently harm national recreational enclaves. The Government claimed that the alleged chain of causation was too attenuated to confer standing on the students. The court, however, responded in a

---

59/ For a less timid criticism of the Supreme Court's opinions on standing, see K. C. Davis, Administrative Law Treatise, 1982 Supplement 325-370 (1982).

60/ 405 U.S. 727 (1972).

61/ 412 U.S. 669 (1973).

footnote that a "trifle" of injury in fact is enough. 62/ Although subsequent cases 63/ cast some doubt on whether SCRAP I will be followed in the future, no case has directly reversed that decision, and it remains a leading precedent in the environmental area.

Thus, it is possible to briefly answer the question posed in this Part in this way: When violations of NEPA are alleged, anyone who can claim at least a "trifle" of "injury in fact" has standing to sue.

62/   Id. at 689 n. 14.

63/   See, e.g., Simon v. Eastern Kentucky Welfare Rights Organization, 426 U.S. 26 (1976).

Chapter 3

WATER POLLUTION CONTROL

J. Gordon Arbuckle and Timothy A. Vanderver, Jr.
Attorneys
Patton, Boggs & Blow
Washington, DC

1.0 Introduction – The Historical Perspective

While "modern" federal water pollution control legislation has been on the books at least since 1948, effective enforcement mechanisms are a comparatively recent development. It was not until 1970, with the resurrection of the old "Refuse Act" (33 USC § 407), that industrial dischargers were faced with any real threat of prosecution for their polluting activities. Since that "first step" in 1970, major legislative and administrative actions have resulted in a comprehensive and increasingly effective regulatory program in the water pollution control area. With the development of effective enforcement mechanisms, it is becoming more and more essential for business managers to understand and learn how to cope with this complex regulatory framework. To develop this understanding, it is necessary to have some background in the pre–1972 approach.

1.1 Water Quality Standards

The enforcement approach prior to 1970 was to "protect the public health or welfare" and "enhance the quality of water" through adoption and enforcement, primarily by the states, of "water quality standards." Although theoretically workable, this approach encountered insurmountable problems in most states, including:

-- Inability to determine with precision when a discharge violated applicable standards;
-- Inapplicability of federal-state water quality standards to intrastate waters;
-- Lack of state initiative in making load allocations required for enforceable standards; and
-- Cumbersome enforcement mechanisms and the requirement for state consent.

1.2 Effluent Criteria Under the Refuse Act

Although a few states were able to make the water quality standards approach work, it became clear that an effective nation-wide approach would require implementation of a permit program based on federal minimum "end of pipe" effluent criteria enforce-able directly against the discharger. When legislation proposed in 1969 to provide this mechanism failed to pass, the Administration initiated the Refuse Act Permit Program in late 1970.

The Refuse Act is an archaic 1899 statute designed to protect navigation. It does, however, prohibit all discharges into navigable waters or tributaries thereof unless a permit is obtained from the U.S. Army Corps of Engineers prior to commencing the discharge. By using this authority to require all industrial dischargers to apply for and obtain permits, the granting or denial of which would be based on environmental factors, the Administration was able, for the first time, to pose a credible threat of prosecution. Hundreds of cases were initiated under the Refuse Act, and the Refuse Act program should be considered a major milestone in federal efforts to effectively regulate industrial discharges.

Like the old water quality standards, however, the Refuse Act program had deficiencies which eventually proved fatal:

(1)   The Act itself provided no standards for the grant or denial of permits, and no regulations were ever promulgated to provide such standards. Thus, "violators" were totally at the mercy of the prosecutors and there were many instances of inequitable prosecutions, many appeals, and many reversals;

(2)   There was some question as to whether the penalties provided by the Act were adequate;

(3)   The Act was not applicable to municipal sewers - a major pollution source;

(4)   The Refuse Act did not lend itself to effective administration for pollution control purposes; and

(5)   The relationship of the Refuse Act to more modern environmental statutes, such as NEPA, was not clear and judicial decisions resulting from this lack of clarity eventually brought the entire program to a halt.

1.3 The Need for New Authority

By late 1971 it was clear that enforcement efforts up to that time, while having had a substantial impact, had reached the point of stalemate. It was generally recognized that both industry and the enforcers would benefit from a complete legislative revision of the water pollution control statutes.

1.4 The Clean Water Act

In late 1972, Congress finally passed, over President Nixon's veto, a comprehensive recodification and revision of federal water pollution control law. The 1972 Act, 33 USC § 1251 et seq.--the product of many months of legislative deliberations—sought to establish an effective federal-state regulatory framework preserving the best aspects of both the "Water Quality Standards" and "Effluent Limitations" regulatory approaches. The goals and objectives of the 1972 Act and the mechanisms which the Act provided for enforcing progress towards those goals still function as the basic regulatory framework for the federal-state water pollution control effort.

While the 1972 Act's basic framework proved reasonably effective, many important issues had to be faced in determining exactly how to regulate within that basic framework during the first five years of EPA's implementation of the Act. These issues were dealt with in numerous EPA administrative policy determinations and court decisions which provided the background for an intensive Congressional review of the Act five years after its enactment. As a result of this review, major amendments to the Act (P.L. 95-217) were adopted in 1977 largely focusing on the manner of regulating toxic or "priority" pollutants. Congress revised the Act in 1978, 1980 and 1981. The 1978 Amendments focused on discharges of hazardous substances, and the 1980 and 1981 Amendments concentrated primarily on the federal grant programs for publicly-owned treatment works.

In this chapter we will outline the regulatory framework established by the Clean Water Act, as amended, discuss some of the major questions faced in the process of implementation and compliance, and analyze the impacts which the program has had.

2.0 The Federal-State Water Pollution Control Program - Overview

The regulatory program established under the Clean Water Act, as amended, has two basic elements—a statement of goals and objectives and a system of regulatory mechanisms calculated to achieve those goals and objectives.

2.1 Goals and Objectives

The Act's stated objective (Section 101) is to "restore and maintain the chemical, physical and biological integrity of the nation's waters." To achieve that objective, the Act establishes as "national goals": (1) achieving a level of water quality which "provides for the protection and propagation of fish, shellfish, and wildlife" and "for recreation in and on the water" by July 1, 1983; and (2) eliminating the discharge of pollutants into U.S. waters by 1985. These "national goals" are not mere verbiage but, as will be demonstrated, are a very significant factor in determining the stringency of the limitations which will be imposed.

2.2 Mechanisms for Achieving Goals and Objectives

The principal mechanism for achievement of the goals and objectives propounded originally by the 1972 Act is a system for imposing effluent limitations on or otherwise preventing discharges of "pollutants" into any "waters of the United States" from any "point source." This system includes the following five basic elements:

(1) A permit program (the National Pollutant Discharge Elimination System—NPDES) requiring dischargers to disclose the volume and nature of their discharges, authorizing EPA to specify the limitations to be imposed on such discharges, imposing on dischargers an obligation to monitor and report as to their compliance or non-compliance with the limitations so imposed, and authorizing EPA enforcement in the event of non-compliance.

(2) A system of technology-based effluent limits establishing base-level or minimum treatment required to be achieved by direct industrial dischargers (existing and new sources) and publicly owned treatment works (POTWs) and a complementary system of pretreatment requirements applicable to dischargers to publicly owned treatment works.

(3) A program for imposing more stringent limits in permits where such limits are necessary to achieve water quality standards or objectives.

(4) A set of specific provisions applicable to certain pollutant discharges of particular concern or special character (e.g., accidental or intentional discharges of oil or hazardous polluting substances, discharges of toxic chemicals creating risks to human health, and non-process discharges such as contaminated plant site runoff); and

(5) A grant program to fund POTW attainment of the applicable requirements.

Although these basic elements are readily understandable from a broad-brush perspective, a full understanding of the Act's requirements necessitates careful study of the many definitional issues and detailed policy determinations which have evolved during the process of implementing the Act.

3.0   Permitting Under The National Pollutant Discharge Elimination System

As noted, the Act's primary mechanism for imposing limitations on pollutant discharge is a nationwide permit program established under Section 402 and referred to as the National Pollutant Discharge Elimination System (NPDES). EPA's present regulations make the NPDES permit program the vehicle for consolidating permit issuance under most other EPA-administered permit programs, including RCRA, the Safe Drinking Water Act, and portions of the Clean Air Act, 40 CFR Parts 121-125. This section will consider three basic permit program issues—the program's scope of applicability, the procedures followed in permit issuance, and the nature of the conditions normally included in permits.

3.1 Program Scope and Applicability

Under the NPDES program, any person responsible for the discharge of a pollutant or pollutants into any waters of the United States from any point source must apply for and obtain a permit.

Although the definition of pollutant in Section 502(6) of the Act includes only the materials specifically listed in that section 1/ the definition is nevertheless quite broad and has been broadly interpreted to include virtually all waste material, whether or not that material has value at the time it is discharged.

The term discharge of a pollutant or pollutants under the Act is defined in Section 502(12) to mean the addition of any pollutant to waters of the United States from any point source. The Act's requirement that there must be an addition of a pollutant in order for an activity to constitute a discharge has been successfully utilized in some situations to preclude the imposition of limitations on the discharge of materials in a waste stream which are present only by reason of presence in intake waters, if the intake water is drawn from the same body of water into which the discharge is made and if the pollutants present in the intake water are not removed by the discharger as part of his usual operations (see NPDES regulations, §§ 122.15(a)(5)(iv), (v); 122.63(h).

The point source element of the discharge definition has been one of the most difficult aspects of the permit program's implementation process. The Act defines the term "point source" to include "any discernable, confined and discrete conveyance,...from which pollutants are or may be discharged." The "may be" language is important because it means that permits are required for facilities such as surface waste impoundments from which discharges are not normally anticipated except under unusual but foreseeable conditions such as excessive rainfall. The "discrete conveyance" language of the definition is so comprehensive as to cover a number of types of discharges, such as storm sewers, irrigation flows and the like, which are not really amenable to efficient regulation through the issuance of permits. For this reason, a number of statutory and administrative exemptions from the point source definition or the scope of the permit program have been adopted. These include irrigation return flows, the discharge of sewage from vessels and

---

1/   Dredged spoil, solid waste, incinerator residue, sewage, garbage, sewage sludge, munitions, chemical wastes, biological materials, radioactive materials, heat, wrecked or discarded equipment, rock, sand, cellar dirt and industrial, municipal, and agricultural waste discharged into water.

effluent from properly functioning marine engines, certain agricultural and silvicultural discharges, and certain discharges of dredged or fill material regulated under Section 404 of the Act.

EPA's regulations also provide an exemption from the individual permit requirement for certain discharges of non-process waste water into separate storm sewer systems, which will be covered by "general" permits. See NPDES regulations, § 122.57. This exemption is not available, however, where the waste water prior to discharge has been contaminated by contact with aggregations of waste, raw materials or pollutant contaminated soil at an industrial or commercial site. The precise scope of the exclusion, therefore, is a matter of considerable difficulty and careful consideration is required prior to any decision not to apply for a permit for stormwater discharges.

The term waters of the United States is defined by the EPA regulations (40 CFR § 122.3) to include (1) navigable waters; (2) tributaries of navigable waters; (3) interstate waters; and (4) intrastate lakes, rivers and streams (a) used by interstate travelers for recreation and other purposes, or (b) which are a source of fish or shellfish sold in interstate commerce, or (c) which are utilized for industrial purposes by industries engaged in interstate commerce. The intent of this definition is to cover all waters over which the broadest constitutional interpretation would allow the federal government to exercise jurisdiction. NRDC v. Callaway 392 F.Supp. 685 (D.D.C. 1975). The definition clearly covers wetlands. Few exclusions to the definition have been recognized and those which have been accepted to date seem to be limited to situations where the waterway in question is wholly confined on the property of the discharger, does not result in any flow beyond the property line, and is not available for significant public use.

One remaining major issue is the extent to which discharges to publicly or privately owned sewage systems constitute discharges to waters of the United States so as to be subject to the NPDES permit requirement. It is fairly well accepted that a discharge to a sewage system which is not connected to an operable treatment works is a discharge subject to the NPDES program, but that a discharge to a publicly owned treatment works which is capable of meeting its effluent limits is excluded from the NPDES permit requirement (40 CFR § 122.51(c)(2)). Discharges to a publicly owned treatment works not capable of meeting the applicable requirements applicable to it under the Clean Water Act are not subject to permit requirements, although the proposed NPDES permit regulations would have required permits. There are flexible permit requirements for discharges to privately owned treatment works which give EPA substantial discretion to consolidate or issue separate permits as needed to meet effluent standards.

To summarize, though there are important exclusions, the scope of the NPDES permit program is exceedingly broad and the basic intent is to cover all pollutants discharged from all facilities into virtually all waters in the U.S. including, potentially, some conveyances to public and private treatment systems.

3.2 Permitting Procedures

Under Section 402 of the Clean Water Act, EPA is the issuing authority for all NPDES permits in a state until such time as the state elects to take over program administration and obtains EPA approval of its program. Approximately two-thirds of the states have approved NPDES programs and function as the issuing authorities for permits in their jurisdictions. Where the state is the issuing authority, permitting procedures are generally comparable to the EPA procedures discussed below, with certain exceptions. For example, the states, unlike EPA, are not required to provide for an evidentiary hearing, though many do. Where the state is the issuing authority, procedures for judicial review of permit issuance are those provided under the state administrative procedure act rather than under the Clean Water Act and the Federal Administrative Procedure Act. State permit issuance is not a federal action subject to the requirements of the National Environmental Policy Act (see Chesapeake Bay Foundation, Inc. v. Virginia State Water Control Bd., 453 F. Supp. 122 (E.D.Va. 1978)).

Permits issued by states are subject to review by EPA and a state permit may not be issued if the Administrator of EPA objects within 90 days after the state's proposed issuance. The Administrator must state the reasons in support of his objections and must provide a statement of the limitations and conditions which would be included in the permit if it were to be issued by EPA. States are entitled to a public hearing regarding the Administrator's objections and if the objections are not resolved, at the hearing or otherwise, the Administrator can issue the permit. EPA has the authority to withdraw its approval of a state program and take over the entire program administration if it finds that the state is not carrying out the program in accordance with the requirements of the Act.

Procedures for permit issuance are generally as follows: A permit application, on the appropriate form, must be submitted to the EPA regional administrator (or the state, if it is the issuing authority) at least 180 days in advance of the date on which a proposed discharge is to commence or the expiration of the present permit as the case may be. Where EPA is the issuing authority, it will require, for new dischargers, submission of a new source questionnaire before it will process the permit application. This questionnaire serves as the basis for an EPA determination as to whether the facility is a "new source." If the facility is determined to be a new source, the applicant will be required to prepare an environmental assessment for EPA's use in determining whether an environmental impact statement is required by the National Environmental Policy Act.

After the application is filed, the district engineer of the Corps of Engineers must be given an opportunity to review the application to evaluate the impact of permit issuance upon anchorage and navigation. Other federal agencies, and specifically the Fish and Wildlife Service of the Department of the Interior and the National Marine Fisheries Service of the Department of Commerce, are provided a similar opportunity to comment on the application.

Where EPA is the issuing authority, the state in which the discharge will occur must be provided with an opportunity to review the application. Based on that review, the state is asked to certify, pursuant to Section 401 of the Act, that the permitted discharge will comply with applicable provisions of Sections 301, 302, 303, 306, and 307 of the Act. Since provisions in Sections 301 and 303 deal with the question of compliance with state water quality standards, the state, in effect, is asked to certify that the discharge in question will comply with all limitations necessary to meet water quality standards, treatment standards, or schedules of compliance established pursuant to any state law or regulations.

Although the applicable regulations would appear to require the applicant for an NPDES permit to provide EPA with the required certification, in practice EPA forwards applications received without a certification to the appropriate state and keeps the state advised throughout the permit proceedings. If a state does not either certify or deny certification within a reasonable time after the receipt of the permit application, it will be deemed to have waived the certification requirement. Because this time period starts to run on the state's receipt of an application, it is advisable for the applicant to send a copy of the application to the state rather than waiting for EPA to do so. EPA is barred from issuing any NPDES permit unless the state has either certified the permit or waived its right to certify.

In processing the application, the issuing authority makes tentative determinations as to whether a permit should be issued, and, if so, as to the required effluent limitations, schedules of compliance, monitoring requirements and so forth. These tentative determinations are organized into a draft permit and the discharger is normally given an opportunity to review and comment on this draft. The public is given notice of the permit application proceeding and the issuing authority's preliminary determinations with respect thereto. 2/

2/   If a variance request or other effort to secure relaxation of generally applicable effuent limits is indicated, it is appropriate to submit the request at this point in the proceedings. If this is done, a stay of further action on the permit, pending disposition of the request, would be appropriate.

The regulations provide for a period of not less than 30 days during which the public may submit written comments and/or request that a public hearing be held. The issuing authority is required to hold a public hearing if there is a significant degree of public interest in a proposed permit or group of permits. The public must be notified of such hearings and interested persons must be given at least 30 days in which to prepare for the hearings. Following the public hearing, the issuing authority issues a final determination regarding permit issuance after taking into account the comments received. Where the final determination is substantially unchanged from the tentative determination outlined in the original public notice, the issuing authority must forward a copy of the determination to any person who submitted written comments regarding the permit. Where the issuing authority's decision substantially changes the tentative determinations and draft permit, public notice must be given.

Within thirty days following the date of the notice of final determination, any interested person may request an evidentiary hearing or a legal review to reconsider the determination.

The granting of an evidentiary hearing or legal review stays the effective date of all contested provisions of the permit. The hearing is an on-the-record quasi-judicial proceeding presided over by a "judicial officer" who shall not be employed in the Office of Enforcement or the Office of Water and Waste Management, and shall not participate in the consideration or decision of any case in which he or she performed investigative or prosecutorial functions, or which is factually related to such a case. Section 124.72(a).

The decision reached on the basis of the evidentiary hearing may be appealed to the EPA Administrator. Where EPA is the issuing authority, the entire permit issuance proceeding, of course, is subject to judicial review under the Administrative Procedure Act. Where the state is the issuing authority, the state administrative procedure act probably governs.

Contested provisions of the permit become effective, and a final permit is issued, upon completion of these review proceedings. The issuance of a permit under the Clean Water Act will be deemed to fulfill the permit requirements of the Refuse Act of 1899, as well as those under the Act itself except for requirements under Section 307(a) covering discharge of toxic pollutants presenting human health risks. It should be noted, however, that issuance of a permit does not mean that no further action will be required during the permit term. As the permit makes clear, additional applications must be filed and processed whenever modifications to the facility or method of operation will result in changes to the discharge. Thus, keeping permits up-to-date will often be a continuous endeavor.

3.3 Permit Conditions

An NPDES permit performs two basic functions in the Clean Water Act regulatory process. It establishes with specificity the level of performance which the discharger must maintain and it places on the discharger an affirmative obligation to report to the cognizant authorities when that level of performance is not achieved. Many of the conditions typically included in industrial permits are either negotiable or susceptible to legal attack. Accordingly, proposed permit conditions should not be accepted without question. They should be carefully analyzed and, if burdensome and unjustified, they should be contested. The more significant permit conditions are discussed below.

Monitoring and Reporting—The monitoring requirements in an NPDES permit are of critical importance. The effectiveness of the permit program in assuring compliance with applicable effluent limitations, water quality standards, pretreatment standards and other requirements established pursuant to the 1972 Act will depend, in major part, on the effectiveness of monitoring and data maintenance requirements included in permits pursuant to Section 308. 3/ Under that section, EPA is authorized to require the owner or operator of any point source to establish and maintain specified records, make specified reports, install, use and maintain monitoring equipment and methods, take specified samples, and provide other information which EPA may reasonably require. As with the permit program in general, the states have the opportunity to administer their own monitoring programs and, upon obtaining EPA's approval of an appropriate monitoring program, the state becomes the monitoring authority for all point sources within its jurisdiction.

The enforcing authority will have the right to enter the premises of the discharger at any reasonable time, inspect the records required to be maintained, take test samples and so forth. All data obtained under Section 308 is required to be open to the public except to the extent non-disclosure is necessary to protect trade secrets.

Section 122.63 of the NPDES regulations specifies the manner in which effluent limitations are to be included in permits and thus imposed on permittees. The monitoring requirements in various sections of Part 122 are intended to assure compliance with the limits included in permits pursuant to § 122.63. Under these provisions, limits are to be imposed and monitoring is to take place at the point of discharge except in limited situations where monitoring at point of discharge is impracticable or infeasible. The regulations do

---

3/   Public treatment works subject to the Act's permit requirements must also impose monitoring requirements on industrial discharges into their facilities.

provide the permit issuer with authority to require monitoring of internal waste streams in certain situations such as where the final discharge point is inaccessible, where wastes at the point of discharge are so diluted as to make monitoring impracticable, or where interference among pollutants at the point of discharge would prevent detection or analysis. A permittee is required to monitor, as specified in his permit, to determine (1) compliance with the limitations on amounts, concentrations or other pollutant measures specified in the permit, (2) the total volume of effluent discharged from each discharge point and (3) otherwise as required by the permit.

The permit must include requirements for maintenance and proper installation of the monitoring equipment, must specify monitoring methods and frequencies adequate to provide reliable data regarding the volume of flow and quantity of pollutants discharged, and must specify the test methodology to be utilized in analyzing the samples taken. The regulations put the burden on the applicant, if he believes that the monitoring requirements specified in a draft permit are inadequate to yield accurate data, to request additional monitoring requirements which are sufficient to achieve an acceptable degree of accuracy. Compliance with the effluent limits set in the permit will be assessed through application of the monitoring methods which the permit provides. Thus, unless inadequate monitoring requirements are contested during the permit issuance procedures, it may be difficult to use alleged inadequacy as a defense in any later enforcement action.

Monitoring records, including charts from continuous monitoring devices and calibration and maintenance records, must be maintained for a minimum period of three years with automatic extensions of that period being provided throughout the course of any unresolved litigation regarding discharges pursuant to the permit or the effluent guidelines included therein. Extensions may also be requested by the permit issuing authority.

The results of monitoring must be reported periodically to the permit issuing authority on forms provided by the authority. Frequency reporting is governed by the terms of each individual permit and must be at least annual. In addition to the periodic reporting requirement, § 122.18 of the regulations requires non-compliance reporting on a quarterly basis, and certain toxic discharges must be reported within 24 hours. § 122.62(g). 4/ Failure to properly monitor and report is a violation of the permit and any person who knowingly makes any false statement in monitoring records, monitoring reports, or compliance or non-compliance notifications is subject upon conviction to both substantial fines and criminal penalties.

4/ The non-compliance reporting requirements are specific and detailed and should be carefully reviewed by all permittees.

It is evident from the foregoing that the monitoring requirements may occupy a considerable amount of employee time, require
the installation of sophisticated sampling devices, extensive analysis
and testing, and detailed recordkeeping and reporting. A severe
strain may be placed on the capacities of private test laboratories
qualified to perform these services particularly as the "toxics strategy" is implemented. Many companies may find themselves compelled to develop additional in-house technical capability in order to
meet the Section 308 requirements as imposed in the permit.

Schedules of Compliance—Although the Act itself establishes
firm deadlines for the achievement of the required levels of treatment, the issuing authority has considerable latitude to require
compliance or interim steps towards compliance at earlier dates.
The Act also provides some latitude for extending compliance deadlines in certain situations, as where compliance is dependent on
connection to a yet-to-be constructed public treatment works or
where use of innovative technology is involved. In view of these
potential variables, careful consideration of proposed schedules is
definitely advisable.

Effluent Limitations—In situations where a permit is issued
prior to the publication of effluent limitations for the particular
industrial category or subcategory applicable to the facility being
permitted, there is considerable flexibility in the determination of
the precise effluent limitations which will be mandated by the
permit since the limits, in this interim period, are to be based on
"engineering judgment." Even after promulgation of limitations, the
applicant may seek modification of limits in the permit pursuant to
the variance clause, and there is also considerable opportunity for
the permitting authority to impose discharge limitations more
stringent than the "base-level" effluent guidelines, where necessary
to meet water quality standards, water quality related effluent
limitations, the requirements of state planning processes, or other
applicable limitations. Thus, there is considerable room for discussion regarding limits to be imposed in permits and a careful engineering analysis of proposed permit limits is definitely required.

Additional Effluent Limitations—To date, NPDES permits
have normally specified four or five pollutants as being subject to
effluent limitations; a far greater number will be included in future
permits as a result of EPA's toxics strategy, which is discussed
below. EPA's NPDES permit application and related regulations
(§ 122.53) require extensive waste stream analysis in order to file
permit applications, extensive cataloging in the application of
virtually all chemicals in the waste stream, and imposition of controls on the discharge of those chemicals. Many of these requirements have been suspended by the Reagan Administration. Implementation of these requirements will complicate the permit process
even further and require more extensive monitoring than was the
case.

Duration and Revocation—Permits may be valid for terms of up to five years, 5/ and may be subject to revocation or modification based on a very minimal showing of "cause." A company's interest, in connection with the permit process will generally be best served by obtaining a permit with the maximum duration and with as much specificity as is obtainable in regard to the possible grounds of revocation or modification. On the permit's expiration, the permittee, in order to obtain reissuance, must demonstrate compliance with any more stringent criteria which have been promulgated during the term of the original permit. The application for reissuance should be filed well in advance of the existing permit's expiration date.

Other—Depending on the precise nature of the applicant's operation, consideration might be given to bypass and upset provisions, start-up period exclusions and so forth. Those who will be responsible for complying with the permits are well advised to make every reasonable effort to predict potential compliance problems and discuss them fully during the permit issuance process rather than in later enforcement proceedings.

4.0 Establishing the Limitations for Inclusion in the Permit—Technology and Water Quality-Based Limits

The most difficult questions which EPA has faced in the development of the Clean Water Act program have involved the establishment of limits to be imposed in the permits issued under the NPDES mechanism. As previously noted, the Act contemplates a two-part approach: (1) nationwide base-level treatment to be established through an assessment of what is technologically achievable and (2) more stringent treatment requirements for specific plants where necessary to achieve water quality objectives for the particular body of water into which that plant discharges. While this concept seems simple, its execution requires answers to questions which have proved exceedingly complex:

— What specific pollutants should be addressed in establishing the limitations?
— How can technology-based effluent limits adequately take into account all factors relevant to the

---

5/   However, EPA regulations require that permits for the 34 industry categories now subject to review for establishment of toxics oriented BAT limits (see Part 4.1) either (a) be short-term permits expiring before the deadline for achievement of the new BAT limits or (b) include a "reopener clause" authorizing imposition of the new limits in the permit.

question of what is achievable and how can plant-
to-plant variability be accommodated?
--   What are the mechanics for deciding when more
stringent limitations are required to meet water
quality objectives and how do we get the necessary
analyses performed prior to making permit issuance
decisions?

These questions and the process by which they have been answered
furnish the subject matter for this section.

4.1 Pollutants to be Addressed

Although the Act is broadly inclusive in its definition of
pollutants which are subject to regulation and permitting, it did not,
prior to 1977, furnish adequate guidance as to the level of detail
with which pollutants should be categorized in developing the effluent limits which the Act required. For that reason, and perhaps
because of the tremendous schedule pressure which the unrealistic
1972 Act deadlines imposed, EPA, in developing the system of
limitations required by the Act, focused almost entirely on gross or
"conventional" measures of pollutants such as biochemical oxygen
demand (BOD), Suspended Solids (SS) and acidity and alkalinity
(pH). As long as this approach was followed, EPA's basic system of
effluent limits and permit requirements was unable to take into
account the fact that some pollutants (organic chemicals, heavy
metals, pesticides and so forth) might be deserving of more concern
and more stringent regulation than the solids and oxygen demanding
materials contained in conventional wastes. Regulation of "toxic"
pollutants was thought to be the exclusive province of Section 307
(a) of the Act, which authorized EPA to identify and regulate, on a
chemical-by-chemical rather than industry-to-industry basis, substances which it could prove to have toxic effects on identified
organisms in affected waters.

Because of the stringent burden of proof and extensive procedures which the pre-1977 Section 307 required, EPA was not
successful in establishing under that section a meaningful program
to control the discharge of toxic pollutants. Only a limited number
of substances were identified as toxic substances. Long delays were
encountered before final effluent limits were adopted for any of
them.

The absence of an effective toxics strategy under the 1972
Act resulted in litigation against EPA by the Natural Resources
Defense Council, an environmental organization. That litigation was
settled, and in the process of settlement, EPA and the environmental litigants developed an overall policy which focuses all of the
regulatory mechanisms provided by the 1972 Act upon the primary
objective of effectively regulating the discharge of toxic or priority
pollutants.   In developing this policy, the parties identified the

pollutants which would be the primary subject of regulation, the industries which would be the primary concern in applying the regulations, and the methodology for applying the regulatory tools which the Act provides pursuant to an overall toxic-oriented strategy. The agreements reached in these negotiations were embodied in a settlement decree in the case (NRDC v. Train, 8 E.R.C. 2120 (D.D.C. 1976)) and that decree has become the manifesto for toxics strategy under the Clean Water Act.

The decree mandates full utilization of all the available regulatory tools under the Act with a specific focus on the identified "priority pollutants." Pursuant to the decree, EPA must develop a program to regulate the discharge of 65 categories of "priority pollutants" (including at least 129 specific chemical substances--see Annex A, which is attached) by 34 industry categories which cover over 700 subcategories. More than 70 percent of the nation's industry will be affected by the decree. The 34 industry categories are listed in Annex B.

The consent decree required adoption of best available technology effluent limitations for each priority pollutant in each industrial category by June 30, 1983. These limitations had to be applicable to at least 95 percent of the point sources in each identified industry category or subcategory. Similar technology-oriented requirements must be adopted for new sources and sources discharging into publicly owned treatment works. The basis for excluding a category of point sources from the new toxic focused system of technology-based effluent limitations was narrowly circumscribed. A category could be excluded from regulation under the decree only if:

-- equivalent or greater protection is already provided by a presently effective effluent limit (e.g., a Section 307 limitation or prohibition on the specific chemical in question);

-- the specific pollutant in question is present in the industry effluent only by reason of the presence of that pollutant in intake waters. Except in the case of pretreatment requirements, this basis for exclusion is subject to the further limitation that the water body which is the source of such intake waters must be the same water body as the one to which the discharge occurs; and

-- the pollutant is either not present in the industry discharge or is present only in trace amounts not likely to cause toxic effects to any identifiable organism.

In addition to this new, stringent toxic pollutant focused set of industry-by-industry effluent limits, the consent decree made specific provision for full implementation of the waterway segment-by-segment approach. It required EPA to make provision for applying more stringent requirements for the identified priority pollutants where necessary to achieve water quality objectives; to publish a new criteria document on health and aquatic life effects of the identified priority pollutants by June 30, 1978; and to have in effect a "specific and substantial" program for determining when limits more stringent than the industry-by-industry technology-based effluent limits are required.

All NPDES permits issued or renewed after January 1, 1978 were required to make specific provision for modification to comply with these new effluent limits as they are developed.

Thus, the NRDC consent decree provided a judicial mandate for full utilization of the Water Act enforcement mechanisms in a carefully formulated toxics or priority pollutant-focused program.

The 1977 Amendments adopted this mandate and enacted it into the Federal statutory law. The Amendments:

— adopt the consent decree list of priority pollutants as the list of toxic substances to be given primary emphasis in the implementation of the Water Act (This list of toxic substances is reproduced as Annex A.);

— require adoption of best available technology effluent limitations for each listed substance by July 1, 1980;

— require compliance with these BAT effluent limitations by July 1, 1984 (instead of July 1, 1983, as required by the consent decree);

— permit EPA to add to or remove from the list of "toxic" substances (Although the Act provides no specific criterion for making such additions or deletions, the Conference Committee Report states that a decision by the Administrator to add or remove a substance from the list is final unless it is based on arbitrary and capricious action);

— require compliance with BAT effluent limitations for toxic pollutants subsequently added to the list within three years of the establishment of the limitations;

— provide a new system for upgrading and enforcing pretreatment regulations based on both the effluent limitations on the discharge from publicly owned treatment works and the intended use of the sludge from the facilities;

— authorize EPA to adopt regulations establishing best management practices to control the discharge of the listed pollutants in the form of runoff or other uncontrolled discharges from industrial plant sites, parking lots and so forth;

— require effluent limitations based on best available technology for other non-conventional pollutants by July 1, 1987; and

— require the Administrator to publish information related to the factors necessary to maintain fish, shellfish and wildlife in waterway segments.

In short, the 1977 Amendments confirm and institutionalize the consent decree with some modifications.

Congress' action in amending the Act does not eliminate the function of the consent decree in spelling out in more detail EPA's obligations in regard to implementation of a toxics strategy under the amended Act. On March 9, 1979, after further extensive negotiations, the consent decree was amended to reflect the changes made by the 1977 Amendments and to respond to the operational problems perceived by EPA since the decree was originally issued in 1976. These modifications to the consent decree reflect the 1977 Amendments' extension of the time for compliance with effluent limitations reflecting best available technology to June 30, 1984. They clarify EPA's responsibility regarding the development of direct discharge and pretreatment standards for pollutants other than those specifically included on the priority pollutant list. The modification also extended the deadlines for the development of technology-based effluent limitations for the 34 industrial categories and expanded the permissible bases upon which EPA may exclude substances from regulation pursuant to the consent decree. These deadlines were extended somewhat in May 1982, but the District Court rejected EPA's bid for extensions of up to thirty months.

This expanded authority to exclude results primarily from a new definition of trace amounts. "Trace amounts" which can be excluded from regulation include (i) substances not detectable by analytical methodology, (ii) pollutants detectable in discharges from only a small number of sources within a subcategory and unique to those specific subcategories, (iii) substances present in amounts too small to be reduced by known technologies, and (iv) pollutants controlled by technologies upon which other limitations are based. The Administrator is also authorized to exclude pollutants from coverage under the direct discharge effluent limitations if the amount and toxicity of such pollutants within a category or subcategory does not, in his judgment, justify the development of regulations having nationwide applicability.

The basis for excluding pollutants from the applicability of pretreatment standards is similarly expanded. EPA is authorized to make such exclusions when it finds that the amount and toxicity of all incompatible pollutants discharged by a category or subcategory taken together is so small that regulations of nationwide applicability governing pretreatment of those pollutants is not justified.

In the water quality standards area, the modified consent decree makes more specific the program required for identifying bodies of water as to which the technology-based effluent limitations are inadequate to protect toxic-related water quality objectives. Under the modified decree, the evaluation program must include a process for identifying specific portions of waters contaminated by discharges of toxic pollutants, the pollutants present, the concentrations found, and the sources. In making this determination, EPA is specifically required to survey a substantial number of portions of navigable waters, to develop a process for identifying toxic pollutants which should have nationwide or regional controls, and to establish a process for developing and implementing the necessary control strategies for reducing or eliminating the discharges of toxic pollutants in these specific waterway segments. The affected waters were to be identified by EPA by July 1, 1981; by December 1981, EPA was to publish a strategy for reducing or eliminating the toxic discharges to these designated waters, including the legal authority to be used to enforce the program and a schedule for implementation. EPA has not met the schedule and has yet to publish the necessary control strategies.

It seems clear that the consent decree as confirmed by the 1977 Amendments and modified pursuant thereto will result in a major transformation of the entire Clean Water Act program. The toxics strategy has changed from a relatively minor Water Act specialty to the driving force behind the program. The industry-by-industry technology-based effluent limitations will be transformed from limited requirements focused on three or four conventional pollutants to a very specific system of limitations potentially applicable to 129 or more different pollutants for each industry category. Water quality standards, heretofore of relatively little concern to industry, must be more fully implemented with a toxics orientation.

These difficult questions must be addressed in the face of severe time pressures and of the likelihood of continuing litigation and continuing legislative initiatives. Against this background, we will now turn to a more detailed consideration of EPA's process for the development of technology and water quality-based effluent limitations.

4.2 Required Level of Treatment—Technology-Based Limits for "Existing" Direct Discharges

Section 301(b) of the 1972 Act provided for the establishment of nationally applicable technology-based effluent limitations on an industry-by-industry basis. These effluent limitations were to establish a nationwide base-level of treatment for existing direct discharge sources in every significant industrial category. This level of treatment was to be achieved in two phases. For "existing" 6/ industrial discharges, Section 301 directs the achievement:

> by July 1, 1977, of effluent limitations which will require application of the best practicable control technology currently available, and by July 1, 1983 of effluent limitations which will require application of the best available technology economically achievable.

Best practicable technology (BPT) was defined generally by EPA as the "average of the best existing performance by well-operated plants within each industrial category or subcategory." The word "control" emphasized Congress' expectation that, in establishing the 1977 effluent guidelines, EPA would emphasize end-of-pipe treatment rather than in-plant control measures. However, Section 304(b)(1) of the Act makes it clear that the alternative of in-plant process changes may be considered, at least for the purpose of determining whether a proposed effluent limitation is "practicable." The word "practicable," when read together with the provisions of Section 304(b)(1)(B), requires that effluent limitations be justifiable in terms of the "total cost of (industry-wide) application of (the required) technology in relation to the effluent reduction benefits to be achieved." This determination is to take into account a number of specific factors such as the age of the equipment and facilities involved, the process employed, and non-water quality environmental impacts. Thus, in developing the BPT limitations, EPA was required to make what amounted to a cost-benefit balancing test that took into account a broad range of specific engineering factors relating to the ability of plants within a category or subcategory to achieve the limits. The BPT definition was essentially

---

6/   The Act's "existing discharge" provisions will in fact apply to some newly constructed facilities since they cover any source for which a new source performance standard (see Part 4.3) has not been proposed.

unchanged by the 1977 Amendments. It is the basis upon which the limits in the first round NPDES permits were developed and continues to be applicable to those permits as well as to EPA's efforts to develop the few BPT limits yet to be established and to any modifications proposed to the existing limits.

EPA defined best available technology (BAT) as the "very best control and treatment measures that have been or are capable of being achieved." The agency can consider in-plant process changes in addition to end-of-pipe treatment measures in establishing these 1983 limitations. Although EPA is required to consider the cost of achieving the required effluent reduction in determining whether a BAT limitation is economically achievable, it is not required to balance cost against effluent reduction benefit as it is in the case of the BPT standards. The engineering factors required to be considered—age of equipment and facility, process employed, process changes, non-water quality environmental impacts and so forth—are the same for BAT as for BPT.

The BAT definition was essentially unchanged by the 1977 Amendments but its scope of applicability was radically altered and its date for attainment was extended. Under the 1977 Amendments, the BAT effluent limitations are to focus primarily on the priority pollutants listed in the NRDC consent decree and on additional toxic pollutants identified pursuant to Section 307(a) of the Act. These new priority and toxic pollutant-oriented best available technology effluent limitations are to be adopted in accordance with a detailed time schedule established by the consent decree as modified 7/ and are required to be complied with by July 1, 1984 for the pollutants identified in the consent decree. For pollutants not listed in the consent decree but identified as toxic pollutants under Section 307(a)(1) of the Act, compliance with BAT effluent limits is required no later than three years after the date on which the limitations are established.

The "conventional" pollutant measures, which were the primary focus of EPA's pre-1977 BAT effluent limitations are specifically excluded from the scope of coverage of the BAT limits provided by the 1977 Amendments. Those pollutants are subject to an entirely new treatment standard established for the first time in the 1977 Amendments—"Best Conventional Pollutant Control Technology."

The "Best Conventional Technology" effluent limitations are, like the BPT and BAT limitations, to be adopted on an industry-by-industry basis but are to apply for each affected industry only to pollutants which are identified as "conventional." The 1977 Amendments specifically included within the definition of "conventional

_____

7/   There have been several schedule modifications.

pollutants" biological oxygen demand (BOD), suspended solids (SS), fecal coliform bacteria, and pH. EPA is authorized to include additional pollutants within the conventional pollutants definition, and, pursuant to that authorization, has identified or proposed to identify chemical oxygen demand (COD), residual chlorine, and phosphorus. Thus far, EPA has added only oil and grease to the statutory list of conventional pollutants. The Act specifically excludes heat from the conventional pollutant definition. The Best Conventional Technology limitations are to be adopted by EPA based on a consideration of the reasonableness of the relationship between the cost of attaining a reduction in effluents and the effluent reduction benefits which will result. The cost of providing treatment to comply with these limits is expected by the Congress to be generally comparable to the cost of achieving the secondary treatment limitation for publicly owned treatment works. As with BPT and BAT limits, EPA is required, in adopting Best Conventional Technology effluent limits, to take into consideration factors such as the age of the equipment and facilities involved, the process employed, engineering aspects, process changes and non-water quality environmental impacts (including energy requirements).

The Congress anticipated that EPA, in developing the Best Conventional Technology limits, would conduct a review of the old BAT limits for conventional pollutants and reduce the stringency of such limits to the extent indicated by the economic justification and cost comparability with secondary treatment requirements of the Best Conventional Technology definition in the 1977 Amendments. As might have been expected, EPA, in conducting this review, determined for the most part that the old BAT limits for conventional pollutants met the new Best Conventional Technology limits. Thus, though EPA made some adjustment of the pre-1977 BAT to date limits for some industries (e.g., a number of categories of the food processing industry), for most industries the first result of the 1977 Amendments was to convert the old BAT limits into Best Conventional Technology limits. Under the 1977 Amendments, compliance with Best Conventional Technology effluent limitations must be achieved by July 1, 1984.

EPA's first effort at developing BCT regulations was reversed because the Agency failed to adequately consider cost-effectiveness in the development of these rules. American Paper Institute v. EPA, 660 F.2d 954 (4th Cir. 1981). EPA has recently proposed new regulations, which appear to be far less costly than the original rules. In many industry categories, EPA's new methodology results in BCT limitations no more stringent than those established for BPT.

The last of the three categories of technology-based effluent limits for existing industry direct discharges which the 1977 Amendments provide is the system of effluent limitations to be adopted for "nonconventional nontoxic" pollutants. This is essentially an "everything else" category which applies to all pollutants other than those identified as priority pollutants, toxic pollutants or conventional pollutants under the preceding sections of Section 301. The 1977 Amendments appear to require compliance with best available technology effluent limits to be adopted for these pollutants by July 1, 1984 or three years after the date the limitations are established by EPA regulations, whichever is later, but in no case later than July 1, 1987. Though this section of the Act would appear to contemplate that EPA will have adopted effluent limitations for all pollutants by July 1, 1987 at the latest, it is probably unreasonable to expect the Agency to accomplish this objective. Further, in light of the fact that EPA is authorized to add pollutants to the lists of toxic and conventional pollutants from time to time, it is questionable whether the nonconventional pollutants provision is necessary or even helpful. Full implementation of the provision is unlikely and its eventual deletion would appear to be advisable.

4.3 Required Level of Treatment—Technology-Based Limits for "New Source" Direct Discharges

The establishment of effluent limitations for "new sources" (defined as any facility the construction of which is commenced "after the publication of proposed regulations" prescribing an applicable standard of performance) is separately dealt with in Section 306 of the Act. Although the general approach for establishment of new source performance standards under Section 306 is similar to the approach for the establishment of Section 301 effluent limitations (discussed in the previous section) there are significant differences both as to the level of treatment required and the manner of applying the limitations established.

Section 306(a)(1) of the Act defines the term "standard of performance" as "a standard for the control of the discharge of pollutants which reflects the greatest degree of effluent reduction...achievable through application of the best available demonstrated control technology, processes, operating methods, and other alternatives, including, where practicable, standards permitting no discharge of pollutants" (emphasis added). The primary difference between this criteria and the Section 301 criteria discussed in the previous section lies in the fact that, under Section 306, EPA is specifically required to consider not only pollution control and abatement processes and techniques, but also various alternative production processes, operating methods, in-plant control procedures and so forth. Accordingly, in the establishment of Section 306 New Source Performance Standards, alternatives or supplements to end-of-pipe treatment will be emphasized. Production process alternatives, which, though less economic, may have a significantly reduced pollution potential may, as a practical matter, be required.

A second major difference regarding criteria for development of new source performance standards is the absence of the kind of

requirements for detailed consideration of economic and technological factors which are established by Section 304 for existing
source effluent limitations procedures. The absence of such required considerations reflects a presumption that if a source is yet
to be constructed, there is much greater flexibility to alter total
facility design so as to be capable of achieving stringent effluent
limitations. Thus EPA has far greater discretion in the promulgation
of new source performance standards than it does with respect to
existing sources.

A third, and major, factor to be taken into account when
considering the applicability of new source performance standards is
that the Act provides virtually no flexibility for moderating the
impact of those standards when applied to specific facilities. The
fundamental factors variance and other modification authorities
provided by the Act are not applicable in the new source situation
and, accordingly, strict conformity with the new soure performance
standards, where applicable, is essential.

Finally, where EPA is the issuing authority, the issuance of a
permit for a new source discharge is a federal action subject to the
review requirements of the National Environmental Policy Act.
Thus, where the issuance of a new source discharge permit is found
to be a major action with a significant effect on the environment, an
environmental impact statement will be required. The result will be
both substantial delay in the issuance of the new source permit and
the potential inclusion of stringent requirements in permits which
are issued.

Because the determination as to whether a facility is a new
source has such a substantial impact, both in terms of the stringency
of the treatment standards applied and the length of time required
in order to obtain a permit, the question of precisely when a facility
"commences construction" for purposes of determining whether new
source performance standards are applicable has been a source of
major controversy. This issue is addressed in considerable detail in
§ 122.66 of EPA's NPDES regulations (cited above) and has also been
extensively considered in court decisions and in opinions of EPA's
General Counsel. The question of when construction is commenced
is nevertheless a very difficult factual issue and companies planning
new facilities should carefully review this issue with counsel early in
the planning process.

Section 306 does offer both to new sources and to new dischargers which are not new sources one important protection which
is not available to existing sources under Section 301. Section 306
specifically provides that any new facility constructed to meet all
applicable new source standards of performance in effect as of the
time it is constructed, may not be subjected to any more stringent
standards for ten years from the date construction is completed or
for the period of depreciation under the Internal Revenue Code,
whichever is shorter. This protection from more stringent standards

of performance, as EPA construes the Act, is not applicable to any more stringent permit conditions which are not technology-based, e.g., it is not applicable to conditions based on water quality standards or toxic pollutant chemical-based prohibitions or on effluent standards under Section 307(a) or to any new permit conditions which are applicable to pollutants not controlled by the applicable new source performance standards with which the facility complied at the time of construction. It should be noted that, on the expiration of the ten-year protection period, immediate compliance with the standards in effect at the time of such expiration will be required. No implementation period for compliance with those standards will be allowed.

4.4   Required Level of Treatment—Technology-Based Limits for Indirect Dischargers (Pre-Treatment)

Industrial facilities that discharge into publicly owned works (POTWs) are not directly subject to the direct discharge treatment standards under Sections 301 and 306, which are discussed above, but are subject to comparable treatment requirements (pretreatment standards) adopted pursuant to Section 307(b) of the Act. Pretreatment standards are calculated to achieve two basic objectives: (1) to protect the operation of publicly owned treatment works and (2) to prevent the discharge of pollutants which pass through publicly owned treatment works without receiving adequate treatment. The dual objectives of the pretreatment program result in a two-part system of controls under the applicable EPA regulations, 40 CFR Part 403.

The first part of the pretreatment regulations focuses primarily on the objective of preventing the discharge into POTWs of pollutants which will interfere with or prevent the proper operation of the receiving treatment works. Consistent with this basic objective, the generally applicable pretreatment requirements (40 CFR § 403.5) are applicable to all pollutants discharged into a publicly owned treatment works which might interfere with the facility's operation. This "protection" standard takes the form of a prohibition on the introduction into any publicly owned treatment works of:

(i)   Pollutants which create a fire or explosion hazard in the POTW;

(ii)   Nondomestic discharges with a pH lower than 5.0 unless the works is specifically designed to accommodate such discharges;

(iii)   Solid or viscous pollutants which obstruct the flow in a sewer system;

(iv)   Discharges of such volume and concentration that they upset the treatment process and cause a permit violation (e.g., oxygen demanding pollutants such as BOD); and

(v)   Heat in amounts which will inhibit biological
        activity in the POTW resulting in interference,
        but in no case heat in such quantities that the
        temperature influent at the treatment works
        exceeds 40°C (104°F) unless the works are
        designed to accommodate such heat.

The second major objective of the pretreatment regulations—preventing the discharge in the publicly owned treatment works of pollutants which pass through those treatment works without receiving adequate treatment—is to be achieved by "categorical" pretreatment regulations. These categorical regulations are applicable only to "incompatible" pollutants—e.g., pollutants other than biochemical oxygen demand, suspended solids, pH and fecal coliform bacteria, and which are not adequately treated in the normal publicly owned treatment works treatment process. 8/ These categorical pretreatment regulations, like the new BAT regulations and new source performance standards, are to focus primarily on the 34 industries and 65 toxic pollutant categories specified in the NRDC consent decree. For each discharger into a publicly owned treatment works, they are intended to achieve a level of treatment prior to discharge from the publicly owned treatment works equivalent to that which would have been provided had the industrial facility discharged those pollutants directly.

Accordingly, the industrial facility discharging into a publicly owned treatment works will be required to achieve, in meeting the applicable pretreatment limits, a level of treatment performance equivalent to the applicable BAT effluent limitations or new source performance standards unless the receiving POTW has an approved pretreatment program and requests revision of the applicable pretreatment limit based on the POTW's demonstrated capability to remove that pollutant in its treatment process. In order to qualify for a revision, the POTW must provide complete, consistent removal of each pollutant for which a discharge limit revision is sought, and its sludge use or disposal practices must, at the time of the application and thereafter, remain in compliance with all applicable criteria, guidelines and regulations for sludge use and disposal. EPA is in the process of simplifying the regulations for granting indirect dischargers credit for the pollutant removals achieved by POTWs.

Pretreatment requirements are directly enforceable by EPA and states with NPDES permit issuance authority, but the EPA regulations contemplate eventual delegation of primary enforcement

---

8/   Additional pollutants may be identified as "compatible" for a
      particular treatment works if it can be shown that the facility
      in question adequately treats those pollutants.

responsibility to individual POTWs with EPA and the states receding to a backup role.

Under the regulations, any POTW (or combination of POTWs operated by the same authority) having a total design flow greater than five million gallons per day must, if it receives incompatible industrial waste, develop and implement a pretreatment program within three years after its next issued NPDES permit and no later than July 1, 1983. A POTW must have an approved pretreatment program in order to seek modification of the categorical pretreatment standards to reflect its treatment capabilities (40 CFR § 403.8(a)). POTW programs must meet funding, personnel, legal, and procedural criteria sufficient to ensure that the POTW's enforcement responsibilities can be carried out. Once the program is developed and approved, the POTW will be responsible for enforcement of the national pretreatment standards. A POTW may exercise enforcement authority through a number of methods including contracts, joint powers agreements, ordinances, or otherwise.

Finally, pretreatment regulations establish extensive reporting requirements, for both industrial users and POTWs in order to monitor and demonstrate compliance with categorical pretreatment standards.

The pretreatment regulations will have a major impact on all industries subject to categorical pretreatment standards, as well as on other industrial users of POTWs which will have to comply with prohibited discharge requirements.

4.5 Technology-Based Treatment Standards for Industrial Dischargers Dealing with Process Variability

As the technology-based effluent limits become more complex and address many more pollutants, adopting effluent limitations which properly take into account all of the factors listed in Section 304 of the Act as required considerations in the development of such limitations will obviously become much more difficult. The likelihood of having effluent limitations adopted without consideration of special circumstances applicable to particular plants or categories of plants in an industry will therefore become much greater and valid application of technology-based effluent limits will, in many cases, demand some mechanism by which plant-to-plant variations can be taken into account.

The mechanisms to permit plant-to-plant flexibility which are specifically provided by the Act are exceedingly limited in scope. Section 301(c) grants the Administrator authority to modify the 1984 BAT requirements or the related pretreatment requirements if it can be shown that the economic capability of the discharger necessitates less stringent limitations. A further prerequisite to such a modification is a showing that it will result in further progress toward elimination of the discharge of pollutants. Though this basis for granting a variance is reasonably broad, the circumstances in which it can be granted are strictly limited. The Section 301(c) variance does not apply to the "Best Conventional Technology" effluent limitations, and Section 301(l) of the Act precludes the modification of any effluent limitation regulating a toxic or priority pollutant. Accordingly, the Section 301(c) variance authority applies only to the "nonconventional nontoxic" pollutants and, in view of this fact, the utility of this authority is exceedingly limited.

Section 301(g), which is also applicable to the nonconventional nontoxic pollutants (excluding heat), requires the Administrator to modify BAT or pretreatment limits based on a showing by the discharger that the requirement as modified will result at a minimum in compliance with the 1977 BPT requirements, that the modification of the requirements will not result in any additional requirements on any other point or non-point source of pollutants, and that the modification will not interfere with the attainment or maintenance of a level of water quality which will assure protection of public water supplies and fishable and swimmable waters. For this type of variance, an application must be filed within 270 days after publication of the effluent guidelines from which a variance is sought or from the date of enactment of the 1977 Amendments.

The final statutory basis for modification of BAT effluent limits and pretreatment standards is set forth in Section 301(k). That subsection authorizes the Administrator or state issuing authority to issue a permit providing for compliance by July 1,1987 rather than 1984 if a source seeks to achieve the applicable limits through the use of innovative technology which has the potential for industry-wide application and has a substantial likelihood of achieving greater effluent reduction than the effluent limitations or will result in significantly lower costs. It is unclear whether this innovative technology variance may be granted for toxic pollutant limits in view of the prohibition against modification of toxic pollutant effluent limitations set forth in Section 301(l).

With respect to the 1977 BPT effluent limits, the Act provides only one basis for extending the time for compliance. Direct dischargers which planned to comply with direct discharge requirements by tying in to a publicly owned treatment works but were unable to achieve compliance by the 1977 deadline because the POTW was not constructed can, under carefully limited circumstances, obtain permit revisions to allow additional time until the POTW is operational or until July 1, 1983, whichever is earlier.

Although the statutory variance authority is of limited utility, EPA has provided, by administrative interpretation, a variance mechanism which promises to be much more helpful. This administrative variance has come to be referred to as the "fundamental factors" variance and was initially applied to the 1977 BPT effluent limitations through the inclusion in each set of effluent limitations regulations of a variance clause. This clause allowed a discharger to demonstrate that the limitations should not apply to its facility because of the existence of factors which were fundamentally different from those considered by EPA in the process of developing the effluent limitations.

The scope of the required variance clause was expanded in the case of Appalachian Power Company v. Train, 545 F.2d 1351 (4th Cir. 1976), and the necessity of some sort of variance mechanism was confirmed by the Supreme Court in the Dupont case, 430 U.S. 112 (1977). The need for a fundamental factors variance is inherent in the nature of the process for development of effluent limitations under the Clean Water Act and pursuant to the provisions of the Federal Administrative Procedures Act. Since it is virtually impossible to fully consider all of the factors required to be considered by Section 304 of the Act for every plant or type of plant in every industrial category, there must be some mechanism for taking into account factors not fully considered in the regulation development process at the time the effluent limitations are applied in a permit to a particular facility.

In recognition of this fact, EPA, in the pretreatment regulations and NPDES permit program regulations discussed above, has expanded the circumstances in which the fundamental factors variance is applicable. It is now available with respect to the categorical pretreatment regulations, as well as for all of the technology-based effluent limits for existing sources. It is not available for new source performance standards (on the theory that a facility yet to be constructed has considerable design flexibility and is not constrained by the numerous existing factors which may affect attainable treatment levels) or to water quality-related effluent limitations. In order to obtain a fundamental factors variance, the discharger must bear the burden of showing that factors applicable to this facility are fundamentally different from those considered in the development of the effluent limitations guidelines. Factors which § 125.31 of the regulations allow to be considered as fundamentally different are:

(1)   The nature or quality of the pollutants contained in the raw waste load of the applicant's process waste water;

(2)   The volume of the discharger's process waste water and effluent discharged;

(3)   Non-water quality environmental impacts of control and treatment of the discharger's raw waste load (are these impacts fundamentally more adverse than those considered during the development of national limits?);

(4)   Energy requirements of the application of control and treatment technology (are they fundamentally greater than those assessed in developing national limits?);

(5) Age, size, land availability and configuration as they relate to the discharger's equipment or facilities, processes employed; engineering aspects of the application of control technology; and

(6) Cost of compliance with required control technology (is it "wholly out of proportion" to the removal costs considered in developing national limits?).

If it finds that a fundamentally different factor exists, EPA may adopt alternative effluent limitations for the facility in question. It should be noted that those limits may be either more or less stringent than the effluent limitations with respect to which the variance is granted.

The fundamental factors variance is not available simply because the cost of compliance with BPT limitations would force plant closure. EPA v. National Crushed Stone Association, 449 U.S. 64 (1980). Instead, the costs of BPT compliance are relevant in deciding if fundamentally different factors exist at a plant and, if so, whether the alternate effluent limitations are as cost-effective as those imposed on the industry in general. Weyerhauser Co. v. Costle, 590 F.2nd 1011, 1036 (D.C. Cir. 1978).

Finally, it should be noted that although the fundamental factors variance is an important mechanism and will become increasingly so as effluent limitations become more detailed and address more pollutants, its potential availability does not reduce the necessity for careful monitoring of the development process for applicable effluent limitations to assure that the factors which are considered during that process are properly assessed and applied. The fundamental factors variance is available only for factors not considered in the development process. The only meaningful relief available for improper application of factors considered during the development process is an appeal to the courts. Unless this appeal is taken within 90 days after the applicable effluent limits are finally published, the right to raise these issues will be waived.

4.6 Technology-Based Treatment Standards—Publicly Owned Treatment Works

For discharges from publicly owned treatment works (POTWs), Section 301 directs the achievement: by July 1, 1977, of (1) effluent limitations based on secondary treatment, as defined by EPA and (2) any more stringent limitations are necessary to comply with water quality standards or treatment standards imposed by state law 9/, and by July 1, 1983, the adoption of waste management techniques which provide for the application of best practicable waste treatment technology over the life of the treatment works. 10/

In 1973, EPA published final regulations defining "secondary treatment" for purposes of Section 301, 40 CFR Part 133. The effluent levels prescribed by these regulations are as follows:

	% Removal	Concentration—mg/1 Monthly Average	Weekly Average
BOD (5 day)	85	30	45
S.S.	85	30	45
Coliform		200/100 ml.	400/100 ml.

pH	6.0 to 9.0

The regulations make special provision for upwards revision of the "secondary treatment" effluent limits (1) where necessary to take into account storm water infiltration into combined sewers during wet weather periods; and (2) where necessary to take into account the fact that the Section 301 and Section 306 effluent limitations applicable to major industrial dischargers into the treatment works (those exceeding 10% of the design flow) would permit an industrial user to directly discharge greater concentrations than those set forth in the table. In the latter case, the permitted discharge from the POTW which is attributable to the industrial waste

---

9/   The 1977 Amendments provide for extension of the 1977 secondary treatment and other deadlines where, because of lack of federal funding or otherwise, planned facilities have not been completed. The extension shall be to the earliest date on which funding can be provided and construction completed but no later than July 1983. Industrial dischargers whose permits require discharge to a treatment works and who had enforceable contracts for such discharge or who were included in a treatment works facility plan filed with a grant application may be granted an extension on much the same basis as the treatment works itself.

10/   The Best Practicable Waste Treatment Technology requirement has been construed by EPA to mean secondary treatment unless special circumstances applicable to a particular facility indicate that a higher level of treatment is more cost effective or required to meet water quality criteria.

received for treatment may be increased to equal, but not exceed, that which would be permitted, under the applicable effluent limitations, if the industrial facility were discharging directly into a waterway.

In the 1981 Amendments, Congress revised the definition of secondary treatment so that such biological treatment facilities as oxidation ponds, lagoons, and ditches and trickling filters are deemed to be the equivalent of secondary treatment. Section 304(d)(4). The Administrator is to publish design guidance to assure that water quality is not adversely affected by this definitional change.

The relative stringency of these effluent limitations and the fact that, under the 1972 Act, public treatment facilities were, for the first time subjected to effective and directly enforceable federal effluent limitations and permit requirements, gave municipal authorities a strong mandate to rigorously enforce flow and concentration limitations on industrial users of their systems. In many cases, the "pretreatment requirements" imposed by municipal authorities pursuant to this mandate have been far more stringent than the federal pretreatment standards discussed above. In addition, as noted below, the increasing need for high levels of performance by POTWs result in new or upgraded facilities which can drastically increase the cost to industry of waste treatment services.

4.7   More Stringent Treatment Required to Meet Water Quality-Related Effluent Limitations

As has been noted, the technology-based effluent limitations discussed above function as nationwide minimum or base level treatment standards. The Act provides two separate mechanisms for the imposition of more stringent requirements where dictated by the need to protect or maintain water quality in specific bodies of water.

Section 301(b)(1)(C) of the Act requires both industrial dischargers and POTWs to achieve, no later than July 1, 1977, any effluent limitations more stringent than the minimum technology-based standards which may be necessary to meet applicable federal-state water quality standards. This requirement is incorporated into permits issued by EPA through the state certification requirement under Section 401 of the Act. (See Part 3.2 above.)

Section 302 of the Act authorizes EPA directly to establish effluent criteria more stringent than the applicable BAT limits where necessary for the attainment or maintenance in a specific body of water quality which "shall assure protection of public water supplies, agriculture and industrial uses, and the protection and propagation of a balanced population of shellfish, fish and wildlife, and allow recreational activities in and on the water..." EPA has interpreted this Section 302 authority as providing a selective tool for the Agency to impose more stringent requirements where necessary to protect important water resources. Although this section has received little if any use to date, it does have great potential impact in that it authorizes EPA to adopt its own effluent limitations for any body of water as to which a state fails or refuses to adopt water quality standards sufficient to maintain fishing and swimming uses.

The water quality standards and water quality-related effluent limitations imposed by these two mechanisms have substantial potential for requiring levels of treatment considerably higher than those required by the technology-related effluent limits in areas of heavy discharge concentration, in waters where very stringent quality standards have been established, and in waters with limited assimilative capacity. This potential impact is exacerbated by the fact that there is no provision for the grant of variances from the Section 301 water quality standards. The requirement for compliance with water quality standards is inflexible and mandatory. The impact of this requirement will depend to a considerable extent on the resolution of a number of major policy questions now being addressed by EPA.

The procedures for setting water quality standards are quite complex. States, acting pursuant to the procedures set out in 40 CFR § 35-1550, hold public hearings every three years for the purpose of revising and reviewing state water quality standards. EPA does not set specific minimums for state standards; instead the rules require that such standards protect public health, § 35-1550(b)(1), specify and protect appropriate water uses (e.g., water supply, fish, wildlife), § 35-1550(b)(2), and set specific criteria to attain these ends, § 35-1550(b)(3). The state standards must attain the Clean Water Act's goal of fishable, swimmable waters wherever attainable, and must, at a minimum, maintain the uses designated in the standards and current uses. § 35-1550(c). In addition, no degradation of "outstanding national resource" waters, such as those in National and State parks, is to be permitted. § 35.1550(e).

In October 1982, EPA proposed to change this standard-setting process drastically. 47 Fed. Reg. 49234 (Oct. 29, 1982). The proposed rules would focus state attention on water quality standards for "priority" water bodies, i.e., those where existing water quality standards require the imposition of controls beyond those required by BPT, BCT, and BAT standards for industry and POTWs. States are to review existing use designations for these water bodies, in order to determine if existing designations make sense in light of natural limitations on the water body such as natural concentrations of pollutants, low-flow or intermittent flow conditions, dams and other physical conditions which would make attainment of the designated use (e.g., cold water fishery) impossible. The proposed rule also permits cost-benefit analysis of the additional controls beyond BAT which would be required to attain the designation. Designated uses may not be downgraded if the water body is in fact used for those purposes now. The provisions in existing rules concerning "outstanding national resource" waters would be deleted. The proposed rules emphasize state, rather than EPA, decisionmaking about water quality. These changes are controversial and may be altered significantly before final promulgation. Further, the effect of these revisions will depend in large part on the mechanisms used to translate standards for receiving waters into end-of-pipe effluent limitations imposed on dischargers.

Perhaps more important than the proposed use designations discussed above is EPA's proposal regarding the pollutants required to be addressed by state water quality standards. In the past, EPA has published criteria for a number of pollutants of specific concern in its publication "Quality Criteria for Water," July 1976, the so-called Red Book. These criteria have recently been rescinded, and EPA has announced its intention to issue a Water Quality Standards Handbook before a final rule is published on state water quality standards. Although these criteria have, to some extent, served as guidance in the implementation of state water quality standards programs, they have, to date, had no direct regulatory impact since states have been specifically required to adopt water quality standards for each of the pollutants listed in the criteria document. As a result, most states have placed primary emphasis in their water quality standards programs on conventional measures of pollutants such as dissolved oxygen, pH and fecal coliform bacteria, and very few states have had a substantial program for the establishment of water quality standards for heavy metals, pesticides and other non-conventional or toxic pollutants.

Pursuant to the NRDC consent decree, EPA is now proposing to revise the present policy. It will adopt criteria for the priority pollutants listed in the consent decree in addition to those now covered in the Red Book.

The present criteria have serious deficiencies. The Red Book was essentially a literature survey which took the lowest concentration of a chemical that has been shown to cause mortality or other adverse effects on fish or aquatic organisms. It then applied an estimated arbitrary safety factor to arrive at a concentration limit (expressed in milligrams or micrograms per liter) to be achieved in the receiving water body. These criteria were translated to water quality standards, and effluent limitations from affected point sources would then be determined on the basis of these limits.

The criteria documents were generally deficient in detailed consideration of variations in receiving waters, variations of species, required safety factors and so forth. It is not clear whether EPA's new standards handbook will remedy these deficiencies. Accordingly, the likelihood of treatment requirements for particular discharges based on inadequate scientific information is becoming increasingly likely.

Those policy revisions discussed above, which will increase the stringency of water quality standards and make water quality standards applicable to a much broader range of pollutants, can have a substantial impact only if mechanisms are developed for translating the standards for receiving waters into end-of-pipe effluent limitations to be imposed on dischargers. The system provided by Section 303, whereby states are required to inventory all waters within their jurisdictions, identify those waters as to which BAT effluent limits are inadequate to promote and maintain compliance with water quality standards (water-quality-limited segments), establish maximum loadings for the water quality limited segments, and provide a system for allocating those maximum loadings among all dischargers to the affected waters, has not yet been fully implemented due to the extreme technical difficulty of carrying out the modeling and other studies required to accomplish these tasks.

Because of this non-implementation of the Section 303 planning process, water quality-related effluent limitations have often not been included in permits when they should have been. When they have been included in permits, only rough calculations and judgmental estimates for a few pollutants have formed the basis for inclusion. This situation is clearly going to change. EPA is obligated under the NRDC consent decree to develop a specific and substantial program for incorporating water quality-related effluent limitations for the toxic pollutants into permits. As a result of this commitment and of the fact that more 303 plans will be completed with the passage of time, the system for incorporating water quality-related effluent limits into permits has to become more and more effective.

In addition, EPA, in its NPDES permit regulations, has developed a mechanism for placing much of the burden of completing required studies on the person proposing to discharge. This mechanism, set out in § 122.52 of the regulations, would require any new source or new discharger who proposes discharging into a water-quality limited segment to submit with the permit application a demonstration that there are sufficient remaining load allocations to allow the discharge and that the facility is entitled to those allocations. For discharges to water-quality limited segments, the issuing authority cannot issue a permit unless it finds that the facility will not cause or contribute to the violation of water quality standards applicable to the water into which the discharge is made. These requirements can be expected to result in a system similar to that now applicable to the location of new facilities in nonattainment areas under the Clean Air Act, where pressure for new industrial growth results in the imposition of increasingly stringent requirements on existing sources in order to permit new facilities without violation of applicable standards.

EPA has borrowed another concept from the Clean Air Act—the "bubble"—for use in the water pollution context. Under one recent proposal, EPA would permit facilities to cumulate the discharges from different outfalls of the plant and meet a single effluent limitation, rather than outfall-by-outfall limitations. The original proposal is limited to steel plants, with the idea being that it will be expanded to other industries if it proves workable. This approach may lead to appreciable cost savings depending on whether it can be used in water-quality limited areas and whether it applies to toxic pollutants.

In summary, it seems clear that, both as to industrial direct discharge and pretreatment requirements, water quality standards on certain bodies of water can be expected, during the next five to ten years, to have a significant impact in increasing the stringency of treatment requirements to be imposed on industrial and other facilities. The new toxics orientation of the water quality standards, together with the policy changes and enforcement mechanisms discussed above, merit careful consideration by potentially affected companies. Those companies would be well advised to participate actively in state proceedings related to the review and revision of existing water quality standards and the carrying out of the Section 303 planning process. EPA's proceedings in connection with the finalization of its new water quality standards policy and the extension and upgrading of existing water quality criteria are deserving of equal, if not greater, attention if we are to assure that water quality-related effluent limits, when they are applied, will be applied on the basis of adequate scientific knowledge and reasonable safety factors.

5.0 Controlling Non-Process-Related Waste Discharges

Although the system of effluent limits imposed through the NPDES permit program is an effective means of regulating waste discharges which result from normal industrial or municipal processes and which are amenable to treatment prior to discharge, this system is clearly not an appropriate means of regulating and controlling accidental and unanticipated discharges or discharges which, by their nature, are not subject to confinement and treatment (e.g., area-wide or plant site runoff). For this latter class of discharges, the focus of regulation must be on preventing the discharge (in the case of the accidental spill) or on minimizing the volume of pollutants carried (in the case of area-wide and plant site runoff). In recognition of this circumstance and of the fact that accidental spills and "non-point source" discharges are responsible for a very large percentage of the total pollutants introduced into the nation's waterways, the Act provides a number of mechanisms, supplemental to the NPDES permit program, to control discharges which are unrelated to industrial process wastes. This system of supplemental regulatory controls is the subject of this section and the next one.

5.1 Controlling Area-Wide Non-Point Source Pollution—Section 208 Planning

The primary mechanism contemplated by the Clean Water Act for controlling area-wide non-point source pollution is the planning and regulatory program created by Section 208. This section would require each state to identify areas of the state which, due to urban industrial concentrations or other factors, have substantial water quality control problems. For each of these designated "waste treatment management areas," a representative of state and local officials would be identified and charged with the responsibility of developing a comprehensive area-wide plan for solving the area's water quality control problems.

After several years, however, Congress stopped funding the development and implementation of 208 plans. As a consequence, little progress has been made under Section 208 since Fiscal Year 1980. Nonetheless, a brief discussion of this program is warranted, both because of its innovative, comprehensive approach and because it could be revitalized.

Under Section 208, an EPA-approved planning organization would be eligible for federal grants to develop and implement a comprehensive planning program. The plans developed pursuant to Section 208 must be consistent with the Act's other planning requirements (the Section 303 continuing planning process and Section 201 waste treatment management plans) and are to provide both a general plan and a regulatory approach for dealing with important regional pollution control issues. The plan must include a program providing for regulation of the location, construction and modification of any facilities that might result in a discharge within the planning area.

For purposes of controlling area-wide and non-point source pollution, a plan must include a process to identify sources of non-point pollution within the planning area, including agricultural and silvicultural activities, surface or underground mine runoff (from both active and abandoned mines), construction activity, land disposal operations, and irrigation. For these identified sources, the plan must also include control measures such as management practices and land use requirements to minimize each activity's pollution potential. The control requirements developed under the 208 planning process may be enforced by the designated agency or by the Governor of the state.

Despite the primary emphasis on non-point source discharges, 208 plans can have applicability in other areas. For example, the plans are required to include a program for regulating the location, construction and modification of any facility that may result in a discharge. This provision provides authorization for a pre-construction permit review provision that could impose constraints on the siting of new facilities beyond those imposed by the NPDES permitting process. The plans, which must address applicable water quality standards, could also substantially affect the location of municipal treatment works.

If a 208 plan is approved and implemented, it will have significant impacts on all waste discharges within the waste treatment management area. NPDES permits may not be issued if they conflict with an approved plan. The plans will contain waste load allocations based on water quality criteria which will significantly affect a number of permits. Finally, grants for publicly-owned treatment works are to be given only for facilities which conform to the applicable plan.

5.2 Stormwater Discharges and Best Management Practices

As noted above (see Part 3.1), the question of whether stormwater discharge outlets are "point sources" has proved to be a difficult definitional issue. Following litigation on this question, EPA was forced to revise its approach. The major outlines of this revised approach are set out below.

The first element of the revised approach concerns stormwater discharges which have been contaminated by contact with wastes, raw materials or pollutant-contaminated soil from land or facilities used for industrial or commercial activities. Such discharges are subject to an individual NPDES permit and will normally be subjected to effluent limitations and monitoring requirements substantially identical to those imposed on other industrial discharges.

EPA's regulations define all other storm sewers in urbanized areas as point sources and would subject them to the NPDES program. Except in limited circumstances, however, such sewers will only require "general" NPDES permits. A "general" permit will authorize all stormwater discharges which fall within certain parameters (such as amounts of pollutants discharged); no permit applications or other processing will be required for discharges which fall within these parameters. This general permit system is the primary mechanism for regulating plant site runoff where toxic and hazardous pollutants are not involved.

In the 1977 Amendments, Congress added authority for regulating contamination of stormwater discharges by toxic and hazardous pollutants. Section 304(e) authorizes EPA to require the control, through "Best Management Practices," of toxic pollutants resulting from ancillary industrial activities and to prescribe regulations to control plant site runoff, spillage or leaks, and sludge or waste disposal. The legislative history of this provision indicates that Congress anticipated that EPA's regulations would specify treatment requirements, operating procedures, and other management practices by classes and categories of point source discharges.

EPA proposed sweeping regulations to implement the best management practices provisions of Section 304(e), 43 Federal Register 39282 (September 1, 1978), but issued final regulations of more modest scope. 40 CFR Part 125, Subpart K. Both the proposed and final regulations, however, attempt to apply the BMP requirements on an across-the-board basis, instead of by categories. This administrative short-cut may lead to difficulties in the operation of the BMP program.

The final regulations emphasize BMPs of a procedural nature (especially preventive maintenance and housekeeping) and BMPs requiring only minor construction. EPA stated that these regulations are the first of two or more steps; Spill Prevention, Control and Countermeasure (SPCC) plans for hazardous substances (which have been proposed but never promulgated) and possibly additional BMP provisions are scheduled as regulatory requirements in the future.

The existing BMP requirements are applicable to all dischargers who use, manufacture, store, handle or discharge any pollutant listed as toxic under Section 307 or as hazardous under Section 311 for all ancillary manufacturing operations which may result in significant amounts of toxic or hazardous pollutants reaching waters of the U.S. Any BMPs required by a Section 304(e) effluent limitations guideline must be expressly incorporated into an NPDES permit and BMPs may be so incorporated if EPA or the State agency determines this to be "necessary to carry out the provisions of the Act..." These requirements appear to have been specifically contemplated by Congress when it added the BMP provisions in 1977.

In addition, the regulations require the permittee to develop a "Best Management Practices program," which must be submitted as part of the permit application and which will be subject to all permit issuance procedures. This program must be written, must establish toxic and hazardous substances control objectives, and must establish specific BMPs to meet these objectives. The program must also address a number of points concerning ancillary activities such as materials inventory and compatibility, employee training, visual inspections, preventive maintenance, housekeeping, and security.

It is clear that these requirements will impose considerable administrative burdens on affected permittees. Permittees will also have to incur costs, which may be considerable in some cases, in order to comply. Further, some discussion of the BMP regulations, as originally proposed, is in order since these are the best guide as to what will be contained in any additional BMP requirements.

As proposed, the BMP regulations would require affected permittees to prepare a BMP plan which would be incorporated into the facility permit so that any violation of the plan would also be a violation of the NPDES permit. The plan would have to incorporate any applicable hazardous substances SPCC plan. As with the existing regulations, specific control objectives and specific best management practices to meet these objectives would have to be established. Finally, and perhaps most important, the plan would have to address a number of problem areas such as liquid and raw material storage areas, plant site runoff, and so forth. EPA indicated that addressing these problem areas adequately could involve major construction requirements.

Compliance with the BMP regulations, as proposed, could obviously be an expensive undertaking. Further, there is no assurance that this sweeping approach will prove cost effective or that it is necessary. These considerations are likely to prevent the promulgation by EPA of any additional BMP regulations, at least during the Reagan Administration.

6.0 Oil and Hazardous Substances

Section 311 of the 1972 Act established an extensive regulatory scheme for dealing with accidental or intentional discharges of oil and hazardous substances. The 1977 Amendments modified Section 311 in several ways, principally with respect to the limits on the liability of a discharger of oil or of hazardous substances. Congress further amended Section 311 in 1978, primarily in order to make the section's provisions with respect to hazardous substances more workable. In 1980, Congress enacted the Comprehensive Environmental Response, Compensation and Liability Act (CERCLA), which has significantly expanded EPA's authority and resources to clean up hazardous wastes listed under Section 311. Spills of petroleum products continue to be regulated solely under Section 311 of the Clean Water Act.

Although oil and hazardous substances are covered by the same Clean Water Act provisions, they have traditionally been treated separately by EPA. The following discusion analyzes each in turn.

6.1 Oil

The Act prohibits the discharge of "harmful quantities" of oil into navigable waters. EPA regulations (40 CFR § 110.3) have defined the term "harmful quantities" to cover all discharges which "violate applicable water quality standards or cause a film or sheen upon the surface of the water..." Thus virtually all discharges of oil are prohibited. 11/

Industry's responsibility under this section has several facets. Owners and operators of large oil (including animal or vegetable oil) storage facilities (1,320 gallons above ground or 42,000 gallons below ground) must comply with EPA regulations (40

11/ It is arguable that the oils and greases contained in an NPDES permitted discharge are not covered by the Section 311 limitations and reporting requirements. However, many NPDES permits contain a condition making it clear that the permit does not in any way excuse Section 311 compliance.

CFR Part 112) which seek to minimize the probability than an oil spill will occur by requiring the development, implementation and maintenance of Spill Prevention, Control and Countermeasure (SPCC) Plans. Plan implementation is often a matter of considerable expense, since the installation of containment structures, maintenance of inspection procedures, and other preventive measures are often necessary plan elements. Failure to prepare and maintain a plan in accordance with the regulations subjects the violator to civil penalties of up to $5,000 for each day of violation. 40 CFR Part 114. Similar, but more stringent, planning and accident avoidance requirements are applicable under Coast Guard regulations governing vessels and oil transfer operations associated therewith. 33 CFR Parts 154-157.

In addition, vessels must establish evidence of financial responsibility to meet potential liability under Section 311. Section 311(p)(1). The financial responsibility which must be evidenced is the greater of $125 per gross ton or $125,000 for inland oil barges, and $150 per gross ton for other vessels. Financial responsibility may be established by insurance, surety bonds or qualification as a self-insurer.

If, despite compliance with the spill avoidance procedures discussed above, a spill does occur, additional obligations arise. The owner or operator of the source from which the discharge originates must immediately report the discharge to the Coast Guard and/or EPA. 33 CFR § 153.203; 40 CFR § 110.9. Failure to comply with this requirement results, upon conviction, in a fine of up to $10,000 and/or imprisonment for not more than one year. Section 311(b) (5). It should be kept in mind that this reporting requirement is broadly construed and may apply to oil spills which originate several miles inland (e.g., if the spill goes into a storm sewer which outlets to navigable waters).

In addition to giving notice, the discharger must either contain and clean up the spill or pay the cost of clean up efforts by responsible government agencies. Sections 311(c), 311(f). Section 311(f) limits the discharger's liability for the government's actual removal costs to $50 million unless there is willful negligence or willful misconduct in which case there is no limit on liability. EPA is authorized to establish lower limits of liability for facilities having small storage capacity (1000 barrels or less). Generally, effective private clean up measures are less costly than similar efforts by the government and, in addition, those efforts are of considerable practical importance in mitigation of civil penalties discussed below.

The discharger's final obligation is to pay a civil penalty of not more than $5,000 for each spill. Section 311(b)(6). Although the Coast Guard (which is the agency administering the penalties section) must assess a penalty, it has considerable discretion to reduce the amount of the penalty based on the size of the business of the

discharger, the effect of the penalty on his ability to continue in
business, and the gravity of the violation. The Act provides the
right to notice and a hearing in connection with civil penalty assessments and there was case law to the effect that the notice given by
the discharger must not be utilized as a means of obtaining information to serve as the basis for assessing a civil penalty. 12/ That case
law was not accepted by the Coast Guard however, and upon appeal
the LeBoeuf case was reversed.

6.2 Hazardous Substances

Although, as noted above, Section 311 governs the discharge
of hazardous substances as well as of oil, EPA was much slower in
implementing the hazardous substances provision. It finally promulgated hazardous substances regulations in March 1978 and indicated
that they would become effective during the summer. Before the
regulations became effective, however, a U.S. District Court enjoined significant parts of them so that they could not go into effect. Congress responded to the court's action by amending Section
311 to simplify and clarify its provisions. Pub. L. 95-576 (November
2, 1978). The 1978 Amendments were directed toward the two most
significant problems identified by the court: the elements necessary
to establish what was to be considered a harmful quantity and the
relationship of Section 311 to the NPDES program.

Pursuant to these Amendments, EPA has designated approximately 300 substances as hazardous and thus subject to the Section
311 program. 40 CFR Part 116. In addition, the Agency has designated quantities of these substances that may be harmful (called a
"reportable quantity"). 40 CFR Part 117. Hazardous substances are
placed in one of five categories: X, A, B, C, D. A harmful quantity
of a category X substance is one pound, of a category A substance is
10 pounds, of a category B substance is 100 pounds, of a category C
substance is 1000 pounds, and of a category D substance is 5000
pounds.

The second principal feature of EPA's hazardous substance
regulations is the exclusion of discharges made in compliance with
an NPDES permit. Since a primary purpose of the Amendments was
to limit Section 311 to "classic" hazardous substance spills, the
regulations specify that they are not applicable to chronic discharges of designated substances if the discharge complies with an
NPDES permit. 40 CFR § 117.12. Such discharges, of course,
remain subject to regulation under the NPDES program.

Further, if an NPDES facility has intermittent, anticipated
spills of hazardous substances (i.e., into plant drainage ditches), it

12/   United States v. LeBoeuf Bros. Towing Co., 377 F. Supp. 558
(E.D.La. 1974),reversed 537 F.2d 149 (5th Cir. 1976).

should determine whether these discharges ought to be brought within the terms of its NPDES permit. The regulations give the facility the option of having such discharges regulated through the NPDES program or pursuant to Section 311.

Discharges of hazardous substances may also reach navigable waters through municipal sewers and publicly owned treatment works. Discharges from industrial facilities to a POTW are not covered by the regulations at present. The regulations do apply to all discharges of reportable quantities of hazardous substances to POTWs by mobile source such as trucks unless the discharger has met certain requirements. 40 CFR § 117.13.

A facility owner or operator who spills a harmful quantity of a hazardous substance must report the spill; failure to do so will subject it to criminal penalties. If there is a spill, the violator is also subject to a fine of up to $5000. In lieu of this fine, EPA can seek a penalty through a civil action in Federal courts; this penalty can range up to $50,000 or up to $250,000 if the discharge was the result of willful negligence or willful misconduct within the privity and knowledge of the owner/operator.

Finally, it should be noted that the reporting requirements for spills of hazardous substances (as well as other defined wastes) have been substantially supplemented by CERCLA. For a fuller description of these requirements, see Chapter 10.

The nature of these regulations and the potential penalties thereunder place a premium on developing compliance procedures before a spill occurs. A facility should first be evaluated to determine whether it discharges, or might discharge, a reportable quantity of any hazardous substance to the waters of the United States. If there is a risk of such a discharge, the exemptions established by the regulations should be considered in order to determine if they will be applicable to the potential discharge. If no exemption is available, it may be advisable to develop a program to prevent such discharges. Further it is essential to implement a contingency plan capable of assuring a prompt and appropriate response in the event of a non-exempt reportable discharge.

7.0 Other Critical Elements of the Water Act Program

In addition to the features of the Water Act program described above, there are several other important elements which must be discussed if the overall program is to be understood as a coherent whole. These elements are described below.

7.1 Abatement Actions and Sanctions

In order to assure compliance with the regulatory program, Congress established extensive provisions to deal with violations of the Act. Dischargers who fail to obtain permits under the Act or who violate the Act's effluent limitations, pretreatment requirements, or monitoring provisions, or any permit conditions required to implement these may be proceeded against under the Refuse Act of 1899, under the Clean Water Act (although there is at least some question as to whether the Section 309 sanctions apply to a failure to obtain a permit), and under the state laws providing for implementation of the NPDES program. All of the foregoing sanctions may be pursued concurrently, although it is likely that EPA will defer to state enforcement action if such actions are expeditiously commenced. As the emphasis of the regulatory program moves from the establishment of standards and the issuance of permits to concerns about compliance with the terms of standards and permits, provisions for dealing with violations will become more and more important.

EPA has a number of enforcement options under the Water Act: (1) issuance of a compliance order; (2) obtaining injunctive relief under Section 309; (3) seeking civil penalties; and (4) initiating criminal prosecution. In addition, Sierra Club v. Train, 557 F.2d 485 (5th Cir. 1977), held that EPA can elect to take no formal enforcement action at all. Should EPA decide not to take any formal action, it can either ignore a violation as being de minimis or attempt to resolve the violation by informal procedures.

Compliance orders are administrative orders by which EPA directs the violator to come into compliance with the applicable statutory, regulatory, or permit term. These orders are subject to judicial review.

EPA's second option, obtaining injunctive relief pursuant to Section 504, is applicable to discharges which present an imminent and substantial endangerment to the health, welfare or livelihood of persons. In such circumstances, EPA is empowered to bring suit in a U.S. district court to immediately stop the discharge of pollutants causing such a situation.

EPA can also seek injunctive relief under Section 309(b). The U.S. district court hearing such an action has jurisdiction to restrain the violation of any condition or limitation which implements Sections 301, 302, 306, 307, 308, 318, and 405 and to require compliance with the condition or limitation.

Violations of these same sections or of permit conditions implementing these sections can also be punished by civil penalties of up to $10,000 for each day of violation. Finally, any person who "wilfully or negligently" violates such provisions or permit conditions (and any person who violates a properly issued administrative order will certainly meet the test) is subject to fines of $2,500 to $25,000 per day of violation or imprisonment of up to a year or both. "Responsible corporate officers" are subject to the same fines and penal sanctions as their companies. Fines are doubled for second time offenders. The Act also provides fines and imprisonment for willful false statements of incorrect entries in any information required to be filed or maintained under the Act.

In addition to these EPA weapons, those states which have assumed NPDES permit responsibility are also responsible for enforcement. These states have their own enforcement laws, policies and personnel, all of which may be quite different from those of EPA. The situation is further complicated by the fact that EPA does not always agree with state enforcement decisions. If it does not, Section 309(a)(1) permits it to intervene to assure that "appropriate" enforcement action is taken.

From the foregoing, it is obvious that a great deal of discretion is involved in decisions about whether and how to enforce the Act. A discharger who is or may be faced with a potential enforcement action for a violation of the Act or of a permit issued thereunder (and this category includes almost every discharger) must be aware of this discretion and must be prepared to deal with it in the most effective manner possible. This will be discussed below but two efforts by EPA to prescribe the manner in which its discretion should be utilized deserve brief mention first.

An early effort to establish guidelines for the exercise of EPA discretion was an EPA memorandum concerning settlement of civil penalty enforcement cases. This memorandum established a number of principles to govern the determination of the acceptable dollar amount at which a civil penalty proceeding can be settled instead of being taken to trial. Any discharger facing a civil penalty action should review this memorandum with care; it was published in the June 10, 1977 "Current Developments" section of the BNA Environment Reporter.

A second effort to guide EPA's enforcement discretion is a recent EPA memorandum concerning criminal enforcement priorities. This memorandum identifies factors to be considered in deciding whether to bring criminal proceedings, including the intent of the alleged violator, the threat to human health caused by the violation, the effect on EPA's regulatory programs (e.g., falsification of monitoring data), deterrence, and the compliance history of the alleged violator. The memo lists highly specific violations under the Clean Water Act and other statutes in the order of their importance. See the reproduction of this memorandum in the October 22, 1982 "Current Developments" section of the BNA Environment Reporter. EPA has added a significant criminal enforcement staff for the first time so that these enforcement priorities will be more than a dead letter. Consequently, it may be appropriate to focus compliance efforts on avoiding these sorts of violations.

This broad discretion on the part of EPA and the states calls for a different approach by potential violators than would be the case if there were some system of automatic penalties. The primary element of such an approach will be for a discharger to invest as much time and effort with all relevant agencies as is necessary. When several parts of EPA and several different state agencies are involved, there is no assurance that they are pursuing a coherent strategy or, indeed, are even talking to each other. Thus the discharger must be prepared to keep all federal and state agencies fully informed, preferably in a way that will ensure the most favorable processing of any potential violations. In doing this, the discharger should attempt to accomplish the following three goals:

-- Convince the relevant enforcement agencies of its good faith. Since the enforcement agencies will not, for the forseeable future, be able to move against every violation, criteria will have to be used in deciding who to move against. One of these criteria will almost always be whether the violator has been acting in good faith or bad faith.

-- The discharger must be especially aware of any particular circumstances that may be relevant. Discharges which may create public health problems, or create unique environmental impacts, or which are likely to be the subject of adverse publicity must be recognized and, to the degree possible, special efforts should be made to avoid discharges of such substances.

-- The discharger must cultivate a highly refined sense of "when to fight and when to switch." Some enforcement actions require defending; others may be best dealt with by compromise and settlement.

These guidelines are not a panacea to the problems involved in dealing with potential enforcement actions. However, they can serve to ameliorate some of the uncertainty surrounding the present enforcement system.

7.2 Citizen Suits

Section 505 of the Act provides an additional impetus to vigorous enforcement of the Act's provisions. It authorizes any person "having an interest which is or may be adversely affected" to commence civil actions either against a discharger, for violation of any effluent standard or limitation under the Act, or against EPA for failure to proceed expeditiously to enforce the Act's provisions. Experience under the Refuse Act program indicates that citizen suit provisions are highly effective in increasing the number of enforcement actions brought. While the 1972 Act, unlike the Refuse Act, does not make provision for the payment of a "bounty" to the moving citizen, it does make specific provision for the payment of attorney and expert witness fees. This latter provision will likely be of more assistance to environmental action groups than was the bounty provision under the Refuse Act.

It should therefore be anticipated that Section 505 will greatly facilitate the bringing of citizens' suits where an appropriate
interest can be shown. A number of such suits have already been
brought against EPA and other government agencies; an increasing
number of such suits against dischargers should be anticipated in the
future.

The citizen's suit provision will likely result in a vigorous
enforcement attitude on the part of EPA and a great deal of leverage for environmentalists in forcing abatement of pollution problems
which become a matter of significant public concern.

7.3. Provisions Having Special Applicability

7.3.1 Discharges to Ground Waters

One by-product of the Clean Air Act and the Clean Water
Act has been increased pressure to dispose of waste materials on or
below land and the consequential increased threat of groundwater
contamination. However, underground aquifers is one class of water
bodies which is not included in the Act's definition of "waters of the
United States."   Thus, although the Act, in Section 402(b)(1)(D),
requires states, as a precondition to approval of their NPDES programs, to "control the discharge of pollutants into wells," it gives
EPA no direct authority to regulate disposal of pollutants by sub-
surface injection.

Although EPA initially sought to regulate underground discharges pursuant to the Clean Water Act, it met with mixed
results.   The courts disagreed as to whether EPA had authority to
regulate disposal into wells under that statute.   See United States
Steel v. Train, 556 F.2d 822 (7th Cir. 1977), and Exxon Corp. v.
Train, 554 F.2d 1310 (5th Cir. 1977).   EPA is now relying on the
authority of the Safe Drinking Water Act (SDWA), 42 USC § 300 et
seq., to regulate such discharges and is encouraging the states to
develop underground injection control programs pursuant to 40 CFR
Part 146.

Part C of the SDWA applies to injection wells. However, well
injection is broadly defined as the:

> subsurface implacement of fluids through a bored,
> drilled or driven well; or through a dug well, where the
> depth is greater than the largest surface dimension.

Thus, the state underground injection programs will have broad
applicability.

Pending adoption by the state of underground injection control programs, EPA is regulating the injection of hazardous wastes
under the Resource Conservation and Recovery Act. Waste lagoons
and ponds will continue to be regulated by EPA and the states pursuant to the hazardous waste program.

Thus, many companies which had been exempt from waste-water discharge regulation under the Clean Water Act because they did not discharge to navigable waters will now be subjected to requirements governing wastewater discharges pursuant to the Safe Drinking Water Act and the Resource Conservation and Recovery Act.

7.3.2 Dredged or Fill Material

Section 404 of the Clean Water Act has had a very substantial, and undoubtedly unintended, effect on development in areas adjacent to navigable waters. The section was intended to reduce the stringency of limitations on the disposal of dredged or fill material into navigable water by granting the Corps of Engineers the authority to designate disposal areas and issue permits to discharge dredged and fill material therein rather than making such discharges subject to the general permit program provided by Sections 301, 304, 402 of the Act. Unfortunately, the section has had just the opposite effect due primarily to the following three factors:

--   Section 404 has been construed to extend to all waters of the United States, N.R.D.C. v. Callaway, 392 F. Supp. 685 (D.D.C. 1975). Accordingly, the Corps permit program under Section 404 is applicable to many dredge and fill projects which would not have required permits under prior law;

--   The Corps has construed Section 404 broadly, so as to cover not only disposal of dredged or fill material, as the section would seem to contemplate, but also the emplacement of dredge or fill material for development purposes and the construction of structures (33 CFR Part 209); and

--   Section 511 of the Act, which passed both houses in a form which made it clear that NEPA would not be applicable to Corps permits under Section 404, was revised in conference to cover only permits issued by the EPA Administrator. Thus, Section 404 permits, unlike most other permits under the Act, may be subject to NEPA review requirements.

For these reasons, Section 404, which was passed with a view to facilitating the Corps of Engineers' dredging programs, has become the basis for a massive new system of regulation applicable to virtually all construction or development activities along any waterway or in wetland areas. This is a development similar in the scope of its impact to the "discovery" of the Refuse Act of 1899 (see Part 1.2 above).

Congress responded to this situation by extensively revising Section 404 in the 1977 Amendments. After lengthy debate, the decision was made to utilize the framework that had developed as a result of the three factors described above and to modify it by adding new provisions which ameliorate the difficulties created by administrative and judicial interpretations of the section. Although the Amendments may eventually make it somewhat easier to obtain dredge and fill permits, the requirements for permits will generally remain more stringent than was intended when the 1972 Act was passed.

The principal change was to authorize the states to establish permit programs for dredge and fill activities in non-navigable waters. 13/ In order to establish such a program, a state must comply with extensive requirements prescribed by the Act and must obtain EPA's approval of the program. There are also requirements for the state's operation of its program, including a requirement that a copy of each permit application and each proposed permit be sent to EPA. EPA, the Corps of Engineers, and the U.S. Fish and Wildlife Service have the right to comment on applications and proposed permits, and provision is made for the situation in which EPA objects to issuance of a permit. Section 208 was also revised to assure that dredge and fill activities are considered in the water pollution control planning process.

A second change authorized the Corps of Engineers (or a state having an approved program) to issue "general" permits for specified categories of activities involving the discharge of dredge and fill materials. To issue such a permit, there must be a finding that the activities in the category are similar in nature and will have minimal adverse effects. Any activity covered by a general permit can be conducted without obtaining an individual Section 404 permit so long as the requirements and standards set forth in the general permit are complied with. The Corps has recently expanded the scope of its general permit program to reduce the regulatory burden on a number of activities which involve incidental dredge or fill work. 33 CFR Parts 320-330.

Finally, new Section 404(f) exempts certain dredge and fill discharges from regulation under Section 404 if specified effects on navigable waters are avoided. The activities thus excluded from the scope of Section 404 include maintenance operations, the construction of temporary sedimentation basins, temporary farm, forest and mining roads, and several types of agricultural activities.

13/   It is generally thought that, if a state does establish its own program, it will not be subject to NEPA constraints in its permit issuing activities.

7.3.3 Ocean Discharge Criteria

Section 403(c) of the Act directed EPA to promulgate guidelines for determining the effects of pollution discharges on ocean water quality and other aesthetic, recreational, and economic values of the oceans. No permit for an ocean discharge may be issued unless the permit issuing authority determines that the discharge will not cause unreasonable degradation of the environment, and permit conditions may be imposed to insure that such degradation will not occur. 40 CFR Part 125, Subpart M.

The 1981 Amendments to the Clean Water Act extended the time for municipalities to apply for waivers of secondary treatment requirements for ocean discharges. Pub. L. 97-117. In some circumstances, primary treatment may also be waived. EPA has announced that it will process municipal waiver applications in groups from the same geographic areas.

7.3.4 Thermal Discharges

Although heat is a pollutant and thereby subject to technology-based effluent limitations imposed on industrial dischargers and POTWs, it has unique features so Congress included special provisions to protect against unnecessary control of heat. If the discharger can show that the technology based effluent limitations under Section 301 or under a new source performance standard are more stringent than necessary to assure protection and propagation of a balanced, indigenous population of shellfish, fish and wildlife in and on the body of water where the discharge is to occur, the Administrator or state may adjust the effluent limitation to a less stringent level, which will still assure such protection and propagation. This is the only section of the Act where water quality considerations can provide a variance from the otherwise minimum technology-based standards.

This provision--Section 316--is particularly important to power plants because heat is such a significant part of their discharge and because EPA established a "no-discharge" BAT requirement for heat. Even though this effluent limitation was overturned by the courts, Appalachian Power Co. v. Train, 545 F.2d 1351 (4th Cir. 1976), permit issuers most often initially propose no-discharge of heat as an effluent limitation under Section 402(a).

Section 316 proceedings are quite complex; EPA requires substantial amounts of scientific data. There are difficult questions regarding what is the "indigenous" population; when a population is "balanced;" and how heat will in fact affect the aquatic organisms. Nonetheless, this provision does provide useful additional protection for thermal dischargers.

8.0 The EPA Construction Grants Program

In light of the stringent treatment requirements imposed by the 1972 Act on publicly-owned treatment works, it was obvious that a major federal assistance program would be required to enable municipalities to construct the facilities necessary to comply with the new effluent limitation. The construction grant program which the 1972 Act established in response to this need is the largest public works program now being funded by the federal government. Although the grants program, as originally enacted, was thought of as a short-term program to fund initial compliance during the first five years of the Act's effectiveness, and although there have been persistent efforts to cut back the program's funding, it seems likely, at this writing, that a substantial grants program will continue to exist for the forseeable future.

Under the grant program, the federal share of the cost of approved treatment works was 75 percent, but was decreased to 55 percent in 1981. 14/ This is supplemented in most instances by a 15 percent state grant so that at present, the grantee local government generally pays only 10 percent of the eligible costs of the total facility. The Act and EPA's implementing regulations (40 CFR Part 35, Subpart E) impose substantial conditions governing factors such as the share of capital and operating costs which industrial users must pay, the eligibility of different parts of the plant and related sewer systems and so forth. The objective is to assure that grants will fund the construction of plants which will meet applicable treatment limits in a cost effective manner. These conditions can have very substantial impacts on users of publicly-owned treatment works. These impacts are discussed below.

8.1 The Cost Recovery Program

When the 1972 Act was enacted, Congress feared that the substantial grant assistance available to municipalities could function as an indirect subsidy to industrial users of the funded treatment works and that this subsidy would give users of POTWs an unfair competitive advantage over direct dischargers. Accordingly , Section 204 of the Act required, as a condition to federal construction grant assistance, that the applicant demonstrate that it:

> has made provisions for the payment by the industrial users of the treatment works, of that portion of the costs of construction of such treatments works which is allocable to the treatment of such industrial wastes to

---

14/   The federal share may be increased to 85 percent for grants made between September 30, 1978 and October 1, 1981 where the eligible publicly-owned treatment works proposes to utilize innovative or alternate waste water treatment processes identified in section 201(g)(5).

the extent attributable to the federal share of the cost
of construction. [Emphasis added.]

From the industrial user's viewpoint, the industrial cost recovery (ICR) requirement converted the construction "grant" to the
equivalent of a long-term, no-interest loan. However, ICR proved
quite difficult to administer and in order to carry out this program,
EPA published detailed and complex guidelines.

As a consequence of the numerous administrative problems
with the ICR program, Congress in 1977 declared an 18-month
moratorium on ICR payments, and ordered a thorough study of the
program. After the moratorium was extended for an additional
year, Congress abolished the ICR program in 1980, as it was clear
that the administrative cost substantially offset payments to the
Treasury. Until the Act was further amended in 1981, the industrial
cost exclusion (ICE) provisions of the 1980 Amendments prohibited
including the cost of treating industrial wastes in the grant program. ICE was abolished, however, by the 1981 Amendments.

Some local communities continue to assess ICR payments
even though they are no longer required by Federal law. Such local
ICR requirements are of questionable legality under the statutes of
several states.

8.2 User Charges

As the cost recovery regulations define industrial users'
proportionate share of the capital cost of new, grant funded treatment facilities, the user charge regulations establish requirements
to be met by a municipal system for industrial sharing of the annual
operating and maintenance charges of such facilities. Section 204 of
the Act requires, as a condition of federal construction grant assistance, a finding that the applicant has adopted or will adopt:

a system of charges to assure that each recipient of
waste treatment services within the applicant's jurisdiction...will pay its proportional share...of the costs of
operation and maintenance (including replacement 15/
of any waste treatment services provided by the applicant.

15/ The term "replacement" has been defined by EPA to mean
"expenditures for...equipment...which are necessary to maintain...capacity and performance during the service life of the
treatment works..."

The EPA regulations (40 CFR § 35-929-1) elaborate on the statutory requirement for proportionate distribution 16/ of O&M costs as follows:

> A grantee's user charge system based on actual use (or estimated use) of waste water treatment services may be approved if each user (or user class) pays its proportionate share of operation and maintenance (including replacement) costs of treatment works within the grantee's service area, based on the user's proportionate contribution to the total waste water loading from all users (or user classes).
>
> To insure proportional distribution of operation and maintenance costs to each user (or user class), the user's contribution shall be based on factors such as strength, volume, and delivery flow rate characteristics.

Quantity discounts to large volume users are not acceptable. EPA's philosophy is that savings resulting from economies of scale should be apportioned to all users or user classes. This would not, however, appear to preclude recognition of the fact that some large volume users are able to provide efficiencies to the treatment facility to which they discharge through flow equalization or other measures to control delivery flow rate. User charges may be established based on a percentage of the charge for water usage only in cases where the water charges are based on a constant cost per unit of consumption and thus may be reasonably reflective of the amount

---

16/   The 1977 Amendments included a provision authorizing applicants which, prior to enactment of the Amendments, used a system of dedicated ad valorem taxes as a basis for funding costs of operation and maintenance of their facilities, to continue such system as the user charge system for their facility, with respect to small residential users as defined by EPA. EPA has defined a small residential user to include industrial users which introduce no more than the equivalent of 25,000 gallons per day of domestic sanitary waste to the treatment works. All industrial users whose flows exceed the 25,000 gallon per day domestic equivalent limit and all users of systems not having in effect an acceptable ad valorem system on the effective date of the 1977 Amendments are required to pay user charges based on actual use. The authorization to use ad valorem tax systems for user charge collection applies only where the system results in a proportionate distribution of costs.

of wastewater discharged. The regulations also specifically provide that an industrial user which discharges, to a treatment works, wastewater containing toxic pollutants that cause an increase in the cost of managing the effluent or sludge from the treatment works, must pay for those increased costs. Finally, it should be noted that user charges, unlike cost recovery payments, are to be based on actual use of the facility and not on reserved shares, as is sometimes erroneously asserted by some municipalities.

Appendix B to EPA's regulations sets forth in more detail the guidelines for user charge computations and provides sample formulae for use in that connection. Although the guidelines are reasonably understandable, they are technical in nature. There is considerable potential for misapplication, particularly by small municipalities. A company which is a substantial contributor to a treatment works would thus be well advised to pay close attention to the municipality's determination of the user charge system which it will adopt.

As indicated above, the treatment works operator is obligated to develop a user charge mechanism, which will require each user to pay its proportionate share of the cost of waste treatment. This obligation is not fulfilled if, due to the selection of an inappropriate or defective formula or improper application of the formula selected, industrial users are required to subsidize waste treatment services performed for other users of the system. EPA approval of any planned federal construction grant application could, if necessary, be contested on that basis.

The basic approach in discussions with the POTW operating entity should be to make certain that the formula adopted (1) gives recognition to economies, other than economies of scale, which may be inherent in the nature of the company's discharge (e.g., the discharge may occur at non-peak periods, it may be low in suspended solids as compared to domestic sewage and so forth) and (2) does not give excessive weight to characteristics of the company's discharge, such as BOD content, which do result in additional treatment costs. For example, if the treatment works is primarily flow dependent, a high surcharge based on strength of effluent may well be inappropriate. Numerous other technical questions such as the following may arise and should be addressed:

If the industrial user pretreats its effluent so that its strength is less than that of domestic waste, shouldn't it be entitled to a cheaper rate?

Shouldn't an industrial user's charge be reduced if it holds its effluent for discharge at non-peak flow periods, thereby contributing to the efficiency of the treatment works?

If the particular type of industrial effluent makes the treatment works operate more efficiently, shouldn't that factor be recognized?

If an industrial user's wastes are phosphorous and nitro-gen-deficient, isn't it inappropriate to require that user to pay the portion of plant operation and maintenance expense allocable to removal of those pollutants?

If a substantial portion of the plant capacity is for treatment of water flowing into the system during periods of rainfall due to infiltration and inflow, shouldn't costs allocable to the treatment of this waste-water be primarily allocated to residential connections which are the primary cause of this circumstance?

These and many other similar questions are commonly an-swered at the local level in connection with the locality's devel-opment of the user charge system which will be proposed for EPA acceptance. Since user charges are becoming an increasingly impor-tant component of industrial users' total cost of waste treatment services provided by POTWs, the importance of being alert to the proposal of ordinances establishing new user charge systems and of raising questions such as these cannot be over-emphasized.

8.3 Cost Effectiveness and Eligibility

As is evident from the preceding sections, facilities which utilize publicly-owned treatment works as a means of waste disposal have an immediate and substantial interest in minimizing the costs of constructing and operating such works. While the POTW owner-grantee is similarly motivated, these public officials are often not highly sophisticated in the waste treatment area and need help, in the form of effective public and industry participation, to assure that their waste treatment program is the most cost-effective that can be obtained. Thus, though the statute (Section 212(2)(B)) does clearly require that grant-eligible facilities be demonstrated to be the most cost-efficient alternative for compliance with applicable effluent limits over the facility's useful life, we have seen numerous examples, over the first years of the program's existence, of plants being designed to achieve levels of treatment beyond that required by the applicable permit limits, with capacities in excess of that necessary to serve foreseeable needs and so forth. The procedures mandated for the development of Section 201 facilities plans, the preparation of environmental assessments related thereto, and the conduct of value engineering studies do provide both industry and concerned citizens with considerable opportunities to avoid this

occurrence in their areas through the presentation of well–substantiated comments and criticism. Such participation is clearly beneficial not only to the concerned users but also in terms of facilitating
achievement of the basic objectives of the construction grant program.

The final issue which should be considered in any effort to
minimize the cost of industrial participation in a grant-funded
POTW program is the question of whether all or only some of the
elements of the POTW are eligible for federal grant funding. Treatment works costs which are found to be ineligible must be fully
funded by the grantee, through a bond issue or otherwise, and industrial users are generally called upon to pay their proportionate share
of the cost of amortizing the required bonds. Thus, where a portion
of the facilities is found to be ineligible, industrial users will be
called upon to pay, not only the costs of the treatment works over
its useful life, but also their share of the bond interest on that
facility.

Consistent with the general objective of minimizing expenditure of federal grant funds, EPA has narrowly interpreted the
Act's eligibility provisions as they apply to treatment facilities
designed to handle industrial wastes. Thus though the Act's definition of treatment works would appear to apply to facilities which
handle industrial wastes, EPA's regulations specify that allowable
projects do not include "(1) costs of interceptor or collector lines
constructed exclusively or almost exclusively to serve industrial
users or (2) costs allocable to the treatment for control or removal
of pollutants in wastewater introduced into the treatment works by
industrial users, unless the applicant is required to remove such
pollutants introduced from non-industrial sources." The scope of
this exclusion in individual circumstances is subject to considerable
interpretation and there are also considerable legal questions
regarding the statutory authorization for this provision. Its application does merit careful attention in a number of situations. 17/

8.4 Construction Grants—Summary

The factors referenced above make it clear that users of
POTWs are no longer insulated from very substantial costs resulting
from the need to achieve compliance with the Clean Water Act and

---

17/ The 1977 Amendments do make provision for funding of pri-
vately-owned treatment works serving commercial users where
it can be demonstrated that such a facility is the most cost-
effective way of providing waste treatment services and
governmental entities have certified that the facility will be
operated and maintained consistent with the requirements of
the Act (Section 202(h)).

requirements thereunder. In many circumstances, publicly-owned treatment works can be a relatively expensive way of meeting the Act's objectives and the economics of alternative on-site treatment and direct discharge should be carefully examined before making or continuing commitments to rely on a POTW as a method of compliance.

9.0 Pollution Control Planning in the Current Regulatory Climate

Compliance with the complex regulatory requirements outlined above would be a difficult and costly proposition even under the best of circumstances. These difficulties are compounded by the fact that the current regulatory climate is one where overall enforcement policies and standards of compliance are not fully developed. In many cases, the questions of how the law will be interpreted and enforced are not amenable to predictable answers. Though the Act does offer the basic framework to permit informed management decisions, the input necessary to establish a regulatory climate where reliable judgments can be made is dependent in major part on the exercise of initiative by the companies which are subject to regulation.

9.1 EPA Standards Development Programs

The suitability and practicability of the standards and regulations which EPA promulgates under the Act are dependent on EPA's thorough understanding of the processes and products to be regulated, the availability of detailed and reliable data on the applicability and limits of available treatment technology, and careful consideration of the economic and environmental impacts involved. Except for industry inputs, most standards (whether done by EPA in-house or through outside contractors) tend to be based principally on technical data readily obtainable through review of existing literature. In some cases, this data is outdated, unreliable or inadequate. Thus, absent effective and technically documented participation by industry spokesmen, the standards which EPA promulgates are likely to have unanticipated effects when applied to real world conditions. Particular process or design factors may not have been considered and may be inequitable when applied to a specific plant or product.

Thus, early and active participation in the standards development process, either directly or through appropriate industry organizations, is advisable. Although EPA has completed the first ground of standards development, the toxics strategy will continue to require such participation. Such participation could properly involve the following steps:

(1) Assess the probability that standards which will be applicable to your company's operations will be promulgated.

(2) Determine the procedure which will be followed in developing the standard, the contemplated time schedule, and the areas under consideration where data available to EPA may be deficient.

(3) Assess the standards development procedure to determine whether it provides for taking into account any unusual aspects of your plant process or product design. Make comments to EPA and any private contractor involved as to how the procedure could be improved.

(4) Consider the possibility of arranging a mechanism, through the appropriate industry organization, for making available to EPA and/or the appropriate private contractor any relevant technical data possessed by companies in the industry which is unpublished or otherwise not generally accessible.

(5) If the time schedule permits, consider the desirability of industry sponsored research or analytical projects to fill gaps in existing data on available technology or environmental and economic impact. In this connection, consideration should be given to consulting with EPA on the structuring of the project and exploring the possibility of EPA involvement in the conduct of the project.

(6) After a proposed standard is published in the Federal Register, the company or its spokesmen should participate in the usual comment procedure and consider the possibility of obtaining judicial review if the standard, as finally promulgated, is still untenable. In this connection, it should be kept in mind that if objections to standards are not timely asserted in judicial review proceedings, then they are waived. Further, it is generally more palatable to litigate a standard at a time when your company does not stand accused of a violation.

9.2 Negotiation of Permit Conditions

Whether a company's authorization to discharge is in the form of an NPDES permit for direct discharge into a waterway or a contractual authorization from a municipality for use of its public treatment facilities, it should be kept in mind, at the time their permit or authorization is obtained, that its terms and conditions may be every bit as important, in terms of impact on profits, as a major corporate contract. Accordingly, pollution control managers should take great pains to determine the areas in which the Act leaves room for negotiation and, based on a careful assessment of the company's long-term interests, should negotiate actively in an effort to obtain favorable permit terms and conditions. These negotiations will be more important and much more complicated if toxic pollutants are involved.

9.3 Discussions With Regional Office and State Officials

No matter how good the standards are or how carefully permits are drawn, there will inevitably be situations where companies are forced to make major investment decisions which are affected by unreasonable uncertainties in determining the applicable environmental control requirements. In these circumstances, serious consideration should be given to obtaining advance guidance from the appropriate EPA regional office and/or state enforcement personnel—whether or not the applicable statute makes provision for obtaining such guidance. A written indication that the cognizant authority has reviewed your proposal and found it acceptable, while perhaps not legally binding, can be of great future benefit. If the proposal is not acceptable to EPA or the state, it may be better to find that out before money has been spent. The chances of acceptance are generally far greater when the company goes to the regulator, rather than the other way around.

9.4 State and Local Planning Activities

Industry would also be well advised to pay considerable attention to the substantial planning requirements which are imposed by the Act on state and local governments. The state and regional water quality implementation plans, continuing planning processes and areawide waste treatment management plans may well be as important as federal rules and regulations in determining a company's future abatement costs. If properly carried out, these planning processes can be of immeasurable aid to business planners in predicting and planning for the future.

10.0 Conclusion

The period since enactment of the 1972 Act has been a time of intensive questioning regarding the basic legal underpinnings of the program. Now, with some of these very basic questions regarding the Act's regulatory approach having been answered, we are in the midst of a regulatory effort of a scope and magnitude which would have been inconceivable ten years ago. As this effort is carried out, it seems clear that the regulations will become more complex, compliance more costly, and monitoring to assure and document compliance a much more difficult matter. Under these circumstances, it is obvious that the development of a workable and effective program will require the best efforts of both the regulators and the parties to be regulated. EPA, for its own part, must establish priorities and allow both industry and its own enforcement personnel to concentrate their attention on resolving the problems which are most significant in terms of impact on human health and the environment. We must not spend our time, money and effort identifying and monitoring pollutants which are present in inconsequential amounts and to which significant portions of our population are not exposed.

Industry, for its part, must make every effort to avoid the tremendous expenditure of time and effort which has been experienced in litigation to resolve EPA mistakes and omissions by participating fully and intelligently in applicable procedures for the development of effluent limitations, water quality criteria, management plans and the like. With this kind of cooperative effort there is at least some hope for achieving a regulatory environment in which a company can intelligently plan for compliance with water pollution control requirements—when the requirements established are (1) predictable and understandable; (2) equally applicable to and equitably enforced against all companies; (3) technologically and economically feasible; (4) announced sufficiently in advance of effectiveness to permit lead time for compliance; and (5) constant for a reasonable period of time after final adoption.

We have now reached the point of general awareness that the cost of pollution abatement requirements often constitutes a very substantial portion of the total cost of many companies' final product and where the effectiveness with which a company plans its pollution control program may determine the extent to which the company remains competitive in its industry. Achievement and maintenance of a regulatory climate which facilitates intelligent planning is the best, and perhaps the only way of achieving the pollution control objectives announced by Congress when it passed the 1972 Act. It is to be hoped that both regulators and those regulated will be able to avoid unnecessary adversary tendencies, face up to the real regulatory issues, and develop a program which reasonably and cost-effectively achieves essential water quality objectives without major economic or social dislocation.

ANNEX A — SECTION 307 — TOXIC POLLUTANTS

Acenaphthene
Acrolein
Acrylonitrile
Aldrin/Dieldrin
Antimony and compounds*
Arsenic and compounds
Asbestos
Benzene
Benzidine
Beryllium and compounds
Cadmium and compounds
Carbon tetrachloride
Chlordane (technical mixture and metabolites)
Chlorinated benzenes (other than dichlorobenzenes)
Chlorinated ethanes (including 1,2-dichloroethane, 1,1,1-ethane and
    hexachloroethane)
Chlorinated naphthalene
Chlorinated phenols (other than those listed elsewhere; includes
    trichlorophenols and chlorinated cresols)
Chloroalkyl ethers (chloromethyl, chloroethyl, and mixed ethers)
Chloroform
2-chlorophenol
Chromium and compounds
Copper and compounds
Cyanides
DDT and metabolites
Dichlorobenzenes (1,2-, 1,3-, and 1,4-dichlorobenzenes)
Dichlorobenzinine
Dichloroethylenes (1,1-and 1,2-dichloroethylene)
2,4-dichlorophenol
Dichloropropane and dichloropropene
2,4-dimethylphenol
Dinitrotoluene
Diphenylhydrazine
Endosulfan and metabolites
Endrin and metabolites
Ethylbenzene
Fluoranthene

---

*   The term "compounds" shall include organic and inorganic
       compounds.

ANNEX A (continued)

Haloethers (other than those listed elsewhere; includes chlorophenyl-
    phenyl ethers, bromophenylphenyl ether, bis (dischloroiso-
    propyl) ether, bis-(chloroethoxy) methane and polychlorinated
    diphenyl ethers)
Halomethanes (other than those listed elsewhere; includes methylene
    chloride methylchloride, methylbromide, bromoform, dichloro-
    bromomethane,   trichlorofluoromethane,   dichlorodifluoro-
    methane)
Heptachlor and metabolites
Hexachlorobutadiene
Hexachlorocyclohexane (all isomers)
Hexachlorocyclopentadiene
Isophorone
Lead and compounds
Mercury and comounds
Naphthalene
Nickel and compounds
Nitrobenzene
Nitrophenols (including 2,4-dinitrophenol, dinitrocresol)
Nitrosamines
Pentachlorophenol
Phenol
Phthalate esters
Polychlorinated biphenyls (PCBs)
Polynuclear aromatic hydrocarbons (including benzanthracenes,
    benzo-pyrenes, benzofluoranthene, chrysenes, dibenzanthra-
    cenes, and indenopyrenes)
Selenium and compounds
Silver and compounds
2,3,7,8-Tetrachlorodibenzo-p-dioxin (TCDD)
Tetrachloroethylene
Thallium and compounds
Toluene
Toxaphene
Trichloroethylene
Vinyl chloride
Zinc and compounds

ANNEX B

1. Adhesives and Sealants
2. Aluminum Forming
3. Asbestos Manufacturing
4. Auto and Other Laundries
5. Battery Manufacturing
6. Coal Mining
7. Coil Coating
8. Copper Forming
9. Electric and Electronic Components
10. Electroplating
11. Explosives Manufacturing
12. Ferroalloys
13. Foundries
14. Gum and Wood Chemicals
15. Inorganic Chemicals Manufacturing
16. Iron and Steel Manufacturing
17. Leather Tanning and Finishing
18. Mechanical Products Manufacturing
19. Nonferrous Metals Manufacturing
20. Ore Mining
21. Organic Chemicals Manufacturing
22. Pesticides
23. Petroleum Refining
24. Pharmaceutical Preparations
25. Photographic Equipment and Supplies
26. Plastic and Synthetic Materials Manufacturing
27. Plastic Processing
28. Porcelain Enamelling
29. Printing and Publishing
30. Pulp and Paperboard Mills
31. Soap and Detergent Manufacturing
32. Steam Electric Power Plants
33. Textile Mills
34. Timber Products Processing

Chapter 4

AIR POLLUTION CONTROL

G. William Frick [1]
Attorney
Lathrop, Koontz, Righter, Clagett & Norquist
Washington, DC

1.0 Introduction

Although generally described as environmental legislation, the Federal Clean Air Act (42 USC § 7401 et seq.) was enacted primarily because of growing recognition, by the Congress as well as the general public, of the serious adverse public health effects that result from air pollution. Certain environmental effects, such as reduced visibility, are readily apparent and, to a certain extent, easy to control; early air pollution control efforts focused on those problems through ordinances against black smoke and open burning. The most serious problems, however, are more insidious and require longer time periods to become apparent, e.g., impaired breathing functions, cancer, lower crop yields, premature deterioration of paint and building materials.

The less immediate, less visible effects of air pollution also make it more difficult to develop public support for the enormous cost associated with air pollution control efforts. As with most "police power" functions, air pollution control was initially left to the states and local governments. However, the political and economic obstacles to controlling sources of air pollution proved too difficult for them to overcome and the need for federal control efforts became apparent. The demand for a comprehensive federal

---

[1] Former General Counsel, U.S. Environmental Protection Agency. This chapter is a revision and update of versions written for previous editions of the Environmental Law Handbook by Robert L. Baum, Esq. and Michael A. James, Esq. to whom credit should be given for their contribution.

attack on the program also reflected a growing recognition that air pollution does not honor political boundaries and individual members of the public have no way to protect themselves against the hazards in the air they breathe.

The Clean Air Act of 1970 (P.L. 91-604), along with the major amendments adopted in the Clean Air Act Amendments of 1977 (P.L. 95-95), constitute a significant step forward in the nation's attack on the emission into the air of harmful pollutants. It creates a wide ranging, coordinated federal/state scheme of regulation that now pervades our social order and national economy, and affects virtually every citizen in the country. Consequently, with its impact on so many commercial and private activities, it is important that persons occupying executive or professional positions in industry and persons responsible for public policy have a basic understanding of its provisions.

2.0 History

The first "Clean Air Act" was passed in 1963. 2/ It provided for grants to air pollution control agencies and contained the first federal regulatory authority. The latter consisted of an abatement conference procedure, to be used in very limited circumstances. Although a number of abatement conferences were held around the country and some control efforts begun as a result of them, the air pollution problem was growing faster than federal, state and local efforts and abilities to control it.

In 1965, Congress amended the Act to add Title II, The Motor Vehicle Air Pollution Control Act (P.L. 89-272, 79 Stat. 991), which authorized federal emission standards for new vehicles. In 1967, Congress considerably broadened the Act with respect to stationary source control. The 1967 Amendments gave the federal government authority to adopt emission control regulations in designated areas which had air pollution problems. It also provided a system of limited federal enforcement.

In late 1970, after extensive hearings and debate, the Congress determined that drastic changes in the governmental response to air pollution were required and a totally restructured federal/state scheme was adopted in the Clean Air Act Amendments of 1970. While continuing to look to state and local governments as the primary focus of regulatory efforts, Congress provided the newly created Federal Environmental Protection Agency (EPA) with authority to establish, in accordance with specific Congressional directives, the minimum air quality and regulatory goals the states

---

2/   In 1955, the "Air Pollution Control--Research and Technical Assistance Act," P.L. 84-159, 69 Stat. 322, had been enacted, but it contained no regulatory authority.

and locals were to achieve. Congress also took the unusual step of establishing very stringent, and in many cases unrealistic, deadlines for action by the state and federal government. Where states failed to satisfy the Congressional expectations, EPA was directed to take specific regulatory actions. Furthermore, in addition to a more vigorous new motor vehicle control program with Congressionally adopted emission limitations, the 1970 Act provided for certain national emission standards that would be applicable regardless of air quality or the substantive governmental requirements in the area where the source was located.

3.0 Establishment of Air Quality Standards

3.1 Air Quality Criteria

Section 108 of the Act requires that the EPA Administrator publish a list of pollutants which he determines have adverse effects on public health or welfare, and which are emitted from numerous and diverse stationary or mobile sources. The "listing" of a pollutant sets in motion the process for establishing ambient air quality standards for such a pollutant. Although the Administrator of EPA considered the determination to list a pollutant to be discretionary, that flexibility was diminished by the court decision in NRDC v. Train, 411 F. Supp. 864 (S.D. N.Y.) aff'd 545 F. 2d 320 (2nd Cir. 1976), which required the Administrator to list lead. For each pollutant, a "criteria" document must be compiled and published by the Administrator. The criteria are scientific compendia of the studies documenting adverse effects of specific pollutants at various concentrations in the ambient air. In setting ambient air quality standards for the nation, i.e., prescribing the levels of air quality which the law requires to be attained and which determine the degree of control needed for individual sources, the Administrator is required to base his judgment solely on information in the criteria documents.

Section 108 also requires that, simultaneously with the issuance of criteria, the Administrator issue documents describing techniques for controlling the criteria pollutants. The information in these documents describes the various methods of reducing or eliminating emissions of the pollutant in question, as well as the costs of those methods.

The 1977 Amendments imposed a specific requirement that EPA issue a criteria document for nitrogen oxides, covering short term exposure effects of nitrogen dioxide and various suspect carcinogenic derivatives of oxides of nitrogen.

3.2 National Ambient Air Quality Standards

Under Section 109 of the law, the Administrator is to establish "national ambient air quality standards" (NAAQS) for each pollutant for which he issues a criteria document under Section

108. The NAAQS are of two types. The "primary" NAAQS for a pollutant is to be set at the level of air quality which, based on the criteria "and allowing an adequate margin of safety," will protect the public health. [§ 109(b)(1)]

Two points concerning the primary standards are important. First, the language and history of the Act make it clear that the standards are to be set at levels which protect not only the normal healthy majority of the population, but even especially sensitive persons with pre-existing illnesses or conditions which pollution might exacerbate, although not cause. The second, and perhaps more significant point, is that the primary NAAQS are to be established solely on a strictly scientific basis using the data in the criteria documents; cost, technical feasibility or any other factor than public health cannot be considered in setting the standards. Such factors cannot be the basis for either a legal challenge to the standard or an excuse for failure to attain it. Because of the Act's rigid requirements for achievement of the primary NAAQS, there is growing concern that the primary NAAQS should be set only after some consideration of the benefits that would result as compared with the overall cost to society of achieving the standards. This is particularly an issue with respect to pollutants that have significant natural sources, such as particulates and ozone.

The secondary NAAQS [§ 109(b)(2)] is that level of air quality which protects the public welfare from any known or anticipated adverse effects. "Public welfare" [§ 302(h)] encompasses essentially all parts of the environment other than human health that might be affected by an air pollutant, e.g., soil, crops, vegetation, animals, manmade materials, visibility, and personal comfort and well-being. In short, the secondary standard is to protect against any type of adverse effect, even if it could not be scientifically shown to affect man's physiological well-being in any narrow medical sense. The requirement of secondary standards was based on the knowledge that, in some cases, air pollutants had adverse effects on materials, vegetation, or visibility at levels lower than those which could be shown to directly affect human health.

Ambient standards for six pollutants were promulgated by EPA on April 30, 1971. 3/ The six were sulfur dioxide (SO_2), particulate matter, carbon monoxide (CO), hydrocarbons (HC), nitrogen dioxide (NO_2), and photochemical oxidants. On February 8, 1979, (44 Fed. Reg. 8202 et seq.), EPA redesignated the oxidants NAAQS to an ozone standard and increased the level by 50%. In the case of the last four NAAQS, generally associated with emissions from mobile sources, the secondary standards are the same as the primary, because no studies had revealed effects on welfare from these

---

3/   40 CFR Part 50.

pollutants at levels which did not affect human health. However, for SO_2 and particulate matter, generally associated with emissions from stationary sources, secondary standards were set at more stringent levels than the primary, because effects on vegetation and visibility had been identified at levels which had not been shown to be harmful man.

Hydrocarbons were originally included in the NAAQS because they contribute to the formation of ozone. As a class, hydrocarbons alone do not cause direct health or welfare effects at ambient levels. The hydrocarbon NAAQS was only to be used as a guide for determining achievement of the ozone NAAQS. As part of its review of the hydrocarbon criteria, EPA determined that there was no quantitative relationship between hydrocarbon levels and ozone, and EPA revoked the NAAQS on January 5, 1983. 48 Fed. Reg. 628. Hydrocarbon emissions, however, will still be controlled as part of the ozone NAAQS control strategy.

Pursuant to court order, EPA established NAAQS for lead on October 5, 1978 (43 Fed. Reg. 46258). Although previously regulated only as a fuel additive, regulations on stationary sources will now be imposed.

Despite the importance of the NAAQS in what follows under the Act, only one portion of one standard from the original six NAAQS was challenged in the Courts. In the course of a lawsuit by Kennecott Copper Corporation, 4/ EPA withdrew a portion of the secondary standards for sulfur dioxide. Otherwise, the April 30, 1972, NAAQS's remain essentially in effect.

In the 1977 Amendments, Congress directed the Agency to completely review all the criteria documents and NAAQS and to make appropriate revisions to the NAAQS by the end of 1980. Even before this requirement was enacted, EPA had begun a reassessment of the NAAQS for photochemical oxidants which resulted in the February 8, 1979, revision. The 1977 Act also required EPA to develop a NO_2 NAAQS for short term exposures. Such a standard could necessitate new control strategies for areas that are meeting the current annual NO_2 standard.

Despite their critical importance to the scheme of the Clean Air Act, NAAQS are not directly enforceable. They are the controlling force behind the development and implementation of emission limitations and other controls pursuant to other sections of the statute. It is those requirements that the government actually enforces against polluters rather than asserting that a source is violating an NAAQS.

The NAAQS establish ceilings for individual pollutant concentrations that should not be exceeded anywhere in the United

---

4/ Kennecott Copper Corp. v. EPA, 462 F.2d 846 (D.C. Cir. 1972).

States. They, therefore, determine the degree of control that will be imposed on existing sources and the restrictions on location of new sources, depending on whether air quality is better than or worse than the NAAQS in the particular area where the source is or will be located.

3.3 Air Quality Control Regions

Prior to the 1970 Clean Air Act, Congress had recognized the difficulties States and their sometimes relatively autonomous political subdivision had in coordinating efforts to control air pollution. Consequently, in the 1967 Act, the Secretary of Health, Education and Welfare was directed to designate "Air Quality Control Regions" (AQCR's). These are interstate or intrastate areas which, because of common meteorological, industrial and socioeconomic factors, should be treated as a single unit for the purpose of air pollution control. The concept of ignoring jurisdictional boundaries in order to treat regional air pollution problems was preserved in the 1970 law. The 1970 Amendments required the entire country to be divided into AQCR's. 5/

The 1977 Amendments to the Act (Public Law 95-95, August 7, 1977) reduced the significance of the AQCR's by requiring the States to identify, and EPA to designate formally, areas of the country which meet NAAQS national ambient air quality standards, do not meet NAAQS, or for which there are insufficient data to place them in either of those categories. Many of the areas have been designated on the basis of county boundaries. 6/ Some are determined by the area around a single point source that is affected by that source. "Air quality maintenance areas" have also been designated that are not coterminous with AQCR's.

Classification of an area determines what actions the state and EPA will be required to take to regulate air pollution from existing and new emission sources. Areas are classified for each pollutant for which a national ambient air quality standard is in effect, on the basis of monitoring data to the extent possible.

4.0 State Implementation Plans (SIP's)

4.1 Content of SIP

The key regulatory section of the Act is Section 110. It implements the Congressional philosophy that "prevention and control of air pollution at its source is the primary responsibility of

---

5/   The 247 AQCR's designated by HEW and EPA are identified in the Code of Federal Regulations (hereafter CFR) in Title 40, Part 81.

6/   43 Fed. Reg. 8962, March 3, 1978.

state and local governments" 7/ and provides a structure under
which state and local governments are expected to establish the
regulatory framework necessary to achieve the NAAQS through
their jurisdictions. However, it also directs the EPA to impose the
necessary regulations if state and local governments fail to meet the
Act's directives.

The structure of Section 110 is as follows. Within nine
months of the promulgation of an NAAQS, each state, after public
hearings, is to submit to the Administrator of EPA for his approval a
plan for implementation of the NAAQS in every AQCR in the state.
8/ Under the timetable in the 1970 Act, state implementation plans
were due on January 30, 1972. The law gives the Administrator of
EPA four months to approve or disapprove the SIP. If a state fails
to submit a plan or submits a plan which the Administrator deems to
be inadequate, the Administrator must promulgate federal regulations to substitute for or supplement that portion of the state's plan.
[§ 110(c)] Approval of a state plan makes its provisions enforceable by the federal government as well as the state. 9/

A SIP consists of a description of the air quality in each
AQCR, an emissions inventory of sources that emit each pollutant
covered by an NAAQS, emission limitations and compliance schedules applicable to each source that will reduce pollutant emissions so
that the total pollutant contribution is below that necessary to
achieve the NAAQS, a permit program for review of new source
construction to insure new emissions will not cause a violation of
NAAQS, monitoring and reporting requirements, and enforcement
procedures. All of those elements comprise the control strategy of
the SIP for satisfying the goal of the Act to achieve a level of air
quality throughout the country that will protect both public health
and the public welfare.

In the SIP's submitted in 1972 for attainment of the original
six NAAQS, states were given substantial flexibility to choose which
sources to regulate, and to vary the degree of control among
sources; because air quality varied greatly throughout the country,
the emission limitations necessarily varied substantially. Some
areas already had air quality better than NAAQS while others had
such serious problems that they still have not achieved one or more
s0andards seven years later, and there is some question whether
certain areas will ever achieve it. While states still have great
flexibility, the 1977 Amendments established additional conditions

---

7/   § 101(a)(3).

8/   EPA's minimum requirements for approvable state plans are
      set forth in 40 CFR Part 51.

9/   See 40 CFR Part 52.

on the minimum requirements that states must impose, particularly in areas that have not yet achieved the NAAQS. Part D of Title 1 of the Clean Air Act requires states to revise their SIP's, to impose reasonably available control technology (RACT) on existing sources, and to impose rigorous requirements on new sources in nonattainment areas, including requiring them to obtain offsets from other sources equivalent to the emissions to be added by the new source.

The Act requires that the SIP attain the primary standards "as expeditiously as practicable," but in no event later than three years from the date of plan approval. Section 110(e) permits, if the Governor requests at the time the plan is submitted, up to two additional years for attainment of a primary standard upon a showing that three years is inadequate despite application of all available measures. Since most states, in 1972, assumed standards could be met within the three-year period, particularly because of an apparently unlimited, cheap supply of "clean" oil, relatively few states asked for the additional two years.

SIP's are to provide for attainment of the secondary standard within a "reasonable time." The term "reasonable time" is not defined in the Act and states can consider technological and economic problems in deciding on an appropriate date for achievement of the welfare standard. 10/ Although the provisions of Section 110 in the 1970 Act were relatively simple and straightforward, the development and adoption of effective emission controls involved complex technical, economic and political decisions, and many states failed to submit SIP's that could be approved in their entirety. Unfortunately, even when approved, or substitute EPA regulations promulgated, a large number of plans failed to achieve the NAAQS for one or more pollutants in some regions of the state. Consequently, Congress in its 1977 Amendments imposed more demanding provisions in Section 110 to reinvigorate the SIP program.

In the 1977 Amendments, Congress retained all of the above requirements and added several others. By August 7, 1978, States were to submit SIP revisions that require each major source to pay fees sufficient to cover the states' cost of handling any construction or operating permit for the source, require state permit and enforcement boards to restructure their memberships and make public disclosures to prevent conflicts of interests, provide for prevention of interference with other states' air quality, require consultation with local governments and federal land managers in

---

10/ EPA by regulation indicated that, where controls were reasonably available, a "reasonable time" for achievement of the secondary standards for sulfur oxides and particulates would be three years, unless the state could show that good cause exists for choosing a later date. 40 CFR 51.13(b)(1) and (2).

carrying out major SIP functions, and provide for notification to the public areas not meeting the NAAQS.

The most significant addition to the SIP process adopted by the 1977 Amendments relates to areas that did not achieve the NAAQS within the statutory deadlines, so called "nonattainment areas." Although much attention has been directed toward the provisions applicable to new sources in nonattainment areas, discussed below along with the SIP provisions applicable to review new sources in clean air areas to prevent significant deterioration of air quality, the 1977 Amendments also imposed additional SIP requirements on existing sources. Recognizing that many SIP's were inadequate and had not achieved all the NAAQS in all areas of the country, Congress required all SIP's to be reviewed; where standards were still violated, revised SIP's were to be submitted by January 1, 1979. Congress extended the original deadlines to December 31, 1982, with additional time to December 31, 1987, available in certain circumstances to achieve NAAQS for ozone or CO. To gain that additional time, however, the states have to adopt significantly more stringent SIP provisions.

In addition to the significant new source review provisions, all existing sources must be required to install, at a minimum, "reasonably available control technology." [§ 172] In order to extend the time to 1987 for ozone and CO, which are primarily related to automobiles, states must adopt a vehicle inspection and maintenance program and adopt such other vehicle control measures as may be necessary. States must also show "reasonable further progress" toward achievement of the NAAQS, which is defined in Section 171 as the accomplishment of "annual incremental reductions in emissions." As an "incentive" to states to adopt these more stringent provisions, Congress provided that if revised SIP provisions are not adopted and approved by EPA by June 30, 1979, there was to be no construction in the state of new or modified sources of the air pollutants for which NAAQS are exceeded. [§ 110(a)(2)(I)] Although EPA has made a number of interpretations of the regulations and the statute to prevent the construction ban from stiffling economic growth, the ban has gone into effect in a number of areas around the country and has limited construction in some places. The difficult decisions involved delayed state action and many SIP's were not revised by the June 30, 1979, deadline. On December 31, 1982, many areas of the country lacked approved SIP's and still violated a least one NAAQS.

With the failure of the 97th Congress to amend the Clean Air Act to provide an extension of its December 31, 1982 deadlines, EPA faced the prospect of administering the statute with the severe penalties adopted in the Clean Air Act Amendments of 1977. EPA has stated that the failure of states to have adequate plans achieving the standards by December 31, 1982, requires that it impose the construction ban and take steps to terminate federal highway funds and air grant money for nonattainment areas in the state. The extent to which EPA must immediately impose these sanctions is in sharp dispute, although interpretations of the law may be affected by the political implications of imposition of the sanctions. Possible extension of the deadlines and adjustments in the method for imposing sanctions will be considered during debate over amendments to the Clean Air Act in 1983.

The Congress did address one deadline problem in the Steel Industry Compliance Extension Act, P.L. 97-23 (July 17, 1981) whereby it provided in an amendment to § 113(e) that steel production facilities may have their compliance date extended to as late as December 31, 1985. The company must show that the funds to be used for compliance with environmental requirements are needed and will be used for investment in production facilities to improve efficiency and productivity.

4.1.1 Role of Technology and Economics

The principal industry court challenges to the first SIP's involved whether EPA, in determining whether to approve the SIP, must consider the technological and economic feasibility of the measures in the plan. EPA took the position that the statutory requirement that primary NAAQS be achieved within three years overrode any considerations based on cost or availability of technology; sources could always be shut down. Moreover, § 116 gives a state the right to adopt any requirements it wants, even more stringent than necessary to achieve the NAAQS. Consequently, if the plan when properly enforced would result in achievement of the NAAQS, EPA would approve it regardless of any misgivings it might have regarding the technological or economic feasibility of the particular approach chosen by the state. EPA further argued that review of these issues must be accomplished at the state level where the principal responsibility lies or, in a limited fashion, in federal enforcement actions.

Ultimately, the Supreme Court decided unanimously in favor of EPA's position that Section 110 does not require EPA to engage in a review of technological or economic feasibility when considering SIP's for approval [Union Electric Company v. EPA, 427 U.S. 246 (1976)]. The Court read the Act to necessitate a review of each SIP only to determine whether it meets the requirements explicit in Section 110, i.e., that it includes specific measures and insures the attainment and maintenance of the NAAQS. The opinion noted that challenges concerning technological and economic feasibility could be made at the state level through administrative and judicial channels, and suggested that a source might obtain some review on its particular feasibility problems should the SIP be enforced against it in federal district court. The Court chose specifically not to decide what consideration EPA must give to technological or economic feasibility when it promulgates SIP measures.

Union Electric was a particularly important decision because, under the 1977 Amendments, states were required to submit for EPA approval major revisions of many SIP's. While Union Electric should discourage most challenges to EPA's approvals based on economics and technology, some arguments still may be raised [see Bunker Hill Co. v. EPA, 572 F.2d 1286 (9th Cir. 1977)] and Court challenges to SIP's at the state level can be expected to be more numerous.

EPA has attempted to provide sources with the ability to choose the most cost effective means to meet emission require-ments by authorizing various "emissions trading" approaches. See 47 Fed. Reg. 15076, et seq.; April 7, 1982. This policy allows a state and a source to use various techniques to achieve the goals of the statute but in a more cost effective manner. The "bubble" policy allows a source which is subject to several emission limits at the same facility to achieve different reductions at various emission points (higher than required in some cases and lower than required in others) as long as the total emissions from the plant are no higher than would have occurred if the facility met all of the requirements as imposed. With respect to new sources, EPA authorizes "netting" whereby intra-plant offsets can be used to avoid new source review; "offsets" where reductions can be obtained from other facilities, which were not otherwise required to achieve those reductions, to offset emissions of another company; and "banking," whereby an accounting system can be developed which will allow a source, which for business reasons reduces emissions to utilize those reductions as offsets for future emissions increases.

4.1.2 Use of Dispersion Techniques

One of the major debates that arose during implementation of the 1970 Act is whether SIP's may reply on techniques other than continuous emission reduction to demonstrate attainment of the NAAQS. To some extent, any air quality management program relies upon the natural dispersion capacities of the meteorology and topography of the area being managed. However, many sources, particularly isolated facilities, proposed to monitor meteorological conditions and curtail operations and emissions intermittently, thereby preventing NAAQS from being exceeded, even where tech-nology or other means of achieving continuous emission control were available. A related approach was to rely upon tall stacks to dis-perse emissions which might otherwise be controlled by available techology.

These two questions were addressed in three major lawsuits brought by industry and by environmental groups. 11/ The courts uniformly held that dispersion dependent techniques such as inter-

---

11/   NRDC v. Train, 489 F.2d 390 (5th Cir. 1974); Big Rivers Electric Cooperative v. Train, 523 F.2d 16 (6th Cir. 1975); Kennecott Copper Corp. v. Train, 526 F.2d 1149 (9th Cir. 1975).

mittent control and tall stacks are permissible to attain NAAQS under Section 110 of the Act only if all available constant emission controls are first applied.

In Section 123 of the 1977 Act, Congress attempted to finally resolve the tall stack and intermittent controls issues. Continuous emission controls must be applied, except nonferrous smelters and fuel-burning sources ordered to burn coal instead of oil or gas will be allowed on a limited basis to rely on intermittent controls to allow attainment of NAAQS. The Section allows SIP's to give credit in their control strategies to stack heights representing "good engineering practice" (GEP), but not for the height of the stack above GEP. EPA published regulations defining "good engineering practice" on February 8, 1982 (47 Fed. Reg. 5864 et seq.). The regulations generally provide that a source will be given credit for emissions from a stack 2-1/2 times the height of nearby structures. EPA also allows a minimum height of 65 meters. EPA will allow a higher stack for unusual topographcal situations when necessary to avoid downwash or prevent adverse impacts.

4.1.3 Transportation Control Plans

When SIP's were submitted in January of 1972, it was clear that the standards for automobile related pollutants (HC, CO, Oxidents, and NO_2) could not always be met through conventional means of control on stationary sources. As newer cars, subject to more stringent emission standards, replaced the older "dirtier" car population, improvements in air quality could be predicted. That improvement, plus control of certain stationary sources would, in many areas, achieve the standards. But, in a significant number of metropolitan areas, such controls were inadequate to correct the problem.

Since neither EPA nor the states had any real experience in coping with this problem, in 1972 the Agency permitted states with problems to submit plans which merely quantified the problems, and permitted them an additional year to submit a plan for solving it. A court eventually held that, although "the Administrator acted in the best of faith in attempting to comply with the difficult responsibilities imposed on him...," the extension was illegal. 12/ As a result, EPA was forced to promulgate requirements that the states impose strategies for lowering concentrations of automobile pollutants by insuring the cars in use are maintained properly and by reducing the use of cars. These groups of measures are known as Transportation Control Plans (TCP's). Since the states, almost without exception, did not adopt TCP's, the Administrator was required by the Act to do so and began promulgating TCP's in late 1973.

12/ NRDC v. EPA, 475 F. 2d 968 (D.C. Cir. 1972).

The TCP's created more controversy than any other single action of the Agency. They did, however, dramatize the extent of the mobile source air pollution problem, and the types and extent of the sacrifices which must be made if the health standards are to be achieved. TCP's included the following types of measures: exclusive bus and bicycle lanes; bridge tolls; area-wide computer systems to identify and bring together potential car poolers; surcharges on parking spaces in urban areas to force people for economic reasons to look to alternative means of transportation; state inspection and maintenance systems; requirements that older cars be retrofitted with devices to reduce emissions; requirements for improvements of mass transit systems, and finally, where achievement of the standards could not be reliably predicted, gas rationing to whatever extent necessary to reduce vehicle miles traveled in the problem areas. 13/

It soon became clear that the states and the general public were not ready to support such pervasive measures that intruded into almost all areas of public activity, even though reducing vehicle miles traveled was clearly necessary for reaching air quality goals and also consistent with other national needs during the energy crisis of 1974. The significant public support for air pollution controls quickly faded when it became apparent that improved air quality could only come about with restrictions on America's most cherished possessions, its automobiles. Congress reacted to the public mood and, in connection with energy legislation, 14/ adopted provisions of law that deferred any EPA regulations regarding parking management. It also revoked EPA's authority to impose parking surcharges. The need for TCP's to achieve the NAAQS for automobile-generated pollutants in urban areas has not gone away. Although the debate on TCP's has been allowed to die down, it will surface again with the revised SIP's for nonattainment areas. Even with a 1987 deadline, some TCP measures will have to be adopted and it remains to be seen whether the public attitude has become more accepting toward restrictions on their freedom to use automobiles.

4.1.4 Maintenance of Ambient Air Quality Standards

The Act requires that SIP's assure maintenance of NAAQS's as well as attainment. While EPA's regulations governing SIP content required states to take account of projected growth in develop-

---

13/ A good example of a comprehensive TCP is the one first proposed for Boston, 38 Fed. Reg. 30960, Nov. 8, 1973. This plan contains virtually every measure which EPA believed feasible to reduce car use. Other TCP's contained these types of measures plus gas rationing.

14/ The "Energy Supply and Environmental Coordination Act of 1974," P.L. 93-319, June 22, 1974.

ing their plans, most SIP's submitted to EPA in 1972 reflected the lack of time and expertise necessary to build growth considerations.

An environmental group challenged EPA's approvals of the plans on this ground and EPA conceded that its one required mechanism for assisting maintenance efforts--preconstruction review of new and modified stationary sources--was not sufficiently comprehensive to enable SIP's to maintain NAAQS. In 1974, EPA added requirements that the plans include provisions for long term maintenance measures and for review of indirect sources. EPA required states to identify those areas which had the potential for exceeding a NAAQS within 10 years, called air quality maintenance areas (AQMA's). Once such AQMA's are designated, states must submit SIP provisions that will maintain the NAAQS for a period of 10 years. Ideally, the state would consider the expected and/or desired growth and determine what limitations should be established to insure the needed air quality. While review of new sources on a case-by-case basis in itself can prevent an ambient standard from being exceeded, without planning it necessarily operates on a first-come, first-served basis. The 10 year maintenance plans were designed to avoid this. As a practical matter, however, such maintenance plans are designed to alert the state to the possibility of violations occuring because of growth in the area and to establish a procedure whereby the state will respond to that threat with appropriate SIP revisions.

While the air quality maintenance plan requirements remain in effect and are specifically referred to in the 1977 Amendments to Section 110(a)(2)(B), state resources in the SIP area will in all likelihood be devoted to the development of plan revisions incorporating measures for prevention of significant deterioration and for attainment in current nonattainment areas rather than implementing the maintenance requirements.

4.1.5 Indirect Source Review

As part of the settlement of a lawsuit with the Natural Resources Defense Council, EPA extended its new source review requirements to so-called "complex" or "indirect" sources. 15/ Certain sources, such as shopping centers, highways or sports arenas, do not emit pollutants in significant quantities but attract automobiles which can cause high pollutant concentrations. Accordingly, to insure maintenance of certain standards, e.g., carbon monoxide, it is appropriate to prevent facilities which attract sources of that pollutant from being built in certain areas, or to require them to be designed in such a way that vehicle concentrations will not cause the ambient standard for CO to be violated.

15/   40 CFR 52.21 (Feb. 25, 1974).

Basically, the regulations required review in larger cities of new facilities that would provide parking for 1000 or more cars, for increases of 500 parking places in existing facilities, and for a new highway that within 10 years would be expected to be used by 20,000 vehicles per day. Outside of the larger cities, the triggering numbers were larger. The regulations also covered the construction or modification of new airports.

The reaction was immediate and strong. Commercial interests, primarily developers of large shopping centers, united in an all-out effort to resist this expansion of regulatory authority. Their arguments were strengthened by the fact that the "problem" was created by the automobile, a pollution source over which their new regulators, viz., EPA, had control.

In response to criticism of the indirect source program generated by shopping center and other commercial interests, Congress included in EPA's appropriation bill for several years a restriction on the use of any funds to enforce parking management regulations. In the 1977 Amendments, Congress barred EPA from engaging in any indirect source review, except for federally-funded highways and airports, but reserved to the states the right to have indirect source programs in their SIP's.

4.1.6 Variances

Historically, the chief regulatory means by which states postponed the requirement that a source comply with applicable requirements was by the granting of a variance. One of the first issues litigated under the 1970 Act was whether and to what extent a state could allow variances to requirements included as part of an approved SIP.

EPA took the position that a variance could be approved so long as it would not interfere with attainment of the NAAQS. If interference with the standards was shown, the source had to proceed under Section 110(f) of the Act, which involved a lengthy formal hearing process.

The Natural Resources Defense Council challenged this approach, claiming that all variances to regulations included in a SIP had to be issued by means of Section 110(f). After seven United States Courts of Appeals arrived at three different views as to the legality of EPA's interpretation of the Act, the Supreme Court heard the case and decided in favor of EPA's position. 16/

The outcome of the debate is that states may grant a variance which can be approved by EPA as a revision to the SIP if the source's emissions will not interfere with attainment or maintenance of the NAAQS's. However, many major sources will not be able to meet this test. The handling of major noncomplying sources is

---

16/   Train v. NRDC, 421 U.S. 60 (1975).

currently through enforcement actions, either federally under Section 113 of the Act, or by the states, although the 1977 Amendments placed significant new restraints on EPA's administrative handling of non-complying sources.

4.2 New Source Review in Nonattainment Areas

Section 110(a)(2)(D) requires SIP's to include a program for preconstruction review of new or modified stationary sources to insure that such sources will not interfere with attainment or maintenance of NAAQS. After the date for achievement of the ambient standards passed, it became difficult to justify allowing construction of any new facilities in light of this mandate; any new facility emitting a pollutant for which NAAQS were violated would obviously "interfere" with attainment. To prevent a "no growth" situation in such areas, EPA issued a ruling on December 21, 1976, indicating how it interpreted this section. 17/ The primary conditions imposed before a new source could be constructed was that a reduction in emissions be obtained from existing sources, whether owned by the applicant or not, which would not otherwise have occurred and which would provide a more than one-for-one offset to the emissions from the new or modified facility.

This "offset" policy also required the source to install the "best available control technology," (BACT) which was generally new source performance standards, because it was seeking to locate in an area with serious air pollution problems. The policy was controversial because it brought attention to the inherent conflict between achievement of air quality goals and economic growth. Yet, ironically, the offset policy strained the language of the Act and was adopted by EPA in an effort to prevent the Act from imposing more drastic curtailment on growth.

Despite the initial success of the offset policy, EPA felt strongly that Congress needed to address directly the growth issue in the Act. After adopting a very limited scheme for dealing with growth in the 1976 Amendments, which never became law, Congress approached the issue with a comprehensive program in the 1977 Amendments. This program, set forth in Sections 171-178, was the major dividend in the legislative delay from 1976 to 1977.

The 1977 Amendments adopted the EPA offset policy as a starting point, except that the baseline for determining offsets will be the applicable SIP rather than the "reasonably available control technology" test in the EPA regulations. EPA is to apply its offset policy until states adopt revised SIP provisions incorporating a preconstruction review program as set forth in Section 172. EPA

17/   41 Fed. Reg. 55524-30.

revised its offset policy on January 16, 1979, 18/ to reflect the changes made by the Congress in the 1977 Amendments. That policy will be effective until July 1, 1979, when state procedures are to be in place. The policy continues to apply to new sources, or modifications to existing sources, with the potential to emit more than 100 tons of a pollutant. In another significant change, EPA authorized states to allow the "banking" of emissions offsets; this will allow a source that reduces emissions, beyond that necessary under the SIP, to save the emission reductions as offsets against future expansion. Such an approach may give rise to the first marketing of "pollution rights."

The statutory program required by Section 172 to be included in all SIP's for areas not achieving NAAQS must provide for a permit program for all new or modified sources with the potential (design capacity) to emit one hundred tons or more per year of a given pollutant. The preconstruction review is to determine whether the source will be in compliance with applicable SIP requirements and will meet the specific requirements applicable to nonattainment areas.

The definition of "source" for purposes of determining new source review in nonattainment areas was made narrower than the definition for PSD areas due to concern that the Agency should review more sources in areas that were not achieving the standards. EPA, therefore, defined source to include even a single piece of process equipment, which minimized opportunities for intra-source offsets. 45 Fed. Reg. 52746; August 7, 1980. In order to allow more flexibility to sources in nonattainment areas to utilize the bubble approach to compliance, EPA on October 14, 1981, revised the nonattainment requirements to employ the same definition of "source" as in PSD areas. 47 Fed. Reg. 50766. That decision was overturned, however, in NRDC v. Gorsuch, 17 ERC 1825 (D.C. Cir. 1982). The court held that EPA's decision was inconsistent with the nonattainment requirements of the statute and with the court's previous decision in Asarco, Inc. v. EPA, 578 F.2d 319 (D.C. Cir. 1978) where the court held that a bubble concept is impermissible when the Congressional objective was improvement, rather than simple preservation, of existing air quality. The Supreme Court has been asked to review the NRDC decision.

In addition to the procedural review, these sources must be controlled to a level reflecting the "lowest achievable emission rate," (LAER) which is a defined term meaning the most stringent emission standard in any SIP (unless it is shown to be unachievable) or the lowest emissions any source in the same category has achieved in practice. A new source cannot receive a permit unless other sources owned or operated by the applicant in the state are

---

18/   44 Fed. Reg. 3274, et seq.

meeting all applicable emission limits or at least meeting all compliance schedule steps.   For a source to satisy the statutory
requirement that after it starts operation there will be "reasonable
further progress" towards achievement of the NAAQS that is being
violated, it must obtain permanent enforceable emission reductions
at its own facilities or from other sources, or the revised SIP must
include provisions that curtail other sources so that allowances for
growth have been built into the control strategy.

     If a state fails to meet these requirements, there can be
serious consequences for growth in nonattainment areas.   Section
110 was amended in 1977 to require that unless a SIP meets the
nonattainment requirements of the Act, "no major stationary source
shall be constructed or modified" in the area if it will emit the
nonattaining pollutant. 19/ This provision was meant to spur states
toward the kind of planning and strategy development that effective
air quality management demands.   There is very little time for the
planning and regulatory processes to be accomplished, however.

     In addition to the prohibition on new facilities if states do not
adopt adequate revisions to SIP's to implement the nonattainment
requirements, there are other sanctions built into the nonattainment
program.   States can lose further federal highway funds if transportation control measures would be necessary for attainment. [§176
(a)].   A state's failure to implement its SIP after the same date will
subject it to cutoff of EPA Clean Air Act grants.   [§ 176(b)].
Finally, the entire federal government is directed by Section 176 (c)
not to fund, approve, license or permit any activity that is inconsistent with an applicable SIP.

4.3 Prevention of Significant Deterioration (PSD)

     On December 5, 1974, EPA promulgated regulations designed
to prevent significant deterioration of air quality in areas of the
country where ambient standards are already being met. 20/ The
Sierra Club had challenged EPA's determination that it had no
authority to regulate in this area on the grounds that the Section
101(b)(1) statement of purpose indicated the Act was to "protect and
enhance" the quality of the nation's air resources, and the Act should
not allow the air in pristine areas to be polluted, even up to the
levels of the relatively stringent secondary standards.   In litigation
which reached the Supreme Court, Sierra Club won its case when the

---

19/   § 110(a)(2)(I).

20/   30 Fed. Reg. 42510.

Court divided 4 to 4. 21/ This had the effect of affirming the lower court decisions, holding not only that EPA had such authority but also was required to issue implementing regulations.

From its proposed regulation on July 16, 1973, through public hearings, reproposals, meetings with states and citizen groups and the expenditure of enormous amounts of internal resources to develop the final regulations, EPA attempted to strike a balance between a sound environmental principle, and the difficulties in its implementation. Without any Congressional guidance, the EPA struggled to develop a system that would satisfy the court yet not stop all growth in clean air areas.

EPA's final regulations were immediately the subject of litigation, both by environmental groups, who considered the regulations inadequate, and by other interests, who considered the regulations more stringent than necessary. EPA's regulations allowed state and local governments to determine what degradation would be "significant" in terms of local conditions. Specifically, the regulations provided for three types of areas with certain "increments" of additional pollution allowed in each. Class I areas were those in which the increments of permissible deterioration were so low that they effectively precluded any substantial growth. The increments for Class II areas were designed to allow moderate, controlled growth in these areas; all areas in the country were initially classified as Class II. The Class III areas allowed additional pollution up to the secondary standard. The only pollutants covered by the regulations were SO_2 and particulate matter.

On August 2, 1976, the United States Court of Appeals for the District of Columbia Circuit upheld the regulations in their entirety. Sierra Club, et al. v. EPA, 540 F.2d 1114 (D.C. Cir. 1976). The Supreme Court agreed to review the case but, before briefs were filed. Congress adopted the 1977 Amendments which included a specific national policy to prevent significant deterioration and detailed how that policy is to be implemented.

What Congress has done is to expand upon the approach taken in EPA's initial regulations. The classes of areas have now been congressionally established, with certain national parks irrevocably categorized as Class I and the rest of the country classified as Class II. The limited amounts of additional pollution that will be allowed in each area are set forth in Section 163, and are more restrictive

---

21/ In Sierra Club v. Ruckelshaus, 344 F. Supp. 253 (D.D.C. 1972), affirmed sub nom. Fri v. Sierra Club, 412 U.S. 541 (1973), the District Court enjoined EPA from approving portions of state implementation plans that did not provide for prevention of any significant deterioration of air quality in those regions that have air cleaner than the secondary ambient air quality standards.

than EPA's regulations; although only increments for SO_2 and particulates are established, EPA was directed to develop increments
for other pollutants within two years from the date of enactment of
the 1977 Amendments. but which it has never done. A preconstruction review is required for any source in one of 28 specified categories with the potential to emit more than 100 tons per year of any
pollutant, or any other source that has the potential to emit 250 tons
per year. In addition to not exceeding the increments, these new
sources must use "best available control technology" (BACT) which
is to be determined on a case-by-case basis (although nothing less
stringent than NSPS will be allowed); BACT must be met for all
pollutants regulated by the Act, not just NAAQS pollutants.
    Consistency with the increments is predicted by use of diffu-
sion modeling applied to a baseline, which is the concentration of
the pollutant involved on the date of the first application for a
permit in the area. Proposed sources will be required to conduct
monitoring to assist EPA or the state in identifying baseline concentrations.
    States and Indian governing bodies are permitted to reclassify
the Class II areas if they follow detailed procedural requirements
which emphasize public involvement, consideration of competing
interests, and the approval of local governing bodies. Certain federal lands may not be reclassified to Class III.
    EPA promulgated regulations specifying application of the
new statutory PSD requirements on June 19, 1978. 22/ EPA's regulations were challenged by environmental groups and various industries. They were upheld in part but remanded in part by the United
States Court of Appeals for the District of Columbia Circuit in
Alabama Power Company v. Costle, 13 ERC 1993 (D.C. Cir. 1980);
see also, 13 ERC 1225. EPA then made a substantial change in its
regulations and published a new round of final regulations on August
7, 1980. (45 Fed. Reg. 52676, et seq.).
    The PSD program is administered primarily through review of
new sources and modifications to existing sources. Each state
implementation plan is to have provisions that require review of
such sources. Where they do not, EPA administers a permit system,
established in 40 CFR § 52.21. A source will have to undergo new
source review if it is a major emitting facility and it has the "potential to emit" more than 100 tons of any pollutant regulated by the
Clean Air Act, not just sulfur dioxide or particulates. (The amount
is 250 tons for sources other than the 28 specific categories, noted
above.) "Potential to emit" means the maximum design capacity of
the source after application of pollution controls. For a modification to undergo review, it must be a modification of an existing
major stationary source which creates a "significant net increase" in

---

22/   43 Fed. Reg. 26380, et seq.

emissions of a pollutant regulated under the Clean Air Act. The Alabama Power decision required EPA to define "significant net increase" for each pollutant, which EPA has done in 40 CFR § 52.21 (b)(23). Fugitive emissions will not be calculated in determining potential to emit unless they are specifically designated by EPA by regulation. EPA has done so for the 28 listed categories of sources. 40 CFR § 52.21(i)(4)(vii).

In determining the "source" to which the regulations apply, EPA will examine the largest grouping of pollutant-emitting activities located on contiguous or adjacent properties which are under the control of the same person and within the same sic code major group. 40 CFR §52.21(b)(6). The definition of source is important because new source review applies only to a net increase in emissions from the source. If emissions can be reduced at other locations within the source to levels below 100 tons, new source review may be avoided. Thus, the larger number of emitting activities which constitute the source, the greater possibilities for offsets.

If a source is subject to new source review, it will have to make several demonstrations before it will be allowed to construct. First, it must show that it will not cause a violation of NAAQS. Second, it must show that any emission of particulates or sulfur dioxide will not cause a violation of the statutory PSD increments. Third, it must show that it will employ "best available control technology" (BACT) at the facility. This is defined in §165(a)(4) of the Act as a case-by-case determination of the maximum emission reduction achievable by the facility for each pollutant regulated by the Clean Air Act, taking into consideration cost, energy, non-air environmental impacts, and other factors. BACT cannot be less stringent than NSPS. Design, equipment and operational standards or work practices may be mandated as part of BACT. It is important to note that even though the PSD program has focused on particulates and SO_2, it is a much broader program and is designed to minimize increases in pollutant loadings of all pollutants regulated by the Act to preserve air quality as well as provide maximum room for future growth. For this reason, BACT is required for each pollutant emitted by the source in greater than de minimus amounts once it is determined that BACT applies.

Under the 1977 Amendments' scheme, public hearings are required on applications for permits. An applicant must make a technical showing on the proposed source's emissions effect on visibility and vegetation and describe any general growth in the area which may result from the source's existence. These requirements, and the BACT and air quality monitoring requirements discussed above, are certain to mean that the PSD permit process will be more lengthy now than under EPA's 1974 regulations. Congress recognized this and extended the 90-day period for permit approval to one year.

The comprehensive preconstruction review programs developed for nonattainment areas and PSD areas mean that all major new source construction, or modifications to existing sources, will undergo careful scrutiny. Because air quality will be either better than or worse than NAAQS in all areas, the source will be subject to one or the other of these reviews for every pollutant for which there is an NAAQS, and in many cases will be subject to both reviews. In addition to the review for impact on ambient air concentrations, the new or modified source will have to install minimum levels of control equipment based on available technology rather than ambient air considerations. New source performance standards are no longer the most stringent technological standards that may be applied, although they remain the minimum level of control in both situations. Finally, despite EPA's and the states' efforts to administer those programs with flexibility and awareness of the need for economic growth, the opportunities for opponents of projects to delay or thwart construction projects are significant. Moreover, it is the limited "increments" that control allowable growth in PSD areas, not NAAQS, and the air resources available for new construction can be quickly used up. Careful planning for new facilities with a healthy respect for the significance of these provisions is essential for companies planning expansion.

4.4 Energy Related Authority

4.4.1 Conversions to Coal

Due to the problems the country experienced in the 1974 energy crises, amendments to the Clean Air Act were enacted as part of the Energy Supply and Environmental Coordination Act of 1974 (ESECA). 23/ This was part of a Congressional program to convert major consumers of fuel to burning coal rather than oil or natural gas.

Under Section 119 of the amended Clean Air Act, the Administrator was given authority to extend the date for final compliance in the applicable SIP for sources ordered by the Federal Energy Administration (FEA) to convert coal on a long-term basis, if the coal available to the source was not of sufficient quality to result in prompt compliance with the SIP. The Administrator was to impose conditions to insure that the NAAQS would not be violated and to place the source on an enforceable schedule to comply with the applicable emission limitation as soon as possible.

Section 119 of ESECA has now been rescinded and coal conversions are ordered at the direction of the Department of Energy pursuant to the Powerplant and Industrial Fuel Use Act of 1978 (P.L. 95-260). Exemptions from such conversion orders are available where environmental requirements, including those imposed by the Clean Air Act, would be violated.

23/ P.L. 93-319 (June 22, 1974).

The 1977 Amendments transferred the Clean Air Act program for coal conversions to the enforcement provisions of the Act. A new Section 113(d)(5) authorized EPA to issue orders which allow converting sources to delay compliance with applicable SIP emission limits until the end of 1980. The order can be extended for five additional years for a source that cannot comply by 1980.

4.4.2 Energy Emergency Provisions

In the 1977 Amendments, Congress for the first time provided states with a process for suspending SIP requirements when energy is in extremely short supply. This authority, a new Section 110(f), was used in seven states in the winter of 1977-78 when the coal miners' strike caused a virtual halt to supplies of Eastern coal.

To emphasize the gravity it attached to cutbacks in pollution control, the Congress required that the President declare a regional energy emergency before any suspensions of control requirements may be issued to fuel-burning sources. After this declaration, a governor may issue source-by-source suspensions if energy shortages in a source's vicinity are causing serious unemployment or threatening residential heating. These suspensions may last up to four months unless the President sets a shorter term for his declaration or unless the Administrator of EPA determines that the governor's findings were erroneous.

5.0 National Stationary Source Emission Standards

The Clean Air Act provides authority for nationally applicable emission standards that are imposed regardless of the quality of ambient air in the particular location where the source is located. New source performance standards (NSPS) under § 111 are technology-based while national emission standards for hazardous pollutants (NESHAP) under § 112 are based on health protection.

5.1 New Source Performance Standards

Section 111 authorizes the Administrator to identify those sources which "...contribute significantly to air pollution which causes or contributes to the endangerment of the public health or welfare." For such sources, he is to set emission standards applicable to the new sources of the types identified, as well as to modifications of existing sources of that type. The standards are to be at levels which the Administrator determines are based on the "degree of emission reduction achievable" through the best technology "the Administrator determines has been "adequately demonstrated." In making such a determination the Administrator is to take into account the cost of meeting the standards and to find that the costs are not unreasonable.

As originally conceived, the NSPS provision had two purposes. First, it reflected the Congressional view that new plants had the greatest flexibility to be designed to incorporate the latest, most effective pollution control technology. Second, it expressed a policy of requiring the same degree of control on all new sources in a particular category regardless of where they are located, thereby preventing states from soliciting industry with lenient air pollution requirements and creating "pollution havens." The NSPS also conserve air resources for future growth.

With the development of the programs to prevent significant deterioration and for nonattainment areas, the purposes of NSPS have changed substantially. In many cases, NSPS may be only a point of departure for determining BACT or LAER for a new source--although NSPS will always apply as a ceiling on emissions in those determinations.

The importance that Congress continues to attach to NSPS was emphasized by the 1977 Act's requirement that, within one year after enactment, EPA must list all major stationary source categories for which NSPS have not been established and must set NSPS for those categories over the following four years. States were given the right to petition EPA to include additional source categories on the list and to revise NSPS when improved control technologies are developed. The NSPS apply to any new facility or modification of an existing facility that commence construction after the date of proposal of the NSPS.

The most controversial amendment to Section 111 in the 1977 Amendments requires EPA to set NSPS for fossil fuel burning sources, including electric utility plants, that would require a nationwide percentage reduction of the pollutants which would have been emitted had the fuel been burned without emission controls. Precombustion removal of pollutants, mainly sulfur, may be credited toward the reduction requirement. This provision would require flue gas desulfurization (scrubbers) or other technology to be installed in all cases. Use of low sulfur coal, even that clean enough to meet the current NSPS without expensive desulfurization, would be effectively precluded. The requirement would affect coals from Western mines primarily, and would increase the cost of new Western and Midwestern power plants. EPA's NSPS for power plants were revised on June 11, 1979 (44 Fed. Reg. 33580) and challenged by both industry and environmental groups. EPA's implementation of the percentage reduction requirement was upheld, including EPA's decision to establish different percentage reduction requirements depending upon the sulfur content of the fuel being burned. (The required percentage reduction varied between 70% and 90%.) See, Sierra Club v. Costle, 15 ERC 2137 (D.C. Cir. 1981).

In response to repeated requests from EPA, Congress included in Section 111 authority for EPA to set NSPS as design, equipment, work practice or operational standards where numerical emission limitations would be infeasible. EPA must allow alternative control methods if they are equally effective, and must revise the NSPS to numerical limits if it becomes feasible to do so.

A little-noticed but increasingly important part of Section 111 is subsection (d), which requires the states to regulate emissions from existing sources in any source category for which EPA sets NSPS for new and modified sources. This requirement applies only to pollutants not covered by NAAQS, such as sulfuric acid mist and fluorides. States are now in the process of developing standards for those pollutants under control technology guidelines established by EPA. EPA must approve each state's standards or establish its own substitute standards—an approach patterned on the SIP's.

5.2 Hazardous Emission Standards

The problem of particularly dangerous air pollutants which are not emitted by a sufficiently wide range of sources to justify an NAAQS, and establishment of SIP's, is dealt with by emission standards for hazardous pollutants pursuant to § 112. The pollutants to be covered by § 112 are those which "...may reasonably be anticipated to result in an increase in mortality, or an increase in serious irreversible, or incapaciting reversible illness." In the Senate Report on the 1970 Amendments, a number of such substances were identified as candidates for control under this section. Asbestos, beryllium and mercury standards were promulgated on April 6, 1973, for the most significant source categories. 24/ On October 21, 1976, standards were established for vinyl chloride emissions from plastics industry plants. EPA has also listed benzene, radionuclides and arsenic, and is developing NESHAP's for these pollutants. Listing of coke oven emissions, cadmium, and acrylonitrite is under consideration.

The criteria for establishing NESHAP's are that they be set at a level adequate to protect the public health with an ample margin of safety; the Act does not specifically authorize the Administrator to consider costs or availability of control technology.

In reality, EPA does review the costs involved and the availability of technology to control emissions to the desired level. EPA gives less consideration to those factors than in other regulatory decisions under the Act, but absent an overwhelming health hazard, EPA will be reluctant to shut down an industry by requiring zero emissions. For example, EPA has taken the approach of announcing as a goal a zero emissions limit for one hazardous pollutant, vinyl chloride. Attainment of that goal, however, would depend on development of control technology that is not prohibitively expensive.

Unlike NSPS, NESHAP's apply to existing as well as new sources. The latter must comply at the time of commencement of operations. Existing sources, however, may apply for a period of up to two years to comply with the standards.

Enforcement of the asbestos standard presents a significant problem. Because of the impossibility of measuring asbestos at the site of emissions, the standards for spraying asbestos and for demoli-

---

24/ 40 CFR Part 61.

tion of buildings containing asbestos insulation are written as prohibitions or specifications of work practices rather than numerical emission limits. The standards were challenged in enforcement proceedings on the grounds that only numerical emission standards are authorized by Section 112. The Supreme Court ultimately ruled that work practices were not authorized by § 112. 25/

Prior to the Supreme Court's decision, the 1977 Amendments revised Section 112 to authorize the EPA to set design, equipment, work practice or operational standards where numerical emission limits would not be practicable, such as in the case of asbestos. Nevertheless, in the Adamo decision, both the majority (five Justices) and minority (four Justices) took the unusual approach of appearing to look ahead to the new amendment and find a technical flaw that may make enforcement under that authority difficult or impossible.

Much of EPA's difficulty in administering § 112 flows from its inflexible terms. Standards are to be established which provide "an ample margin of safety" and there is no express authority to take into consideration economic and technological feasibility. Many people argue that there is no threshhold level for carcinogens and exposure of any amount could potentially produce cancer. Therefore, if implemented literally, § 112 could require zero emissions of suspect carcinogens. In 1979, EPA floated a proposed policy for regulation of airborne carcinogens which would take into consideration the risk presented in determining whether standards more rigorous than best available technology (which included considerations of economic and technological feasibility) were necessary. 44 Fed. Reg. 58642; Oct. 10, 1979. The policy produced substantial comment but no real agreement on the most feasible approach. EPA and the Congress are still searching for a regulatory approach that would protect against the major risks presented by airborne carcinogens, if any, yet without unreasonable adverse impacts on business.

Because EPA has promulgated such a limited number of NESHAP's EPA has received substantial criticism from the environmental community and certain members of Congress. Several legislative proposals have been made which would require EPA to make final decisions on approximately 40 pollutants, primarily suspect carcinogens, over a several year period. Failure of EPA to act, under some proposals, would result in the pollutant automatically being listed as a matter of law and force EPA to set standards.

6.0 Information Gathering Authority

Any agency charged with responsibility for carrying out or overseeing important regulatory programs must have commensurate authority to obtain the information relevant to those programs. In

---

25/   Adamo Wrecking Co. v. United States, 98 S. Ct. 566 (1977).

Section 114 of the 1970 Act, Congress gave EPA broad powers to obtain information necessary to the development and enforcement of standards and other regulations for the programs under Title I of the Act, especially Sections 110 through 113 and 120. This authority includes the ability for EPA to require a source owner to test the source's emissions to enter the premises of the source to emission test or to inspect aspects of the source's operations relevant to its emissions. EPA may also require source owners to maintain records and submit reports regarding their emissions and controls. EPA's authority to obtain information was upheld as constitutional in U.S. v. Tivian Laboratories, Inc., 12 ERC 1568 (1st Cir. 1978).

Although the Supreme Court decision overturning the Occupational Safety and Health Administration's warrantless searches in Marshall v. Barlow's, Inc. (98 S.Ct. 1816 (1978), arguably could have affected EPA's authority, the Agency as a general policy has adopted the practice of obtaining search warrants where voluntary inspection is refused.

7.0 Enforcement Authority

The Act sets forth a relatively simple procedure for federal enforcement of applicable implementation plans and other specified requirements of the Act. 26/ Where EPA finds a violation, it issues, through the appropriate EPA regional office, a "Notice of Violation." The Notice describes the specific violation and is sent to the alleged violator, as well as to any appropriate state or local control agency. If the violation continues for more than 30 days after the Notice issues, EPA may either commence a civil action (for an injunction) or issue an administrative order to the source. Any order must allow the source a reasonable time to comply, taking into consideration any good faith efforts to comply and the seriousness of the violation. Under the 1970 Act, EPA's practice was to issue orders with final compliance dates beyond the date for attainment of the standards, provided the schedule was as expeditious as practicable.

Notices of violation are not required where EPA finds violations of NSPS, hazardous emission standards, or certain reporting requirements. In these cases, the Administrator may immediately issue an administrative order or bring an appropriate civil action. The absence of a notice of violation requirement here makes it relatively clear that notice in the SIP context is designed not to assist the violator but to give the state an opportunity to begin the action instead of EPA.

Section 113 also provides that where the Administrator finds that violations in a state are so widespread that it appears the state generally is failing to enforce its plan, he may so notify the state

---

26/ § 113(a).

and initiate a period of federally assumed enforcement. This period continues until the Administrator determines that the state has resumed the needed enforcement activities. The EPA has not yet had occasion to implement this portion of the section, but it does enforce the implementation plans which it promulgates.

Paragraph (c) of Section 113 authorizes criminal penalties for "knowing" violations of the law. Violations which (1) occur during a period of federally assumed enforcement, (2) occur more than 30 days after receipt of a Notice of Violation or (3) consist of a failure to comply with an order issued by the Administrator are considered to be "knowing" violations. In addition, persons who knowingly violate the New Source Performance Standards of Section 111 or the Hazardous Emission Standards of Section 112 are subject to the criminal sanction.

For the "knowing" offenses, the law authorizes a fine of not more than $25,000 per day and/or imprisonment for up to one year. For subsequent convictions, the sanctions are doubled. In Section 113(c)(2), a $10,000 fine and/or imprisonment for up to 6 months is authorized for the making of false statements or tampering with monitoring devices required by the Act.

At the request of EPA, Congress included in the 1977 Amendments authority to seek from a court civil penalties up to $25,000 per day of violation. Civil penalties were attractive to the Agency because a court can consider them outside the complexities of a criminal trial.

7.1 Compliance Orders and Noncompliance Penalties

The 1977 Amendments made two major changes in the enforcement practices of EPA. Expressing dissatisfaction with EPA's practice of avoiding the strict deadlines of the Act through enforcement orders, Congress provided that the Administrator cannot authorize noncompliance through enforcement orders except pursuant to the "delayed compliance order" (DCO) procedures of §113(d). [§ 110(i)]. Such DCO's may be issued only until July 1, 1979, or three years from the date the SIP requires compliance. Public participation in the issuance of the DCO is required. Although a DCO will insulate a source from further enforcement actions under the Act, it will not, except in limited circumstances, excuse the source from payment of noncompliance penalties under § 120. Certain sources using innovative technology or subject to coal conversion orders may be given additional time for compliance. This restriction on EPA's authority to issue enforcement orders, coupled with the directive in § 113(b) requiring the Administrator to bring civil actions against major stationary source violators, means there will be increased emphasis on litigation, including consent decrees, to enforce the Clean Air Act.

The second major change in enforcement strategy under the Act was the adoption of Section 120 which provides for fines to be paid by noncomplying sources that are calculated to take away the economic advantage of noncompliance. Section 120 is the first attempt by Congress to build into a major regulatory program a scheme wherein economic disincentives are to be used to complement a traditional standards-based regulatory structure. The section's fundamental policy is to recover as a penalty any economic costs a source owner or operator may be avoiding by not making the capital outlays or operation and maintenance expenditures that would be necessary to comply with an SIP or Sections 111 or 112 standards.

Although the noncompliance penalty program was heralded as being an effective alternative to traditional enforcement systems, interest in the program has slackened considerably. Congress declined to include a similar provision in the Clean Water Act Amendments of 1977. EPA's regulations (40 CFR Part 66) became effective October 27, 1980. Upon notification by EPA that penalties are being assessed under the regulations, the source is to compute its own fine based upon a complex computer analysis which is made part of the regulations. This analysis requires information from the company on approximately 15 different variables, including capital cost, debt service, operation and maintenance expenses. The complexity of the process, however, has proved to be a deterrent and EPA has considered using it in only a very limited number of situations. Future use of the procedure also appears limited.

Any major source which in the future is covered by a SIP for the first time, or has a major new requirement imposed, would have three years from the imposition of the requirement before noncompliance penalties would apply.

8.0 Emergency Authority

As is the case with most public health protection statutes, the Clean Air Act recognizes that on occasion the normal regulatory procedures may be inadequate and that extraordinary measures may have to be taken to protect public health. For this purpose, the Act's Section 303 authorizes the Adminstrator to seek a federal court order directing any type of air pollution source to stop emitting, or to take other appropriate action, when he finds that air pollution is "presenting an imminent and substantial endangerment to the health of persons." The 1977 Amendments added authority to issue a short-term administrative order to begin abatement actions while a lawsuit is being prepared.

This authority, designed principally to deal with air pollution episodes occurring when stagnant meteorological conditions prevent normal dispersion of pollutants by the wind, has been invoked only once, in Birmingham, Alabama. However, EPA personnel have been ready in several other cities when episodes have occurred to take necessary legal action if the state or local agency response proved inadequate.

9.0 Ozone Protection

In 1975, scientists began to announce the results of studies on depletion of the ozone layer in the stratosphere. Ozone, which is part of the photochemical oxidants complex and injurious to human health when breathed, is essential to screen out harmful ultraviolet radiation that can cause skin cancers and reduced crop yields at excessive exposures.

The chemical agents implicated in the ozone depletion phenomena are the halogenated compounds known as "halocarbons." Though stable in the lower atmosphere, scientists believe they become unstable in sunlight in the atmosphere and react with ozone, forming new compounds, thereby depleting the ozone available for screening. These halocarbons are in widespread use, as aerosol propellants, refrigerants, and foaming agents, and are released in the atmosphere when aerosol-packaged products are used and through leakage or destruction of refrigeration equipment.

Congress became concerned in 1976 that the available data showed that slow but predictable ozone layer depletion was probably occurring. The Toxic Substances Control Act (TSCA), passed that year, included regulatory authority broad enough to allow EPA to deal with halocarbons. Nevertheless, the 1977 Amendments to the Clean Air Act added a new regulatory scheme designed specifically for the regulation of halocarbons, and required numerous federal agencies to participate in a study of the problems, culminating in a report to Congress two years after the enactment of the Amendments.

The regulatory approach prescribed in the new Sections 150-159 is relatively simple, as contrasted with the complex scientific questions involved. The Administrator may issue regulations controlling halocarbons or "any substance, practice, process, or activity" that affects the stratosphere, if the effect "may reasonably be anticipated to endanger public health or welfare." Any regulatory activity is to be deferred until after the report mentioned above is filed, unless EPA obtains information before that time which would be sufficient to make the required findings about effects on the stratosphere and risks to health or welfare.

Before the 1977 Amendments became law, EPA and other federal agencies had already begun regulating halocarbon use as an aerosol propellant. EPA used its authority under TSCA. Congress provided in the Amendments that this activity should go on without interference, but made it clear that future regulation should be under the Clean Air Act scheme.

10.0 Motor Vehicle Emission Control

10.1 Introduction

Since 1965, the federal government has had authority to set emission standards applicable to new motor vehicles and engines. Standards are to be set for pollutants which the Administrator determines "...cause, or contribute to, air pollution which may reasonably be anticipated to endanger public health and welfare." Limitations on emissions of hydrocarbons and carbon monoxide were applied to the 1968 model year vehicles and all subsequent model years. An emission standard for oxides of nitrogen went into effect beginning with 1973.

10.2 Statutory Standards and Suspension

With the knowledge that motor vehicle pollutants constituted the single most difficult air pollution problem facing the nation, and noting the limited progress in abating it, Congress in 1970 took the unusual step of actually prescribing the standards to be applied in order to attain and maintain air quality protective of health in urban areas heavily impacted by automobile pollution. The law 27/ required a 90% reduction of hydrocarbons and carbon monoxide from allowable emissions in 1970, and a 90% reduction in nitrogen oxides emissions from levels measured from 1971 model year vehicles. The 90% reductions in HC and CO were to be achieved in 1975, and the NO_x reductions in 1976. In each case, the Administrator was permitted to suspend for one additional year the 90% reduction requirements if he found, after public hearing, that the needed technology was not available. In addition, the manufacturer applying for the suspension must have made good faith efforts to meet the standards.

Manufacturers applied for the suspension of the 1975 standards at the first opportunity, viz. January, 1972. After evaluation of the extensive written and oral information submitted, EPA determined that the manufacturers had failed to prove that technology was not available, and accordingly denied the one year suspension. The manufacturers took their case to the United States Court of Appeals. The Court assessed in detail the technical and policy aspects of the problem, 28/ and found that EPA had not adequately supported its conclusion that the standards could be met. Specifically, EPA had not adequately considered whether the available technology, catalytic mufflers, would be available in sufficient quantities to meet market demands.

Subsequent to the decision, EPA held new hearings and granted a suspension. Then, in accordance with the statutory mandate, EPA set interim standards which (although not equal to the 90% reduction desired by Congress) were quite stringent.

With the passage of the Energy Supply and Environmental Coordination Act in 1974, Congress re-examined the statutory

---

27/   § 202(a)(1) and (2).

28/   International Harvester v. Ruckelshaus, 478 F.2d 615 (D.C. Cir. 1973).

standards and determined, for fuel conservation purposes, to set back its stringent hydrocarbon and CO standards to model year 1977. Nitrogen oxides standards were also postponed one year. In both cases, an opportunity for a one year suspension was again provided.

Acting under that authority, in March 1975, the Administrator suspended the standards, based on his determination that the automobile manufacturers' proposed use of catalytic emission controls with air pumps to meet the stringent standards posed a risk of creating high sulfuric acid emissions and that the suspension would provide time to analyze the possible severity of such risk. With the suspension, the Administrator issued interim standards preserving the existing standards for model year 1977.

The biggest controversy that developed during Congress' consideration of the 1977 Amendments was the automobile emission standards and the timetable for implementing them. Congress took up where it had left off in 1970. There was little question that Congress would set the standards and not leave the job to EPA; the debates focused heavily on fuel economy consequences of different sets of standards, particularly standards for oxides of nitrogen.

What emerged from these often heated discussions was basically another postponement of what were once the 1975 statutory standards. The hydrocarbon standard was set back to model year 1980; the carbon monoxide level deferred to 1981 with the potential of an administrative suspension for two more years. Only for oxides of nitrogen was there a significant loosening of the stringent number originally set for the 1976 models. Section 202 now prescribes a 1.0 grams per vehicle mile standard beginning in model year 1981, although this can be relaxed slightly by EPA for an innovative technology or for diesel powered automobiles. In 1983, Congress will again consider relaxation and postponement of the statutory standards.

In the 1977 Amendments, Congress for the first time took charge of standard setting for heavy duty vehicles, i.e., larger trucks, a field they had previously left to EPA's discretion. EPA was left with the authority to substitute standards reflecting what the best available technology can achieve, if the statutory standards prove infeasible.

Probably the most interesting aspect of the Amendments' treatment of heavy duty vehicles is the provision in Section 206(g) for a "nonconformance penalty." This would allow trucks to be certified and sold if they did not exceed the standard by more than a margin set by EPA, if the manufacturer paid a nonconformance penalty. The penalties would be set by EPA so as to remove any competitive advantage (probably through lower fuel use) that trucks not meeting the standards might have, and EPA would have to increase the penalties "periodically." This scheme is the second instance in the Act where an economic incentive program has been added to complement the traditional regulatory scheme.

10.3 Certification

Under the Clean Air Act, no manufacturer may introduce vehicles subject to emission standards into commerce, unless they have been certified by EPA to conform to the standards. 29/ The certification procedure consists of a lengthy test on prototype vehicles. Most of these tests are conducted by a manufacturer at its own facility, but a few are sent to EPA's laboratory at Ann Arbor, Michigan for confirmatory testing. A limited number of cars are run to 50,000 miles and their emissions tested periodically to determine the durability of the vehicles' emission controls. A "deterioration factor" is determined by observation of the increase in emissions from the 4,000 mile test to the 50,000 mile test. This factor is then applied to a single test on a somewhat larger group of the same "family" of cars. This procedure indicates whether or not a proto- type vehicle has been designed to meet the standards for the useful life of the vehicle. 30/

If the tests are successful, a certificate of conformity cover- ing that type of engine/vehicle combination is issued. The manufac- turer is then free to begin producing cars built the same as the certified prototypes. Certification demonstrates that the manufac- turer can build a vehicle capable of meeting the standards, but tests on vehicles in ordinary use have shown that emissions typically do not meet the standards.

10.4 Compliance by Production Vehicles

Certification verifies the capability of prototype to comply with the applicable emission standards, but provides little assurance that production vehicles will comply either at the time of their manufacture or thereafter, when operated and maintained by their owners. At the time Congress was considering the 1970 Act, it was presented with data showing significant failure of compliance by vehicles in use, and decided to adopt measures to enable EPA and the vehicle owners to ensure vehicles' compliance throughout their useful life.

The provisions adopted required compliance by vehicles through a "useful life" of 5 years or 50,000 miles, required manufac- turers to warrant against defects and that vehicles would comply for the useful life period, authorized EPA to require manufacturers to recall vehicles found not to comply for the specified period, and authorized EPA to test production vehicles on the assembly line and to revoke the certificate conformity as to any noncomplying vehi- cle. Unfortunately, subsequent studies of in use vehicles do not

---

29/ § 203 sets forth the "prohibited acts" under Title II of the Clean Air Act, Emission Standards for Moving Sources.

30/ § 206: 40 CFR Part 86.

indicate the durability of the emission controls has significantly increased.

10.4.1 Assembly Line Testing

Section 207(b) authorizes the Administrator to conduct assembly line testing of new vehicles. If, based on such tests, he determines that certain vehicles do not conform to the regulations, he can suspend or revoke the certificate of conformity covering the class of vehicles, until such time as the manufacturer has corrected the deficiency. The manufacturer is entitled to a hearing on the determination by the Administrator, and may appeal to the United States Court of Appeals if the final administrative decision goes against him.

The absence of a "short" test for assembly line cars has, until recently, precluded EPA from implementing this section. However, the Agency has developed an assembly line testing program called Selective Enforcement Audit (SEA). 31/ This program uses the lengthy federal test procedure, but only on limited numbers of production vehicles.

Very briefly, SEA functions as follows: EPA orders a manufacturer to conduct tests on a relatively small number of cars chosen at random on the assembly line. If those tests indicate that the cars are meeting standards, the program with respect to that line of vehicles terminates. If, however, the tests indicate that there is a question about compliance, the size of the sample would be increased and testing would continue. A sufficient number of vehicles will be tested to support a valid judgment as to the status of the entire class of cars. If the judgment is that the class is not meeting the standards, the certificate of conformity is revoked, and no vehicles covered by that certificate may be marketed.

10.4.2 Warranties

The Act's imposition of statutory warranties was perhaps a "first" in the history of regulatory legislation. It represents an attempt to make the regulated industry directly responsible to the people who purchase its products.

Section 207(a) requires the manufacturer to warrant to the owner that the vehicle is designed, built, and equipped to conform at the time of sale with applicable standards, and that it is free from defects in materials and workmanship which would cause noncompliance. Both of these warranties carry with them rather substantial problems of proof for the owner, and have not proved to be effective remedies.

31/ The Selective Enforcement Audit Program was promulgated on July 28, 1976. 41 Fed. Reg. 31472.

A potentially more important check on emissions is under Section 207(b), which requires a manufacturer to warrant that the vehicle will perform in compliance with the applicable standards for its useful life. The section predicates implementation of the warranty on the development of a short test which would correlate with the lengthy test used at the certification stage and which could be carried out expeditiously at state, local, or federal testing stations. The certification test covers various modes of operation, and it has only recently been possible to make significant progress toward developing a correlating short test.

When this obstacle is overcome, the performance warranty can be implemented, but even then it is conditioned by the statute to be applicable only if (1) the vehicle was maintained and operated in accordance with the maintenance instructions supplied to the owner by the manufacturer, and (2) the nonconformity resulted in the owner having to bear a penalty or sanction. If these requirements are satisfied, the manufacturer must, at no cost to the purchaser, bring the car back into conformity. What the section means is that even with the short test, manufacturers will not have to fix cars at their expense, until such time as state or local inspection programs are in place. Only a few of these programs are underway.

10.4.3 Recall

Section 207(c) gives the Administrator authority to order manufacturers to recall and repair or modify groups of vehicles which exceed the emission standards when in actual use. The manufacturer has the right to a hearing for the purpose of contesting EPA's finding that his vehicles do not meet standards. These are formal hearings before an Administrative Law Judge.

In the past two years, EPA has required several manufacturers to recall thousands of automobiles for failure to meet the standards to which they were certified. Generally, the needed repair or replacement was readily identifiable, and only one recall order was contested through the hearing appeal route.

It is too early in the operation of the recall program to predict whether most car owners will bring in their vehicles for repair in response to a pollution control related recall.

10.4.4 Vehicle Inspection

The 1970 Act evidenced a great deal of Congressional enthusiasm for motor vehicle inspection programs. The Act (§ 210) authorized federal grants to states to encourage their development, required that state implementation plans include them where necessary, and made the Section 207(b) performance warranty dependent on their existence.

This emphasis is understandable, since it is widely believe that a properly designed and operated I & M program, that includes requirements for necessary maintenance on noncomplying cars, is one of the most cost-effective means of holding automobile emissions in check. Development of these programs has been very slow, however, largely because of inadequate funding and lack of public support.

EPA's attempts, as part of the transportation control plans, to require states to adopt and carry out inspection and maintenance programs, were challenged in court by virtually every affected state. The several United States Courts of Appeals which considered these challenges took different positions on the legality of the requirements, and the Supreme Court refused to issue a decision because of a technical problem with EPA's regulation imposing the requirement.

The 1977 Amendments mandate vehicle inspection and maintenance for areas that cannot meet NAAQS for motor vehicle related pollutants by the end of 1982. It does not appear that Congress has become less convinced of the merit of this type of program, but it has allowed states the possibility of more time to accept the idea and develop programs suited to their needs.

10.5 Enforcement

Enforcement of the motor vehicle regulatory program is exclusively through the courts. The Act provides for injunctive relief to stop violations (§ 204) and for civil penalties of up to $10,000 per violation per vehicle (§ 205). A few large civil penalties have been imposed on manufacturers in violation.

11.0 Fuel and Fuel Additive Provisions

11.1 Registration

The Congress expressed its concern with the possible harmful effects of the byproducts of fuel additives, which are so widely used in gasoline, by including in the 1967 Act a requirement that fuel additives be registered with the government for purposes of gathering information about their composition and combinations. This program, which was quite limited and not implemented until regulations were issued in 1970, was broadened considerably in Section 211 of the 1970 Act. The registration requirement was extended to fuels as well as additives, and additional provisions authorized EPA to require information on the products and byproducts of the combustion of fuels and additives, as well as on their effects on health, welfare, and motor vehicle emission control systems. Congress' purpose was to enable EPA to make judgments which might lead to regulation under the Act or point to the need for further legislation.

Regulations implementing the revised registration program were issued in November of 1975, 32/ and the registrations are made by the filing of the required information by the manufacturers

---

32/   40 CFR Part 79, 40 Fed. Reg. 52009.

involved. Largely because of EPA's failure to develop test protocols, however, very little analysis has been done by fuel or additive
manufacturers or EPA on the fuel and additives registered, or their
combustion byproducts. The 1977 Act includes amendments to
Section 211 that attempt to expedite the gathering of information
on possible health or welfare effects or effects on emission control
systems. Testing was made a prerequisite to registration (and,
therefore, marketing), and currently registered products must be
tested within four years.

EPA's authority is not without limits, however. The use of
additives in motor oil was held to be outside the scope of Section
211. 33/

11.2 Regulatory Authority

The law authorizes two approaches to the control or prohibition of automobile fuels and fuel additives. Under Section 211(c)
(1)(B), the Administrator is authorized to regulate the manufacture
or sale of motor vehicle fuels or additives, if he finds that products
of the additives will impair, to a significant degree, the performance
of an existing or proposed emission control device.

EPA determined that in order to attempt to meet the stringent 1975 standards, automobile manufacturers primarily intended
to rely on the catalytic converter--a device which is "poisoned," i.e.
rendered ineffective, by lead. As a result of this finding, the
Agency promulgated regulations, 34/ which require that there be one
grade of unleaded gasoline generally available throughout the country at the larger gasoline stations. 35/

Because lead free gasoline production uses more crude oil to
increase the octane of the fuel to meet minimum car requirements,
there is increasing pressure on EPA to defer the 1979 deadline for
meeting the 0.5 grams per gallon limit to conserve dwindling supplies of crude oil. EPA's decision to bar use of MMT, a partial
substitute for lead as a fuel additive, has also been critized. Political and practical problems of fuel supply coupled with increasing
regulation of stationary sources of lead in SIP's may produce some
relaxation on control of fuel additives.

In paragraph (A) of Section 211(c)(1), the Administrator is
also given authority to control the use of fuel additives, if he finds

---

33/ Lubrizol Corp. v. EPA, 562 F.2d 807 (D.C. Cir. 1977).

34/ 40 CFR Part 80.

35/ In addition to various labeling requirements, the Part 80
     regulations require that the unleaded gasoline be dispensed
     from a special nozzle, and that cars with catalytic converters
     have gasoline inlets designed to mate with the special nozzles.

they will "endanger the public health or welfare." EPA determined that lead emitted from automobiles as a result of the use of leaded gasoline posed an endangerment to public health, particularly among urban children. On December 6, 1973, 36/ EPA adopted regulations that required the gradual phasing down of the amount of lead used in leaded gasoline. The schedule called for a maximum of 1.7 grams per gallon on January 1, 1975, and then reduced annually the allowable amount to 0.5 grams per gallon by 1979. Small refineries (50,000 barrels per day of gasoline or less) owned by small refiners (total capacity of 137,500 barrels per day of gasoline or less) were provided additional time to meet the 0.5 grams per gallon standard. In § 211(g) of the Act, Congress determined that these smaller firms might have greater difficulty in raising capital or making other necessary capital investments and should be given until 1982, a three year extension, to meet the standards. Those facilities were required to meet interim levels based upon a statutory scale depending on their size. EPA regulations implementing § 211(g) were promulgated August 7, 1979, (44 Fed. Reg. 53146) in 40 CFR § 80.20(b).

The controversy over whether or not lead emitted from motor vehicles affects human health was and is a heated one. The regulations were challenged in the United States Court of Appeals for the District of Columbia, which set aside the regulations. However, upon EPA's motion, the Court of Appeals agreed to have all nine members of the Court consider the case. A final decision upholding the regulations was issued in March 1976. 37/ Enforcement of the regulations was reinstated after the Supreme Court declined to review the case.

In response to requests by small refiners and other firms (including lead manufacturers) affected by the lead phasedown regulations, EPA requested comment in early 1982 on whether the final lead phasedown requirement should be retained or other adjustments made in the requirements. A number of firms argued that the natural reduction in leaded gasoline production due to the market demand of unleaded gasoline of the national vehicle population which requires unleaded gasoline makes a mandatory restriction on lead usage unnecessary. Small refiners argued that final compliance with the requirement was not necessary for public health reasons and would impose unreasonable adverse economic effects on small refineries. Modifications to the lead phasedown regulations were one of the recommendations of the Vice President's Task Force on Regulatory Reform.

36/   40 CFR 80.20.

37/   Ethel Corp. v. EPA, 541 F.2d 1 (D.C. Cir. 1976), cert. denied, 426 U.S. 941.

EPA's request for public comment produced a large number of comments from environmental groups, the affected industry, and other interested parties. After considering the comments, EPA withdrew its February proposal and reproposed changes to the regulations. 47 Fed. Reg. 38070, et seq. (August 27, 1982). Based on the earlier comments, EPA determined that there was a continuing need for regulation of lead as a fuel additive on public health grounds. EPA determined that it would make the requirement more stringent by establishing a 1.10 gram per gallon standard for leaded gasoline only. (With the 0.5 gpg total gasoline production average, the actual lead content of leaded gasoline would be much higher depending on the percentage of unleaded and leaded gasoline produced by the individual refinery; unleaded gasoline is limited by EPA regulations to .05 grams per gallon.) EPA determined that by 1990 the leaded gasoline restriction would result in approximately 34% greater lead reduction than the existing standard. Final regulations were promulgated on October 29, 1982 (47 Fed. Reg. 49322, et seq.)

With respect to small refineries, although EPA had proposed to allow them an alternative, higher lead standard, EPA determined after considering comments submitted that small refineries should also be required to meet the 1.1 grams per leaded gallon standard. EPA found that concerns for public health and the disruption of competition within the refining industry caused by a dual standard justified its requiring all facilities to meet the same requirement. EPA did grant an approximately eight-month extension of time for compliance. The final regulations became effective November 1, 1982.

12.0 Aircraft Emission Control

Section 231 empowers the Administrator to establish emission standards for aircraft and aircraft engines, following the regulatory pattern set forth in Section 202(a) for motor vehicles. Before setting standards, EPA was required to conduct a study of the effects of aircraft emission on air quality and the technological feasibility of controls.

As a result of the study, EPA concluded that although aircraft emissions did not have major impact throughout AQCR's they were significant contributors to high concentrations in and around airport sites, because of their ground operations as well as takeoffs and landings. Accordingly, EPA established emission standards for most classes of new aircraft and aircraft engines and for the most significant emitters among existing aircraft and engines. [38]/

These standards, which can be issued only if the Secretary of Transportation agrees that they do not create safety problems, are

---

[38]/   40 CFR Part 87.

required by the Act to be enforced by the Department of Transportation, which has issued regulations for that purpose.

13.0 Citizens Suits

Congress was aware of the immense task of policing regulations applicable to thousands of sources, as well as the historical apparent lack of enthusiasm on the part of the enforcers; in 1970 it offered the public opportunity to assist in the process through citizen suits. Section 304 of the Act authorizes two types of suits by citizens. Under Section 304(a)(1), a person may sue any other person, including the United States government or other political jurisdictions, alleged to be in violation of emission standards or limitations, or enforcement orders issued by the Administrator or a state. In short, Section 304 is designed to make the Act enforceable in federal district courts by anyone with the interest and resources to do so.

Information concerning violations should be readily available to interested citizens. Section 110(a)(2)(f) requires that sources periodically report emission data to the state, and that such reports must be available to the public. Section 114, which authorizes the Administrator to inspect sources and require reports, specifically exempts "emission data" 39/ from information which might be withheld from the public on the grounds that it constitutes a trade secret. Again, in Section 208, emission data on motor vehicles is excluded from restrictions which might otherwise allow it to be withheld from public disclosure.

The 1977 Act expanded the jurisdiction of the federal district courts to hear citizens suits. Citizens can now sue to enforce most of the major requirements imposed when the Act, as opposed to just emission standards and limitations. The Act does not specifically authorize citizens to seek penalties or damages.

While citizen suits against polluters have not yet been a major factor under the law, paragraph (a)(2) of Section 304 has had enormous impact. Under this authority, citizens are authorized to bring actions against the Administrator of EPA, "...where there is alleged a failure...to perform any act or duty under this Act which is not discretionary..." In those few words, Congress established a mechanism by which the judicial branch of the government would, if asked, oversee a portion of EPA's implementation of the law.

It was a citizen suit in California 40/ which forced EPA to propose a transportation control plan for the South Coast Basin which included a provision requiring in excess of 80% gas rationing. It was under the citizen suit provision that the Sierra Club success-

---

39/ Section 114(c).

40/ City of Riverside v. Ruckelhaus, 4 ERC 1728 (C.D. Cal. 1972).

fully litigated the issue of significant deterioration. There are other examples where suits under this section have forced the Agency to act at a time, and sometimes in a manner, it would not have chosen.

Citizens are required to give 60 days notice, before bringing a § 304 suit, to the Administrator of EPA, the state and the violator. If EPA or the state is diligently prosecuting an enforcement action against the violator, the citizen may intervene in the litigation.

14.0 Judicial Review

Because of the importance and the controversial nature of most of EPA's regulatory decisions implementing the Clean Air Act, most decisions are challenged in court by environmentalists, by industry or both. Court decisions have played a crucial role in determining the direction of EPA's implementation of the Act as well as insuring that an adequate technical case has been made by EPA for regulation.

Courts often view their role as one of partnership with EPA in developing the law and procedures implementing this significant legislation and actively grapple with the difficult policy issues surrounding EPA's regulatory decisions to protect public health when scientific knowledge is still uncertain, e.g. Ethel Corp. v. EPA, supra. Consequently, Section 307(b) of the Act is a key element in the overall implementation of the statute. To expedite the reaching of final decisions on EPA's regulations, in view of the short statutory deadlines, Congress provided for direct review of most regulations in the United States Courts of Appeals and required that challenges be brought within certain time limits.

The 1970 Act required persons who wished to challenge an Agency action to file a petition for review in the appropriate Court of Appeals within 30 days after the action was taken. The courts have upheld this time limit on judicial review by dismissing late petitions. In the 1977 Amendments, Congress lengthened the dead-line to 60 days. Congress also endorsed the absolute cutoff that bars attacks on a regulation, as a defense in an enforcement action if the issue could have been raised in the Court of Appeals. The 1977 Act also ratified a court's decision that, in order to get judicial review after the deadline, a person must petition the Agency showing new information not available when the EPA action was being developed.

In the review by the court, a three judge panel of the court examines the record compiled by the Agency in the course of taking the action, to determine whether the action was arbitrary or capricious. This "arbitrary, capricious" test, experience has shown, can be the basis of an extremely searching inquiry into all facets of an EPA decision; it can be the basis for substitution by the judges of their judgments for those made by the Agency or it can support a quite superficial inquiry into the Agency's rationale. Courts have taken all of these approaches in the many decisions issued since the passage of the 1970 Act.

The court's review also includes a determination about whether the Agency's action exceeded its authority under the Act and whether proper procedures were followed in taking the action.

The Congress provided in the 1977 Amendments that EPA actions of national applicability and effect are to be reviewed in the Court of Appeals for the District of Columbia Circuit. This provision codified a growing body of judicial decisions and is important to EPA because issues often cannot be settled for years if petitioners may obtain review in a number of the twelve Courts of Appeals. Differences among the circuits are not unusual, and the only solution is U.S. Supreme Court review, which is always a lengthy process.

15.0 Acid Rain

One of the most controversial issues that is not dealt with directly by the Clean Air Act is the problem of acid deposition or "acid rain." For some time there has been growing evidence that lakes and streams, primarily in the northeast portion of the United States and in Canada are becoming more acidic causing a reduction, or in some cases total elimination, of fish and other life in those bodies of water. Acid deposition is also suspected of reducing forest productivity. Many people believe that the increasing acidity is due to long range atmospheric transport of sulfur emissions, principally from power plants in the mid-West. The sulfur dioxide is carried by winds aloft until the sulfur precipitates as sulfates in the rain where it causes adverse effects to the land and water. There is, however, intense scientific and political debate over the causes of acid rain, the contribution of power plants, and the appropriate methods for addressing the problem, (e.g., reduction in sulfur emissions or treatment of lakes and land to neutralize the acid). A ten-year study of acid rain was authorized by the Congress under the auspices of the National Academy of Science. The Clean Air Act provisions were not drafted with this type of pollution problem in mind; they are premised on state by state control strategies and the identification of specific sources which contribute to a particular pollution problem. EPA has generally held that it lacks authority under the Act to address the problem directly.

The National Commission on Air Quality recommended increased authority for EPA to regulate long range transport and recommended that there be a significant reduction by 1990 in sulfur dioxide emissions. Canada has also pressed vigorously for controls by the federal government on power plant emissions. A number of proposals have been considered by the Congress to address acid rain. These range from stepped-up research to major regulatory programs. The most comprehensive statutory proposal would require specific reductions, (e.g., 10 million tons of sulfur dioxide) from sources, primarily power plants within 31 eastern states. The exact form of increased authority for EPA to address the problem of acid rain will be hotly contested but it is probable, due to the strong political and public pressure for action on this issue, that the next substantive amendments to the Clean Air Act will contain some provision on acid rain.

Chapter 5

RESOURCE CONSERVATION AND RECOVERY ACT

Thomas F. P. Sullivan [1]
Attorney and President
Government Institutes, Inc.
Rockville, MD

1.0 Solid and Hazardous Wastes

Solid and hazardous wastes are creating more concerns every year. In addition to the traditional problems of economics, technology and personnel, the field now requires that business and government officials have knowledge of a broad range of complex legal and regulatory matters.

Many types of legal issues are involved. Generally, the legal issues are nuisance, negligence, trespass, property rights, zoning, and local ordinances. The fundamental legal principles which are regularly encountered in this field were described in Chapter 1. Other chapters of this book have covered such possible concerns as: air pollution from incinerators; land use problems in the development of landfills; water pollution from run-off; offshore dumping; and noise from equipment operation, among other related concerns.

In this chapter the focus is on the Federal and state efforts in solid waste, hazardous waste and resource recovery under the

---

1/ The Author is indebted to Tom Watson, Ridgway M. Hall, Jr., Jeffrey J. Davidson and David R. Case of the Washington law firm Crowell & Moring who authored the Hazardous Waste Handbook 4th Edition, Government Institutes, 1982. This chapter relies heavily on that book. For anyone wishing additional information on hazardous waste, the Hazardous Waste Handbook is a 652-page text which is recommended as a comprehensive analysis of hazardous waste laws and regulations.

Resource Conservation and Recovery Act. 2/ In a separate chapter, the related Comprehensive Environmental Response, Compensation and Liability Act, also known as Superfund, is described.

The public concern with hazardous wastes disposal has thrust this area into the national spotlight. This national focus coupled with the broad impact of the Resource Conservation and Recovery Act will make this one of the "hottest" topics of the 1980's.

2.0 Solid Waste Disposal and Resource Recovery Act

The first Federal legislative endeavor in solid waste was in 1965 when the U.S. Congress enacted the Solid Waste Disposal Act, 3/ which was subsequently amended in 1970 and 1973 by the Resource Recovery Act. 4/ This law initiated a Federal role in solid waste and resource recovery by authorizing the Federal Government to:

(1)   promote the demonstration, construction and application of solid waste management and resource recovery systems;
(2)   provide technical and financial assistance to state and local government and interstate agencies in the planning and development of resource recovery and disposal programs;
(3)   promote a national research and development program for improved methods of collection, separation, recovery and recycling as well as environmentally safe disposal of nonrecoverable residue;
(4)   provide guidelines for collection, transport, separation, recovery and disposal systems; and
(5)   provide for training grants in design, operation and maintenance of disposal systems.

The Solid Waste Disposal and Resource Recovery Act, unlike the Clean Air Act or the Federal Water Pollution Control Act, did not contain standards or timetables for compliance. However, guidelines were authorized but these were mandatory only for the Federal Government. Since the Federal Government is so large and operates numerous facilities, the guidelines were envisioned to have a significant impact on the solid waste and resource recovery fields as "trendsetters."

2/   Public Law 94-580, 42 U.S.C § 6901 et seq.

3/   P.L. 89-272 (1965).

4/   P.L. 91-512 (1970) and P.L. 93-14 (1973).

These guidelines, published in Title 40 of the Code of Federal Regulations, Parts 240, 241, 243, 244, 245, 246 and 247, cover: (1) incineration (thermal processing); (2) operation of sanitary landfills; (3) storage and collection; (4) beverage containers; (5) resource recovery facilities; (6) source separation; and (7) procurement, which is advisory only.

The guidelines are applicable to Federal agencies and their contractors, if they have jurisdiction over Federal real property which involves them in solid waste disposal activities. They are also applicable to Federal agencies which generate solid wastes or issue permits or licenses for disposal.

These guidelines have been continued by the Resource Conservation and Recovery Act which reauthorized them. The Resource Conservation and Recovery Act (RCRA) passed by the Congress in September 1976, however, so expands the Federal involvement in the field that the impact of these guidelines is overshadowed by the hazardous waste programs created by RCRA.

3.0 Resource Conservation and Recovery Act of 1976 (RCRA)

In a last minute flurry of activity during the early Fall of 1976, the 94th Congress enacted a major law, the Resource Conservation and Recovery Act. In June 1976 the Senate had enacted its version (S. 2150). The House held hearings on proposed legislation but seemed to be overwhelmed by the number of solid waste bills that were offered. Finally, in the closing days of the Congress a bill that represented a composite of many of the key concepts that had been proposed in the House was enacted. Since there was not sufficient time to have a conference with the Senate, the House chose the expeditious route of enacting a bill with the Senate title. It was then returned to the Senate for enactment and then sent to the President for his signature. 5/

The key point to remember is that there is little legislative history on RCRA and the available information provides little on the intent of Congress. Several important areas of interpretation are still being debated within EPA, many years after enactment of RCRA. This is due at least partially to vague and very broad statutory language which is inadequately explained by the legislative history. In the amendments to RCRA by the Quiet Communities Act

---

5/   For a comprehensive review of the legislative history with personal insights into the last-minute passage, see a paper by former House Commerce Committee Counsel William L. Kovacs contained in the book Resource Conservation and Recovery Act: A Compliance Analysis, published by Government Institutes, Washington, D.C., 1979.

of 1978, 6/ and the Solid Waste Disposal Act Amendments of 1980, 7/ Congress declined to resolve some of the major outstanding issues of interpretation. Therefore, EPA has been left largely on its own in making key decisions with respect to the RCRA hazardous waste program.

The Resource Conservation and Recovery Act of 1976 is a multifaceted approach toward solving the problems associated with the estimated 6 billion tons of solid wastes generated each year, and the problems resulting from the anticipated annual increases in the volume of such waste. RCRA greatly expanded the role of the Federal Government in the field of solid waste disposal management with particular emphasis on the regulation of hazardous waste.

In summary, RCRA: (1) continues the Federal facilities guideline program established under the 1970 Solid Waste Disposal Act; (2) creates a major new Federal hazardous waste regulatory program; (3) prohibits the practice of open dumping; (4) encourages through Federal aid, state and regional solid waste management planning; (5) provides for extensive grants and information programs. RCRA replaced the '65 and '70 Acts.

RCRA is divided into 8 subtitles, A through H, and these are described in the following sections.

4.0 General Provisions

4.1 Objectives of RCRA

The general provisions, Subtitle A, contain the objectives of this law. 8/ The eight objectives set forth the basic thrust of the statute, which is to promote the protection of health and the environment and to conserve valuable material and energy resources by:

(1)   providing technical and financial assistance to state and local governments and interstate agencies for the development of solid waste management plans (including resource recovery and resource conservation systems)...

(2)   providing training grants...

(3)   prohibiting future open dumping on the land and requiring the conversion of existing open dumps...

6/   42 U.S.C. § 6901 et seq.

7/   P.L. 96-482, 94 Stat. 2334 (23 October 1980).

8/   RCRA, § 1003.

(4)   regulating the treatment, storage, transportation, and disposal of hazardous wastes...

(5)   providing for the promulgation of guidelines...

(6)   promoting a national research and development program for improved solid waste management and resource conservation techniques...

(7)   promoting the demonstration, construction, and application of solid waste management, resource recovery, and resource conservation systems...

(8)   establishing a cooperative effort among the Federal, State, and local governments and private enterprise in order to recover valuable materials and energy from solid waste.

4.2 Definitions

Definitions of the key words are generally most critical to the proper interpretation of a statute.   One definition of great importance to understanding RCRA is the broad definition of solid waste. 9/   The definition in Section 1004(27) is: "The term 'solid waste' means any garbage, refuse, sludge from a waste treatment plant, water supply treatment plant or air pollution control facility...."   This would not be a bad definition if the legislative draftsmen had stopped here.   However, they couldn't contain themselves to only regulating solids but decided to encompass a great deal more of the physical world by adding "...and other discarded material, including solid, liquid, semisolid, or contained gaseous materials resulting from industrial, commercial, mining and agriculture activities and from community activities but does not include solid or dissolved material in domestic sewage, or solid or dissolved materials in irrigation return flows or industrial discharges which are point sources subject to permits under section 402 of the Federal Water Pollution Control Act, as amended (86 Stat. 880), or source, special nuclear, or byproduct material as defined by the Atomic Energy Act of 1954, as amended (68 Stat. 923).

Many will be surprised to learn that for RCRA purposes certain liquids or contained gases are solids by definition of the U.S. Congress.

The regulatory program of RCRA is contained in Subtitle C and covers the management of those solid wastes categorized as hazardous.   The Act provides the following definition of hazardous wastes:

9/   RCRA, § 1004.

"The term 'hazardous waste' means a solid waste, or combination of solid wastes, which because of its quantity, concentration, or physical, chemical, or infectious characteristics may—

"(A) cause, or significantly contribute to an increase in mortality or an increase in serious irreversible, or incapacitating reversible illness; or

"(B) pose a substantial present or potential hazard to human health or the environment when improperly treated, stored, transported, or disposed of, or otherwise managed" (Section 1004(5)).

The scope of the hazardous waste regulatory program is primarily determined by EPA's application of these definitions.

4.3 Guidelines

Subtitle A 10/ includes the directive for EPA to develop suggested guidelines to assist state and local governments in solid waste management. These suggested guidelines are to :

(1)   provide technical and economic descriptions of the level of performance available from various practices;

(2)   describe levels of performance including methods and degrees of control for public health, protection of ground and surface waters from leachates, protection of waters from runoff, protection of air quality, disease and vector control, safety and aesthetics; and

(3)   provide minimum criteria to enable the states to define those solid waste management practices which constitute the open dumping of solid waste or hazardous waste and are to be prohibited. The criteria are of importance because they are the basis for a national program of enormous proportions to eliminate open dumping. (The proposed classification criteria were published and are discussed in Section 7.0 of this chapter.)

According to EPA's interpretation, this is the basic authority for the continuation of the Federal facilities guidelines also.

10/   RCRA § 1008.

5.0 Office of Solid Waste and Authorities

RCRA's Subtitle B 11/ legislatively established the Office of Solid Waste within EPA and authorizes the Administrator to implement this Act. This subtitle also gives EPA authority to provide technical and financial assistance to the states, and regional or local agencies through resource recovery and conservation panels. It gives a 5 percent grant toward the purchase price of tire shredders, requires that an annual report be submitted to Congress, and provides the general authorization of funds for EPA.

EPA's annual RCRA report to the Congress is a most informative document for those interested in keeping informed about developments in this field.

6.0 Hazardous Waste Management

The "heart" of RCRA is the hazardous waste program mandated by Subtitle C (Sections 3001 through 3013). The intent of this Congressional directive is to control hazardous wastes from the time they are generated until they are properly disposed. This is called a "cradle to grave" regulatory program.

The RCRA program does not encompass past (pre-RCRA) disposal sites and their clean-up. Congress enacted the Comprehensive Environmental Response, Compensation and Liability Act, known either as CERCLA or Superfund, 12/ to handle the clean-up of hazardous waste sites such as the infamous Love Canal and other such environmental hazards. Generally speaking, RCRA regulates active disposal sites and Superfund is directed to those inactive hazardous waste disposal sites that pose an environmental or health threat. See Chapter 10 for a description of the CERCLA or Superfund program.

RCRA Subtitle C mandates a comprehensive set of regulations that cover:

(1) the determination of what hazardous wastes are (identification)
(2) procedures and forms for notifying EPA if you are involved with hazardous wastes (notification)
(3) requirements for generators of hazardous wastes
(4) transporter requirements
(5) requirements for treatment, storage or disposal
(6) permit program

11/   Subtitle B is RCRA §§ 2001 through 2006.

12/   P.L. 96-510, 42 U.S.C. §§ 9601 et seq. 1981.

(7)   inspection and enforcement
(8)   state program conditions.

Each of these segments will be covered in the following sections.

6.1 Identification of Hazardous Wastes

The identification of a hazardous waste first requires a determination whether the particular material is a solid waste. This determination is initially based on the definition of a solid waste. (See Section 4.2 of this chapter.) The definition includes a wide variety of wastes and excludes some others.

The most important aspect of EPA's current implementing definition of the term "solid waste" is its expansive interpretation of the phrase "other discarded material" which is contained in the statutory definition. EPA had difficulty drafting a definition of this phrase. Materials which are in fact thrown away are "wastes" and should clearly be regulated. Furthermore, EPA found that "garbage, refuse, or sludge" are materials which are presumptively destined to be thrown away and, therefore, should be regulated as a solid waste. 13/

For all other materials, EPA focused on whether the material is occasionally thrown away. Consequently, EPA defined the term "other waste material" as:

> any solid, liquid, semi-solid, or contained gaseous material resulting from industrial, commercial, mining or agricultural operations, or from community activities which:
>
> (1)   is discarded or is being accumulated, stored or physically, chemically or biologically treated prior to being discarded; or
> (2)   has served its original intended use and sometimes is discarded; or
> (3)   is a manufacturing or mining by-product and sometimes is discarded." (Emphasis added.) 14/

"Discarded" material is defined as one which: is abandoned [and not used, re-used, reclaimed or recycled] by being:

13/   See 45 FR 33093.

14/   40 CFR 261.2 (b).

(1)   disposed of; or
(2)   burned or incinerated, except where the material is being burned as a fuel for the purpose of recovering usable energy; or
(3)   physically, chemically, or biologically treated (other than burned or incinerated) in lieu of or prior to being disposed of. (Emphasis added.) 15/

These two interlocking definitions of the statutory term "other discarded material" result in EPA regulating a universe of materials which may not be commonly understood to be "wastes" for a particular industry or company. Only two types of materials are clearly not a solid waste. The first category includes materials which are primarily products of a particular manufacturing or mining process or which are considered intermediate products. The second category includes those materials (other than garbage, refuse, or sludge) which are always used, reused, reclaimed or recycled. Such second category of materials are, by definition, not "discarded" materials and, therefore, are not solid wastes.

Once a material is found to be a solid waste, the next question is: is it a "hazardous waste?" EPA's regulations automatically exempt certain solid wastes from being considered hazardous wastes. Generally these regulatory exemptions include:

(1)   household waste;
(2)   agricultural wastes which are returned to the ground as fertilizer;
(3)   mining overburden returned to the mine site;
(4)   utility wastes from coal combustion;
(5)   oil and natural gas exploration drilling waste;
(6)   wastes from the extraction, benefaction, and processing of ores and minerals, including coal;
(7)   cement kiln dust wastes;
(8)   arsenical-treated wood wastes generated by end users of such wood;
(9)   certain chromium-bearing wastes. 16/

15/   40 CFR 261.2(c).

16/   40 CFR 261.4(b), 45 FR 33120, 45 FR 72037 (30 October 1980), 45 FR 76620 (19 November 1980), 45 FR 78531 (25 November 1980).

These exemptions have qualifying conditions and are subject to occasional clarification by EPA. So, the reader is cautioned that this determination of what wastes are hazardous is often rather difficult because all the circumstances and conditions must be considered.

The household waste exemption is intended to apply to waste streams generated by consumers at the household level but also includes waste streams from hotels, motels, mobile residences, and pumpings from household septic tanks. 17/

EPA has also provided some limited regulatory exemptions under particularly defined circumstances such as for hazardous waste that is generated in a product or raw material storage tank, transport vehicle, pipeline or manufacturing process unit. EPA has also exempted waste samples and other samples collected for monitoring and testing. 18/

If a solid waste material does not qualify for one of the many exemptions, it will be deemed a hazardous waste if it:

(1)   is listed as a hazardous waste by EPA in 40 CFR Part 261, Subpart D, and has not been delisted,

(2)   is a mixture of a listed waste and a solid waste and has not been delisted, or

(3)   exhibits any of the four hazardous waste charac-teristics identified in 40 CFR Part 261, Subpart C. 19/

The lists, characteristics and "mixture rule" are described in the following sections.

6.1.1 Hazardous Waste Lists

EPA has established three hazardous wastes lists:

(1)   hazardous wastes from nonspecific sources [40 CFR 261.31] (e.g., spent nonhalogenated solvents, toluene, methyl ethyl ketone...);

17/   See 45 FR 33099. Household wastes that are mixed with hazardous wastes may result in the mixture being deemed a hazardous waste.

18/   A comprehensive description of all the regulatory exemptions is beyond the scope of this text, so the reader is referred to the Hazardous Waste Handbook for a detailed discussion. See footnote 1.

19/   40 CFR 261.3(a).

(2)   hazardous wastes from specific sources [40 CFR 261.32] (e.g., bottom sediment sludge from the treatment of waste waters from wood preserving); and

(3)   discarded commercial chemical products, and all off-specification species, containers, and spill residues thereof. [40 CFR 261.33] 20/

The first two hazardous waste lists are largely self-explanatory. A company need only compare its solid waste stream to the lists to determine if it manages a hazardous waste.

The third list sets forth commercial chemicals which, if discarded, must be treated as hazardous wastes. This hazardous waste list actually consists of two distinct lists. One list sets forth chemicals deemed toxic and, therefore, hazardous if discarded [40 CFR 261.33(f)]. These are regulated like the other listed hazardous wastes. A second list contains wastes which EPA identifies as acutely hazardous (40 CFR 261.33(e)). They are subject to a more rigorous small generator exclusion limitation discussed in 6.3.1 of this chapter.

Hazardous waste regulation under the commercial chemical list is expected to be triggered most often when a company decides to reduce inventory and discards a listed commercial chemical product in its pure form.

A common scenario which will trigger the commercial chemical list is an accidental spill situation. 21/ If a listed commercial chemical is spilled, the spilled chemical and any contaminated material, i.e., dirt and other residue, is likely to be discarded and thus becomes a hazardous waste and must be managed as such. Therefore, even companies which generally do not discard or intend to discard any of the commercial chemical products on the list must be prepared to comply with the RCRA hazardous waste regulations in the event of an accidental spill. 22/

20/   45 FR 33122-27, 45 FR 47833-36 (16 July 1980); 45 FR 72039 (30 October 1980); 45 FR 74890 (12 November 1980); 45 FR 78541-44 (25 November 1980); 46 FR 27476-77 (20 May 1981).

21/   40 CFR 261.33(d), 45 FR 78541 (25 November 1980), 46 FR 27477 (20 May 1981).

22/   See 45 FR 76629 (19 November 1980).

6.1.2 Hazardous Waste Characteristics 23/

RCRA provides that EPA may identify hazardous wastes by simply establishing characteristics of hazardous wastes. Thus, if an unlisted solid waste exhibits a hazardous waste characteristic, it is still regulated under the RCRA hazardous waste program.

EPA has established four hazardous waste characteristics. All persons who generate a solid waste have the responsibility to ascertain whether their wastes exhibit one or more of these characteristics:

    (1)   Ignitability
    (2)   Corrosivity
    (3)   Reactivity
    (4)   EP Toxicity

6.1.2.1 Ignitability

The hazardous waste characteristic of ignitability was established to identify solid wastes capable during routine handling of causing a fire or exacerbating a fire once started. A solid waste is deemed to exhibit the characteristic of ignitability if it meets with one of the following four descriptions. First, it is a liquid, other than an aqueous solution containing less than 24 percent alcohol by volume, with a flash point of less than 60 degrees centigrade (140°F). Second, it is a nonliquid which under normal conditions can cause fire through friction, absorption of moisture or spontaneous chemical changes and burns so vigorously when ignited that it creates a hazard. Third, it is an ignitable compressed gas as defined by the DOT regulations set forth at 49 CFR 173.300. Finally, it is an oxidizer as defined by the DOT regulations set forth at 49 CFR 173.151.

6.1.2.2. Corrosivity

The hazardous waste characteristic of corrosivity was established because EPA believed that wastes capable of corroding metal could escape their own containers and liberate other wastes. In addition, wastes with a pH at either the high or low end of the scale can harm human tissue and aquatic life and may react dangerously with other wastes. Therefore, EPA determined that any solid waste is deemed to exhibit the characteristic of corrosivity if it is (1) aqueous and has a pH of less than or equal to 2.0 or greater than or equal to 12.5, or (2) a liquid and corrodes steel at a rate greater than 6.35 millimeters (.250 inches) per year under specified testing procedures.

23/   40 CFR 261.20.

6.1.2.3 Reactivity

EPA established the hazardous waste characteristic of re-activity to regulate wastes which are extremely unstable and have a tendency to react violently or explode during stages of its management. The regulation lists several situations where this may happen which warrant specific consideration (e.g., the behavior of the substance when mixed with water, when heated, etc.). Instead of developing a precise scientific description of this characteristic, EPA has promulgated a descriptive, prose definition of reactivity under the view that suitable test protocols for measuring reactivity are unavailable.

6.1.2.4 Extraction Procedure (EP) Toxicity

EPA decided that one of the most significant dangers posed by hazardous wastes stems from the leaching of toxic constituents of land-disposed solid wastes into groundwater. Consequently, the extraction procedure toxicity characteristic is designed to identify wastes which are likely to leach hazardous concentrations of specific toxic constituents into groundwater under improper management conditions.

To implement the EP toxicity characteristic, EPA established a mandatory testing procedure which extracts the toxic constituents for a solid waste in a manner which EPA believes will stimulate the leaching action which occurs in landfills. The EP testing protocol is described in detail in 40 CFR Part 261, Appendix II.

The EP toxicity testing protocol subjects a representative sample of a solid waste to an acidic leaching medium. The testing protocol requires the mixing of a solid waste with an acetic acid solution with a pH of 5.0 (plus or minus 0.2) for a period of 24 hours. Then, the extract from the mixing is tested to determine whether it contains any of the contaminants identified in the National Interim Primary Drinking Water Standards promulgated under the Safe Drinking Water Act. The potency of any such leach-ate is likely to be attentuated between the time it would presumably migrate from a landfill and actually contaminate a groundwater supply and thus EPA chose a dilution factor of 100.

6.1.3 Mixtures of Hazardous Wastes and Solid Wastes

It is important to note that EPA treats mixtures of a non-listed hazardous waste and a solid waste differently than it does a mixture of a listed hazardous waste and a solid waste. A mixture including a listed hazardous waste and a solid waste is treated as a hazardous waste unless such a mixture qualifies for an exemption. 24/ A mixture including a non-listed hazardous waste and a solid

---

24/   See 40 CFR 261.3(a)(2), 46 FR 56588-89 (17 November 1981).

waste will be deemed hazardous only if the entire mixture exhibits one of the four hazardous waste characteristics.

This distinction between mixtures, including a listed waste or a nonlisted waste is known as the "mixture rule."

6.1.4 Used, Reused, Recycled or Reclaimed Hazardous Wastes

EPA, in the 19 May 1980 regulations made two important decisions pertaining to hazardous wastes which are used, reused, recycled or reclaimed. First, EPA asserted jurisdiction over such materials despite objections that such regulation would thwart the resource recovery goals of RCRA. 25/ Second, EPA agreed that most of the hazardous waste program regulations that it was promulgating on 19 May 1980 were not appropriate to the management activities associated with hazardous wastes which are used, reused, recycled, or reclaimed. Thus, EPA promulgated special regulatory provisions for such wastes which temporarily exempt them from the hazardous waste program. 26/

The special requirements provisions state that non-listed hazardous wastes are exempt from hazardous waste regulation so long as the hazardous waste is:

(1) being beneficially used or re-used or legitimately recycled or reclaimed.

(2) being accumulated, stored or physically, chemically or biologically treated prior to beneficial use or re-use or legitimate recycling or reclamation.

Listed hazardous wastes, mixtures including listed hazardous wastes, and sludges which are transported or stored prior to use, reuse, recycling, or reclamation are subject to the transportation and storage requirements of the hazardous waste program.

6.2 Notification of Hazardous Waste Management Activities

RCRA Section 3010(a) requires that any person who manages a hazardous waste (i.e., generators, transporters, owners, or operators of T/S/D facilities) must file a notification with EPA. EPA published EPA Form 8700-12 as a Section 3010(a) notification form, explained the notification requirements, and included instructions for completing the form. 27/

25/   45 FR 33092.

26/   40 CFR 261.6.

27/   45 FR 12746 (26 February 1980).

EPA Form 8700-12 requires only a bare minimum of information. The reporting company must identify itself, its location and the EPA identification number for the listed hazardous wastes and for the non-listed hazardous wastes (e.g., toxic, reactive) it manages. It is important to remember that notifications are required to be filed for each site (e.g., plant) at which there is hazardous waste management activity because RCRA is a specific facility or site specific regulatory program.

6.3 Generators of Hazardous Waste

The legislative history of RCRA clearly indicates that the statute was not intended to prohibit the generation of hazardous waste but to regulate the management of any hazardous waste from the moment that it is generated.

EPA's regulations define the term "generator" as:

"Any person, by site, whose act or process produces hazardous waste identified or listed in Part 261 of this Chapter" or whose act first causes hazardous waste to become subject to regulation. 28/

EPA has said that they respect any arrangement made by private parties which assigns generator duties among different parties but will reserve the right to hold the owner, operator, and any third party whose act first causes the waste to become subject to regulation jointly and severally liable for satisfaction of the generator duties for each plant site. 29/

The definition of a "generator" refers explicitly to the particular site of generation. Thus, a corporation with several plants must evaluate and comply with the generator requirements individually for each facility.

6.3.1 Small Generators

The regulations identifying hazardous waste also establish special, less rigorous requirements for those generators of hazardous waste which produce waste in small quantities. 30/ EPA decided that it was administratively infeasible to immediately regulate the estimated 300,000 generators of hazardous waste. EPA's small

---

28/   40 CFR 260.10(a)(26).

29/   45 FR 72026 (30 October 1980).

30/   40 CFR 261.5, 45 FR 76623 (19 November 1980), 46 FR 27476 (20 May 1981).

generator requirements are based on lack of administrative resources which compel the agency to direct its efforts to large generators. A background document on this subject states that the
small generator eligibility requirements will be narrowed sometime
between 1983 and 1985.

The small generator requirements provide that if a generator
produces a total of less than 1,000 kilograms (kg) of hazardous
wastes in a calendar month, then it is subject only to minimal requirements under the hazardous waste program. A small generator
must "ensure" that its hazardous waste is treated or disposed of in a
facility permitted, licensed, or registered by a state to manage
municipal or industrial solid wastes, or in a facility which beneficially uses or reuses or legitimately recycles or reclaims the
waste. If a small generator stores its hazardous waste on-site, it
may not accumulate more than a total of 1,000 kg at any time.

The 1,000 kg generation limit is lowered to 1 kg per month
for hazardous wastes which are found on the list of acutely hazardous wastes (e.g., acutely hazardous commercial chemical products). 31/

EPA has interpreted the regulations as applying to a total of
all hazardous wastes. Thus, if a generator has three different hazardous wastes produced in monthly quantities of 300 kg, 600 kg, and
200 kg, the small generator exclusion would not apply.

Some companies may move into and out of the small generator provision as monthly production rates change.

Both the U.S. Congress and EPA envision leaving 1000 kg
generation limit to 100 kg or lower sometime in the next few
years. This would result in many additional sites or facilities being
regulated. So, any generators currently exempted as "small generators" must carefully monitor legislative and regulatory developments.

6.3.2 Requirements Imposed Upon Generators

Generators of hazardous wastes, that are not exempted,
generally have the following requirements:

(1) Recordkeeping that identifies the quantity,
     constituents, and disposition of hazardous wastes;

31/   40 CFR 261.5(e)(1), 45 FR 76623 (19 November 1980). Note
       that in the future, EPA may identify listed hazardous wastes
       from specific or non-specific sources as acutely hazardous and
       subject such wastes to the lower small generator exclusion
       level. 40 CFR 261.30(d), 45 FR 74892 (12 November 1980).

(2)   Labeling of containers used to store, transport, or dispose of hazardous wastes;

(3)   Use of appropriate containers;

(4)   Furnishing of information regarding a generator's hazardous waste to persons who transport, treat, store, or dispose of such waste;

(5)   Use of a manifest system and any other reasonable means necessary to assure the proper disposal of hazardous wastes; and

(6)   Submission of reports to EPA or the authorized state agency that identify the quantity and disposition of hazardous wastes.

Perhaps the most important duty imposed upon a generator is the obligation to determine whether any of its solid waste is a "hazardous waste." 32/

Every generator of a hazardous waste must obtain an EPA Identification Number before the waste can be transported, treated, stored, or disposed. 33/ In addition, a generator is required to have its hazardous waste transported, treated, stored, and disposed by persons who also have obtained their EPA Identification Numbers. 34/

6.3.3 Recordkeeping

The purpose of the manifest is to track the handling of a hazardous waste from the moment it is generated to the site of its final disposition. The manifest is the basis of the recordkeeping system. The manifest stands as a record of all who handle a particular hazardous waste and as a blueprint for accountability in the event that a quantity of hazardous waste is misplaced.

The generator must prepare a sufficient number of copies of the manifest so that all parties listed on the manifest as handling the hazardous waste will be provided with a copy and a copy will be returned to the generator from the T/S/D facility.

Generators are required to keep three types of records. 35/ First, a copy of each signed manifest must be kept for a period of three years from the date of acceptance of the waste by the initial

---

32/   40 CFR 262.11.

33/   40 CFR 262.12.

34/   40 CFR 262.12(c).

35/   40 CFR 262.40.

transporter. Second, copies of reports required to be filed with EPA (the biennial reports and the exception reports) must also be kept for three years from the date such report was due. EPA changed the annual report to a biennial report requirement. Finally, the records of any test results, waste analyses, or determinations must be kept for three years from the date the waste was last sent to a T/S/D facility on-site or off-site. This last requirement only applies to test results pertaining to a waste which is deemed to be a hazardous waste.

An exception report is required in the event that a generator does not receive a manifest back in a timely or properly executed manner. The regulations specifically provide that a generator must contact the transporter and/or the T/S/D facility to determine what happened to the manifest and the hazardous waste. If, after the 45th day, the generator has not received a manifest with the proper signature from the T/S/D facility, the generator must submit an exception report to the EPA Regional Administrator.

6.3.4 90–Day Storage Exemption

A generator is allowed to store its hazardous wastes on-site for a period of up to 90 days without having to obtain a permit for their storage facility. This provision recognizes that a generator cannot be expected to immediately transport off-site the hazardous waste which it may generate on a daily basis. However, EPA has imposed requirements for this temporary on-site storage.

6.3.5 Labels and Containers

A generator must properly prepare the waste for transportation off-site. EPA adopted the DOT regulations with respect to the packaging, labeling, marking, and placarding. In addition to the DOT regulations, EPA requires that any container of 110 gallons or less must be specifically marked with the generator's name, address, manifest document number, and the words:

> Hazardous waste - federal law prohibits improper disposal. If found contact the nearest police or public safety authority or the United States Environmental Protection Agency.

6.4 Transporters of Hazardous Wastes

RCRA regulates any person who transports hazardous wastes, whether in interstate or intrastate commerce. Thus, the reach of RCRA includes not only shippers and common carriers of hazardous wastes, but also the private company that occasionally transports hazardous wastes on its own trucks solely within its home state. RCRA has resulted in the regulation of transporters who previously were not subject to the regulations issued by the U.S. Department of

Transportation under the Hazardous Materials Transportation Act (HMTA).

EPA promulgated standards for all transporters of hazardous wastes on 19 May 1980, 40 CFR Part 263. These standards are closely coordinated with the DOT standards under HMTA. For the most part, EPA's regulations incorporate and require compliance with the DOT provisions on labeling, marking, placarding, using proper containers, and reporting discharges.

Persons moving hazardous waste which is subject to the small generator provisions, or which qualifies for the special provisions for recycled waste, need not comply with the transporter regulations at this time.

6.4.1 On-Site versus Off-Site

Anyone who moves a hazardous waste that is required to be manifested off the site where it is generated, or the site where it is being treated, stored and disposed of, will be subject to the transporter standards. The only person not covered are generators or operators of T/S/D facilities who engage in on-site transportation of their hazardous waste. Once a generator or a T/S/D facility operator moves its hazardous waste off-site—which can be just a few hundred feet down a public road—he is then considered a transporter and must comply with the regulations.

6.4.2 Transporter Requirements

All transporters subject to the regulations must obtain an EPA Identification Number prior to transporting any hazardous waste.

A transporter may only accept hazardous waste which is accompanied by a manifest signed by the generator. The transporter himself must sign the manifest and return one copy to the generator before leaving the generator's property. At all times the transporter must keep the manifest with the hazardous waste. When the transporter delivers the waste to another transporter or to the designated T/S/D facility, he must (1) date the manifest and obtain the signature of the next transporter or the T/S/D facility operator, (2) retain one copy of the manifest for his own records, and (3) give the remaining copies to the person receiving the waste.

Note that there are special requirements which apply to rail or water transporters of hazardous waste, and those who transport hazardous waste outside of the United States. 36/

If the transporter is unable to deliver the waste in accordance with the manifest, he must contact the generator for further instructions and revise the manifest accordingly.

36/   40 CFR 263.20(f).

The regulations also impose certain recordkeeping requirements. 37/ The transporter must keep the executed copy of the
manifest for a period of three years.

Transporters of hazardous wastes may also become subject to
the Part 262 requirements for generators if, for example, the transporter mixes hazardous wastes of different DOT descriptions by
placing them into a single container. Also, a hazardous waste which
accumulates in a transport vehicle or vessel or a product or raw
material pipeline will trigger the generator standards when the
waste is removed.

EPA has made clear that a transporter who holds a hazardous
waste for up to ten days should not be considered to be storing hazardous waste, and should not be required to obtain a RCRA permit.
The transporter must obtain a permit for storage of hazardous
wastes beyond the 10 day exemption.

6.4.3 Hazardous Waste Discharges

The regulations provide that if an accidental or intentional
discharge of a hazardous waste occurs during transportation, the
transporter is responsible for its clean up.

In the event of a discharge, the transporter must take immediate action to protect human health and the environment, including treatment or containment of the spill and notification of
local police and fire departments.

EPA has specifically incorporated DOT's discharge reporting
requirements into the RCRA regulations. 38/ The DOT regulations
identify the situations in which telephone reporting of the discharge
and the filing of a written report are required.

6.4.4 Enforcement

Transporters are subject to both DOT and EPA enforcement.
EPA will be primarily responsible for monitoring compliance by
generators and T/S/D facilities with the RCRA requirements. DOT
will conduct an ongoing program of inspections of transporters to
monitor their compliance. DOT will immediately advise EPA of
"any possible" violations of the RCRA transporter regulations so
that EPA can take enforcement action. In addition, EPA intends to
bring enforcement actions against transporters where the transportation of hazardous wastes is ancillary to treatment, storage or
disposal of such wastes.

37/   40 CFR 263.22.

38/   See 49 CFR 171.15 and 171.16 (1979).

6.5 Treatment, Storage, and Disposal (T/S/D)

The term "T/S/D" is commonly used to refer to the three different hazardous waste management activities that are regulated under RCRA Section 3004, and which thus require a permit under RCRA Section 3005.

A facility will be regulated as a "treatment" facility with respect to the hazardous waste it handles if the operator utilizes:

> any method, technique, or process, including neutral-
> ization, designed to change the physical, chemical, or
> biological character or composition of any hazardous
> waste so as to neutralize such waste, or so as to recover
> energy or material resources from the waste, or so as to
> render such waste nonhazardous, or less hazardous;
> safer to transport, store or dispose of; or amenable for
> recovery, amenable for storage, or reduced in volume.
> 39/

This definition is obviously very broad, and will cover even the most commonplace treatment activities such as neutralizing or dewatering hazardous wastes.

A facility will be regulated as a "storage" facility if it is used to engage in:

> the holding of hazarous waste for a temporary period, at
> the end of which the hazardous waste is treated,
> disposed of, or stored elsewhere. 40/

An operator's activities will be regulated as "disposal" if the facility is used for:

> the discharge, deposit, injection, dumping, spilling, leak-
> ing, or placing of any solid waste or hazardous waste
> into or on any land or water so that such solid waste or
> hazardous waste or any constituent thereof may enter
> the environment or be emitted into the air or discharged
> into any waters, including ground waters. 41/

Practical application of these definitions is often difficult. Therefore, sensible application must be sought from EPA.

39/   40 CFR 260.10(a).

40/   Id.

41/   Id.

6.5.1 Active/Inactive Facility

EPA has determined that Congresss intended RCRA to apply primarily to hazardous waste activities that take place after the effective date of the Subtitle C regulations, i.e., 19 November 1980, and not to abandoned sites or past disposal practices. 42/ Consequently, T/S/D facilities rendered "inactive" as of 19 November 1980 were able to avoid the RCRA standards. Any T/S/D facility that was "active" after that date must now be in compliance with the hazardous waste program.

6.5.2 Interim and Permitted Facilities

RCRA establishes initially two categories of T/S/D facilities: (1) interim status facilities that do not need individually-issued permits to continue operating while EPA puts the RCRA permit scheme in place, and (2) permitted facilities which include new T/S/D facilities and facilities that did not qualify for interim status, both of which must first obtain RCRA permits to begin or continue operations.

To qualify for interim status, a facility must satisfy the three-part statutory test in RCRA Section 3005(e) of:

(1)   being in existence on 19 November 1980,
(2)   notifying EPA pursuant to RCRA Section 3010(a) of its hazardous waste management activities, and
(3)   filing an application for a permit.

A facility's interim status will end when EPA promulgates permanent technical standards applicable to that facility so that EPA, or a state with an approved program, can request a permit application from the facility and issue an effective permit.

All other T/S/D facilities, including new facilities that were not "in existence" on 19 November 1980 and facilities that have otherwise failed to qualify for interim status, must obtain an individual RCRA permit.

6.5.3 Exempt T/S/D's

The following T/S/D facilities or hazardous waste activities are exempted altogether from both the interim status and permanent program standards: 43/

42/   See 45 FR 33170.

43/   40 CFR 265.1(c), 264.1(c), as amended, 47 FR 8306 (25 February 1982).

(1)   Facilities that dispose of hazardous waste by means of ocean disposal pursuant to a permit issued under the Marine Protection, Research, and Sanctuaries Act.

(2)   The disposal of hazardous waste by underground injection pursuant to a permit issued under the Safe Drinking Water Act.

(3)   A publicly owned treatment work (POTW) which treats or stores hazardous wastes which are delivered to the POTW by a transport vehicle or vessel or through a pipe.

(4)   T/S/D facilities which operate under a state hazardous waste program authorized pursuant to RCRA Section 3006.

(5)   Facilities authorized by a state to manage industrial or municipal solid waste, if the only hazardous waste handled by such a facility is otherwise excluded from regulation pursuant to the special requirements for small generators.

(6)   A facility which treats or stores hazardous wastes that are subject to the special requirement for hazardous wastes which are used, reused, recycled, or reclaimed.

(7)   On-site accumulation of hazardous waste by generators for 90 days or less.

(8)   Farmers which dispose of waste pesticides from their own use in compliance with 40 CFR 262.51.

(9)   Owners or operators of a "totally enclosed treatment facility."

(10)   Owners and operators of elementary neutralization units and wastewater treatment units.

(11)   Persons taking immediate action to treat and contain spills.

(12)   Transporters storing manifested wastes approved in containers at a transfer facility for 10 days or less.

(13) The act of adding absorbent material to hazardous waste in a container or the inverse, adding hazardous waste to absorbent material in a container, to reduce the amount of free liquids in the container, if the materials are added when wastes are first placed in the container.

6.5.4 Standards of General Applicability

Both the interim and permanent regulations for T/S/D facilities include standards of general applicability (e.g., personnel training, security, financial responsibility) as well as specific design and operating standards for each different type of T/S/D facility (e.g., storage tanks, landfills, incinerators).

Under both the interim and permanent programs, operators are required to have an EPA identification number.

In order to properly manage a hazardous waste, an operator of a T/S/D facility must have sufficient knowledge of the particular waste being handled. Consequently, the regulations require the operator to obtain or conduct a detailed chemical and physical analysis of a representative sample of a hazardous waste before the waste is treated, stored, or disposed of at the facility.

To prevent unknowing entry, and to minimize the potential for unauthorized entry of people or livestock to the active portion of a T/S/D facility, operators must install a security system. This may be either a 24-hour surveillance system or a barrier around the facility and a means to control entry, and posted "Danger" signs.

Operators are required to prepare and implement an inspection plan specifically tailored to the circumstances at their facility.

T/S/D facility personnel are required to have expertise in the areas to which they are assigned, thus reducing the chances that a mistake due to lack of training might lead to an environmental accident. The training may be by formal classroom instruction or on-the-job training. The program must be directed by a person trained in hazardous waste management procedures.

The regulations specifically require that special precautions be taken to prevent accidental ignition or reaction of ignitable or reactive wastes.

Requirements for the handling of ignitable, reactive, and incompatible wastes are largely common sense practices. Specific requirements regarding the mixing of ignitable, reactive, or incompatible wastes are also included in the regulations.

Operators of permitted facilities must document their compliance with the regulations concerning management of ignitable, reactive or incompatible wastes.

Permitted facilities to be sited in areas prone to seismic activity or floodplains are subject to location standards designed to reduce the additional risks posed by these facilities.

Regulations for preparedness and prevention have been promulgated to minimize the possibility and effect of an explosion, spill, or fire at a T/S/D facility. Facilities must have, unless unnecessary due to the nature of the wastes handled, the following equipment:

(1) an internal alarm or communications system,
(2) a device capable of summoning emergency assistance from local agencies,
(3) fire and spill control equipment, and
(4) decontamination equipment.

Operators are required to have a contingency plan for the facility designed to minimize hazards to human health and the environment in the event of an actual explosion, fire, or unplanned release of hazardous wastes.

Upon receipt of a manifested shipment of hazardous waste, the operator of a T/S/D facility must immediately sign, date, and give to the transporter a copy of the manifest prepared by the generator. Within 30 days, the operator must return another copy of the manifest to the generator.

A key provision of the regulations is the requirement that all T/S/D facilities maintain a complete operating record until closure.

There are basic reports which the T/S/D facility operator is obligated to file with the EPA Regional Administrator. One report is the "unmanifested waste" report which the operator must file within 15 days of accepting any hazardous waste that is not accompanied by the required manifest.

There are in addition certain specialized reports that must be filed in specific circumstances. For example, reports must be filed in the event of a hazardous waste release, fire, or explosion.

There are general closure requirements applicable to all T/S/D facilities, and additional requirements for each specific type of facility.

Financial responsiblity requirements have been established in both the interim and permanent standards to ensure that funds for closure and post-closure are available.

The regulations also require operators to obtain liability insurance to provide coverage during the operating life of a facility for claims arising out of injuries to persons or property which result from hazardous waste management operations.

6.5.5 Standards for Specific Types of T/S/D Facilities

The standards discussed above are generally applicable to all T/S/D facilities, from the simple container storage facility to the most complex landfill. EPA has also promulgated specific standards for each of ten different types of T/S/D facilities that constitute the universe of facilities regulated under RCRA.

The ten types of T/S/D facilities regulated are:

(1)   Containers
(2)   Tanks
(3)   Surface Impoundments
(4)   Waste Piles
(5)   Land Treatment Units
(6)   Landfills
(7)   Incinerators
(8)   Thermal Treatment Units
(9)   Chemical, Physical, and Biological
       Treatment Units
(10) Underground Injection Wells

If the reader wishes further information on the detailed requirements for each of these ten types then the reader can review the
Code of Federal Regulations, Title 40, Part 264 or see the Hazardous Waste Handbook, 4th Edition, Chapter 6.

6.5.6 Standards for Special Types of T/S/D Facilities

EPA has proposed certain limited requirements for special
types of T/S/D facilities. Although at this time the proposal only
encompasses wastewater treatment and elementary neutralization,
EPA plans to add other special regulatory requirements which will
govern additional types of T/S/D facilities and/or specific hazardous
wastes in the future.

6.6 Permits

RCRA requires every owner or operator of a T/S/D facility to
obtain a permit. EPA has implemented a regulatory scheme for
conferring "interim status" on qualifying existing T/S/D facilities
whereby these facilities may continue operations without having
been issued a site-specific permit. 44/
A new facility or an existing facility that failed to qualify for
interim status must obtain a permit before commencing operations.
The regulations contain a two-step approach to the permitting process. A Part A application, containing certain basic information about the facility, must be filed as soon as a facility
becomes subject to the hazardous waste regulatory program. For
most existing facilities, this was 19 November 1980. The filing of a
Part A application was a condition to qualify for interim status. A
Part B application, requiring substantially more detailed

44/   See the discussion of the interim status standards for T/S/D
       facilities in 40 CFR Part 265.

information, may not be filed until after the effective date of applicable Phase II T/S/D regulations.

Permit applications will be requested and final permits will be issued by states authorized under RCRA to administer their own programs, and by the EPA Regional Administrator in all other states. Permit issuance must be based on a determination that the T/S/D facility is in compliance with all requirements of RCRA.

EPA established the substantive requirements and procedures for RCRA permits in 40 CFR Parts 122, 123 and 124 as part of the Agency's consolidated permit regulations. The consolidated permit regulations apply to the National Pollutant Discharge Elimination System (NPDES) under the Clean Water Act; the Underground Injection Control program (UIC) under the Safe Drinking Water Act; the dredge or fill program under Section 404 of the Clean Water Act; the Prevention of Significant Deterioration (PSD) program under the Clean Air Act (for EPA-issued permits only); and hazardous waste management program under RCRA.

Part 122 establishes definitions and basic permit requirements for EPA-administered RCRA, UIC, and NPDES programs. It spells out in detail who must apply for a permit; how a permit is issued; what terms, conditions, and schedules of compliance must be incorporated into the permit; when and how monitoring and reporting of permit compliance must be performed; when permits may be revised, reissued, or terminated; and what special requirements apply to certain types of industries.

Part 124 establishes the procedures for processing and issuing permits under all regulatory programs administered by EPA including RCRA. It includes procedures for preparing draft permits, public hearings, and final decisions.

6.7 State's Hazardous Waste Program

States are authorized by RCRA to develop and carry out their own hazardous waste programs in lieu of the federal program administered by EPA.

States with legislative authority for hazardous waste programs on 24 October 1982 may first obtain "interim authorization" from EPA to carry out their programs.

Regardless of whether a state receives interim authorization, any state may apply for "final authorization" to administer the RCRA hazardous waste program. In order to substitute for the federal program, the state program operating under final authorization must have standards which are "equivalent" to the EPA regulations, provide for adequate enforcement, and are consistent with federal or state program applicable in other states.

As of early 1983, all but 18 states had been granted Phase I interim authorization. EPA anticipates that 35 to 40 states will operate RCRA hazardous waste regulatory programs.

6.8 Inspection and Enforcement

RCRA provides that any officer, employee or representative of EPA or of a state with an authorized hazardous waste program may inspect the premises and records of any person who generates, stores, treats, transports, disposes, or otherwise handles hazardous waste. EPA's inspection authority extends to persons or sites which have handled hazardous wastes in the past but no longer do so.

The owner/operator must provide government officials access to records and property relating to the wastes for inspection purposes. Copying and sampling are authorized.

EPA's inspection program commenced 19 November 1980, the effective date of the hazardous waste regulations. By the end of 1982 EPA had already inspected over 1000 generation and disposal facilities. This pace is expected to increase during subsequent years.

The constitutionality of this inspection provision is questionable. Since this Section 3007 of RCRA apparently violates the U.S. Constitution's protection against unreasonable searches, EPA inspectors are cautioned to seek a warrant if their inspection is challenged. All organizations should have a company policy and procedure for handling inspections properly and it should include consideration of whether or not a warrant should be required.

There are several types of enforcement actions available to EPA under RCRA. These include administrative orders, civil and criminal penalties, and injunctive relief.

Under RCRA whenever EPA determines that any person is violating Subtitle C of RCRA (including any regulation or permit issued thereunder), the agency has two options. First, it may issue an order requiring compliance immediately or within a specified time period. Alternatively, EPA may seek injunctive relief against the violator through a civil action filed in a U.S. District Court.

Any person who violates any requirement of Subtitle C is liable for a civil penalty of up to $25,000 for each day of violation, regardless of whether the person had been served with a compliance order. A person subject to RCRA can not rely on EPA to tell him when he is in violation, then take the required corrective action, and thus avoid a penalty.

RCRA imposes criminal liability of up to $50,000, two years imprisonment, or both. The 1980 Amendments added a totally new type of criminal sanction know as "knowing endangerment." The purpose of this sanction is to provide substantial felony penalties for certain life-threatening conduct. Here, an individual faces a fine of up to $250,000 and/or up to five years' imprisonment. An organizational defendent is subject to a maximum fine of $1 million. A rigorous and strict enforcement program is expected because of the national concern for hazardous wastes and the resulting political pressures for action against those responsible.

7.0 State or Regional Solid Waste Plans

Regulation of non-hazardous waste is the responsibility of the states pursuant to Subtitle D of RCRA. The Federal involvement is limited to establishing minimum criteria that would prescribe the best practicable controls and monitoring requirements on solid waste disposal facilities.   Compliance with the minimum requirements determines whether a facility is classified as an "open dump" or not. Disposal of solid waste in "open dumps", (i.e., those facilities not meeting the criteria) is prohibited. Existing dumps are given five years in order to make modifications that will allow them to meet the requirements, and it is the state's responsibility to insure that such upgrading occurs or the open dumps are closed.

The basic flaw in this strategy, however, is the absence of any enforcement authority for the ban on open dumps. EPA's enforcement authority only covers hazardous wastes. EPA cannot take any steps against a person disposing of non-hazardous wastes in an open dump or against the state for failing to close open dumping, other than terminating certain grant funds available to the state under RCRA.

Because the definition of solid waste includes hazardous as well as non-hazardous waste, a facility which receives both types of wastes would have to meet the Subtitle C criteria as well as the Subtitle D requirements. This presumably will encourage the development of facilities just for disposal of non-hazardous waste, but the breadth of EPA's proposed designation of hazardous waste may make it difficult for facilities to insure that hazardous wastes are not in fact being disposed of at the site.

RCRA envisions that the state, with the help of Federal grant funds, will develop regional solid waste management plans. The program is patterned on Section 208 of the Clean Water Act and relies upon a comprehensive regional planning approach to solving solid waste problems. The state would be responsible for identifying appropriate management areas, developing regional plans through the use of local and regional authorities, inventoring and closing or upgrading existing open dumps, and generally assessing the need for additional solid waste disposal capacity in the area.

Of particular significance is a requirement that states not have any bans on the importation of waste for storage, treatment or disposal, or have requirements that are substantially dissimilar from other disposal practices that would discourage the free movement of wastes across state lines. Although enforcement of this requirement may be difficult, in light of the limited enforcement authority available to EPA, it does evidence a Congressional policy for a national approach to solid waste disposal and prevents localities from shielding themselves from disposal to the detriment of other jurisdictions.

8.0 Role of the Department of Commerce

Subtitle E gives the Department of Commerce (DOC) some responsibilities: (a) develop standards for substituting secondary materials for virgin materials; (b) develop markets for recovered materials; and (c) for the promotion of resource recovery technology generally.

The authorities given to DOC are similiar to those assigned to EPA in other sections of the Act, specifically Subtitle H, Research, Development, Demonstrations and Information. DOC and EPA are supposed to work together but the DOC has not received sufficient funding to support a major role.

9.0 Federal Responsibilities

Subtitle F requires that all Federal agencies and instrumentalities comply with all Federal, state, interstate, and local requirements stemming from RCRA unless exempted by the President. This includes the guidelines promulgated under Subtitle A. (See Section 4.3 of this chapter.)

This also requires the Federal Government to institute a procurement policy which encourages the purchase of recoverable materials when available at reasonable prices and which, because of their performance, can be substituted for virgin materials.

10.0 Citizen Participation and Other Provisions

Subtitle G provides for citizen participation in RCRA and some other interesting provisions.

Citizen suits are envisioned by Congress and many others as a key enforcement tool for environmental protection. RCRA's provisions for citizens suits and judicial review are modeled on the Clean Air Act.

These provide that any person may bring a civil action against any alleged violator of the Act's requirements or against the Administrator for a failure to perform a nondiscretionary duty. Further, any person may petition the EPA Administrator for promulgation, amendment or repeal of any regulation. Public participation is to "be provided for, encouraged and assisted by the Administrator and the State." Most importantly, RCRA authorizes the courts to award costs including attorneys' fees to any party.

10.1 Imminent and Substantial Endangerment Under RCRA

The EPA may bring suits to restrain an imminent and substantial endangerment to health or the environment.

EPA issued a memorandum on 25 January 1980, defining "imminent and substantial endangerment" as posing a "risk of harm" or "potential harm" but not requiring proof of actual harm. 45/ This interpretation was upheld in United States v. Vertac Chemical Corp., 489 F. Supp. 870 (E.D. Ark. 1980), the first published decision interpreting RCRA Section 7003. In issuing a preliminary injunction to contain the migration of dioxin from landfills and a treatment basin into a creek, the court held that under the endangerment provisions of both RCRA and the Clean Water Act harm need only be threatened rather than actually occurring. As a result of this decision, the imminent and substantial endangerment provision should see wide use as an enforcement tool in the future.

10.2 Employee Protection and Other Provisions
A provision is provided in RCRA to protect employees who file, institute or cause to be filed or who testify in any proceedings under RCRA. These employees can not be fired for that fact.

Subtitle G also contains the general authority for EPA to make grants and contracts in support of the objectives of RCRA and requires EPA to study training and personnel needs in the field.

11.0 Research, Development, Demonstration, and Information
In cooperation with Federal, state, and interstate authorities, private agencies and institutions and individuals, EPA is directed to conduct, encourage and promote the coordination of research, investigations, experiments, training, demonstrations, surveys, public education programs and studies relating to: the protection of health; planning, financing and operation of waste management systems including resource recovery; improvements in methodology of waste disposal and resource recovery; methods for remedying damages by earlier or existing landfills; and methods for rendering landfills safe for purposes of construction and other uses.

EPA is directed to carry out a number of special studies including the following subjects: small-scale and low technology approaches to resource recovery; front-end separation for materials recovery; mining waste; sludge; and airport landfills.

A cabinet level committee chaired by the Administrator of EPA is mandated to investigate the impact on resource recovery and conservation of: (a) incentives and disincentives, including existing public policies such as tax credits and depletion allowances; (b) restricting the manufacture or use of certain categories of consumer products; (c) application of a charge on consumer products to reflect the cost of solid waste management services.

45/   Memorandum dated 25 January 1980, from Douglas MacMillian, Acting Director of EPA's Hazardous Waste Enforcement Task Force, to Regional Enforcement Division Directors and others.

12.0   Implementation of the Resource Conservation and Recovery Act

Financial and human resource constraints will require the development of specific priorities and phasing for RCRA implementation. We forecast that controlling hazardous waste disposal will be the highest priority activity in the RCRA implementation during the 1980's. This activity will provide stimulus for resource conservation and recovery by increasing the costs of disposal. As the cost of disposal escalates because of RCRA, many firms will seek to change processes so as to eliminate or minimize waste. Others will look for markets to recycle the materials because the economics of recycling will become advantageous as RCRA increases costs.

Industrial wastes will receive priority emphasis for all solid waste management activities, particularly those of a regulatory nature. This is due to the relatively greater toxicity and quantity of such wastes.

Encouragement of state implementation is a high priority activity and incentives will be provided for that purpose. Achievement of the objectives of both Subtitles C and D depend upon the establishment and implementation of state programs (both for the regulation of disposal and for resource recovery and conservation). Financial and technical assistance for the development of state programs will be maximized.

There are five major tools which will be used to meet the goals and objectives of RCRA; regulations, economic incentives, research and development, technical assistance and public participation.

13.0   Enforcement of the Resource Conservation and Recovery Act

RCRA only provides for Federal enforcement of disposal of hazardous wastes. For other solid wastes, the Federal role prescribed in RCRA is to establish criteria for characterizing disposal operations which adversely affect health and the environment. The application and enforcement of the criteria is the responsibility of the states. Most states can be expected to move aggressively, others will not. The major Federal lever to bring about disposal controls is financial and technical assistance to the states.

Hazardous waste disposal as regulated under RCRA provides EPA with the authority to inspect facilities which handle hazardous wastes, and to have access to all records kept pursuant to the other sections of RCRA. The authority to inspect is a major element of the compliance monitoring and permitting programs. Hazardous waste management facilities will be inspected before a permit is granted, and all hazardous waste handlers (including the facilities) will be inspected on a continuing basis for compliance monitoring. Inspections will also serve as a means of gathering additional data on the technology of hazardous waste management. This information will be used to update the regulations as necessary, and to apply the most current standards to the control of hazardous wastes for the best protection of public health and the environment.

14.0 State and Local Activity

The majority of operations and activity in resource recovery and solid waste are of a local nature. These endeavors, with which we are familiar, involve local legal issues that have for the most part been covered in Chapter 1. There are some highlights of a national interest which we will describe in the next three sections.

14.1 Interstate Commerce and Solid Waste

Some states have moved to ban the importation of wastes as have their political subdivisions. These actions have raised serious questions relative to restraint of trade and interference with inter-state commerce. In Chapter 1, the U.S. Constitution's Commerce Clause limitations are described. A major case was decided by the U.S. Supreme Court on the issue of interference with interstate commerce and RCRA. The case, City of Philadelphia v. New Jersey, 46/ held that a New Jersey statute barring disposal within the state of solid waste originating or collected outside the state (e.g., New York City and Philadelphia) did violate the Commerce Clause of the U.S. Constitution. The Supreme Court ruled that it was immaterial whether the legislative purpose was to protect New Jersey's environment or its economy. This may not be accomplished by discriminating against articles of commerce coming from outside the State unless there is some reason, apart from their origin, to treat them differently. A State may not attempt to isolate itself from a problem common to many by erecting a barrier against the movement of interstate trade, by imposing on out-of-state commercial interests the full burden of conserving New Jersey's remaining landfill space.

The New Jersey statute cannot be likened to a quarantine law which bans importation of articles of commerce because of their innate harmfulness and not because of their origin. Though New Jersey concedes that out-of-state waste is no different from domestic waste, it has banned the former while leaving its landfill sites open to the latter, thus trying to saddle those outside the State with the entire burden of slowing the flow of wastes into New Jersey's remaining landfill sites.

46/   11 ERC 1770, 437 U.S. 617 (U.S. Sup. Ct. 1978).

It is interesting to note that the U.S. Court of Appeals upheld the constitutionality of the Chicago ordinance banning the sale of detergents containing phosphates. 47/ A similar result favorable to the legislation was reached when the famous Oregon "Bottle Bill" was upheld as not being such an interference with interstate commerce as to violate the Commerce Clause. 48/

14.2 "Bottle Bills"

For the past several years, the issue of legislation and regulations of beverage containers has been discussed at many public levels throughout the U.S. On the state level the Aluminum Association claims that over 1,000 container bills have been introduced in state legislatures since 1969. Several dozen local proposals to restrict beverage containers have also been introduced.

The key legislation on the state level has been the Oregon "Bottle Bill" which was passed on October 1, 1972. This Oregon law provides that all beer and soft drink containers sold in the state are required to carry refund values of 2 or 5 cents. Cans with pull-tab openers were banned outright. Disagreement continues over the effectiveness of the "Oregon type" legislation. Among the industry and labor arguments are that if this type of legislation becomes popular it will cause unemployment among producers of disposables and force the creation of regional industries rather than nationwide industries.

Citizens of Colorado, Maine, Massachusetts and Michigan voted on similar proposals in 1976. Michigan and Maine voted to follow the Oregon lead. Colorado and Massachusetts rejected the concept. On the Federal level numerous bills have been introduced but with no success. This area seems to be charged with emotionalism on both sides of the argument and what will happen in the future is anyone's guess.

14.3 Solid Waste Facility Siting

The history of citizen resistance to the siting of solid waste facilities is extensive and consistent. Such opposition is the nearly-unbroken rule rather than the exception. A number of communities have been unable to overcome citizen opposition to the siting of a landfill or other solid waste management facility. This opposition is not usually centered upon erroneous or disputed data regarding the adequacy of the proposed facility with respect to public health or

---

47/   Procter & Gamble v. Chicago, 7 ERC 1328 (7th Cir. 1975).

48/   American Can Co. v. Oregon Liquor Control Commission, 517 P2d 691, 4 ERC 1584 (Ore. Cir. Ct. 1973).

adequacy of the proposed facility with respect to public health or the environment. It is not a legal or regulatory problem—although sometimes, so characterized. It instead demonstrates an educational and attitudinal problem which solid waste management officials will find to be a pivotal constraint and issue in developing solutions to current problems of solid waste facility siting.

15.0 Prospectus

Passage of RCRA marked the start of a new era for management of hazardous and solid waste disposal and development of resource recovery systems. However, the implementation of RCRA is not going to be accomplished in a few years. This is a program that will undoubtedly occupy the attention of concerned people in government and out of government for the foreseeable future.

Chapter 6

TOXIC SUBSTANCES

Marshall Lee Miller
Attorney
Reid & Priest
Washington, DC

1.0 Introduction

The problem of hazardous chemicals, including pesticides, is acquiring increasing importance with the public realization that thousands of carcinogenic (cancer-causing), teratogenic (birth defect-causing) and mutagenic (genetic-damaging) substances are present in our environment. Both the World Health Organization and the National Cancer Institute estimate that between 60 and 90 percent of cancers are environmentally induced. 1/ The Toxic Substances Control Act (TSCA) of 1976 provides EPA with authority to require testing of chemical substances, both new and old, entering the environment and to regulate them where necessary. This authority supplements sections of existing toxic substances laws, such as Section 112 of the Clean Air Act, 2/ Section 307 of the Water Act, 3/ and Section 6 of the Occupational Safety and Health Act, 4/ which already provide regulatory control over toxic substances.

1/   See for example, WHO Reports on Cancer, cited in In Re Shell, 6 ERC 2047, 2051. The term "environment," of course, encompasses a wide range of possible exposures from industrial chemicals to food and cosmic radiation.

2/   Clean Air Act, 42 U.S.C. § 1857 et seq., PL 91-604 (1970).

3/   Federal Water Pollution Control Act, 33 U.S.C. § 1251 et seq. PL 92-500 (1972).

4/   29 U.S.C. § 651 et seq., PL 91-596, 84 Stat. 1950 (1970).

2.0 Problem of Unregulated Chemicals

Prior to the passage of the Toxic Substances Control Act of 1976, there was no general federal requirement that the thousands of new chemicals developed each year be tested for their potential environmental or health effects before they were introduced into commerce.   An estimated two million chemical compounds have been recognized, with some 250,000 additional substances now being developed each year. 5/ While most such chemicals never reach the market, EPA calculates that approximately a thousand of these new chemicals will be produced annually in commercial quantities.   Of these, only a fraction are subject to mandatory testing requirements under the Pesticide Act (FIFRA) or the Food, Drug and Cosmetic Act (FDCA). 6/

Recent tragic experiences illustrate the hazards of this lack of testing. In the late 1960's, there arose national concern over the widespread contamination of food, water, and soil by certain highly toxic compounds of organic mercury. By 1972 the government had authority (under the Clean Air Act and the Federal Water Pollution Control Act) to control direct emissions of mercury into the environment, but there was no federal authority to require testing of the effects of various mercuric compounds or to regulate the multiple uses of mercury in industrial, commercial, and consumer products.

Another episode in the early 1970's involved polycholorinated biphenyls (PCBs), used in such diverse applications as printing inks and hydraulic fluids. PCBs are similar to DDT, Aldrin-Dieldrin, and other chlorinated hydrocarbons in their pervasiveness and persistence in the environment and in their suspected carcinogenicity.

A host of other chemicals have also received recent public attention. A partial list includes asbestos, lead (including tetraethyl lead), arsenic, fluorocarbons (freon), nitrosamines, methyl butyl ketone, cadmium, and fluorides.

Vinyl chloride was involved in one of the most publicized episodes. In January 1975, a link was confirmed between worker exposure to vinyl choride monomer (VCM) and a rare form of cancer, angiosarcoma of the liver. Except for the extreme rarity of this

---

5/   New York Times, 8 July 1975.

6/   Only three federal statutes give the government authority to require chemical manufacturers to test their products. They are the Federal Insecticide, Fungicide and Rodenticide Act, as amended (7 U.S.C. § 135 et seq.), dealing with pesticides: the Federal Food, Drug and Cosmetic Act, (21 U.S.C. § 321 et seq.) requiring testing of drugs and food additives: and Section 211 of the Clean Air Act (42 U.S.C. § 1857 et seq.), providing authority to require testing of fuel additives.

disease and the unusual number of workers in whom it was found, the carcinogenic properties of VCM might have remained undetected. Medical experts now fear that it may also result in damage to the brain and other key organs. An OSHA standard in 1975 set a permissible limit at one part per million (1 ppm) but not before three decades of workers had been exposed to levels as high as several hundred parts per million. 7/

The incident which contributed directly to the passage of TSCA was the discovery in mid-1975 that workers in a small Virginia manufacturing plant had sustained severe neurological and reproductive damage from exposure to the chemical Kepone. Federal and state health agencies were widely criticized for failure to prevent this tragedy. The head of one agency responded, "We could accomplish a great deal if we were able to keep track of what toxic chemicals are entering our environment. Toxic substances legislation . . . is therefore an important need." 8/   While Kepone may not actually be a good example of this need (as a pesticide, it had long been screened and registered with EPA), the national attention engendered by such tragedies finally prodded Congress to enact the Toxic Substances Control Act.

3.0 The Need for a Toxic Substances Control Act

Prior to the passage of the Toxic Substances Act, significant gaps existed in the federal government's authority to test and regulate problem chemicals. The Clean Air Act, the Federal Water Pollution Control Act, and other laws dealt with chemical substances only when they entered the environment as wastes (emissions to the air or discharges to the water). In many cases controls could not be easily fashioned or required without severe economic consequences. Toxic substances legislation, which provides testing well before a chemical reaches the production phase, overcomes this difficulty.

Other statutes, such as the Occupational Safety and Health Act and the Consumer Product Safety Act, deal only with one phase of the chemical's existence (worker exposure or direct consumer

---

7/   OSHA "Vinyl Chloride Standard," 29 CFR 1910, 1017. This was upheld unanimously by the Court of Appeals in Society of Plastics Industry v. U.S. Dept. of Labor, 509 F. 2d 131 (2nd Cir. 1975); and the Supreme Court denied certiorari, sub. nom. Firestone Plastics Co. v. U.S. Dept. of Labor, 95 S. Ct. 1998 (1975).

8/   Testimony of the Assistant Secretary of Labor for OSHA before a Subcommittee of the Senate Committee on Agriculture and Forestry (2 February 1976).

exposure) and contain no authority to address environmental hazards. While both of these statutes are clearly needed, the life cycle of a chemical, from production to ultimate disposal, provides many opportunities for its escape into the environment and human exposure, and federal authority to deal with the overall cycle is fragmented. The Toxic Substances Control Act is designed to fill these gaps, both in regulatory powers and authority to require that tests be conducted before the human or environmental exposure occurs.

4.0 Legislative Background

In 1970 the President's Council on Environmental Quality (CEQ) recommended that the Administrator of EPA be empowered "to restrict the use or distribution of any substance which he finds is hazardous to human health or to the environment." 9/ This was incorporated in the President's Message to Congress on the Environment in February 1971. 10/ Both the House and Senate passed toxic substances bills during the 92nd Congress, but the House acted too late in the session to permit a resolution of the differences between the two bills. In the 93rd Congress, both houses approved toxic substances legislation, but were unable to reach a compromise in conference.

The 94th Congress, beginning January 1975, considered a variety of toxic substances legislative proposals. A bill similar to that passed by the Senate in the previous Congress was introduced as S.776 by Senators John V. Tunney (D-Cal.), Philip Hart (D-Mich.) and Warren Magnuson (D-Wash.). After considerable debate, the Senate Committee on Commerce reported out a modified bill, S.3149, which incorporated many of the basic principles of S.776 but in a substantially redrafted form. This bill was passed by the Senate on 26 March 1975, by a vote of 60-13, with only three significant amendments.

Three different bills were introduced in the House. One, H.R.7229, sponsored by Congressman Robert Eckhardt (D-Tex.), was reported with amendments from the Subcommittee on Commerce and Finance to the full House Commerce Committee. The Ford Administration, however, actively supported a more limited bill (H.R.12336) sponsored by Representative John McCollister (R-Neb.). This bill resembled House-passed legislation of previous years and had the support of most of the chemical industry. A third bill, introduced by Rep. William Broadhead (D-Mich.), was the most expansive of these and was supported by organizations such as Ralph

---

9/   See CEQ, Environmental Quality, August 1971, p. 306.

10/   Ibid., appendix F.

Nader's Health Research Group. The House passed a compromise
measure (H.R.14032) on 23 August 1976. 11/
On 28 September 1976, the House and Senate agreed on a
final version of the Toxic Substances Control Bill, which was enacted on 11 October 1976 and signed into law by the President. It
became effective, with one exception, on 1 January 1977. 12/

5.0 Toxic Substances Control Act of 1976
The Toxic Substances Control Act (TSCA) has two main
regulatory features:
First, acquisition of sufficient information by EPA to identify
and evaluate potential hazards from chemical substances;
Second, regulation of the production, use, distribution, and
disposal of such substances where necessary. The principal provisions of the Act are described in the following sections.

6.0 Premanufacture Notification—Statutory Provisions
The heart of TSCA is the requirement for premanufacture
notification (PMN). Under Section 5 a manufacturer must notify
EPA ninety days before producing a new chemical substance, defined
as any chemical not listed on a specially compiled inventory list
(discussed later). Notification is also necessary even for older
chemicals, already on that list, if the Administrator concludes that
there is a significant new use which increases human or environmental exposure. 13/ In either case, EPA may extend the notification processing period by an additional ninety days, but the

---

11/ See H.R. 94-1341, accompanying H.R.14032, and the
Conference Report at 94-1679; S.R. 94-698 and the Senate
Conference Report, 94-1302.

12/ The exception is Section 4(f), which takes effect two years
later. Actually, without implementing regulations, none of
the sections had immediate force on 1 January 1977 except
for Section 8(e) requiring the reporting of significant adverse
effects.

13/ TSCA § 5(a). The criteria the Administrator must consider
for a new use determination ("SNUR"—Significant New Use
Regulation) include the expected production volume, increased quantity or duration of human and environmental
exposure, and hazards of manufacturing and distribution.

reasons for requiring longer consideration may be challenged in court. 14/

Many companies may wish to notify EPA well before the ninety day period in order to forestall last-minute delays in marketing. There are disadvantages to this, however: Competitors will thereby be tipped off to the company's marketing plans, and EPA has warned that PMN data submitted too far in advance may be rejected as lacking sufficient certainty of the ultimate intention to manufacture.

Within five days of receiving the notice, EPA must publish in the Federal Register an item identifying the chemical substance, listing its intended uses, and a description of the toxicological tests required to demonstrate that there will be no "unreasonable risk of injury to health or the environment." 15/

If the Administrator decides that the data submitted is "insufficient to permit a reasoned evaluation" and that the chemical may pose a risk to man or the environment, he may restrict or even prohibit any aspect of the chemical's production or distribution. Such an order, however, must be issued no later than 45 days before the expiration of the notification period, meaning that the Agency must respond very quickly. The manufacturer then has 30 days to submit specific objections to the order. 16/

Finally, for those chemicals on the priority list for which special testing is required, the Administrator is required to publish in the Federal Register his reason for not taking action to limit production and use, before the end of notification period. 17/

By statute, Section 5 was to take effect thirty days after the publication of the inventory list, which was due in November 1977. Since this did not occur until the summer of 1979, implementation of the manufacturing notification requirements was long delayed.

14/   TSCA § 5(c). Such a challenge is subject to the disclosure restrictions of Section 14.

15/   TSCA §§ 6(d) and 5(d)(2). The five days exclude weekends and legal holidays, the name of the company itself need not be disclosed in the FR, but EPA will make it available upon request.

16/   TSCA § 5(e)(1). This description, although complex, is nevertheless an oversimplification.

17/   TSCA § 5(g). This publication, however, is not a prerequisite for the production or marketing of the product.

6.1 Proposed PMN Regulations

In January 1979, EPA proposed voluminous PMN regulations, 18/ which required not only the submission of data specified by Congress in Section 5(d) but also extensive reporting and record-keeping derived presumably from Section 8. The proposed requirements would include complete flow charts of the production process, a risk assessment of production and distribution, certification that processors and consumers have been notified regarding the chemical's properties, detailed information on hourly emissions and effluents, and approximately 110 pages of forms with other requirements. 19/

The EPA-commissioned Arthur D. Little, Inc., study on the economic burden of complying with the proposed PMN regulations estimated that the paperwork alone would cost from $2500 to $41,000, depending on the assumptions. Preparation would also require hundreds of hours, exclusive of the still unknown testing costs. The report concluded that at $10,000 per chemical for PMN, half of the new chemicals normally introduced each year would not be released. At $40,000, 90% would not be introduced. 20/ The effects on small companies, which are responsible for a disproportionate amount of chemical innovation, 21/ would be disasterous if they are not granted some relief. 22/ The irony is that the original EPA estimates on PMN costs, made before passage of the Act, were

---

18/   44 FR 2242, 10 January 1979.

19/   See also EPA, "Explanatory Appendix: Premanufacture Notice Forms", January 1979; "Support Document: Premanufacture Notification Requirements and Review Procedures", January 1979; and "TSCA: Questions and Answers on the Proposed PMN Regulations", February 1979.

20/   EPA, "Impact of TSCA Proposed PMN Requirements", December 1978, p. 13.

21/   Ibid, p. III-18.

22/   Statement of Ervin Colton, CERAC Inc. of Milwaukee, at EPA PMN hearing 13 February 1979, p.5. The definition of small business in the proposal was annual sales of one million dollars, compared with five million under Section 8. Also, the one thousand pound presumption for exempt R & D was dropped entirely under the proposed Section 5 regulations.

negligible. They assumed that companies would be required to submit information which most would have available anyway. 23/

In October 1979, EPA responded to public criticism of its voluminous notification regulations by issuing a new PMN proposal. 24/ This eliminated or made optional many previous Agency demands for "a considerable amount of information that is not related to EPA's decision-making." EPA claimed this revised rule would reduce mandatory PMN compliance costs to a $1200 - $8900 range per chemical, provided neither health questions nor confidentiality was raised. Despite requests, the October reproposal again did not provide special treatment for low-volume substances of, say, less than one metric ton a year, but EPA did specifically request additional comments on this issue. An exemption from supplementary reporting was provided for small business, defined as companies with annual sales below one million dollars, 25/ and they were promised extra latitude in answering many of the PMN information forms with "not available."

No final PMN regulations have yet been issued.

6.2 Interim PMN Policy

In November 1980, just after the presidential election, the Carter Administration published a revised interim policy to be followed until final rules were promulgated. 26/ With the advent of the Reagan Administration, a much-simplified PMN procedure was promised that would minimize the burden on the reporting industries, but this shorter version did not prove any easier to prepare. As of early 1983, no final regulation has yet appeared.

Meanwhile companies are complying with Section 5 as best they can, given EPA's shifting attitudes. This means submitting a notification and hoping the Agency will not find it inadequate in whole or in part.

23/   Letter from Gary H. Baise, Director of EPA's Office of Legislation, to Senator John V. Tunney (D-Calif.), no date but approximately June 1973, reprinted in Senate Commerce Committee Report No. 93-254 on S.426, pp. 50-51.

24/   44 FR 59764, October 1979.

25/   The figure under Section 8(b) was five times higher, while under 8(a) a proposal set the level as thirty million.

26/   45 F.R. 74378, 7 November 1980.

6.3 Proposed Testing Guidelines Under Section 5

In March 1979, EPA issued proposed guidelines for testing under Section 5. 27/ Although TSCA's testing rules are to be issued under Section 4, EPA took this additional step because of widespread industry concern that Section 5(e) might be used to delay production indefinitely. Under that section, the Administrator is empowered to seek an injunction to prevent the manufacture or distribution of a substance for which data is insufficient and from which there might be an unreasonable risk. Producers therefore wished to know what data EPA would regard as sufficient. Their concern was heightened by a provision in the proposed PMN regulation that the 90-day clock would stop on a notice found to be deficient in some respect. 28/ Despite Agency denials, many companies feared that this was an imaginative loophole created to extend the statutory 90/180-day notice period and thereby to convert the process into a certification program akin to FIFRA or FDA.

6.4 PMN Exemption: Section 5(h)(4)

The statute provides that the Administration can exempt a manufacturer of a new substance from all or part of PMN if he decides that its production, distribution, use, and disposal "will not present an unreasonable risk of injury to health or the environment." 29/

In 1980, Polaroid requested EPA for a blanket exemption on minor changes made from time to time in the formulation of instant photographic film. 30/ After similar requests from other companies, prolonged debate, and an initial rejection of the exemption by the White House's Office of Management and Budget (OMB) as too restrictive, 31/ the Agency finally approved the first Section 5(h)(4) exemption in a rule published in June 1982. 32/

In July 1982, in response to industry petitions, EPA proposed other rules under Section 5(h)(4) which would exempt about half of

---

27/   44 FR 16240, 16 March 1979.

28/   44 FR 2242 at 2272, proposing 40 CFR § 720.34.

29/   TSCA § 5(h)(4).

30/   See BNA, Chemical Reporter (17 October 1980), p. 913.

31/   Ibid, 23 October 1981, p. 803; 30 October 1981, p. 819.

32/   47 FR 24308, 4 June 1982.

all new chemicals produced in the U.S. 33/ They would provide that manufacture of certain polymers, chemicals used solely at the plant site, and low volume chemicals (defined generally by the companies as 25 thousand pounds anually). 34/ For chemicals produced in volumes under one thousand kilos a year, only a brief notice need be submitted to EPA under the polymer exemption proposal: namely, manufacturer's name, location, chemical identity, and the polymer's molecular weight; another category of polymers, those produced in quantities of between one thousand and ten thousand kilograms annually, would have to submit somewhat more information for an abbreviated 14-day PMN. Environmentalists, such as the NRDC predictably reacted with alarm to the proposals. 35/

6.5 Significant New Use Regulations (SNURs)
Although commonly forgotten, Section 5's PMN requirements apply not only to new chemicals but to significant new uses of existing chemicals or even an appreciable increase in their utilization for an existing purpose. According to Section 5(a)(2), relevant factors include:

(A)   the projected volume of manufacturing and processing of a chemical substance,
(B)   the extent to which a use changes the type or form of exposure of human beings or the environment to a chemical substance,
(C)   the extent to which a use increases the magnitude and duration of exposure of human beings or the environment to a chemical substance, and
(D)   the reasonably anticipated manner and methods of manufacturing, processing, distribution in commerce, and disposal of a chemical substance.

33/   47 FR 32609, 28 July 1982.

34/   Section 26 provides that action taken for a single chemical may also be taken for a group; so, to grant a broad Section 5(h)(4) exemption, EPA must follow the rulemaking procedures of TSCA § 6(c)(2) and (3). Within five days of receipt EPA under Section 5(d)(2) must publish in the Federal Register, subject to Section 14 provisions on confidentiality, information on the new substance and its uses. Section 5(c) allows a 90-day extension period, if necessary for good cause, subject to section 5(e) and (f) regulatory triggers.

35/   BNA, Chemical Reporter (30 July 1982), p. 555.

Determining when a use is a new one, especially for a chemical already having scores of applications, can be difficult. EPA found that drafting rules concerning a multitude of such situations was even harder than anticipated. After several unsuccessful attempts, the Agency decided to issue SNURs on an ad hoc basis. Then, after a pattern perhaps developed, regulations could be prepared.

EPA therefore examined approximately thirty different chemicals with purported new uses, and on 19 November 1980 issued its first SNUR on N-methanesulfonyl-p-toluenesulfonamide. Despite evidence of some adverse effects, exposure was considered minimal because annual production for this use was only four hundred pounds a year. The manufacturer was required to give the Agency 90-days notice if it should increase production over one thousand pounds (450 kg) a year or change the use. 36/

The significance of its first SNUR was muted, however, by the accompanying explanation from senior EPA officials, such as Deputy Assistant Administrator Warren Muir, that it was not a good example of what they expected in future SNURs. This uniqueness was reinforced when the incoming Reagan Administration indicated its own misgivings about the program. Referring to the candidates for SNUR, Muir's successor, Don Clay, expressed doubt that most of the hundred then suggested were actually sufficiently hazardous enough to warrant special treatment; perhaps Section 8(a) reporting requirements (discussed below) might be more appropriate. 37/ The Chemical Manufacturers Association (CMA) favors this latter approach. 38/

For whatever reason, EPA still has done little to implement Section 5(a), either by general rule or on a substance-by-substance basis.

6.6 Rejection of PMNs

In December 1979, EPA rejected its first PMN because of inadequate information concerning production volume, disposal methods, and other essentials. The company, which EPA declined to identify, responded that it had assumed only the facts set forth in Section 5(d)(2) were needed. 39/ The reply is unconvincing because Section 5(d)(1) specifying the data required refers directly to the information listed in Section 8(a)(2).

36/   BNA, Chemical Reporter (28 November 1980), p. 1105.

37/   E.g., ibid, 18 September 1981, p. 555.

38/   Ibid., 8 January 1982, p. 1045; 26 February 1982, p. 1223.

39/   BNA, Chemical Reporter, (4 January 1980), p. 1557.

EPA officials lamented the scarcity of information provided in the early PMNs but, as already discussed, preferred to deal with the problem on ad hoc basis. 40/ For example, the Agency would review the submitted toxicological data and, after critical remarks, would induce the affected company to withdraw its notification, either permanently or pending further submissions or tests. 41/

A more formalistic procedure is provided in the lengthy Sections 5(e) and (f) of the Act. If the Administrator determines that there could be environmental risk and that the information provided is inadequate to make a "reasoned evaluation," he may prohibit chemical production. 42/ If the Agency decides that there is an actual indication of hazard, rather than simply insufficient evidence to rebut, Section 5(f) provides that it may prohibit, limit, or otherwise restrict production or use, as set forth in various portions of Section 6. 43/

The first Section 5(e) notice, announced in April 1980, proposed delaying the manufacture of six new but questionable chemicals. The firm dropped its manufacturing plans shortly thereafter. 44/ In September 1980, EPA issued another order to block production of a new chemical pending development of additional information on its human health rules. 45/ That has been the pattern, and to date no manufacturer, foreign 46/ or domestic, has contested the determinations in federal district court, as permitted in Section 5(f). 47/

It is still not clear under the law what happens next, for the statute is ambiguous, there are as yet no court decisions, and the legislative history offers two inconsistent views. Senator Warren Magnuson (D-Wash.) explained that the House-Senate compromise

---

40/   Ibid, 25 January 1980, p. 1636.

41/   See, for example, ibid., 14 November 1980, p. 1057.

42/   TSCA § 5(e).

43/   TSCA § 5(f), esp. (f)(2) referring to TSCA §§ 6(a) and 6(d)(2)(B).

44/   BNA, Chemical Reporter (25 April 1980), pg. 91.

45/   BNA, Chemical Reporter (5 September 1980), p. 753.

46/   BNA, Chemical Reporter (16 October 1981), p. 787.

47/   TSCA § 5(f)(3)(B).

language here was based on procedure in the FDA law, 48/ whereby
the Agency could determine if the objections had merit: "If the
Administrator determines that valid objections have been filed, then
he is required either to seek an injunction or to dismiss the order. If
he decides that the objections are not reasonable, then the proposed
order becomes effective upon the expiration of the premarket
notification." 49/   Rep. James T. Broyhill (R-N.C.), on the other
hand, informed the House that a company objection, no matter how
frivolous, blocks the effect of the Administrator's order and forces
him to resort to a federal district court for injunctive relief. 50/

When EPA concludes that there is sufficient information to
classify a chemical as an unreasonable risk, it may issue a proposed
order restricting manufacture, processing, or distribution. It may
also directly seek an injunction which, like the above procedure for
insufficient data, is also necessary if a company challenges the
prospective order. 51/

7.0 Inventory List: Section 8(b)

Because the notification rules apply primarily to new chemical substances, there must be a list available of pre-existing chemicals. Under Section 8(b), EPA is therefore required to compile an
inventory of chemicals manufactured or processed in the United
States. This does not cover every chemical ever produced but is
limited to those substances produced within the three-year period
preceding the promulgation of applicable regulations, namely since 1
January 1975. 52/

The statute required that this list be prepared and published
"not later than 315 days after the effective date of this Act." This

---

48/   Food, Drug, and Cosmetic Act § 701(e); See also Pfizer v.
        Richardson, 434 F. 2d 536 (2nd Cir. 1970).

49/   122 Congressional Record 16803.   28 September 1976: See
        TSCA § 5(e)(2).   The Senate interpretation seems more
        consistent with the actual language of the Act and is probably
        the approach which EPA will adopt.

50/   Ibid., H-11344.

51/   TSCA § 5(f). See also the section in this chapter on Enforce-
        ment, Part 11.0.

52/   TSCA § 8(b). The regulations according to Section 8(a) were
        supposed to have appeared 180 days after the effective date
        or 1 July 1977. However, they were signed on 12 December
        1977 effective 1 July 1978.

11 November 1977 deadline proved far too optimistic for the inventory reporting regulations were not even published until late December 1977, six weeks later. 53/ This gave chemical companies until 1 May 1978 to submit their products for inclusion in the inventory, finally scheduled for publication in June 1979. 54/ Processors and importers had an additional 210 days to report any other chemicals, and only after was that a final revised inventory list published. 55/ This process thus turned into a rather lengthy one, which consequently, considerably delayed the implementation of other parts of the Act, particularly premarket notification. 56/

Any substance not reported for the Inventory by 30 August 1980 must undergo premanufacture review before it may be manufactured or imported for a commercial purpose. This applies even if a producer can demonstrate that a substance was, in fact, produced before then. The converse, however, does not hold true: EPA has

---

53/   42 FR 64572, 23 December 1977. Regulations were first proposed on 9 March 1977 (42 FR 13130) and after modification were reproposed on 2 August 1977 (42 FR 39182).

54/   Some manufacturers complained that EPA itself should have compiled the basic inventory list and then asked chemical companies only to fill in any gaps. This proposal was rejected as infeasible. See, e.g. Appendix A, Comment 2, 42 FR 64580.

55/   42 FR 64572, 23 December 1977.

56/   EPA published inventory reporting regulations on 23 December 1977 (42 FR 64572) and supplemented them on 6 March 1978 (43 FR 9254) and on 17 April 1978 (43 FR 16178). In October 1978 (43 FR 49688), a policy for revised inventory reporting was published. Then, in May 1979, distribution of the initial inventory list, containing over 44,000 chemical substances, began.

A second inventory reporting period lasting 210 days began on 1 June 1979. During this period, a person who processes or uses a chemical substance for a commercial purpose or imports a chemical substance as part of a mixture or article may report a chemical substance that was not included on the published Initial Inventory, if the substance was manufactured, processed, or imported for a commercial purpose since 1 January 1975. The notice of availability of a cumulative supplement and revised inventory was published in the Federal Register on 29 July 1980 (45 FR 5544).

removed from the list certain substances, notably ones involved in synthetic fuels, which it claims were improperly registered as commercial products, and hence "grandfathered," when in fact they were only in research and development at the time. 57/

The obligation to report does not extend to all companies dealing with chemical substances. By regulation, EPA limits this to manufacturers and others with (a) over thirty percent (by weight) of their products classified under SIC code categories 28 or 2911; 58/ or (b) the total chemical production or importation exceeding one million pounds; or (c) special reporting for any substances produced in quantities over a hundred thousand pounds at one site in 1977. 59/

Small manufacturers, defined in the regulations under Section 8 as those with total sales less than five million dollars, were given a limited exemption from some of the reporting requirements. 60/ They were required to submit a list of substances produced but did not need to give production volumes, except for chemicals produced in excess of a hundred thousand pounds, nor separate volume figures for each plant site. This rather trivial exemption is not available to small companies owned or controlled by a larger, non-eligible company. 61/

Another exemption is for chemical substances produced in "small quantities for purposes of scientific experimentation or analysis or chemical research." The regulation declares a legal presumption that any chemical produced in a quantity of under a thousand pounds annually is for research and development and may therefore not be reported on the inventory, unless the producer can

---

57/   BNA, Chemical Reporter (7 August 1981), p. 428; (18 June 1982, p. 390).

58/   40 CFR § 710.3(a). SIC is the abbreviation for "Standard Industrial Classification."

59/   As elsewhere in the Act, production includes manufacturing, processing, or importing.

60/   For Section 5 purposes, however, EPA initially proposed defining small business by total sales of less than one million dollars, 44 FR 2242, 10 January 1979.

61/   40 CFR § 710.2(x). The original Section 8 proposal defined small business as a company having total sales under a hundred thousand dollars. 42 FR 39191 (2 August 1977), EPA officials later confided that this unreasonably low figure was never really serious.

demonstrate otherwise. 62/ A subsequent EPA regulation attempted to clarify this question by suggesting that a manufacturer request his customers to certify that a chemical is not used for purposes other than R & D. 63/

A third exclusion is for "mixtures" which are not considered to be "chemical substances" under Section 8(b). A mixture is defined as any combination of substances which is not the result of chemical reaction and which does not occur in nature. 64/ Remember, however, that mixtures are only excluded from some of the requirements of TSCA; they may still be subject, for example, to the provisions of Sections 4 and 5. 65/

Also exempt from inventory requirements are naturally occuring substances, tobacco, food and food additives, and other chemicals such as drugs and pesticides which are regulated under other federal environmental acts. 66/

The essential point is, however, that exclusion from the inventory reporting requirements was a mixed blessing. Since placing a substance on the list "grandfathered" it from future PMN requirements, except for significant new uses, it was obviously a benefit for a producer or processor to have everything possible in the inventory.

EPA intends periodically to update the inventory list to include products for which notification forms have been submitted. The most recent compilation, listing 58,000 substances, was released in June 1982. Future manufacturers can therefore consult the

---

62/   40 CFR § 710.2(y). Section 8(b) of the Statute says, "The Administrator shall not include in such list any chemical substance which is manufactured only in small quantities (as defined by the Administrator by rule) solely for purposes of scientific experimentation or analysis of, such substance or other substance, including such research or analysis for the development of a product."

63/   43 FR 9254, 9255, 6 March 1978.

64/   TSCA §§ 3 and 8(b). See also 122 Congressional Record H-11020 (23 September 1976).

65/   TSCA §§ 4(a) and 5(a).

66/   The general exemptions from the definition of "chemical substance" under the Act are set forth in § 3(2)(B). EPA has issued several further clarifications on inventory coverage, such as for natural gas streams (43 FR 16178, 17 April 1978) and natural latex (43 FR 9254, 6 March 1978).

revised list and know that no futher notification to EPA is required, unless special testing under Section 4 is necessary.

8.0 Reporting Requirements

8.1 Section 8(a)

Under Section 8(a) of TSCA, the Administrator must promulgate rules under which each person who "manufactures or processes or proposes to manufacture or process a chemical substance" must keep records and make reports to the Administrator as is deemed necessary for the effective enforcement of the Act. The Administrator may require such information as molecular structure, categories of use, amounts produced, description of by-products, disposal methods, and all existing data concerning the environment and health effects of each substance. Manufacturers and processors are persons who manufacture or process chemicals for "commercial purposes."

Section 8 generally exempts small manufacturers or processors from the provisions but they may be subject under certain circumstances. 67/ In the case of manufacturers or processors of mixtures or of small quantities of research and development chemicals, reports and records may be required to the extent "necessary for the enforcement of this Act."

8.2 Proposed 8(a) Regulation, 1980

Rules governing Section 8(a) were to be promulgated no later than 180 days after TSCA went into effect. However, the proposed rules were not published until 29 February 1980, 68/ more than 2 1/2 years after the deadline for final rules.

The proposal required chemical manufacturers, including miners and importers, and some processors to report production and exposure-related data on approximately 2300 chemicals, chosen because of toxicity or exposure levels. EPA intended to use this data for preliminary risk assessment and for ranking chemicals.

The proposed rules contained two phases of reporting. First, manufacturers and importers of the chemicals listed had to answer several questions including questions on customer use. Second, if they were unable to report customer use, EPA could require customers to submit information.

67/   Section 8(a)(3)(A)(ii).

68/   45 FR 13646.

Under the Section 8(a) proposal, small manufacturers are defined as:

(1)   total sales for all products at all sites together of less than $30 million for the reportable year, and

(2)   production volume at each site for the chemical reported less than 100,000 pounds (45,400 kilograms) for the reportable year.

In October 1980, EPA proposed a generic small business reporting exemption under Section 8(a). This eliminated all record-keeping requirements for qualifying companies, unless they planned to manufacture or process (a) a substance subject to a Section 4 testing rule, (discused below), (b) a substance categorized as an unreasonable risk under Section 5(b)(4), or (c) a restriction substance under Section 6, or (d) one subject to a Section 5(e) rule for additional testing information. 69/

In a planned subsequent rulemaking, the Agency wanted to propose Section 8(a) reporting rules for the follow-up of selected new chemicals after they had passed through the PMN process.

8.3 Section 8(a) Final Regulations

The final Section 8(a) regulation, when issued in June 1982 70/ cut the reporting list down drastically from almost 2,300 to only around 245 chemicals. Manufacturers must report production, release and exposure data, which will then be used to determine which chemicals deserved further testing.

EPA also published concurrently a 3-part proposed rule under Section 8(a), requiring processors to report on the listed 250 chemicals whenever the manufacturers' reports fail to account for use of 80% of the substance. The proposal added another fifty chemicals for consideration for inclusion in the final list. 71/

8.4 Reporting of Health and Safety Studies: Section 8(d)

Section 8(d) requires the Administrator to promulgate rules requiring any person who manufactures, processes, or distributes in

---

69/   45 FR 66180, 6 October 1980.

70/   47 FR 26992, 22 June 1982.

71/   47 FR 26992, 22 June 1982; BNA Chemical Reporter 25 June 1982, pp. 412 and 423ff; 2 April 1982, p. 3.

commerce any chemical substance or mixture to submit to the Administrator

    (1)   lists of health and safety studies (A) conducted or initiated by or for such person with respect to such substance or mixture at any time, (B) known to such person, or (C) reasonably ascertainable by such person, except that the Administrator may exclude certain types or categories of studies from the requirements of this subsection if the Administration finds that submission of lists of such studies are unnecessary to carry out the purposes of this Act; and

    (2)   copies of any study contained on a list submitted pursuant to paragraph (1) or otherwise known by such person. 72/

In July 1978 EPA promulgated rules governing this subsection of TSCA 73/ requiring manufacturers, processors, or persons distributing in commerce the chemicals on the first Interagency Testing Committee priority list to submit lists and copies of health and safety studies on those chemicals. 74/

The Manufacturing Chemists Association filed a petition requesting EPA to amend or repeal the rule in September 1978. EPA rejected the petition, with minor exceptions. 75/

On 15 September 1978, the Dow Chemical Company filed a petition for review of the rule in the U.S. Court of Appeals for the Third Circuit, questioning EPA's authority to obtain studies on chemicals manufactured or processed for research and development purposes, since it was claimed such chemicals are not manufactured or processed for "commercial purposes", or on chemicals from companies that do not manufacture, process or distribute those chemicals. In addition, Dow asserted that EPA had not provided adequate notice and fair opportunity to comment on some of the provisions of the rule.

72/   TSCA § 8(d)(1) and 8(d)(2).

73/   43 FR 30984, 18 July 1978.

74/   Two minor corrections were made to the rule shortly thereafter (43 FR 36249, 16 August 1978 and 43 FR 41205, 15 September 1978).

75/   43 FR 56724, 4 December 1978.

Although the Court denied Dow's challenge of EPA's authority on 24 August 1979 76/ and EPA itself had no doubt that the provisions of the rule were within the Agency's statutory authority, EPA decided that Dow had raised substantial questions on whether adequate notice and comment were provided with respect to some provisions of the rule. Therefore the rule was revoked on 31 January 1979. 77/

A new proposed rule was published in the Federal Register on 31 December 1979 78/ requiring reporting of lists and copies of studies on all chemicals included in the 18 July rule, as well as additional chemicals recommended by the ITC and other chemicals separately selected by EPA. The Agency specifically requested comment on whether it should exercise authority to obtain copies of studies on substances from persons in possession of such studies whether or not they manufacture, process, or distribute the substances. The proposal also established an obligation to list on-going studies for five years after a chemical appears on the Section 8(d) list.

The final rule, which appeared in September 1982, 79/ after extensive public comment, somewhat reduced the reporting requirements set forth in the earlier rule.

First, the sweeping definitions of "known to" or in the "possession" of, were replaced with a procedural definition that would better indicate when an extensive search could be considered final, for purposes of the Act. Companies, henceforth, need only search "the company files in which they ordinarily keep studies and records kept by employees whose assigned duty is to advise the company on health and environmental effects of chemicals." 80/ This search may be limited to records developed after 31 December 1979, when the revised rule 8(d) was proposed.

However, companies which manufactured a chemical within the past ten years, even if they are not currently doing so, are obliged to submit copies of studies but need not provide lists of other known studies. This could be helpful where say, a company's research uncovered that one of its chemicals was potentially harmful and therefore discontinued it, although other manufacturers continued production unaware.

76/   Dow Chemical Co. v. EPA, 605 F. 2d 673 (3rd Cir. 1979).

77/   44 FR 6099.

78/   44 FR 77470.

79/   47 FR 38780, 2 September 1982 40 CFR Part 716.

80/   Ibid.

Distributors are exempted from Section 8(d) reporting by this revised regulation. They do not normally conduct studies anyway, and a review of all submissions under the provisions of the Section 8(d) rule indicated none were from distributors.

Also exempted were seven types of studies that the Agency had not found useful in assessing risks but which were burdensome to compile. These exceptions include studies of impurities (which would presumably exempt reports on hazardous dioxin impurities), published studies, and studies submitted previously to EPA or on non-confidential basis to another federal agency.

EPA declined, however, to retreat from its previous position that research and development studies are nevertheless "for commercial purposes" and therefore reportable. The Agency's contention had been judically approved, making a subsequent change more difficult. The final rule nevertheless relies on a different argument, namely that the purpose of Section 8(d) "is to give the Agency access to information from which it can assess the nature and significance of chemical hazards and risks. TSCA is intended to address these hazards and risks to health or the environment whether or not the chemicals are desired commercial products." 81/

8.5 Reports of Health and Safety Studies

Companies routinely test their chemical products for efficiency and safety. Section 8(d) directs that EPA issue rules requiring any person manufacturing, etc., a chemical to provide the Agency with copies of such health and safety studies. 82/ But the rule is broader than just that. If the company has copies of, knows of, or reasonably could ascertain that other experimental reports or studies exist regardless who performed or conducted them, it must also provide copies or lists of those reports. 83/

The Administrator is given the statutory authority to exclude certain categories of studies, however, if he determines they are "unnecessary to carry out the purposes of this Act." 84/

This seemingly straightforward section has been the source of considerable controversy. This included a query from a major industry-supported but independent testing lab which had important studies; since it was not a manufacturer, however, it contended it had no obligation under Section 8(d) to report them to EPA. (The information was, of course, provided to EPA in due course.)

81/   Ibid., p. 38781.

82/   TSCA § 8(d)(1)(A).

83/   TSCA § 8(d)(1)(B), (C), and 8(d)(2).

84/   TSCA § 8(d)(1)(C).

A chemical company challenged an obligation to report studies conducted for research and development on substances produced in small quantities and not offered for sale. The company contended that the statutory definition of "manufacture" under Section 8 meant "manufacture or process for commercial purposes" and that this excluded R & D. 85/ The Court of Appeals held, however, that Section 8(d) embraced such limited manufacture and, therefore, EPA was authorized to seek the data. 86/

In September 1982 EPA issued a final rule requiring companies to provide the Agency with unpublished studies. 87/ The specifically requested information on forty chemicals and chemical categories—39 recommended for Section 4(e) testing by the eight-agency Federal Interagency Testing Committee (ITC) through June 1981 (actually about 175 substances), plus asbestos added by EPA. 88/

At the same time, the Agency proposed adding another 65 chemicals more recently by the ITC. 89/

9.0 Hazard Reporting Requirements

9.1 Substantial Risk Notification: Section 8(e)

The sweeping general notification requirements of TSCA could swamp EPA with far more data than it could initially absorb. For the next few years, until comprehensive screening criteria are established, this could mean that information on potentially hazardous substances would languish unanalyzed in EPA files while some chemical tragedy occurs. Indeed, this suggests that notification—the key feature of the entire statute—may require a scientific sophistication that may not be developed for many years.

If health effects cannot be confidently predicted in advance, then EPA must learn of them as soon as they are discovered. Section 8(e) places upon chemical manufacturers, etc., the responsibility for reporting any indication of adverse effect. In the words of the Act, any person

> who obtains information which reasonably supports the conclusion that such substance or mixture presents a

---

85/   TSCA § 8(f).

86/   Dow Chemical Co. v. EPA, 605 F. 2nd 673 (3rd Cir. 1979).

87/   47 FR 38780, 2 September 1982.

88/   See this Chapter, Paragraph 10.3.

89/   47 FR 38800, 2 September 1982.

substantial risk of injury to health or the environment shall immediately inform the Administrator of such information unless such person has actual knowledge that the Administrator has been adequately informed of such information. 90/

Such a reporting requirement is not unprecedented. Section 6 of FIFRA has a similar provision for "factual information regarding unreasonable, adverse effects on the environment. 91/ However, FIFRA's use of the word "unreasonable" assumes, perhaps unrealistically, that the manufacturer himself will make an adverse risk-benefit analysis and then report it. TSCA insists that any evidence of "substantial risk" must be reported. Hard and unmistakable evidence is not required; instead any "information which reasonably supports the conclusion" of possible substantial risk must be reported. Failure to report may subject any individual or company to civil penalties and even criminal prosecution. 92/

EPA issued regulations implementing § 8(e) in March 1978. 93/ This placed upon corporation presidents and other top officials the responsibility for ensuring that adverse information is reported. 94/ The regulations state, however, that

> An employing organization may relieve its individual officers and employees of any responsibility for

---

90/   TSCA § 8(e).

91/   FIFRA § 6(a)(2).   A more formal system of five-year postmarket surveillance is suggested in the proposed FDA law revisions submitted to Congress in March 1978.   FDA Proposal § 108(g).

92/   TSCA §§ 15(3), 16, and 17. It is interesting to note that in the first major criminal case against a company (Velsicol) for failure to disclose adverse data on the pesticides chlordane and heptachlor, the Justice Department chose to use the general federal criminal laws rather than FIFRA § 6(a)(2).

93/   43 FR 11110, 16 March 1978.

94/   This is not an empty threat. The Supreme Court held that a chief executive officer was personally and criminally liable under federal health laws for not preventing rodent contamination of food in one of his warehouses, even though he had delegated responsibility to a corporate vice president. U.S. v. Park, 421 US 658 (1975); See also U.S. v. Dotterweich, 320 US 277 (1943).

reporting substantial-risk information directly to EPA by establishing, internally publicizing, and affirmatively implementing procedures for employee submission and corporate processing of pertinent information. 95/

In defining substantial risk, the regulation excludes from consideration the "economic or social benefits of use, or cost of restricting use." Moreover the regulation takes a strongly health protectionist view by directing that the extent of exposure is to be given little weight in assessing human health risks, since "the mere fact the implicated chemical is in commerce constitutes sufficient evidence of exposure." 96/

9.2 Significant Adverse Reactions: Section 8(c)
Under Section 8(c) of TSCA, any person who manufactures, etc., any chemical substance or mixture shall maintain records of "significant adverse reactions" alleged to have been caused by the chemical. Those records relating to possible health reactions of employees must be kept for thirty years, during which time they may be inspected by or submitted to anyone he designates. All other recorded allegations need be preserved for only five years.

A comparison of Section 8(c) indicates that both the standard of proof and the required response is appreciably lower than for Section 8(e).

	TSCA § 8(c)	TSCA § 8(e)
Trigger	"Significant" adverse reactions"	Substantial risk of injury"
Evidence	"Alleged"	"Information" which reasonably supports the conclusion
Response	Record and retain for 5 or 30 years	Notify EPA immediately
Regulation	Final: 1982	Final: 1978

95/   43 FR 11110, supra, Section II.

96/   Ibid. at 11111, Section V.

The proposal, published by EPA in July 1980 97/ defined "significant adverse reactions" as "reactions which may indicate a tendency of a chemical substance or mixture to cause long-lasting irreversible damage to health or the environment." Second, all manufacturers, processors and chemical distributors—except retailers—were included in the rule (an estimated 580,000 firms). And third, oral as well as written allegations were required to be recorded.

The final version in September 1982 98/ reflected the Reagan Administration's desire for less burdensome regulations. First, the definition was changed to place more emphasis on the word "significant":

> Significant adverse reactions are reactions that may indicate a tendency of a chemical substance or mixture to cause long-lasting or irreversible damage to health or the environment.

Moreover, only previously "unknown" effects need be recorded. This borrows a concept from Section 8(e) that may be appropriate there, where the goal is to inform EPA of new hazards, but is not fitting in a section that essentially provides for a log of health problems and complaints.

Second, the requirement to record oral allegations is dropped, although realistically that is the form in which most worker complaints would be made. Third, only processors in certain SIC code industries (namely, SIC categories 28 and 2911) are covered, while manufacturers of "naturally-occurring" substances are exempted entirely. This reduces the number of affected firms by over 98% to only 10,000. And fourth, while the statute gave EPA an alternative of record inspection or submission, the final regulation opted for the former, with no automatic reporting requirement.

10.0 Testing Requirements

10.1 General Testing Requirements: Section 4(a)

Section 4(a) of TSCA permits EPA to require the testing of any chemicals, both old and new, if an unreasonable risk to health or the environment is suspected. 99/ Testing may also be required if a

---

97/   45 FR 47008, 11 July 1980.

98/   47 FR 38780, 2 September 1982; see also EPA Concept Paper on Section 8(c), 8 July 1982.

99/   TSCA § 4(a)(1)(A).

chemical will be produced in such quantities that significant human or environmental exposure could result. 100/

Mixtures are also subject to the above rules, but only when the effects cannot be determined or predicted by testing the individual chemical substances which comprise the mixture. 101/ This will reduce the testing burden, particularly for small producers and formulators.

Note that not all questionable chemicals need be tested—only those for which EPA makes a specific determination that additional data is necessary and issues a formal testing standard. This standard may prescribe the biochemical effects to be investigated, the tests to be conducted, and even the experimental protocols to be followed. 102/ The statute itself, in Section 4(b), details many of the studies that may be required, including carcinogenicity, mutagenicity, teratogenicity, behavioral modification, synergism, and various degrees of toxicity. Moreover, EPA must review each testing standard at least once a year and revise them where warranted. 103/

In setting these testing standards, the EPA Administrator is to consider the relative costs and availability of facilities and personnel, and the period within which they can reasonably be performed. 104/ This little-noticed provision can have considerable future significance, for the present animal testing capability in this country could be saturated by a sudden increase in demand.

EPA's effort to develop test standards under Section 27 is presently encountering serious technical difficulties. Consequently, publication of these important protocols could be delayed. 105/

A company intending to run tests on a chemical for which EPA has issued no standard under Section 4(a) but may do so in the future, can formally request from EPA testing rules for that

---

100/   TSCA § 4(a)(1)(B).

101/   TSCA § 4(a)(2).

102/   This rulemaking is subject to the Administrative Procedure Act, 5 U.S.C. § 551, including requirements for a transcript.

103/   TSCA § 4(b)(2). An earlier bill required EPA to propose test protocols within one year of enactment but this was not in the final version. See Senate Committee on Commerce, "Toxic Substance Control Act of 1973, Report on S.426," (D.C: G.P.O., 1973), p. 7.

104/   TSCA § 4(b)(1).

105/   TSCA § 27.

product. 106/ This could help avoid later charges that the tests were inadequate or otherwise not in conformity with EPA requirements. It would also help a company in litigation with OSHA or other parties, even if no Section 4(a) rule is ever issued.

In 1981, for example, EPA took 14 test rule actions and decided not to regulate testing on three other chemicals. 107/ This was overshadowed, however, by the Reagan Administration's penchant for voluntary testing over required rules, despite charges from environmental groups that it undermines TSCA. 108/

10.2 Testing Reimbursement

Because toxicological testing is so expansive, TSCA borrowed from the pesticide act a provision for sharing of testing costs. 109/ The reimbursement period is generally five years from date of submission but may be modified by the Administrator to conform to the time necessary to develop such data. 110/ If the manufacturers cannot decide among themselves a proper allocation of costs, the Administrator—as formerly in FIFRA—is required to adjudicate the dispute after consultation with the Attorney General and the Federal Trade Commission. 111/ Sharing such data exempts subsequent producers from having to conduct or submit duplicative test results.

The Agency has proposed a reimbursement rule under Section 4 which will share the cost of testing between producers in proportion to their production volume. The proposal also suggests a mechanism for adjudicating disputes on cost claims. 112/

10.3 Priority List for Chemical Testing

There are tens of thousands of potentially toxic substances. Congress recognized that if EPA tried simultaneously to regulate all

---

106/   TSCA § 4(g).   EPA has sixty days to grant or deny the petition.   Then, if granted, it has only seventy-five days to issue test standards; if denied, the Agency must publish reasons for the denial in the Federal Register.

107/   BNA, Chemical Reporter, 26 March 1982, p. 1323.

108/   Ibid., 9 July 1982, p. 468.

109/   FIFRA § 3(c)(1)(D), 7 U.S.C. § 136a(C)(1)(D).   This issue is discussed later, in the chapter on Pesticides.

110/   TSCA § 4(c)(3)(B).

111/   TSCA § 4(c).

112/   BNA, Chemical Reporter, 11 June 1982, p. 349.

of them with its limited resources, it might actually accomplish nothing. 113/ This was important, for an earlier Agency attempt to keep short the first list of regulated toxic substances under Section 307 of the Clean Water Act had failed when challenged by environmentalists in court. 114/

Section 4(e) of the Act therefore provided for a priority list of chemicals for testing and directed that it "may not, at any time, exceed 50." 115/ The "list of 50" may contain groups of chemicals as well as individual substances. This permits considerable expansion of the list's scope, if the Administrator so desires. There is a likelihood that the final list will leave a number of vacancies that can be filled if important new chemical hazards are discovered.

The procedure for preparing this list is spelled out in great detail: a committee of eight members, each from a designated government agency, 116/ was given until the end of September 1977 to submit a candidate slate, based on toxicity and exposure, to EPA Administrator for public comment and his final decision. 117/ Within twelve months he must either initiate a rulemaking under Section 4(a) or publish the reasons why not. 118/

The preparation of the inventory priority list began with an initial list of approximately 3650 chemicals compiled from nineteen

---

113/   Congressional authorization for the first year of TSCA implementation was originally only ten million dollars, a fraction of the sum allocated for other EPA programs at their inception. This has since been substantially increased. See TSCA § 29.

114/   N.R.D.C. v. Train, 8 ERC 2120 (D.D.C. 1976).

115/   TSCA § 4(e)(1)(A).

116/   These include EPA, OSHA, CEQ, NIOSH, NIEHS, NCI, NSF, and the Department of Commerce. Several other agencies overlooked by the statute, such as FDA, have unofficially become a part of the committee. Others include the Consumer Product Safety Commission (CPSC), and the Department of Defense and Interior. Members serve four years, may not have any financial interest, or accept employment for one year from anyone subject to TSCA.

117/   TSCA § 4(e)(2). The priority list is supposed to be updated every six months.

118/   TSCA § 4(e)(1)(B).   One observer, who believed the nine month period was too long, had earlier described the process as confirmation of Parkinson's law that work expands to fit the time. He was over-optimistic.

scientific sources. Next, substances under the jurisdiction of other federal laws, such as pesticides and drugs, were deleted. These and other deletions led to a Master File of 1700, which was then screened for production volume and population exposure to produce a Preliminary List of 330 chemicals which was published in July 1977. This list was in turn reduced to a candidate list of eighty.

In October 1977 the Interagency Testing Committee (ITC) nominated the first group of ten substances (six categories of chemicals and four individual substances) to the Administrator. 119/ A second set of eight recommendations (four categories and four individual substances) was submitted in April 1978. 120/

The third report of the ITC recommended the addition of three substances (two categories of chemicals and one individual substance) in October 1978. 121/ Twelve new substances (one category of chemicals and eleven individual substances) were added in April 1979. 122/

In October 1978, twelve months after the publication of the initial priority list, EPA decided it was not yet prepared to issue rules by the statutory deadline, so it withdrew that first group and declared that it would postpone testing rule-making until appropriate standards were developed. 123/ This action has been widely criticized and on 8 May 1979, the National Resources Defense

---

119/   42 FR 55026, 12 October 1977. This group included alkyl epoxides and phthalates, chlorinated benzenes and paraffins, chloromethane, cresols, hexachlorobutadiene, nitrobenzene, toluene, and xylenes.

120/   43 FR 16684, 19 April 1978. This listed acylamide, aryl phospates, chlorinated naphthalenes, dichloromethane, halogenated alkyl epoxides, polychlorinated terphenyls, pyridine, and 1,1,1-trichloroethane.

121/   43 FR 50630, 30 October 1978. This group listed dichloropropane, glycidol and its derivatives, and chlorinated benzenes--tri, tetra, and penta.

122/   3 Chemical Regulation Reporter, 4 May 1979, p. 110. This list includes acetonitrile, aniline and chloro-, bromo-, and nitroanilines; antimony; antimony sulfide; antimony trioxide; cyclohexanone; hexachlorocyclopentadiene; isophorone; mesityl oxide; 4,4-methylenedianiline; methyl ethyl ketone; and methyl isobutyl ketone.

123/   43 FR 50134, 26 October 1978.

Council (NRDC) instituted an eventually successful suit against EPA for failure to develop testing rules on the initial ITC recommendations. 124/

The chairman of the ITC under the Reagan Administration, Elizabeth Weinburger, announced in March 1982 that the committee would no longer examine broad categories of chemicals, but half of the forty now listed are categories rather than individual substances. 125/

The TSCA Section 4(e) Priority List
October 1982

Chemicals and Groups Designated for Response
Within 12 Months

Entry	Date of Designation
1. Acetonitrile**	April 1979
2. Acrylamide (environmental effects)**	April 1978
3. Alkyl epoxides	October 1979
4. Aniline and bromo-, chloro-, and/or nitroanilines	April 1978
5. Antimony (metal)**	April 1979
6. Antimony (sulfide)**	April 1979
7. Antimony trioxide**	April 1979
8. Aryl phosphates	April 1978
9. Biphenyl	April 1982
10. Bis(2-ethylhexyl) terephthalate	October 1982
11. Chlorinated benzenes, mono- and, di- (environmental effects)	October 1977
12. Chlorinated benzenes, tri-, tetra-, and penta-(environmental effects)	October 1978
13. Cresols	October 1977
14. Cyclohexanone	April 1979
15. Dibutyltin bis(isooctyl maleate)	October 1982
16. Dibutyltin bis(isooctyl mercaptoacetate	October 1982
17. Dibutyltin bis(lauryl mercaptide)	October 1982
18. Dibutyltin dilaurate	October 1979
19. 1,2-Dichloropropane	October 1978

124/ N.R.D.C. v. Costle, 14 ERC 1858 (S.D. N.Y. 1980).

125/ BNA, Chemical Reporter, 26 March 1982, p. 1323.

20.	Dimethyltin bis(isooctyl mercaptoacetate	October 1982
21.	1,3-Dioxolane	October 1982
22.	Ethyltoluene	April 1982
23.	Formamide	April 1982
24.	Glycidol and its derivatives	October 1978
25.	Halogenated alkyl epoxides	April 1978
26.	Hexachloro- 1,3-butadiene**	October 1977
27.	Hexachlorocyclopentadiene**	April 1979
28.	Hydroquinone	November 1979
29.	Isophorone**	April 1979
30.	Mesityl oxide	April 1979
31.	4,4'-Methylenedianiline	April 1979
32.	Methyl ethyl ketone**	April 1979
33.	Methyl isobutyl ketone**	April 1979
34.	Monobutyltin tris(isooctyl mercaptoacetate)	October 1982
35.	Monomethyltin tris(isooctyl mercaptoacetate)	October 1982
36.	Pyridine**	April 1978
37.	Quinone	November 1979
38.	4-(1,1,3,3,-Tetramethylbutyl) phenol	October 1982
39.	Toluene**	October 1977
40.	1,2,4-Trimethylbenzene	April 1982
41.	Tris(2-ethylhexyl) trimellitate	October 1982
42.	Xylenes**	October 1977

Other Recommended Chemicals and Groups

	Entry	Date of Recommendation
1.	Carbofuran intermediates	October 1982
2.	Trimethylbenzenes* (except 1,2,4-Trimethyl-benzene; see 40 in list above)	April 1982

*   see May 25, 1982 (47 FR 22594(G))
** In compliance with the EPA affidavit to a federal court, a Federal Register disposition notice is expected to be signed by the EPA Administrator on or before December 31, 1982.

11.0 EPA's Enforcement Role

EPA is given broad authority to take whatever measures are deemed necessary to restrict chemicals suspected of posing harm to man or the environment. The procedures are modeled basically on the pesticide act, although there are several important differences.

Like FIFRA, there is a regulatory distinction between substances presenting unreasonable risks (Section 6) and those more severe cases which constitute an imminent hazard (Section 7). 126/

The TSCA borrows its definition of hazard for invoking "cancellation" directly from FIFRA: "unreasonable risk of injury to health or the environment." 127/ There is, however, one small change--the phrase is preceded by the words "presents or will present." This was added to avoid the interpretation that "risk" meant a certainty of harm, as had been proposed by an appellate court panel (later reversed) in a case under § 211 of the Clean Air Act. 128/

Section 6 authority is not limited to removing a chemical from the market. It may also include limiting the amount that can be produced, prohibiting or limiting specific uses considered most hazardous, requiring labels and warnings, mandating extensive manufacturing and monitoring records, controlling disposal, "or otherwise regulating any manner or method of commercial use of such substance or mixture." Restrictions may even be applied to some geographical areas and not to others. Quality controls in manufacturing or processing may be required if there is a potential problem of highly toxic impurities, such as TCDD in the herbicide 2,4,5-T. The manufacturer or processor may be required to replace or repurchase products held to constitute a hazard. 129/

The regulations for implementing Section 6 rulemakings were issued in final in December 1977. 130/ These emphasized flexible procedures, rather than strict adherence to the Administrative Procedure Act, although a limited right of cross examination is provided. Subpoena authority is also available, although to be used sparingly.

126/ Compare FIFRA §§ 6(b) and 6(c) with TSCA §§ 6 and 7. Note that while TSCA does not use the terms "cancellation" or "suspension" since there is no registration to cancel or suspend as under FIFRA, these are nevertheless convenient terms to use for the process in Section 6 and 7.

127/ TSCA § 6(a).

128/ Ethyl Corp. v. EPA, 7 ERC 1353 (CADC 1975): reversed en banc by 541 F. 2d 1, 8 ERC 1785 (CADC 1976); cert. denied 426 US 941, 8 ERC 220 (1976). Section 112 of the Clean Air Act authorizes regulation of potentially harmful fuel additives, especially lead.

129/ TSCA § 6(a) and (b).

130/ 40 CFR part 750, 2 December 1977.

EPA's recent enforcement record has been much criticized, due to a dramatic drop in referrals to the Justice Department. PCB fines, however, have been considerable for failing to inspect, label, or for maintaining leaking equipment.

11.1 PCB and CFC

One of the most controversial chemicals EPA has had to deal with is polychlorinated biphenyls (PCBs). Congress sought to insure that EPA would confront the problem by specifically mandating action and a regulatory timetable in Section 6(e). This unusual step prodded EPA into banning some uses of PCBs in 1977 and most production and use in April 1979. 131/ EPA estimates that the new more stringent standard will bring nearly a million additional pounds of PCBs under control. 132/

Another widely publicized chemical group is the chlorofluoro-carbons. On 17 March 1978, EPA promulgated final regulations prohibiting almost all of the manufacturing, processing, and distribution of chlorofluorocarbons for those aerosol propellent uses subject to TSCA. 133/ These regulations became effective 15 October 1978.

11.2 Imminent Hazards: Section 7

The standard for "suspension" actions under Section 7 of TSCA is, as with pesticides, an "imminent hazard." This is defined somewhat more stringently than in FIFRA, however, as "a chemical substance or mixture which presents an imminent and unreasonable risk of serious or widespread injury to health or the environment. 134/

EPA may also take action during premarket notification where there is insufficient information to evaluate health or environmental effects. The Agency must go to court in order to halt the manufacture or prohibit a specific use of a substance, if the manufacturer objects to the proposed EPA ban, or where there is adequate evidence that the substance presents an unreasonable risk. 135/

131/ 3 Chemical Regulation Reporter, 20 April 1979, p. 49. See also Preamble to EPA Final Rules for PCBs Manuf., 17 April 1979.

132/ BNA, Chemical Regulation Reporter, 6 April 1979, p. 3.

133/ 43 FR 55241, 27 November 1978.

134/ TSCA § 7(f).

135/ TSCA § 5(f).

Unlike FIFRA, enforcement orders under TSCA cannot be issued solely on the Agency's own authority, challengeable only before the court of appeals. If a proposed restrictive rule is contested, EPA must seek an injunction from a federal district court, which will itself determine whether there is sufficient basis for legal action. EPA may also initiate a civil suit in district court to seize an imminently hazardous chemical. 136/ Judicial review of final EPA orders is limited to the circuit of courts of appeals, which must determine whether the Agency action is supported by substantial evidence on the record as a whole. 137/

The rulemaking procedures adopted assure manufacturers of a full range of due process safeguards, including reasonable hearing procedures, the right of cross-examination during rulemaking, and the right of appeal. EPA's authority to propose an immediately effective rule to ban or limit manufacture of an existing chemical is limited by the requirement that it first obtain a court injunction based on the same legal criteria as applied in cases of imminent hazard. Therefore, a substantial degree of proof is required, procedural safeguards afforded, and assurance provided that EPA cannot act without good cause.

While the Agency has used its Section 6 authority sparingly apart from the specific instance of Section 6(e) PCB regulation, it has not used Section 7 at all yet.

12.0 PCB Regulation

The regulation of polychlorinated biphenyls (PCBs) is an anomaly. Nowhere else in the environmental laws is a substance banned by name, although there have been occasional requirements that EPA examine specific substances--such as asbestos, mercury, beryllium and cadmium under Clean Air Act § 112--for possible eventual regulation. Because of perennial dissatisfaction with various Agency actions, Congress has discussed utilizing this device further, either to restrict additional chemicals or, especially with FDA on sacchain, to prevent regulators from restricting a chemical. Thus, the PCB issue is interesting not only because of the broad public attention it has received but also as a possible regulatory precedent for future actions.

PCBs have been used as transformer fluids and dielectics, but their darker side was not revealed until a tragic episode in Japan in 1969. Cooking oil somehow became contaminated with PCB leaking from a transformer. This resulted in deaths, central nervous system damage, serious stomach and liver disorders, and possibly cancer.

136/ TSCA § 7(a), (b) see also § 6(c),(d).

137/ TSCA § 19.

Immediate steps were taken in Japan to prevent this problem from recurring. No action was taken in the United States, however, until several more years and several serious incidents later.

PCBs are ubiquitous in the environment. They are stable even at high temperatures, and may not break down into non-toxic compounds for many years. PCBs sealed in a transformer may last 15, 20, or perhaps 25 years before needing replacement because of eventual leaks.

Following a number of episodes in Michigan and elsewhere (actually due largely to the unrelated polybrominated biphenyls) Congressman John Dingell (D-Mich.) and other representatives inserted Section 6(e) into the final version of TSCA. It provided for a schedule which would first stop PCB manufacture and then gradually curtail its use. EPA, as usual, missed most of the deadlines but did finally issue a series of regulations implementing the statute.

Section 6(e) directs EPA to phase-out PCB manufacture and use according to a statutorily-mandated timetable. After one year from the passage of the Act (that is, by October 1977) no one may manufacture, process, distribute, or use any PCB except in "a totally enclosed manner." 138/ Unless the Administrator finds no unreasonable risk, 139/ no one may manufacture PCBs at all after two years, nor distribute it after 2 1/2 years. 140/ If needed, the Administrator may utilize any other provision of TSCA or of any other federal law to regulate PCBs. 141/

At the time of enactment, these provisions seemed to pose no problem. There was only one remaining PCB manufacturer in the United States and it intended to abandon the business. Utilities and other owners of PCB-filled electric transformers and capacitors were permitted to maintain their equipment for its working life, provided it did not leak or require major servicing. Congressmen could therefore vote for tough regulation of unpopular PCBs a month before national elections, without any appreciable political risk.

EPA's initial regulations addressed four categories: PCB transformers (those having over 500 parts per million of PCB in the transformer fluid); PCB contaminated transformers (having between 50 and 500 parts per million); and a category not specifically defined except by exclusion, which would be non-PCB transformers, defined

---

138/   Defined in TSCA § 6(e)(2)(C).

139/   See TSCA § 6(e)(3)(B).

140/   TSCA § 6(e)(3).

141/   TSCA § 6(e)(5).

as those less than 50 parts per million. The fourth category, not discussed here, was railroad transformers.

Such transformers were required to be appropriately labeled, standards were set for transport of PCB, and disposal of techniques were outlined including incineration.

The statute exempted transformers and other uses that were "totally enclosed." If a transformer were not "totally enclosed," it must be banned. But how would EPA know, and did a tiny, well-contained leak of a thimblefull a year constitute a non-enclosed use requiring tens of thousands of dollars for equipment replacement? First of all, there is a problem called "sweating"—a fancy word EPA likes for small leaks, and in March 1980 it requested comments on the extent "weeping" or "sweating" was a problem for PCB trans-formers. The answers the Agency received were quite varied, ranging from estimates of 80-90% sweating to a fraction of that. EPA decided not to issue regulations, hoping the issue would just fade away.

An environmental group, the Environmental Defense Fund (EDF), brought suit against EPA's 1978 and 1979 implementing regulations 142/ and persuaded the court of appeals to strike them down as "unsupported by the record." 143/ Because of the broad nature of the suit, this meant that EDF won not only on the issue that prompted the suit, namely a desire for stringent inspection and maintenance of electrical equipment, but on most other issues as well. This included the 50 ppm cut off level for regulation, which was admittedly arbitrary but reflected the consensus of author-ities. And that led to problem number two.

Many chemical processes involving aromatics and chlorine were found to produce small but measureable traces of PCBs as unintended by products. This could affect up to a quarter of all American chemical operations, most of whom did not (and probably still do not) realize they were vulnerable to EPA enforcement or citizens' suits for "manufacturing" PCBs in violation of the law.

After a series of chemical and electrical industry surveys, EPA proposals, 144/ and public hearings, EPA decided to issue three

---

142/   43 FR 7150, 17 February 1978; 44 FR 31542, 31 May 1979.

143/   Environmental Defense Fund v. EPA, 636 F. 2d 1267, 15 ERC 1081 (CADC, 1980).

144/   See 47 FR 24976, 8 June 1982.

sets of regulations. 145/ Rule One, published in August 1982, 146/ applied to electric transformers and capacitors. It prohibits PCB-filled equipment near food and feed after October 1985 (the proposed rule allowed indefinite use, subject to weekly self-inspections), authorized most other electrical equipment for the remainder of its useful life, subject to (for large transformers) a quarterly self-inspection, allowed storage for disposal of non-leaking equipment outside of qualified storage facilities, and provided for retaining three years of maintenance records.

Rule Two, issued in October 1982, 147/ exempted by product manufacture which took place entirely within closed systems or separated as designated waste for disposal by EPA-approved methods. Although originally requested by the companies, the lengthy final version was opposed because it promised an "exemption" for which few if any companies could honestly qualify.

Rule Three, applying generally to the incidental by-product problem in the chemical industry, is currently in preparation.

A related question involved in protracted litigation is whether monochlorinated biphenyls are polychlorinated biphenyls. Despite linguistic and persistence arguments, EPA decided they were and brought a major enforcement action against a leading company. The company's challenge to the regulations was dismissed for lack of jurisdiction, 148/ then pursued through a protracted series of hearings and appeals within EPA. The Agency judicial officer, Ron McCallum, ruled in July 1982 that the company had indeed violated the PCB rules and that the courts of appeals, not an enforcement proceeding, was the proper forum for a challenge to the definition of PCB. 149/

The once-simple PCB issue remains a troublesome one, because of this lawsuit and its consequences, because the Agency was

---

145/ Ironically, despite the Reagan Administration's expressed preference for agreements instead of edicts the Agency rebuffed a negotiated settlement proposed in late 1982 by an unusual coalition of chemical industry and environmentalist groups.

146/ 47 FR 37342, 25 August 1982.

147/ 47 FR 46980, 21 October 1982.

148/ Dow Chemical Co. v. Costle, 484 F. Supp. 101 (D.C. Del., 1980).

149/ BNA, Chemical Reporter, 20 August 1982, p. 645; see also 30 July 1982, p. 558.

long unwilling to make decisions on incineration and on other disposal techniques, and because the problem is technically and legally more complex than anyone imagined. Meanwhile, Congress has grown impatient with the delays. As it pointed out rather bitterly to EPA on the eve of the current litigation, even four years after decisive action was ordered on PCBs, 99% of that chemical in the United States is still in existence.

13.0 Confidentiality

Since a principal function of TSCA is the collection of voluminous information on chemical substances, concern for the protection of genuine trade secrets continues to be a hotly debated topic.

Section 14 provides that EPA may not release any information which is not exempt from mandatory disclosure under the Freedom of Information Act (FOIA). 150/ This excludes "trade secrets and commercial or financial information obtained from a person and privileged or confidential." 151/ TSCA does not prohibit the disclosure of health and safety studies nor, of course, the release of information to federal officials in the performance of their duties. Data may also be disclosed to protect "against an unreasonable risk of injury to health or the environment" in a legal proceeding. There is interestingly no allowance for release of information to state health authorities, despite the lessons of the Kepone tragedy, although perhaps they could qualify by being made "contractors with the United States." 152/

EPA's general regulations for dealing with FOIA requests under its various statutes were issued in September 1976. 153/ Although they tend strongly to favor disclosure, EPA had relatively few business secrets in its files, so industry has had few objections so far to these procedures. The exception is pesticides regulation, which for several years has been entangled by litigation over release of data. 154/

Some chemical industry representatives have complained that existing laws are not sufficiently protective of confidential business

---

150/   TSCA § 14(a).

151/   Administrative Procedure Act § 2, 5 U.S.C. § 552(b)(4).

152/   TSCA § 14(b) and (a); see also 40 CFR § 2.301(h), 43 FR 2637, 18 January 1978.

153/   41 FR 36902, 1 September 1976.

154/   Mobay Chemical Corp v. Train, F. Supp., 8 ERC 1227 (D.C. W. Mich. 1975); dismissed per curiam U.S., 8 January 1979.

information. The president of the Manufacturing Chemists Association, for example, has expressed concern that as long as the trade secret exemption under the FOIA remains permissive, "there is no assurance that privately developed information submitted to the government in confidence will not be disclosed." 155/

EPA modified some portions of the original March 1977 inventory reporting proposal 156/ to assuage certain industry fears, such as by deleting the requirement that a toxicological bibliography be submitted. 157/ The Agency has also established a task force to establish computer security precautions to protect information submitted or stored on magnetic tape. 158/

Polaroid Corporation challenged the adequacy of protection provided for chemical trade secrets which the company was required to furnish EPA under the reporting regulations. 159/ In June 1978 a U.S. district judge denied the request that Polaroid be excused from reporting the information, but also issued an injunction ordering EPA not to disclose the information outside the Agency.

Then on 8 September 1978, EPA issued amendments to its confidential business information regulations 160/ providing substantial protection for TSCA confidential information and providing for notice to affected businesses before confidential information is disclosed outside EPA. 161/ Polaroid withdrew its suit and the Court order was vacated. The problem of confidentiality nevertheless will continue to be a sensitive issue for the foreseeable future.

155/ Letter from former MCA President William J. Driver to Sen. James Abourezk (D-S.D.), Chairman of the Administrative Practice and Procedure Subcommittee of the Senate Judiciary Committee, 18 January 1978, quoted in BNA Environment Reporter, 1978, p. 1468.

156/ 42 FR 13130, 9 March 1977.

157/ 42 FR 39182, 39188, 2 August 1977, reproposing 40 CFR 710.7(e).

158/ See, e.g., 42 FR 53804, 53805, 3 October 1977; 43 FR 1836, 12 January 1978.

159/ Polaroid Corp. v. Costle, No. 78-11335 (D.C. Mass. 1978).

160/ 40 CFR Part 2, 43 FR 3997, 8 September 1978.

161/ This provision for notification to the company was already set forth in Section 14(c) of the statute.

EPA has consistently insisted that requests for confidentality be accompanied by an explanation to why it is needed. Merely calling something a trade secret does not make it so. However, the first policy issued by the Reagan Administration on Section 5 provided that under PMN a manufacturer could withhold data as confidential without providing a rationale. 162/

14.0 Citizen Enforcement and Legal Fees

Private citizens are allowed, even encouraged, to participate in TSCA administrative and judicial proceedings. 163/ Section 21 provides that any person may petition the Administrator to take action on rules under Sections 4-8, excepting imminent hazard determinations under Section 7, the Administrator then has 90 days either to grant or deny the petition. If he denies the petition, a citizen may initiate civil action in a federal district court. 164/

Citizens may also file suit under Section 20 to compel the Administrator to perform any non-discretionary duty, or against anyone including the government alleged to be in violation of any rules issued under Sections 4-6. The plaintiff, however, must give EPA the traditional 60 days notice before he may commence his litigation. 165/

The exclusion of Section 7 from both the citizens petition and citizens suit sections is particularly striking, considering that the imminent hazard area of FIFRA has been a prime focus of activity by environmental groups.

Attorney and witness fees may be awarded by the courts to persons litigating under TSCA. There is no requirement that the person's legal position has prevailed, or that such an award be limited to so-called public interest groups, although that is surely its main concern. The statutory test is simply that costs and reasonable

---

162/ BNA, Chemical Reporter, 7 February 1982, p. 443.

163/ The citizen participation sections were missing in whole or part from earlier versions of TSCA. For example, H.R. 5356 of 1973 had neither section, while the Senate bill (S.426) had a citizens suit provision (§ 19) but only an oblique reference to citizen petitions (§ 24a). See House Report 93-360 (1973) and Senate Report 93-254 (1973).

164/ TSCA § 21.

165/ TSCA § 20.

fees may be granted "if the court determines that such an award is appropriate." 166/

15.0 Relationship of TSCA to Other Federal Laws

TSCA was enacted to fill gaps left by other laws, but Congress was also concerned that it not lead to jurisdictional conflicts with other agenices or even between different divisions of EPA. There was no wish to see a repetition of the bitter OSHA-EPA dispute of 1973 over pesticide re-entry standards. 167/ Consequently, Section 9 sets forth in some detail the coordination procedures to be followed when two health regulatory laws overlap.

If the EPA Administrator determines that another law not administered by EPA would be more appropriate for regulating a given hazard, he must submit a description of the situation to that agency for action. The receiving agency must then take whatever regulatory measures it deems necessary, or reply in the Federal Register with a "detailed statement" why no action is warranted. There the matter rests, whether EPA is in accord with the decision or not. (A citizen suit against the second agency is nevertheless possible.) EPA cannot thereafter bring an enforcement action of its own under Sections 6 or 7 concerning that hazard. 168/

For other laws administered under EPA, the Administrator is given the flexibility to apply them where they would be most useful or to rely on the provisions of TSCA. He is not relieved of the procedural or substantive requirements in those other laws, however, if he chooses to rely on them. 169/

Finally, Congress added a special provision concerning OSHA, stating the EPA's exercise of authority under TSCA did not

---

166/   TSCA § 19(d).

167/   Under pressure of lawsuit by a migrant farmworkers' group, OSHA sought in spring 1973 to assert jurisdiction over conditions of fieldworker exposure to pesticides. This account is related in the chapter on Pesticides, Section 9.5.

168/   TSCA § 9(a). EPA could try to circumvent this bar by first initiating an enforcement action and then sending the notification to the other agency, but this Section 9(a)(3) "loophole" seems insufficiently broad for that gambit to succeed.

169/   TSCA § 9(b). At least theroretically, the application of the doctrine to all laws "administered in whole or in part by the Administration" also includes the Food, Drug, and Cosmetic Act. See the chapter on Pesticides, Section 9.1.

constitute a preemption of OSHA jurisdiction under OSH Act Section 4. 170/

15.1 Existing Toxic Substances Laws

The term "toxic substance" has become so identified with this new Act that one often forgets there is considerable legislation dealing with chemical substances already on the books. In one sense, almost all of the recent environmental laws have in fact been directed at toxic substances.

One generally excludes from the term "toxic substance" the six original air pollutants regulated by EPA under Sections 108-110 of the Clear Air Act; carbon monoxide, hydrocarbons, photochemical oxidant, sulfur dioxide, nitrogen oxides, and particulate matter. In sufficient concentrations most of these substances can be immediately deadly and all have serious long-term effects on health. They tend, however, to be the ubiquitous products of combustion, the waste products of an industrial society, and their control necessitates a general national policy that cuts across many diverse industries. Similarly, a number of the substances controlled under the water pollution laws are usually excluded from the definition, including suspended soil particles and decaying organic products which adversely affect the biological oxygen demand (BOD) of the water.

15.2 Clean Air Act

Section 112 of the Clean Air Act, entitled "National Emission Standards for Hazardous Air Pollutants," is specifically directed toward toxic substances. Although this provision has so far been used only for asbestos, mercury, beryllium, and vinyl chloride, it could develop into one of the most important parts of the Act. Arsenic and benzene are currently under consideration for regulation under this section. One reason for its infrequent use is its deliberate omission of economic or technical feasibility in standard setting; the only relevant factor for the Administrator is "the level which in his judgement provides an ample margin of safety to protect the public health from such hazardous air pollutants." 171/ EPA tacitly ignored this unusual provision in the vinyl chloride deliberations 172/ and this, if deemed successful, may lead to greater use of this

---

170/   TSCA § 9(c); OSH Act § 4(b)(1).

171/   Clear Air Act, § 112(b)(1)(B).

172/   EPA, "Proposed Standard for Vinyl Chloride", 16 December 1975.

section in the future. 173/

15.3 Water Pollution Act

Another key law is Section 307 of the Water Pollution Act entitled "Toxic and Pre-treatment Effluent Standards." 174/ This provides specifically for the listing and setting of standards with an "ample margin of safety" for hazardous chemicals discharged into the nation's waterways. In September 1973 EPA listed nine chemicals, mostly pesticides, on this list, including DDT, Aldrin-Dieldrin, PCBs, Toxaphene, and cadmium and mercury compounds. 175/ Effluent standards for these substances do not apply to all industries but only to about two dozen broad categories such as non-ferrous metal smelters textile manufacturers, and agricultural fertilizer manufacturing. 176/ By the consent decree between EPA and the Natural Resources Defense Council in June 1976, a total of 65 substances comprising several hundred individual chemicals was added to the Section 307 list. 177/ This decree was subsequently written into the 1977 Amendments to the Clean Water Act. 178/

Under Section 311 entitled "Oil and Hazardous Substance Liability", EPA is to regulate "spills" of hazardous substances into the nation's waterways and coastal zones. The Administrator is required to list those elements and compounds which should be

---

173/ The original Clean Air bill considered by Congress had two toxic substances sections—the present one for extreme hazards and a milder version allowing economic considerations for the less serious toxic pollutants. The House-Senate Conference Committee in 1970 dropped the latter section from the final bill without giving any reason.

174/ Federal Water Pollution Control Act, § 307, 33 U.S.C. § 1317.

175/ 38 FR 24342, 7 September 1975. The rules of practice under § 307 were amended by 41 FR 1765, 12 January 1976.

176/ For more detailed information, see Chapter 3 on Water Pollution Control.

177/ N.R.D.C. v. Train, 8 ERC 2120 (D.D.C. 1976); see also N.R.D.C. v. Train, 510 F.2d 692 (D.C. Cir. 1974).

178/ PL 95-217. There has been some dispute about the degree to which Congress incorporated the consent decree into the amendments. Rep. Ray Roberts (D-Tex.) insisted that it didn't, or at least modified it considerably; Sen. Edmund Muskie (D-Me) said that it did. The latter view is preferred.

designated "hazardous substances". Within 180 days of this designation he is to establish a unit of measurement and a monetary penalty for the discharge of a unit into the water. EPA finally proposed such a list in December 1975. It announced that although the Act authorizes the imposition of fines up to five million dollars, the Agency would voluntarily limit penalties to $5000 unless gross negligence by the polluter is demonstrated. 179/

The Administator also has emergency authority under Section 504 of the Water Act to seek to enjoin any person from discharging any pollutants which are "presenting an imminent and substantial endangerment to health or welfare." 180/ This section has rarely been invoked by EPA, despite numerous situations for which it would be appropriate.

15.4 Occupational Safety and Health Administration

The Occupational Safety and Health Act, although not usually regarded as a toxic substance act, is potentially the most important statute in the field. 181/ Although limited to occupational situations, the Act covers over 80 million workers, many of whom have much greater exposure to highly toxic chemicals than they are ever likely to encounter in the general environment. Section 6 of the Act 182/ requires OSHA to set strict health standards at a level "which most adequately assures, to the extent feasible, on the basis of the best available evidence, that no employee will suffer material impairment of health or functional capacity even if such employee has regular exposure to the hazard dealt with by such standard for the period of his working life. 183/ This Act, if fully implemented, could have a tremendous effect.

In the nine years since the passage of this Act, however, OSHA has put out only six final health standards--asbestos, vinyl chloride, coke oven, arsenic, benzene, and a group of carcinogens. In late 1975, after a change in OSHA's top management, standards were proposed for ten other substances, including lead, beryllium, and trichloroethylene. Final standards for others are pending. In

---

179/   EPA, Notice of Proposed Rulemaking, Designation of Hazardous Substances, 40 FR 59960-60017 (30 December 1975). 40 CFR Parts 116-19

180/   Federal Water Pollution Control Act § 504, 33 U.S.C. § 1364.

181/   29 U.S.C. § 651 et seq., PL 91-596, 84 Stat. 1590.

182/   OSH Act § 6, 29 U.S.C. § 655.

183/   OSH Act § 6(b)(5).

addition, OSHA has a list of approximately 400 substances with threshold limits adopted from the recommended lists of private industrial hygiene organizations. 184/

15.5 Consumer Product Safety Commission
The Consumer Product Safety Act and related statutes such as the Hazardous Substances Act administered by the Consumer Product Safety Commission (CPSC) also confer jurisdiction over certain forms of toxic substances. One should note, however, that "hazardous substances" as used in this act includes devices and equipment, and thus is much broader than the term toxic substances. Furthermore, the CPSC may address only human safety questions derived from the use of consumer products, and thus it has no authority over environmental problems. In the past, the CPSC has exhibited little activity in the chemical area, except for limited involvement in cases concerning two spray can propellants, vinyl chloride and freon, and a fumbled effort on asbestos hair dryers. It issued a detailed cancer policy document modeled closely on that proposed by OSHA but was forced to withdraw it in April 1979 because of procedural deficiencies.

16.0 The Proposed Federal Cancer Policy
The proposed Federal Cancer Policy, initiated by OSHA in October 1977, considered by all four health regulatory agencies-- OSHA, EPA, FDA, and CPSC--and currently on hold by the Reagan Administration, could potentially have more effect on toxic chemical control than the better-known Toxic Substances Control Act. This cancer policy, if effectively applied, could directly impact hundreds or thousands of chemical substances throughout American industry.

16.1 Goals of Proposed Federal Cancer Policy
The three goals hoped to be reached through OSHA's proposed Federal Cancer Policy are (1) to avoid repetitious scientific debate at OSHA hearings and ad hoc decisions on health standards involving carcinogens, (2) to streamline OSHA's ponderous standard setting process by "prefabricating" the essential elements of several alternative versions, and (3) ultimately to harmonize the policies of the four health regulatory agencies. The regulatory requirements, derived from the cancer principles, spell out monitoring and medical tests in rigorous detail and set a goal of reducing levels of "confirmed" carcinogens to near zero.

184/   These are being reviewed as part of the Standards Completion Process to convert the bare threshold numbers into a full standard with monitoring, medical, and other requirements.

16.2 Background of the Policy

Efforts to develop a cancer policy at both OSHA and EPA date from the Aldrin-Dieldrin pesticide suspension decision at EPA in October 1974. This set forth tentative principles of carcinogenicity which the Agency could apply to future regulatory cases. 185/ EPA subsequently established a task force to analyze this fledgling policy and recommended a final version. The focus shifted to OSHA in 1975 with the transfer of several former EPA officials to that agency. In January 1976 a lengthy OSHA draft proposal was widely circulated, but the change of administrations forestalled its issuance. Finally, the proposal, different in only a few details from the version prepared nine months earlier, was signed by the head of OSHA on 28 September 1977 and subsequently appeared in the Federal Register on 4 October 1977, entitled "Identification, Classification and Regulation of Toxic Substances Posing a Potential Occupational Carcinogenic Risk." 186/

16.3 Scientific Principles of the Cancer Policy

The proposed policy takes a hardline approach to carcinogens, namely that exposure should be reduced to zero, or as close to zero as feasible. If safer alternative chemicals are available, they should be substituted.

The leading scientific policy conclusions in the proposal are as follows:

1. A carcinogen is defined as a substance or condition which increases the incidence of generally irreversible benign or malignant tumors, reduces the latency period, or produces unusual tumors in animals or man.
2. The results of cancer tests on animals, particularly rodents and other animals, are relevant to human exposure. ("Any substance which is shown to cause tumors in animals should be considered carcinogenic and, therefore, a potential cancer hazard for man.")
3. A threshold or "no effect" level may theoretically exist for carcinogens but this has not been conclusively demonstrated; and, even so, it would have to be determined separately for each substance. Therefore, the only safe level is zero.
4. Most carcinogens are neither species-specific nor organ-specific.

185/   In Re Shell, 6 ERC 2047 (1974).

186/   42 FR 54148, 4 October 1977.

5. A substance may be termed a confirmed carcinogen after replicated tests in only one species. ("If carcinogens are not species-specific, it logically follows that the demonstration of carcinogenic effect in more than one species is not absolutely necessary for finding of carcinogenicity.") Note that EPA has recently commented that under some circumstances even replication should be waived as unnecessary.

6. In evaluating test data, no distinction will be made between benign and malignant tumors. ("The Agency proposes to place as much weight on an experiment in which only benign tumors are observed, as upon experiments in which both malignant and benign tumors are induced.")

7. Positive test results, (i.e., indicators that a substance is carcinogenic) outweigh negative findings.

8. Chemical structural similarity of a suspect chemical to a known carcinogen may be a guide for testing priority but is itself insufficient to classify the former as a carcinogen.

9. Induced tumors appearing in animals at the point of application, or due to physical rather than chemical effect, may be disregarded.

10. The administration of high doses is a methodological device necessary for finding gross effects in small test samples. "Consequently, a substance that will induce cancer in experimental animals at any dose level, no matter how high or low, should be treated with great caution."

11. The Ames test or other in vitro experiments using non-mammalian species are not an appropriate basis for regulatory action, but positive results plus carcinogenicity in one mammalian species may be.

12. Human epidemiological studies are generally an insensitive indicator of carcinogenicity, unless the study is exhaustively controlled or the particular cancer is quite unusual (e.g., angiosarcoma from vinyl chloride).

16.4 Implementation Regulations of the Cancer Policy

The implementation regulations and model standards (Part II) are an attempt to convert the scientific principles discussed above into full OSHA standards through a modular format. There are five such formats:

1. Category I—Emergency Temporary Standard for Confirmed Carcinogen.

   • Lowest levels feasible within the six-month period of the ETS.
   • Most of the medical surveillance, waste disposal, recordkeeping, and other precautions required under a permanent standard, allowing for the short compliance period.

2. Category I—Permanent Standard for Confirmed Carcinogen.

   - Level set at zero exposure or as low as feasible.
   - Feasibility not really defined in the entire document, nor is it clear whether it is limited to technological feasibility, as OSHA insists, or can also include economic risk-benefit calculations.
   - A full battery of monitoring, medical and protective equipment requirements designed to safeguard employees from exposure to carcinogens in the workplace.
   - This category can be triggered by a finding of carcinogenicity in tests with two animal species, one species if replicated, one species unreplicated if accompanied by a positive in vitro test, or other evidence determined sufficient by the Secretary of Labor.
   - These regulations are unusually specific, dealing in detail with everything from the laundering of work clothes to the application of cosmetics by employees in the workplace.

3. Category II—Suspected Carcinogens

   - This category can be applied to all the toxics substances for which the data is "suggestive" of carcinogenicity but for which the tests for Category I are either not met or partially rebutted.
   - The Standard level will be set sufficient to prevent acute or chronic non-carcinogenic effects.
   - Most of the medical, monitoring, and other requirements applicable to Category I are required.

4. Category III—Acquitted Chemicals (or "Guilt Unproved")

   - This class encompasses substances which have either been cleared of suspicion of carcinogenicity, or which still deserve some additional research.

5. Category IV—Foreign Toxic Substances

   - This provision is merely an attempt to close the loophole by which a toxic substance for which no federal standard exists could be imported to the U.S. from abroad.
   - As in Category III, no special regulations other than publication are provided for this group.

In July 1980, as the final step in the implementation of the policy, OSHA brought out a long, tentative list of cancer candidates for regulation. 187/ In its final version, the candidate list of the substances numbered 204; half were borrowed from an EPA compilation by its Carcinogen Assessment Group (CAG), while the remaining half were submitted by an outside consulting firm on contract to OSHA. 188/ The plan was to select up to twenty for the development of full health standards, ten for Category I and ten for Category II.

The Reagan Administration, under considerable business pressure, put a hold on the cancer policy within days of its coming to office. In December 1981 OSHA announced that it was subjecting the entire issue to extensive review, 189/ and in July 1983 the Agency published a notice suspending the candidate project pending further review by OSHA and, though not mentioned, the development of a government-wide policy 190/ currently under consideration by a committee headed by White House Science Advisor, George Keyworth. The principal reason for this stay was concern that the process could constitute a blacklist of chemicals and cause undo alarm.

17.0 Conclusion

The Toxic Substances Control Act has gotten off to a slow start, due in part to the delay in filling top EPA positions. 191/ The ponderous pace did not accelerate thereafter, however, so the Act may require an entire decade to implement fully. We should recognize the considerable administrative burden this cumbersome statute

---

187/   OSHA Press Release, 14 July 1978.

188/   45 FR 53672, 12 August 1980.

189/   OSHA Press Release, 31 December 1981; 47 FR 187, 5 January 1982.

190/   48 FR 241, 4 January 1983. See also Administrative Conference of U.S., Recommendation 82-5, "Federal Regulation of Cancer-Causing Chemicals", 18 June 1982.

191/   See, for example, the story entitled, "Search for Toxic Chemicals in Environment Gets A Slow Start, Is Proving Difficult and Expensive," Wall Street Journal, 9 May 1978, p. 48. Similar criticism, almost a year later, arose from Congressional oversight hearings before the House Subcommittee on Consumer Protection on 8 March 1979.

places on EPA; the Agency needs not only technical expertise but also extensive managerial and legal resources.

For the immediate future TSCA will be essentially an information-gathering act, although the Administrator has promised soon to initiate legal proceedings under Section 6 against a number of particularly hazardous substances. The concurrent slow-downs at OSHA, FDA, and the CPSC have created a back pressure which could create an impetus for change in the next several years. Even if this occurs, however, past experience is not comforting that the new Administration will be any more proficient than its predecessors.

Nevertheless, in the long run, the importance of TSCA is likely to expand gradually, much as the requirements of FIFRA and the FDA Act increased substantially long after their enactment.

Chapter 7

FEDERAL REGULATION OF PESTICIDES

Marshall Lee Miller
Attorney
Reid & Priest
Washington, DC

1.0 Background to the Federal Regulation of Pesticides

The benefits of pesticides, herbicides, rodenticides, and other economic poisons are well known. They have done much to spare us from the ravages of disease, crop infestations, noxious animals, and choking weeds. In the last twenty years, however, beginning with Rachel Carson's Silent Spring 1/, there has been a growing awareness of the hazards, as well as the benefits of these chemicals, which may be harmful to man and the balance of nature. The ability to balance these often conflicting effects is hampered by our lack of understanding of adverse side effects, a problem which will become even more acute during the next few years as EPA investigations shift from the major pesticides, on which an appreciable amount of research has been conducted, to those for which data is relatively sparse.

1.1 Early Efforts at Pesticide Regulations

Although chemical pesticides have been subject to some degree of federal control since the Insecticide Act of 1910 2/, the relatively insignificant usage of pesticides before World War II made regulation a matter of low priority. This act was primarily concerned with protecting consumers from ineffective products or deceptive labeling, and contained neither a federal registration requirement nor any significant safety standards.

The war enormously stimulated the development and use of pesticides. The resulting benefits to health and farm production

---

1/ Rachel Carson, Silent Spring (New York, 1962).

2/ 36 Stat. 331 (1910).

made pesticides a necessity and transformed the agricultural chemical industry into a major sector of the economy. In 1947 Congress responded to the situation by enacting the more comprehensive Federal Insecticide, Fungicide, and Rodenticide Act (FIFRA), 3/ requiring that pesticides distributed in interstate commerce be registered with the U.S. Department of Agriculture (USDA) and containing a rudimentary labeling provision. The Act, like its predecessor, was more concerned with product efficacy than with safety, but the statute did declare pesticides "misbranded" if they were necessarily harmful to man, animals, or vegetation (except weeds) even when properly used. 4/

Three major defects in the new law soon became evident. First, the registration process was largely an empty formality since the Secretary of Agriculture could not refuse registration even to a chemical he deems highly dangerous; he could register "under protest," but this had no legal effect on the registrant's ability to manufacture or distribute the chemical. Second, there was no regulatory control over the use of a pesticide contrary to its label, as long as the label itself complied with the statutory requirements. Third, the Secretary's only remedy against a hazardous product was a legal action for misbranding or adulteration, and--this was crucial--the difficult burden of proof was on him.

The statute nevertheless remained unchanged for seventeen years. Pesticides were not then a matter of public concern and the USDA was under little pressure to tighten regulatory control. Only a handful of registrations under protest were made during that period, and virtually all these actions involved minor companies with ineffective products. The one notable case in this area involving a fraudulently ineffective product was lost by the USDA at the district court level and mooted by the Court of Appeals. 5/

In 1964 the USDA persuaded Congress to remedy two of these three defects: the registration system was revised to permit the Secretary to refuse to register a new product or to cancel an existing registration, and the burden of proof for safety and effectiveness was placed on the registrant. 6/ This considerably strengthened the

---

3/   61 Stat. 190 (1974).

4/   Old FIFRA (pre-1972)§2(z)(2)(d). See H. Rep. 313 (80th Cong., 1st Sess.). 1947 U.S. Code Cong. Serv. 1200, 1201.

5/   Victrylite Candle Co. v. Brannan, 201 F.2d 206 (D.C. Cir. 1952).

6/   Act of 12 May 1964, PL 88-30S, 78 Stat. 190. There were other, less significant, amendments in 1959 (73 Stat. 286) and 1961 (75 Stat. 18, 42).

Act but made little difference in practice. The Pesticide Registration Division, a section of USDA's Agricultural Research Service, was understaffed—in 1966 the only toxicologist on the staff was the division's director—and the division was buried deep in a bureaucracy primarily concerned with promoting agriculture and facilitating the registration of pesticides. The cancellation procedure was seldom is ever used, 7/ and there was still no legal sanction against a consumer's applying the chemical for a delisted use.

The growth of the environmental movement in the late 1960's, with its concern about the widespread use of agricultural chemicals, overwhelmed the meager resources of the Pesticide Division. Environmental groups filed a barrage of law suits demanding the cancellation or suspension of a host of major pesticides such as DDT, Aldrin-Dieldrin, and the herbicide 2,4,5-T. This hectic and bewildering situation demanded a new approach to pesticide regulations.

1.2 Creation of the Environmental Protection Agency

On 2 December 1970, President Nixon signed Reorganization Order No. 3 8/ creating the Environmental Protection Agency (EPA), and assigned to it the functions and many of the personnel previously under Interior, Agriculture, and other government departments. EPA inherited from USDA not only the Pesticides Division but also the environmental law suits against the Secretary of Agriculture. Thus, within the first two or three months the new Agency was compelled to make a number of tough regulatory decisions. The EPA's outlook was considerably influenced by judicial decisions in several of the cases it had inherited from USDA or, concerning pesticide residues, from the Food and Drug Administration of the Department of Health, Education, and Welfare (HEW), now the Department of Health and Human Services (HHS). These court decisions consistently held that the responsible federal agencies had not sufficiently examined the health and environmental problems associated with pesticide use. These helped to shape—one might even say force—EPA's pesticide policy during its formative period. 9/

EPA's first policy determination, issued by Administrator William Ruckelshaus in early 1971 in response to a court order, was

---

7/ Instead, a Pesticide Registration notice would be sent ordering the removal of one or more listed uses from the registration.

8/ Reorganization Order No. 3 of 1970, §2(a)(1), 1970 U.S. Code Cong. Ad. News 2996, 2998, 91st Cong. 2nd Sess.

9/ These cases will be discussed in a later section, (9.1).

the "Statement of the Reasons Underlying the Decision on Cancellation and Suspension of DDT 2,4,5-T, and Aldrin-Dieldrin," usually called the 18th of March Statement. This order declared that pesticides would no longer be given only perfunctory review at registration nor be virtually immune from examination thereafter, and reemphasized that the statutory burden of proving a product safe rested with the chemical industry. This meant that EPA and the agricultural chemical industry would henceforth need additional resources for more intensive scientific review.

2.0 Pesticide Statute

2.1 Key Provisions of the Federal Insecticide, Fungicide and Rodenticide Act

The Federal Insecticide, Fungicide, and Rodenticide Act (FIFRA), 10/ as amended by the Federal Environmental Pesticide Control Act (FEPCA) of October 1972 11/ and the FIFRA Amendments of 1975 12/ 1978 13/ and 1980 14/ is a complex statute. Terms may have a meaning different from, or even directly contrary to, normal English usage. The term "suspension", for example, really means an immediate ban on a pesticide, while the harsher-sounding term "cancellation" indicates only the initiation of administrative proceedings which can drag on for years. There are five key features of the FIFRA; the other points will be discussed more fully in a subsequent section.

The Amendments to FIFRA reflect Congressional, industry and environmentalist concern about federal control of pesticide distribution, sale, and use. The 1972 Amendments amounted to a virtual rewriting of the law. EPA was given expanded authority over field use of pesticides and several categories of registration were created which give EPA more flexibility in fashioning appropriate control over pesticides. The 1975 Amendments are significant not for what they actually changed but because of the motivations that prompted them. These Amendments were viewed by many as, at best, unnecessary and, at worst, a further encumbrance upon an already complicated administrative procedure. EPA was required to consult with the Department of Agriculture and Agricultural

---

10/ 7 U.S.C. § 135, et seq.

11/ PL 92-516, 86 Stat. 973, 21 October 1972.

12/ PL 94-140, 28 November 1975.

13/ PL 95-396, 92 Stat. 819, 30 September 1978.

14/ PL 96-539, 94 Stat. 3194, 17 December 1980.

Committees of Congress before issuing proposed or final standards regarding pesticides. EPA also got the authority to require that farmers take exams before being certified as applicators.

The 1978 Amendments reflected the near-collapse of EPA's pesticide registration program. EPA was given the authority to conditionally register a pesticide pending study of the product's safety and was given the ability to perform generic reviews without requiring compensation for use of a company's data. The 1980 Amendments provided for a two-house veto over EPA rules or regulations and required the Administrator to obtain Scientific Advisory Review (SAR) of suspension actions after they were initiated.

2.2 Registration Procedures

All new pesticide products used in the United States, with minor exceptions, must first be registered with EPA. This involves the submittal of the complete formula, a proposed label, and "full description of the tests made and the results thereof upon which the claims are based." 15/ The Administrator must approve the registration if the following conditions are met:

> (A) its composition is such as to warrant the proposed claim for it;
> (B) its labeling and other materials required to be submitted comply with the requirements of this act;
> (C) it will perform its intended function without unreasonable adverse effects on the environment; and
> (D) when use in accordance with widespread and commonly recognized practice it will not generally cause unreasonable adverse effects on the environment. 16/

The operative phrase in the above criteria is "unreasonable adverse effects on the environment" which was added to the Act in 1972. This phrase is defined elsewhere in FIFRA as meaning "any unreasonable risk to man or the environment, taking into account the economic, social, and environmental costs and benefits of the use of the pesticide." 17/

15/   1 FIFRA § 3(c)(1), 7 U.S.C. § 136(c)(1).

16/   FIFRA § 3(c)(5), 7 U.S.C. § 136a(c)(5).

17/   FIFRA § 2(bb), 7 U.S.C. § 136(bb). The 1975 amendments, as will be discussed, added the specific requirement that decisions also include consideration of their impact on various aspects of the agricultural economy.

This controversial expression, which appears also in the cancellation-suspension section of the Act, 18/ disturbed some environmentalists who feared that the word "unreasonable" plus the consideration of social and economic factors would undermine the effectiveness of the cancellation procedure, but experience to date has not indicated a problem.

The registration is not valid for all uses of a particular chemical. Each registration specifies the crops and insects on which it may be applied, and each use must be supported by research data on safety and efficacy. Registrations are for a five-year period, after which they automatically expire unless an interested party petitions for renewal and, if requested by EPA, provides additional data indicating the safety of the product. 19/ For the past several years, pre-EPA registrations have been coming up for renewal under much stricter standards than when originally issued. The agricultural chemical companies have justifiably complained that the increased burden of registration is discouraging the development of new pesticides, but there seems no responsible alternative.

2.3 Federal Control Over Pesticide Use

Until 1972 the government had no control over the actual use of a pesticide once it had left a manufacturer or distributor properly labeled. Thus, for example, a chemical which would be perfectly safe for use on a dry field might be environmentally hazardous if applied in a marshy area, and a chemical acceptable for use on one crop might leave dangerous residues on another. The EPA's only recourse (other than occasional subtle hints to the producer) was to cancel the entire registration -- obviously too unwieldy a weapon to constitute a normal means of enforcement. A second problem was that a potential chemical might be too dangerous for general use but could be used safely by trained personnel. There was, however, no legal mechanism for limiting its use only to qualified individuals.

Because of these problems, both environmentalists and the industry agreed that EPA should be given more flexibility than merely the choice between cancelling or approving a pesticide. Congress therefore provided for the classification of pesticides into general and restricted categories, 20/ with the latter group available only to Certified Applicators. There are several categories of

---

18/   FIFRA § 6, 7 U.S.C. § 136d.

19/   FIFRA § 6(a), 7 U.S.C. § 136d(a).

20/   FIFRA § 3(d), 7 U.S.C. § 136a(d).

applicators, including private applicators and commercial applicators who use or supervise the application of pesticides on property other than their own. A pesticide label permitting use only "under the direct supervision of a Certified Applicator" means that the chemical is to be applied under the instructions and control of a Certified Applicator who, however, is not required to be physically present when and where the pesticide is applied.

The additional flexibility of the certification program was a principal reason the industry eventually supported the 1972 Amendments to FIFRA, but some environmentalists were concerned that the program might become a farce, especially when administered by certain states. Certification standards are prescribed by the EPA, as are requirements for periodic reporting to EPA, but any state desiring to establish its own certification program may do so if the Administrator determines that it satisfies the guidelines and statutory criteria. 21/

The efficacy of the entire certification program, however, has become questionable as a result of the 1975 Amendments to FIFRA, for example, these considerably loosened the procedures for certification by forbidding EPA to demand any examinations of an applicant's knowledge. 22/ These Amendments will be discussed more fully in a separate section. There is a possibility that some states may license anyone who applies, but EPA requirements for periodic reporting and inspection provide some degree of control, and there should be no objection to every farmer becoming a Certified Applicator if he is willing to undergo training.

Finally, since 1972 it has been unlawful either "to make available for use, or to use, any registered pesticide classified for restricted use for some or all purposes other than in accordance with" the registration and applicable regulations. 23/ Stiff penalties for violations of these restrictions include fines up to $25,000 and imprisonment for up to a year. 24/

2.4 Cancellation

While the registration process may be the foundation of the FIFRA, cancellation represents the cutting edge of the law and attracts the most public attention. Cancellation is used to initiate review of a substance suspected of being a "substantial question of

---

21/   FIFRA § 4, 7 U.S.C. § 136b.

22/   PL 94-140 § 5, amending FIFRA § 4(a)(1).

23/   FIFRA § 12(a)(2)(F), 7 U.S.C. § 136(a)(2)(F).

24/   FIFRA § 14, 7 U.S.C. § 136 1.

safety" to man or the environment. 25/ During the pendency of the proceedings the product may be freely manufactured and shipped in commerce. A cancellation order, although final if not challenged within 30 days, usually leads to a public hearing or scientific review committee, or both, and is quite protracted—a matter of years rather than months. A recommended decision from the agency hearing examiner (now called the administrative law judge) goes to the Administrator or his delegated representative, the Chief Agency Judicial Officer, for a final determination on the cancellation. If sustained, this would ban the product from shipment or use in the United States. 26/

Even under the old FIFRA 27/ it became clear that there were several quite different types of cancellation. First, there was a cancellation when a substance was, in EPA's opinion, a highly probable threat to man or the environment but for which there was not yet sufficient evidence to warrant immediate suspension. Second, there could be a cancellation when scientific tests indicated some cause for concern and a public hearing or scientific advisory committee was desired to explore the issue more thoroughly. And third, there could be a cancellation issued in response to a citizens' suit when a fact-finding hearing was desired to enable both critics and defenders of the pesticide to present their arguments. These distinctions, although not found in the statute, were nevertheless quite important. State authorities, for example, would often recommend that farmers cease using a cancelled product which they thought had been declared unsafe, although EPA may have considered the action in category two or three above. Conversely, there were occasions when the EPA wanted to communicate its great concern over the continued use of a product without resorting to suspension.

This problem is not resolved completely by the amended FIFRA, but two levels of action are distinguished: "The Administrator may issue a notice of his intent either (1) to cancel its registration or to change its classification together with the reasons (including the factual basis) for his action, or (2) to hold a hearing to determine whether or not its registration should be cancelled or its

---

25/   EDF v. Ruckelshaus, 439 F.2d 584, 591-92, 2 ERC 1114, 1119 (D.C. Cir. 1971).

26/   The scientific review committee and other features of this process will be discussed later in more detail.

27/   The cancellation-suspension section of the old Act was § 4(c); it is § 6 of the post-1972 FIFRA.

classification changed." 28/ This revision of the law may not have solved EPA's communications problem with local officials, but it does provide a statutory basis for a distinction which the EPA was intent on making.

2.5 Suspension
A suspension order, despite its misleading name, is an immediate ban on the production and distribution of a pesticide. It is mandated when a product constitutes an "imminent hazard" to man or the environment, 29/ and may be invoked at any stage of the cancellation proceeding or even before a cancellation procedure has been initiated. According to the 18th of March Statement, "an imminent hazard may be declared at any point in the chain of events which may ultimately result in harm to the public." 30/ There are two types of suspension orders: an ordinary suspension order and an emergency suspension order.

2.5.1 Ordinary Suspension
The purpose of an ordinary suspension is to prevent an imminent hazard during the time required for cancellation or change in classification proceedings. An ordinary suspension proceeding is initiated when the Administrator issues notice to the registrant that he is suspending use of the pesticide. This notice must include the Administrator's findings pertaining to the question of imminent hazard. The registrant may request an expedited hearing within five days of receipt of the Administrator's notice. If no hearing is requested, the suspension order can take effect and the order is not reviewable by a court. 31/
Suspension procedurally "resembles...the judicial proceedings on a contested motion for a preliminary injuction," 32/ hence the tentative connotation of the term, and remains in effect until the

---

28/ FIFRA § 6(b), 7 U.S.C. § 136d(b). Note that the Administrator himself may request a hearing, a power which he did not have under the old FIFRA, although arguably he assumed this authority in his August 1971 cancellation order on 2,4,5-T.

29/ FIFRA § 6(c), 7 U.S.C. § 136d(c).

30/ See 18 March 1971 Statement, p.6. A suspension order must be accompanied by a cancellation order if one is not then outstanding. FIFRA § 6(b), 7 U.S.C. § 136d(b).

31/ FIFRA § 6(c), 7 U.S.C. § 136d(c).

32/ EDF v. EPA 465 F. 2d 538, 4 ERC 1523, 1530 (D.C. Cir. 1972).

cancellation hearing is completed and a final decision is issued by the Administrator. 33/ This does not actually accord with reality but has been the consistent theme of judicial decisions since the Agency's inception. According to this view, the function of a suspension order is not to reach a definitive decision on the registration of a pesticide but to grant temporary, interim relief. 34/ The Circuit Court of Appeals for the District of Columbia has repeatedly stated this view: "The function of the suspension decision is to make a preliminary assessment of evidence and probabilities, not an ultimate resolution of difficult issues", 35/ and "the suspension order thus operates to afford interim relief during the course of the lengthy administrative proceedings." 36/

The court of appeals has emphasized that "imminent hazard" does not refer only to the danger of immediate disaster: "We must caution against any approach to the term 'imminent hazard', used in the statute, that restricts it to a concept of crises." 37/ In another case, the court declared that the Secretary of Agriculture:

> has concluded that the most important element of an 'imminent hazard to the public' is a serious threat to public health, that a hazard may be 'imminent' even if its impact will not be apparent for many years, and that the 'public' protected by the suspension provision includes fish and wildlife. These interpretations all seem consistent with the statutory language and purpose. 38/

33/   Nor-Am v. Hardin, 435 F. 2d 1151, 2 ERC 1016 (7th Cir. 1970), cert. denied 402 U.S. 935 (1971).

34/   See, In re Shell Chemical, Opinion of the Administrator, pp. 8-11, 6 ERC 2047 at 2050 (1974).

35/   EDF v. EPA, supra, 465 F. 2d at 537, 4 ERC at 1529.

36/   EDF v. Ruckelshaus, supra, 439 F. 2d at 589, 2 ERC at 1115.

37/   EDF v. EPA, supra, 465 F. 2d at 540, 4 ERC at 1531.

38/   EDF v. Ruckelshaus, supra, 439 F. 2d at 597, 2 ERC at 1121-22.

2.5.2 Emergency Suspension

An emergency suspension differs from an ordinary suspension in that the registrant is not given notice or the opportunity for an expedited hearing prior to the suspension order taking effect. The registrant is, however, entitled to an expedited hearing to determine the propriety of the emergency suspension. The Administrator can only use this procedure when he determines that an emergency exists which does not allow him to hold a hearing before suspending use of a pesticide. 39/

EPA first used the emergency suspension procedure in 1979 when it suspended the sale and use of 2,4,5-T and Silvex for specified uses. EPA issued the emergency suspension orders based on its judgement that exposure to the pesticides created an immediate and unreasonable risk to human health. EPA's action was reviewed by a Michigan district court in Dow Chemical Co. v. Blum. 40/ Where the plaintiffs petitioned for judicial review of EPA's decision and a stay of the emergency suspension orders. In upholding EPA's order, the court analogized the emergency suspension order to a temporary restraining order and defined the term emergency as a "substantial likelihood that serious harm will be experienced during the three or four months required in any realistic projection of the administrative suspension process." 41/ The court held that this standard requires the Administrator to examine five factors: (1) the seriousness of the threatened harm; (2) the immediacy of the threatened harm; (3) the probability that the threatened harm would result; (4) the benefits to the public of the continued use of the pesticides in question during the suspension process; and (5) the nature and extent of the information before the Administrator at the time he makes his decision. The court also held that an emergency suspension order may be overturned only if it was arbitrary, capricious, or an abuse of discretion or if it was not "issued in accordance with the procedures established by law." 42/

39/ § 6(c)(3), 7 U.S.C. § 136d(c)(3).

40/ 469 F. Supp. 892, 13 ERC 1129 (E.D. Mich 1979).

41/ Ibid. at 902, 13 ERC at 1135.

42/ Ibid. The court stated that it arrived at its decision to uphold EPA's order "with great reluctance" and would not have ordered the emergency suspension orders on the basis of the information before EPA, but was not empowered to substitute its judgement for that of EPA's. 469 F. Supp. at 907, 13 ERC at 1140.

2.6 Balancing Test in FIFRA

The balancing of risks versus benefits lies at the heart of the FIFRA, and its importance warrants a separate discussion. There are some who feel that certain types of pesticides, particularly carcinogens, should be forbidden per se as done under the Delaney Amendment to the Food, Drug, and Cosmetics Act. 43/ FIFRA does not require this inflexibility, although the courts have cautioned that it "places a heavy burden on any administrative officer to explain the basis for his decision to permit the continued use of a chemical known to produce cancer in experimental animals." 44/ EPA Administrator Russell Train in 1974 noted this in his decision regarding Aldrin-Dieldrin:

> Since Aldrin-Dieldrin has been found to be car-cinogenic in mice and probably carcinogenic in rats, and to present a high risk of cancer to man, it is arguable that any use of Aldrin-Dieldrin, however significant or beneficial in social or economic terms, cannot be justified, even for the limited period of time until the completion of the cancellation proceedings.
>
> As indicated in Part I of this opinion, however, it is appropriate that the possible benefits of Aldrin-Dieldrin or the absence of such benefits, be considered in this proceeding. Nevertheless, it is apparent that any benefits attributable to Aldrin-Dieldrin must be of high order to affect the findings on carcinogenicity. 45/

The balancing that is applied during the registration process and, more formally, during the cancellation proceedings is deter-mining whether there are "unreasonable adverse effects on the environment," taking into consideration the "economic, social, and environmental costs and benefits of the use of any pesticide." 46/

In a suspension proceeding, however, the FIFRA does not require a balancing of environmental risks and benefits. It has nevertheless been EPA's policy since its inception to conduct such an analysis, although in practice the benefits would obviously need to be considerable to balance a finding of "imminent hazard." One

---

43/ FDCA § 409(c)(3)(A), 21 U.S.C. § 348(c)(3)(A). The relationship between the FIFRA and the FDCA will be discussed later in more detail.

44/ EDF v. Ruckelshaus, supra, 439 F. 2d at 596, 2 ERC at 1121.

45/ In re Shell Chemical, supra., 32, 6 ERC at 2057.

46/ FIFRA §§ 2(bb), 3(c)(5), and 6(b), 7 U.S.C. § 136(bb), 136a(c)(5), and 136d.

Administrator noted that "the Agency traditionally has considered
benefits as well as risks . . . and, in [his] opinion, should continue to
do so." 47/

3.0 Trade Secrets
One issue in FIFRA that has generated considerable controversy involves the treatment of trade secrets. 48/ The judicial
protection of commercial trade secrets has gradually eroded during
the past few years. Courts discovered that many so-called trade
secrets were in fact widely known throughout the industry and did
not merit confidential status. 49/ Section 10 of FIFRA, added in the
1972 Amendments, provides that trade secrets should not be released but, if the Administrator proposes to release them, he should
provide notice to the company to enable it to seek a declaratory
judgement in the appropriate district court. 50/

It is, of course, desirable that university scientists and others
outside industry and government should be able to conduct tests on
the effects of various pesticides. In one case debated by the Agency
for several years, a Georgia professor needed to know the chemical
composition of a particular pesticide to conduct certain medical
experiments. Should the EPA or a court furnish this information to
a bona fide researcher, with or without appropriate safeguards to
preserve confidentiality? EPA resolved that question in the experi-
menter's favor after an investigation revealed that the chemical
composition in fact was not a trade secret within the industry, but
the underlying question has yet to be resolved.

Section 10 provides that "when necessary to carry out the
provisions of this Act, information relating to formulas of products

---

47/ In re Shell Chemical, supra, p.11, 6 ERC at 2050-51, upheld
unanimously by the D.C. Court of Appeals in EDF v. EPA, 510
F.2d 1292, 7 ERC 1689 (4 April 1975). This practice was also
judicially approved in an unrelated case with the same name,
EDF v. EPA, supra, 465 F. 2d at 540, 4 ERC at 1530.

48/ FIFRA § 10, 7 U.S.C. § 136h. Trade secrets have proved to be
a major source of contention in the implementation of the
Toxic Substances Control Act.

49/ This is true not merely in the pesticide area but also, for
example, in the Clean Air Act under Section 211 pertaining to
gasoline additives, where an EPA review several years ago
concluded that most of the hundreds of so-called trade secrets
relating to additives in gasoline were in fact either common
knowledge in the industry or were easily discoverable by back-
engineering.

50/ FIFRA § 10 (c), 7 U.S.C. § 136h(c).

acquired by authorization of this Act may be revealed to any federal agency consulted and may be revealed at a public hearing or in findings of fact issued by the Administrator. 51/ Consequently, if the public interest requires, whatever that means, a registrant must assume that the formula for his product can be made available, although in practice this may not occur very often.

Because of the controversy surrounding the disclosure of trade secrets, Congress amended FIFRA in 1975 and 1978. The 1975 Amendments 52/ cleaned up an ambiguity created by the 1972 Amendments by specifying that the new use restrictions applied only to data submitted on or after 1 January 1970. The definition of trade secrets was left to the Administrator.

EPA took the position that the 1972 and 1975 Amendments restricted use and disclosure of only a narrow range of data, such as formulas and manufacturing processes, but not hazard and efficacy data. However, the industry challenged this view with some initial success. 53/ In 1978, Congress again amended Section 10 to limit trade secrets protection to formulas and manufacturing processes, thus reflecting EPA's position. 54/

In Union Carbide Agricultural Products Company v. Costle, 55/ the Second Circuit overturned an injunction that Union Carbide obtained to prevent EPA from disclosing confidential research data under Section 3 of FIFRA. The appeals court held that the lower court applied the wrong legal test in evaluating the plaintiff's request; and that the moving party must show "likelihood of success" on the merits, which Union Carbide did not do. 56/

Union Carbide asserted that disclosure of the data effected a taking of its property, but the Second Circuit expressed doubts that

---

51/ FIFRA § 10(b), 7 U.S.C. § 136h(b). Note that state agencies are not mentioned.

52/ PL 94-140, 89 Stat. 75 (1975).

53/ Mobay Chemical Corp. v. Costle, 447 F. Supp 811, 12 ERC 1228 (W.D. Mo. 1978), appeal dismissed 439 U.S. 320, reh denied 440 U.S. 940 (1979); Chevron Chemical Co. v. Costle, 443 F. Supp 1024 (N.D. Cal. 1978).

54/ PL 95-396, 92 Stat. 812.

55/ 632 F. 2d 1014, 15 ERC 1113 (2nd Cir. 1980) cert. denied 450 U.S. 996.

56/ Ibid. at 1018, 15 ERC at 1115. The 1978 Amendments to FIFRA passed during the pendency of the suit so the plaintiff amended his complaint to attack the new provisions on constitutional grounds.

such a taking occurred, noting that a distinction must be made between EPA's use of the data and disclosure to the public. Even if there was a taking, the court stated that Union Carbide must establish that it was without an adequate remedy under the Tucker Act. 57/

In Chevron Chemical Co. v. Costle, 58/ a Delaware district court held that FIFRA authorizes EPA's consideration of pre-1970 data for subsequent registrations. It also held that Congress found the use of the data would be a taking for a public, rather than private, purpose. Since FIFRA did not preclude a Tucker Act remedy, the court found that retroactive application of the 1978 Amendments did not violate the plaintiff's due process rights.

On appeal, the Third Circuit upheld the district court's decision and clarified the nature of the plaintiff's property rights in its data. 59/ The appeals court found that Congress rejected the idea that there was a common law property right of exclusive use for materials in the government's files prior to 1 January 1970; according to the court, the 1978 Amendments, which did not extend the compensation provision to pre-1970 data, was implicit rejection of the exclusive use doctrine for that data. The Third Circuit also held that Chevron's property right on the pre-1970 data was based on 18 U.S.C. § 1905 which does not confer a private right of action; it only creates a standard by which to judge the legality of an agency's disclosures. That standard is the right of non-disclosure, not of non-use. 60/

4.0 1972 Amendments to FIFRA

The Amendments to FIFRA in 1972 which are known as the Federal Environmental Pesticides Control Act (FEPCA) 61/ and amounted to a virtual rewriting of the law. They were considered necessary to (1) strengthen the enforcement provisions of FIFRA, (2) shift the legal emphasis from labeling and efficacy to health and environment, (3) provide for greater flexibility in controlling

---

57/ 28 U.S.C. § 1491. The Tucker Act provides compensation for private property taken for public purposes, thus satisfying the Fifth Amendment requirement that the federal government compensate owners when it takes their property.

58/ 499 F. Supp. 732, injunction denied, 499 F. Supp. 745, affirmed 641 F. 2d 104 (3rd Cir. 1981), cert. denied 452 U.S. 961.

59/ 641 F. 2d 104, 16 ERC 2004 (3rd. Cir. 1981), cert. denied 452 U.S. 961.

60/ Id. at 114, 16 ERC at 2013.

61/ PL 92-516, 86 Stat. 973, 21 October 1972.

dangerous chemicals, (4) extend the scope of federal law to cover intrastate registrations and the specific uses of a given pesticide, and (5) streamline the administrative appeals process. Three of the principal changes made by the new law—EPA's expanded authority over field use, the creation of several categories of registration, and trade secrets—have already been discussed. The following discussion will consider other important features of the 1972 Amendments to FIFRA.

4.1 Indemnities

Section 15 provides financial compensation to registrants and applicators owning quantities of pesticides who are unable to use them because of cancellation or suspension. This section, although rarely if ever invoked, was the most controversial in the entire Act. The Amendment's industry supporters threatened to block passage of the entire 1972 legislation if this section were not attached. Public interest groups complained that it would force taxpayers to indemnify manufacturers for inadequate testing and would encourage the production of unsafe chemicals.

As a partial compromise, a clause was added to bar indemnification to any person who "had knowledge of facts which, in themselves, would have shown that such pesticide did not meet the requirements" for registration and continued thereafter to produce such pesticide without giving notice of such facts to the Administrator. 62/ Even under the most expedited Agency procedures, that saving clause may disqualify registrants and manufacturers in virtually all cancellation and suspension actions.

The real purpose of the indemnity provision, according to agriculture chemical lobbyists, was not to compensate manufacturers or even retailers and farmers, but to deter EPA from cancellation and suspension actions. A wide-spread belief in the farming community was that EPA would be reluctant to act if it were forced to buy up large quantities of a banned chemical, using funds from EPA's general budget to indemnify pesticide companies and users. This is, of course, somewhat naive. Federal agencies do not, and should not, make decisions involving human safety and the environment because of such factors; but to the degree that it provides an incentive to the EPA to consider its own budget, rather than the public welfare, it is poor policy.

There is one situation in which the section may influence EPA action. Following a suspension or final cancellation order, the Agency has traditionally not attempted to recall or stop the use of those amounts already in distribution. This tradition, which arose before the passage of the 1972 Amendments, stemmed from the

62/ FIFRA § 15(a), 7 U.S.C. § 136m(a).

hazards of bulk disposal 63/ and the training time needed before
alternative pesticides could be used, but it may now have become
standard Agency practice. 64/ It is uncertain how much Section 15
unconsciously encourages this practice of condoning the continued
use of a chemical which it has declared an imminent hazard.

4.2 "Featherbedding" or "Me–Too" Registrants

The second most contested provision in the 1972 FEPCA,
after the question of indemnities, was the issue of "featherbedding"
on registration. The original version in the House stated that "data
submitted in support of an application shall not, without permission
of the applicant, be considered by the Administrator in the support
of any other application for registration." 65/ Supporters of the
provision, basically the larger manufacturers, claimed that it prevented one company from "free-loading" on the expensive scientific
data produced by another company; environmentalists dubbed this
the "mice extermination amendment" for requiring subsequent
registrants to needlessly duplicate the laboratory experiments of the
first registrant.

The groups finally found an acceptable compromise allowing
subsequent registrants to reimburse the initial registrant for reliance on its data, adding to the above language the words: "unless
such other applicant shall first offer to pay reasonable compensation
for producing the test data to be relied upon." 66/ The section
provides that disputes over the amount of compensation should be
decided by the Administrator, but the 1975 Amendments removed
the unfortunate clause which ensured that the original registrant
should have nothing to lose by appealing to a district court since "in
no event shall the amount of payment determined by the court be
less than that determined by the Administrator." 67/ The 1978
Amendments removed the unwelcome task from the Administrator
entirely by providing for mediation by the Federal Mediation &

63/ Recall and disposal will be discussed later.

64/ See in re Shell Chemical, supra, p. 2, 6 ERC at 2061. Note,
however that in this case the cutoff date was the issuance of
the Notice of Intent to Suspend, not the date of the final
suspension several months later.

65/ FIFRA § 3(c)(1)(D), 7 U.S.C. § 136a(c)(1)(D).

66/ Ibid.

67/ Ibid. This portion was deleted by PL 94-140 § 12.

Conciliation Service. 68/ The 1975 Amendments also pushed back the effective date of the compensation provision from October 1972, the date of the enactment of the FEPCA Amendments, to 1 January 1970. 69/

The data compensation provision has created many problems in the registration process. Pesticide manufacturers brought several lawsuits to determine the breadth of this provision, the proper use of the data, and the amount of compensation that a manufacturer is entitled to for use of its data.

In Amchem Products, Inc. v. GAF Corp., 70/ the primary issue before the U.S. Court of Appeals for the Fifth Circuit was the effective date of the 1972 Amendments. The plaintiff, a manufacturer of a plant growth regulator, challenged the subsequent registration of the substance by another manufacturer on the grounds that the plaintiff had not been compensated for use of its data on which the registration was based.

In district court, EPA and the second manufacturer successfully argued that the effective date of the compensation provision was controlled by Section 4(c)(1) of FEPCA 71/ which required EPA to promulgate regulations governing registrations within two years. Since EPA did not promulgate regulations covering compensation until after the second manufacturer filed its application, the second manufacturer argued that the compensation provision did not apply. 72/

The Fifth Circuit reversed the district court's interpretation, holding that Section 4(c)(1) neither deferred the effective date of the FEPCA Amendments nor gave EPA any discretion to activate provisions of the Act by delaying promulgation of implementing

---

68/ PL 95-396 § 2(2), 92 Stat. 819.

69/ PL 94-140, § 12, amending FIFRA § 3(c)(1)(D).   The 1972 amendments had not actually specified an effective date but most authorities assumed it was the date of enactment.

70/ 594 F. 2d 470 (5th Cir. 1979), reh. denied 602 F. 2d 724 (5th Cir. 1979).

71/ FEPCA § 4(a), 86 Stat. 998, 999.

72/ Amchem Products, Inc. v. GAF Corp., 391 F. Supp 124, 7 ERC 1877 (N.D. Ga. 1975). The taking issue also arises under cases interpreting the 1978 Amendments.

regulations. 73/ The Fifth Circuit also rejected the defendant's argument that the compensation provision applied only to data submitted for the first time by the plaintiff after the FEPCA Amendments became law. The court held that construing the provision to apply to data already in EPA's possession would satisfy Congressional intent to "[put] an end to free rides" by subsequent applications. 74/

In Mobay Chemical v. EPA, 75/ Mobay Chemical sued EPA claiming that EPA's use of its registration data prior to 1970 which was not compensatable under FIFRA was a taking for private use and invalid under the Fifth Amendment. Mobay did not base its claim on FIFRA, but rather the Due Process Clause of the Constitution, claiming that it was deprived of its right to exclusive use of its property. The district court for the Western District of Missouri upheld the 1972 Amendment on the grounds that § 3 of FIFRA was enacted under the Commerce Clause and that Congress's concern with preventing costly duplicative testing was reasonably related to a legitimate purpose. The court also noted that EPA's use of the data did not create a deprivation of property which rose to the level of a taking.

On appeal, the U.S. Supreme Court dismissed the case on procedural grounds. The Court held that since FIFRA did not address EPA's use of pre-1970 data, the plaintiff's challenge was to "agency practice, not the statute." 76/ Since the three judge district court panel had been improperly convened, the court held that it did not have jurisdiction to hear the appeal.

In the case In Re Ciba-Geigy Corp. v. Farmland Industries, Inc., 77/ EPA set out criteria to be applied in determining what constitutes reasonable compensation under § 3(c). Plaintiff Ciba-Geigy claimed that it was entitled to $8.11 million in compensation

---

73/   594 F. 2d at 475.

74/   Ibid. at 482. In 1975, this provision was again amended to provide that only "data submitted on or after Jan. 1970" was covered by the section.

75/   447 F. Supp. 811, 12 ERC 1572 (W. D. Mo. 1975).

76/   439 U.S. 320, 12 ERC 1581 (per curiam) (1979).

77/   Initial Decision, FIFRA Comp. Dockets Nos. 33, 34 and 41 (19 August 1980).

from Farmland Industries for the latter's use of test data to register three pesticides. The defendant argued that it should pay only a proportional share of the actual cost of producing the data based on its share of the market for the products, approximately $49,000. The plaintiff contended that reasonable compensation should be based on the standards used in licensing technical knowledge; an amount equal to the cost of reproducing the data plus a royalty on gross sales for three years.

The administrative law judge hearing the case ruled that a cost-royalty formula was closer to Congress's intent to avoid unnecessary testing costs. He concluded that the reasonable compensation provision was not intended to provide reward for research and development as the plaintiff's formula would do. The fairest compensatory formula, according to the judge, was using the data producer's cost adjusted for inflation and the defendant's market share two or three years after initial registration. Although no reward for research and development was created, this compensation formula does create an incentive to research because the benefits gained from decreased costs of subsequent registrants outweighs the disadvantages of decreasing the original data producer's projects.

4.3 Essentiality in Registration

Another registration change obtained by the pesticide industry was a prohibition against EPA refusing to register a substance because it served no useful or necessary purpose. This was not a dispute as to whether, under both the old and new FIFRA, a registration application must demonstrate that a product would "perform its intended function." 78/ The agricultural chemical companies, however, were apprehensive that EPA might refuse to register a new product because an old one satisfactorily performed its intended function. These fears were largely groundless, for EPA's best interest lay in as much duplication of pesticides as reasonably possible, since the existence of a similar but safer chemical facilitates the removal of a hazardous pesticide from the market. There was therefore little objection to this non-essential Amendment on "essentiality."

78/ FIFRA § 3(c)(5)(D), 7 U.S.C. § 136a(c)(5)(D).

4.4 Intrastate Registrations

One important difference between the old and new laws is that under the old FIFRA, 79/ federal authority did not extend to intrastate use and shipment of pesticides with state registrations. This meant that federal authority could be avoided simply by having a manufacturing plant in the principal agricultural states. The new FIFRA 80/ broadens the registration requirement to include any person in any state who sells or distributes pesticides.

The states do retain some authority under Section 24 "to regulate the sale or use of any pesticide or device in the state, but only if and to the extent the regulation does not permit any sale or use prohibited by this Act." 81/ States, furthermore, cannot have labeling and packaging requirements different from those required by the Act--a measure which was popular among some chemical manufacturers who feared that each state might have different labeling requirements. It also seems to exclude a feature common to several of the other environmental laws whereby states may impose stricter requirements than federal on pesticide use within their jurisdiction.

Finally, the section gives a state the authority, subject to certification by the EPA, to register pesticides for limited local use to treat sudden and limited pest infestations, without the time and administrative burden required by a full EPA certification. 82/

The fears of pesticide manufacturers that the states would impose more stringent labeling requirements were justified in spite of the 1972 Amendments. California imposed additional data requirements under its restricted-use registration. In National Agricultural Chemicals Association v. Rominger, 83/ a California district court declined to issue a preliminary injunction against the state's regulations on the grounds that there was no Congressional

---

79/   Old FIFRA § 4(a).

80/   FIFRA § 3(a), 7 U.S.C. § 136a(a).

81/   FIFRA § 24(a), 7 U.S.C. § 136v(a).

82/   FIFRA § 24(c), 7 U.S.C. § 136m(a).

83/   500 F. Supp 465, 15 ERC 1039 (E.D. Cal. 1980).

mandate to occupy the field when Section 24 was enacted, thus there was no federal preemption of restricted-use registrations. 84/

4.5 Scientific Advisory Committees

An important issue for EPA in the 1972 legislation was a revision of the role of scientific advisory committees in the cancellation-suspension process. 85/ According to the old FIFRA, a registrant challenging a cancellation order could request either a public hearing or a scientific advisory committee; and, in practice, cases involving several registrants usually resulted in both. EPA was also strongly dissatisfied with the vague and often contradictory reports of the advisory committees.

In the 1972 Amendments to FIFRA, the advisory committee was transformed into an adjunct of the hearing process, resolving those scientific questions which the administrative law judge or the parties determined were essential to the final decision by the Administrator. This enables the advisory committee to consider questions of scientific fact while the public hearing is in process, rather than in a separate proceeding with long delays and divisions of responsibility. By meeting outside of the public hearing, the scientists can also avoid being subject to cross examination and other unpopular legal burdens.

The advisory process, however, was again made more formalistic by the 1975 Amendments. The use of a scientific advisory committee is now mandated both for cancellation actions (where they are usually requested anyway) and for any general pesticide regulations; and the composition and selection process for the committee is set forth in considerable detail. 86/

In 1980, Section 25(d) was amended to allow the chairman of a Scientific Advisory Committee to create temporary subpanels on specific projects. 87/ Section 25(d) was also amended to require the Administrator to submit any decision to suspend the registration of a

---

84/ The court also dismissed challenges to two other provisions of the California laws for lack of ripeness. These challenges were claims that the statute improperly allowed the state to set residue tolerances different from EPA tolerances and that certain labeling requirements for insecticides were improperly imposed.

85/ See FIFRA § 6(d), 7 U.S.C. § 136d(d).

86/ PL 94-140, § 7, amending FIFRA § 25. A more detailed analysis of the 1975 changes appears in 5.0.

87/ PL 96-539, 94 Stat. 3195.

pesticide to a scientific advisory panel (SAP) for its comment. 88/
The Amendment does not alter the Administrator's authority to issue
a suspension notice prior to SAP review, it only requires him to
obtain SAP review after the suspension is initiated.   The 1980
Amendments also require the Administrator to issue written procedures for independent peer review of the design, protocol and
conduct of major studies conducted under FIFRA.   The latter two
Amendments are outgrowths of the General Accounting Office
(GAO) study of EPA's controversial decision to suspend 2,4,5-T on an
emergency basis.   GAO reviewed EPA's decision and concluded that
EPA did not have clearly defined peer review procedures.   The
Amendments were enacted to require EPA to proceed on the basis of
validated scientific information and to avoid another 2,4,5-T
controversy. 89/

4.6 Standing for Registration, Appeals and Subpoenas
        The old FIFRA assumed that only registrants would be inter-
ested in the continuation of a product's registration or the setting of
public hearings and scientific advisory committees. It was increasingly evident, however, that this unintended exclusion of both users
and environmentalists needed revision.
        A registrant, when faced with cancellation, might prefer not
to contest those minor categories of use which it regarded as financially insignificant but which a user might regard as necessary for
the protection of his crops.   The law was therefore amended by
FEPCA to allow not only registrants but any "other interested
person with the concurrence of the registrant" to request continuation of the registration. 90/ While this Amendment remedies the
problem of legal standing, it does not provide the resources and data
which a user would need to support his renewal application. 91/
        Another problem of standing relates to the right of environ-
mental and consumer groups to utilize the administrative procedures

---

88/   Id.

89/   No. 96-1020, 96th Cong., 2d Sess. (1980) p.4.

90/   FIFRA § 6(a)(1), 7 U.S.C. § 136d(a)(1). See also McGill v. GPA,
      593 F. 2d 631, 13 ERC 1156 (5th Cir. 1979).

91/   A good example is the Aldrin-Dieldrin suspension proceeding,
      in which the registrant was almost solely interested in the use
      for crops, while the USDA had to join the proceeding to insure
      that other registrations were properly represented. This USDA
      action under the new FIFRA, however, was necessary not
      because the users now lacked legal standing, but presumably
      because they lacked adequate resources. In re Shell Chemical,
      supra, 6 ERC 2047.

under cancellation–suspension. The old FIFRA did not clearly provide for such groups to request a public hearing or scientific
advisory hearing, even though they could obtain judicial review in
the court of appeals as a "person who would be adversely affected by
such order." 92/ The new Act does not specifically give citizens'
groups the right to request a public hearing, but the Administrator
himself is now empowered to call a hearing which he might do at the
request of such a group. Furthermore, as already discussed, all
interested parties may request consent of the administrative law
judge to refer scientific questions to a special committee of the
National Academy of Sciences for determination, a right which did
not exist before.

, The administrative law judge plays a key role in these proceedings, for his approval is necessary for advisory committee
referrals and for the power of subpoena, which is given not to the
parties but to him. 93/ It was Congress' intent to allow the judge
just sufficient discretion to eliminate frivolous or irrelevant issues,
hence the statutory language that "upon a showing of relevance and
reasonable scope of evidence sought by any party to a public hearing, the hearing examiner shall issue a subpoena to compel testimony
or production of documents from any person." 94/ Some commentators, however, have expressed concern that a judge may have
excessive latitude to deny reasonable requests. 95/

The issue of standing came up in Environmental Defense Fund
v. Costle 96/ when the D.C. Circuit upheld EPA's denial of standing
for an environmental group which requested a Section 6(d) cancellation hearing for the continued use of chlorobenzilate in four
states. The Environmental Defense Fund (EDF) requested the

92/   Old FIFRA § 4(d). The standing environmental groups to
      contest governmental actions in general is quite complex. See,
      for example, Sierra Club v. Morton, 405 U.S. 345, 3 ERC 2039
      (1972).

93/   See the EPA Rules of Practice 40 CFR § 164.21, 38 FR 19378
      (1973) and U.S. v. Allen, 494 F. Supp 107 (W.D. Wisc. 1980).

94/   FIFRA § 6(d), 7 U.S.C. § 136d(d).

95/   See, for example, William A. Butler, "Federal Pesticide Law,"
      in Erica L. Dolgin and Thomas G. P. Guilbert, Federal Environ-
      mental Law (St. Paul, Minn., West Publishing Co., 1974), p.
      1256.

96/   631 F. 2d 922, 15 ERC 1217 (D.C. Cir. 1980), cert. denied 449
      U.S. 1112.

hearing after the Administrator issued a Notice of Intent to Cancel the registration of chlorobenzilate for all uses other than citrus spraying in four states. The Administrator denied the hearing holding that FIFRA was not structured for the purpose of entertaining objections by persons having no real interest in stopping the cancellation from going into effect, but who object to the agency's refusal to propose actions. 97/   The D.C. Circuit upheld the Administrator's decision that EDF was not an "adversely affected" party under Section 6(d) stating that a 6(d) hearing may be used only to stop a cancellation proceeding, not initiate one. The proper procedure for EDF in seeking review of EPA's decision to retain the registration for citrus users was to challenge the notice provisions permitting the limited use in district court under Section 16(a) of FIFRA. 98/

4.7 Judicial Appeals

Under the old FIFRA 99/ appeals from decisions of the Administrator went to the United States court of appeals. According to Section 16 of the amended FIFRA, however, appeals under some circumstances may go to a federal district court. Agency "refusals to cancel or suspend registrations, or to change classifications not following a hearing, and other final agency actions not committed to agency discretion by law are judicially reviewable in the district courts." 100/ District courts are also given the authority to "enforce and to prevent and restrain violations of, this act." 101/ Other appeals go to the court of appeals.

This change provoked considerable controversy in the EPA during the legislative process. The rationale for change was that courts of appeals are not designed to develop a record if none existed from the proceeding below. It thus seemed logical that in those instances where a record was developed, after public hearing or otherwise, the appeal should be to the court of appeals, whereas

---

97/   Final Decision, FIFRA Docket No. 411 (20 August 1979) at 12–22.

98/   631 F. 2d at 935, 15 ERC at 1229. This case is also noteworthy for its treatment of judicial review under Section 16(b): See discussion on Judicial Review in 4.2.

99/   Old FIFRA § 4(d).

100/   FIFRA § 16(a), 7 U.S.C. § 136n(a).

101/   FIFRA § 16(c), 7 U.S.C. § 136n(c).

in cases where there was no record for the court to review the matter should go to a district court for findings of fact.

Unfortunately, this creates a certain ambiguity which a party might utilize to prolong the judicial review process. In one case that predated the amended FIFRA, an aggrieved registrant appealed to a district court judge whose record for eccentricity was almost legendary although he had no jurisdiction whatsoever over the matter. It was almost two years before an order of the court of appeals could be obtained to overturn an injunction which he had issued against the Agency. 102/ The legal process would have taken considerably longer if the statutory exclusion of the district court from jurisdiction had been less explicit.

Section 16 has been the focus of two courts of appeals decisions which reached contrary holdings on the issue of whether the federal courts or the courts of appeals have jurisdiction to review the denial of a request for a FIFRA Section 6(d) hearing on a notice of cancellation. In Environmental Defense Fund v. Costle, 103/ the D.C. Circuit held that if an administrative record exists in support of a denial of a hearing request, jurisdiction lies exclusively with the courts of appeals. In AMVAC Chemical Corp. v. EPA, 104/ a divided Ninth Circuit rejected the D.C. Circuit's analysis and held that a denial of a hearing was a procedural action and not an "order" following a "public hearing" within the meaning of Section 16(b). Hence, judicial review of hearing request denials lies in the district courts.

The Ninth Circuit attempted to distinguish the Environmental Defense Fund case because the Environmental Defense Fund petitioners had the opportunity to present their arguments to a Scientific Advisory Panel and the petitioner in AMVAC did not have such an opportunity. 105/ This distinction is rather unpersuasive because the record on which the D.C. Circuit relied included only the proceedings and pleadings on the procedural question of judicial review. Consequently, these two cases present conflicting interpretations of Section 16(b) which may cause procedural nightmares for future review of EPA actions.

102/   Pax Co. v. U.S., 454 F. 2d 93, 3 ERC 1591 (10th Cir. 1972).

103/   631 F. 2d 922, 15 ERC 1217 (D.C. Cir. 1980) cert. denied 449 U.S. 1112. This case is also important for its treatment of standing, discussed in the previous subsection.

104/   653 F. 2d 1260, 15 ERC 1467 (9th Cir. 1980) as amended 5 February 1981, reh. denied, 10 April 1981.

105/   Ibid. at 1265.

4.8 Exports and Imports

The old FIFRA 106/ provided that imports should be subject to the same requirements of testing and registration as American products. Section 17 of the new FIFRA kept this provision 107/ and, at the urging of the chemical industry, also retained the controversial provision excluding U.S. exports from the Act, other than for certain record keeping requirements. 108/

There were two reasons for this. First, the agricultural chemical producers, seeing the market for some of their products such as chlorinated hydrocarbons drying up in this country, wished to continue exporting the products abroad. They argued that foreign producers would not be stopped from manufacturing these chemicals and they wished to continue to compete, as well as to keep in operation profitable product lines.

A secondary but more compelling reason was that cancellation decisions made in the United States are based upon a risk-benefit analysis that might have little relevance to conditions abroad. For example, DDT is neither needed nor, because of insect resistance, very useful for the control of malaria in the United States. The situation in, say Ceylon, however, may be quite different (although resistance is becoming an increasing problem there as well) and should be considered separately.

One problem with this approach is that persistent pesticides may be distributed by oceans and the atmosphere in a world-wide circulation pattern that does not stop at national boundaries. A second problem is that there is no requirement that foreign purchasers relying on EPA registration as proof of a product's safety be notified of cancellation-suspension proceedings. Only after a final Agency decision--which may take years--is the State Department legally required to inform foreign governments. 109/ The 1978 Amendments do add a requirement that such exports be labeled that they are "not registered for use in the U.S." 110/

In 1980 EPA issued a final policy statement on labeling requirements. 111/ Under the 1978 Amendments, pesticides which are manufactured for export must have bilingual labeling which

---

106/ Old FIFRA § 10.

107/ FIFRA § 17(c), 7 U.S.C. § 136o(c). The old FIFRA provisions on exports is § 3(a)(5)(b).

108/ See FIFRA § 8, 7 U.S.C. § 136f.

109/ FIFRA § 17(b), 7 U.S.C. § 136o(b).

110/ FIFRA § 17(a)(2), 7 U.S.C. § 136o(e)(f). See also 44 FR 4358, 19 January 1979.

111/ 45 FR 50274, 28 July 1980.

identify the product and protect persons who come into contact with it. If the pesticide is not registered for use in the United States, the exporter must obtain a statement from the foreign purchaser acknowledging its unregistered status. 112/

The policy statement implements these new requirements by requiring exported products to bear labels containing an EPA establishment number; a use classification statement; the identity of the producer as well as information about whether the pesticide is registered for use in the United States. In the case of highly toxic pesticides, a skull and crossbones must appear and the word "poison" along with a statement of practical treatment written bilingually. 113/

The policy statement also requires that a foreign purchaser of an unregistered pesticide sign a statement showing it understands that the pesticide is not registered for use in the United States. The exporter must receive the acknowledgement before the product is released for shipment and submit it to EPA within seven days of receipt. EPA then transmits the acknowledgements to the appropriate foreign officials via the State Department. The acknowledgement procedure applies only to the first annual shipment of an unregistered pesticide to a producer; subsequent shipments of the product to the same producer do not need to comply with the acknowledgement process. 114/

On 15 January 1981, President Carter signed Executive Order 12264 establishing procedures for the export of banned or significantly restricted substances from the United States. 115/ The comprehensive policy was designed to make present statutory controls over exports more consistent and effective. The cornerstone was a provision requiring that foreign importing countries be notified of the importation of a restricted or banned substance. One of the most restrictive provisions and one that reportedly caused the most disagreement between the federal agencies involved in the policy directed the Department of Commerce to develop regulations for licensing exports of hazardous wastes. The order applied to pesticides, chemicals, drugs, and other products which were restricted in some way by federal statute.

112/   PL 95-396, 92 Stat 833; codified at 7 U.S.C. § 136(o).

113/   45 FR at 50274, 50278, 28 July 1980.

114/   Ibid. at 50276-77.

115/   46 FR 4659, 19 January 1981.

The policy was short-lived because President Reagan rescinded it on 17 February 1981 shortly after he took office. 116/ President Reagan sought instead a review of existing U.S. export controls. The recission resulted in no real changes in the notification requirements under Section 17 of FIFRA.

4.9 Disposal and Recall

An important question following a cancellation or suspension action is whether to recall those products already in commerce. 117/ "Misbranded" pesticides may be confiscated, and on several occasions EPA has ordered manufacturers to recall a pesticide when the hazard so warranted, but for both practical and administrative reasons cancellation-suspension orders have generally provided that banned pesticides may be used until supplies are exhausted, without being subject to recall. 118/ It may seem inconsistent to ban a substance as an imminent hazard and yet allow quantities already on the market to be sold, but repeated challenges by environmentalist groups have been unsuccessful. 119/

This policy was thought necessary, for example, in the mercury pesticides case when EPA scientists concluded that the recall of certain mercuric compounds would result in a concentration more harmful to the environment than permitting the remaining supplies to be thinly spread around the country. In the DDT case the Administrator decided that his final cancellation order would not go into effect for six months to ensure the availability of adequate supplies of alternative pesticides (organophosphates which can be very hazardous to untrained applicators) and to allow time for training and educational programs to prevent misuse of the new chemicals.

116/ 46 FR 12943, 19 February 1981.

117/ FIFRA §§ 19 and 25, 7 U.S.C. §§ 136q and 136w. See also the previous discussion of indemnities.

118/ Compare the recall authority of the Consumer Product Safety Commission under Section 15 of its Hazardous Substance Act, 15 U.S.C. § 1274, PL91-113, which makes recall almost mandatory. The Consumer Product Safety Act, Section 15, on the other hand, provides several options, 15 U.S.C. 2064, PL 92-573.

119/ See, e.g. EDF v. EPA 510 F.2d 1292, 7 ERC 1689 (D.C. Cir. 1975).

EPA promulgated regulations for the storage and disposal of pesticides in May 1974 120/ and proposed others which were never implemented. 121/ These detailed the appropriate conditions for incinerations, soil injection, and other means of disposal, established procedures for shipment back to the manufacturers or to the federal government, directed that transportation costs should be borne by the owner of the pesticide, and provided standards for storage. The regulations devote considerable attention to the disposal problem of pesticide containers, which have caused a significant proportion of accidental poisonings.

4.10 Experimental Use Permits

FIFRA 122/ provides for experimental use permits for registered pesticides. 123/ The purpose of this seemingly innocuous section is to permit a registration applicant to conduct tests and "accumulate information necessary to register a pesticide under Section 3." 124/ This provision, however, has already been used in at least one successful effort to evade a FIFRA cancellation-suspension order. Under strong political pressure from Western sheep interests and their Congressional spokesmen, EPA granted a Section 5 permit for the limited use of certain banned predacides and devices including the "coyote getter." 125/

In March 1974 EPA proposed regulations for experimental permits, noting that in the one-year period from October 1972 to October 1973 almost 100 experimental permits were issued authorizing the use of a total of 1.5 million pounds of pesticides, and this figure did not include substantial experimental use of federal and

---

120/   39 FR 15236, 1 May 1974, 40 CFR § 165.

121/   39 FR 36874, 15 October 1974.

122/   FIFRA § 5, U.S.C. § 136c.

123/   The 1975 Amendments added a specific provision for agricultural research agencies, public or private.

124/   FIFRA § 5(a), 7 U.S.C. § 136c(a).

125/   EPA's pesticide regulatory decisions have generally been little affected by such outside pressures, but this action was one of the three exceptions of the rule. The others were an emergency permit for DDT use in the Pacific Northwest, and the protracted deliberations on the ant-killer Mirex.

state agencies. 126/ These regulations, which became final on 30 April 1975 provide for tighter control over experimental use, including that by governmental agencies, 127/ but did not close the loophole entirely.

EPA issued final regulations on 18 July 1979 under which a state may develop its own experimental permits program. 128/ A state, by submitting a plan which meets the requirements of EPA's regulations, may receive authorization to issue experimental use permits to potential registrants under 24(c) of FIFRA (restricted use registration), agricultural or educational research agencies, and certified applicators for use of a restricted use pesticide.

Permits cannot be issued by a state for a pesticide containing ingredients subject to an EPA cancellation or suspension order, or a notice of intent to cancel or suspend or which are not found in any EPA registered product. 129/ The regulations also contain strict limitations on the production and use of a pesticide. Periodic reports must be submitted by the permittee to the state detailing the progress of the research or restricted use. In addition, permits cannot be issued for more than three years.

5.0 1975 Amendments to FIFRA

Congress' 1975 Amendments to the FIFRA are significant not for what they actually changed but because of the motivations that prompted them. The Amendments themselves were viewed by many as, at best, unnecessary and, at worst, a further encumbrance upon an already complicated administrative procedure. They did, however, indicate a strong desire on the part of Congress—or at least their respective agriculture committees—to restrict EPA's authority to regulate pesticides. The situation was summarized by an editorial in a Washington, D.C., newspaper captioned, "Trying to Hogtie the EPA." 130/

126/ 39 FR 11306, 27 March 1974, 40 CFR § 172.

127/ Ibid. The regulations point out that, except in limited circumstances, the amended FIFRA "does not grant a blanket exemption to federal or state agencies."

128/ 44 FR at 41783, 18 July 1978; 40 CFR § 172.20.

129/ 44 FR at 41788. States may, however, issue permits for products containing ingredients subject to the Rebuttable Presumption Against Review process (RPAR).

130/ The Washington Star, 8 October 1975.

5.1 Need For FIFRA Renewal

The authorization for FIFRA under the 1972 Act was limited to three years. 131/ Congress was therefore provided the opportunity in 1975 to review the strengths and shortcomings of the 1972 legislation, even though some portions of that law were not scheduled to go into effect until four years after enactment. 132/ This review, however, also provided a chance for those, both within and without Congress who believed that EPA had been given too much authority, to seek to redress the balance.

Some environmentalists feared that the Agriculture Committee would allow the bill to lapse altogether, which would have created some uncertainty as to whether the entire FIFRA would have been abolished or merely the 1972 Amendments. Practically speaking, it probably would not have made any difference, as EPA could not have administered any part of the law without Congressional authorization of funds. This eventually, however, probably would have created a backlash in favor of the environmentalists and led to much more stringent laws than the House Agricultural Committee or the agricultural chemical industry desired.

Authorization was therefore granted for FIFRA, but the extension was only for one year (to 30 September 1976) rather than the two-year period which EPA originally sought. The reason for this limitation, according to the official House report, was "to give it [Congress] an opportunity to continue to exercise effective oversight activities over its [EPA's] operations," particularly in view of the controversies that had been generated in many of its activities. 133/

5.2 Controversy over USDA's Veto of EPA

The most spirited debate in the Committee hearings was over an Amendment submitted by Representative Bob Poage (D-Tex), the former Chairman of the House Agriculture Committee. The Poage-Wampler Amendment would have permitted the Secretary of Agriculture to veto EPA actions cancelling or suspending a registration, changing the classification of a pesticide, or issuing regulations.

131/ FIFRA § 27. Actually the term for the Act was less than three years since the Act finally went into effect in October 1972 and the authorization expired 30 June 1975.

132/ One such example is EPA's authority under § 27 to require that a pesticide be registered for use only by a certified applicator.

133/ House Report No. 94-497, "Extension and Amendment of the FIFRA, as Amended," 19 September 1975, for H.R. 8841, p. 5.

The proposed Amendment provided no criteria or legal requirements which the Secretary had to meet before such a veto, nor was it necessary for the Secretary to consider the extensive record developed by EPA for the Administrator's decision. Moreover, although less than half of EPA pesticides relate to Agriculture, 134/ the Secretary would have been granted authority to block EPA actions on all of them. The Amendment would have also severely compromised the administering of the Act by fragmenting the authority over pesticides between the two agencies. 135/ There was some sentiment in Congress for restoring jurisdiction over pesticides to USDA, but the Department's poor prior record discouraged serious consideration of this idea. 136/

5.3 Requirement of Consultation By EPA With USDA

Congress decided instead to require that EPA engage in formal consultation with USDA and with the Agricultural Committees of the House and Senate before issuing proposals or final standards regarding pesticides. This amends Section 6(b) of the FIFRA to provide that EPA should give 60 days' notice to the Secretary of Agriculture before a notice is made public. The Secretary then must respond within 30 days, and these comments, along with the response of the EPA Administrator, are published in the Federal Register. According to the House report, "this represents a real change from present procedures . . . it would have much the same effect as the public exposure of an environmental impact statement. . . ." 137/ These consultations, however, are not required in the event of an imminent hazard to human health for which a suspension order under Section 6(c) is warranted. 138/

This Amendment makes sense only if one assumes either that USDA had not been contacted regularly by EPA before making major

---

134/ See the statement of Russell E. Train, Administrator, EPA before the Senate Agriculture Committee, reprinted in the Senate Report No. 94-452, "Extension of the FIFRA," 10 November 1975, to accompany H. R. 8841, p. 18.

135/ This difficult situation also exists between EPA and FAA, although in that instance the roles are reversed. See the chapter on Noise in this book.

136/ See House Report No. 94-497, p.7.

137/ House Report No. 94-497, p.6. These time deadlines may be by agreement between the Administrator and the secretary, PL 94-140, § 1.

138/ FIFRA, § 6(c), 7 U.S.C. § 136d(c).

decisions in the past, or if it is believed (as the above House report seems to indicate) that USDA's objections to EPA actions had not been given sufficient public attention. Neither assumption is really accurate. The Amendment does, however, place USDA in the potentially embarrassing situation of having to respond formally within an unreasonably short period to EPA proposals. The Department of Agriculture was previously in the politically desirable position of being able to criticize EPA actions without having to provide detailed explanation or supportable objections. 139/

At the same time that the Administrator provides a copy of any proposed regulations to the Secretary of Agriculture, he is also required to provide copies to the respective House and Senate Agricultural Committees. The practical impact of this requirement is that Congress is provided an opportunity to communicate displeasure to the Administrator before a proposal is issued without necessarily having to subject these comments to scrutiny in the public record. 140/

5.4 Scientific Advisory Committees

One of the reforms of the 1972 Amendments had been to streamline the Scientific Advisory Committee process so that Committee deliberations could proceed simultaneously with the administrative hearing, thereby saving time and making them a part of the fact-finding and evaluation system rather than a separate procedure. The 1975 Amendments require that the Administrator submit proposed and final regulations to a specially constituted scientific advisory panel, separate from the regular Scientific Advisory Committees, at the same time that he provides copies to the Secretary of Agriculture and to the two agricultural committees of Congress. The advisory committee then has 30 days in which to respond. Membership on this committee is prescribed in unusual detail. The Administrator can select seven members from a group

---

139/ The requirement for EPA to consult with USDA is the reverse of the situation regarding small watersheds under PL 566, whereby EPA can formally object to USDA's approval of small watersheds, although USDA does not have to accept the objections. House Report No. 94-497, p.6. A similar authority is found in EPA's right to object to FAA decisions which might affect emissions into the ambient air.

140/ EPA has often required that Congressional communications after the issuance of a proposal be placed on the public record; and where this was not done, as in the DDT proceedings, environmental groups successfully sued to ensure that these contacts and written comments are made public.

of 12 nominees, six nominated by the National Science Foundation, and six by the National Institutes of Health. 141/

One might question the value of yet another advisory committee when, as Administrator Train has pointed out, "EPA is already awash in scientific advisory panels." 142/ After all, the statute already provides for a separate scientific advisory committee under the auspices of the National Academy of Sciences for each pesticide cancellation action. EPA has also had, since its inception, a Science Advisory Board (formerly called the Hazardous Materials Advisory Committee) and the Administrator has recently created a Pesticides Policy Advisory Committee. Furthermore, one might question how effective the new advisory committee will be, given its 30-day time limit, considering that the present advisory committees at EPA and other agencies have great difficulty in producing creditable reports under schedules permitting four months of review or longer.

5.5 Economic Impact On Agriculture Statement

The 1975 Amendments also reflected the increasing trend in government toward requiring impact statements before regulations can be issued. Congress, borrowing from the environmental impact statement process 143/ and the economic impact statement requirements, 144/ mandated in the new Amendment that the Administrator, when deciding to issue a proposal, "shall include among those factors to be taken into account the impact of the action proposed in such notice on production and prices of agricultural commodities, retail food prices, and otherwise on the agricultural economy." 145/

The necessity for this new legal provision is questionable since the balancing of risks and benefits is at the heart of FIFRA.

141/ PL 94-140, § 7, amending FIFRA § 25(d), 7 U.S.C. § 136w.

142/ Statement of EPA Administrator Russell Train to the Senate Agricultural Committee, reprinted in Senate Report No. 94-452, p.18. This concern apparently did not prevent Congress from amending FIFRA in 1980 to allow the chairman of a SAP to create subpanels. See discussion of 1980 Amendments, infra.

143/ National Environmental Policy Act, § 102(2)(c), 42 U.S.C. §§ 4321 et seq. (1969); see also 36 FR 7724 (1971) and 38 FR 20549 (1973).

144/ Presidential Executive Order No. 11821, 29 November 1974.

145/ PL 94-104, § 1, amending FIFRA § 6(b), 7 U.S.C. § 136d.

No one at EPA or anywhere else has contended that the agricultural benefits of pesticides should not be taken into consideration in this balancing equation. In fact, although the courts have stated that EPA legally need not consider benefits in suspension actions involving an imminent hazard to human health and the environment, EPA from the beginning has always made the agricultural factor an essential element in its determinations. 146/ The committees themselves were vague about the actual need for this legislation. The Senate stated, "The Committee concurs in the House position that EPA has not always given adequate consideration to agriculture in its decisions. This concern was also expressed by many witnesses appearing before the Committee." 147/ However, the House position, at least as indicated in their official committee report, suggests less certainty: "The Committee believes that the [present] statutory test is a sound one and that changes are not needed in the formula. There was, however, a strong belief among many witnesses that the impact on the agrcultural economy of decisions in EPA was not fully developed by EPA and was not given sufficient recognition." 148/

5.6 Self-Certification of Private Applicators

The clearest illustration of Congress' altered view toward FIFRA is their treatment of the certification program which had been a major reason for the enactment of the 1972 Amendments. This law provided that the pesticides which might be too harmful to the applicators or to the environment if indiscriminately used could continue to be applied by farmers and pesticide operators who had received special training in avoiding these problems.

The program had run into resistance from the beginning from farmers who resented the requirement that they be trained to use chemicals on their own property. As stated in the House report, "The Committee does not see the need for a farmer who would be treating his own farm as he has done for many years to have to go to the county seat or elsewhere for a special training program to get certified." 149/ The changed law does not remove the examination requirement from commercial applicators, who apply pesticides to

---

146/   See the discussion of this in paragraph 2.6 of this chapter.

147/   Senate Report No. 94-452, p.9.

148/   House Report No. 94-497, p.6.

149/   House Report No. 94-497, p.9.

property other than their own. 150/ It does create an exemption, however, which covers not only the farmer who is applying pesticides to his own land but also his employees. And it must be remembered that the hazards are not necessarily limited to the applicator; organophosphates, which are nerve gases, may be highly toxic to the applicators, but many other substances if improperly used may run off to threaten neighboring farms or the environment in general. The amended law does not seem to recognize this latter problem.

The 1975 Amendments also removed the authority of the Administrator to require, under state plans submitted for his approval, that farmers take exams before being certified. In other words, EPA may require a training program but may not require a final examination to determine if the information has been learned. 151/ In the opinion of the House Agriculture Committee, "The farmer would be more aware of the dangers of restricted use pesticides if each time he makes a purchase he is given a self-certification form to read and sign." 152/

The report continues, "at the time of purchase of a pesticide, the dealer goes through the information on the label with the prospective buyer and satisfies himself that the buyer understands the limited uses prescribed by the label. Once the dealer is satisfied that the buyer understands the label clearly, he provides the buyer with a certification form for signature in which the buyer certifies he understands the restricted use of the pesticide and will conduct himself accordingly. The dealer is checked periodically to assure that he is informed on the use of the various pesticides that he is licensed to sell and is properly instructing buyers. 153/

6.0 1978 Amendments to FIFRA

6.1 Conditional Registration
The near-collapse of EPA's pesticide registration process prompted creation of a system of conditional registration or reregistration. This could be applied when certain data on a product's

---

150/ See the definition of commercial applicator in FIFRA § 2(e).

151/ States may themselves require an examination of certified applicators but, under the amended FIFRA, EPA could not make this a prerequisite for state plan approval. See PL 94-140 § 5, amending FIFRA § 4, 7 U.S.C. 136b. See also Senate Report No. 94-452, pp. 7-8.

152/ House Report No. 94-497, p.9.

153/ Ibid, at 9-10.

safety had either not yet been supplied to EPA or had not yet been analyzed to ensure, according to FIFRA § 3(a)(5)(D), that "it will perform its intended function without unreasonable adverse effects on the environment."

Three kinds of conditional registrations are authorized by § 6 of the 1978 law which amends FIFRA § 3(c) with a new section entitled "Registration Under Special Circumstances:" pesticides identical or very similar to currently registered products; new uses to existing pesticide registrations; and pesticides containing active ingredients not contained in any currently registered pesticide for which data need be obtained for registration. These conditional registrations must be conducted on a case-by-case basis, with the last type of conditional registration further limited both by duration and by the requirement that the "use of the pesticide is in the public interest." Conditional registration is prohibited if a Notice of Rebuttable Presumption Against Registration (RPAR) has been issued for the pesticide. And the proposed new use involves use on a minor food or feed crop for which there is an effective registered pesticide not subject to a RPAR proceeding.

Cancellation of conditional registrations must be followed by a public hearing, if requested, within 75 days of the request, but must be limited to the issue of whether the registrant has fulfilled its conditions for the registration. 154/

EPA published final regulations implementing conditional registration on 11 May 1979. 155/

6.2 Generic Pesticide Review

EPA has long complained that registration and, especially, reregistration reviews should be conducted for entire classes of chemicals rather than being limited to examining each particular registration as it comes up for five-year renewal. This authority has always existed under FIFRA, but a district court decision in 1975 156/ on compensation for data made this so complicated that the plan was dropped pending a legislative solution.

The Amendment that finally emerged under this label in Section 4 of the 1978 Act, however, is considerably different in scope: "No applicant for registration of a pesticide who proposes to purchase a registered pesticide from another producer in order to formulate such purchased pesticide into an end-use product shall be

154/   § 12 of 1978 Act, amending FIFRA § 6.

155/   44 FR 27932, 11 May 1979.

156/   Mobay Chemical Corp. v. Train, 394 F. Supp 1342, 8 ERC 1227 (W.D. Mo. 1975).

required to (i) submit or cite data pertaining to the safety of such purchased product; or (ii) offer to pay reasonable compensation . . . for the use of any such data." 157/

In September 1978, EPA listed 40 chemicals contained in 21,000 pesticides to which it intended to apply generic review within the next two years. This included kelthane, azides, warfarin, naphthalene, and boric acid. 158/

6.3 Greater State Authority

Several sections of the 1978 Amendments reflect Congress' intent to give the states greater responsibility in regulating pesticides. This includes not only training and cooperative agreements, but also increasing federal delegation over such matters as intrastate registrations and enforcement. 159/ The EPA Administrator, however, retains overall supervisory responsibility and ultimate veto authority.

Because some states, such as California have promulgated stringent guidelines for pesticide regulations, there has been proposed legislation to limit state authority under Section 24 to gather data about a pesticide for state registration. 160/ Pesticide manufacturers have complained for several years that state registration procedure, which may require additional studies and data gathering, are time-consuming and costly. There have been no changes in Section 24 yet; however, Congress may limit the regulatory authority of the states in future legislation.

6.4 Compensation and Confidentiality

The already overlong FIFRA provisions on the procedures for compensating other firms for their scientific test data are made even more lengthy and complex. One improvement, however, is shifting the arbitrator role from the EPA Administrator to the Federal Mediation and Conciliation Service. 161/ As with TSCA, the controversy over trade secrets will continue to be one of the most

---

157/ 1978 Act, amending FIFRA § 3(c)(2).

158/ BNA 2 Chemical Regulation Reporter, 29 September 1978, pp. 1157-1158.

159/ §§ 21-27 of 1978 Act.

160/ See Hearings Before the House Agricultural Committee, Federal Insecticide, Fungicide, and Rodenticide Act Amendments, H.R. 5203, Serial No. 97-R, (1982).

161/ § 2 of 1978 Act, amending FIFRA § 3.

troublesome in the law.   The new Amendments do clarify EPA's authority to disclose ecological and toxicological data to the public. 162/

6.5 Efficacy

The requirements for test data on a pesticide's efficacy are now made discretionary for EPA. This does not change the present practice very much, because efficacy information has been increasingly less important over the past few years. But the provision is interesting because it marks a complete reversal from the original purpose of federal pesticide legislation earlier in this century, which was to protect farmers from "snake oil" pesticide claims. 163/

7.0 1980 Amendments to FIFRA

FIFRA was amended again in 1980, but the Amendments make only minor changes in Section 25 of the Act. These changes are briefly described in the following two sections.

7.1 Two–House Congressional Veto Over EPA Regulations

The 1980 Amendments amended Section 25(a) to provide a two–house Congressional veto over EPA rules or regulations. 164/ Under the Amendments, the Administrator is required to submit to each house of Congress new FIFRA regulations. If Congress adopts a concurrent resolution disapproving the new regulation within 90 days of its promulgation it will not become effective. However, if neither house disapproves the regulation after 60 days and the appropriate committee of neither house has reported out a disapproving regulation, the regulation becomes effective.

The constitutionality of Congressional vetoes of administrative rules is unsettled. The Supreme Court has at least one case pending before it on one–house vetoes. 165/ Two–House vetoes have not been the subject of litigation as of this writing.

162/   § 15 of 1978 Act, amending FIFRA § 10. The trade secrets provision is discussed in 3.0, infra.

163/   § 5 of 1978 Act, Amending FIFRA § 3 (c)(5).

164/   PL 96–539, 94 Stat. 3194, 3195 amending 7 U.S.C. § 136w(4).

165/   Chadha v. Immigration & Naturalization Service, 634 F. 2d 408 (9th Cir. 1980), cert. granted, 102 S. Ct. 87 (1981), restored to calendar for reargument, 102 S. Ct. 3507 (1982).

7.2   Changes in the Function and Design of the Scientific Advisory Panel (SAP)

Section 25(d) of FIFRA was amended by the insertion of two provisions.   One authorizes the chairman of the FIFRA Scientific Advisory Panel (SAP) to create subpanels. 166/ The other provision requires the Administrator to submit emergency suspension orders to the SAP for review of the environmental impacts of the suspension. 167/

The 1980 Amendments also adds Section 25(e) to the Act which requires the Administrator to issue written procedures for independent peer review of the design and conduct of major studies performed by EPA. 168/   This provision is an outgrowth of the General Accounting Office (GAO) study of EPA's decision to issue an emergency suspension for 2,4,5-T. GAO concluded that EPA did not have clearly defined peer review procedures and that such procedures were necessary to bolster public confidence in EPA's decision. 169/

8.0 Legal Cases

The usual way to understand a legal field is first to read the statute and then to read the cases involved. This is much less helpful in understanding the FIFRA, however, for several reasons. First, the FIFRA, especially the old FIFRA, had a very complicated legal framework in which the practice had for many years necessarily deviated from the apparent scope of the statute. One such instance was the shift from a mere labeling statute, in which harmful substances would be removed as "mislabeled," to one where the health and safety issues were in the forefront. Second, the scientific issues involved in determinations of carcinogenicity, teratogenicity, subacute effects, and the sophisticated chains of causation affecting the environment are understandably not simple matters for a court to follow. Third, as a result, the courts have only hesitantly postulated adjudicatory principle, and some of these if taken literally have been too unrealistic for the Agency to follow. Decisions tend either to be declarations of deference to administrative expertise or remands for further elucidation of a point troubling the court.

166/   PL 96-539, 94 Stat. 3194, amending 7 U.S.C. 136w(a).

167/   Ibid.

168/   PL 96-539, 94 Stat. 3195 adding § 25(e), 7 U.S.C. § 136w(e).

169/   H.R. No. 96-1020, 96th Cong., 2d Sess. (1980), pp. 4, 8.

8.1 Basic Cases

The early cases, originating in the period before EPA's creation, generally resulted in court determinations that the responsible federal agency had not sufficiently examined the health and environmental problems.

A leading case in this respect is the 1970 Court of Appeals decision by Judge Bazelon in Environmental Defense Fund v. Hardin, 170/ which not only gave legal standing to environmental groups under the FIFRA but also determined that the Secretary of Agriculture's failure to take prompt action on a request for suspension of the registration of DDT was tantamount to a denial of suspension and therefore was suitable for judicial review. 171/

That same year the Seventh Circuit Court of Appeals held en banc in Nor-Am v. Hardin 172/ that a pesticide registrant could not enjoin a suspension order by the Secretary of Agriculture, since the administrative remedies, namely the full cancellation proceedings, had not been exhausted: "The emergency suspension becomes final only if unopposed or affirmed in whole or in part, by subsequent decisions based upon a full and formal consideration. 173/ An underlying reason for the court's action, which reversed a three-judge Court of Appeals panel in the same circuit, 174/ was the realization that the suspension procedure, which had been designed to deal with imminent hazards to the public, could effectively be short-circuited by injunctions. In the court's view, therefore, a suspension decision is only equivalent of a temporary injunction which shall hold until the full cancellation proceedings are completed. 175/

170/   428 F. 2d 1083, 1 ERC 1347 (D.C. Cir. 1970).

171/   As there was no administrative record underlying the Secretary's inaction, however, the court remanded the issue to the Department of Agriculture" to provide the court with a record necessary for meaningful appellate review."

172/   435 F. 2d 1151, 2 ERC 1016 (en banc) (7th Cir., en banc, 1970).

173/   Ibid. at 1157, 2 ERC at 1019.

174/   435 F. 2d 1133, 1 ERC 1460 (7th Cir. 1970).

175/   435 F. 2d at 1160-1161.

One of the most important of the earlier cases was EDF v. Ruckelshaus. 176/ The court in another opinion by Judge Bazelon found that the Secretary of Agriculture failed to take prompt action on a request for the interim suspension of DDT registration but that the Secretary's findings of fact, such as the risk of cancer and its toxic effect on certain animals, implicitly constituted a finding of "substantial question concerning the safety of DDT" which the court declared warranted a cancellation decision. The suspension issue was remanded once again for further consideration.

The decision is worthy of attention on two additional points. First, Judge Bazelon made the sweeping statement that "the FIFRA requires the Secretary to issue notices and thereby initiate the administrative process whenever there is a substantial question about the safety of the registered pesticide . . . The statutory scheme contemplates that these questions will be explored in the full light of a public hearing and not resolved behind the closed doors of the Secretary." 177/ Second, the court approved the findings of the Secretary that a hazard may be "imminent" even if its effect would not become realized for many years, as is the case with most carcinogens, and that the "public" protected by the suspension provision includes fish and wildlife in the environment as well as narrow threat to human health. 178/

Wellford v. Ruckelshaus, 179/ another case inherited by EPA from USDA, involved a partial remand of the Secretary of Agriculture's decision concerning suspension and cancellation of certain uses of the herbicide 2,4,5-T for use around the home, in aquatic areas, and on food crops. This case is primarily important for its articulation of certain procedural ground. It agreed with the contention that suspension is only "a matter of interim relief," 180/ and stated that the criteria for suspension during an administrative

---

176/ EDF v. Ruckelshaus, 439 F. 2d 584, 2 ERC 1114 (D.C. Cir. 1971). This was a sequel to the earlier EDF v. Hardin case, supra, but the name of the Administrator of EPA was substituted for the Secretary of Agriculture since the authority of USDA had been transferred to the EPA the month before.

177/ Ibid. at 594, 2 ERC at 1119. Because there may be a "substantial question of safety" about most pesticides, administrative necessity has forced EPA to interpret this as requiring cancellation of only the most harmful chemicals.

178/ Ibid. at 597, 2 ERC at 1121-22.

179/ 439 F. 2d 598, 2 ERC 1123 (D.C. Cir. 1971).

180/ Ibid. at 601, 2 ERC at 1124.

process involved the Secretary's first determining "what harm, if any, is likely to flow from the use of the product during the course of administrative proceedings. He must consider both the magnitude of the anticipated harm and the likelihood that it would occur. Then, on the basis of that factual determination, he must decide whether anticipated harm amounts to an 'imminent hazard to the public.' " 181/

8.2 Label Restrictions: Theory and Practice

One of the most interesting pesticide cases, In re Stearns, 182/ raised the question whether a chemical could be banned that was too toxic to be safely used around the home but which nevertheless was labeled properly with cautionary statements and symbols such as the skull and crossbones. "Stearn's Electric Paste," a phosphorous rat and roach killer, was so potent that even a small portion of a tube could kill a child and a larger dose would be fatal to an adult. There was no known antidote. An incomplete survey of state health officials indicated several dozen deaths and many serious accidents, most involving young children. Because of this hazard and the existence of safer substitutes, the USDA cancelled the registration of the paste in May 1969, before the creation of EPA, and a USDA Judical Officer upheld this action in January 1971 by relying on the provision in the old FIFRA that "the term misbranded shall apply . . . to any economic poison . . . if the labeling accompanying it does not contain directions for use which are necessary and, if complied with, adequate for the protection of the public." 183/

A year and a half later, however, the Seventh Circuit Court of Appeals concluded that the statutory test for misbranding was whether a product was safe when used in conformity with the label directions, not whether abuse or misuse was inevitable. The court was impressed with the conspicuous "poison" markings and contended that "disregard of such a simple warning would constitute gross negligence." 184/ The hazard of young children left the court unmoved: "such tragedies are a common occurrence in today's

---

181/ Ibid. at 602, 2 ERC at 1125.

182/ 2 ERC 1364 (Opinion of Judicial Officer, USDA, 1971); Stearns Electric Paste Company v. EPA, 461 F. 2d 293, 4 ERC 1164 (7th Cir. 1972).

183/ Old FIFRA § 2(z)2(c).

184/ Stearns Electric Paste, supra, 461 F. 2d at 310, 4 ERC at 1175.

complex society and must be appraised as discompassionately as possible." 185/ The cancellation order was set aside.

On the same day, that same panel of the Seventh Circuit also decided Continental Chemiste v. Ruckelshaus, 186/ involving a Lindane (benezene hexachloride) vaporizer, which when lighted emitted a cloud lethal to many insect pests. Studies by USDA demonstrated that these devices in the home produced residues of Lindane on food which "posed a threat to human health." 187/ The vaporizers were registered only for use in commercial and industrial establishments, not for home use, but the registrant's advertising and marketing techniques were specifically designed to promote sales to private consumers. The court declined to rule this illegal, deciding the case on another issue to be discussed later.

The issue was confronted more decisively by the Eighth Circuit a year later in another Lindane case, Southern National v. EPA. 188/ The registrants challenged a proposed EPA label reading in part "Not for use or sale to drug stores, supermarkets, or hardware stores or other establishments that sell insecticides to consumers. Not for sale to or use in food handling, processing or serving establishments." 189/ In EPA's opinion, acceptance of such a label would avoid the necessity of cancelling the entire registration. The court questioned whether EPA was within the scope of its powers under the (old) FIFRA in placing the burden on the manufacturer to discourage distribution to homes but nevertheless sustained the Agency action in all respects.

EPA's policy position, under both the old and new FIFRA, is that if there are safer alternatives to a product which arguably constitutes a substantial question of safety, the hazardous product should be removed from the market. This attitude was clearly expressed In re King Paint, 190/ concerning a paint additive that was toxic to humans but rather ineffective as a pesticide. The Judicial Officer, after reviewing the benefits and alternatives, concluded,

---

185/   Ibid. at 308, 4 ERC at 1174.

186/   461 F. 2d 331, 4 ERC 1181 (7th Cir. 1972).

187/   See 461 F. 2d at 333, 4 ERC at 1182.

188/   470 F. 2d 194, 4 ERC 1881 (8th Cir. 1972). This case was decided about a month after the enactment of the new FIFRA on 21 October 1972, but that law was not applied here.

189/   Ibid. at 196, 4 ERC at 1882.

190/   2 ERC 1819, (Opinion of EPA Judicial Officer, 1971).

the fact "that many hazardous substances find their way into the homes and all too frequently into the hands of children — is no justificiation for exposing the consumer to another source of accidents." 191/ Since less toxic and more effective alternatives existed; the registration was cancelled and this decision was not appealed. This Agency position has implicity been approved by subsequent judicial decisions, except for Stearns, for it is difficult to argue the benefits of retaining a hazardous chemical when preferable alternatives exist.

8.3 Administrator's Flexibility

The courts have recognized tht the EPA in many cases is operating on the frontiers of scientific knowledge. One leading decision, EDF V. EPA, 192/ noted that "it is not an agency in the doldrums of the routine or familiar." 193/ The issues are highly technical, the available scientific data may be inadequate, and "the concept of the safety of the products is an evolving one which is constantly being further refined in light of our increasing knowledge." 194/

> Environmental law marks out a domain where knowledge is hard to obtain and appraise, even in the administrative corridors; in the courtrooms, difficulties of understanding are multiplied. But there is a will in the courts to study and understand what the agency puts before us. And there is a will to respect the Agency's choices if it has taken a hard look at its hard problems. We emphasize again the judicial toleration of wide flexibility for response to developing situations. . . . The Court's concern is for elucidation of basis, not for restriction of EPA's latitude. 195/

8.3.1 Concerning The Scientific Advisory Committee

In emphasizing the Administrator's regulatory flexibility, the courts have rejected the contention that he must "rubber stamp" the

---

191/   Ibid. at 1824.

192/   465 F. 2d 528, 4 ERC 1523 (D.C. Cir. 1972).

193/   Ibid. at 541, 4 ERC at 1531.

194/   Ibid. at 535 n.5, 4 ERC at 1527, quoting with approval EPA's 18th of March Statement.

195/   Ibid. at 541, 4 ERC at 1531-32.

findings of the Scientific Advisory Committee or the Administrative Law Judge. This is illustrated by Dow Chemical v. Ruckelshaus 196/ concerning the herbicide 2,4,5-T. In 1970 the USDA suspended some uses of the chemical and cancelled others because of the high risk that it, or a contaminant known as TCDD, had proved a potent teratogen in laboratory tests. Most of these uses were not challenged, but Dow did contest the cancellation on rice. A Scientific Advisory Committee convoked by EPA concluded that the "confused aggregate of observations indicated registrations should be maintained" but that there remained serious questions needing further extensive research. The Administrator reviewed the report in considerable detail and concluded that a "substantial question of safety" existed sufficient to justify an administrative hearing; in the meantime, the cancellation was maintained. 197/ Dow appealed, but the Court of Appeals for the Eighth Circuit held that the Administrator was not compelled to follow the recommendations of the advisory committee if he had justifiable basis for doing otherwise. 198/

8.3.2 Concerning The Administrative Law Judge
The Administrator is also not bound by findings of the Administrative Law Judge. This conclusion follows the general principle of administrative law that a hearing examiner's decision should be

---

196/ 477 F. 2d 1317, 5 ERC 1244 (8th Cir. 1973).

197/ The deficiencies in the advisory report, which was poorly reasoned and internally inconsistent, contributed to the Agency's skepticism towards this system of information collection and analysis. The advisory process was improved considerably, however, by providing better staff support to the committee and making them an adjunct of the hearing process.

198/ This case is better remembered for its unconscionable delay of the administrative process. Dow appealed first to a district court in Arkansas and obtained an injunction against further EPA action on 2,4,5-T, although the statute explicitly excluded district courts from jurisdiction. The Eighth Circuit reversed, noting that the court below lacked jurisdiction and that in any case Dow was not entitled to an injunction during a period when "the cancellation orders have no effect on Dow's right to ship and market its product until the administration cancellation process has been completed." Ibid. at 1326, 5 ERC at 1250.

accorded only the deference it merits. As the Supreme Court said in Universal Camera, "we do not require that the examiner's findings be given more weight than in reason and in light of judicial experience they deserve." 199/ Only if the decision-maker arbitrarily and capriciously ignored the findings of an examiner, or if the credibility of witnesses was crucial to the case—a situation that rarely exists in an administrative hearing—would a different conclusion be indicated. In the DDT case, the court noted that demeanor was not particularly important, adding that "examiner himself had no particular expertise, for he was a coal mine accident specialist" borrowed from the Department of Interior. 200/

8.3.3 National Environmental Policy Act

The EPA is also not bound by the National Environmental Policy Act (NEPA) 201/ to file Environmental Impact Statements on its pesticide decisions, since the procedures under the FIFRA are an adequate substitute. Although the strict language of NEPA states that all agencies of the federal government should file impact statements, this law was enacted before EPA existed, and courts almost unanimously have found that there is little logic in requiring an agency whose sole function is protection of environment to file a statement obliging it to take into consideration environmental factors. 202/ Courts nevertheless hesitated to grant a blanket exemption to EPA, preferring to stress that EPA actions are mandated by a given statute, although this justification has not exempted certain non-environmental agencies; or they have noted that EPA procedures for articulating its position and providing for public comment were an adequate substitute for the same procedures under NEPA. The court in EDF V. EPA ("DDT case") discussed all these factors: 203/

> We conclude that where an agency is engaged primarily in an examination of environmental questions, where substantive and procedural standards

---

199/ Universal Camera Corp. v. NLRB, 340 U.S. 474 (1951).

200/ EDF v. EPA (DDT case), 489 F.2d 1247, 1253, 6 ERC 1112, 1117 (D.C. Cir. 1973).

201/ 42 U.S.C. § 4331 et seq., 83 Stat. 852.

202/ For example, Essex Chemical Corp., v. Ruckelshaus, 486 F. 2d 427 , 5 ERC 1820 (D.C. Cir. 1973), Portland Cement Assn. v. Ruckelshaus, 486 F. 2d at 375, 5 ERC 1593 (D.C. Cir. 1973).

203/ EDF v. EPA, 489 F. 2d at 1257, 6 ERC at 1119.

ensure full and adequate consideration of environmental issues, then formal compliance with NEPA is
not necessary, but functional compliance is sufficient.   We are not formulating a broad exemption
from NEPA for all environmental agencies or even for
all environmentally protective regulatory actions of
such agencies. Instead, we delineate a narrow exemption from the literal requirements for those actions
which are undertaken pursuant to sufficient safeguards
so that the purpose and policies behind NEPA will
necessarily be fulfilled. The EPA action here meets
this standard, and hence this challenge to the EPA
action is rejected.

9.0 Pesticide Regulation Under Other Federal Statutes

Pesticides are not regulated solely under the FIFRA. They
may also involve regulatory authority under the Food, Drug and
Cosmetic Act (FDCA), under the statutes of several other federal
agencies, and under other environmental laws administered by EPA.

9.1 Pesticides Under the Food, Drug & Cosmetics Act

One important function of EPA regarding pesticides is not
derived from the FIFRA--the setting of tolerances for pesticide
residues in food. This authority, originally granted to the Food and
Drug Administration under the Food, Drug and Cosmetic Act, 204/
was transferred to EPA by the 1970 Reorganization Plan establishing
the Agency and, more specifically, by subsequent detailed memos of
agreement between EPA and FDA.

The reorganization plan provided that EPA should set tolerances and "monitor compliance," while the Secretary of HEW would
continue to enforce compliance. The Amendments to FIFRA in 1972
also invested EPA with authority to prevent misuse of registered
pesticides.   Under Section 408 of the FDCA, the Administrator
issues regulations exempting any pesticides for which a tolerance is
unnecessary to protect the public health. 205/ Otherwise, he "shall
promulgate regulations establishing tolerances with respect to . . .
pesticide chemicals which are not generally recognized among
experts . . . as safe for use . . . to the extent necessary to protect
the public health." 206/

Pesticide residues are present in most meats, fruits, and
vegetables whether or not chemicals are applied to them. DDT, for

---

204/   FDCA § 408, 21 U.S.C. § 346a, et seq.

205/   FDCA § 408(c), 21 U.S.C. § 346a(c).

206/   FDCA § 408(b)(c), 21 U.S.C. § 346(b) and (c).

example, is detectable in most foods, even in mothers' milk. Before registration of a pesticide, a residue tolerance must be set for the maximum level at which that chemical can be safely ingested. Tolerances are usually set at two orders of magnitude (one-hundredth) below the level at which the pesticide has demonstrated an effect on experimental animals. 207/ Some particularly hazardous chemicals are set at "zero residue," but this is causing an increasing problem as the detection capability of analytical equipment is improved. 208/

EPA's pesticide jurisdiction is supposed to cover only residues resulting from a chemical's use as a pesticide but not exposure resulting from, say, dust blowing from a factory (this may be covered by EPA's Clean Air Act) or a truck carrying the chemicals. 209/ In two major cases involving HCB (hexachlorobenzene) contamination of cattle in Louisiana and sheep in the Rocky Mountains, the HCB was blown from open trucks onto pasture land while being transported from one point to another. EPA assumed responsibility for these cases because the tolerance problems regarding health are really the same whether the chemical entered the food as a result of agricultural use or for some other reason, and FDA was only too glad to oblige.

Several of the pesticide tolerance cases involved DDT. The leading pre-EPA case was Environmental Defense Fund v. HEW. 210/ EDF proposed that the Secretary of HEW establish a "zero tolerance" for DDT residues in raw agricultural commodities, as they could potentially cause cancer in human beings. 211/ The D.C. Circuit pointed out that the Delaney Amendment, 212/ banning all "additives" found to induce cancer when ingested by man or

---

207/   This is an oversimplification: the tolerance margin depends on the particular effects of the chemical.

208/   This problem of the so-called "zero level" exists in other health laws as well; the recent Department of Labor standard on vinyl chloride, for example, set a "no detectable level" arbitrarily defined as one part per million (ppm), plus or minus one-half of a ppm.

209/   FDCA § 306, 21 U.S.C. § 336.

210/   428 F. 2d 1083, 1 ERC 1341 (D.C. Cir. 1970).

211/   FDCA § 408, 21 U.S.C. 301.

212/   FDCA § 409(c)(3)(A), 21 U.S.C. § 348(c)(3)(A), of 1958. See also H.R. Rep. No. 1761, 86th Cong., 2d Sess., Appendix 2 (1960) U.S. Code Cong. & Ad. News 2887, 2936.

animal, "did not apply to pesticide chemicals, although it did indicate strong Congressional concern with potential carcinogens.

The question of whether DDT was a food "additive" in fish within the meaning of the FDCA was raised again in U.S. v. Ewing Bros. 213/ The Seventh Circuit explained that prior to the Delaney Amendment the term did not cover substances present in the raw product and unchanged by processing, but after 1958 the definition was expanded so a single tolerance could cover both raw and processed foods. Since DDT was an additive and EPA had not issued a tolerance, DDT was theoretically a food adulterative and contaminated items were liable to seizure. 214/

This could mean, however, that most foods could be seized as adulterated, including the Great Lakes fish at issue in Ewing. Realizing this in 1969, the FDA had established an interim action level of 5 ppm DDT in fish, thereby excluding all but the most contaminated samples. 215/ This procedure was approved by the Seventh Circuit Court of Appeals in U.S. v. Goodman, 216/ which held that the Commissioner of FDA had "specific statutory authority in the Act empowering him to refrain from prosecuting minor violations," 217/ and that this permitted him to set and enforce action levels in lieu of totally prohibiting the distribution of any food containing DDT at any level.

9.2 Clean Air Act of 1970

Pesticides in the air may be regulated under Section 112 of the Clean Air Act pertaining to hazardous air pollutants. A hazardous pollutant is defined as one for which "no ambient air quality

---

213/   502 F. 2d 715, 6 ERC 2073 (7th Cir. 1974).

214/   Under FDCA § 402(a)(2)(C), 21 U.S.C. § 342(a)(2)(C), this affects only a substance that "is not generally recognized among experts . . . as having been adequately shown . . . to be safe under the conditions of its intended use . . . " See FDCA § 201(s), 21 U.S.C. § 321(s). Without a tolerance, "the presence of the DDT causes fish to be adulterated without any proof that it is actually unfit as food." 6 ERC 2073, 2077.

215/   Action levels and enforcement, unlike tolerance setting, remain a prerogative of FDA under Section 306 of the FDCA, 21 U.S.C. § 336.

216/   486 F. 2d 847, 5 ERC 1969 (7th Cir. 1973).

217/   Ibid. at 855, 5 ERC at 1974; FDCA § 306, 21 U.S.C. § 336, U.S. v. 1500 Cases, 245 F. 2d 208, 210-11 (7th Cir. 1956); U.S. v. 484 Bags, 423 F. 2d 839, 841 (5th Cir. 1970).

standard is applicable and which in the judgment of the Administrator may cause, or contribute to, an increase in mortality or an increase in severe irreversible, or incapacitating reversible illness." 218/ EPA publishes a list of hazardous air pollutants from time to time and, once a pollutant is listed, proposed regulations establishing stationary source emission standards must be issued unless the substance is conclusively shown to be safe. This section has so far not been applied to pesticides but could acquire more significance in the future.

9.3 Federal Water Pollution Control Act of 1972

The Water Act as amended in 1972 219/ has at least three provisions applicable to pesticides. Under Section 301, pesticide manufacturers and formulators, like all other industrial enterprises, must apply for discharge permits if they release effluents into any body of water. These point sources of pollution must apply the "best practicable control technology" by 1977 and by 1983 must use "the best available control technology." 220/

Hazardous and ubiquitous pesticides may be controlled under Section 307 governing "toxic substances." 221/ Within one year of the listing of a chemical as a "toxic substance," the special discharge standards set for it must be achieved. There was originally some dispute whether pesticides should properly be regulated under this section because, unless they are part of a discharge from an industrial concern, they generally derive from non-point sources such as runoff from fields and therefore could be controlled under a third provision, § 208, which is largely under the jurisdiction of the states. 222/

EPA's principal function under Section 208 is to identify and oversee problems of agricultural pollution, regulated at the state and local level. By 1977, according to the Statute, state authorities were to have formulated control programs for the protection of

---

218/   Clean Air Act, § 112(a)(1), 42 U.S.C. § 1857c–7(a)(1) (1970).

219/   Federal Water Pollution Control Act Amendments of 1972 (FWPCA), 33 U.S.C. § 1251 et seq., 86 Stat. 816 (1972).

220/   FWPCA § 301, 33 U.S.C. § 1311.

221/   FWPCA § 307, 33 U.S.C. § 1317. The criteria for this list is given in 38 FR 18044 (1973).

222/   EPA, however, has not followed this reasoning. The present § 307 list of 299 toxic pollutants contains many of the major pesticides. See NRDC v. Train (D.C. Cir. 1976) 8 ERC 2120.

water quality, pesticides and other agricultural pollutants such as feed-lots. 223/

9.4 Solid Waste Disposal Acts

The EPA had very limited authority under Section 204 of the Solid Waste Disposal Act, as amended by the Resource Recovery Act of 1970, 224/ to conduct research, training, demonstrations and other activities regarding pesticides storage and disposal. 225/ Enactment of the Resource Conservation and Recovery Act (RCRA) in October 1976 gave EPA an important tool for controlling the disposal of pesticides, particularly the waste from pesticide manufacture. 226/ The role of RCRA is described in detail in a separate chapter of this Handbook.

9.5 Occupational Safety and Health Act

The EPA and the Department of Labor share somewhat overlapping authority under FIFRA and the Occupational Safety and Health Act (OSHA) 227/ for the protection of agricultural workers from pesticide hazards. This produced a heated inter-agency conflict during the first half of 1973, although the FIFRA and its legislative history clearly indicated that the EPA had primary responsibility for promulgating re-entry and other protective standards in this area, and that OSHA specifically yielded to existing standards by other federal agencies. 228/ The question was finally settled by the White House in EPA's favor after a court had enjoined Labor's

---

223/ FWPCA § 208, 33 U.S.C. § 1288.

224/ 42 U.S.C. § 3251 et seq., 79 Stat. 997 (1965), 84 Stat. 1227 (1970); RCRA § 204, 42 U.S.C. § 3253.

225/ RCRA § 212, 42 U.S.C. 3241. Under the Solid Waste Disposal Act, guidelines applicable only to federal agencies have been issued regarding pesticide storage and disposal pertaining to Sections 19 and 25 of the FIFRA. 39 FR 15236, 1 May 1974, and proposed regs., 39 FR 36847, 15 October 1974. See also RCRA § 209, 42 U.S.C. § 3254c.

226/ PL 94-580, 42 U.S.C. 6801 (21 October 1976).

227/ 29 U.S.C. § 651, et seq., 84 Stat. 1590.

228/ OSHA § 6, 29 U.S.C. § 655.

own proposed standards. 229/ Both agencies now seem relatively satisfied with the arrangement. Some farm worker groups, however, still contend that the protective standards on EPA pesticide labels are weak and seldom enforced, and that only California and a few other states have adequate statutory and enforcement programs. It may be that local standards, with some federal monitoring of their effectiveness, would be the preferable approach, since the safe re-entry period after spraying can vary dramatically depending on humidity and other local conditions.

9.6 Federal Hazardous Substances Act

The Federal Hazardous Substances Act of 1970 230/ regulates hazardous substances in interstate commerce. However, pesticides subject to the FIFRA and the FDCA have been specifically exempted by regulation 231/ from the definition of the term "hazardous substance." This statute is administered by the Consumer Product Safety Commission (CPSC) which also administers the Poison Prevention Packaging Control Act of 1970, 232/ designed to protect children from pesticides and other harmful substances. It is not yet clear how EPA and the CPSC will divide their overlapping authority in this area. EPA might welcome the involvement of CPSC in this limited portion of the pesticide area to the extent that its own hands are tied by the Court of Appeals decision in the Stearns Paste case. 233/

9.7 Federal Pesticide Monitoring Programs

The FDA and USDA assist EPA in monitoring pesticide residues in food. The FDA conducts frequent spot checks and an annual Market Basket Survey in which pesticide residues are analyzed in a representative sampling of grocery items. The FDA's Poison Control Center also compiles current statistics on chemical poisoning. The USDA's Animal and Plant Health Inspection Service conducts spot checks on pesticides in meats and poultry based on samples taken at slaughter houses throughout the country.

229/   Florida Peach Growers Assn. v. Dept. of Labor, 489 F. 2d 120, (5th Cir. 1974).

230/   15 U.S.C. § 1261 et seq., 84 Stat. 1673.

231/   16 CFR § 1500 3(b)(4)(ii).

232/   15 U.S.C. § 1471 et seq., 84 Stat. 1670.

233/   U.S. v. Stearns Electric Paste, supra.

The Department of Interior samples pesticide residues in fish and performs experiments to determine the effects of pesticides which may be introduced into the aquatic environment. The Geological Survey Division of Interior also conducts periodic nationwide water sampling for pesticides and other contaminants. The National Oceanic Atmospheric Administration (NOAA) under the Department of Commerce monitors aquatic area for pesticide levels, and the Department of Transportation's Office of Hazardous Substances records accidents involving pesticides in shipment and distribution.

10.0 The RPAR Process

The most important new area in pesticides involves the contested reregistration process, usually termed the Rebuttable Presumption Against Registration (RPAR).

Many pesticides are coming up for renewal that were originally registered under the USDA or the early days of EPA when the standards for review were less strict. These will have to be given much closer scrutiny this time. This is mandated by the 1972 Amendments to FIFRA, which directed EPA to assess the risks of all pesticides by October 1976. 234/ (This deadline was missed, as was a Congressional extension to October 1977.)

Since there are over thirty thousand registrations, EPA realized early that it could not give adequate individual attention to each one, so it sought a procedural shortcut. The obvious solution was to examine in detail only those for which serious adverse data was alleged. Furthermore, since the law placed the burden of proof on the proponent of registration, this feature was naturally incorporated in the new process. 235/

From this uncontroversial basis developed a most controversial program. As set forth in Section 162.11 of the pesticide regulations, 236/ "a rebuttable presumption shall arise . . . upon a determination by the Administrator that the pesticide meets or exceeds any of the criteria for risk set forth in subparagraph (3)." These criteria are extraordinarily detailed; for example, under acute toxicity they specify "an acute dermal LD_{50} of 6g/kg, 'or' an inhalation LC_{50} of 0.04mg/liter or less as formulated." 237/ Chronic toxic effects, such as oncogenicity (cancer) and mutagenicity, are also listed.

234/   Section 4(c)(2) of 61 Stat. 163, 7 U.S.C. § 135.

235/   Most of the plan was worked out at an EPA conference in Easton, Md., in the summer of 1974.

236/   40 CFR § 162.11; 40 FR 28268, 3 July 1975; as amended by 40 FR 32329 and 42746.

237/   40 CFR § 162.11 (3)(i)(A)(2) and (A)(3).

The regulations call for EPA then to notify the registrant that a rebuttable presumption exists against the pesticide and allow 45 days (extendable to 105 days) for him to submit scientific data rebutting the allegations of risk. The burden of proof is on him to demonstrate that the product, if used correctly, is not likely to result in any significant adverse, acute, or chronic effects. 238/ If the question is not resolved at this point, a public hearing may be held to assess the balance of risks and benefits.

In practice, the Agency has established a multistage review process, beginning with the placing of a pesticide on a lengthy suspect list and then a pre-RPAR review of all available scientific literature and test data to determine whether any risk criteria are met. Even this preliminary step can have serious economic consequences, and the chemical industry complains:

> the pesticide suffers in the marketplace because people have a tendency to back away when a possible RPAR is mentioned and is put into "limbo" as far as registration is concerned. Even a label Amendment is out of the question as long as RPAR is threatened. 239/

The original RPAR candidate list contained 45 classes of pesticides, of which 24 were still undergoing pre-RPAR review at the end of 1977. 240/ An additional 23 new chemicals were added to the pre-RPAR list on December 1977. 241/ Many more suspect pesticides were scheduled for inclusion on subsequent pre-RPAR.

The Reagan Administration has initiated a new policy with respect to RPAR's which will supposedly streamline the process. 242/ Registrants requested a preliminary initial review process, so that chemicals only entered the formal RPAR process when clear

---

238/ 40 CFR § 162.11 (a)(4).

239/ "A Trojan Horse Named RPAR," Farm Chemicals, August 1977.

240/ Six others had been voluntarily cancelled by the registrants, 12 had been RPAR'ed, and 2 were returned to the registration process. Letter of EPA Administrator Douglas M. Costle to Sen. Edward M. Kennedy, 4 November 1977, reprinted in BNA, Chemical Regulation Reporter, p. 1277.

241/ BNA, Chemical Regulation Reporter, 23 December 1977, p. 1493.

242/ Ibid. 9 July 1982, pp. 506-510.

risk problems were established.   They also sought expedited
decisionmaking once RPAR was triggered.   As a result, EPA proposed to revise its policy to include more opportunity of negotiations
between EPA and a registrant.   EPA also proposed a preliminary risk
assessment before the public evaluation process is initiated.   No new
chemicals have been placed on the RPAR or pre-RPAR review under
the Reagan Administration, and EPA has indicated it will eliminate
its backlog of chemicals under review by the end of 1982. 243/
Since EPA is not known for meeting deadlines, this "end of 1982"
target date is suspect.

243/   Ibid. 16 July 1982, p. 500.

Chapter 8

OCCUPATIONAL SAFETY AND HEALTH ACT [1]

Marshall Lee Miller
Attorney
Reid & Priest
Washington, DC

1.0 Introduction

The U.S. Occupational Safety and Health Administration (OSHA) has been called the most unpopular agency in the federal government. It has justifiably been criticized for confusing regulations, chronic mismanagement, and picayune enforcement. With somewhat less accuracy, business groups have likened it to an American gestapo, while labor unions have denounced it as unresponsive and bureaucratic.

It is not often recognized, however, that OSHA is also perhaps the most important environmental health agency in the government. Even the Environmental Protection Agency (EPA), with far greater resources and public attention, deals with a smaller range of much less hazardous exposures than does OSHA. After all, individuals are more likely to be exposed to high concentrations of dangerous chemicals in their workplaces than in their backyards.

2.0 Comparison of OSHA and EPA

There are several distinct differences between OSHA and EPA. First, OSHA has major responsibility over workplace safety as well as health. Second, OSHA is essentially an enforcement organization, with a majority of its employees as inspectors, performing fifty thousand or more inspections a year. This "highway patrol" function, inspecting and penalizing thousands of businesses large and small, is the major reason for OSHA's substantial unpopularity. At

---

[1] A section-by-section outline of the key provisions of the statute can be found at the end of this chapter as Appendix A.

EPA, on the other hand, inspections and enforcement are a relatively minor part of the operation.

Third, whereas EPA is an independent regulatory agency,
albeit headed by presidential appointees, OSHA is a division of the
Department of Labor. This organizational arrangement provides not
only less prestige and, in theory, less independence for OSHA, but
poses an internal conflict whether OSHA should be primarily a
health or a labor-oriented agency. Nevertheless, OSHA and EPA
regulate different aspects of so many health issues—asbestos, vinyl
chloride cancer policies, hazard labeling, and others—that it is
reasonable to regard them both as overlapping environmental organizations.

3.0 Legislative Framework

OSHA was created in December 1970—the same month as
EPA—with the enactment of the Occupational Safety and Health
Act (OSH Act), 2/ and began official operation in April 1971. When
compared with other environmental acts, the OSH Act is very simple
and well drafted. This does not mean that one necessarily agrees
with the provisions of every section, but it is clearly and concisely
written so that details can be worked out in implementing regulations. And unlike the other environmental laws which have been
amended several times, the OSH Act has not been modified since its
original passage. 3/

3.1 Purpose of the Act

The Act sets an admirable but impossible goal: to assure that
"no employee will suffer material impairment of health or functional
capacity" from a lifetime of occupational exposure. 4/ It does not
require a balancing test nor a risk-benefit determination. The
supplementary phrase in the OSH Act, "to the extent feasible," was
not meant to alter this. This absolutist position, comparable only to
one provision in the Clean Air Act, 5/ reflects Congress' displeasure

---

2/   Occupational Safety and Health Act of 1970, P.L. 91-596, 84
     Stat. 1590.

3/   Its annual appropriations legislation, however, has been
     modified several times to restrict OSHA authority over small
     businesses, farming, hunting, and other subjects.

4/   OSH Act § 6(b)(5), emphasis added.

5/   Clean Air Act § 112, 42 USC § 1857. There is considerable
     controversy whether this section, the National Emission
     Standards for Hazardous Air Pollutants (NESHAPS), was really
     intended by Congress to have this effect.

at previous, flexible state standards which traditionally seemed always to be resolved against workers' health. In fact, the concession to "feasibility" was added almost as an afterthought. 6/

Business groups did obtain two provisions in the law as their price for support. First, industry insisted that states should be encouraged to assume primary responsibility, thereby minimizing the role of the federal OSHA. Second, because of their distrust for the allegedly pro-union bias of the Department of Labor, responsibility for first-level adjudication of violations would be vested in an independent, three-member panel of judges in a separate Occupational Health and Safety Review Commission. Both of these provisions may be mistakes, and (as discussed below) the first has openly been acknowledged as such by many industry leaders.

Congress did reject, however, an industry effort to separate the standard setting authority from the enforcement powers of the new organization. A special role for the National Institute for Occupational Safety and Health (NIOSH) sought to assure it a primary position in the standard-setting process. Thus, the three main roles of OSHA are (1) setting of safety and health standards, (2) their enforcement through federal and state inspectors, and (3) public education and consultation.

3.2 Coverage of the Act

In general, coverage of the Act extends to all employers and their employees in the 50 states and all territories under federal government jurisdiction. 7/ An employer is defined as any "person engaged in a business affecting commerce who has employees but does not include the United States or any State or political subdivision of a State." 8/ Coverage of the Act was clarified by regulations published in the Federal Register on 21 January 1972. 9/ These regulations interpret the coverage as follows:

(1) The term "employer" excludes the United States and states and political subdivisions.
(2) Any employer employing one or more employees is under its jurisdiction, including professionals, such

---

6/ The Supreme Court's consideration of this issue will be discussed in a later section.

7/ OSH Act § 4(a)-4(b)(2).

8/ OSH Act § 3(5). The appropriations language, as mentioned, has excluded several "peripheral" categories of employers in the past few years.

9/ Ibid.

as physicians and lawyers; agricultural employers; and nonprofit and charitable organizations.

(3)   Self-employed persons are not covered.

(4)   Family members operating a farm are not regarded as employees.

(5)   To the extent that religious groups employ workers for secular purposes, they are included in the coverage.

(6)   Domestic household employment activities for private residences are not subject to the requirements of the Act.

(7)   Workplaces already protected by other federal agencies under other federal statutes (discussed later) are also excluded.

4.0 Federal and State Employees

The exclusion of federal and state employees 10/ has been the topic of much discussion and debate. Although Section 19 of the Act designates the responsibility for providing safe and healthful working conditions to the head of each agency and implementing regulations have been published according to various Executive Orders, many commentators feel the individual agencies' programs are inadequate and inconsistent.

In 1980, a new Presidential Executive Order 11/ was issued, which broadened the responsibility of federal agencies for protecting their workers, expanded employee participation in health and safety programs, and designated circumstances under which OSHA will inspect federal facilities. In the operation of their internal OSHA programs, agency heads will have to meet requirements of basic program elements issued by the Department of Labor and will have to comply with OSHA standards for the private sector unless they can justify alternatives.

5.0 Health Standards

Health issues, notably environmental contaminants in the workplace, have increasingly become OSHA'S primary concern over the past few years. Health hazards are much more complex, more difficult to define, and because of the delay in detection, perhaps more dangerous to a larger number of employees. Unlike safety

---

10/   Ibid, 37 FR 929, 21 January 1972, 29 CFR § 1975.

11/   Executive Order 12196, signed 26 February 1980, 45 FR 12769, superseding E.O. 11807 of 28 September 1974.

hazards, the effects of health hazards may be slow, cumulative, irreversible, and complicated by non-occupational factors.

If a machine is unequipped with safety devices and maims a worker, the danger is clearly and easily identified and the solution usually obvious. However, if workers are exposed for several years to a chemical that is later found to be carcinogenic, there may be little help for those exposed.

In the nation's workplaces there are tens of thousands of toxic chemicals, many of which are significant enough to warrant regulation. Yet OSHA only has a list of 400 substances with simple threshold limits adopted from the recommended lists of private industrial hygiene organizations.

The promulgation of health standards involves many complex concepts. To be complete, each standard needs medical surveillance requirements, recordkeeping, monitoring, and multiple physical reviews, just to mention a few. At the present rate, promulgation of standards on every existing toxic substance could take centuries. OSHA has explored various generic or categorical approaches to standard setting, but so far these have been poorly organized.

6.0 Slow Pace of Standards Development: The Noise Example

Many of the criticisms lodged against OSHA stem from the slow standard setting process, and those complaints are generally valid. A good example of footdragging by the agency is its attempt to issue a noise standard. The Labor Department began regulating noise as far back as 1968 under the Walsh-Healy Public Contracts Act of 1936. 12/ With the creation of OSHA, responsibility for noise regulation was transferred to that agency, and in 1972 NOISH submitted a criteria document, which led to an OSHA proposed standard for 85 dB(A) (decibels). 13/ Issuance of the final revised OSHA noise standard has been promised for so long that predictions are no longer taken seriously. For instance, in October 1976, an OSHA official stated that a standard for noise regulation would be published within three months. 14/

In the meantime, labor leaders were complaining about the delay, hinting that political motives were responsible. 15/ In January 1977, a new administration assumed office that was

---

12/   41 USC §§ 35-45.

13/   NOISH, "Criteria Document on Noise," 18 October 1972.

14/   BNA, Noise Regulations Reporter, no. 64, 25 October 1976, pp. A34-35.

15/   Ibid., no. 63, 11 October 1976, pp. AA-1 et seq.

considered to be more friendly to organized labor; but three years later, they still had not released the long-awaited, or long-dreaded, noise standard. The administrator of OSHA indicated in July 1977 that a task force was being established and that the standard would be ready by "early 1978." 16/ It was not, however, and OSHA did not even reopen the rulemaking record to introduce new information and updated cost data until April 1980. 17/ On 16 January 1981, a hearing conservation program was developed, 18/ but the main noise standard is now not expected in this decade and even the present new standard is being reviewed for modifications.

7.0 Standard Setting

To meet the objectives defined in the Act, three different standard setting procedures were established. These three standard setting procedures, are:

(1) Consensus Standards, Section 6(a).
(2) Permanent Standards, Section 6(b).
(3) Emergency Temporary Standards, Section 6(c).

We can all recognize the amount of time that could be expended in this process. There are thousands of chemical substances, electrical problems, fire hazards, and many other dangerous situations prevalent in the workplace for which standards needed to be developed.

7.1 Consensus Standards: Section 6(a)

Congress realized that OSHA would need standards to enforce while it was developing its own. Section 6(a) allowed the agency, for a two-year period which ended on 25 April 1973, to adopt standards developed by other federal agencies or to adopt consensus standards of various industry or private associations. This wholesale adoption pleased industry and removed some of the burden from OSHA, at least temporarily. When the agency found a conflict between any existing national consensus standard and an established federal standard, it was to promulgate the standard affording the greater protection to affected employees. This hurried initial standards package was published for the most part in June 1974. 19/ This has

---

16/ Ibid., no. 83, 18 July 1977, p. A-25.

17/ 45 FR 26366, 18 April 1980.

18/ 46 FR 4161, 16 January 1981, amending 29 CFR § 1910.95.

19/ 39 FR 23502, 27 June 1974.

resulted in a list of several hundred common toxic chemicals, such as hydrogen cyanide, with maximum permitted air concentrations specified in parts per million (PPM) and in milligrams per cubic meter (mg/M^3).

There are several problems inherent in these standards. First, these threshold values are the only elements to the standard. There are no required warning labels, monitoring, medical record-keeping, nor do they distinguish between 8-hour, 15-minute, peak, annual average, and other periods of exposure. Second, being thresholds, they are based on the implicit assumption that there are universal no-effect levels, below which a worker is safe. This is a controversial subject. There may conceivably be a no-effect level for each individual, with a broad average for a large population, but the scientific data is not able to determine what it might be. Moreover, with carcinogens, the prevailing view is that there may be no threshold: the dose-response curve continues down to zero.

Third, most of the standards were originally established not on the basis of firm scientific evidence but, as the name implies, on the basis of consensus among various industry and governmental hygienists. These various lists had been around for years, with no urgency to keep them current. By the time they were adopted by OSHA, many were out of date. They are now frozen in time, probably for decades, until OSHA goes through the full Section 6(b) process, described below.

Whatever the disadvantages, Congress was undoubtedly correct in requiring the compilation of such a list. Otherwise, there would have been no OSHA health standards at the beginning; there are virtually no others even now.

7.1.1 Standards Completion Process

The Agency has attempted to deal with one of the above objections to the Standards Completion Process for the 6(a) standards. Over a number of years, OSHA has taken a half-dozen or more threshold standards and added various medical, monitoring, and other requirements. The numbers themselves cannot be updated, for legal reasons, but at least a broader range of protection is offered to exposed workers.

7.2 Permanent Standards: Section 6(b)

Permanent standards must now be developed pursuant to Section 6(b). This is the present standard setting process. Permanent standards may be initiated by a well-publicized tragedy, court action, new scientific studies, or (usually) the receipt of a criteria document from the National Institute of Occupation Safety and Health (NIOSH), an organization described in Section 13.0 of this Chapter. The criteria document is a compilation of all the scientific reports on a particular chemical, including epidemiological and animal studies, along with a recommendation to OSHA for a standard. The recommendation, based supposedly only on scientific health considerations, includes suggested exposure limits (8-hour average, peaks, etc.) and appropriate medical monitoring, labeling, and other prescriptions.

Congress apparently assumed that NIOSH would be the standard-setting arm of OSHA although the two are in different government departments (HHS and Labor, respectively). Theoretically, OSHA would take the recommendations from NIOSH, factor in engineering and technical feasibility, and them promulgate as similar a standard as possible. However, the system has never worked this way. Instead, OSHA's own standards office has regarded NIOSH's contribution as just one step in the process—and not one entitled to a great deal of deference. Criteria documents vary considerably in quality, depending in part on to whom they were subcontracted, but another problem is that too often they are insufficiently discriminating in evaluating questionable studies. That is, one study is regarded as good as any other study, without regard to the quality of the data or the validity of the protocols. Of course, another factor in OSHA's attitude just might be the "not invented here" syndrome.

Following receipt of the criteria document, or some other initiating action, OSHA will study the evidence and, in theory, publish a proposed standard. Most candidate standards never get this far: the hundreds of NIOSH documents, labor union petitions, and other serious recommendations have resulted in (depending on the count) only slightly over a dozen health standards since 1970. [20]

The proposed standard is then subjected to public comment for a 60 or 90 day period, after which the reactions are analyzed and (usually) informal public hearings are scheduled. In a few controversial instances, there may be more than one series of hearings and comments. Then come the post-hearing comments, which are perhaps the most important presentations by the parties. After considerable further study, a final standard is eventually promulgated. The entire process could be accomplished in under a year, but in practice it takes a minimum of several years and possibly even decades.

Even when issued in "final," the process may not be completed. Some standards are obviously defective. The present asbestos standard for example, does not even acknowledge the

---

[20] This meager number does not reflect OSHA's scientific judgment that the other candidates are unworthy or that the Agency has sharply different priorities, although these may be partial factors. More important reasons are: poor leadership, technical inexperience, and a bit of politics.

substance as a human carcinogen. It was reproposed as such in late 1975, but the revised version has yet to be promulgated. 21/

Under the Reagan Administration, another form of revision has developed. Standards which have become final and survived legal challenge all the way up to the Supreme Court, such as cotton dust and lead standards, have nevertheless been called into question. 22/ With this revision caveat, the following is a list of the nine final health standards which OSHA has promulgated to date:

(1) Asbestos 23/

(2) "14 carcinogens" 24/

-4-nitrobiphynyl 25/

-alpha-nephthylamine 26/

-methyl chloromethyl ether 27/

-3,3'-dichlorolenzidine 28/

-bis-chloromethyl ether 29/

-beta-naphthylamine 30/

21/ The standard is now not expected before the end of 1983, if then, according to OSHA Health Standards Director, Leonard Nance, as reported by Gershon Fishbein, "Occupational Health and Safety Letter," 22 September 1982.

22/ 47 FR 5906, 9 February 1982 - "While the agency has determined that the application of cost-benefit analysis to this standard is precluded by the Supreme Court's decision, the agency has concluded that it is totally appropriate to reexamine new health data and alternative compliance approaches, as well as matters relevant to the implementation and enforcement of the cotton dust standard." 47 FR 26557, 18 June 1982—"OSHA is currently undertaking a thorough reconsideration of the lead standard...."

23/ 29 C.F.R. § 1910.100.
24/ 29 C.F.R. § 1910.100.
25/ § 1310.1003.
26/ § 1310.1004.
27/ § 1910.1006.
28/ § 1910.1007.
29/ § 1910.1008.
30/ § 1910.1009.

-benzidine 31/

-4-aminodiphenyl 32/

-ethyleneimine 33/

-beta-propiolactone 34/

-2-acetylaminofluorene 35/

-4-dimethylaminoazobenzene 36/

-N-nitrosodimethylamine 37/

-(MOCA--stayed by court action)

(3)   vinyl chloride 38/

(4)   inorganic arsenic 39/

(5)   lead 40/

(6)   coke oven emissions 41/

(7)   cotton dust 42/

(8)   1,,2-dibromo-3-chloropropane 43/

(9)   acrylonitrile 44/

7.3. Emergency Temporary Standards

The statute also provides for a third standard-setting approach, specified for emergency circumstances where the normal, ponderous rulemaking procedure would be too slow. Section 6(c) gives the Agency authority to issue an emergency temporary standard (ETS) if necessary to protect workers from exposure to "grave danger" posed by substances "determined to be toxic or physically harmful or from

---

31/   § 1910.1010.
32/   § 1910.1011.
33/   § 1910.1012.
34/   § 1910.1013.
35/   § 1910.1014.
36/   § 1910.1015.
37/   § 1910.1016.
38/   § 1910.1017.
39/   § 1910.1018.
40/   § 1910.1025.
41/   § 1910.1029.
42/   § 1910.104.
43/   § 1910.1044.
44/   § 1910.1045.

new hazards." [OSHA Act § 6(c)(1)]. Such standards are effective immediately upon publication in the Federal Register. An ETS is only valid, however, for six months. OSHA is thus under considerable pressure to conduct an expedited rulemaking for a permanent standard before the ETS lapses. For this reason, a quest for an emergency standard is the preferred route for labor unions or other groups seeking a new OSHA standard. In fact, most of the existing 6(b) standards began as emergency standards under Section 6(c).

8.0 Safety Standards

This chapter emphasizes the health aspects of OSHA. Most press attention and the Agency's own emphasis since the mid-1970s has been on health standards. Nevertheless, OSHA is also an occupational safety organization. The two parts of the organization are quite distinct: there are separate inspectors and standards offices for each, and the two groups are different in terms of background, education, and age. There are also far more safety than health inspectors.

Safety hazards are those aspects of the work environment which, in general, cause harm of an immediate and sometimes violent nature, such as burns, electrical shock, cuts, broken bones, loss of limbs or eyesight, and even death. The distinction from health is usually obvious, with mechanical and electrical considered as safety problems while chemicals are considered health problems. Only noise is difficult to categorize; it is classified as a health problem.

The Section 6(a) adoption of national consensus and other federal standards, created chaos in the safety area. It was one thing for companies to follow guidelines that, in many cases, had not been modified in years; it was another thing for those guidelines actually to be written down as law. The Act provided two years for OSHA to produce standards derived from these existing standards; the Agency should have gone through these standards, simplified them, deleted the ridiculous and unnecessary ones, and promulgated final regulations that actually identified and eliminated hazards to workers. But it did not happen that way.

Almost all of these so-called "Mickey Mouse" standards were safety regulations, such as the requirement that fire extinguishers had to be attached to the wall exactly so many inches above the floor. Undertrained OSHA inspectors often failed to recognize major hazards while citing industries for minor violations "which were highly visible, but not necessarily related to serious hazards to workers' safety and health." 45/

45/ Statement of Basil Whiting, Deputy Assistant Secretary of Labor for OSHA, before the Committee on Labor on Human Resources, U.S. Senate, 21 March 1980, pp. 5-6.

At a conference on Occupational Safety and Health Regulations in 1978, then Deputy Director of the Safety Standards Program at OSHA, John Proctor, stated:

> New standards will be needed to fill major gaps and respond to priority needs disclosed by work injury data or safety research into the causes of injury as well as the means of control or elimination of hazards and risks. The ability to anticipate the potential hazards of new technology or to advance the state of the art for engineering controls and means of safeguarding of exposed employees will be a major goal for OSHA's safety standards staff. 46/

Section 6(g) of the OSH Act directs OSHA to establish priorities based on the needs of specific "industries, trades, crafts, occupations, businesses, workplaces, or work environments." The Senate report accompanying the OSH Act stated that the agency's emphasis initially should be put on industries where the need was determined to be most compelling. 47/ "OSHA's early attempts to target inspections, however, were sporadic and, for the most part, unsuccessful." 48/ The situation has improved somewhat in recent years, for both health and safety, in part because of the recent requirement that some priority scheme be used that could justify search warrants, if requested under the Barlow decision. 49/

9.0 Areas Covered by the Standards
To give the reader an idea of the areas covered by the standards, the following is a subpart listing from the Code of Federal Regulations, Part 1910, Occupational Safety and Health Standards. The health standards are contained in Subpart Z and the others are

---

46/ Proceedings of the Occupational Health and Safety Regulations Seminar (Washington, D.C.: Government Institutes, 10-11 April 1978), p. 15.

47/ For the legislative history of the Act, see especially the Conference Report 91-1765 of 16 December 1970, as well as H.R. 91-1291 and S. Rpt. 91-1282.

48/ Basil Whiting Statement, op.cit., p. 4.

49/ Marshall v. Barlow's Inc., 436 U.S. 307 (1978).

safety related except for Subparts A, B and C which cover both.
The <u>Code of Federal Regulations</u> is offered for sale by the U.S.
Government Printing Office.

Subpart A - General (purpose and scope, definitions,
            applicability of standards, etc.)

Subpart B - Adoption and Extension of Established
            Federal Standards (construction work,
            ship repairing, longshoring, etc.)

Subpart C - General Safety and Health Provisions
            (preservation of records)

Subpart D - Walking-Working Surfaces (guarding
            floor and wall openings, portable lad-
            ders, requirements for scaffolding, etc.)

Subpart E - Means of Egress (definitions, specific
            means by occupancy, sources of stan-
            dards, etc.)

Subpart F - Powered Platforms, Manlifts, and Vehi-
            cle-Mounted Work Platforms (elevating
            and rotating work platforms, standards
            organizations, etc.)

Subpart G - Occupational Health and Environmental
            Control (ventilation, noise exposure,
            radiation, etc.)

Subpart H - Hazardous Materials (compressed gases,
            flammables, storage of petroleum
            gases, effective dates, etc.)

Subpart I - Personal Protective Equipment (eye and
            face, respiratory, electrical devices,
            etc.)

Subpart J - General Environmental Controls (sani-
            tation, labor camps, safety color code
            for hazards, etc.)

Subpart K - Medical and First Aid (medical serv-
            ices, sources of standards)

Subpart L - Fire Protection (fire supression equip-
            ment, hose and sprinkler systems, fire
            brigades, etc.)

Subpart M - Compressed Gas and Compressed Air
            Equipment (inspection of gas cylinders,
            safety relief devices, etc.)

Subpart N - Materials Handling and Storage (pow-
            ered industrial trucks, cranes, heli-
            copters, etc.)

Subpart O - Machinery and Machine Guarding
            (requirements for all machines, wood-
            working machinery, wheels, mills, etc.)

Subpart P - Hand and Portable Powered Tools and
            Other Hand-Held Equipment (guarding

of portable power tools, sources of standards, etc.)

Subpart	Q -	Welding, Cutting and Brazing (definitions, sources of standards, etc.)
Subpart	R -	Special Industries (pulp, paper and paperboard mills, textiles, laundry machinery, telecommunications, etc.)
Subpart	S-	Electrical (application, National Electrical Code)
Subpart	T -	Commercial Diving Operations (qualification of team, pre- and post-dive procedures, equipment, etc.)
Subpart	U-Y-	[Reserved]
Subpart	Z -	Toxic and Hazardous Substances (air contaminants, asbestos, vinyl chloride, lead, benzene, etc.)

10.0 Variances

10.1 Temporary Variances

Section 6(b)6(A) of the OSH Act establishes a procedure by which any employer may apply for a "temporary order granting a variance from a standard or any provision thereof." According to the Act, the variance will be approved when OSHA determines that the requirements have been met and establishes that (1) the employer is unable to meet the standard "because of unavailability of professional or technical personnel or of materials and equipment," or because alterations of facilities cannot be completed in time; (2) that he is "taking all available steps to safeguard" his workers against the hazard covered by the standard for which he is applying for a variance; and (3) he has an "effective program for coming into compliance with the standard as quickly as practicable." 50/

This temporary order may be granted only after employees have been notified and, if requested, there has been sufficient opportunity for hearing. The variance may not remain in effect for more than one year with the possibility of only two six-month renewals. 51/ The overriding factor an employer must demonstrate for a temporary variance is good faith. 52/

50/   OSH Act § 7(b)(6)(A).

51/   Ibid.

52/   E. Klein, Variances, in Proceedings of the Occupational Health and Safety Regulations Seminar, (Washington D.C.: Government Institutes), p. 74.

10.2 Permanent Variances

Permanent variances can be issued under Sec. 6(d) of the OSH Act. A permanent variance may be granted to an employer who has demonstrated "by a preponderance" of evidence that the "conditions, practices, means, methods, operations or processes used or proposed to be used" will provide a safe and healthful workplace as effectively as would compliance with the standard.

11.0 Compliance and Inspections

11.1 Field Structure

The Department of Labor (DOL) has divided the territory subject to the OSH Act into ten federal regions (EPA also uses the same boundaries), each containing from four to nine area offices. When an area office is not necessary because of a lack of industrial activity, district offices or field stations are established. Each region is headed by a regional administrator; each area by an area director. In the field, compliance officers represent area offices and inspect industrial sites in their vicinity.

11.2 Role of Inspections

The only way to determine compliance by employers is inspections, but inspecting all the workplaces covered by the OSH Act would require decades. Each year there are over fifty-thousand federal inspections, and twice as many state inspections, but there are several million workplaces. Obviously, a priority system for high-hazard occupations is necessary, along with random inspections just to keep everyone "on his toes."

11.3 Training and Competency of Inspectors

There has been a major problem with OSHA inspectors in the past—the training program has not adequately prepared them. In the early days there was tremendous pressure from the unions to get an inspection force on the job as soon as possible, so training was minimal. Inspectors would walk into a plant where kepone dust was so thick workers could not see across the room, and, because there was no standard as such, would not think there was a problem. Yet had there been a fire extinguisher in the wrong place, and had the inspector been able to see it through the haze, he would have cited the plant for safety violation.

Competency among staff has markedly improved since the early days of the program. Both in-house training efforts by OSHA and increased numbers of professional training programs conducted by colleges and universities have contributed to these improvements. There is also

a greater sensitivity towards workers and their representatives. 53/

11.4 Citations

If the inspector discovers a hazard in the workplace, a citation is in order. Citations can be serious, nonserious, willful, or
repeated. A serious violation is found if there is "substantial probability that death or serious physical harm could result from a
condition which exists, or from one or more practices, means,
methods, operations, or processes which have been adopted by or are
in use, in such place of employment unless the employer did not,
and could not with the exercise of reasonable diligence, know of the
presence of the violation." 54/ A penalty is mandatory for a serious
violation; a nonserious violation is discretionary.   Even several
nonserious violations considered together do not make up a serious
violation unless the combination somehow would be likely to lead to
death or serious physical harm to an employee.

11.5 Willful Violations

The Administration has a powerful weapon with which to
threaten those employers who are careless of, or indifferent to,
their obligations under the Act. Any employer who is aware of a
hazardous condition in his plant, yet makes no effort to rectify it,
may be held to be a willful violator and penalized as such. A "willful" violation is "properly defined as an act or omission which
occurs consciously, intentionally, deliberately or voluntarily as
distinguished from accidentally." 55/

> The critical element of proof necessary is that of know-
> ledge....OSHA would have to establish that the employer
> was aware that a hazardous condition existed and then
> took no reasonable steps to eliminate the condition. 56/

Penalties for willful violations considerably exceed those for serious
or nonserious violations; a penalty of $10,000 may be assessed for
each violation.

53/   Statement of Lane Kirkland, President, AFL-CIO, before the
      Senate Committee on Labor and Human Resources on Over-
      sight of the Occupational Safety and Health Act, 1 April 1980.

54/   OSH Act § 17(k).

55/   Guidebook to Occupational Safety and Health (Chicago: CCH,
      1974), p. 149.

56/   OSH Act § 17(d).

11.6 Repeat Violations

The same penalty may be applied for repeated violations, with each day being in theory a separate violation. A citation for a repeated violation cannot be issued unless the employer has been cited for a violation, has abated the violation, and has thereafter again violated the same standard or permitted the same hazard to exist in his plant. In the case of a company having multiple sites or plants, in different states or OSHA regions, the issue of repeatedness is more complex. OSHA has changed its definitions several times, and the policy is not yet firm.

When enough time has been allowed for the correction of a violation, OSHA may reinspect the plant to verify compliance with issued citation. If the employer has failed to abate, a penalty of up to $1000 per day will be assessed "for each day during which such failure or violation continues." 57/

12.0 State OSHA Program

12.1 The Concept

The OSH Act requires OSHA to encourage the states to develop and operate their own job safety and health programs, which must be "at least as effective as" the federal program. 58/ Until effective state programs are approved, federal enforcement of standards promulgated by OSHA preempt state enforcement. 59/ State laws remain in effect when no federal standard exists.

Before approving a submitted state plan, OSHA must make certain that the state can meet criteria established in the Act. 60/ Once a plan is in effect, the secretary may exercise "authority...until he determines, on the basis of actual operations under the State plan, that the criteria set forth are being applied. 61/ But he cannot make such a determination for three years after the plan's approval. OSHA may continue to evaluate the state's performance in carrying out the program even after a state plan has been approved. If a state fails to comply, the approval can be withdrawn, but only after the agency has given due notice and opportunity for a hearing.

57/ Ibid.

58/ OSH Act §§ 2(b)(11) and 18 (c)(2).

59/ OSH Act § 18(a).

60/ OSH Act § 18(c)(1) - (c)(8).

61/ OSH Act § 18(c).

12.2 Critiques

The program has not worked as anticipated, although almost half the states have their own system. Industry has cooled to the local concept, which requires multi-state companies to contend with a variety of state laws and regulations instead of a uniform federal plan. Moreover, state OSHAs are often considerably larger than the local federal force, so there can be more inspections. Organized labor has never liked the state concept, because of its poor experience with the previous local organizations and a realization that its strength could more easily be exercised in one location—Washington, D.C.--than in all fifty states and territorial capitals. This has meant, ironically, that some of the better state programs, in areas where unions had the most influence, were among the first rejected by state legislators under strong union pressure.

Organized labor and industry are not alone in their criticism of the state programs. Health research groups, OSHA's own national advisory committee (NACOSH), and some of the states themselves have also voiced disapproval of the state program policy. Ineffective operations at the state level, disparity in federal funding, and lack of the necessary research capability are just a few of the criticisms lodged. 62/

> OSHA had not developed articulate, coherent programs
> for achieving fully effective enforcement. State plans,
> in other words, are likely to be defective because they
> have been formed around defective criteria. OSHA must
> now go back and redo, to a certain extent, those criteria
> and reevaluate the state plans. 63/

There is some defense of state control, however. "To the extent that local control increases the responsiveness of programs to the specific needs of people in that area, this [a state plan] is a potentially good policy." 64/ But reevaluation and revision will be necessary in the next several years if OSHA's policy for state programs is to be accepted by all the factions involved.

62/ Robert Hayden, "Federal and State Roles" in Proceedings of the Occupational Health and Safety Regulation Seminar, (Washington, D.C.: Government Institutes, 1978) pp. 9-10.

63/ Ibid., p. 11.

64/ Nicholas A. Ashford, Crisis in the Workplace: Occupational Disease and Inquiry (Boston: MIT Press, 1976) p. 231.

13.0 Consultation

Employers subject to OSHA regulation, particularly small employers, need on-site consultation to determine what must be done to bring their workplaces into compliance with the requirements of the OSH Act. These consultations should be free from citations or penalties. As in so many other areas of OSHA regulation, there has been a great deal of controversy surrounding the consultation process. Union leaders have always feared that OSHA could become merely an educational institution rather than one with effective enforcement. But Section 21(c) of the Act does mandate consultation with employers and employees "as to effective means of preventing occupational injuries and illnesses." 65/

Along with the consultation provisions, the statute provides for "programs for the education and training of employers and employees in the recognition, avoidance, and prevention of unsafe or unhealthful working conditions in employments covered" by the Act. 66/ OSHA produces brochures and films to educate employees about possible hazards in their workplaces. But, there are problems at every stage of the information process, from generation to utilization. It can be an overwhelming task to generate all the information needed for a particular hazard. But even when useful and pertinent information is gathered and disseminated, decision-makers may be slow in using it.

In 1979, OSHA instituted a New Directions Training and Education Program which made available up to $2.7 million in grants to support the development and strengthening of occupational safety and health competence in business, employee, and educational organizations. This program supported a broad range of activities, such as training in hazard identification and control; workplace risk assessment; medical screening and recordkeeping; and liaison work with OSHA, the National Institute for Occupational Safety and Health, and other agencies. "The goal of the program was to allow unions and other groups to become financially self-sufficient in supporting comprehensive health and safety programs." 67/ This program, criticized by some as a payoff to constituent groups, especially labor unions, has been a natural target of Reagan Administration budget cutters, but the concept of increased consultation has been given even greater emphasis.

65/ OSH Act § 21(c)(2).

66/ OSH Act § 21(c)(1).

67/ U.S. Department of Labor, "OSHA News," 12 April 1978.

There is also a provision that state plans may include on-site consultation with employers and employees to encourage voluntary compliance. 68/ The personnel engaged in these activities must be separate from the inspection personnel and their existence must not detract from the federal enforcement effort. These consultants not only point out violations, but also give abatement advice.

14.0 Overlapping Jurisdiction

There are other agencies involved with statutory responsibilities that affect occupational safety and health. These agencies indirectly regulate safety and health matters in their attempt to protect public safety.

One example of an overlapping agency is the Department of Transportation and its constituent agencies, such as the Federal Railroad Administration and the Federal Aviation Administration. These agencies promulgate rules concerned with the safety of transportation crews and maintenance personnel, as well as the traveling public, and consequently overlap similar responsibilities of OSHA.

Section 4(b)(1) of the OSH Act states that when other federal agencies "exercise statutory authority to prescribe or enforce standards or regulations affecting occupational safety or health," the OSH Act will not apply to the working conditions addressed by those standards. Memorandums of understanding (MOUs) between these agencies and OSHA have eliminated much of the earlier conflict.

The Environmental Protection Agency is the organization that overlaps most frequently with OSHA. When a toxic substance regulation is passed by EPA, OSHA is affected if that substance is one that appears in the workplace. For instance, both agencies are concerned with pesticides, EPA with the general environmental issues surrounding the pesticides and OSHA with some aspects of the agricultural workers who use them. During the first half of 1973, there was a heated interagency conflict over field reentry standards for pesticides (see Chapter 7 on Pesticides), a struggle which spilled over into the courts and eventually had to be settled by the White House in EPA's favor. 69/

Thus, although the health regulatory agencies generally function in a well-defined area, overlap does occur. As another

---

68/   29 CFR § 1902.4 (c)(2)(xiii).

69/   Florida Peach Growers Assn. v. Dept. of Labor, 489 F.2d 120 (5th Cir. 1974). To avoid this type of confrontation, in 1976 Congress provided in Section 9 of the Toxic Substances Control Act the detailed coordination procedures to be followed when jurisdictional overlap occurs.

example, there are toxic regulations under Section 307 of the Federal Water Pollution Control Act, Section 112 of the Clean Air Act, and under statutes of the FDA and CPSC. These regulatory agencies realized the need for coordination, particularly when dealing with something as pervasive as toxic substances, and under the Carter Administration combined their efforts into an interagency working group called the Interagency Regulatory Liaison group (IRLG). Although the IRLG was abolished at the beginning of the Reagan Administration, the concept of interagency working groups is a good one. The federal agencies involved in regulation should rid themselves of the antagonism and rivalry of the past and cooperate with one another to meet the needs of the public.

15.0 Occupational Safety and Health Review Commission

The OSH Act established the Occupational Safety and Health Review Commission (OSHRC) as "an independent quasi-judicial review board" 70/ consisting of three members appointed by the President to six year terms. Any enforcement actions of OSHA that are challenged must be reviewed and ruled upon by the Commission. 71/

Any failure to challenge a citation within 15 days of issuance automatically results in an action of the Review Commission to uphold the citation. This decision by default is not subject to review by any court or agency. When an employer challenges a citation, the abatement period, or the penalty proposed, the Commission designates a hearing examiner who hears the case; makes a determination to affirm, modify or vacate the citation or penalty; and reports his finding to the Commission. 72/

> The report of the hearing examiner shall become the final order of the Commission within thirty days after such report by the hearing examiner, unless within such period any Commission member has directed that such report shall be reviewed by the Commission. 73/

The employer or Agency may then seek a review of the decision in a federal appeals court.

70/   Ashford, Crisis, p. 145.

71/   OSH Act § 12(a)-(b).

72/   OSH Act § 12(j).

73/   Ibid.

One of the major problems with the Review Commission is the question of its jurisdiction. "The question has arisen of the extent to which the Commission should conduct itself as though it were a court rather than a more traditional administrative agency." 74/ The Commission cannot look to other independent agencies in the government for a resolution of this problem "because its duties and its legislative history have little in common with the others." 75/ It cannot conduct investigations, initiate suits, or prosecute; therefore, it is best understood as an administrative agency with the limited duty of "adjudicating those cases brought before it by employers and employees who seek review of the enforcement actions taken by OSHA and the Secretary of Labor." 76/

Another problem inherent in the organization of the Commission is the separation from the Administration. There has been a question of where the authority of the Administration ends and the authority of the Commission begins. Because of the autonomous nature of the Commission, it cannot always count on the support of the Administration. In fact, OSHA has generally ignored Review Commission decisions, and few inspectors are even aware of the Commission interpretations on various regulations.

16.0 National Institute of Occupational Safety and Health

Under the Act, the Bureau of Safety and Health Services in the Health Services and Mental Health Administration was restructured to become the National Institute for Occupational Safety and Health (NIOSH) so as to carry out HEW's responsibilities under the Act. 77/ (HEW--The Department of Health, Education, and Welfare--has since become the Department of Health and Human Services.) Since mid-1971, NIOSH has claimed the training and research functions of the Act, along with its primary function of recommending standards.

For this latter task, NIOSH provides recommended standards to OSHA in the form of criteria documents for particular hazards. These are compilations and evaluations of all available relevant information from scientific, medical, and (occasionally) engineering research.

74/ Ashford, Crisis, p. 145.

75/ Ibid. pp. 281-82.

76/ Ibid.

77/ OSH Act § 22(a).

The order of hazards selected for criteria development
is determined several years in advance by a NIOSH
priority system based on severity of response, population at risk, existence of a current standard, and advice
from federal agencies (including OSHA) as well as
involved professional groups. 78/

The criteria document may actually have some value apart
from its role in standards-making. Even though they do not have the
force of law, they are widely distributed to industry, organized
labor, universities, and private research groups as a basis to control
hazards. The criteria documents also serve as a "basis for setting
international permissible limits for occupational exposures." 79/
    To the extent that certain criteria documents may be defi-
cient, as discussed earlier, this expansive role for them among
laymen poses a real problem. This problem may unfortunately
become worse, as NIOSH declines in both funds and morale. Nevertheless, there is benefit in having the two organizations separate.
OSHA has been able to take action on some matters, such as clarify-
ing that carbon black is not a carcinogen, which NIOSH was bureau-
cratically unable to resolve. 80/ And NIOSH has not hesitated to
criticize OSHA for regulatory decisions, such as issuing no standard
on formaldehyde, which the former believed was scientifically
untenable. 81/

17.0 Reprisals Against Worker Complaints: Section 11(c)
    Congress assumed that the workers in a given workplace would
be best aquainted with the hazards there. It therefore statutorily
encouraged prompt OSHA response to worker complaints of violations. 82/ And since this system could be undermined if employers
penalized complaining employees, the Act in Section 11(c) provides
sanctions against such retaliation or discrimination:

78/ John F. Finklea, "The Role of NIOSH in the Standards Process,"
     in Proceedings of the Occupational Health and Safety
     Regulation Seminar, p. 38.

79/ Ibid, p. 39.

80/ Letter from John Miles, Enforcement Chief, to author,
     November 1982.

81/ See G. Fishbein, op. cit., 8 June 1982.

82/ OSH Act § 8(f)(1).

No person shall discharge or in any manner discriminate against any employee because such employee has filed any complaint or instituted or caused to be instituted any proceeding under or related to this Act or has testified or is about to testify in any such proceeding or because of the exercise by such employee on behalf of himself or others of any right afforded by this Act. 83/

If discrimination occurs, particularly if an employee is fired, a special OSHA team intervenes to obtain reinstatement, back wages, or—if return to the company is undesirable--a cash settlement for the worker. If agreement cannot be reached, the Agency resorts to litigation.

This entire system has not worked as expected. First, the worker complaints have suprisingly not been a very fruitful source of health and safety information. Far too many of the complaints came in bunches, coinciding with labor disputes in a particular plant. OSHA has therefore finally abandoned its policy of trying to investigate every complaint.

Second, the 11(c) process has worked slowly and uncertainly, so even though an employee may receive vindication, the months (or more) of delay and anguish are a strong disincentive for workers to report hazards. Third, it is often difficult to determine whether a malcontented worker was fired for informing OSHA or for a number of other issues which might cloud the employer-employee relationship. Does the complaint have to be the sole cause of dismissal or discrimination, or can some (fairly arbitrary) allocation be made.

Fourth, there is continuing controversy over whether 11(c) should protect workers complaining of hazards to other than OSHA, even if the direct or indirect result is an OSHA inspection. In the Kepone case of 1975, an employee complained of hazardous chemicals to his supervisor, was fired, and only then went to OSHA. Not only was he declared unprotected by the Act, but his complaint, no longer being a worker complaint, was not even investigated at the time. 84/

A related current issue is whether an employee who reports a hazard to the press, whose ensuing publicity triggers an OSHA investigation, was protected by 11(c). Recently, OSHA regional officials decided in favor of the worker and won the subsequent

---

83/   OSH Act § 11(c)(1).

84/   See Marshall Lee Miller "Report on OSHA," submitted to Assistant Secretary Bingham, 20 January 1976, pp. 4-5.

litigation in federal district court. The Solicitor of Labor, however, disagreed and attempted in late 1982 to withdraw the Agency from a winning position. 85/

For all these reasons, therefore, a worker must still complain at his peril.

18.0 Constitutional Challenges: The Barlow Case

Litigants have challenged OSHA's constitutionality on virtually every conceivable grounds from the First Amendment to the Fourteenth.

The one case that has succeeded has led to the requirement of a search warrant, if demanded, for OSHA inspectors. For diverse reasons, however, this decision has not had appreciable impact.

In sustaining the challenge by a businessman from Pocatello, Idaho, the Supreme Court in Marshall v. Barlow's Inc. 86/ decided that the Fourth Amendment to the Constitution, providing for search warrants, was applicable to OSHA. Section 8(a) of the Act, in which Congress had authorized warrantless searches was held unconstitutional. There are circumstances in which warrants are not required, such as federal inspection of liquor dealers, 87/ gun dealers, 88/ automobiles near international borders, 89/ and in other matters with a long history of federal involvement. And despite the political furor over OSHA, even the John Birch Society has not objected to elevator and food inspectors. Since governmental regulation of working conditions arguably has a firmer historical basis than those other areas, which also have definitive constitutional limits, 90/ requiring a search warrant for inspecting working conditions was not an inevitable result for the court to react.

While the court held OSHA inspectors are required to obtain search warrants if denied entry to inspect, it added that OSHA need meet only a very minimal "probable cause" requirement under the Fourth Amendment in order to obtain them. As Justice White explained:

85/   Washington Post, "About Face Considered in OSHA Suit," 20 October 1982.

86/   436 U.S. 307 (1978).

87/   Colonnade Catering Corp. v. U.S., 397 U.S. 72 (1970).

88/   U.S. v. Biswell, 406 U.S. 311 (1972).

89/   U.S. v. Ramsey, 431 U.S. 606 (1977).

90/   U.S. Constitution, Amendments II and XXI.

Probable cause in the criminal sense is not required.
For purposes of an administrative search such as this,
probable cause justifying the issuance of a warrant may
be based not only on specific evidence of an existing
violation but also on a showing that "reasonable legislative or administrative standards for conducting an...in-
spection are satisfied with respect to a particular
[establishment]. 91/

Moreover, if too many companies demanded warrants, so that
the inspection program was seriously impaired, the Court indicated
it might reconsider its ruling. This ironically would make enjoyment
of a Constitutional right partly contingent on few attempting to
exercise it. It is therefore not surprising that commentators, both
liberals and conservatives, were critical of the decision. Conservative columnist James J. Kilpatrick declared flatly:

If the Supreme Court's decision in the Barlow case was a
"great victory," as Congressman George Hansen pro-
claims it, let us ask heaven to protect us from another
such victory anytime soon. 92/

91/   Marshall v. Barlow's Inc., supra, quoting Camara v. Municipal
      Court, 387 U.S. 523 at 538 (1967).

92/   Washington Star, 2 June 1978.

APPENDIX A

OUTLINE OF KEY PROVISIONS
OCCUPATIONAL SAFETY AND HEALTH ACT OF 1970

PL 91-596, 84 Stat. 1590, 29 U.S.C.
(29 December 1970)

§ 1 Title: Occupational Safety and Health Act of 1970

§ 2 Findings and Purpose
   (a)   States findings—injuries are "a substantial burden upon...interstate commerce" because of lost wages, medical expenses, and compensation
   (b)   States purpose—"to assure so far as possible every working man or woman in the Nation safe and healthful working conditions"
   (b)   (3)   Authorizes Secretary of Labor to set mandatory standards—(also § 2 (b) (9))
   (b)   (7)   "By providing medical criteria which will assure insofar as practicable that no employee will suffer diminished health, functional capacity, or life expectancy as a result of his work experience"
   (b)   (9)   "By providing for the development and promulgation of occupational safety and health standards"
   (b)   (10) Establishes enforcement program and prohibits advance notice of any inspection
   (b)   (11) Authorizes state programs, provides grants, encourages improvements in administration and experimental projects

§ 3 Definitions
   (1)   (5)   "Employer"—anyone, excluding U.S. or local governments, who has employees
   (8)   O.S.&H. "standard"—practices, methods, etc., "reasonably necessary or appropriate" for safe and healthful employment
   (9)   "National consensus standard"—(1) adopted by a "nationally recognized standards-producing organization" under circumstances (2) giving interested persons chance to comment and (3) designated as such by Secretary of Labor
   (10) "Established Federal standard"—any U.S. agency standard or law, as of enactment date

§ 4 <u>Applicability</u>

(b)   (1)   Excludes AEC authority (42 U.S.C. 2021 under AEC Act § 274)

(b)   (2)   Supersedes Walsh-Healy Act (41 U.S.C. 35 <u>et seq.</u>), Service Contract Act of 1965, etc., but those standards deemed to be issued under this Act

(b)   (4)   "Nothing in this Act shall be construed to supersede or in any manner affect any workmen's compensation law or to enlarge or diminish or affect any manner the common law or statutory rights, duties, or liabilities of employers and employees under any law...."

§ 5 <u>Duties</u>

(a)   (1)   General Duty Clause: "Each employer shall furnish to each of his employees employment...which are free of recognized hazards that are causing or are likely to cause death or serious physical harm to his employees"

(a)   (2)   Employer shall comply with standards issued under the Act

(b)   Employees shall comply with standards applicable to him

§ 6 <u>Standards</u>

(a)   Secretary to promulgate national consensus and established federal standards on occupational safety and health within 2 years of effective date of Act [21 April 1973 cutoff], without regard for APA procedures; if conflict of standards select most protective rule

(b)   Rules may be modified or promulgated as follows—

(b)   (1)   NIOSH recommendation, possible advisory committee recommendation for standard to be published within 90-days (limit extendable to 270 days)

(b)   (2)   Proposal and comment to be published within 30 days, advisory committee 60 days after report

(b)   (3)   Hearing set 30 days after end of comment period, if requested

(b)   (4)   Rule to be issued within 60 days of hearing completion, with effective date not more than 90 days later

(b)   (5)   Secretary shall set standard "which most adequately assures, to the extent feasible, on the basis of the best available evidence, that no employee will suffer material impairment of health or functional capacity even if such employee has regular exposure to the hazard...for the period of his working life." The primary consideration is the "attainment of the highest degree of health and safety protection for the employee" but other factors include the "feasibility" of the standard. Performance (rather than design) standards preferred, if possible.

(b) (6) Applications for variances from standards (temporary)

(b) (7) Labels, protective equipment, medical examinations and other items to be in standard

(b) (8) Explanation required when standard differs substantially from consensus standard

(c) Emergency standards for "grave danger" available within 6 months after publication of emergency standards but effective until superseded

(d) Applications for variances from standards (permanent)

(f) Provides for legal challenge to a standard to be filed within 60 days. Filing of petition not to operate as a stay of standard unless court so orders. Test for judicial review: "The determination of the Secretary shall be conclusive if supported by substantial evidence in the record considered as a whole." (See also § 11 "Judicial Review" for non-standards.)

§ 7 Advisory Committees

(a) Establishes National Advisory Committee on Occupational Safety and Health (NACOSH)

(b) Appoints special advisory committees of up to 15 members to be chosen for standard-setting

§ 8 Inspections and Recordkeeping

(a) Authorizes Secretary to inspect working places upon presentation of credentials and at reasonable times

(b) Provides for witnesses and evidence in inspections and investigations

(c) Empowers Secretary of Labor or of HEW [now HHS, Health and Human Services] to require records and posting of notices, reports of injuries, exposure to toxic substances, and warnings to employees

(d) Directs authorities to minimize the burden to small businesses

(e) Allows employer and employee representatives to accompany inspector

(f) Allows employees to request inspection of violation or imminent hazard

(g) Authorizes Secretary to respond to § 8 (f) if he believes such danger exists

§ 9 Citations
  (a) Details procedure for OSHA issuing citations for viola-
       tions and setting abatement procedures; de minimis
       violations need not be cited
  (b) Requires posting of citation
  (c) Sets limit of 6 months on citations after violation (§ 9
       (c))

§ 10 Enforcement Procedures
  (a) Notifies employer he has 15 days to contest citation,
       otherwise a final order is not reviewable
  (b) Sets procedure if employer fails to correct violation
  (c) Sets procedure for contesting citations with Review
       Commission (5 U.S.C. 554, excl. (a) (3))

§ 11 Judicial Review
  (a) Allows review of court of appeals within 60 days but no
       automatic stay (§ 11 (b) gives appeal rights to Secretary
       of Labor)
  (c) Prohibits discharge or discrimination against complain-
       ing worker
  (2) Allows 30 days after violation to file complaint
  (3) Allows DOL response within 90 days

§ 12 Review Commission
  (a) Establishes 3 member commission named by President
  (b) Sets terms to run 6 years
  (f) Sets quorum of 2
  (h) Compels witnesses to appear, testify and produce
       evidence
  (j) Appoints hearing examiners who are to produce report
       which will be final within 30 days

§ 13 Counteraction of Imminent Dangers
  (a) Gives jurisdiction to district courts to restrain
       conditions where a danger could "reasonably be
       expected to cause death or serious physical harm
       immediately"
  (d) Gives right of a citizen suit against Secretary of Labor
       for mandamus

§ 14 Representation in Litigation
       Allows Solicitor of Labor to represent Secretary in civil
       litigation (cf. 28 U.S.C. 518 (a) exception)

§ 15 Confidentiality of Trade Secrets
       Protects trade secrets (18 U.S.C. § 1905) but allows
       disclosure to officials and in regulatory proceedings

§ 16 <u>Variances for National Defense</u>
Provides variances, tolerances, and exemptions "to avoid serious impairment of the national defense" after due process
Limits effect to 6 months unless notice and hearing opportunity given to affected employees

§ 17 <u>Penalties</u>
(a) Willful or repeat violations--civil penalty up to $10,000 for each violation
(b) Serious violation--civil penalty up to $1,000 per violation
(c) Non-serious--civil penalty up to $1,000
(d) Failure to correct violation after citation—civil penalty up to $1,000 a day
(e) Willful violation resulting in death--$10,000 fine and up to 6 months prison; on subsequent convictions, $20,000 and one year, or both
(f) Tip off of inspectors coming--fine of $1,000 and/or 6 months in prison
(g) False statements--$10,000 and 6 months prison
(h) Violation of 18 U.S.C. 1111 or 1114 resulting in death of official--liable for imprisonment up to life
(i) Violation of posting requirements—$1,000 per violation
(j) Commission's authority to assess all civil penalties, considering size of business; gravity of violation, good faith of employer; previous violations
(k) Definition of "serious" violation: "serious probability" of death or serious injury and that employer knew or should have known of the violation
(l) Specifies civil penalties are to be paid to U.S. Treasury

§ 18 <u>State Plans</u>
(a) State not preempted where no federal § 6 standard exists
(b) Gives state authority to develop own OSHA programs
(c) Provides for procedures and requirements for approving a state plan
(d) Gives opportunity for state to have notice and hearing if plan rejected
(e) Allows three-year probation period after state plan approved
(f) Affirms federal supervision of state's effectiveness and authority to withdraw plan approval
(g) Gives court of appeals review of OSHA approval or rejection decisions
(h) Allows federal-state agreements on partial enforcement pending § 18 (b) decision

§ 19 Federal Safety Programs

(a)   Establishes responsibility of federal agencies to maintain effective safety programs

(b)   OSHA report to be submitted annually to President and Congress

(c)   Amendment of 5 U.S.C. § 7902 (c) (1)

(d)   Gives OSHA access to records of federal agencies unless to be kept secret for national interest

§ 20 Research

(a)   (1)   Directs Secretary of HEW, [HHS] after consultation with OSHA, to provide grants, research, and other activities

(a)   (6)   Authorizes HEW [HHS] to develop and update a list of toxic substances

(a)   (7)   Directs Secretary to conduct and publish studies of chronic or low-level exposures

(b)   Authorizes HEW [HHS] to make § 8 inspections

(e)   Delegates functions of Secretary to NIOSH

§ 21 Training and Education

(a)   Directs Secretary to provide educational programs, grants, and contracts by qualified personnel

(c)   Provides for education and consultation programs with employees and employers

§ 22 NIOSH

(a)   Establishes National Institute of Occupational Safety and Health at HEW [HHS]

(b)   Specifies a 6-year term for Director

§ 23 State Grants

(a)   Authorizes funding for § 18 state programs development

(d)   Designates appropriate state agency by governor

(f)   Establishes federal share may not exceed 90 percent of application for approval

(g)   Provides for continuing grants to states approved under § 18 limited to 50 percent

§ 24 Statistics

(a)   Establishes responsibility of Labor Department and HEW [HHS] to develop occupational safety statistics

(b)   Authorizes federal grants and contracts

Chapter 9

NOISE

Marshall Lee Miller
Attorney
Reid & Priest
Washington, DC
Former Deputy Administrator, OSHA

1.0 Introduction

Noise is such an integral part of life that we take for granted all but the harshest abuse of our eardrums. This seemingly simple subject is one we all feel we understand. Where we might be awed by the intricacies of toxic chemicals or the complexity of ambient air equation models, we all feel confident that we understand noise. It is, after all, a loud piece of machinery, or a sonic boom, or a blaring stereo next door. Noise can be a nuisance and for generations the law has treated it as merely that. If the din became too oppressive, one could seek remedy in a court of law to restrain another from violating the right to enjoyment of one's property. 1/

But what once might have been considered merely a nuisance is now seen, with intensive industrialization and the increasing crowding of modern life, to be one of the most pervasive health problems of our society. There has also been a growing awareness of the technical complexity of noise. The scientific debates about the physical effects of noise have become just as controversial and replete with jargon as those concerning teratogenic chemicals or biological oxygen demand. In fact, a prominent acoustical scientist recently urged his colleagues to use simpler terms so that laymen could continue to follow the debate. Because the traditional common law remedies have proved inadequate to deal with these developments, there has been since 1970 an increasing resort to federal regulation.

1/ For a fuller discussion of this, see the sections on Torts and Nuisance in Chapter 1 of this book.

1.1 The Characteristics of Sound

Sound intensity is measured in decibels. The zero on the decibel scale is based on the lowest sound level that the healthy human ear can detect. Decibels are not linear units like miles or pounds; rather, they are representative points on a sharply rising, logarithmic curve. Each ten units represents an increase of tenfold, twenty units means a hundredfold (10 x 10), thirty units a thousand-fold (10 x 10 x 10), and so on. Thus, one hundred decibels is 10 billion times as intense as one decibel. This system is used because the human ear can detect such a wide range of acoustical energy that otherwise units in the trillions might be required.

For comparison, the rustle of leaves is rated at 10 decibels, a typical office has about 50 decibels of background noise, moderate traffic noise ranges around 70 decibels, pneumatic drills and heavy trucks at 15 meters range between 80 and 90, and a jet takeoff at 60 meters is 120 or greater. Sound levels are measured at their source, unless otherwise specified, because their intensity is inversely proportional to the square of the distance from that source. 2/

A second important element of noise is frequency or pitch, which is the rate of vibrations of the sound wave. 3/ This is measured in cycles per second and expressed in Hertz (Hz). The audible frequency range of sound is often taken to be between 20 Hz and 20,000 Hz. The ability to hear frequencies declines with age (presbycusis), 4/ and most adults are limited to the range below 12-15,000 Hz. Some music experts, however, believe we can still "sense" sounds beyond those we can hear.

Sound perception is affected by such factors as background noise level, distance, repetitiveness, tone components, duration, number of sources, insulation, and subjective receiver factors including both conscious and subconscious responses. For outdoor sound there are variables such as baffles, terrain, wind direction and

---

2/ Certain EPA standards, such as for aircraft and trucks, provide that noise measurements be taken at a specified distance from the source. This will be discussed later in this chapter.

3/ There is technically a slight difference between these two concepts.

4/ Some authorities believe that presbycusis is less a natural concomitant of aging than the result of years of aural abuse. See statement of Jack Westman, Department of Psychiatry, University of Wisconsin Medical School, Madison, Wisconsin, before the Senate Subcommittee on Government Regulations, Small Business Committee, 23 July 1975, p.2.

velocity, atmospheric pressure and temperature. Interior sound, in addition to most of these variables, also involves the reverberative and reflective characteristics of various building materials and fixtures, the size and shape of a room, and the absorptive characteristics of its furnishings.

There have been a number of scientific efforts to combine factors such as loudness and duration in one numerical scale which will indicate the degree of human annoyance. One useful scale, the Effective Perceived Noise Level (EPNL), is based upon the relative curve of human discomfort to high frequency sounds such as aircraft or truck engine changes in acceleration. This is then adjusted for the duration and presence of discrete tones such as the whine or scream of jet operations. 5/

2.0 Biological Effects of Noise

It has long been recognized that painfully loud sound can produce deafness or impaired hearing; the biophysical mechanisms by which this occurs and the conditions under which individuals are susceptible have yet to be fully explained scientifically. We are also now beginning to realize that noise can harm body organs other than the ears, as well as produce psychological effects which many have long suspected.

2.1 Physical Effects

There is a continuing controversy over definitions of deafness. First, there is a need to distinguish between temporary effects following loud noise from which the ear can easily recover (Temporary Threshold Shift, TTS), and those effects which involve permanent loss of some degree of hearing (Noise Induced Permanent Threshold Shift, NIPTS).

Second, there is a question as to what degree of hearing loss should be considered a serious impairment. There is some scientific feeling that the general population should be protected against a permanent impairment (NIPTS) of more than five decibels, which represents a considerable decrease in aural perceptiveness. 6/ There

---

5/ Noise measurement is a complex subject on which the above provides only some of the basic terminology. See, for example, the basic EPA noise criteria document: "Public Health and Welfare Criteria for Noise," 27 July 1973, EPA document, No. 550/9-73-002.

6/ See, for example, testimony of Daniel L. Johnson, Aerospace Medical Research Laboratory, Wright-Patterson AFB, Ohio, in OSHA Noise Hearings, Washington, D.C., 27 June 1975, transcript 765.

ENVIRONMENTAL LAW HANDBOOK

are others, however, who believe that substantial impairment does not take place until hearing loss reaches 25 decibel attenuation. 7/ This does not represent the beginning of hearing impairment or a satisfactory policy goal but rather is the point at which a severe, compensable handicap is defined. A person with such a hearing loss would be able to understand only 50 percent of monosyllabic words spoken in a quiet room and only 90 percent of all sentences. 8/

Third, at what frequency should hearing impairment be measured? After all, the ability to hear the higher frequencies is usually lost first. For a proper appreciation of musical harmonics, it is thought important to hear the frequencies between 10,000 and 15,000 Hz which is within the upper range of most normal individuals. The current debate, however, centers around a far more modest expectation: whether good hearing between 2,000 and 4,000 Hz is essential for proper understanding of spoken words. In some of the OSHA noise hearings, the director of that agency's standards office testified in favor of measurements only up to 2,000 Hz, describing those as the "speech frequencies," and defining impairment as a 25 decibel loss in that frequency range. 9/ Witnesses from EPA and NIOSH, on the other hand, have repeatedly emphasized the measurement of hearing loss "in the critical frequencies above 2,000 Hz, which are the soonest and most severely affected by exposure to noise." These frequencies, according to an EPA analysis of the proposed OSHA standard, "are as important as those below 1,900 Hz for determining the intelligibility of speech." 10/

These distinctions, while seemingly technical or trivial, can have important policy consequences. It will be a balancing of the risks to workers against the equally speculative cost to industry that

---

7/ Some scientists have even argued that a hearing impairment should not be considered serious until the loss is 50 decibels or more. W. Dixon Ward, Department of Otolaryngology, Chief, Hearing Research Laboratory, University of Minnesota, testifying on behalf of the American Iron and Steel Institute, OSHA Noise Hearings, 1 July 1975, transcript 1047.

8/ Statement of Joseph H. Hafkenschiel, Economist, Communication Workers of America, Testimony at the OSHA Noise Hearings, July 1975.

9/ Statement of Dan Boyd, then Director of Standards for OSHA, OSHA Noise Hearings, 23 June 1975, transcript p. 13.

10/ EPA review and report, "Proposed OSHA Occupational Noise Exposure Regulation," 39 FR 43802, 18 December 1974.

will determine where OSHA will set its important noise standard and what standards EPA and other federal agencies will promulgate for other segments of the economy.

2.2 Physiological Effects

The harmful effects of noise are not limited to the auditory system. We are all aware that a sharp sudden noise can cause the adrenaline to flow. Modern man is subject not to occasional stresses but to an unrelenting bombardment of noise which keeps his body on alert. This stress is not something that exists only in the mind, a synonym for a "nervous" condition. This assumption has been corrected by Dr. Jean Taché of the University of Montreal who has declared, "Now, to most people, stress is something bearing a psychological connotation. Stress is something in our heads. I would like to say that stress is something that happens in our body. During stress, the size of our organs change, they are modified; the adrenal is enlarged, the lymphatic system increases in size. So stress is not something merely in our heads, it is something that happens in our body." 11/

These manifestations can be demonstrated objectively by scientific measurements. A hormone, CRF, is secreted by the hypothalmus which stimulates the production of ACTH by the pituitary. This activates the adrenals producing corticoids which in turn moblize the entire body for a fight-flight situation. Stress, therefore, is not merely a situation which can be diagnosed only by a psychiatrist; it can also be determined quite objectively by, for example, measuring the corticoid level in the blood or the urine. 12/

The effect of these stress hormones on the cardiovascular system is well known. The arteries constrict, raising the blood pressure and placing greater strain on the heart. It is not possible to determine precisely what percentage of coronaries and strokes, if any, might be due in part to the effects of noise. These effects, according to one authority, "are likely to be distributed over a large number of common individual cardiovascular and other maladies whose causation is complex and attributable to other factors as well. Nonetheless, cardiovascular diseases are such a massive problem in our society that even if noise increases the incidence or severity by only a small percentage in the exposed population this

---

11/ Statement of Jean Taché, Institute of Experimental Medicine and Surgery, University of Montreal, Canada, before the Senate Small Business Committee, op. cit., p.23.

12/ Ibid., pp. 23-24.

would be a very substantial adverse effect. Major cardiovascular diseases account for well over half the deaths in the United States, currently somewhat over a million people per year." 13/
Continuous noise, by putting the body under stress, can lead to irritation and fatigue. This can be the case even if the noise is not at an uncomfortably high level, provided it is loud and relatively continuous. Some observers believe that these tensions can lead to distractions and a generally higher injury rate, although this point must await further studies for verification. There is more substantial evidence that noise can reduce efficiency and promote absenteeism, either because of its physical symptoms or because it is a distraction factor among workers subjected to excessive noise levels. 14/
Finally, animal tests suggest that noise may cause yet another barely explored medical hazard. Pregnant mice exposed to high noise levels produced offspring whose skeletal systems were incompletely developed and had a greater susceptibility to gastric ulcers and other gastrointestinal diseases. 15/

3.0 OSHA Regulation of Noise
Most of the severe noise problems are encountered in the occupational context. The former head of EPA's Noise Office has acknowledged, "As far as hearing loss or impairment is concerned, there is absolutely no question that the workplace represents the most serious exposure for the largest group." 16/ The leading standards and enforcement responsibility for noise is thus the Occupational Safety and Health Administration (OSHA) in the Department of Labor.

13/ Statement of Nicholas A. Ashford, Center for Policy Alternatives, MIT, Cambridge, Mass., before the Senate Small Business Committee, p. 249.

14/ This will be discussed in more detail in the section on the Economic Costs and Benefits of Noise Regulation by OSHA.

15/ Statement of Jean Taché, supra, p.26. Recent studies in California suggest that exactly the same effects—spina bifida, cleft palate, and anencephaly—may be produced in humans, see Washington Post, 20 February 1978.

16/ Statement of Alvin F. Meyer, EPA, Senate Small Business Committee, op. cit., p. 119.

3.1 The Present OSHA Standard

The Labor Department first began regulating noise under statutes of limited applicability, the most noted being the Walsh-Healey Public Contracts Act of 1936, 17/ which affected employees under private supply contracts with the federal government.

Under this statute, on 20 September 1968 the Department proposed for comment an 85 decibel (dB(A)) standard for an eight-hour working day. 18/ This level was adopted as the final standard on 17 January 1969, although companies with an effective hearing conservation program were allowed 92 dB(A) until 1 January 1971. The effective date of the regulation was thirty days from the date of publication. 19/

Just before the effective date, however, on 14 February 1969, the initiation date was postponed three months. 20/ No reason for the delay was given, but the Department later acknowledged that it was due to the advent of the Nixon Administration on 20 January 1969. 21/ When the standard finally appeared on 20 May 1969, it differed considerably from the original version. In particular, it established a maximum permissible eight-hour level of 90 dB(A). 22/

In December 1970, with the creation of OSHA, this protection was extended to cover all nongovernmental employees in the United States. 23/

17/   41 U.S.C. §§ 35-45. Similar noise exposure limits were issued under the (McNamara-O'Hara) Service Contract Act of 1965, 41 U.S.C. § 351 et seq.

18/   33 FR 14258 (1968). The A-scale attempts to relate loudness in decibels to the varying sensitivity of the human ear at different frequencies.

19/   34 FR 788 (1969), revising 41 CFR 50-204.

20/   34 FR 2207 (1969).

21/   See the preamble to the 20 May 1969 promulgation, infra.

22/   34 FR 7946(1969), esp. 7948-49.

23/   OSH Act § 6(a), 29 U.S.C. § 655(a). The effective date of the Act was April 1971. For two years, OSHA could also adopt other "established federal standards" which might be relevant to safety and health but which had not automatically been adopted under OSHA, and "national consensus standards," set forth by private standard-setting associations. This period ended in April 1973.

This standard is the one still being enforced today by OSHA. This standard provides, in addition to a noise exposure limit of 90 decibels, a doubling rate of five decibels. This means that for an increase of every five decibels in the sound level, the exposure time must be cut in half. For example, exposure at 90 decibels is permitted for eight hours, at 95 for four hours, and at 100 for two hours.

PERMISSIBLE NOISE EXPOSURE LIMITS 24/

Duration Per Day In Hours	Sound Level 90 dB(A) Standard	Hypothetical 85 dB(A) For Comparison 25/
8	90	85
6	92	87
4	95	90
3	97	92
2	100	95
1 1/2	102	97
1	105	100
1/2	110	102
1/4 or less	115	105

The standard also provides for a maximum sound level for impact or impulsive noise of 140 decibels, 26/ and a limit for continuous noise at 115 decibels for a fifteen minute period. As in other OSHA standards, employers are required first to control noise by engineering changes and administrative controls. Only if these methods prove infeasible should employers resort to the use of

---

24/   Table G-16 in 29 CFR 1910.95.

25/   Note that the 85 dB(A) column is hypothetical, prepared by the author, which also assumes a 5 decibel doubling rate. It is not a part of the Table G-16 or the official standard, although it might eventually become OSHA's noise standard.

26/   One hundred such 140 dB(A) impacts a day would be allowed with a tenfold increase number each decrease of ten decibels, and ten thousand at 120 decibels. This level, while startlingly high, is in accord with recommendations by the American Conference of Government Industrial Hygienists (ACGIH) and the American Industrial Hygiene Association (AIHA). See BNA, Noise Reporter, 9 June 1975, A-14.

personal protective equipment such as earmuffs and earplugs, along with a hearing conservation program. 27/

3.2 Enforcement

OSHA's enforcement of the present noise standard, although criticized as less than strict, 28/ has exceeded that of many other OSHA health standards. Generally, OSHA inspectors do not make separate inspections for noise, as they might do for toxic chemicals or particular safety hazards, but the ubiquitous nature of noise and its ease of detectability lead to the high citation rate. In 1975, for example, OSHA inspectors cited over 2,400 violations of the noise standard and imposed over a hundred thousand dollars in penalties. These figures, although still inadequate, constituted 4.3 percent of all health citations. This compares with a total of only 51 OSHA citations (0.09 percent) for dangerous carcinogenic chemical hazards. 29/

OSHA can impose both civil and criminal penalties for noise violations. For serious offenses, defined as those liable to cause "death or serious physical harm," the maximum fine is one thousand dollars per incident (the average is approximately half that). Repeated or willful offenses may be punished by fines as high as ten thousand dollars per violation. 30/ Most noise violations, however, are treated as "non-serious", for which the average fine on a first offense is around fifteen dollars.

3.3 OSHA Noise Hearings

OSHA's present standard, adopted from a regulation under a prior statute, is only an interim measure. Congress never intended that the temporary consensus and other federal standards adopted by

---

27/ OSHA, "Guidelines to the Occupational Noise Standard," 1971. See also, 29 CFR 1910.95.

28/ Testimony of Nicholas Ashford, MIT, Senate Small Business Committee, op. cit., p. 253. He testified then that "I think it would be fair to say that, from looking at the compliance history in the noise area by OSHA that there has not been a strict enforcement of the standard."

29/ OSHA, unpublished computer readout of 1975 inspections, 19 February 1976. See also OSHA Press Release, 25 February 1976. The carcinogen category is defined for these calculations as those standards in 29 CFR 1910.1003-1016.

30/ OSH Act § 17, 29 U.S.C. § 666.

OSHA in 1970 would remain the standards for the indefinite future. The procedure established under Section 6(b) of the OSHA statute is that the National Institute of Occupational Safety and Health (NIOSH), a branch of the Department of Health, Education, and Welfare (HEW), prepare criteria documents outlining all the relevant scientific information about the health effects of a particular substance or condition. This document is then forwarded to OSHA which conducts its own analysis of the criteria document and other relevant scientific information, often with the help of a special scientific advisory committee, and considers the technological and economic feasibility factors which are beyond NIOSH's statutory purview. OSHA then proposes a standard as a basis for discussions at subsequent public hearings. The proposal is subsequently modified, if deemed necessary, and the final standard is issued. 31/

NIOSH sent its noise criteria document to OSHA on 14 August 1972. 32/ A Standards Advisory Committee on Noise was appointed. 33/ Sixteen months after receipt of the criteria document, the Advisory Committee transmitted its comments and recommendations to the OSHA Standards office on 20 December 1973. The Standards office, after another ten months of deliberation and preparation, issued on 18 October 1974 a proposed occupational noise exposure standard. 34/

OSHA proposed retention of the 90 dB(A) noise level, a peak impulse exposure at 140 decibels, a five decibel doubling rate, and provisions for employee monitoring and audiometric testing with specific recordkeeping provisions. The limited changes in the proposal prompted some critics to wonder why OSHA had bothered to initiate the time-consuming rulemaking procedure.

31/ OSHA's standard setting record is not beyond reproach. Although there are thousands of toxic substances for which no standards exist and NIOSH has submitted a dozen or more criteria documents each year for OSHA consideration, OSHA has averaged less than one final standard a year since its creation, and these generally have been the result of court action or emergency procedures.

32/ This is in accordance with OSH Act § 29(a)(3), 29 U.S.C. § 669.

33/ OSH Act § 76, 29 U.S.C. § 656, requires representation from labor unions, management, government and independent experts.

34/ 39 FR 37773, 24 October 1974.

EPA immediately objected to the OSHA proposal. This was not officiousness by EPA but a duty under Section 4(c)(2) of the Noise Control Act of 1972, 35/ which gave EPA the chief coordinating responsibility for noise within the Administration. Under this statute, EPA Administrator Russell Train notified OSHA on 6 December 1974 that EPA "believes that the proposed regulation does not protect the public health and welfare to the extent required and feasible." 36/ EPA argued that an eight-hour work day exposure standard of 85 dB(A) was more consistent with available scientific evidence. In fact, EPA argued that its scientific data "support a level of 75 dB(A) for an ultimate health goal; EPA believes that the reduction to 85 dB(A) is an important step toward this goal." 37/

EPA also contended that the OSHA-proposed doubling rate of five decibels had no scientific justification; the proper rate, based on the total amount of acoustic energy, should have been three decibels. In addition, EPA criticized OSHA's reliance on audiometric monitoring, since individual variations and the crudeness of measurement techniques could allow a threshold shift as great as 35 decibels before a worker was informed of his hearing loss. 38/

The OSHA public hearing on the proposed noise standard began in June 1975 and continued for several weeks. A team of representatives from the EPA noise office, headed by Alvin Myer, testified strongly against the OSHA proposal, but the anticipated bitter clash between the two agencies never occurred. OSHA's position was not as adamant as it had sometimes been described. OSHA had never held, as some had portrayed, that a 90 decibel standard would protect against all adverse health effects. This misconception arose partially from OSHA's deliberate vagueness, but the proposal document itself clearly stated the following:

> With regard to the risk of hearing loss, OSHA recognizes that comparatively more workers would be at lower risk at 85 dB(A) than at 90 dB(A). However, we also recognize the technical feasibility problems and the economic impact associated with an 85 dB(A) requirement as reflected in the Bolt, Beranek and Newman study and in

---

35/   PL 92-574, 86 Stat. 1236, 42 U.S.C. § 4903(c)(2).

36/   EPA, "Proposed OSHA Occupational Noise Exposure Regulation," 39 FR 43802.

37/   Ibid.

38/   Ibid., p. 43808.

the draft environmental impact statement. Therefore, OSHA proposes to keep the level at 90 dB(A) until empirical data and information on the health risks, feasibility, and economic impact indicate the practicality and necessity of an 85 dB(A) requirement. 39/

3.4 Economic and Technical Feasibility

The major controversy between EPA and OSHA was the medical and technical basis of the proposed 90 dB(A) standard. EPA pointed out that NIOSH, while favoring a standard of 85, had stated it "reluctantly concurs" with the 90 decibel proposal. 40/ EPA pointed out that this concurrence was solely the result of NIOSH deferring to OSHA's judgment on economic and technical feasibility, as set forth in Section 20 of the OSHA statute, 41/ and was not an independent conclusion by NIOSH that attainment of noise levels below 90 decibels was generally technically infeasible. 42/

Neither EPA, OSHA, nor any outside experts were really sure just what was attainable and at what cost. OSHA commissioned a sweeping economic impact study to determine the anticipated cost of complying with both 90 decibel and 85 decibel standards. This study by Bolt, Beranek and Newman (BBN) estimated that the cost for attaining a 90 dB(A) level would be about $13 billion--even though this had been the federal standard for a number of years--and that the added cost for reaching the 85 decibel level would be $18 billion. 43/

The benefits of a lower noise standard are even more controversial. The BBN study estimated that a reduction from 90 decibels to 85 decibels would reduce by 770,000 the number of workers who

---

39/   OSHA, "Proposed Occupational Noise Exposure," 39 FR 3773, 24 October 1974.

40/   See NIOSH Criteria Document, "Occupational Exposure to Noise," p. II-3.

41/   OSH Act, § 20(a)(3), 29 U.S.C. § 669(a)(3).

42/   EPA, "Proposed OSHA Occupational Noise Exposure Regulation," 39 FR 43802, 18 December 1974.

43/   Bolt, Beranek and Newman, Inc., Cambridge, Mass., "Impact of Noise at the Workplace," Report No. 2671. See also OSHA Noise Hearings, transcript p. 281 et seq.

would have extreme hearing loss at retirement age. 44/ The reduction from 90 to 85 decibels would also provide protection to an additional 8.2 million workers who would otherwise face serious but not disabling hearing losses over their working life. 45/

The economic costs of this hearing loss cannot, of course, be estimated precisely, partially because of the difficulty in assigning dollar values to human losses. Attempts to quantify some of the data by using workmen's compensation awards (although they are notoriously low) produced estimates in the billions of dollars. 46/ A more interesting, if more speculative, estimate involves estimating the cost of increased absenteeism as a result of annoying noise. The Frye Report calculated that if absenteeism could be reduced one day per year for those workers exposed to noise levels over 85 decibels, a reasonable assumption, this would add $2 billion a year to the GNP. 47/

There have also been attempts to calculate the social costs of irritation annoyance from noise. It is generally accepted that workers prefer quiet working surroundings to the strain of enduring noise levels of 90 decibels or higher. One study took 10 cents an hour as the minimum differential that a worker would accept and 50 cents as a maximum. These computations produced an annoyance estimate ranging from $3 to $14 billion a year. Compliance with a 90 dB(A) standard would produce a yearly benefit of (using the high figure) $3 billion, while attaining an 85 decibel level would yield $4.6 billion. 48/

Another authority has estimated that the benefits to workers from reducing noise-related tension to 85 decibels would be between

---

44/ Bolt, Beranek and Newman Report, p. 37.

45/ See Bolt, Beranek and Newman Report, Tables III and IV.

46/ See statement of Nicholas Ashford, OSHA Noise Hearings, 23 July 1975, transcript, p. 84.

47/ U.S. Department of Health, Education and Welfare(HEW), Public Health Service, Protecting the Health of 80 Million Americans, 1965. The Frye estimate has been recomputed for 1976 figures. See also Ashford statement in OSHA hearings, transcript, p. 85; and Ashford statement before Senate Small Business Committee, op. cit., p. 252.

48/ Ashford, OSHA Noise Hearings, transcript, pp. 87-90.

$5.2 and $13 billion and at least another $11 billion for hearing preservation. 49/

3.5 Hearing Protection Devices

A major issue faced by OSHA is the efficacy of hearing protection devices such as ear plugs and muffs. Industry representatives argued that they should be allowed to meet the OSHA noise standard, whether 85 or 90 decibels, in any way possible. This could mean providing personal protective equipment, rather than reducing the general noise level in an industry. According to one company spokesman, the same or better protection to employees could be provided by ear protectors at a fraction of the cost: "the question must be raised as a matter of public policy whether the benefits to be attained from engineering controls justify the allocation of scarce capital to projects that are non-productive." 50/ Union representatives, on the other hand, point to numerous studies and testimony that this reasonable approach has often not worked well in practice. 51/ This problem has also arisen in enforcement proceedings before the Review Commission and the courts.

3.6 The Feasibility and Balancing Debate

Current OSHA noise enforcement, and the eventual new noise standard, will be largely determined by the outcome of a continuing legal debate over feasibility and balancing. The important issues include the following:

(1)   Can OSHA legally consider economic factors in setting health or safety standards levels?
(2)   If so, is this consideration limited only to extreme circumstances?
(3)   Does the Occupational Safety and Health Act provide for a balancing of costs and benefits in setting standards?

49/   This, he suggested, however, would still total less than the BBN cost estimates. Robert Stewart Smith, The Occupational Safety and Health Act: Its Goals and Achievements (Washington, D.C.: American Enterprise Institute, 1976), p. 51.

50/   Edwin H. Tootham, Senior Noise Control Engineer, Bethlehem Steel, OSHA Noise Hearings, 1 July 1975, pp. 1117 and 1126.

51/   See, for example, the testimony of David Metz, Chairman, Speech and Hearing Department, Cleveland State University, on behalf of OSHA, OSHA Noise Hearings, 24 June 1975, p. 176 et seq.

(4)   Can OSHA mandate engineering controls although
      they alone would still not attain the standard?
(5)   And, can OSHA require engineering controls even
      if personal protective equipment (such as ear
      plugs) could effectively reduce noise to a safe
      level and at a much lower cost?

Although these questions have been extensively litigated
before the Occupational Safety and Health Review Commission
(OSHRC) and the courts, no definitive answers have yet emerged,
even for issue number one. This is due to a difference of opinion
between several circuit courts of appeals over the interpretation of
"feasibility" in Section 6(b)(5) of the Act.

One must remember that the OSHA legislation was originally
seen by Congress in rather absolutist terms: any standard promulgated should be one "which most adequately assumes . . . that no
employee will suffer material impairment of health." Only late in
the debate was the Department of Labor able to insert the phrase
"to the extent feasible" into the text. This was intended to prevent
companies having to close because unattainable standards were
imposed on them, but it was not spelled out to what extent economic
as well as technical feasibility was included. 52/

Two federal circuits have held that economic factors are
included, but to a limited degree. In Industrial Union Department,
AFL v. Hodgson, the D.C. Circuit accepted that economic realities
affected the meaning of "feasible," but only to the extent that "a
standard that is prohibitively expensive is not 'feasible.' " 53/ It was
Congress' intent, the court added, that this term would prevent a
standard unreasonably "requiring protective devices unavailable
under existing technology or by making financial viability generally
impossible." The court warned, however, that this doctrine should
not be used by companies to avoid needed improvements in their
workplaces:

52/   This account of the behind-the-scenes machinations is based
      largely on the views of the late Congressman William Steiger
      (R-Wisc.), a principal author of the act, and of Lawrence Sil-
      berman, then Solicitor of Labor. The legislative history is
      relatively unhelpful on this subject. See, for example, hearings
      before the Select Subcommittee on Labor, Committee on
      Education and Labor, "Occupational Safety and Health Act of
      1969," two vols., 1969.

53/   499 F.2d 467, 1 OSHC 1631 (D.C. Cir. 1974).

Standards may be economically feasible even though, from the standpoint of employers, they are financially burdensome and affect profit margins adversely. Nor does the concept of economic feasibility necessarily guarantee the continued existence of individual employers. 54/

A similar view was adopted by the Second Circuit in The Society of the Plastics Industry v. OSHA, written by Justice Clark, who cited approvingly the case above. 55/ He held that "feasible" meant not only that which is attainable technologically and economically now, but also that which might reasonably be achievable in the future. In this case, which concerned strict emissions controls on vinyl chloride, he declared that OSHA may impose "standards which require improvements in existing technologies or which require the development of new technology, and . . . is not limited to issuing standards based solely on devices already fully developed." 56/

Neither court undertook any risk-benefit analysis, such as attempting to compare the hundreds of millions of dollars needed to control vinyl chloride with the lives lost to angiosarcoma of the liver. Those who have attempted to develop such equations have generally concluded the task is undoable, at least for most such chronic health effects. 57/

A third federal appeals court, however, has taken a strongly contrary position in a case specifically involving noise. In Turner Co. v. Secretary of Labor, the Seventh Circuit Court of Appeals decided that the $30,000 cost of abating a noise hazard should be weighed against the health damage to workers, taking into consideration the availability of personal protective equipment to mitigate the risk. 58/

54/   1 OSHC 1631 at 1639.

55/   509 F.2d 1301, 2 OSHC 1496 (2d Circ. 1975), cert. den. 421 US 992.

56/   509 F.2d at 1309, 2 OSHC at 1502 (2d Cir. 1975).

57/   See, for example, the conclusions of the National Academy of Sciences report, "Government Regulation of Chemicals in the Environment," 1975.

58/   561 F.2d 82, 5 OSHC 1970. (7th Circ. 1977). The Occupational Safety and Health Review Commission (OSHRC) decisions on Turner and the related Continental Can case can be found at 4 OSHC 1554 (1976) and 4 OSHC 1541 (1976), respectively.

This holding is not unreasonable, but it is based on a highly tenuous interpretation of the law. The court, without providing any clear rationale for its view, held that "the word 'feasible' as contained in 29 CFR § 1910.95(6)(1) must be given its ordinary and common sense meaning of 'practicable.'" (This may be so but is of no analytical value.) From this the court concluded:

> Accordingly, the Commission erred when it failed to consider the relative cost of implementing engineering controls . . . versus the effectiveness of an existing personal protective equipment program utilizing fitted earplugs. 59/

This interpretation does not follow from the analysis. In fact, since the Turner Company had both the financial resources and the technical capability to abate the noise problem, compliance with the regulation would appear to be "practicable." The court, however, considered this term to mean that a cost-benefit computation should be made.

Because of these differing interpretations of the law, OSHA's enforcement of its noise standard was inevitably affected. The Supreme Court's decisions on benzene and cotton dust (discussed in the OSHA Chapter) have helped to clarify the parameters of feasibility roughly along the lines OSHA had advocated.

3.7 The Long-Anticipated OSHA Noise Standard

Issuance of the final revised OSHA noise standard has been promised for so long that predictions are no longer taken seriously. In May 1976, for example, a senior OSHA official declared that the standard should be published sometime that year. In October, another OSHA spokesman said it would be issued within three months.

Meanwhile, several labor leaders hinted darkly that sinister political motives were responsible for the delay, 60/ and one union

---

59/   5 OSHC 1790 at 1791.

60/   In 1972, the then-head of OSHA, George Guenther, wrote a memo to the Under Secretary of Labor indicating that the organization would trim its sails during the Presidential election campaign. This memo, uncovered a year later, became a favorite topic for union leaders charging the Agency with crass political sellouts. This criticism was specifically leveled at OSHA on noise by Eric Frumin of the Amalgamated Clothing and Textile Workers Union in October 1976.

brought suit unsuccessfully to require publication of the noise standard within thirty days. In January 1977, a different political party considered friendlier to labor assumed control of OSHA. The head of OSHA promised in July 1977 that it would be ready by "early 1978." It was not, however, and when she left office four years later it too had not released the long-awaited, or long-dreaded, noise standard.

This delay is due partly, of course, to the extraordinary complexity of the subject. But many of the issues for which additional information is sought are also ones for which it is probably unobtainable in the foreseeable future. Thus, it is correct that a standard could be issued within three months of a decision on several important questions.

A more important reason for the delay, therefore, is the hesitation of OSHA's leadership, both past and present, to promulgate a standard with such explosive political consequences for themselves and the Agency. This caution is warranted, but countervailing pressures mean the decision cannot be postponed indefinitely.

4.0 Environmental Protection Agency Authority

Although OSHA has the primary responsibility for controlling most noise sources in the environment, the Environmental Protection Agency (EPA) has been given statutory authority to oversee federal actions toward noise pollution in general. EPA also has responsibility for a number of environmental noise pollutant sources, ranging from snowmobiles to aviation (in concert with the Federal Aviation Administration), which are of significant national concern.

The Reagan Administration came into office in 1981 determined to eliminate the entire EPA noise program, which then numbered about 110 people. On 17 February 1981, the White House's Office of Management and Budget (OMB) issued a "no appeal" directive to phase out the office; the only choice was the timing, either six or eighteen months. Two years later, the staff numbered 2 1/2 people, and most of the regulatory programs were rescinded. 61/ The Administration was not able to eliminate them entirely, however, because certain strong industry groups and their congressional supporters wanted federal preemption of a multiplicity of inconsistent and possibly stricter standards. The Noise Act itself was left in place.

61/   Charles Elkins, former director of EPA's Noise Office, 28 January 1983.

4.1 The Noise Act of 1970

The 1970 Congress enacted the Noise Pollution and Abatement Act, a short act of two sections which was attached as Title IV to the Clean Air Act enacted in the same year. 62/ It directed EPA to establish an Office of Noise Abatement and Control. This office was not then granted any regulatory authority but was to thoroughly investigate the effects of noise on the public health and welfare, to identify major noise sources, and to determine seven statutorily-specified effects of noise. These include the following:

- effects at various levels;
- projected growth of noise levels in urban areas through the year 2000;
- the psychological and physiological effect on humans;
- effects of sporadic extreme noise (such as jet noise near airports) as compared with constant noise;
- effect on wildlife and property (including values);
- effect of sonic booms on property (including values); and
- such other matters as may be of interest in the public welfare. 63/

This information was to be used in the preparation of recommendations to Congress within one year for further legislation on the abatement of noise pollution. 64/

4.2 The Noise Control Act of 1972

The Noise Control Act of 1972 65/ set forth the broad goal of protecting all Americans from "noise that jeopardizes their health or

---

62/   PL 91-604, 42 U.S.C. § 1857, et seq.

63/   Clean Air Act of 1970, § 402(a), 42 U.S.C. § 1858(a).

64/   Clean Air Act § 402(b), 42 U.S.C. § 1858(b). EPA, Report to the President and Congress on Noise, 31 December 1971. This was sent to the White House along with 15 detailed technical reports on noise effects, noise measurement, and other problems.

65/   PL 92-842, 42 U.S.C. §§ 4901, et seq.

welfare." 66/ The bill provides four broad duties for EPA: to serve as a coordinator within the federal government for noise control efforts, to establish noise standards based on scientific criteria documents, to regulate noise emissions from products in commerce, and to provide general information to the public concerning the noise emission of such products.

A primary feature of the Act, and probably a reason for its attracting support from such divergent interests, was that it delineated the bounds between federal and local jurisdiction over noise. The legislation ostensibly placed principal authority for regulating noise with the states and local communities to ensure that the federal government will not become enmeshed in nationwide noise zoning duties. The practical effect of the 1972 Noise Act, however, was precisely the opposite. While the preamble to the Act acknowledges the "primary responsibility for control of noise rests with state and local governments," the major emphasis of the Act is indicated by the phrase that follows: "Federal action is essential to deal with major noise sources in commerce, control of which requires national uniformity of treatment." 67/

There is an interesting contrast here, distinguishing ambient noise and noise sources, between the noise and air laws. Ambient noise, the level of noise in the general environment, is essentially a local problem, while the noise-producing products and machinery are generally those which are used and sold nationally. Under the air pollution laws, however, the ambient levels are set nation-wide by the federal government on health bases, but the sources of air pollution (other than mobile sources) are generally regulated through state authorities under Sections 110 and 111 of the Clean Air Act.

The federal supremacy issue may have been swayed by important commercial interests: while they wanted no regulations for new products, they preferred uniform federal rules to a hodge-podge of state and local regulations. These, they feared, might constitute a serious burden on interstate commerce.

Despite contrasting interests, on 8 November 1978 the Quiet Communities Act was approved extending the provisions of the Noise Control Act of 1972 and amending some sections of the Act to

---

66/   Noise Act § 2(b), 42 U.S.C. § 4092(b).

67/   Noise Act § 2(a)(3). The language on the primacy of local governments is lifted almost literally from the preamble to the Clean Air Act, Section 101(a)(3), where it has been retained through successive amendments even though the section has increasingly become an anachronism.

put more of the burden on state and local governments. Section 14 was expanded to focus more attention on state and local governments providing them with the funds to develop and disseminate information, to conduct and finance research, to purchase monitoring equipment, and in other ways to facilitate the development and enforcement of noise control standards. Nevertheless, the Quiet Communities Act provides that no actions, plans or programs should be "inconsistent with existing Federal authority . . . to regulate sources of noise in interstate commerce." 68/

4.3 Noise Sources and Criteria

In a procedure also modeled after the Clean Air Act, 69/ EPA was required to publish within nine months, i.e., July 1973, noise criteria identifying the effects on health and welfare of different forms and levels of noise. There was also a requirement in the Act for a second report three months later indicating what levels of ambient noise were adequate "to protect the public health and welfare with an adequate margin of safety." 70/

The next report, due 18 months after the enactment of the Act, i.e., April 1974, called for the identification of those specific products or classes of products which are major noise sources. 71/ This report included information on control techniques, economic and technical feasibility data, and alternative noise control methods. 72/ This list was to be revised and supplemented from time to time and published in the Federal Register along with supporting criteria documents. 73/

4.4 Setting of Noise Emission Standards

Following the identification of the principal noise sources that are "feasible and are requisite to protect the public health and

---

68/   Quiet Communities Act, PL 95-609, § 2.

69/   See Clean Air Act § 108, 42 U.S.C. 1857c(3).

70/   Noise Act § 5(a)(2).   This second report was essentially superfluous.

71/   This requirement was not in fact met until a further thirteen months later.

72/   Noise Act § 5(b).

73/   Noise Act § 5(c). Regulatory actions taken by EPA under this and other sections of the Act will be discussed later in this chapter.

welfare," 74/ the Administrator was directed to take into account in determining both feasibility and advisability, "the magnitude and conditions of use of such products (alone or in combination with other noise sources), the degree of noise reduction achievable through the application of the best available technology, and the cost of compliance." 75/

EPA was required to propose noise emission standards within 18 months of enactment for those products or classes of products identified under Section 5(b) as major noise sources, if EPA found such standards were feasible and if the products fell in one of the following categories:

    (i) Construction equipment
    (ii) Transportation equipment (including recre ational vehicles and related equipment)
    (iii) Any motor or engine (including any equipment of which an engine or motor is an integral part)
    (iv) Electrical or electronic equipment 76/

Once a standard was proposed for a noise source, final regulations were to be issued within six months unless the Administrator determined that noise emission standards were not feasible for such products. 77/ This congressional device to hasten the administrative process by a rigorous burden of proof is found in few other environmental statutes. 78/

In May 1975 EPA identified a number of products for Section 6 standards, including (1) buses, (2) wheel and crawler tractors, (3) motorcycles, (4) solid waste compactor trucks, and (5) truck-mounted refrigerators. 79/

It should be noted that while the standard procedure for developing standards under Section 6 derives from the identification

---

74/   Noise Act § 6(b).

75/   Noise Act § 6(c)(1).

76/   Ibid.

77/   Noise Act § 6(a)(3).

78/   The most notable are Section 112(b)(1)(B) of the Clean Air Act regarding hazardous air pollutants and Section 307(a)(2) of the Water Pollution Act covering toxic effluent standards.

79/   40 FR 23105, 28 May 1975.

of the product as a major noise source under Section 5, EPA has the authority to impose noise standards on any product, even though it has not been identified as a major noise source and no control techniques have been set forth. 80/ This provision, therefore, provides an alternative to the congressionally-declared categories under Section 6(a). 81/

Several other features of the standards-setting section merit further brief explanations. First "any such noise emission standards shall be a performance standard." This is consistent with congressional determination in other environmental acts that industry should not be told how to reduce emissions by design standards but rather should be told only what level should be attained to protect public health and welfare and then be allowed to reach it in any fashion desired. This is a reasonable approach, although it ignores those frequent situations in which industry and government agree on what technology is available but disagree on the levels attainable under varying circumstances. 82/

Second, in standards setting EPA is also required to consider the degree of noise reduction possible using best available technology (BAT), considering the cost of compliance. This can be at odds with the requirement for performance standards. What often occurs in practice is that EPA ascertains what is the best available technology, determines from that what level is achievable under normal circumstances, and then sets a performance standard at that level. Thus, standards are often set on the basis of design criteria but are converted into performance standards.

Third, the requirement to take into consideration the magnitude and use of the product, either by itself or in combination with other noise sources, may result in more severe noise reductions in certain cases because of the likelihood that a number of machines or devices will be operating simultaneously.

4.5 Federal, State and Local Jurisdiction Under Section 6

The noise emission standards under Section 6 affect state and local authority over noise only in one sense: local jurisdictions are preempted from imposing their own noise emission standards on new products for which federal standards apply, unless these standards are identical with federal standards. (The term "new product"

80/ Noise Act § 6(b).

81/ Noise Act § 6(a)(1)(C).

82/ This was the situation, for example, in EPA air standards involving both mercury and asbestos, and with OSHA standards on the coal tar pitch volatiles (CTPV) from coke ovens.

means, for practical purposes, virtually any product.) 83/ For those products for which EPA has not yet issued standards, local standards, if any, would continue to apply without preemption. Moreover, local governments would retain their authority "to regulate use, operation, or movement of products—except aircraft—without regard to preemption." 84/

During the legislative debates prior to enactment of the Noise Bill, the Nixon Administration had favored a complete preemption of state authority once a federal emission standard had been set (unless the local standard was identical) to prevent impeding the nationwide distribution of products. The House declined to accept total state preemption: while states were preempted from regulating products not yet sold to a consumer, they could control noise from products once they had reached their ultimate user. 85/ In 1978, the Quiet Communities Act amended Section 6 of the original act giving states or political subdivisions thereof the right to petition the Administrator to revise a federal standard on the grounds that a more stringent standard is necessary to protect public health and welfare. 86/

Some consideration was given by Congress to a federal ambient noise standard, similar to the ambient procedure under the Clean Air Act. 87/ This was rejected, however, because such a standard "would, in effect, put the federal government in the position of establishing land use zoning requirements on the basis of noise—i.e., noise levels to be permitted in residential areas, in business areas, in manufacturing and residential areas, and within those areas for

---

83/ § 3(5) defines "new product" as "(a) a product the equitable or legal title of which has never been transferred to an ultimate purchaser, or (b) a product which is imported or offered for importation in the United States and which is manufactured after the effective date of regulation under § 6 or § 8 which would have been applicable to such product had it been manufactured in the United States."

84/ House Committee on Interstate and Foreign Commerce, "Legislative History of Noise Control Act of 1972," March 1972 pp. 8-9, interpreting Noise Act § 6(e).

85/ E.L. Dolgin and T.G.P. Guilbert, Editors, Federal Environmental Law (St. Paul, Minn.: West Publishing Co., 1974).

86/ PL 95-609, § 5.

87/ Clean Air Act §§ 108-110.

different times of the day or night. It is the committee's view that
this function is one more properly that of the States and their political subdivisions. . . ." 88/

4.6 Warranties
After a standard has been issued, Section 6(d)(1) requires the
manufacturer to warrant to the purchaser that the product was
designed and built to conform with the noise standard at the time of
sale. He does not necessarily warrant that the product will conform
to the standard over its useful life, although EPA might so require.
This warranty makes available to the producer the normal defenses
of wear and tear of the product, misuse, and lack of proper maintenance.
However, where a product is inherently defective, any cost
obligation incurred by the dealer to correct the defect must be
borne by the manufacturer. The transfer of any such cost obligation
from the manufacturer to any dealer through a franchise or other
agreement is prohibited. In spite of this prohibition, it would appear
that where the responsibility for product performance over a period
of time might be involved, this might still fall within the normal
arrangements a manufacturer may have with his dealer.

4.7 Advertising Restrictions
In an obvious attempt to keep the manufacturers from ex-
ploiting the cost aspects of noise control, Section 6(d)(3) requires
that if a manufacturer advertises that his product includes valuable
or costly noise emission control devices or systems, such claims are
subject to verification by the Bureau of Labor Statistics. Access
may be afforded to the manufacturer's books, documents, papers and
records. To forestall such investigations, manufacturers' advertising
will probably focus on performance, compliance with standards, and
other benefits, but not refer to cost or value of the noise emission
control devices or systems.

4.8 Labeling
In Section 8 the EPA Administrator is required by regulation
to designate any product (or class thereof) which (1) emits noise
capable of adversely affecting the public health and welfare or (2) is
sold wholly or in part on the basis of its effectiveness in reducing
noise. The prospective user must be informed of the level of noise
the product emits or its effectiveness in reducing noise.

88/ House Commerce Committee, "Legislative History of Noise
Control Act of 1972," supra, p.9.

The labeling approach is based on the premise that it constitutes a partial alternative to setting often-arbitrary numerical
standards or the outright banning of harmful products. It assumes
that consumers will prefer less hazardous products to those which
are more hazardous, if they are properly informed of the facts. Or
if they prefer the more hazardous, because of lower cost or for some
other reason, at least they will have had the opportunity to exercise
an informed choice.

Although an advance notice of proposed rulemaking was
published in December 1974, 89/ a general labeling proposal was not
signed until 10 June 1977. It sets forth the criteria for eventual
selection of candidate products for labeling. They should also be
coordinated with other federal agencies, such as the Consumer
Product Safety Commission, which also have labeling requirements. 90/

The labeling preemption provision is somewhat vague. 91/
The state or political subdivision is not prevented from regulating
product labeling or information in any way which does not conflict
with EPA regulations. In other words, the state or political subdivision cannot require information of the type required by EPA to be
given in a form different from that prescribed by EPA. The Director of EPA's Noise Office declared then that local jurisdictions
would indeed be encouraged to instigate their own labeling
programs, even though this could have been a serious burden to
trade. 92/

With the virtual demise of EPA's noise program, however, this
proposal and other regulatory initiatives have been suspended.

4.9 Development of Low–Noise–Emission Products

Low–noise–emission products (LNEP) are defined in Section 15
as any products which emit noise in amounts significantly below the
levels specified in noise emission standards applicable at the time of
procurement. EPA is empowered to set up procedures to determine
which products qualify and to certify them for use in the federal

---

89/ BNA, Noise Reporter, 9 December 1974, A-12.

90/ The Department of Commerce adopted in May 1977 an experi-
     mental volunteer labeling program and invited companies to
     participate. See 42 FR 26647. The Home Appliance Manufac-
     turers objected to this plan, claiming it would be costly and
     would add to already overcrowded labels.

91/ Noise Act § 8(c).

92/ See BNA, Noise Reporter, 27 September 1976, A-1.

government, if the General Services Administration finds the cost of the product less than that of one for which it would be substituted. Any statutory price limitations would be waived. 93/

In May 1977, EPA proposed LNEP standards for heavy and medium trucks and for portable air compressors. 94/ A month later, the GSA actually completed an LNEP purchase of quieter push power mowers. 95/

4.10 Prohibitions and Penalties

The Noise Act makes illegal the manufacture, distribution, or importation of any new product produced after the effective date of a regulation under either Section 6 (noise standards) or Section 8 (noise labeling information). The Act also prohibits the removal or rendering inoperative of noise control devices prior to sale of the product to an ultimate purchaser, 96/ or "the use of a product after such device or element of design has been removed or rendered inoperative by any person." 97/

Section 11 of the Act prescribes fines and imprisonment for willful violations of Section 10. In the original Act these sanctions were as high as $25,000 and imprisonment for up to one year, or both, for first violations. The penalty for subsequent violations could reach $50,000 and imprisonment for up to two years. 98/ However, the Quiet Communities Act of 1978 reduced these limits to a maximum of "$10,000 per day of such violation." 99/

4.11 Control of Transportation Noise

Congress recognized in the Noise Act that the primary sources of noise, other than machinery, were the vehicles involved in

---

93/   Final regulations on procurement were issued in 1974. 39 FR 6670.

94/   42 FR 27442, 27 May 1977.

95/   Reported in BNA, Noise Reporter, 25 April 1977, A-6.

96/   "Ultimate purchaser" is defined as "the first person who in good faith purchases a product for purposes other than resale." Noise Act § 3(4).

97/   Noise Act § 10(a).

98/   Noise Act § 11(a). As in many other acts, each day of a violation may constitute a separate offense under this section, see § 11(b).

99/   PL 95-609, §4, Amending Noise Act § 11(a)(2).

general transportation. Thus, while Congress provided one section (Section 6) covering general machinery and motors, three detailed sections were incorporated into the Act to deal with aircraft noise (Section 7), railroad noise (Section 19), and noise from motor carriers (Section 18). EPA is thus given authority in areas where other federal agencies such as the Federal Aviation Administration (FAA) and the Federal Railroad Administration (FRA) normally exercise sole jurisdiction. Moreover, to the extent that these and other federal agencies have not issued standards and regulations protecting their workers from occupational noise, OSHA has authority under its statute to regulate and enforce its own standards. 100/

4.12 Aviation Noise

Congress' primary concern in the transportation area, as reflected in the legislative history, was with aviation noise. 101/ EPA's regulatory involvement has accordingly been much more extensive in this area, as we shall see in a separate section later. 102/ In 1968 Congress had given the FAA, which is responsible for airline safety, the additional responsibility of regulating aircraft and airport noise. 103/ The 1972 Noise Control Act added to this authority but also extended EPA's authority into the area. The Administration had recommended that EPA be given veto power over all noise standards and regulations issued by the FAA. Some environmentalists favored giving EPA even fuller power, allowing the EPA Administrator to set aviation noise standards directly.

100/ OSHA Act § 4(b)(1). This authority has not been without legal challenge; in the railroad area, for example, the highest courts have several times considered cases unsuccessfully brought to deny OSHA's jurisdiction to inspect railroad property. The FRA has general jurisdiction in the area but has not issued comprehensive occupational standards.

101/ House Committee on Interstate and Foreign Commerce, "Legislative History of Noise Control Act of 1972," March 1972.

102/ The 1971 EPA Noise hearings revealed that public complaints about noise from aircraft surpassed those from any other source. EPA estimated in its 1971 report to the President, supra, that over 7 million Americans were burdened with aircraft noise.

103/ 1968 Amendment to the Federal Aviation Act of 1958, § 611, 49 U.S.C. § 1431.

Congress rejected both these positions, because it felt that EPA lacked the requisite technical expertise concerning aircraft and engine design. Instead, the 1972 Act provides for joint regulatory authority for FAA and EPA, although the former retains the leading role. 104/

The basic statutory provision is Section 7 of the Noise Control Act of 1972, along with its Section 7(b) which amends Section 611 of the Federal Aviation Act of 1958. Section 7 provided that within nine months after the enactment of the Noise Act, EPA should conduct a detailed and comprehensive study of the adequacy of FAA standards and controls on flight operations and on aircraft, and the available means of reducing the cumulative noise exposure around airports. This important study was sent to the respective committees of the House and Senate on 31 July 1973. 105/

Section 7(b) of the Act amended Section 611 of the Federal Aviation Act to provide that the Administrator of the FAA "shall prescribe and amend such rules and regulations as he may find necessary to provide for the control and abatement of aircraft noise and sonic boom" and shall consult with others to determine what actions are necessary and whether they are "economically reasonable, technologically practicable, and appropriate for the particular type of aircraft, aircraft engine," etc., for application. 106/ The 1972 Amendments specified that the FAA must consult with EPA before taking any regulatory actions on noise.

A more significant authority for EPA is the right to propose noise regulations which the FAA must consider and within 30 days publish a notice of proposed rulemaking. Within a further 60 days FAA must hold a public hearing and after a reasonable time and after further consultation with EPA, the FAA must prescribe the regulations in whole or in part or detail its reasons for not doing so. 107/ If EPA believes that the action taken by the FAA "does not protect the public health and welfare from aircraft noise or sonic boom," EPA may request the FAA to reconsider its conclusions and

---

104/   House Commerce Committee, "Legislative History of Noise Control Act of 1972," supra, p.9.

105/   EPA, "Report on Aircraft-Airport Noise," July 1973; this was subsequently published as Senate Committee on Public Works, "Report on Aircraft-Airport Noise," series 93-8, 1973.

106/   FAA § 611(b)(1) and § 611(d)(4), 49 U.S.C. § 1431(b)(1) and § 1431(d)(4).

107/   FAA § 611(c)(1).

report in writing to EPA in detail as to why the original recommendations were not followed. This already lengthy process may then be followed by publication in the Federal Register, additional consultations, the preparation of a supplemental environmental report, and a list of additional factors for consideration. 108/ The final decision remains with FAA subject to court challenge, but the FAA is given every procedural incentive to heed EPA recommendations.

Another requirement under Section 611 is that the FAA not issue any certificates for previously unmarketed aircraft "for which substantial noise abatement can be achieved by prescribing standards and regulations" unless the FAA has in fact issued regulations which apply to that type of aircraft. 109/

4.13 Railroad and Motor Carrier Noise Standards

These almost identical two sections, Section 17 and Section 18 of the Noise Act, were apparently considered of marginal importance by Congress. This conclusion is suggested by the legislative history, in which the House report dealt at length with aviation noise but neglected even to mention the two sections as key items in the summary of legislation. 110/ Nevertheless, these two sections have been the object of considerable activity by the EPA Noise Office. Both sections provide that within nine months of the enactment of the statute, EPA should propose noise emission regulations with specific emission standards for railway and motor carriers engaged in interstate commerce. After years of delay, at the request of the railroad companies, the U.S. Court of Appeals of District of Columbia ordered publication of final regulations by 22 February 1979. 111/ However, EPA only issued the proposed regulations on 17 April 1979. 112/ These regulations, when finally issued, are to be in

---

108/   FAA § 611(c)(2), (3), and § 611(d).

109/   FAA § 611(b)(2). The first certification regulations for aircraft noise were issued in December 1969 as Part 36 of the Federal Aircraft Regulations (FAR 36), see 34 FR 453 (1969).

110/   See House Committee on Interstate Foreign Commerce, "Legislative History of Noise Control Act of 1972," March 1972.

111/   Association of American Railroads v. Costle, (D.C. Cir. 1977) 565 F.2d 1310.

112/   44 FR 22960, proposing amendment of 40 CFR 201.

addition to those issued under Section 6 of the statute, and are based on the best available technology (BAT) considering the cost of compliance. 113/

Legislative history indicates that in enacting these two sections Congress may have been more interested in preempting state and local authority than in establishing a federal program. Both of these industries would have been greatly hampered if local regulations could impede their ability to operate in interstate commerce. 114/ According to Section 17(c)(1) (and its twin Section 18(c)(1)), "no state or political subdivision thereof may adopt or enforce any standard applicable to noise emissions resulting in the operation of the same equipment of facility or such carrier unless such standard is identical to a standard applicable to noise emissions resulting from such operations prescribed by any regulation under this section." 115/

A state may still prescribe noise controls which are incidental to other legitimate functions of local government, such as traffic control and licensing regulations, as long as these do not conflict with federal regulations. Also, if particular local conditions require special regulations by state or community, these may be promulgated with the approval of the EPA Administrator after consultation with the Secretary of Transportation. 116/

4.14 EPA's Coordination Role Within the Federal Government

EPA's primary role under the Noise Act, other than the setting of standards, is to act as the coordinator of all federal activities relating to noise. This means first of all that EPA oversees federal agencies' compliance with Section 4(a) of the Act, which directs all federal agencies to "carry out the programs within their control in such a manner to further the policy" set forth in Section 2(b) of promoting an environment free from noise hazards to health or welfare. 117/ This procedure and admonition closely resemble that under the National Environmental Policy Act (NEPA)

113/   Noise Act §§ 17(a)(1) and 18(a)(1).

114/   See Senate Report No. 92-1160, 92nd Cong., 2d Sess. (1972), pp. 8 and 19.

115/   Noise Act §§ 17(c)(1) and 18(c)(1).

116/   Noise Act §§ 17(c)(2) and 18(c)(2).

117/   Noise Act § 4(a) and 2(b).

directing all federal agencies to promote that Act's goal of environmental protection. 118/

The EPA Administrator is given direct authority to coordinate the activities of all federal agencies relating to noise
research and control, and these agencies are directed to provide him
with whatever information he requests. 119/ Moreover, if any
federal agency issues a noise regulation or standard which the EPA
Administrator feels "does not protect the public health and welfare
to the extent he believes to be required and feasible," he may
request that agency to review that action and report to him on the
"advisability of revising such standard or regulation to provide such
protection." These detailed findings may be published in the Federal
Register, along with supporting documents and detailed statements
of findings. The final authority remains with the proposing agency,
but the availability of public analysis and comment gives EPA considerable leverage with a recalcitrant agency.

EPA's most notable use of this authority has been in its
disagreement with OSHA over the proposed new occupational noise
emission standard, which EPA felt was too high to sufficiently
protect workers' health. 120/ A similar provision in Section 7 of the
Act makes the Federal Aviation Administration (FAA) even more
subject to EPA challenge on aviation noise regulations.

EPA is also required under Section 4 to publish periodic status
reports on the progress and activities of other federal agencies in
noise research and control. This gives EPA the additional sanction
of subjecting unresponsive agencies to the full glare of public criticism. 121/

5.0 Quiet Communities Act of 1978

The Quiet Communities Act of 1978 122/ extended the Noise
Control Act of 1972 for one year and amended some of the sections
in order to provide state and local governments with funds to promote the development of noise control programs on a local level as

118/   See NEPA § 101, 42 U.S.C. § 4321 (1969).

119/   Noise Act § 4(c)(1).

120/   Noise Act § 4(c)(2).

121/   Noise Act § 4(c)(3).

122/   PL 95-609, 92 Stat. 3079, 42 U.S.C. 4901 (8 November 1978).

long as no actions or programs are inconsistent with federal regulations. 123/
Other than placing more responsibility on state and local governments, the principal changes made by the Quiet Communities Act were: (1) the penalty for violations of Section 10 was reduced from a maximum of $25,000 to a maximum of $10,000 per day, for the first violation; 124/ and (2) the states or political subdivisions thereof were afforded the right to petition the administrator to revise federal regulations on the grounds that a more rigid standard should be imposed to protect the health and welfare of the public. 125/

6.0 Current Regulatory Actions on Noise
Regulatory agencies, principally EPA and the Department of Transportation, have taken actions which affect important industries. These include aviation (both aircraft and airports), motor carriers, heavy equipment, and new products.

6.1 Regulatory Activity Concerning Noise in the Aviation Industry
FAA and EPA have attempted to lower the noise levels around airports by reducing the emissions level from aircraft through retrofit, by the introduction of quieter aircraft, and by the introduction of new operating procedures such as takeoff and landing regulations at airports.
Federal Aviation Regulation (FAR) 36 was introduced in 1969 to cover aircraft thought "most likely to raise the aircraft noise levels in airport neighborhoods." This regulation covered most types of aircraft but not those currently in use or for which a certificate had already been issued. 126/
The regulation set noise levels for approach, takeoff, and sideline measurements based on weight, with the larger aircraft allowed higher noise levels. 127/

123/   Ibid., § 2, Amending Noise Act § 14(c).

124/   Ibid., § 4, Amending Noise Act § 11(a).

125/   Ibid., § 5, Amending Noise Act § 6(f).

126/   34 FR 453. It did not cover supersonic transports, vertical and short takeoff landing aircraft (V/STOL), and non-jet business and pleasure aircraft.

127/   FAR 36, appendix C.

FAR 36 specifies a measurement system whereby noise levels are monitored one mile from the beginning of the runway on approach, three and one-half miles from the beginning of the runway on takeoff, and approximately 0.3 of a mile to the side of the runway. These measurements can be converted into a special decibel reading designed to approximate the discomfort to which the human observer would be subjected. This Effective Perceived Noise Level (EPNdB) scale includes the noise level, frequency, duration, and the occurrence of strong tones. (In practice, this scale gives a reading 10 to 15 decibels higher than the standard dB(A) measurement used by OSHA.)

In October 1976, EPA proposed that all new aircraft, both subsonic and supersonic, certified after January 1980, would have to be 6 to 18 decibels quieter than present aircraft. The recommended numbers for takeoff, landing, and sideline measurements were derived by simple subtraction from the average of seventeen aircraft sampled. 128/ FAA, however, in June 1978 decided to set different standards for the two types of aircraft. 129/

6.2 Retrofit Of Existing Aircraft

The 1969 FAR 36 noise standards were not designed to result in substantial noise reductions in existing aircraft. After years of debate, on 9 February 1976 the FAA proposed lowering the permissible noise levels from all transport aircraft and all single engine turbo jet aircraft. 130/ The proposed rule would lower the permissible noise levels by up to 10 EPNdB on takeoff, 9 EPNdB on sideline, and 4 EPNdB on landing. 131/

This debate regarding retrofit of existing aircraft, through such means as quieter engines and sound absorbing material, has been one of the most controversial issues at both FAA and the EPA Noise Office. The aviation industry has generally favored the phase-out of older aircraft from U.S. fleets. The shakey financial position of American Airlines in recent years has made them increasingly

---

128/ Aviation Week and Space Technology, 11 October 1976, pp. 24-25.

129/ 43 FR 28406, 29 June 1978.

130/ The original notice of proposed rulemaking, published on 5 November 1975, was more limited in its scope of application.

131/ FAA, Notice 75-378, Docket No. 15131, as amended 9 February 1976; BNA, Noise Regulation Reporter, 16 February 1976, A-5.

reluctant to spend the funds necessary for improved, quieter air-craft; but this has also served to reduce the phase-out rate of older aircraft to two percent a year. At this rate, even by 1990 half of the aircraft will fail to meet the modest FAR 36 standards.

For this reason, the former FAA Administrator, John L. McLucas, endorsed retrofit of existing aircraft, along with ongoing replacement, as a necessary and cost effective means of reducing aircraft noise. 132/ The price tag on this proposal was about $1 billion for retrofit of U.S. aircraft and $250 million for retrofit of foreign jets. The benefit-cost ratio, McLucas estimated, would still be over two-to-one, and the cost would amount to less than two-tenths of one percent of the total operating cost during the year the maximum number of planes would be retrofitted.

The Secretary of Transportation announced on 18 November 1976 that existing aircraft would be given until the beginning of 1985 to comply with FAA noise regulations under FAR 36. The issue of financial options for the necessary retrofits, however, was reserved for further study. 133/

6.3 Airports and Aircraft Operating Procedures
Airport operators in the United States have been among the strongest proponents of aircraft retrofit, because they have borne much public criticism for excessive aviation noise. In 1962, the U.S. Supreme Court declared in Griggs v. Allegheny County that the airport operator, usually a local government agency, is responsible for securing sufficient land and easements around the airport to ensure the proper functioning of airport facility. Failure to do so, with resultant noise disruption to the neighboring community, makes the operators of the airport—not the federal government—responsible for any damages. 134/

In September 1975, a California Superior Court ruled that those subjected to high levels of aircraft noise may sue for mental and emotional distress, and that the same plaintiffs may sue repeat-

---

132/ John L. McLucas, FAA Administrator, statement before the House Public Works Aviation Subcommittee, 26 February 1976, reported in BNA, Noise Regulation Reporter, 1 March 1976, A-18.

133/ BNA, Environmental Reporter, 26 November 1976, p. 1102.

134/ 369 U.S. 84 (1962). In a dissent, Justices Black and Frankfurter argued that "the United States, not the Greater Pittsburgh Airport, has 'taken' the airspace over Griggs' property necessary for flight." Ibid. at 91.

398 ENVIRONMENTAL LAW HANDBOOK

edly if the noise continued. 135/ Some authorities have expressed the fear that this could lead to the closing of the long-embattled Los Angeles Airport and perhaps scores of others around the country.

The position of the airport operators has been particularly confused since 1973 when the Supreme Court held 5 to 4 in City of Burbank v. Lockheed Air Terminal that local communities could not use their general "police" powers to control airport noise. 136/ According to the Court, the comprehensive 1972 Noise Act gave authority over aircraft noise to the FAA and EPA, thereby pre- empting state and local officials.

In October 1980 the U.S. Supreme Court declined an appeal of a California State Supreme Court decision, thereby upholding its finding that the federal government's preemption of aircraft noise standards nevertheless did not bar suit for nuisance by a property owners' association against a local airport authority. 137/

In February 1974 EPA proposed that airport operators submit noise abatement plans to the FAA. Failure to comply could mean loss of federal financial support and possibly even the airport's operating certificate. 138/ The FAA, however, seriously questioned the desirability of regulating airports, arguing that this was a com- plex and cumbersome approach to a problem better solved by making quieter aircraft.

In July 1975 the FAA declared its intention of formulating a national airport noise policy and requested comments by 1 January 1976. The Agency outlined four possible policy options: to allow airport operators to develop programs for noise abatement without any constraints from the FAA; to develop a federal airport noise abatement plan, in which the airport operator would play no part and for which he would assume no responsibility; to allow operators to develop abatement plans, with subsequent approval by FAA and possibly EPA; and a continuation of the present policy of reducing aircraft noise at its source--the airplane--and leaving to airport

---

135/ Greater Westchester Homeowners' Association v. City of Los Angeles, 30 September 1974, report in BNA, Noise Reporter, 13 October 1973, A-29.

136/ 411 U.S. 624 (1973). The dissent by Justice Rehnquist is the better legal argument, but the policy issues are much harder to call.

137/ Los Angeles v. Greater Winchester Homeowners' Association, U.S., 14 ERC 1074 (1980).

138/ 39 FR 6142 (1974).

operators the right to take whatever additional measures they felt
necessary for operating procedures. Of these choices, the FAA
seemed to lean heavily toward the fourth option, but hearings were
scheduled for public comment in at least 20 cities around the country. 139/
        The FAA has nevertheless proposed a partial noise solution
using changes in aircraft takeoff and landing procedures. This would
be a further development of the FAA's 1972 recommended "get-em-
high earlier" takeoff procedure. So on 20 March 1974 FAA issued an
advance notice of proposed rulemaking calling for a change in landing procedures that would incorporate the "two segment" landing
method. This plan, which involves a rapid descent from altitude and
then a gradual landing approach, rather than the more common
steady gradual descent, has already been used by Northwest Airlines
and Air California with considerable success. Not only has landing
noise been reduced by 16 decibels, 140/ but there has been a real
fuel saving of approximately four million gallons a year for Northwest. 141/
        Some experts, however, have questioned the safety of this
two segment approach. 142/ One official of the Air Transport
Association (ATA), commenting on the proliferation of noise abatement flight procedures, urged the FAA to standardize the system.
"We have been begging them to do it." 143/
        In August 1976, the State of Illinois threatened suit against
the FAA to compel action one way or the other on EPA's numerous
proposals for airport and aircraft noise abatement. Included in the
list were recommendations for minimum altitudes (December 1974),

139/   40 FR 28844, 9 July 1975. The hearing announcements are
       reported in BNA, Noise Reporter, August 1975, A-17; addi-
       tional hearings were announced, Ibid., 10 Nov. 1975, A-19.

140/   Captain J.T. Frederickson, Director, Flying Operations,
       Northwestern Airlines, reported in BNA, Noise Reporter, 23
       June 1975, A-29-30.

141/   Aviation Week and Space Technology, 12 April 1976, pp. 30-
       31; BNA, Noise Reporter, 10 June 1974.

142/   See statement by H.B. Benninghoff, American Airlines,
       testifying for the Air Transport Association, FAA Hearings, 5
       November 1975, reported in BNA, Noise Reporter, 10
       November 1975, A-7-9.

143/   Aviation Week and Space Technology, 12 April 1976, p. 31.

fleet noise level requirements (February 1975), two segment approachs (August 1975), aircraft noise requirements for operating to and from U.S. airports (January 1976), and others. The state attorney explained, "We're trying to get them off their hands." 144/ The FAA, however, declined to prescribe the above EPA proposals. 145/

6.4 DOT's Concorde Decision

Supersonic transports (SST) were expressly excluded from coverage under FAR 36 on the grounds that special rules would have to be designed to deal with this unusual aircraft. The United States dropped the development of the SST for a variety of economic and environmental reasons, but the Anglo-French Concorde and the Soviet Tu-144 were ready for commerical service in early 1976. 146/ The British and French applied for landing rights in New York and Washington, D.C., on a transatlantic route to London and Paris.

There was considerable local and congressional opposition to the granting of these rights, especially from representatives from those two metropolitan areas who characterized the SST as "the noisiest aircraft in the air today." 147/ (A secondary concern was the increase in air pollutants from the aircraft.) Ground monitoring of SST noise indicated that levels were even higher than had originally been indicated: 119.5 EPNdB on takeoff, 116 EPNdB on landing, and 112 EPNdB on sideline. 148/

144/ Ibid., 2 August 1976, pp. 28-29.

145/ EPA Noise Control Program—Progress to Date, April 1979.

146/ Mechanical problems with the Tu-144 kept the aircraft grounded during most of the following years.

147/ See BNA, Noise Reporter, 28 April 1975, A-2.

148/ Ibid., 18 August 1974, A-16. The figures in the FAA Draft Environmental Impact Statement were, respectively, 117.8, 114.9. Moreover, Australian measurements in August 1975 indicated that the production version of the Concorde was significantly noisier than the prototype had been. According to this report, the Concorde was four times louder than the B-707 and eight times louder than the B-747. BNA, Noise Reporter, 29 September 1975, A-25. A somewhat different figure was given by EPA Administrator Train to a Congressional subcommittee on 9 December 1975; he estimated that the Concorde would be twice as loud as the B-707 and four times as loud as the B-747 and DC-10. Ibid., 22 December 1975, A-2.

The level for the Concorde was 129.3, compared with 118.3 for the Boeing 707. 149/
Congressional attempts to ban the SST outright were narrowly defeated in both houses. In the House, an attempted amendment to the aviation appropriations bill was defeated on 10 July 1975 by a vote of 214 to 196. 150/ The Senate, after considerable debate, rejected a similar move sponsored by Senators William Proxmire (D-Wis.) and Birch Bayh (D-Ind.) on 25 July 1975 by a 46 to 44 vote. 151/

Russell Train, then Administrator of EPA, joined the opposition to the Concorde. Although he stressed that his conclusions were preliminary pending a final evaluation of the FAA's environmental impact statement, he declared that approval of landing rights would be inadvisable in New York and "increasingly questionable" in Washington. 152/ Although there were other environmental problems raised by the SST, Train pointed out that his conclusions were based on noise alone, as EPA does not have authority under Section 231 of the Clean Air Act to set air emission standards for SSTs already in production. 153/

Transportation Secretary William T. Coleman had promised a decision on the SST controversy by early February 1976. On 13 January, the last day for receipt of formal comments on the issue, EPA sent him a proposed amendment to FAA noise regulations. EPA proposed to change FAR 91.57 to prohibit non-military SST flights into the United States by any aircraft that did not comply with FAR 36 noise standards as of the end of 1974. This would have prevented all flights to the U.S. by all but three or four existing Concordes. 154/

149/   Ibid., 12 May 1975, A-17.

150/   Ibid., 21 July 1975, A-10.

151/   Ibid., 4 August 1975, A-35.

152/   Testimony of EPA Administrator Russell E. Train, Government Activities and Transportation Subcommittee of the House Government Operations Committee, 9 December 1975, Ibid., 22 December 1975, A-2.

153/   Ibid., A-3.

154/   BNA, Noise Reporter, 19 January 1976, A-10. This EPA proposal was published by DOT as a Notice of Proposed Rulemaking on 12 February 1976. 41 FR 6270, 20 February 1976 .

On 4 February 1976, however, Secretary Coleman overrode these objections and granted "limited landing rights for a demonstration period not to exceed 16 months under certain precise limitations and restrictions." 155/ The Secretary's decision nevertheless contained the following proviso:

> The EIS indicates to me that the marginal impact of six additional flights would be small. Given the subjective nature of human response to noise, however, I must conclude that if any flights at all are justified—that is, if there is sufficient affirmative reason for permitting Concorde flights that we are willing to suffer some environmental effect—those flights should be authorized only on a temporary basis, in order to permit a more intelligent and responsible decision to be made at some point in the future, after we have collected information on the subject response to the Concorde during actual operations. 156/

The matter did not end there. Legal challenges to the decision were brought by environmentalist groups, local governments in the affected states, and by congressmen, who had also introduced legislation to ban the SST. 157/ The most serious threat was posed by the New York Port Authority, which controls Kennedy Airport in New York and which sought to deny SST's access to the airport. 158/

A federal district court in May 1977 found the ban unconstitutional, as contrary to the supremacy clause. This decision was overturned the following month by the Second Circuit, which relied upon the Griggs case mentioned earlier. The Port Authority could set non-discriminatory limits on aircraft noise operations but could not arbitrarily exclude the Concorde. 159/ In October 1977, the Supreme Court denied a stay, thereby allowing flights to commence

---

155/ DOT, "The Secretary's Decision on Concorde Supersonic Transport," 4 February 1976, p.3.

156/ Ibid., p. 50.

157/ BNA, Noise Reporter, 1 March 1976, A-22.

158/ BNA, Noise Reporter, 19 January 1976, A-4.

159/ British Airways Board v. Port Authority, 431 F. Supp. 1216 (1977); reversed 558 F.2d 75 (2d Cir. 1977).

at Kennedy Airport until or unless the local regulations were prepared.

Meanwhile, also in October, the FAA proposed regulations for supersonic aircraft that would allow the present 16 Concordes to operate but would require any beginning operation after January 1980 to meet a limit of 108 EPNdB. 160/

6.5 FAA Noise Certification

The FAA carries out its responsibilities by, in part, certifying various classes of aircraft and providing technical requirements for monitoring.

Under the Reagan Administration the concept of Regulation by Objective (RBO) prompted a review of existing noise standards and the methodology for measuring it. For example, the Aerospace Industries Association (AIA) petitioned for modification of FAR 36 rules on turbojets, set twelve years earlier. It is interesting to note, however, that the request disavowed any intent to weaken the standard. 161/ Citizen suits against airports, discussed earlier are themselves a considerable deterrent to drastic changes upward in noise levels.

7.0 Major Sources of Noise

EPA is required under the Noise Control Act to identify the major sources of noise as the first step in the preparation of noise control regulations. 162/

On 19 June 1974 EPA issued its report identifying the major sources of noise, their levels, and the estimated number of people subjected. EPA also acknowledged that this list is "partially subjective," as many factors other than mere loudness are involved. 163/ The report concluded that urban traffic noise subjects the most people to annoying levels of noise, based on a 24-hour calculation,

---

160/ 42 FR 55176, 13 October 1977. See also 43 FR 28406, 29 June 1978.

161/ 47 FR 47854, 28 October 1982; see Illinois v. Coleman (D.C.D.C., 11 March 1981, No. 76-1961.)

162/ Noise Act § 5(b).

163/ EPA, Identification of Products as Major Sources of Noise, 39 FR 22297 (21 June 1974).

followed by aviation noise and construction equipment noise. 164/
According to the report, medium and heavy duty trucks, motorcycles, and snow-mobiles were the principal transportation noise
sources; and power drivers of rock drills were the most annoying
sources of construction noise. Of these listed products, however,
only two were officially scheduled for regulation under Section 6 as
major sources of noise: medium and heavy duty trucks and portable
air compressors. The other listed products remained candidates for
possible future regulatory action. 165/

    On 20 May 1975 EPA published a second list of products
identified as major noise sources under Section 5(b). These included
motorcycles, buses, wheel and track loaders and wheel and track
dozers, truck transport refrigeration units, and truck-mounted solid
waste compactors as special auxiliary equipment on trucks. 166/
Subsequent administrative procedure, as usual, includes the publication before rulemaking of information on control techniques, costs,
technology, possible labeling requirements, and alternative methods
of noise control. EPA also announced a long list of possible candidates for identification as major noise sources in the immediate
future. These range from almost all forms of surface transpor-

---

164/   Ibid. EPA uses two calculations: the first is the equivalent
       sound level (Leq), which is used to indicate long term hearing
       hazards and day-night sound calculation based on a 24-hour
       period with a 10 dB(A) penalty for sounds occurring at night
       because of their greater annoyance.

165/   EPA has characterized the information gathering and scien-
       tific analysis background to regulation in a slightly different
       fashion. The first step, they consider, was the Title IV
       Report, Report to the President and Congress on Noise, Doc.
       No. 92-63, 92nd Congress, 2nd Session, February 1962; the
       second step was the publication of the "Criteria Document,"
       Public Health and Welfare Criteria for Noise, EPA, 27 July
       1973, pursuant to Section 5(a)(1) of the Noise Control Act of
       1972; and, third, the publication of the "Levels Document,"
       Information on Levels of Environmental Noise Requisite to
       Protect Public Health and Welfare with an Adequate Margin
       of Safety, EPA, March 1974, pursuant to Section 5(a)(2) of the
       Noise Control Act.

166/   40 FR 23105, 28 May 1975.

tation, plus tires, to many types of household appliances from electric toothbrushes to movie projectors.

EPA declared its intention to study a number of particular candidates for possible future identification as major noise sources, including the following: light trucks, motor boats, chain saws, tires, pneumatic and hydraulic tools, power drivers, lawn care equipment, and other special auxiliary equipment on trucks. 167/ Relatively little subsequently appeared on these items, however, except for power mowers.

In December 1982, EPA issued a notice of intent to delete from the list of major noise sources the following items: power lawn mowers, pavement breakers, rock drills, wheel and crawler tractors, buses, and truck transport refrigeration units. This reflected the Reagan Administration's determination to eliminate the program entirely, even if it meant not considering the jackhammer a noisy device. 168/

7.1 Air Compressors

Air compressors were one of the two products first identified by EPA as major noise sources in June 1974. EPA acknowledged at the time that the current technology which relied upon acoustic insulation was not capable of substantially more development but contended that future noise reduction should stress noise source elimination in compressors themselves. 169/

The report noted that insulation had already allowed equipment manufacturers to lower noise levels by a significant 10-20 decibels, depending on whether the units were diesel or gasoline driven.

Because the mean noise levels reported for the "quieted" models ranged around 75 dB(A) (a significant decrease from previous levels of 82 to 92 dB(A)), EPA's first candidate for noise regulation under this section was thus a common but relatively quiet machine, quiet at least in comparison with certain heavy metal shaping machines producing noise levels far in excess of 100 dB(A). 170/

Four months later, EPA proposed a noise emissions standard for compressors with a rated capacity of over 75 cfm (2.1 m^3) of 76

167/ EPA, "Report on the Identification of Products as Major Sources of Noise," 20 May 1975.

168/ 47 FR 54108, 1 December 1982; see also 46 FR 41104, 14 August 1981.

169/ EPA, "Preliminary Cost and Technology Information on Reduction of Portable Air Compressor Noise," June 1974.

170/ Ibid.

dB(A) measured at 7 meters distance. 171/ This standard was expected to benefit approximately 11 percent of the total one million persons severely impacted by construction noise. The cost of this standard, according to EPA estimates, would be approximately $20 million. (Annual sales of air compressors are about $115 million.) 172/

Smaller companies complained that the proposed testing requirements would be a real hardship for them. 173/ Another company representative, on the other hand, noted that the small portable air compressors often made by small companies would be relatively easy to conform to the proposed standard but that larger equipment would become even bulkier and heavier and still might not attain the standard. 174/

EPA held a public hearing on the proposed standard in February 1975 and on 31 December 1975 issued the final regulation. The 76 dB(A) standard was to become effective on 1 January 1978 for compressors with a rated capacity between 75 cfm and 250 cfm; and six months later, on 1 July 1978, for compressors with a capacity over 250 cfm (approximately 7 cubic meters a minute). This extension of the period for compliance, EPA claimed, should have little effect on public health but would reduce the cost of compliance from 16 percent to 12 percent and would avoid the otherwise anticipated 5 percent drop in sales volume. EPA also deferred the requirement that manufacturers certify that their product would meet noise standards for the useful life of the device, pending testing to determine the extent of degradation over time. 175/

In a major deregulation, however, the Reagan Administration in August 1981 included portable air compressors (along with trucks, motorcycles, and garbage trucks) in a proposal to revoke the

---

171/   100 cubic feet per minute (cfm) corresponds to 2.8 m³/min.

172/   EPA Assistant Administrator Roger Strelow, press conference, 22 October 1974.

173/   George Fabian, Jaeger Co., Columbus, Ohio, BNA, Noise Reporter, 11 November 1974, A-11.

174/   Gardner-Denver Co., Quincy, Illinois, Ibid.

175/   EPA, Final Noise Emission Limits for Portable Air Compressors, 31 December 1975, published in the Federal Register 14 January 1976; codified in 40 CFR Part 204.

reporting and record keeping requirements 176/ promulgated in 1976. 177/ Simultaneously, EPA declared its intention to suspend enforcement of these regulations during the period of consideration. 178/ At the end of December 1982, the Agency declared these rules final. 179/

7.2 Trucks

The other major noise source identified by EPA in June 1974 was new medium and heavy duty trucks, defined as vehicles having a gross weight rating over five tons when loaded. 180/ On 2 July 1974, an organization of professional truck drivers (PROD) filed suit in the D.C. District Court seeking to compel EPA to propose regulations on trucks. 181/

In October 1974 EPA proposed an 83 dB(A) noise standard for speeds below 35 mph for model year 1977. This standard was to drop to 80 dB(A) for model year 1981 and to 75 dB(A) by 1983. (Measurements were to be made 50 feet from the center line of traffic.) EPA decided not to propose a regulation for speeds over 50 mph, although a draft proposal a few months earlier had recommended a truck standard of 86 dB(A) at that speed. Because of the uncertainties about tire noise at higher speeds, further action on truck noise must await a resolution of that problem. 182/

EPA's final regulation on truck noise emissions was announced on 13 April 1976. This draft final differed in a number of respects from the proposed regulation issued in October 1974. The final

---

176/   46 FR 41104, 14 August 1981.

177/   40 CFR 205.50 et seq.

178/   46 FR 41057, 14 August 1981.

179/   47 FR 57709, 28 December 1982; 40 CFR 204.

180/   EPA, "Identification of Products as Major Sources of Noise," 19 June 1974, 39 FR 22297 (21 June 1974).

181/   BNA, Noise Reporter, 8 July 1974, A-12.

182/   EPA, Press Release, 13 April 1976. See also EPA, "Proposed Noise Standard for Medium and Heavy Duty Trucks," 22 October 1974, 39 FR 38338, 30 October 1974. Tire and pavement noise could be as significant as the truck noise itself over 40 miles per hour. Crossbar tires were found to be noisier than ribbed treads, and recapped tires ranged 10-15 dB(A) higher.

version postponed for approximately one-half year the 83 dB(A) standard, effective on 1 January 1978, and the 80 dB(A) standard (slated for 1 January 1982). The draft dropped consideration of a 75 dB(A) standard, which had been originally scheduled for 1983, on the basis that further study and research would be necessary for this later period. As with the air compressor standards, the draft regulation also omitted the useful-life provisions from the October proposal which sought to ensure the noise levels did not increase significantly over time.

Administrator Train pointed out that the new standard, although seemingly less stringent than that of Florida and Illinois, was actually more restrictive, because it required that virtually every vehicle meet the standard. This standard, he stated, would slightly increase the initial price of trucks but would reduce the operating costs. 183/

In February 1982, EPA decided to postpone the effective date of the noise emission standard for three years, from 1 January 1983 to 1 January 1986. The level itself remained at 80 dB(A). The deferral, according to the Agency, was to provide economic relief to the distressed industry and allow fuel economy improvements. 184/

7.3 Power Mowers

EPA and the Consumer Product Safety Commission (CPSC) both became embroiled in attempts to regulate noise emissions from power mowers. The CPSC draft proposal in July 1975 called for a limit of 92 dB(A) for walk-behind mowers and 95 dB(A) for riding mowers. This was expected to add a not insubstantial cost of $40 to $112, respectively, to an average machine. The CPSC's interest in power mowers included problems other than noise, particularly the safety hazards. And the need for additional tests on these questions led to several postponements of the planned proposal. 185/

On 12 January 1977 EPA identified power mowers as a major noise source under Section 5(b) and circulated a draft proposal with a standard identical to that originally recommended by CPSC. The Agency estimated that forty million operators were exposed to noise loud enough to cause hearing damage, and twice that number to

---

183/ EPA estimates that this regulation would increase truck prices by about three percent, although this varies with the type and size of the engines. The improved fuel economy, however, was estimated at half a billion a year.

184/ 47 FR 7186, 17 February 1982.

185/ See BNA, Noise Reporter, 19 July 1976, A-11.

annoying noise levels. 186/ The CPSC, faced with the possibility of a jurisdictional dispute with EPA, deleted the noise section from its proposed power mower standard. 187/

The Outdoor Power Equipment Institute challenged EPA's listing of power mowers as major noise sources. District Judge John Sirica dismissed the suit in October 1977 for lack of jurisdiction, pointing out that a Section 5(b) determination was an inseparable part of the Section 6(b) standard-setting process which, under Section 16(a), could only be reviewed by a court of appeals. 188/

The Reagan Administration, however, in December 1982 issued a notice that it did not consider lawn mowers as major noise sources under Section 5, thereby effectively ending plans for regulation in the foreseeable future. 189/

7.4 Garbage Truck Compactors

EPA proposed noise standards on 12 August 1977 for solid waste compactors. This was scheduled to reduce noise by 4 to 8 decibels in 1979, with a standard of 78 dB(A); and the limit would drop to 75 dB(A) on 1 January 1982. The most controversial feature was the requirement that the manufacturers had to certify the equipment would remain in compliance for three years, or 7500 operating hours, after sale to the ultimate purchaser. 190/

The National Solid Waste Management Association claimed EPA lacked the authority to require a three-year assurance period. New York City officials, however, pointed out that they already had stricter standards than the EPA proposal, and these would be preempted once the federal standard became final. 191/

In February 1982, EPA deferred the effective date of the standard (in concert with extension of the truck noise standard) from 1 January 1983 to 1 January 1986. 192/

186/   Leonard Eiserer, ed., Noise Control Report, 17 January 1977, p. 11 and 14 February 1977, p. 265.

187/   Ibid., 18 April 1977, p. 62.

188/   BNA, Noise Reporter, 10 October 1977, A-9.

189/   47 FR 54108, 1 December 1982.

190/   42 FR 43226, 26 August 1977. This feature had caused the delay in issuance of the proposal, which was originally due in November 1976.

191/   BNA, Noise Reporter, 24 October 1977, A-20.

192/   47 FR 7186, 17 February 1982.

7.5 Wheel and Crawler Tractors

Wheel and crawler tractors had been identified as a Section 5(b) major noise source on 28 May 1975. On 23 June 1977, EPA issued a proposed rulemaking on these construction vehicles. This contained the controversial requirement, as above, for an assurance period of five years. 193/ The Construction Industry Manufacturers Association (CIMA) objected to this feature and challenged the justification for tractors' identification as a major noise source. 194/

In December 1982, the Reagan Administration issued a notice of intention to withdraw the proposed regulation. 195/

7.6 Buses

On 29 August 1977 EPA announced a proposed regulation on noise emissions, both interior and exterior, for buses weighing over ten thousand pounds. The limit of 83 dB(A) would take effect for new vehicles on 1 January 1979, then would be reduced to 80 dB(A) in 1983 and 77 dB(A) in 1985. Interior limits for the same period would be 83 dB(A) for 1983 and 80 dB(A) by 1985. School buses are included under this regulation. 196/

7.7 Snowmobiles

A more sensitive issue is the continuing debate over snow-mobiles. These undeniably noisy vehicles have strong political support in the northern states. This has hampered EPA's effort to impose a 78 dB(A) standard at open throttle, measured at 50 feet. At 15 miles per hour, the limit would be 73 dB(A). Snowmobile manufacturers contend that these levels are unnecessarily strict.

On 31 May 1977, EPA's Deputy Administrator Barbara Blum wrote thirty northern governors for advice on whether there should be legal noise regulations on snowmobiles, or merely informational labeling. The latter would have been useful for operators who are subjected to potentially hazardous levels of 90-100 dB(A), but it would not solve the extreme annoyance problem to others. For this reason, such states as New York and Minnesota have stricter stan-

---

193/   42 FR 35804, 11 July 1977.

194/   A similar legal challenge concerning power mowers is discussed above at 7.3.

195/   47 FR 54108, 1 December 1982.

196/   42 FR 45776, 12 September 1972.

dards than the federal proposal. The result of this EPA poll, however, revealed little consensus among "snowbelt" governors. 197/

7.8 Motorcycles

On 28 May 1975, EPA identified motorcycles as a major source of noise in the environment and began preparing noise emission regulations for new motorcycles and new motorcycle replacement exhaust systems distributed in commerce. 198/ On 15 March 1978, EPA proposed regulations which called for "an average 5 decibel reduction in new street motorcycle sound levels by 1985, and a 2 to 9 decibel reduction in sound levels of new offroad motorcycles." 199/ The proposal also included standards for replacement mufflers, which EPA hoped would reduce motorcycle noise "by eliminating the availability of ineffective motorcycle replacement exhaust systems." 200/

EPA also proposed prohibitions against tampering with or reducing the effectiveness of muffler systems. 201/ An amendment to prevent tampering with the noise system, proposed in December 1980, was withdrawn in December 1982. 202/

8.0 EPA Motor Carrier Regulations

EPA issued similar noise emission standards for motor carriers in October 1974. These provided that carriers in interstate commerce should be limited to 90 dB(A) over 35 mph, 86 dB(A) under that speed, and 88 dB(A) in a stationary high revving mode. (All these measurements were based on a distance of 50 feet). This standard became effective, one year from publication, in October 1975. 203/ These regulations were the first issued by EPA under the

---

197/ BNA, Noise Reporter, 6 June 1977, A-19; Ibid., 1 August 1977, A-1.

198/ 40 FR 23105, 28 May 1975.

199/ 43 FR 10822, 15 March 1978.

200/ Ibid.

201/ Ibid.

202/ 45 FR 86694, 31 December 1980; 47 FR 54110, 1 December 1982.

203/ EPA, "Final Interstate Motor Carrier Regulations," 39 FR 38208, 21 October 1974.

Noise Act of 1972 to reach final status, enforceable as part of the noise law.

Once these standards had been issued, it was the responsibility under Section 18 of the Act for the Secretary of Transportation to issue regulations ensuring compliance with these standards. DOT proposed regulations at the end of February 1975, 204/ and on 20 September 1975 issued final regulations. 205/

8.1 EPA Noise Standard For Railroads

EPA proposed noise emission standards for railroads in July 1974. The noise limit for individual locomotives was set at 93 decibels and at 96 decibels for any combination of locomotives. The standard for railroad cars over 45 mph was also set at 93 dB(A), while for speeds below that a standard was proposed at 88 dB(A). (These measurements were to be made 100 feet from the center of the track.) The proposal also recommended that four years after the date of the final standard, the permissible noise level should decrease to 87 dB(A) for a single locomotive and 90 dB(A) for any combination of locomotives under moving conditions. The proposal exempted steam locomotives, most gas turbines and certain electric locomotives; but approximately 27,000 diesel, electric, road, and switcher locomotives were covered. The proposal, furthermore, did not apply to warning devices such as horns or bells or to special purpose equipment such as cranes or mass transit systems. 206/

According to the statute, these proposed regulations by EPA were to be considered and promulgated by DOT within 90 days and would go into effect 270 days after publication. This timetable foundered, however, when the Department of Transportation strongly objected to many features of the EPA proposal. In its official response, DOT contended that the EPA proposal should have included recommendations for active and inert retarders, a limit of 70 dB(A) for mechanical refrigeration cars, and a 75 decibel limit on overall noise emissions during 90 percent of any 24-hour period by October 1978 and 70 decibels by October 1979.

The final rail carrier emission rule did not appear until January 1976, 18 months after the July 1974 proposal. For locomotives

---

204/   DOT, BMCs, "Proposed Regulations on Compliance with EPA Motor Carrier Noise Standards," 40 FR 8658, 28 February 1975.

205/   DOT, BMCs, "Final Regulations on Compliance with EPA Motor Carrier Noise Standards," 40 FR 42432, 20 September 1975.

206/   EPA, Proposed Noise Emission Standard for Railroad Locomotives and Cars, 39 FR 24580, 3 July 1974.

manufactured after 31 December 1979, the standard was set at 90 decibels for locomotives in motion and 87 decibels for those under stationary conditions. The requirement for mufflers applied only to these newer vehicles. Locomotives and railcars produced prior to that were required to follow the "best maintenance practice," described as 96 dB(A) for moving locomotives and 93 dB(A) for stationary ones. For railcars, this best maintenance practice meant 93 dB(A) over 45 miles per hour and 88 dB(A) under that speed.

Finally, the new regulation added a series of measurement criteria, such as ambient noise conditions and test specifications, in response to criticism that the measurement parameter in OSHA's July 1974 proposal could be distorted by a number of such extraneous factors. 207/

The EPA standards, however, left significant areas of railroad operation unregulated. Perhaps because of desire for federal preemption, the Association of American Railroads brought suit to require noise standards for these other areas also. On 23 August 1977 the Court of Appeals for the District of Columbia Circuit agreed, and ordered EPA within a year to propose additional railroad standards. 208/ The additional standards were not even proposed, however, until 17 April 1979. These proposed regulations state specific noise emission standards for facilities and equipment of the nation's interstate rail carriers. 209/

After EPA promulgated several standards, the parties agreed to dismiss on 12 November 1981. The Agency had meanwhile proposed other standards, including one for refrigeration cars and one on railroad property line determinations. In December 1982, these were withdrawn. 210/

Also on 23 August 1977 the Federal Railroad Administration (FRA) issued a final noise enforcement rule to implement EPA's existing noise standards on locomotives and railroad cars. 211/ The regulations, which had been proposed in November 1976, provided

---

207/ EPA, "Final Railroad Noise Emission Standard," 31 December 1975.

208/ Association of American Railroads v. Costle (CADC 1977) Docket No. 76-1353.

209/ 44 FR 22960, 17 April 1979.

210/ 47 FR 54107, 1 December 1982.

211/ 42 FR 42342, amending 49 CFR Part 210.

that locomotives produced after January 1979 should be limited to 90 dB(A) moving and 87 dB(A) stationary. 212/
    EPA had proposed rules allowing states to assure certain responsibilities of a local nature. 213/ Only one locality ever requested consideration under these rules, however, and after seven years the Agency formally withdrew the proposal. 214/ A similar determination involving motor carriers was made at the same time. 215/

212/   BNA, Noise Reporter, 8 November 1976, A-15.

213/   41 FR 52317, 29 November 1976.

214/   47 FR 54313, 2 December 1982.

215/   Ibid.

Chapter 10

COMPREHENSIVE ENVIRONMENTAL RESPONSE, COMPENSATION AND LIABILITY ACT OF 1980 (SUPERFUND) 1/

Ridgway M. Hall, Jr.   and   Thomas F. P. Sullivan
Attorney   Attorney & President
Crowell & Moring   Government Institutes
Washington, DC   Rockville, MD

1.0 Overview

The "Comprehensive Environmental Response, Compensation and Liability Act of 1980," 2/ commonly known as the "Superfund" Act or as CERCLA, 3/ was passed by Congress and signed into law on 11 December 1980. This statute, enacted in the last hours of the 96th Congress, created the first comprehensive Federal emergency authority and industry supported funds to respond to, and pay for, the cost of spills and other releases of hazardous substances.

Superfund establishes two related funds to be used for the immediate removal of any hazardous substance released into the environment from a vessel, or any onshore or offshore facility. The Hazardous Substance Response Fund and the Post-Closure Liability Fund are used by the government to pay cleanup costs and claims resulting from damage to property or the natural environment by the release of hazardous substances.

1/   A more detailed description of this regulatory program is available in Government Institutes' Superfund Notebook (3rd ed. 1982).

2/   Public Law 96-510 (11 December 1980), 42 U.S.C. § 9601 et seq.   Complete text is contained in Government Institutes' Environmental Statutes, pp. 504-548 (1982).

3/   Throughout this chapter we will use the term "Superfund" to refer to this statute.

2.0 "Super" Funds

The Hazardous Substance Response Fund (the "Response Fund") receives 87.5% of its revenue from petroleum and chemical feedstock taxes, with the remaining 12.5% coming from Treasury appropriations. The taxes, imposed as of 1 April 1981, will remain in effect until 30 September 1985, or until $1.38 billion has accumulated in the Response Fund. This Fund is available to respond to releases from any active, and most inactive, sites.

Revenue for the Post-Closure Liability Fund (the "Post-Closure Fund") will come from a tax levied on all hazardous wastes at the time of their receipt at a qualified hazardous waste disposal facility. The tax, imposed beginning on 30 September 1983, will remain in effect until an unobligated balance of $200 million has accumulated in the Post-Closure Fund. It is available to pay cleanup costs of hazardous substances from a facility which has been properly closed in accordance with RCRA requirements.

3.0 Key Purpose

The key purpose of Superfund is to establish a mechanism of response for the immediate cleanup of hazardous waste contamination from an accidental spill or from chronic environmental damage such as is associated with an abandoned hazardous waste disposal site. To achieve the purposes of this Act, certain requirements are placed on all handlers of hazardous waste.

Owners and operators of vessels or facilities handling hazardous wastes are required to show evidence of financial responsibility. This provision ensures that if a hazardous waste is released, the responsible owner, operator or transporter can pay the costs of removing the contaminant and restoring damaged natural resources. Such a release would require immediate notification to the National Response Center (Phone 800/424-8802).

Persons responsible for the release are liable for all costs incurred from the cleanup and restoration of the environment. Only when a financially responsible defendant cannot be found will the Response Fund absorb the costs of removing the released hazardous waste. The law sets forth procedures for making a claim on the Fund when the responsible party is unavailable.

4.0 Agency Responsibilities

Although the law nominally vests most of the response authority with the President, the President has in turn delegated these to various departments and agencies through Executive Order

12316, issued 14 August 1981. 4/ EPA is given overall lead responsibility for implementing the Act. The Coast Guard is responsible
for response actions in the coastal zone, Great Lakes, ports and
harbors. The Department of Defense is responsible for releases
from its vessels and facilities. Evacuation and relocation is handled
by the Federal Emergency Management Agency. 5/ Virtually all
other response action is vested in EPA. Other administrative functions are assigned to the Departments of Transportation, Health and
Human Services, Interior, Treasury, Justice and others.

It should be apparent that there are overlaps and interrela-
tionships between this law and (1) the requirements imposed under
the Resource Conservation and Recovery Act (RCRA) on Treatment,
Storage and Disposal (T/S/D) facilities, and (2) the hazardous substance spill provisions of Section 311 of the Clean Water Act. 6/
One of EPA's first duties in implementing this new law has been to
try to harmonize these relationships to avoid duplication and incon-
sistency.

5.0 Toxic Substances and Disease Registry
An Agency for Toxic Substances and Disease Registry is
established within the U.S. Public Health Service by the Act. This
Agency is to report directly to the Surgeon General of the United
States to help carry out the health-related functions of the Act in
consultation with EPA, FDA, NIOSH, and other federal and state
agencies with an interest in the control of hazardous substances. 7/

4/   46 FR 42237, 20 August 1981.

5/   The Federal Emergency Management Agency was established
      through an executive reorganization to deal with certain
      national emergencies and disasters. See Reorganization Plan
      No. 3 of 1978 (43 FR 41943); Executive Order 12127 of
      March 31, 1979 (44 FR 19367); and Executive Order 12148 of
      July 20, 1979 (44 FR 43239, July 24, 1979). It has major
      responsibilities for implementing the Federal Disaster Relief
      Act of 1974, 42 U.S.C. § 5121 et seq., the Earthquake Hazards
      Reduction Act of 1977, 42 USC. § 7701 et seq., as well as
      responsibilities for the stockpiling of strategic and critical
      materials, emergency broadcasting, federal fire prevention
      activities, responding to flood disasters, and other national
      crises. Its role under Superfund thus far is primarily in the
      area of providing evacuation and relocation assistance.

6/   33 USC § 1321.

7/   Supra Note 2, Superfund, § 104(i).

6.0 Reportable Quantities

Section 101(14) of the Superfund legislation defines a "hazardous substance" as any substance designated as hazardous under Section 311 of the Clean Water Act, any substance designated as hazardous under Superfund Section 102, any hazardous waste which is either listed as hazardous or has hazardous waste characteristics under RCRA, any toxic pollutant listed under Section 307(a) of the Clean Water Act, any hazardous air pollutant listed under Section 112 of the Clean Air Act, and any imminently hazardous chemical substance with which the EPA Administrator has taken action under Section 7 of the Toxic Substances Control Act. The term specifically does not include oil, natural gas, or synthetic gas.

Section 102 authorizes EPA to expand this list by adding any compounds or mixtures which "when released into the environment may present substantial danger to the public health or welfare or the environment." Section 102 also requires EPA to promulgate regulations "establishing that quantity of any hazardous substance the release of which shall be reported pursuant to Section 103" of the Act. Unless and until superseded by these regulations, reportable quantities for hazardous substances listed under Section 311 of the Clean Water Act are those quantities which EPA established for those substances, and for all other substances the reportable quantity is one pound.

Superfund Section 103 requires any person in charge of a vessel or an offshore or onshore facility to immediately notify the National Response Center of any release of any hazardous substance in a reportable quantity. Exempt from the notification requirement is any "federally permitted release." A federally permitted release is any discharge which is in compliance with a permit issued under the Clean Water Act, the Solid Waste Disposal Act (i.e., RCRA), the Marine Protection, Research and Sanctuaries Act of 1972 (commonly known as the "Ocean Dumping Act"), the underground injection control program established under the Safe Drinking Water Act, any Clean Air Act permit or state implementation plan, any discharge to a publicly owned treatment works in compliance with Clean Water Act pretreatment standards, and any discharge authorized under the Atomic Energy Act. This exemption applies whether the permit is issued by a federal, state or local authority. 8/

Failure to notify the National Response Center and any other appropriate government agency of an unpermitted release of a reportable quantity will subject the person in charge of the vessel or facility to a fine of up to $10,000 and imprisonment of up to one year.

8/   Supra Note 2, Superfund § 101(10).

A second important reporting provision requires every person who owned or operated a facility where hazardous substances had been stored, treated or disposed of and which were not permitted or accorded interim status under RCRA to notify EPA of the existence of the facility, and submit an inventory of hazardous substances known to be there as well as any which are known or suspected to have been released there by 9 June 1981. Knowing failure to comply with this requirement also carries a fine of up to $10,000 and imprisonment of up to one year. On 15 April 1981, EPA published a notice as to persons and facilities which must report, and a suggested reporting form. 9/ EPA has since used this information to create a prioritized inventory of potential problem sites.

EPA may issue regulations requiring the keeping of records with respect to such hazardous substances. These records must be retained for 50 years, subject to a waiver by EPA, if a lesser period would be consistent with the purposes of the Act. 10/

7.0 Response and Clean Up Authority

Whenever there is a release of a hazardous substance, the President is authorized to act, consistent with the National Contingency Plan, to remove the hazardous substance and provide appropriate remedial action for environmental protection. 11/ He is not to take such action , however, if he determines that the removal or remedial action will be done properly by the owner or operator of the vessel or facility from which the substance was released. This removal authority extends not only to listed hazardous substances, but to any "pollutant or contaminant" which could adversely affect the environment or human health. As indicated above, nothing in the Act covers oil or gas releases.

In using the Response Fund for this cleanup, the goverment may not go above $1 million, or six months beyond the day of initial response, unless emergency conditions require it. There are also provisions for the state to participate in the funding of such cleanup efforts, as well as in the actual carrying out of the cleanup.

In addition to any other abatement action, the government is authorized to go to the U.S. District Court for the district where any "imminent and substantial endangerment to the public health or welfare or the environment" is occurring or threatened to ask for any appropriate injunctive relief. Willful noncompliance with any

---

9/   46 FR 22144.

10/ Supra Note 2, Superfund, § 103.

11/ Supra Note 2, Superfund, § 104.

such order subjects the violator to a fine of up to $5,000 per day of compliance. 12/

EPA has issued guidelines, in consultation with the Justice Department, for the use of imminent hazard and other enforcement and emergency response authorities for the providing of prompt abatement of hazardous substance incidents. These guidelines explain how the agency intends to coordinate its response actions with the enforcement authorities it has under various statutes. 13/ In general, EPA intends to proceed with identification of potentially responsible parties contemporaneously with site hazard evaluation. EPA will encourage the use of state authorities and personnel for enforcement, if voluntary cleanup arrangements cannot be negotiated with responsible parties. Federal enforcement authorities, of course, will remain an option open to the agency.

8.0 National Contingency Plan

The blueprint for cleanup and remedial action is the National Contingency Plan (NCP) which had been developed orginally under Section 311 of the Clean Water Act. Under Superfund, EPA has revised this Plan to broaden its scope to include landbased facilities with discharges which do not relate in any way to the navigable waters, and to include a new "national hazardous substance response plan which shall establish procedures and standards for responding to releases of hazardous substances, pollutants, and contaminants."14/ Thus essentially all environmental releases of pollutants are at least potentially subject to the NCP unless excluded by law. The NCP includes such matters as:

(1) methods for discovering, reporting, and evaluating hazardous waste disposal facilities;

(2) determining appropriate response methods and equipment;

(3) determining and assigning appropriate roles and responsibilities to various levels of government and government entities in carrying out the plan; and

---

12/ Supra Note 2, Superfund, § 106.

13/ 47 FR 20664, May 13, 1982.

14/ Supra Note 2, Superfund, § 105. The original national contingency plan was set forth at 40 CFR Part 1510, and related primarily to discharges of oil and hazardous substances which affect or may affect the navigable waters. The new Plan is codified at 40 CFR Part 300.

(4)   determining priorities among releases or threatened
      releases for the purpose of taking effective reme-
      dial action.

8.1 Revised National Contingency Plan

Sections 105 and 106 of Superfund required EPA to issue the
Revised National Contingency Plan and emergency response guidelines by 9 June 1981. On 28 July 1981 EPA issued an "Interim Superfund Removal Guidance" document, which provides guidance to on-
scene coordinators and others responsible for removal and remedial
action following a release of hazardous substances. 15/ EPA missed
the statutory deadline for promulgating the NCP and was placed
under a court order to publish the proposed revisions by 15 March
1982 and to publish the final plan by 12 May 1982 in the lawsuit.
Environmental Defense Fund v. Gorsuch, No. 81-2083 (D.D.C.
Feb. 12, 1982, as modified). The revised Plan, formally known as the
National Oil and Hazardous Substances Pollution Contingency Plan,
was finally issued on 16 July 1982. 16/
The NCP is divided into eight subparts:

Subpart A	–	Introduction, scope, and definitions
Subpart B	–	Responsibilities, including federal, state, local and private
Subpart C	–	Organization, coordination and communications
Subpart D	–	Regional and local contingency plans
Subpart E	–	Oil spill response
Subpart F	–	Hazardous substances response
Subpart G	–	Trustees for natural resources
Subpart H	–	Use of dispersants and other chemicals

8.2 National Contingency Plan Scope and Definitions

Subpart A sets forth the scope of the NCP and provides
definitions. The definitions generally follow those in the two
authorizing statutes, but several merit special attention. The term
"Lead Agency" refers to the agency which provides the on-scene
coordinator. In most cases, this will be either EPA or the U.S. Coast
Guard. The "On-Scene Coordinator" (OSC) is the federal official
designated by EPA or the Coast Guard to direct and coordinate
federal responses. Where the response is a planned removal or
remedial action, the duties of the OSC may be transferred to a

---

15/ See notice of availability, 46 FR 40800, 12 August 1981.

16/ 47 FR 31180, 16 July 1982. It goes into effect after 60 days of
     continuous session of Congress.

"responsible official."   All references to the responsibilities and authority of the OSC, therefore, equally apply to the responsible official.

8.3 Responsibilities Under the National Contingency Plan
Subpart B assigns responsibilities among the affected federal agencies and departments and identifies roles for state and local governments and the private sector. It is based upon Executive Orders 11735 and 12316 which delegate responsibilities under Section 311 of the Clean Water Act and Superfund, respectively. All federal, state, and local agencies are directed to cooperate in carrying out orders and in assisting the OSC in any removal, cleanup, or other response action. Further, this subpart sets forth a role that private organizations may play in responding to a release of a hazardous substance. In this regard, it is important to note that if a party intends to seek reimbursement from the Fund for its response authorities, those activities must receive prior approval from the Administration.

Subpart C explains the administrative organizational structure of the response program and sets forth the authorities and responsibilities of the participants. The organizational components of the NCP are discussed in the context of the three types of activity involved: (1) planning and coordination; (2) communication; and (3) on-scene response actions.

8.4 Response Teams
The National Response Team (made up of representatives of at least the 12 federal agencies listed in Section 300.23[b]) is the overall coordinator. The representative from EPA is the chairman, and the representative from the Coast Guard is the vice chairman. The Team is responsible for assuring national preparedness to respond to significant discharges of oil or hazardous substances. Regional Response Teams supplement the National Response Team and carry out response actions at the regional and local levels. The Regional Response Team works together with the federally-designated OSC's for the development of regional and local contingency plans.

EPA and the Coast Guard designate OSC's for all areas in each region. Basically, the Coast Guard appoints the OSC's for coastal areas, and EPA designates the rest. The OSC directs federally-financed response efforts, and coordinates all other federal efforts at the scene of a discharge.

The National Strike Force consists of strike teams established by the Coast Guard on the east, west and gulf coasts to provide emergency assistance. The strike teams will provide assistance to the OSC's on request. They can be supplemented by "emergency task forces" consisting of personnel trained to evaluate, monitor and supervise pollution responses.

An Environmental Response Team is established by EPA to deal with emergencies and lesser problems. These personnel have expertise in biology, chemistry, hydrology, engineering, on-site safety, cleanup techniques, and other skills which may be needed in response actions.

The NCP provides that when an emergency exceeds the response capability of the OSC, transects regional boundaries, or poses substantial threat to the environment, the Regional Response Team may be activated. In more serious situations, notably those with national or international implications, the National Response Team may be activated.

8.5 National Response Center

The National Response Center, located in the offices of the U.S. Coast Guard in Washington, D.C. (telephone 800/424-8802), is the center for all communications. Notice of an oil discharge or a release of a hazardous substance, pollutant, or contaminant should be made immediately to this response center in accordance with Coast Guard regulation.

8.6 Regional Contingency Plan

Subpart D of the NCP requires a regional contingency plan for each "standard federal region." A federal local plan must be developed in all local areas where the Coast Guard furnishes the OSC, and in any other areas where the OSC deems it necessary. The regional contingency plans are to identify information on all useful facilities and resources in the region, and must follow the format of the NCP.

8.7 Oil Removal Under the National Contingency Plan

Subpart E deals with response actions for oil removal. It is divided into four "phases." Phase I is discovery and notification of a discharge. This should be read in conjunction with EPA's regulations concerning the reporting and cleanup of oil spills, 40 CFR Parts 109-114. In Phase II, a preliminary assessment of the oil discharge is made, followed by initiation of action. The OSC must make a reasonable effort to have the responsible party perform removal action voluntarily. If the responsible party does not take such action, or is unavailable, the OSC takes the appropriate response action. Phase III addresses in more detail the containment, countermeasures, cleanup, and disposal actions to be taken by the OSC. Finally, Phase IV deals with the collection of documentation to support cost recovery in connection with the response action. Detailed information must be kept concerning the nature and levels of response action.

Pollution reports must be filed with the national and regional response teams following any major pollution incident.

8.8 Response Actions and Cleanup of Hazardous Substances

Subpart F deals with response actions for releases of hazardous substances. It is divided into seven "phases." Although most of this subpart applies to Fund-financed responses, a substantial part of the requirements also apply to cleanup by responsible parties. (See 300.68 [e]-[j].) These activities apply to both releases of hazardous substances and substantial threats of releases. Phase I is discovery and notification. This should be read in conjunction with the Superfund Section 103(a) reporting requirements and the exemptions under that section for federally-permitted releases.

In Phase II of Subpart F a preliminary assessment of the hazard is made (including identification of the source and the nature of the release). Also, it is determined whether the responsible party is willing and able to take appropriate response action.

Phase III requires immediate removal action when such action is necessary to mitigate significant risks of harm to human life or health or to the environment. A number of specific actions which may be taken are identified, including removal of substances, providing alternate water supplies, sampling and analysis, evacuation, security fences, barriers to the spread of pollutants, and the use of chemical detoxifying agents. Immediate removal action must be terminated after obligation of $1 million or 6 months has elapsed from the date of the initial response, unless it is found that circumstances warrant continued action.

Phase IV requires an evaluation and determination of an appropriate response where circumstances allow planned removal and remedial action. This can be used in lieu of, or after, immediate removal action. It involves a more detailed assessment of the threat of harm and the risks involved.

8.8.1 National Priority List of Problem Sites

In order to make the most of the government's Superfund resources and response capabilities, each state must establish a priority list of problem sites for inclusion on the National Priority List, using a Hazard Ranking System, which considers the magnitude of the harm and the probability of its occurrence.

EPA established an interim priority list of 115 sites in October 1981 and an expanded eligibility list with an additional 45 sites in July 1982 for a total of 160 sites, and began investigation and action at many of them by sending over 700 notice letters to potentially responsible parties. EPA has indicated that litigation will follow if responsible parties fail to take appropriate action. Some federal funds have already been disbursed for emergency cleanup at some of these sites.

EPA published a proposed national priority list of 418 hazard-
ous waste sites, ranked by their potential threat to health and the
environment.   The list was published in the Federal Register of
December 30, 1982.
Most of the sites are located near industrial areas of the
East, Midwest and South. New Jersey, Michigan and Pennsylvania
have the largest number of priority sites. They are all targeted for
cleanup by federal and state governments cooperating under EPA's
Superfund.
The proposed list, when final, will replace the current Interim
Priority List of 160 sites. All but seven sites from the Interim List
are proposed for the final list.

**8.8.2   Removal and Remedial Action Under the National Contin-
gency Plan**
Phase V deals with the planned removal of hazardous substances. To qualify for planned removal the site must present an
emergency situation, or circumstances must be such that there
would be a substantial cost savings by immediate removal response
action. As with immediate removal action, planned removal must be
terminated after $1 million has been obligated or six months has
elapsed from the date of initial response, unless there is a continuing
emergency.   The state involved must request the planned removal.
Like remedial action, planned removal action is authorized only if
the relevant state agrees to pay 10 percent of the response costs, or
50 percent if the state owns the site.
Phase VI involves longer term remedial action. Remedial
action may be arranged through voluntary agreement with the
responsible parties, or by EPA and the state if the responsible parties are unwilling or unable to take the required response action.
Remedial action is normally taken with respect to sites on the
National Priority List. The lead agency is to consider the nature of
the problem and to develop an appropriate remedy, considering all of
the relevant circumstances, including cost-effectiveness and alternate response actions. Finally, Phase VII addresses the collection of
documentation to support cost recovery.

8.8.3 Cleanup Responsibilities Under the National Contingency Plan
In determining the appropriate level of cleanup required the
OSC seems to have the final word. See, e.g., Sections 300.52-300.55
and 300.63-300.68.) While the NCP gives the responsible party an
opportunity to confer with the OSC or the lead agency of whom he is
the representative to determine the appropriate response measures,
there is no mechanism for further administrative review of that
determination in the event that the responsible party and the OSC or
lead agency disagree. This problem is particularly troublesome in

view of Section 107 of Superfund, which provides that a responsible person who fails to respond to the OSC's directive is liable not only for all costs of removal or remedial action incurred by the Government, but also for punitive damages in an additional amount of up to three times the actual response costs if his failure to respond is found to be "without sufficient cause."

EPA has entered into a Memorandum of Understanding with the Coast Guard on accounting for costs incurred by the Coast Guard in supervising or performing cleanup work 17/, and signed a two-year contract with the Corps of Engineers to manage cleanup contracts issued to private companies.

Subpart G of the NCP identifies the official who is the "trustee" of specific natural resources. The trustee may recover damages for the destruction of these resources caused by a discharge of oil or release of a hazardous substance. Subpart H authorizes the use of chemical dispersants provided they appear on EPA's list of accepted dispersants. Use of dispersants not on the list will continue on a case-by-case basis.

9.0 Liability

The owner and operator of a vessel or a facility, and any person who by contract or otherwise agreed to receive hazardous substances for treatment, transport, or disposal, is liable for:

(1) all costs of removal or remedial action incurred by the United States or a state;

(2) any other necessary response costs incurred by any other person;

(3) damages for injury to or destruction of or loss of natural resources.

Where the injury is to natural resources, the President or the authorized representative of any state may act on behalf of the public "as trustee of such natural resources" to recover such damages. The recovered damages are available to restore and rehabilitate the damaged natural resources. 18/

Liability for such amounts is "strict" in the sense that no showing of actual fault is required. Three statutory defenses are allowed, however, where the damage resulted solely from:

17/ 47 FR 4631, 1 February 1982.

18/ Supra Note 2, Superfund, § 107.

(1)   an act of God;
(2)   an act of war;
(3)   an act or omission of a third party, if the defen-
      dant establishes by a preponderance of the
      evidence that he exercised due care and took
      appropriate precautions against foreseeable acts
      or omissions by any such third party and the
      consequences which could foreseeably result
      therefrom. 19/

Maximum liability under these provisions is as follows:

(1)   For any vessel which carries hazardous substance
      as a cargo, $300 per gross ton, or $5 million,
      whichever is greater;
(2)   For any other vessel, $300 per gross ton, or
      $500,000, whichever is greater;
(3)   For any motor vehicle, aircraft, pipeline, or rolling
      stock, $50 million, or such lesser amount as estab-
      lished by regulation (but the ceiling may not be
      less than $5 million or, for releases of hazardous
      substances to the navigable waters, $8 million);
(4)   For any other facility, all response costs plus $50
      million.

These liability ceilings do not apply where the violation resulted
from willful misconduct, or the discharger fails to cooperate in the
cleanup.

The statute is silent on whether liability is to be "joint and
several," so as to allow the government to recover full damages
from one, some, or all potentially liable parties. Of course no
double recovery of the same damages would be allowed. The legislative history indicates that this was a politically sensitive issue which
the sponsors deliberately left to the common law as applied by the
courts. 20/

A "good Samaritan" provision exempts one who renders assistance in cleaning up a spill in accordance with the National
Contingency Plan or at the direction of an on-scene coordinator
from liability, except for gross negligence or willful misconduct.

19/   Supra Note 2, Superfund, §107(b).

20/   See, e.g., 126 Cong. Rec. S 15004 (daily ed. Nov. 24, 1980), and
      127 Cong. Rec. S 9334 (daily ed. Sept. 9, 1981). As of this
      writing, the Justice Department has indicated that it will seek
      to impose joint and several liability under the Act.

There is not liability under these provisions for damages resulting from pesticide applications, which are handled separately under the Federal Insecticide, Fungicide and Rodenticide Act. 21/

It is also provided that where liability under Superfund would run to the owner or operator of a hazardous waste disposal facility which was permitted under RCRA and which has been closed down, such liability may be assumed by the Post-Closure Liability Fund established by Section 232 of Superfund, discussed below. 22/

It is expected that the first source of funds that will be tapped for liability, however, will be the post-closure funds or security (if any) established by the owner or operator of the facility itself.

The Secretary of the Treasury is directed to conduct a study and report to Congress on the feasibility of establishing an optional system of private insurance for post-closure financial responsibility. A draft of this study was submitted to the Congress in 1982 entitled "Hazardous Substances Liability Insurance." It contains a final report on Section 107(k)(4) on post closure requirements and an interim report on Section 301(b) on the adequacy of private insurance.

This document will be followed by a finalized version in 1983, but very few changes are expected to be made. The draft document is supposedly available through the National Technical Information Service in Springfield, Virginia.

10.0 Financial Responsibility

All vessels, facilities (including those regulated by RCRA Subtitle C and other federal laws), and motor carriers must show evidence of financial responsibility, the establishment of which guarantees availability of funds for the removal of hazardous substances in case of their release. 23/ Once financial responsibility is established under Superfund, duplication of financial responsibility under any other state or local law is not required.

10.1 Vessels

Vessel owners and operators bringing into a U.S. port or navigable waters a vessel (except a non-self-propelled barge) over 300 gross tons must establish evidence of financial responsibility of $300 per gross ton or $5,000,000, if it is carrying hazardous

---

21/   7 USC § 136 et seq.

22/   Supra Note 2, Superfund, § 107(k).

23/   Supra Note 2, Superfund, § 108.

substances as cargo. One or any combination of the following will establish financial responsibility: insurance, guarantee, surety bond, or qualification as a self-insurer. Any vessel which fails to produce such evidence of financial responsibility may be denied entrance to or departure from any U.S. port, and subjected to other sanctions as well.

10.2 Facilities

The financial responsibility requirements for facilities are to be promulgated no sooner than 11 December 1985, and are to be phased in over a three- to six-year period thereafter according to the degree and duration of risk, associated with the production, transport, treatment, storage, or disposal of hazardous substances involved. This time lag is to enable the government to coordinate this program with the financial responsibility requirements in effect for treatment, storage and disposal facilities under Part 264 of the RCRA program.

10.3 Motor Carriers

Evidence of financial responsibility requirements for motor carriers will be determined under Section 30 of the Motor Carrier Act of 1980, Public Law 96-296.

10.4 Claims and Penalties

Any claim authorized under Superfund may be asserted directly against the guarantor providing evidence of financial responsibility.

Persons not complying with the financial responsibility requirements will be liable to the U.S. for a civil penalty, not to exceed $10,000 for each day of violation. 24/

11.0 Hazardous Substances Response Fund

11.1 Establishment of the Response Fund

Title II of Superfund, "The Hazardous Substance Response Revenue Act of 1980," amends the Internal Revenue Code of 1954 to impose a tax on petroleum and 42 listed chemicals. 25/ The purpose of this tax is to accumulate 87.5 percent of the total amount of $1.6 billion, or $1.38 billion, into the Hazardous Substance Response Fund. The remaining 12.5 percent will come from general revenue appropriations.

24/ Supra Note 2, Superfund § 109.

25/ Supra Note 2, Superfund, §§ 201-223.

A tax of 79 cents per barrel must be paid on any petroleum product or crude oil imported to the United States, exported from the United States, or produced in the U.S. for use or storage.

The tax on chemicals is set forth in a table listed under new Section 4661(b) of the Internal Revenue Code giving the tax per ton of chemical produced or imported into the United States. The definition of taxable chemical excludes methane and butane used as a fuel, substances derived from coal or used in the production of fertilizer, and sulfuric acid produced as a byproduct of air pollution control. This tax ranges from $.24 to $4.87 per ton of chemical.

The taxes imposed on petroleum products, crude oil, and taxable chemicals became effective on 1 April 1981, and will expire after 30 September 1985, if specified funding levels are met. 26/

In addition to those taxes imposed, the following will be added to the Fund: 27/

(1) amounts recovered as penalties;
(2) one-half of the unobligated balance in the Fund established under Section 311 of the Clean Water Act, and the entire amount appropriated under Section 504(b) of the Clean Water Act;
(3) an authorized appropriation from the Treasury of $44,000,000 per year, for the next five years.

The fund will accrue these amounts until 30 September 1985, or until an existing unobligated balance of $900,000,000 projected by EPA to not drop below $500,000,000 during the following year is in the Fund.

11.2 Fund Uses

Money in the Fund will be used by the President to pay for: 28/

(1) government response costs;
(2) claims by any other person for necessary response costs;
(3) claims resulting from the destruction or loss of natural resources, and the costs of assessing those damages (both short and long-term), including

---

26/   Supra Note 2, Superfund, § 211(a) and (c).

27/   Supra Note 2, Superfund, § 221(b).

28/   Supra Note 2, Superfund, §§ 111, 221(c).

claims originally brought under Section 311 of the
Clean Water Act and not yet satisfied;

(4)   costs of federal or state efforts in restoring,
       replacing or acquiring the equivalent of any
       natural resources damaged;
(5)   costs of a program preventing the recurrence of
       such an incident;
(6)   studies on, and registry of persons exposed to
       hazardous substances;
(7)   purchase and maintenance of response equipment;
       and
(8)   a program protecting the health and safety of
       employees involved in response actions.

There are a number of restrictions on uses of the funds, including
prohibitions on the following uses:

(1)   natural resources injured or destroyed prior to the
       enactment of this Act;
(2)   releases from hazardous waste facilities for which
       liability has been transferred to the Post-Closure
       Liability Fund:
(3)   clean up for an oil spill or release of natural gas;
(4)   expenses associated with injury or loss resulting
       from long-term exposure to ambient concentra-
       tions of air pollutants from multiple or diffuse
       sources; or
(5)   claims in excess of the total money in the Fund at
       any one time.

Note that there is no provision for compensation for death or personal injuries.

11.3 Procedures for Claims Against the Response Fund

No claim may be presented to the Fund until it has first been
presented to any person responsible for the damage, and left unsatis-
fied. Owners and operators of a vessel or facility must settle those
claims asserted against them within 60 days from the time of the
claim. Thereafter the claimant can sue the responsible party or
present his claim to the Fund. The President (or his agent), upon
receipt of a claim against the Fund, will notify the responsible party
or parties and seek to arrange a settlement of the claim. To the
extent such a settlement cannot be achieved, or fails to fairly
satisfy a just claim, the government can pay the claim from the
Fund, and sue the responsible party for the amount so paid. 29/

29/   Supra Note 2, Superfund, §112.

Providing false information in a claim can result in a fine of up to $5,000, imprisonment for one year, or both.

Claims against the Fund must be presented within three years from the time of the discovery of damage from the incident. Persons receiving compensation under Superfund cannot make additional claims under other laws duplicative of those made under Superfund.

12.0 Post-Closure Liability Trust Fund

Beginning on 30 September 1983, a tax will be imposed on any hazardous waste received at a qualified hazardous waste disposal facility so as to create a Post-Closure Liability Trust Fund. 30/ This is a facility which is either permitted or in interim status under RCRA. Any hazardous waste, defined by reference to wastes which are hazardous under RCRA Section 3001 or subject to reporting and recordkeeping requirements of RCRA Sections 3002 and 3004, shall be taxed $2.13 per dry weight ton at the time it is received at a qualified hazardous waste disposal facility. The tax will be imposed on the owner or operator of the facility. It will apply only to those hazardous wastes which will remain at the disposal facility after it is closed. The tax will abate whenever the unobligated balance of this fund exceeds $200,000,000.

This fund can be used for payment of claims for damages similar to those described above for the Response Fund, where the cause of the damage arises after closure of the responsible facility. 31/

13.0 Reports

Four years after Superfund is enacted, the President must submit a comprehensive report to Congress on the experience derived from its implementation. This report will evaluate the performance of such provisions as the tax program, the liability standards, the claims process, and other aspects of the law. Studies are also required on the feasibility of a private insurance plan for owners and operators of vessels and facilities handling hazardous wastes; siting and location of T/S/D facilities; and the adequacy of existing statutory and common law remedies for harm caused by the release of hazardous substances to the environment. 32/

30/   Supra Note 2, Superfund, § 231.

31/   Supra Note 2, Superfund, § 232.

32/   Supra Note 2, Superfund, § 301.

14.0 Regulatory Authority

The President is given broad authority to delegate and assign duties imposed under the Act and to promulgate any regulations necessary to carry out its purposes. 33/ However, Congress added a rather complicated "legislative veto" under which, if both houses of Congress disapprove a regulation within 90 days of continuous session following the date of promulgation of a regulation, the regulation may not take effect. 34/

15.0 Judicial Review

Review of any regulation issued under the Superfund legislation may be obtained only in the U.S. Court of Appeals for the District of Columbia Circuit. Such a petition must be made within 90 days of the date of promulgation of the regulation. All other actions arising under Superfund must be brought in the appropriate U.S. District Court. 35/

16.0 Relationship to Other Laws

Superfund does not preempt any state from imposing any additional liability requirements with respect to the release of hazardous substances. It does provide, however, that anyone who receives compensation for any claim under Superfund is precluded from recovering compensation for the same claim under any other state or federal law. Beyond this, the relationship between Superfund and other laws is somewhat unclear, in that there is the potential for liability on the part of an owner or operator of a facility under several different laws, and it will remain to be seen how these multiple liability provisions will be worked out. 36/

While Section 114 of Superfund provides that states may impose additional liability beyond the liabilities set forth in Superfund regarding the release of hazardous substances, it also provides that:

> Except as provided in this Act, no person may be required to contribute to any fund, the purpose of which is to pay compensation for claims for any costs of response or damages or claims which may be compensated under this title.

33/ Supra Note 2, Superfund, § 115.

34/ Supra Note 2, Superfund, § 305.

35/ Supra Note 2, Superfund, § 113(a), (b).

36/ Supra Note 2, Superfund, § 114.

The Act also seeks to avoid duplicative financial responsibility requirements as well. An interesting issue has been raised as to whether this Section precludes states from implementing their own superfunds based upon fees collected from the regulated community, which have basically the same purpose as the federal Superfund. This issue of federal preemption is being litigated in Exxon Corporation v. Hunt 37/ where industry petitioners are challenging the validity of the New Jersey Spill Compensation and Control Act alleging that it is preempted by the above-quoted language of Section 114. Initially brought before the federal district court, the case was dismissed on jurisdictional grounds because it raised a state tax law question. It was refiled in the New Jersey tax court. The state court ruled that industry could be taxed under both federal and state laws so long as the double tax was not collected and expended on the same project. 38/ The companies have appealed this decision. That lawsuit has potentially far-reaching implications for the ability of states to establish their own superfunds. Related litigation was dismissed by the United States District Court after the Justice Department stipulated with the plaintiffs that the state law was not preempted. Lesniak v. United States, No. 81-977, and Merlino v. United States, No. 81-1914 (D.N.J. Feb. 22, 1982). The stipulation provided that New Jersey could use its funds, without Superfund conflict, for the following purposes: (a) response to oil spills; (b) purely state-cost items not covered by Superfund; (c) state-share cleanup costs; (d) purchase and placement of equipment; (e) restoration of natural resources not covered by Superfund; (f) expenses coverable by Superfund and to be reimbursed from Superfund; and (g) damage claims that would be eligible under Superfund but for which funds are not available.

Superfund contains some conforming amendments to the Clean Water Act, notable relating to Sections 311 and 504. In addition, Section 306 of Superfund provides that each hazardous substance which is listed or designated in Section 101(14) – the comprehensive definition of hazardous substances discussed above – shall within 90 days of passage of the Act be listed as hazardous material under the Hazardous Materials Transportation Act implemented by the Department of Transportation. Thereafter, whenever a new substance is listed under that section, it is also listed as hazardous material under that Act.

37/   D.N.J. Civ. No. 81-1458 M.

38/   S.C. No. 303A-81.

17.0 Assistant Administrator for Solid Waste

Finally, Superfund Section 307 required appointment of an Assistant Administrator for Solid Waste, 39/ which EPA has expanded to "Solid Waste and Emergency Response." This official is responsible not only for implementation of Superfund programs, but for RCRA as well. Under this Assistant Administrator are three Deputy Assistant Administrators, responsible for Superfund, RCRA, and Waste Programs Enforcement, respectively. 40/

39/ This duplicates the mandate of Section 2001(a) of the Resource Conservation and Recovery Act.

40/ See Government Institutes, EPA Guidebook for a detailed description of the function of this organization and current organization charts.

Chapter 11

ENVIRONMENTAL AUDITING

Timothy A. Vanderver, Jr.
Attorney
Patton, Boggs & Blow
Washington, DC 1/

1.0 Introduction

Over the past decade, pollution control laws and regulations in the United States have become increasingly comprehensive and complex. Virtually all forms of environmental pollution are now subject to regulation by the federal government. In many instances, states impose their own pollution control requirements as well. Faced with this regulatory mosaic, many companies--particularly those engaged in manufacturing and/or with multi-plant operations--have adopted a systematic review process to ensure that their operations comply with applicable legal standards. That review process has come generally to be known as "environmental auditing."

It is important to recognize at the outset how an environmental audit differs from ordinary day-to-day environmental management mechanisms. While these mechanisms vary widely, their hallmark is the assignment of responsibility for environmental monitoring and for compliance with permits and other requirements to plant managers or other operating personnel whose primary concern is with production.

By contrast, the audit function is independent of production and is normally carried out by personnel who are unaffiliated with the operation being audited and whose principal or sole responsibility is for the integrity of the audit. The audit function reports to upper-level management and serves as a check on the ability of operating personnel to maintain environmental compliance by means

1/ The author wishes to express his appreciation to Duane A. Siler, Esq. of Patton, Boggs & Blow for his invaluable assistance in preparing this chapter.

437

of the existing day-to-day mechanisms. In this sense, environmental auditing is analogous to traditional financial auditing, in which outside personnel, acting on behalf of management and shareholders, review the company's day-to-day financial transactions for consistency with applicable accounting standards.

At the same time, it must be noted that the term "audit" is much less clearly defined in the environmental context than in the financial.   Environmental auditing remains an imprecise concept subject to many interpretations.   As a consequence, the goals and objectives of any given environmental audit may be unclear unless they are carefully defined in advance. In addition, the absence of a rigid procedure makes it more difficult to carry out an environmental audit than would be the case for a financial audit. On the other hand, because of its inherent flexibility an environmental audit can be designed so as to be of maximum utility to the company for which it is performed.

The concerns which gave rise in recent years to environmental auditing are likely to persist. Despite the Reagan Administration's well-publicized opposition to some provisions of the federal environmental laws and despite the significant changes that some of the Administration's proposals would make, the overall legislative proposals which it put forward in 1981 and 1982 in connection with reauthorization of the Clean Air Act and Clean Water Act are more in the nature of an effort to "fine-tune" those laws than to narrow or relax them substantially. 2/ Similarly, it cannot be assumed that the current approach to enforcement of environmental laws at the federal level will continue indefinitely under this or future administrations. In addition, to the extent that the current Administration realizes its aim of delegating more responsibility to the states, companies with multi-state operations will face a greater variety of legal standards and enforcement philosophies, thus making the task of compliance even more difficult. For all of these reasons, the prospect--at least over the longer term--is for continuing concern about environmental compliance issues. The environmental audit will remain an important tool for addressing this concern.

This chapter is intended as an introduction to the principles and techniques of environmental auditing. Part 2.0 discusses in more detail some of the reasons why companies perform environmental audits. Part 3.0 examines the scope of the audit in relation to the functions it is to serve. Part 4.0 discusses the design of an

---

2/   Opinion polls have revealed broad public support for laws relating to protection of the environment, support which may actually have been solidified by those Administration proposals which have proved controversial.

audit and examines certain methodological issues, including the analytical approach to be used and the preservation of confidentiality. Finally, Part 5.0 discusses the basic steps involved in carrying out a typical audit.

2.0 Reasons for Conducting an Environmental Audit

There are a number of reasons why management may decide to institute an environmental auditing program. First, the consequences of violating environmental laws are potentially very serious, both for the company and for its management. The major federal environmental statutes give the Environmental Protection Agency broad enforcement powers. 3/ At a minimum, EPA may issue administrative orders requiring correction or abatement of a violation. In addition, under most of the statutes, EPA may levy civil penalties of up to $25,000 per day of violation ($50,000 for a second offense), even though the violation may have been entirely unintentional.

Federal laws also provide for criminal prosecution in certain instances. Under the Clean Air Act, one who "knowingly" violates an applicable requirement commits a misdemeanor punishable by a fine of $25,000 per day or by imprisonment for up to one year (both penalties doubled for a second offense). Comparable criminal penalties may be imposed on any person who "willfully or negligently" violates the requirements of the Clean Water Act. The Resource Conservation and Recovery Act establishes similar penalties for those who "knowingly" violate requirements pertaining to management of hazardous waste. In addition, RCRA makes the "knowing endangerment" of another person by such violations a felony punishable by a fine of up to $250,000 and imprisonment for up to two years. 4/

Under the Reagan Administration, EPA has placed increased emphasis on criminal enforcement as a deterrent to violations of the environmental laws. In a memorandum of October 12, 1982, concerning criminal enforcement priorities, the Agency's Associate Administrator, who is responsible for EPA's enforcement policies, observed:

3/ See, e.g., Clean Air Act § 113, Clean Water Act § 309, Resource Conservation and Recovery Act § 3008.

4/ These criminal sanctions apply not only to a company, but also to its responsible employees and officers. Clearly, the provisions for imprisonment make sense only as applied to natural persons.

Criminal case development and referrals will constitute
an important component of EPA's overall enforcement
effort. 5/

The memorandum reflects EPA's effort to increase the effectiveness
of its criminal enforcement program by focusing the Agency's legal
and investigative resources on "cases of the most serious environmental misconduct." The memorandum indicates that EPA is most
likely to seek criminal sanctions in cases which involve knowing or
intentional violations of the law which result in or threaten serious
environmental harm. As the memorandum observes:

Where the offense is deliberate and results in serious
environmental contamination or human health hazard,
the need to achieve deterrence through the application
of strong punitive sanctions will almost always exist.

The memorandum also identifies a subject's history of noncompliance with environmental laws as a strong indicator of the need for
criminal sanctions " to achieve effective individual deterrence."

This emphasis on criminal sanctions and deterrence as an enforcement strategy is a significant development. EPA appears to
have concluded that criminal proceedings, with their strong deterrent effect, are a cost-effective approach to environmental
enforcement. Since it is likely that EPA will be operating under
tight budgetary constraints for the foreseeable future, it is to be
expected that the use of this enforcement tool will indeed increase.

Enforcement actions by EPA are not the only potential source
of liability for noncompliance. Most state environmental statutes
provide for independent enforcement by state authorities. Specific
enforcement provisions of state laws are beyond the scope of this
chapter, but it should be noted that many such laws provide for
severe penalties.

Finally, noncompliance with environmental laws or regulations may be a basis for litigation by private parties. Most of the
major federal environmental statutes provide for private enforcement actions by means of "citizen suits." 6/ Under these provisions,

---

5/   Memorandum from Robert M. Perry, Associate Administrator,
     to Regional Counsels, Regions I-X, (October 12, 1982) re-
     printed in 13 Environment Reporter 859 (October 22, 1982).

6/   See, e.g., Clean Air Act § 304, Clean Water Act § 505,
     Resource Conservation and Recovery Act § 7003, Toxic Sub-
     stances Control Act § 20.

an aggrieved citizen can bring an action in federal court for injunctive relief against any person alleged to be in violation of the statute or its implementing regulations and, if successful, can compel the defendant to reimburse its costs of litigation, including reasonable attorneys' fees. State statutes may also authorize ·citizen suits.

An equally serious concern is the potential for suits by third parties under common law principles such as negligence, nuisance or trespass. Such common law claims are becoming increasing prevalent in connection with the long-term results of pollution-causing activities, principally the disposal of hazardous substances. Evidence that a company's noncompliance with applicable legal requirements contributed to a subsequent environmental hazard could seriously undermine the company's effort to resist liability in such a case.

Avoiding these potentially serious consequences is not a simple task. Environmental laws and regulations, both at the federal and state levels, are quite complex. Moreover, the focus of regulation under those laws varies. For example, the Clean Air Act, Clean Water Act and RCRA all include permit programs. The first two of these statutes allow pollution discharges to the air and water in accordance with emissions limits and effluent guidelines. Under RCRA, by contrast, EPA issues permits to persons who manage hazardous waste but those permits do not allow--and indeed are intended to prevent--any environmental contamination by such wastes.

As a further example, the Clean Air Act and Clean Water Act differ significantly in their approach to authorizing discharges. The Clean Air Act relies on technology-based equipment standards for new sources only. Limits for other sources of air pollution are established by a loading-based approach, i.e., State Implementation Plans which specify emissions limits for individual sources in order to maintain specified standards of ambient air quality. By contrast, the Clean Water Act imposes technology-based standards for all types of discharges to surface waters, with loading-based water quality factors relegated to a minor role. 7/

7/ Further illustrations of the variety among the federal environmental statutes are provided by the Toxic Substances Control Act and the Comprehensive Environmental Response, Compensation and Liability Act of 1980, each of which takes a somewhat unique approach to regulating particular environmental hazards.

Thus, industry is confronted by a potpourri of federal statutes, each of which is concerned with a particular environmental medium and each of which takes a somewhat different approach to controlling pollution. Some statutes require permits; others do not. Under some statutes, compliance with a permit is virtually the only substantive requirement; under others there is an array of additional requirements of which the permittee must be aware.

This complexity is compounded by the existence of different legal requirements under state laws. These may arise in the context of state administration of federal permit programs, including the NPDES discharge permit program under the Clean Water Act, the PSD air pollution permit program under the Clean Air Act, or the hazardous waste facility permit program under RCRA. State programs often include different and/or more stringent requirements than their federal counterparts. Many states also have a body of independent environmental laws and regulations which constitute a second tier of permit and other requirements.

Thus, to be aware of all legal requirements which arise under federal and state regulations is a heavy burden. Heavier still is the burden of operating production facilities in compliance with those requirements. To provide environmental managers with the necessary support to carry out this function, and to check on the effectiveness of those efforts, is the function of the environmental audit.

An audit program also provides important evidence that a company has made a good faith effort to know and comply with applicable legal requirements. In considering what action to take in response to a noncompliance situation, EPA and state authorities usually consider the record of the offending company. If the company has an audit program in place and, even more importantly, has detected and corrected environmental problems as a result of that program, authorities are far less likely to bring an enforcement action. 8/

8/   Under the Reagan Administration, EPA has studied environmental auditing as a potential substitute for government inspection and enforcement. During early 1982, the Agency considered formally adopting a policy whereby companies which conducted environmental audits in accordance with specified standards would be exempt from EPA enforcement actions, provided that, among other things, violations disclosed through the audit process were promptly remedied. At last report, EPA has decided not to proceed with this approach because it might conflict with mandatory enforcement provisions in some statutes.

This showing of good faith could also be important in future litigation wherein third parties seek damages for injuries resulting from an environmental or occupational hazard which the company is alleged to have negligently created. The plethora of claims now pending in the courts alleging improper exposure of employees to asbestos is the first wave of such "toxic tort" litigation. A company's position in defending against such claims will be substantially strengthened if it can show that it exercised due care to protect persons from exposure to known hazards. An environmental audit is one way of documenting such an effort.

While the purpose of an environmental audit is primarily to assure a company's compliance with applicable environmental laws, the audit can help to meet some other important needs as well. For a publicly-held company which must file periodic reports with the Securities and Exchange Commission, an environmental audit provides a means whereby management can be assured that the company has not inadvertently failed to disclose material facts relating to potential environmental liabilities. In recent settlements with several corporations, the SEC has interpreted its existing regulations concerning disclosure of environmental liabilities expansively. In some cases the SEC has required companies to conduct an environmental audit procedure in settlement of administrative or court actions under the federal securities laws.

An environmental audit also can play an important role in corporate acquisitions or mergers. For example, a company which is selling a facility or subsidiary can use an environmental audit to assure a prospective purchaser that the facility or entity is not subject to any known or undisclosed environmental liabilities. Alternatively, the purchaser may conduct an audit to assure itself that the benefits of the acquisition are not outweighted by environmental negatives. Contingent or unknown environmental liabilities also can be a critical factor in a corporate takeover contest. Any company which is contemplating a hostile takeover of another company would be well advised to document its compliance with all environmental laws. If a target company were to discover that an acquiring company had unknown or undisclosed environmental liabilities, it could challenge the takeover on that basis under federal or state securities laws.

3.0 Scope of the Environmental Audit

The scope of an environmental audit depends upon the function it is intended to serve. As discussed above, the essential function of any environmental audit is to provide a report to management on the company's compliance with legal requirements applicable to company activities having environmental impacts. Even this basic report may vary in scope, however, in that it may be concerned with a single plant, with a division or subsidiary, or with an entire company.

The most basic form of audit provides a one-time "snapshot" of the company's compliance status. Because a company's activities frequently change, as do the legal requirements which may apply to those activities, a snapshot audit is of relatively limited value. Thus, the scope of the audit may be broadened in order to find out the reasons why the company is not complying with certain requirements, to predict future problems of noncompliance, and to suggest technical or managerial remedies to prevent recurrence of violations. This broadened audit would examine internal compliance procedures, implementation of company policies, and the past conduct of responsible personnel. Among other things, the audit would investigate whether pollution monitoring has been carried out as required, whether monitoring reports have been timely filed, whether relevant agencies have been notified when environmental incidents occur, whether pollution control equipment has been properly installed and operated, and similar issues. This information could then be used to develop improved internal procedures to reduce the risk of future noncompliance.

The scope of the environmental audit may be expanded further so as to identify potential liabilities resulting from activities which are currently not subject to regulation or which are conducted in accordance with existing legal requirements. Thus, the audit not only could assess the company's current compliance status and indicate how the company's management procedures need to be changed, but could also address the legal ramifications of environmental impacts which are, for the present, consistent with the law.

It has become apparent in recent years that even strict compliance with existing laws may not adequately insure against future liabilities. For example, under Section 107 of CERCLA, generators of hazardous waste are now liable for the cost of cleaning up abandoned hazardous waste sites at which their waste was disposed of. The fact that the generator complied with all applicable legal requirements at the time the waste was deposited at the disposal site is, except possibly in some very limited circumstances, no defense to liability under this statute. New liabilities may also arise under the ever-evolving common law. For example, third parties are increasingly likely to recover damages for personal injury arising out of their exposure to substances which were managed in accordance with all standards which were applicable when the exposure occurred.

An audit can help to manage these risks by identifying potentially hazardous substances which are used in or generated by production processes, particularly those which are known or suspected carcinogens or which have acutely toxic effects. Once these substances are identified, the risks of potential liability and the costs of avoiding such liability can be assessed, and an appropriate strategy for managing the substances can be devised.

In conclusion, the function of the environmental audit will determine its scope. Generally, the more ambitious the audit, the more resource-intensive it will be. Thus, it is necessary to balance the costs of the audit against anticipated benefits. The scope of the audit should be decided in advance, so that the methodology and procedure can be tailored to the audit's purposes. In this respect, as in others discussed below, the planning phase of the audit process is critical to its ultimate success and cost-effectiveness.

4.0 Designing the Environmental Audit

4.1 Audit Methodology

A key issue which must be considered in designing the audit is the method or methods of analysis to be used. There are at least four ways to analyze the environmental consequences of a company's activities:

(1) substance-by-substance analysis of all substances used;
(2) analysis of all unit processes and other components at a given facility;
(3) analysis of methods of disposal utilized at a given facility; and
(4) analysis of applicable legal requirements.

Although they overlap substantially, each analytical approach yields some unique information which will enhance the validity of the audit results. Ideally, all four approaches should be integrated into the audit methodology. Each of them is discussed in more detail below.

4.1.1 Substance-by-Substance Analysis

This method of analysis identifies all regulated substances present at a manufacturing facility and the risks and compliance obligations associated with each substance. This method is particularly appropriate where applicable regulatory requirements focus on particular substances. For example, a large number of industrial waste streams and discarded chemical substances have been "listed" as hazardous wastes in EPA regulations adopted pursuant to RCRA. Similarly, Section 103 of CERCLA requires facilities to notify EPA when they discharge any of a large number of hazardous substances. TSCA regulates the use and management of certain chemicals such as PCBs. If any of the substances identified under these statutes are present at a facility, the audit can focus on whether they are managed in accordance with applicable requirements. In addition, if the audit is designed to identify potential future liabilities arising out of the currently lawful management of hazardous or toxic substances, the substance-by-substance approach is essential.

The first step in this approach is to identify the universe of relevant substances. These may include only substances currently subject to regulation, or may be expanded to include all chemicals which are known or suspected to be carcinogens or are otherwise toxic. Next, an inventory of substances at a given facility should be made, in order to ascertain how many substances from the universe are present. The inventory should cover all substances which enter the facility by any means, including chemicals and other substances used in production, in the laboratory, or anywhere else in the facility. The inventory should also identify all substances which are created by the facility's operations. Finally, substances which are not brought into the facility on an ongoing basis, but which are present from past operations--e.g., PCBs from electrical equipment, or hazardous wastes in abandoned disposal areas--should be identified.

Once the potential problem substances at the facility have been identified, the fate of each of them should be carefully tracked, from the point of introduction into or generation within the plant to the point of ultimate disposition in a product or byproduct or as a waste. To the extent practicable, a materials balance should be calculated for each such substance. Points at which quantities of the substance are lost or discharged prior to ultimate disposition should be identified, and the environmental impacts of those losses described.

Finally, it is necessary to evaluate the facility's compliance with legal requirements which govern the handling of these problem substances, including requirements applicable both to normal operations and to emergency situations. In addition, if the audit is intended broadlly to address future liabilities, some assessment should be made as to the potential future impacts of the substances, even assuming they are currently managed in accordance with existing legal requirements.

4.1.2 Unit Process Analysis

This approach proceeds from an examination of the physical characteristics of a manufacturing facility in order to identify those process areas within the plant from which there is a risk that contaminants may escape to the environment. Each unit process is examined to determine whether it is a closed system, and, if not, at what points within the system pollutants are routinely released or where they may be accidentally discharged. 9/

Unit processes to be examined would include materials reception and handling, in-plant transportation systems, operational processes, product and raw materials storage, and waste disposal operations. The analysis would identify all points or channels through which pollutants are or may be discharged, including smokestacks, vents, wastewater treatment facilities, pipes, sewers, ditches, drainage ponds, spillways, culverts, lagoons, pits, storage areas, incinerators, on-site landfills, injection wells and other waste disposal facilities. It also would examine the way in which materials are handled within a plant, including spillage of raw materials or products, and actual or potential leaks from or within each unit process. After these actual and potential discharges are identified, they can be evaluated against applicable legal requirements, such as permit limits, spill reporting requirements under CERCLA, and regulations under TSCA concerning releases from PCB equipment.

The unit process approach should be comprehensive. That is, all areas within the plant site should be included in one of the unit processes to be examined. No part of the facility should be excluded from this analysis. Thus, nonprocess components such as energy generation facilities or laboratories should be considered a unit process or included within some unit process. Plant areas such as parking lots and grounds should not be overlooked. 10/

4.1.3 Methods of Disposal

This approach focuses on a given plant's methods of waste disposal and compliance problems associated therewith. Under this approach, each waste stream is identified and traced to the point where it is disposed of. This approach is only incidentally concerned

---

9/   Quite similar to the unit process method of analysis is the plant component methodology. The essential difference between the two is that unit process analysis focuses on the processes at a given plant while the plant component methodology looks to the facility's physical components. These two approaches are so similar that performing them both would normally be duplicative. In general, the unit process method is more useful, although there are some situations in which analyzing physical components may be more productive.

10/   In some circumstances, a relatively large number of nonprocess components at a facility may argue for use of the "plant component methodology" discussed in the previous footnote.

with in-plant processes and events prior to the points at which waste streams are produced.

An audit which utilizes this approach would identify all air emissions, water discharges, and disposal of wastes in or on land. Each source of air pollution at the facility would be studied with respect to its characteristics, the type of emissions control equipment used, and the types and quantities of pollutants emitted. For each source, compliance with legal requirements would be assessed. Those requirements would include, among other things, whether the source is in compliance with limits imposed pursuant to the State Implementation Plan or other state regulations, whether the source is subject to federal PSD or nonattainment area permit requirements, whether the source is in compliance with any applicable federal New Source Performance Standard, and whether the source is subject to requirements pursuant to any compliance order.

The audit also would study each discharge of pollutants in wastewater, whether directly to a body of water or to a publicly owned treatment works via a sewer system. With respect to each direct discharge, the audit should identify the receiving water body, the type of wastewater treatment used, and the characteristics of the discharge, including flow, volume and concentrations of toxic, conventional and nonconventional pollutants. Each discharge would be assessed for compliance with the NPDES permit requirement and effluent limitations imposed thereunder. With respect to discharges to a POTW, the audit should identify the POTW, any pretreatment equipment and the characteristics of the wastewater, including flow, volume and concentrations of pollutants (especially toxic pollutants and pollutants which may potentially interfere with the operation of or pass through a POTW).

Finally, the audit would identify each "solid waste" stream subject to regulation under RCRA. The audit would ascertain whether each solid waste generated by a given facility is a "hazardous waste." If so, compliance with EPA hazardous waste management regulations would be asssessed. Among other things, it would be determined whether the waste is wholly or partly exempt from regulation under the "small quantity generator" or "reuse/recycle" exemptions, whether the facility is complying with requirements applicable to generators of hazardous wastes, whether the waste is being transported in accordance with those regulations, and whether the facility at which the waste is treated, stored or disposed of has either an interim status or final RCRA permit and is in compliance with all applicable standards for such facilities.

4.1.4 Legal Requirements Checklist

The starting point for this method of analysis is a survey of relevant environmental laws and regulations. From this survey, a detailed checklist of all legal requirements which are known to or may be applicable to a facility or facilities is assembled. This checklist would include all requirements under any federal or state environmental statute or regulation. The subject facility would then be evaluated against this checklist to determine (a) which requirements are applicable and (b) whether the facility is in compliance with those requirements.

This method of analysis is particularly useful for evaluating compliance with legal requirements concerning management practices and prevention of environmental pollution which may not be fully assessed under the other methods. For example, if a facility handles oil, it may be required to implement a Spill Prevention, Control and Countermeasures Program under Section 311 of the Clean Water Act. Such a requirement deals with potential, rather than actual, waste discharges. Therefore, reliance on a unit process or method of disposal analysis alone might result in a failure to recognize these requirements. The checklist approach assures that all legal requirements are identified and evaluated.

4.2 Analysis of Policy and Organizational Issues

An effective environmental audit generally must examine more than the physical characteristics of a plant, i.e., its inputs, processes, and wastes. The audit must also be designed to address organizational and policy issues as they relate to environmental compliance. Thus, the audit should investigate formal and informal company policies concerning environmental compliance. Among other things, the audit should assemble all written and oral corporate, division or plant-level directives concerning responsibilities for compliance with environmental and occupational safety laws and how those responsibilities are to be carried out. These policy statements may assign responsibility for obtaining permits, conducting monitoring, keeping required records, or filing reports under various environmental statutes. They may also specify lines of organization or chains of command intended to ensure that these responsibilities are discharged. The audit should also inquire into company, division, or plant policies or plans for responding to environmental incidents and/or injury to employees.

Other significant policy issues which the audit may address include the company's view of what employees should do when they become aware of apparent legal violations, the company's policy vis-a-vis employees who submit false reports to the goverment or conceal pertinent information from company officials or the government, and the circumstances, if any, under which the company will assist in the defense of an employee who is prosecuted for alleged legal violations.

4.3 Protecting the Confidentiality of the Audit

The principal disadvantage of an environmental audit is that, by definition, it is designed to discover what may have been previously unknown violations of the law. If the audit reveals a significant environmental problem which then remains uncorrected, the company's legal exposure may be greatly increased. Even if the company takes all appropriate measures to remedy the situation, the government would not be precluded from seeking civil penalties for the period of noncompliance. Nor would the company's corrective action prevent a third party from bringing an action for some future injury caused by the noncompliance situation.

For these reasons, an environmental audit should be designed so that, to the maximum extent possible, a claim of attorney-client privilege can be sustained with respect to the audit report and all information pertaining thereto. If privileged, this information would not be subject to disclosure to an adversary in litigation or in a government investigation. Because the creation of such a privilege is of the utmost importance to the company, careful attention should be given to the rules governing the attorney-client privilege. While there is no way to guarantee that the privilege will apply to any given information, a prudent company will make every effort to bring the audit within the ambit of this privilege.

A complete examination of the law of attorney-client privilege is beyond the scope of this chapter. Anyone who is designing an environmental audit with a view to establishing the privilege should consult counsel for guidance. The following discussion of the prerequisites for an attorney-client privilege is offered only as a general introduction to the area.

Four elements are necessary to establish an attorney-client privilege. First, the privilege applies only to communications between a client and his attorney. In the corporate context, such communications are no longer limited to communications between counsel and corporate employees at the most senior level. This "control group" standard was rejected by the United States Supreme Court in Upjohn Co. v. United States, 499 U.S. 383 (1981). Under that decision, it appears that communications between middle-level or even lower-level employees and corporate counsel are eligible for the privilege, provided that those communications are necessary in order for the attorney to render legal advice, are made pursuant to an investigation which management has ordered counsel to undertake, are made at the direction of management, and are kept confidential. 11/

11/   Note, however, that the Court also observed that: "The privilege only protects disclosure of communications; it does not protect disclosure of the underlying facts by those who communicated with the attorney." 449 U.S. at 395.

The second element of the privilege is that the communication must be made to the attorney in his capacity as a lawyer. Communications which are made to an attorney to obtain business, technical or other nonlegal advice are not covered by the privilege. Thus, in the context of an environmental audit it is important that the company's management clearly document that the purpose of the audit is to seek legal advice about matters within the scope of the audit.

Third, an attorney-client communication must be kept confidential in order to retain its privileged status. It is essential that the attorney who is supervising the audit adopt specific procedures for controlling access to all documents generated during the audit. Those documents should be segregated from other documents and their circulation within the corporation strictly limited. The audit report should be treated as a confidential document and its circulation should be limited, if possible, to top-level management.

Fourth, the attorney-client privilege is destroyed if waived. If attorney-client communications generated during the course of an audit are subsequently disclosed to a government agency, e.g., the Securities and Exchange Commission, they cease to be privileged for other purposes, including environmental enforcement actions. Under some court decisions, even inadvertent disclosure may be deemed a waiver. Therefore, corporate counsel must guard against disclosure of privileged information outside the corporation, as well as its circulation to persons within the company who have no "need to know."

4.4 Composition of Audit Team
The environmental audit usually is performed by a team of people, each contributing his or her own expertise. At a minimum, the team should include legal and technical personnel. Even disregarding the need to place the audit under the direction of legal counsel in order to preserve confidentiality, the environmental lawyer's specialized knowledge of applicable laws and regulations is likely to be indispensable to an effective audit. Just as obvious is the need for technical expertise on the audit team. For this purpose, the team may include an environmental engineer, chemist, or other person with relevant scientific training. It may also be desirable to include a production engineer who can provide an understanding of the production processes at audited facilities.

A preliminary issue is whether the company will rely on in-house personnel or will obtain outside assistance. A number of law firms and consultants have expertise in the area of environmental auditing and can provide an independent review. On the other hand, in-house personnel will have greater familiarity with company operations and will almost certainly be less expensive (especially if only out-of-pocket expenses are considered). Thus, this decision should turn on a company's particular circumstances, such as management's view of the adequacy of in-house resources and of in-house personnel. In addition, the benefits to be obtained from the use of outside experts should be carefully weighed against any additional costs. In any event, a company should consider proposals from an outside expert or experts with respect to the design and conduct of the audit.

A related issue is the extent of participation by personnel affiliated with the facility to be audited. Facility personnel, e.g., the plant manager, can provide valuable information about facility policies and operations. Involvement by facility personnel is also desirable in order to minimize their perception of the audit as an adversary procedure directed against them. Nevertheless, plant personnel involvement must be structured and limited so as to preserve the integrity of the audit process. It is imperative that the audit team remain independent of the audited facility and that it be accountable solely to top-level management.

5.0 Conducting the Environmental Audit

Procedures for conducting environmental audits vary widely. The precise steps to be followed will be dictated by a number of considerations, including the geographic scope of the audit (single facility vs. company-wide), its function (snapshot of present compliance vs. predictor of future compliance), analytical approaches chosen, time allowed for completion, and budgetary constraints. Nevertheless, virtually all environmental audits will include the following steps: (1) design the audit, (2) gather relevant data, (3) analyze data, and (4) report to management. The first step, audit design, is discussed above. The remaining steps in the audit are discussed in more detail below.

5.1 Data Collection

Relevant data about the audit facility usually is collected in two ways. First, facility personnel complete a detailed questionnaire about the site and its operations. After reviewing the information provided in response to the questionnaire, the audit team then conducts a site visit to verify the responses and to obtain additional information.

The audit questionnaire is a critical informational tool. It is the source of most of the information on which the audit report will be based. Therefore, the questionnaire must be developed with great care and facility personnel must understand their obligation to provide complete and accurate responses.

Typically, the audit questionnaire will seek much general information about the facility, including its physical layout, topography, relation to other facilities, age, date of construction, current and previous uses, operating schedules, and expenditures for environmental and occupational safety and health projects.

The questionnaire also will identify plant personnel responsible for environmental compliance and will elicit information about how company policies concerning environmental and occupational safety and health compliance are perceived and executed at the plant level. Finally, the questionnaire will seek information about all environmental emergencies which have occurred over a specified period of time and the plant's response thereto. The questionnaire should also inquire about contingency planning for future emergencies.

In addition to this general information, the questionnaire will seek information relevant to the particular method or methods of analysis being utilized. For example, if the audit is based on a substance-by-substance analysis, the questionnaire will list the universe of relevant substances. Plant personnel will be required to identify those which are present at the site, describe the uses of the substances, track the fate of those substances to the extent known, and provide a materials balance for each such substance. If the audit is based upon analysis of unit processes or waste disposal methods, the questionnaire will request comparably detailed information about these aspects of the facility's operations.

The second step in data collection is a site visit. 12/ The purposes of the site visit are, among other things, to enable the audit team personally to verify the information provided in the questionnaire, to observe the plant layout and operations, and to review plant records for consistency with the questionnaire responses. The site visit also provides an opportunity for the team to interview plant personnel. Persons to be interviewed typically would include at least the plant manager and supervisory personnel responsible for environmental and occupational health and safety compliance. Consideration also should be given to interviewing at least some line employees who are familiar with day-to-day operating practices. Interviews with these personnel can be an invaluable source of information about the adequacy of the plant's compliance procedures.

12/ While important, the site visit is not as important a means of data collection as is a properly designed questionnaire. This is particularly true for audits of several plants in the same industry category. Once the first plant has been visited, little marginal benefit may be obtained from visits to other plants in the absence of indications of trouble. Thus, in some circumstances, site visits may be eliminated from an audit as a means of minimizing costs.

Interviews must be planned and conducted with care. Improperly done, they can aggravate the natural antipathy which may exist between plant management and audit team. Interviews of line employees must remain confidential, but should be conducted in a manner which minimizes plant managers' suspicions toward the audit team. Interviews should not be carried out in an unnecessarily inquisitorial fashion.

5.2 Data Analysis

The next step in the audit is to analyze the information which has been gathered about each audit site. If practicable, the audit team should make a preliminary analysis while still at the site. This will enable factual issues to be resolved while the team still has direct access to the facility's records and personnel. A more thorough analysis can be performed later.

The analytical phase of the audit is of the utmost importance. The audit team must thoroughly understand the scope and function of the audit, as well as the analytical methods being utilized. Depending upon the design of the audit, the audit team's mandate may be simply to identify the applicable legal requirements with which the facility is or is not in compliance. If the scope of the audit is broader--e.g., to recommend remedial measures or modifications in company procedures —the auditors must be aware that this is their responsibility.

5.3 Audit Report

The final step in the audit procedure is to report the findings to management either in writing or orally. A written report is likely to have greater utility as a reference source for further action. However, as discussed above, the confidentiality of any written document cannot be guaranteed. Thus, the audit team may elect to present its most sensitive findings orally.

A related issue concerns the disclosure of audit results to managers of audited facilities. Plant managers understandably have a strong desire to know the results of the audit at the earliest opportunity. However, the audit report is likely to contain information about policy matters appropriately addressed only to corporate management. Moreover, as discussed above, access to the report must be restricted if its confidentiality is to be preserved. For these reasons, the report itself probably should be presented only to corporate management. Such information as should be disclosed to the plant manager or other plant personnel in order to remedy existing violations or improve compliance procedures can be extracted from the report and handled separately.

6.0 Conclusion

Environmental auditing is not a panacea for the problems of assuring compliance with environmental laws.   Nevertheless, a thorough and well-documented review can go far to protect a company and its responsible officials from the threat of civil and criminal penalties.   Further, such a review can significantly aid a company in defending itself against liabilities under both existing and future legal standards.

Chapter 12

LAND USE: MAJOR ISSUES IN THE
CONTROL OF INDUSTRIAL DEVELOPMENT

Timothy A. Vanderver, Jr. and J. Gordon Arbuckle
Attorneys
Patton, Boggs & Blow
Washington, DC

1.0 Introduction

The critical questions in major facilities siting issues are those concerning where a facility is to be located, how the requisite government approvals are to be obtained, and who has the authority to issue these approvals. When faced with the question of properly locating a facility, the industrial planner's response might be that plants should be built where they are most productive from an industrial/economic point of view. Others, however, might respond that plants should be built where they are least costly socially, environmentally and aesthetically. The function of land use law is to provide a mechanism for intelligent resolution of this conflict—achieving the optimum balance between productivity and environmental protection in its broadest sense. To provide such a mechanism, land use law must identify with specificity the approvals that must be obtained, the proper authorities for granting these approvals, and the basis for grant or denial.

The framework which exists today is not reasonably calculated to perform these functions. Major facilities siting decisions are more in the nature of endurance contests than orderly and expeditious administrative procedures. The result is unsatisfactory from all viewpoints. Facilities will be located where they should not be—if the opposition tires easily or runs out of resources—and they often cannot be located where they should be—if local opposition is well funded, aggressive and unwilling to carry its share of the environmental burden.

Obtaining the necessary governmental approvals today requires navigating a maze of exceedingly complex and often contradictory local, state and federal directives. The situation can be briefly summarized as follows. The local government involved ostensibly retains primary responsibility for questions of facility siting. However, local decisionmaking is constrained by a variety of state requirements. These include procedural and substantive legal requirements, and planning programs which may be directed specifically to land use or which may be a part of achieving more general objectives such as air or water pollution control.

The federal government has also intervened in facility siting in a number of ways. Although there are no general federal land use controls or planning, the federal government has encouraged state planning for specified areas (i.e., coastal zone planning) and required state planning and controls concerning land use in order to achieve other environmental objectives. The federal government also impacts on the siting process if specific authorizations, such as dredge and fill permits under Section 404 of the Clean Water Act, are required. Finally, in response to the patchwork situation which has developed, several federal statutes have been enacted during the past ten years to provide procedures for siting particular facilities.

One result of the present situation is that it is almost impossible to ascertain which governmental agency or agencies is responsible for determining whether a given facility should be located at a given site. Instead, the process has become one of seeking an apparently endless series of approvals; failure to obtain even one may jeopardize the project. Careful preparation, perseverance, and luck are necessary for successfully negotiating the numerous pitfalls. This is hardly a satisfactory situation.

The basis for these conclusions and the prospects for correcting present deficiencies are the subjects of this chapter.

2.0 Background and Nature of the Problem
Until quite recently, legal constraints on the use of private property for industrial purposes were relatively minimal. Private rights of action under the common law theories of "private nuisance" or "trespass" (see Chapter 1) have been relatively ineffective due to the difficulty in establishing standing to sue and the severe burden of proof imposed on plaintiffs seeking to demonstrate injury or unreasonable interference with "quiet enjoyment." Government regulatory activities, in the form of "public nuisance" actions (see Chapter 1) or zoning laws, have been almost exclusively a function of local governmental entities and the emphasis has been on the prevention of public health hazards or property uses so incompatible with the established uses of other properties in the same locality as to adversely affect their economic value.

Thus, until the late fifties, control of land use and facilities siting was a purely local matter focused almost entirely on the maintenance of public health and the preservation and enhancement of economic values. Private rights, also defined almost entirely in terms of eminent hazards or economic values, were narrowly defined and difficult to enforce. An industry which was making, or promised to make, a significant contribution to the local economy normally would not have substantial problems with either the local regulators or private litigants as long as it did not create an imminent and substantial health hazard.

Since the late fifties, however, the dynamics of land use control have undergone a radical change. That change could be said to result from general acceptance of these basic premises:

- Economic development at a particular location is not necessarily beneficial; governmental authorities are therefore entitled to restrict or limit development based on broadly defined "public interests" in environmental and even aesthetic values.

- Localized development is not necessarily a matter of purely local concern, but one which may involve regional, state and national interests.

- A property owner does not have a virtually un-limited right to use his property as he pleases: governments and courts are far more willing to impose and uphold "reasonable" restraints on the use of property than was once the case. Further, the definition of what is a "reasonable" restraint has been broadened considerably.

Given acceptance of this basic attitude towards development, two things immediately occur. First, the number of issues which must be addressed and decided upon in any major facilities siting proposal increases exponentially. (E.g., In addition to simple questions such as, "Will it create a substantial health hazard?" or "Will it help the local economy?" numerous complex questions such as "How will it affect the quality of life?" arise and must be answered.) Second, the number of government agencies which must deal with these numer-ous issues also radically increases: siting decisions once made by the city council are now made by the council, the county and regional planning authorities, the state department of environmental protec-tion, state wildlife and historic preservation officials, the Corps of Engineers, EPA, and others.

What emerges from this interplay between the numerous factual and policy issues and exercise of decisionmaking authority by agencies at all levels of government is not, and perhaps cannot be, a coherent body of substantive "Land Use" law. What we have now, as we have seen in connection with recent efforts to build refineries in the Northeastern United States, is bewildering complexity and confusion--where a multimillion dollar project can be defeated on seemingly inconsequential grounds. What we need, at the very least, is a regularized process or system for dealing with the complex interactions between laws and governmental entities which result in constraints on use and development of private property. To some extent, as we will see, there is hope that the necessary procedures will someday be statutorily provided. At present, however, and for the foreseeable future, the complex and difficult questions which arise in connection with major facilities siting decisions must be answered through the ingenuity of industrial planners and their counsel. In the following pages, we will attempt to outline the typical problems which must be faced in siting a major industrial facility and suggest a general approach for dealing with those problems.

3.0 Siting Problems

Table 12-1 provides a generalized matrix of typical decision points involved in any major new facility development or existing facility expansion. A similar, but more specific and more detailed table should be prepared by the facilities planner at the early stages of any development program and detailed assignments of responsibility for obtaining favorable decisions at each critical point should be made. In developing the approach for obtaining siting approval, and at every step along the way, the following general "maxims" should be given careful attention:

- Project approval is nearly impossible if there is strong opposition from the local governmental unit;

- Final disapproval, at any level of government (federal, state or local) can defeat the project; final approval-- from all involved government units--will likely be required before the project may proceed;

- Land use decisions are as much social and political as they are legal--the reasons advanced in opposition to a project may be completely different from the opponent's actual reasons. It is important to identify and deal with the actual reasons whenever possible;

- Finally, and perhaps most important, history demonstrates that major, complex projects are often defeated on relatively inconsequential grounds. Thus the cardinal rule for facility siting is: never ignore any potential criticism, never cut any corner, and never fail to openly discuss the issues with all concerned parties.

With these factors in mind, let us proceed with a more detailed examination of the decision points outlined on the chart.

3.1 Local Issues

Authorizations required from local governmental units are still traditional in form—construction permits, zoning variances, sewer connection permits and so forth. However, there are two basic differences between the local authorization process which exists today and that which existed ten to fifteen years ago. First, decisions by local elected officials can no longer be based solely on the officials' perceptions of the needs of their constituencies, but may be constrained by applicable regional or local land use plans. Second, in view of state and federal involvement in the siting process, the locality's approval of a project will not, as might have been the case ten years ago, be the final word. That decision will be subject to review, scrutiny and possible reversal.

As previously indicated, the major development in the area of regional and local planning has been judicial recognition – in cases like <u>Village of Belle Terre v. Boraas</u>, 416 U.S. 1(1974); <u>Construction Industry Association v. City of Petaluma</u>, 522 F.2d 897 (9th Cir. 1975), cert. denied, 424 U.S. 934; and <u>Golden v. Town of Ramapo</u>, 30 N.Y. 2d 359 (1972)—that localities have great freedom to limit major development within their jurisdiction as long as limitations are imposed pursuant to a comprehensive and rational plan. As will be discussed below, the development of comprehensive planning at the local and regional level has been accelerated by federal planning assistance programs under legislation such as the Coastal Zone Management Act, the Clean Water Act, and the Housing and Community Development Act of 1974. As a result of these factors, local or regional planning can be expected to play an increasing role in foreclosing certain areas from industrial development. Though some efforts have been made to provide for administrative review of adverse local zoning decisions at the state level and there have been some successful challenges of restrictive zoning ordinances in state courts, we seem to be coming to the point where local disapproval of a project, particularly if that disapproval is based on some type of comprehensive plan, is almost invariably fatal to the project. Thus, strong opposition by the local governmental unit should give rise to thoughts of relocating any project which is not totally site dependent. Obtaining the local unit's approval <u>and support</u> should be perhaps the highest priority item in any siting project.

Though the local government's <u>disapproval</u> of a project tends to be irreversible, that rule, as previously indicated, does not hold true where the locality <u>approves</u> the project. Obtaining the requisite permits is only one aspect of the local level efforts in connection with major siting projects. The other task, which is nearly as important and often more difficult, is dealing with the

local minority opposition.   There likely will be such opposition—
whether from oysterman who think their livelihood will be imperiled,
the local retirement community which doesn't want the inflation
that increased employment will bring, the nearby town that thinks
its facilities will be overstressed by a population influx and so
forth.   When land use was purely a local concern, this kind of opposition would not have mattered as long as the local government issued
the required approvals.   Now there are so many forums where objections can be raised that any opposition can cause severe problems
during state and federal deliberations on the project.   Thus, at the
local authorization stage it is important not only to get the necessary approvals, but also to identify all of the sources of opposition
and the "real reasons" for such opposition.   Having identified and
categorized the opposition, it is important, through full and meaningful communication, to alleviate their concerns insofar as possible.
        Local opposition which cannot be neutralized at the local
level will make itself felt in authorization procedures provided by
state and federal statutes and it is at this point that the basis for
opposition begins to be expressed almost exclusively in environmental terms.

3.2 State Law Requirements

        Constraints imposed by state laws on the ability of local
governments to authorize construction of facilities are both procedural and substantive in nature.
        Procedural constraints are usually in the form of a state law,
patterned after the National Environmental Policy Act.   These
statutes typically require that the locality, in granting a construction permit or zoning variance or taking other action to authorize a
significant project, prepare and process a detailed "Environmental
Impact Report" (similar to an impact statement under NEPA).   This
report is commonly circulated through a "clearing-house" procedure
among all state and regional agencies which might have jurisdiction
over the project.   Properly handled, this procedure often becomes a
way of coordinating the various exercises of state agency authority
which are necessary to authorize the project.
        The substantive constraints imposed by state statutes are
almost infinitely variable.   A few states have adopted major facilities siting laws which provide for permitting procedures based on
review and regulation of the location and environmental effects,
from air pollution to noise, of proposed new commercial and industrial developments.   A larger number of states have adopted
wetlands and shoreland protection legislation, which come into play
whenever development in coastal or riverside areas is involved.
These statutes vary greatly in their regulatory requirements; it is a
safe generalization, however, to note that they effectively prohibit
or severely regulate potential projects that would be located in

protected areas. Fish and wildlife protection, historic preservation and a broad range of other types of state programs, which may not immediately seem relevant, may also be of critical importance as, of course, will the state "categorical pollution" control laws--air, water and noise pollution. In short, any major project authorization may involve numerous separate authorizations and a detailed NEPA-type procedure at the state level. If the local opposition remains active, or if regional or national opposition materializes, each of these decision points could become a matter of great difficulty. The state legal-administrative framework must be a matter of major concern in analyzing the prospects of successful completion of any new facility development project.

In an effort to rationalize the confused situation at the state and local level, the American Law Institute has prepared a Model Land Development Code, which covers both land use planning and development controls. The MLDC integrates state and local powers with respect to development controls, but in general does not require planning as a prerequisite to controls. The basic thrust of the Code is to have local governments continue to control development with state intervention at selected points. The two categories in which state intervention is contemplated are Areas of Critical State Concern and Developments of Regional Impact (DRI) or Benefit (DRB).

The provisions concerning the Areas of Critical State Concern, which have been adopted by several states, assert a state interest in environmentally sensitive areas and in areas adjacent to major public facilities. The concept is to prevent local governments from permitting development in such areas that could lead to net negative impacts.

The DRI-DRB provisions are an attempt to elevate major decisions to the state level by providing for a state override of local decisions concerning significant developments. As contained in the Code, the DRI-DRB requirements are somewhat akin to those in NEPA since they require consideration of specified criteria in the decisionmaking process. The Code provides an appeals process for decisions with respect to DRI and DRB; basically, the standard is that any such development must be approved if authorized by the local ordinance and if probable net benefits exceed probable net detriments.

The MLDC is an effort to establish uniform land development controls, primarily at the local level. Insofar as major facilities siting is in issue, the importance of the Code lies not in the provisions concerning local controls nor in the number of states that have adopted it. The critical factor lies in the influence of the MLDC's state-level concepts--Areas of Critical State Concern and Developments of Regional Impact or Benefit. The former shows potential for preventing or delaying development in certain specified areas; the latter could be a means of overcoming local opposition to major projects. To the degree that these concepts gain acceptability, they will have a significant impact on major facilities siting. One way in which such acceptability could be achieved is through federal land use planning legislation (discussed below), since previous bills on this topic have relied heavily on these concepts.

3.3 State and Federal-State Planning

Virtually all of the local and state review, authorization and permitting provisions outlined above are overlaid by a variety of state and federal-state planning programs. Thus, the regulatory framework in most states is a combination between a permitting approach for specific facilities and a generalized planning approach for industrial development. Assurance of compliance with any applicable plans is normally a condition to any authorization to proceed with the project. Assessment of applicable plans is therefore important in the early stages of formulating any major project. Truly effective site development planning would entail the further step of actually participating in the development of plans for the area in which it is planned to locate.

As can readily be seen, state and federal-state planning efforts and development controls lack coherence, particularly as a result of attempting to serve varied and occasionally conflicting objectives. In an effort to remedy this defect, Congress has considered enacting a federal land use planning program several times. The most serious consideration was in 1974, when proposed legislation passed the Senate, but died in the House. This legislation would have established a program encouraging states to adopt a statewide or areawide planning process by use of positive and negative federal inducements. Although largely devoted to assuring the establishment of state land use planning processes, the bills would have required the consideration of certain issues in the process and the inclusion of certain items in the state plan.

General land use planning has been a dormant issue since 1974 as Congress has turned its attention to specific siting legislation, which is discussed in Part 5.0 of this chapter. Further, the present inclination against new federal programs involving grants to the states makes it unlikely that such legislation will be considered again in the near future. Thus, existing state and federal state planning programs will continue to be the key areas of focus for some time.

The general nature of existing planning requirements which may be of concern is as follows.

3.3.1 Statewide Land Use Planning

A few states have enacted generalized land use planning laws which provide for the establishment of regional development plans, designating areas of critical environmental concern, identifying areas which are and are not suitable for industrial development in an attempt to assure that facilities will not be located so as to violate applicable categorical pollution control laws and so forth.

3.3.2 Land Use Planning for Specific Areas

A somewhat larger number of states have adopted legislation providing for stringent planning and regulation of development in areas of particular environmental value—such as coastal areas, wetlands, and the Adirondacks region in New York. The planning and regulatory approach followed in these areas is, as might be expected, more rigorous and less hospitable to industry than the generalized plans discussed above.

The most significant and widespread state programs are those developed under the Federal Coastal Zone Management Act of 1972, which authorized a system of federal grants for developing and administering state coastal management programs. The Act established detailed procedures that must be followed in developing the management program: participation by relevant government agencies and interested groups, public hearings, the adoption of the governmental authority necessary to carry out the management program, and so forth. In addition, the Act requires that each management program include a number of specified elements, such as definition of what constitutes permissible land and water uses within the coastal zone.

Once a state's program has been approved, no federal agency may issue a license or a permit for any activity in the coastal zone unless the state acknowledges (or is presumed to acknowledge) that the proposed activity is consistent with its program. Section 307 (c)(3)(A). If a federal license or permit is required for a facility which may be located in the coastal zone, this provision will impose another potential obstacle. Further, the amount of time necessary for obtaining the state's acknowledgement of consistency will have to be factored into the planning for the facility.

One of the most significant issues concerning the coastal zone is the need for locating some types of energy development (e.g. offshore oil drilling) in these specially protected areas. Congress added Section 308 to the Act in 1976 in an effort to deal with this issue. Section 308 established a coastal energy impact program to encourage planning for coastal energy activities. It also authorized a system of grants, loans and loan guarantees to enable states (1) to develop projects and programs which are necessitated by coastal energy activities and (2) to prevent or ameliorate loss of environmental or recreational resources which would be caused by such activities. Since most coastal states have developed the programs encouraged by Section 308, the federal role in the CEIP is being drastically reduced. The states will be required to bear an increasing share of the funding and administration of their programs. Implementation of the Act is carried out by the coastal states, which include those bordering the Great Lakes. An example of the state legislation which has resulted is the California Coastal Act which has come to be regarded as a model for state implementation of the federal Act.

The California Act establishes a comprehensive scheme of planning and development controls for the coastal zone, which is defined as that area extending from the three-mile limit to a point generally 1000 yards inland of the mean high tide line. The zone may extend much farther inland in some areas and not as far in others. Development is defined quite broadly to include construction, grading, dredging, disposal of any waste, changes in land use, and so forth.

A number of statutory goals govern the implementation of the Act. Perhaps the most important is the principle that conflicts in the planning and permitting process be resolved in a manner which is most protective of significant coastal resources. The Act does recognize that it may be necessary to locate certain industrial and energy facilities in the zone even though they may have adverse impacts on coastal resources. Preferential treatment is to be given to "coastal-dependent" industrial facilities and facility location or expansion at existing sites is encouraged.

Local governments are given primary planning responsibility for the coastal zone, subject to plan review by the regional coastal commissions and certification by the state commission. Once the local coastal program has been certified, the necessary coastal development permits will generally be issued by the local government subject to a limited right of appeal. Coastal development permits can be issued by a different mechanism pending certification of local programs.

The Act appears to have a number of worthwhile features. The statutory provisions which attempt to integrate the coastal zone program with other state and local authorities and, especially, the recognition that other needs may outweigh adverse environmental impacts are important. And the Act appears to take account of the need for development to a far greater extent than the virtual moratorium on major development that preceded its enactment.

3.3.3 Planning for Achievement of Categorical Pollution Control Objectives

In addition to the generalized land planning programs previously outlined, virtually all of the states, at the insistence of federal statutes, have specific programs directed towards achieving objectives of "categorical" pollution control laws like the Clean Air Act and the Clean Water Act. Achieving such objectives through land use controls is complicated by the fact that these objectives are very different from the ordinary objectives of the land use process. The result is that land use planning to attain these objectives, while effective from the narrow perspective of air and/or water quality improvement, does not assure that development occurs in a way that is wise or even environmentally sound.

Until amended in 1977, Section 110 (a)(2)(B) of the Clean Air Act specifically mandated the use of "land use...controls" where necessary to achieve air quality standards. Although that specific requirement was eliminated by the 1977 Amendments, it is evident that, in many respects, the State Implementation Plan (SIP) under the Clean Air Act must be a "land use plan." In particular, siting decisions will be substantially affected by the 1977 Amendments' requirements as to the prevention of significant deterioration (PSD) and nonattainment areas.

The PSD provisions, which apply to those areas whose air quality exceeds the national secondary standards, limit the increases in pollutants in accordance with a statutory scheme for classifying high air quality areas. In addition, every new "major emitting facility" in an affected area must go through an extensive permitting process and obtain a permit which imposes a number of stringent conditions on the facility, including the use of best available control technology and air quality monitoring programs. Finally, protecting visibility in mandatory Class I federal areas is declared a national goal. Obviously, these requirements may impose severe restraints on siting facilities in areas covered by the PSD provisions.

The Amendments also contain provisions for those areas having air pollutants which exceed any national ambient air quality standard. Section 172 now requires that SIPs for nonattainment areas provide for attainment of each national standard as expeditiously as practicable. Although land use controls are not specifically mandated, the Amendments' ambitious goals may compel the use of such controls.

New facilities in nonattainment areas receive detailed consideration in the legislation. Those states which cannot meet the primary standards for carbon monoxide or photochemical oxidants by December 31, 1982 will be required to establish a program which requires, prior to the issuance of permits for new emitting facilities:

"an analysis of alternative sites, sizes, production processes and environmental control techniques for such proposed [facility] which demonstrates that benefits of the proposed [facility] significantly outweigh the environmental and social costs imposed as a result of its location, construction or modification."

As of July 1, 1979, construction of major new facilities which emit nonattainment pollutants is prohibited unless there is an EPA approved plan in place. SIPs for all nonattainment areas must include a permit program for new facilities which is based on a source-by-source or areawide trade-off policy. Unless pollution from existing sources is reduced sufficiently so that total emissions (including emissions from the new facility) are less than before, the new facility will not be permitted. Additionally, the new source must comply with the lowest achievable emission rate and meet certain other requirements.

Finally, federal agencies are prohibited from issuing permits, licenses or any form of assistance for any activity which does not conform to an approved SIP. For those facilities which fall within the nonattainment provisions—roughly those facilities which emit or have the potential to emit 100 tons per year or more of any air pollutant—the procedures and strictures of the 1977 Amendments will significantly affect siting questions.

The Clean Water Act also has significant impacts on development decisions at the state and local level. The most important of the Act's planning provisions, at least in theory, is Section 208, which has been put forward by EPA as an example of what a federal planning provision should be. Others, including the General Accounting Office and the staff of the House Appropriations Committee, have been critical of the 208 program. As a consequence of these criticisms, Congress has declined to fund this program since fiscal year 1980.

Section 208 provides for the establishment of areawide waste treatment planning agencies for "areas which . . . have substantial water quality control problems." Once established, these areawide planning organizations are charged with broad responsibility for developing not only a plan for future construction of necessary waste treatment facilities but also for items such as:

- Establishment of a program to regulate the location, modification and construction of "any facilities" within the area which may result in waste discharges and to assure that industrial or commercial wastes discharged into treatment works meet applicable pretreatment standards;

- Development of a process to identify various nonpoint sources of pollution related to construction activity, mining, agriculture and forestry including procedures and methods "including land use requirements" to control such sources to the extent feasible;

- Development of a process to control underground and on land waste disposal; and

- Identification of measures necessary to carry out the plan, including agencies to construct, operate and maintain required facilities and otherwise carry out the plan.

At the time the plan is approved by the state governor, he designates a management agency or agencies, which can be either existing state agencies or newly created special purpose agencies, to be responsible for implementing the plan for the area in question. Where no planning agency has been designated, the state has the responsibility for developing and implementing plans for the non-designated area.

Section 208 is somewhat unique in that the contemplated result is not only a comprehensive plan, but also an identified method to enforce compliance with the plan and a designated agency responsible for that enforcement. The Act further provides that after a plan is developed, no wastewater discharge permit may be issued nor may any federal construction grant be awarded if it would conflict with the plan. Thus the Act seeks to assure that the plan, once developed, will not be put on the shelf, but will become a valid and viable regulatory mechanism.

The coordinated planning approach of Section 208 has not worked out as anticipated. In the last few years, funding that could have been utilized for 208 planning has been directed to the water quality management plan grants (Section 205) and the pollution control programs of Section 106. These, together with a number of other planning provisions (Section 303 dealing with Water Quality Implementation Plans, Section 209 —Basin Planning, Section 314— Clean Lakes and, indeed, Section 402—the NPDES program itself), will have a substantial impact on planning decisions.

EPA's efforts to prevent the degradation of waters whose quality is better than required by existing standards may also affect industrial facilities siting. Under EPA's "antidegradation" guidelines, a state must develop an antidegradation policy and methods for implementing the policy. Some degradation of high quality water, other than those which constitute an "outstanding natural resource," may be permitted; EPA's guidelines would permit a state to allow limited degradation where economically or socially justified. The policy is being implemented through water quality plans and may also be effectuated through the NPDES program. EPA is currently considering a proposal to relax its antidegradation guidelines. 47 Federal Register 49234 (October 29, 1982). Even if the proposal is adopted, however, the guidelines may restrict the siting of certain types of facilities if they would be dependent on discharges to high quality waters.

Another "categorical" pollution control law which could have some direct impact on land use decisions is the Noise Control Act of 1972. While there are no specific SIP requirements in that Act, it does provide for establishment by EPA of criteria on the effects of noise on the public health and welfare and on available noise control techniques. A few states have adopted laws in the nature of implementation plans, but without any direct EPA involvement, providing for enforcement of ambient noise criteria on an area-by-area basis. They should be considered at early stages of any major siting project.

3.3.4 Other Planning Requirements

There are, of course, numerous other federal and federal-state planning programs ranging from Uniform Relocation Act requirements to Housing and Community Development Act planning grants to flood plain development restrictions, which could have a significant impact on a particular siting proposal. Proposals to site projects on federally owned lands must comply with the land use planning requirements of the Federal Land Policy and Management Act of 1976. Again, it is important in the beginning stages of any major siting proposal to find out what plans are applicable, determine how they might affect the project, and consider how the project might be structured or pursued to avoid or cope with a major problem area.

To summarize this discussion of the existing planning programs, it is fair to say that the present situation is one of overlap and contradiction where it is difficult to determine which plans might be applicable—much less what they require. The involved agencies have made some effort to coordinate the planning programs under their jurisdictions, but there is still a long way to go. In the continuing absence of any national land use policy, a coordinated approach to federal planning programs will be a long and arduous process, but there does seem to be at least some hope for some future element of rationality arising out of the present state of confusion.

3.4 Specific Federal Authorizations

The final stage of the siting process is the issuance of any specific federal authorizations and permits required for construction and operation of the facility. There will be some projects where no specific federal permit is required. Other projects may require eight or ten permits from as many different federal agencies. It is, of course, important at the very outset of any project to know what federal permits will be required and whether the issuance of any of those permits will constitute a "major federal action." Amazingly, however, many companies attempt to shortcut the painstaking analysis required to obtain such knowledge and, as a result, either apply for permits they do not really need or fail to plan for permits that they really do need. This should not happen with proper management and planning.

Obtaining a federal permit or authorization will require satisfaction of a number of environmental requirements. The broadest in scope is NEPA, which is discussed below. The Fish and Wildlife Coordination Act may require the authorizing agency to coordinate with the U.S. Fish and Wildlife Service before taking action. Although other agencies are not required to adopt USFWS recommendations that permits or authorizations not be issued because of potential adverse effects on flora and fauna, such a recommendation will lead to processing delays at the very minimum. Further, some agencies, such as the Corps of Engineers, are strongly suggesting that applicants work out any potential problems with the USFWS before processing begins so that effects on flora and fauna must be taken into account if the Coordination Act is applicable.

The Endangered Species Act of 1973 is having an increasing impact on federal action in this area. In order to implement the Act's goal of protecting and preserving endangered species of animals, birds, fish and plants, the USFWS has promulgated regulations governing any federal action, including permits and authorizations, that have the potential to adversely affect an endangered species or its critical habitat. If the USFWS finds, after consulting with the action agency and conducting biological studies, that such an adverse effect is probable, the proposed federal action will almost certainly be disapproved. Due to widespread dissatisfaction with the operation of the Act, it was amended in 1978 to provide for a procedure for reviewing projects which would otherwise be prohibited because of their adverse effects on an endangered species. If this review reveals that the project meets the rigorous standard for granting an exemption, the project will be permitted in spite of its adverse effects on an endangered species or habitat. The Act was further amended in 1982 to expedite the exemption procedure. Nevertheless, as a general rule, the creation of an adverse effect on an endangered species or its habitat will probably be fatal to the project. Only if the project can be modified to eliminate the adverse effect or relocated to another site will there be any substantial chance of overcoming a finding of probable adverse effect.

NEPA will be involved if issuance of an authorization or a permit constitutes a major federal action. At present, the federal statutes which seem to be most productive of federal authorization requirements that result in NEPA applicability in the generalized industrial siting context are Section 10 of the Rivers and Harbors Act of 1899, which requires a Corps of Engineers permit for building structures or conducting excavation in "navigable waters of the United States," Section 404 of the Clean Water Act, which gives the Corps and EPA authority over the placement of dredged or fill material in any waters of the United States (see Chapter 3), and the wastewater discharge permit program under the Clean Water Act, which provides that NEPA is applicable to the issuance of permits for "new sources" as defined in the Act. However, other federal authorizations (for example, Treasury permits for wineries and breweries) required for specific types of facilities, though seemingly inconsequential, may be sufficient to trigger NEPA and involve all of the environmentally oriented agencies, as well as the general public, in the authorization process.

Once the task of identifying the authorizations required and federal agencies involved is accomplished, there are a number of options for structuring the review process which deserve careful consideration and which might be suggested to the reviewing agencies. In evaluating these options, it should be recognized that there should be a great deal of room left for the development of creative and innovative procedures to minimize duplication and wasted effort without prejudice to the effectiveness of the review process. The major approaches are as follows.

3.4.1 Lead Agency Proceedings

A well-recognized method of preventing unnecessary duplication in situations involving multiple agencies and multiple instances of NEPA applicability is the procedure prescribed by the CEQ regulations in which one involved agency is designated as the "lead agency" and pulls the laboring oar in a single coordinated review proceeding under NEPA. In lead agency proceedings, it is important to assure that there is early agreement on major issues such as the extent of each agency's involvement, the scope of the required impact statement, the timing of agency inputs and so forth. In projects of major scope and complexity, a memorandum of understanding between the concerned agencies may be an appropriate mechanism for achieving such agreement.

3.4.2 Federal-State Coordination

Though less fully explored, there would seem to be considerable potential for reducing duplication between federal NEPA proceedings and proceedings under state and environmental protection or siting laws. In the past, a few federal-state task forces were established to consider regional impacts of critically needed major facilities. State environmental protection acts sometimes provide for acceptance of federal impact statements in fulfillment of state assessment requirements and, in a few instances, federal agencies here accepted comprehensive state assessments as a basis for finding that further review at the federal level was not required.

Federal-state coordination in connection with environmental issues has been given a strong boost by the CEQ regulations. In 40 CFR § 1506.2(b), federal agencies are directed to cooperate with state and local agencies to the fullest extent possible, unless specifically barred from doing so by some other law. Such cooperation is to include joint planning, research, public hearings and environmental assessments. In addition, 40 CFR § 1506.2(c) directs federal agencies—again to the fullest extent possible—to reduce duplication between NEPA and comparable state and local requirements and to prepare joint environmental impact statements.

These new directives should reduce duplication of effort in complying with NEPA and "little NEPAs" and lead to a reduction in time delays.

3.4.3 "Third Party" Contracts

A third innovative approach, which has been utilized by some of the EPA regional offices, is to have environmental assessments prepared by totally independent contractors paid by the applicant but supervised by EPA. This approach, which of course requires the applicant's agreement, can radically telescope the usual two step procedure of having an environmental report prepared by the applicant and then having much of that report redone in the preparation of an independent environmental impact statement by the authorizing agency. In addition to telescoping the time period, this "third party" approach should offer significant advantages from the viewpoint of sustaining the final statement on judicial review.

3.4.4 Legislated Procedures

In truly major siting questions involving facilities of critical national concern (e.g., the Alaska Pipeline, offshore oil ports, deep seabed mining) there may be the possibility of legislative action (similar to the Deepwater Port Act discussed below) to structure and control the review procedures on the project. This is, of course, a difficult and sometimes dangerous approach but one which does merit consideration where serious problems are anticipated.

4.0 Approach Under Existing Law

Though the decisionmaking process which we have described is highly complex and exceedingly unpredictable, it is possible to outline a general approach to siting problems which can work, given extreme care and attention and at least moderately good luck. The basic elements of this approach are as follows.

4.1 Participate in the Land Use Planning Process
As a long range planning and development approach, it <u>does</u> make sense to participate, actively, either directly or through trade or business associations, in states and localities where it may be desirable to locate. Plans being developed today will impact siting decisions for many years in the future and, unless industry partic- ipates, the planning function will be done entirely by governments and environmentally concerned citizens.

4.2 Select Sites and Formulate Plans Based on a Detailed Under- standing of the Siting Process
The site (or preferably alternative sites) should be selected and development plans formulated based on a detailed analysis and understanding of the legal and, at least to some extent, of the political environment in which important decisions will be made. This requires:

- Thorough analysis of likely local opinion, sources and reason for opposition and so forth;

- Identification and analysis of all applicable land use plans and zoning requirements based thereon;

- Identification and analysis of all requirements for authorizations at local, state and federal levels and NEPA or SEPA applicability thereto.

4.3 Structure the Procedure and Climate in Which the Siting Decision Will Be Made
The following general guidelines are usually applicable:

- Keep local decisionmaking as separate as possible from procedural strictures which arise at the state and federal levels, and get the necessary local approvals as early in the game as possible. It is possible and necessary at the local level to deal with the real reasons for opposition and that may be difficult in the context of an environmental review proceeding;

- Use lead agency or clearing-house procedures under NEPA, SEPAs or general state siting laws to coordi- nate the exercise of multiagency jurisdiction and to insure that, at most, the applicant is faced with one federal EIS and one state EIR;

• Consider more innovative coordination procedures to further diminish the problems of duplication of effort and jurisdiction.

4.4 File the Applications

As noted previously, numerous authorizations may be required at the federal and state levels. However, given success in structuring the procedures, there should, at least at the federal level, be only one environmental assessment and that assessment should be considered in a single coordinated review procedure.

For major projects, the basic rule is:

DO NOT STINT ON THE ENVIRONMENTAL
ASSESSMENT DOCUMENT

It is the applicant's basic weapon and also his basic defense. Opponents can be counted on to be super critical and if they can find something significant that the applicant and the responsible agency did not consider, they will get their injunction and delay the project. If, on the other hand, the applicant has prepared an adequate assessment and considered all significant potential impacts and alternative approaches, he should prevail as long as the reviewing agencies do their job.

4.5 Make the Reviewing Agencies Do It Right

The major reason for successful challenges of facilities authorization procedures is the failure of the reviewing agency to do its job. Thus, though there is a major temptation to let the agency cut corners if it is going to issue the required authorization, that temptation should be resisted and the following should definitely be assured:

• The agency must base its draft EIS on its own independent review and there must be a record to show that it has done so.

• The draft must be adequately circulated and the public given an adequate opportunity to comment. The CEQ regulations for processing impact statements must be strictly complied with.

• Issues not addressed in the agency's draft EIS may properly be covered in the public hearings. Comments should be designed to insure that the record is complete.

Through close and careful monitoring of the agency's review process, it should be possible to minimize the risk of bureaucratic oversight and thus assure that the authorization to proceed, once granted, will not be taken away by a court injunction.

4.6 Make Sure That Actual Construction Is in Accordance With Your Authorization and the Final EIS

Despite the fact that the authorization is in hand, there still can be problems if the applicant fails to meet its commitments regarding mitigation of environmental harm or if new grounds for contest are discovered. Thus, the communication, conciliation and general good-neighbor approach should be continued throughout and beyond the construction process and care should be taken to notify and discuss with the cognizant agencies all significant changes in the construction plan.

5.0 Prospects For Change: Specific Siting Legislation

Though the approach outlined above may maximize the chances of success in particular siting propositions, the existing legal framework is inadequate and unnecessarily burdensome and some essential facilities simply cannot be timely authorized within that framework. As noted above, Congress has not seriously considered national land use planning legislation recently. Instead, the focus of Congressional concern with the major facilities siting issue has been process-oriented legislation which establishes detailed procedures for expedited decisions on the siting of a key facility or category of facility.

Examples of process-oriented statutes include the Trans-Alaska Pipeline Authorization Act, the Alaska Natural Gas Transportation Act, and the Deepwater Port Act. Differing situations have led to different legislative approaches: the TAPS Act statutorily mandated the location of the Alyeska pipeline system while most siting legislation focuses on establishing authorization procedures.

5.1 The Deepwater Port Example

The Deepwater Port Act, which became law on January 3, 1975, is perhaps the best example of this type of legislation. It is a response to perceived problems in the siting process for a unique and critically needed type of facility—offshore ports capable of handling supertanker oil shipments—and its major focus is on the procedures for authorization of those facilities. Thus, in many respects, the Act is an experiment to determine whether we can develop procedures which provide for adequate consideration of all potential adverse effects of a project while, at the same time, acceptably dealing with the problems of multiple jurisdictions, overlapping authorities, uncertainties and interminable delays which have to date caused difficulties in major facilities siting proceedings. The experiment involves the following elements.

5.1.1 Time Limitation

In perhaps its most direct attack on previous siting problems, the Act imposes a definite time limit for the completion of each step in the review process. Within 21 days from the filing of an application under the Act, the Secretary must make a finding as to whether the application is "complete." Five days after that determination, a notice must be published in the Federal Register and the timeclock established by the Act starts to run. Theoretically, the required impact statement must be prepared and processed and a final decision on the application reached 330 days after that publication.

5.1.2 Single Coordinated Procedure

Less direct, but perhaps even more revolutionary than the Act's time limit, is its so called "single window" approach for coordinating the federal involvement and, to some extent, the state involvement in the siting and overall review process for deepwater ports. This "single window" approach is basically an elaboration of the "lead agency" approach which has been widely accepted as a way of complying with NEPA requirements in situations where multiple permits or authorization from several federal agencies are required.

The operative provisions of the Act are Section 5(e)(2), which provides that an application filed thereunder

> shall constitute an application for all federal authorizations required for ownership, construction and operation of a deepwater port,

and Section 4(b), which authorizes the Secretary

> . . .upon application and in accordance with the provisions of this Act, to issue . . . a license for the ownership, construction and operation of a deepwater port.

These provisions appear to make it clear that what goes into the "single-window" is one consolidated application and what comes out 356 days later is all federal authorizations required for construction and operation of the port.

The Act attempts to spell out a detailed system for coordinating the inputs of the concerned federal agencies, the public and the states during that 356-day period. It provides for at least one consolidated informal public hearing in the state or states most directly affected and, if necessary to resolve the issues, for a single formal administrative hearing to be held in Washington. It spells out who can and who cannot veto the project (DOT, EPA and "adjacent coastal states" can; others cannot). It establishes specific consultative functions for some agencies, specifically outlines the factors to be considered and findings to be made in the issuance of a license and, in general, does much to avoid the seemingly limitless uncertainties as to who has jurisdiction, what procedures must be followed, what authorizations are required and so forth which have made major facilities siting such a difficult proposition.

5.1.3   One Environmental Impact Statement Based on Identified Criteria

The drafters of the Deepwater Port Act were concerned over the possibility that the involvement of numerous agencies at various stages in the authorization process might be characterized as discrete "major federal actions" giving rise to the need for filing and processing a number of impact statements on a single deepwater port. They sought to eliminate this possibility by providing, in Section 5(f) of the Act, that

> For all timely applications covering a single application area, the Secretary, in cooperation with other involved Federal agencies and departments, shall . . . prepare a single, detailed environmental impact statement, which shall fulfill the requirement of all Federal agencies in carrying out their responsibilities pursuant to this Act to prepare an environmental impact statement.

In addition, the Congress made at least a tentative gesture at resolving one of the major problems of the NEPA impact statement process—the lack of certainty as to the factors which must be "considered" in the review process. It did this by providing, in Section 6 of the Act, for the establishment by the Secretary of "environmental review criteria," consistent with NEPA, to be "used to evaluate a deepwater port" and "considered" in the preparation of the impact statement required by Section 5.

The basic intent of these provisions is to simplify the NEPA process and minimize the threat of litigation based on failure to consider impacts or alternatives by identifying at the outset all factors required to be considered in the NEPA process. This is an exceedingly appealing idea and one which could be very beneficial. Unfortunately, the legislation does not spell it out with the detail and clarity required in order to comfortably rely on these criteria in the preparation of the environmental assessment or impact statement. The Coast Guard, therefore, took a compromise approach. It published general environmental review criteria which do not purport to be an exhaustive catalog of factors to be considered in an

EIS and supplemented those criteria with Guidelines for Preparation of Environmental Assessments identifying in exhaustive detail the information to be supplied by applicants to serve as a basis for the Coast Guard's independent preparation of an EIS on the project. Both the environmental review criteria and the guidelines were subjected to extensive public comment procedures, and, as long as the criteria and guidelines are utilized carefully, there should be no surprises on what either is or is not considered in an EIS on a deepwater port. This careful process of identifying in advance the data to be considered and criteria to be applied should do much to convince any reviewer that the agency has properly fulfilled its responsibility under NEPA.

The three major Deepwater Port Act initiatives outlined above seem to offer a way out of the existing "endurance contest" theory of site authorization proceedings without sacrificing the basic objective of insuring that essential facilities will be constructed and located based on full consideration of impacts and alternatives and in the least objectionable way possible. However, lest the reader be left the impression that specific siting legislation like the Deepwater Port Act is clearly the answer, the problems of the deepwater port experiment must be considered.

5.2 Problems With the Deepwater Port Act Approach

5.2.1 Specific Legislation Begets Stringent Criteria

In today's legislative climate, a new law to control the development of particular types of facilities is an invitation for lawmakers to impose requirements on facilities to insure safety, environmental acceptability and other benefits. Thus, the licensing process for deepwater ports entails items such as an antitrust review, obligations to tear the facility up and take it away after operations are terminated, a best available technology demonstration, stringent construction standards and operating procedures and so forth. All these requirements are far more stringent than those which might have been applicable if it had been possible to get a port authorized without specific siting legislation.

The strict legislative criteria have been paralleled by an administrative tendency to look more carefully at and impose stricter requirements on deepwater ports than would probably have been done in the absence of specific legislation. For example, the antitrust review led to ownership and operational limitations that are far more restrictive than those imposed on other common carriers. These legislative and administrative tendencies should be carefully analyzed by any industry which is likely to become involved in facilities siting legislation proposals. Indeed, these tendencies, unless checked, may prevent widespread use of such legislation as a means of solving siting issues.

5.2.2 "Time Limits" Can Be Illusory

Laws which establish definite timetables for agency action, though rare at the federal level, are not uncommon in the states, and many have found that those time limits are more apparent than real. There is a definite risk of similar problems under federal laws such as the Deepwater Port Act—for example, the regulations provide for stopping the clock when additional information is requested but not forthcoming—and the question of whether the timetable can be enforced is one which is critical to the success of the deepwater port type procedure. The initial deepwater port licenses were issued on schedule, a fact which bodes well for future "time limited" procedures.

5.2.3 It Is Difficult to Enforce the "One Window" Concept

The job of getting 15 or 20 federal agencies to follow the lead agency in exercising their jurisdiction is not an easy one and a breakdown of the "One Window" authorization process would effectively eliminate the beneficial aspects of the Act. "One Window" did work for the initial deepwater port licenses but this is not a basis for assuming that, without careful attention, it will work equally well for other projects.

5.2.4 The "One Environmental Impact Statement" Concept Failed

When it enacted Section 5(f) of the Act, the Congress neglected to say that when it said "one impact statement" it meant one impact statement. Thus, in addition to the impact statement which the Department of the Interior filed when the Administration proposed the legislation, there was an impact statement on the DOT regulations and an impact statement on the licensing process.

The "Identified Criteria" aspect of the bill's approach to impact statements worked reasonably well for the first two license applications. It appears to be a promising approach.

5.3 The Future of the Deepwater Port Approach

Though the Deepwater Port Act experiment has to date been at least a qualified success, it is not a panacea. This conclusion is confirmed by the experience of the first two applications processed under the Act. One applicant accepted a license, constructed the port, and commenced operations; the other declined the license and withdrew from the project. The latter result is largely attributable to requirements imposed as a consequence of the specified statutory procedures.

For the sake of the integrity of future siting procedures, it is hoped that the Deepwater Port Act and subsequent legislation patterned on the example of that Act (such as the Alaska Natural Gas Transportation Act) achieve their purpose fully and gain broad acceptance. The present approach to siting major industrial facilities is deficient and alternatives must be developed. Most of the deficiencies in the deepwater port licensing procedures, as well as those which are developing under ANGTA, may well be attributable to poor legislative drafting and might well be avoided in the future. However, there may not be further opportunities to try the legislated procedures approach unless at least qualified success is achieved in these initial efforts. Thus, both environmentalists and industry have a stake in making certain that these particular siting proceedings result in correct decisions arrived at in an orderly manner based on the right reasons.

If these experiments are successful, we may see their example followed in other critical and site dependent areas such as energy facilities siting and minerals extraction. For certain types of facilities, this approach is the most promising way out of the current siting dilemma.

6.0 Conclusion

While there is some hope that things will get slightly better in the future, the job of coordinating the effort to obtain the necessary authorizations for a new facility will continue to be a difficult one. If industry is to improve its success rate in the facilities siting area, it must recognize that the siting approval process requires at least the same level of careful and specific planning, detailed assignments of responsibility and attention to detail which is customary in closing a major merger or orchestrating a take–over bid. It is hoped that the information provided in this chapter will contribute to an understanding of the problems involved and thereby decrease the number of projects which are halted or substantially delayed due to failure to timely cope with environmentally-based objections.

Table 12-1

Decision Matrix: Environmentally Related Constraints on Construction or Expansion of Major Industrial Facilities

Decision Levels	Decision Points	Factors to be Considered in Risk Analysis	Comments on Strategic Considerations
I. Local Property Owners.	Acquisition of proposed site or firm options thereon.	Resistance to selling and higher prices if proposed use is disclosed. Resentment and possible efforts to set aside sale or option if proposed use is not disclosed.	From the viewpoint of overcoming environmental objections, it is generally best to make full disclosure of intentions at the earliest practicable date. The competing risks of price escalation and resistance to selling may be minimized by preserving site alternatives as long as possible. In circumstances where the proposed use is for a purpose such as power generation, consideration may be given to enlisting governmental aid in site acquisition process.
II. Local Government.	Permit Issuance (Construction, Conditional Use, Sewer Hookup, etc.).	Any applicable state "little NEPA," coastal zone mangement or land use laws. Any applicable local or regional land use plans.	Local level decisionmaking is, in most instances, still primarily political. However, state NEPA or state land use planning laws may impose constraints on purely political decisions.

Table 12-1 (continued)

Decision Levels	Decision Points	Factors to be Considered in Risk Analysis	Comments on Strategic Considerations
	Zoning or Zoning Variances. Taxation and Infrastructure.	Any federal involvement in funding infrastructure which triggers NEPA. Any local political opposition to project.	Environmental concerns make all potential opposition dangerous both in terms of political impact and potential litigation. Thus, all vocal opposition groups should be identifed and, if possible, neutralized. Again, the local climate will likely be enhanced if alternative site options remain viable throughout the decision-making process.
III. State and Regional Bodies.	Any required approvals under coastal zone management or land use legislation or review responsibilities under state "little NEPAs." Any required state permit for construction or operation.	Public hearing procedures at state or regional level may be required in connection with coastal zone or land use approvals. Public hearing procedures are also required in connection with NPDES permit issuance.	Except for truly major projects, state decisions will normally be made by administrative rather than elected officials. Environmentalist opposition, especially from local residents, will nevertheless have a strong influence on this decision-making process. As with the previous decision levels, the presentation of several environmentally justifiable site alternatives will minimize the risk of decisions fatal to the project.

Table 12-1 (continued)

Decision Levels	Decision Points	Factors to be Considered in Risk Analysis	Comments on Strategic Considerations
	Any required state permit certification or approval under NPDES (where the state is the issuing authority) or Clean Air Act implementation plans.	State permits under federal programs may be subject to federal veto, review and/or approval.	
		State decisions may be subject to "little NEPA" requirements.	
	Any assurance of compliance with state noise-control laws.	If federal funding is involved in the project, NEPA itself may apply.	
		Adjacent states may have the right to object if their interests are affected.	
IV. Federal Government.	Any required federal permit or authorization (FERC, ICC, Corps of Engineers, etc.)	NEPA applicability.	With limited exceptions, any federal involvement in the decision-making process will trigger NEPA and the detailed deliberative process which it entails (see Chapter 2).
	Any federal funding participation.	Other precise risks are dependent on the nature of the federal authorization required.	
	Any Clean Air Act review or NPDES permit.		

Table 12-1 (continued)

Decision Levels	Decision Points	Factors to be Considered in Risk Analysis	Comments on Strategic Considerations
V. The Courts.	Common law nuisance or tres-pass litigation.	(See Chapter 1).	The threat of litigation lurks in the background at virtually every decision-making level. Thus, in major site development or facilities expansion plans, all strategic decisions should be made based on full understanding of the implications of such decisions if and when the case comes to court.
	NEPA litigation.	(See Chapter 2).	
	Citizen's suits under the Clean Water Act or the Clean Air Act.	(See Chapters 3 and 4).	
	Citizen's suits under state statutes.		

ABOUT THE AUTHORS

J. Gordon Arbuckle

Mr. Arbuckle is a member of the Washington law firm Patton, Boggs, & Blow. His experience includes representing trade associations, and industrial concerns in connection with the Congressional deliberations which led to adoption of the Federal Water Pollution Control Act, the Ports and Waterways Safety Act and other legislation. He has also been involved in administrative proceedings and litigation under the Water Pollution Control Act, the National Environmental Policy Act, RCRA, TSCA, the Clean Air Act and other state and federal environmental statutes.

G. William Frick

Mr. Frick is a partner in the Washington office of the law firm, Lathrop, Koontz, Righter, Clagett & Norquist where he specializes in environmental matters. His background includes service in the U.S. Environmental Protection Agency Headquarters as Associate General Counsel for Water Quality, Deputy General Counsel and during 1976-77, he was General Counsel of the U.S. EPA. He received his undergraduate and law degrees from Kansas University.

Ridgway M. Hall, Jr.

Mr. Hall is a partner in the Washington, D.C. law firm of Crowell & Moring. Formerly Associate General Counsel of the U.S. Environmental Protection Agency, he now practices environmental law and litigation. He has authored numerous articles on environmental law and is a prominent speaker at seminars and symposia on environmental law and regulatory programs. A magma cum laude graduate of Yale University, Mr. Hall received his law degree from Harvard Law School.

Marshall Lee Miller

Mr. Miller, a partner in the Washington, D.C. office of the law firm of Reid & Priest. He is the former Deputy Administrator of the U.S. Occupational Safety and Health Administration, Department of Labor. His experience includes service as the Special Assistant to

506

the first Administrator of the U.S. Environmental Protection Agency, Chief EPA Judicial Officer and Associate Deputy Attorney General in the U.S. Department of Justice. He has been educated at Harvard, Oxford, Heidelberg, and Yale.

Thomas F. P. Sullivan

Mr. Sullivan has undergraduate degrees from Kenrick Seminary and St. Louis University, and his law degree from Catholic University. He is an attorney in Washington, D.C., who has been in the forefront of the environmental field since the 1960's. Mr. Sullivan has served as editor and author of many books plus being a regular contributing author for "Pollution Engineering" magazine. His lecture credits include numerous environmental engineering conferences and seminars. He also serves as President of Government Institutes, Inc.

Timothy A. Vanderver, Jr.

Mr. Vanderver is a partner in the Washington, D.C. law firm of Patton, Boggs & Blow, and specializes in environmental issues. He is a graduate of Washington & Lee College and Harvard Law School. Mr. Vanderver was awarded the coveted Rhodes Scholarship and as a result achieved his graduate degree in law from Oxford University in England. He has practiced law with the Department of the Interior and the Department of Housing & Urban Development where he specialized in natural resources and land development law.

Books for
Environmental Professionals

New titles to save your company money & enhance your career growth!

1. Environmental Law Handbook, 7th Edition, 1983
A best-seller in the environmental field, this remarkably useful Handbook provides practical information on the major environmental areas with a chapter each on air pollution, water pollution, land use, pesticides, toxic substances, noise, hazardous and solid wastes, CERCLA (Superfund), NEPA, OSHA, plus a single chapter on some of the fundamentals basic to environmental law: environmental torts, constitutional law, considerations, evidence, defenses, who can sue, civil and criminal liability. Sharp, insightful analyses are written in a clear, non-legalese style. **400+ pp., Hardcover**

2. Environmental Statutes
All major environmental laws are finally incorporated into a single, convenient book. The complete text of each statute as currently amended is included with a detailed Table of Contents for your quick referral.
Contents: Clean Air Act as amended; Federal Water Pollution Control Act (Clean Water Act); National Environmental Policy Act; Noise Control Act as amended; Occupational Health and Safety Act; Resource Conservation and Recovery Act as amended; Safe Drinking Water Act as amended; Toxic Substances Control Act; Superfund; and the Used Oil Recycling Act. **601 pp.**

3. Hazardous Material Spills
Learn how major corporations such as Union Carbide, Monsanto and Union Pacific Railroad have established emergency response programs. Discover new techniques and technologies for spills clean-up. Learn how you can prevent needless, dangerous, expensive and embarrassing accidents before they happen. Learn how companies such as yours have cleaned up PCB's, tank car spills, river spills, pesticide and other chemical fires, and how they have managed large-scale evacuations. All from 81 experts who addressed the Sixth Biennial Hazardous Material Spills Conference in April 1982. **510 pp.**

4. EPA Guidebook
Compiled from current EPA documents, this Guidebook provides you with a comprehensive description of the roles and responsibilities of the major EPA offices. Designed for those who need to know which office is responsible for what activities, the Guidebook contains EPA organization charts on both the headquarter and regional levels, plus names of the key contacts and their phone numbers. **166 pp.**

5. Hazardous Wastes Handbook, 4th Ed.
Cut through the confusing red tape surrounding your industrial wastes. Get clear, concise answers which take you step-by-step through the maze of EPA hazardous wastes regulations—the largest environmental program ever undertaken. Handbook carefully analyzes the impact of RCRA and CERCLA on your business and provides practical suggestions—in non-legalese language—on how you can cost-effectively and efficiently comply. The Handbook also contains copies of the major regulations and statutes for easy reference. **656 pp., 3-ring binder**

6. EPA's RCRA Inspection Manual
Developed by EPA to support its inspectors in conducting the complex field inspections fundamental to hazardous waste enforcement. Now you can better understand what compliance is expected of you and how you can most effectively and efficiently comply with the law—*before* the inspector arrives. Contains information-packed descriptions plus checklists covering the key topics that will help you eliminate deficiencies and satisfy an inspection, thereby avoiding civil and criminal penalties. **300 pp.**

7. Environmental Glossary
Records and standardizes more than 3,300 terms, abbreviations and acronyms, compiled directly from the environmental statutes or the code of Federal Regulations. Because of their foundation in the actual environmental legislation or regulations, these definitions are official legal meanings. No working environmental professional or lawyer should be without a copy. Edited by G. William Frick, environmental attorney and former General Counsel of EPA. **301 pp., Hardcover**

8. EPA's TSCA Inspection Manual
Ensure your toxics compliance *before* the inspector arrives! Developed by EPA to support its field inspections. Manual covers such topics as EPA inspector's authorities and responsibilities; inspection procedures; post-inspection activities for the inspector; special procedures; forms; samples; and PCB's enforcement program. **300 pp.**

9. Incineration Systems Course Notebook
Incineration is one of the most promising options for wastes disposal — especially hazardous wastes. This practical Notebook, developed by professional engineer Calvin Brunner, evaluates the state-of-the-art of incineration systems, their costs, environmental considerations, energy considerations, and their relative merits compared to alternative methods of disposal. **411 pp., 3-ring binder**

Guarantee: Your complete satisfaction with any of these books or you may return your order undamaged within 15 days for a full and immediate refund.

Government Institutes, Inc.
966 Hungerford Drive, #24
Rockville, MD (Washington, DC) 20850
(301) 251-9250